# business
# communication
# essentials

## fourth canadian edition

# business
# communication
# essentials

## fourth canadian edition

**Courtland L. Bovée**
Professor of Business Communication
C. Allen Paul Distinguished Chair
Grossmont College

**John V. Thill**
Chairman and Chief Executive Officer
Global Communication Strategies

**Jean A. Scribner**
Program Head, Curriculum
Communication Department
British Columbia Institute of Technology

Toronto

Vice-President, CMPS: Gary Bennett
Editorial Director: Claudine O'Donnell
Acquisitions Editor: David Le Gallais
Marketing Manager: Jennifer Sutton
Project Manager: Kimberley Blakey
Developmental Editor: Jennifer Murray
Manager of Content Development: Suzanne Schaan
Media Developer: Tiffany Palmer
Editorial Production Service: MPS North America, LLC
Compositor: Aptara®, Inc.
Permissions Project Manager: Susan Petrykewycz
Photo Permissions Research: Aptara®, Inc.
Text Permissions Research: Lumina Datamatics
Interior Designer: Aptara®, Inc.
Cover Designer: Aptara®, Inc.
Cover Image: Shutterstock

4   17

**Library and Archives Canada Cataloguing in Publication**
Bovée, Courtland L., author
      Business communication essentials / Courtland L.
Bovée (Professor of Business Communication, C. Allen Paul
Distinguished Chair, Grossmont College), John V. Thill
(Chairman and Chief Executive Officer, Global
Communication Strategies), Jean A. Scribner (Program
Head, Curriculum, Communication Department, British
Columbia Institute of Technology). — Fourth Canadian edition.

Includes bibliographical references and index.
ISBN 978-0-13-350870-3 (pbk.)

      1. Business communication—Textbooks.  I. Scribner, Jean,
author  II. Thill, John V., author  III. Title.

HF5718.B96 2015              651.7          C2014-908460-9

ISBN 978-0-13-350870-3

# Contents in Brief

# Contents

# Preface

No matter what profession you want to pursue, the ability to communicate will be an essential skill—and a skill that employers expect you to have when you enter the workforce. This course introduces you to the fundamental principles of business communication and gives you the opportunity to develop your communication skills. You'll discover how business communication differs from personal and social communication, and you'll see how today's companies are using blogs, social networks, podcasts, virtual worlds, wikis, and other technologies. You'll learn a simple three-step writing process that works for all types of writing and speaking projects, both in college and on the job. Along the way, you'll gain valuable insights into ethics, etiquette, listening, teamwork, and nonverbal communication. Plus, you'll learn effective strategies for the many types of communication challenges you'll face on the job, from routine messages about transactions to complex reports and websites.

*Business Communication Essentials* offers you the opportunity to practise communication skills that will help you get jobs and be promoted in today's workplace. In the words of one Canadian business leader, your communication skills can give you "a sustainable competitive advantage. Technology changes rapidly but your ability to write and speak clearly will support you throughout your career."[1] The new, fourth Canadian edition is student-friendly and features the most extensive end-of-chapter activities available, including questions, exercises, assignments, and cases. Packaged with MyBCommLab, this edition gives you access to tools for building your language skills while you develop your business communication know-how.

## New to This Edition

The key themes and elements in this edition include the following:

**The social communication model.** This edition includes up-to-date coverage of the social communication model that is redefining business communication and reshaping the relationships between companies and their stakeholders. Social media concepts and techniques are integrated throughout the book, from career planning to presentations. Here are some examples:

- Social media questions, activities, and cases appear throughout the book, using Twitter, Facebook, and other media that have been incorprated into the business world.
- Examples of business applications of social media are illustrated and annotated to explain how companies use these tools.
- Infographics and other social–visual communication strategies are explained and illustrated in Chapters 3 and 10.
- The Twitter-enabled backchannel, which is impacting electronic presentations, is covered in Chapter 12.
- Tips on using social networking in the job search process are included in Chapters 13 and 14.

**Compositional modes for electronic media.** For all the benefits they offer, social media and other innovations place new demands on business communicators. This edition gives you practice in nine important modes of writing for electronic media (Chapter 6).

**Personal branding.** As the workforce continues to evolve, taking control of your career is more important than ever. An important first step is clarifying and communicating your *personal brand*, covered in the employment-message chapters (Chapters 13 and 14).

**Storytelling techniques.** Some of the most effective business messages, from advertising to proposals to personal branding, rely on storytelling techniques.

**Full implementation of objective-driven learning.** Every aspect of this textbook is organized by learning objectives, from the chapter content to the end-of-chapter summary and student activities, which makes it easier for you to study, practise, check your progress, and focus on those areas where you need a little extra work.

**New communication cases.** Communication cases give you the opportunity to solve real-world communication challenges using the media skills you'll be expected to have in today's workplace; many of the cases in this edition are new or revised.

**New figures and more annotated model documents.** Dozens of new figures provide examples of the latest trends in business communication. You can now learn from more than 50 annotated model documents, ranging from printed letters and reports to websites, blogs, and social networking sites.

**Real-Time Updates.** This new feature allows students to connect with carefully selected online media items. These elements complement the text's coverage by providing contemporary examples and valuable insights from successful professionals. They can be accessed through MyBCommLab.

# New or Expanded Content

The following topics are revised with new material, or streamlined for more efficient coverage:

### The Communication Context

- Understanding why communication matters
- Communicating as a professional
- Communicating in a world of diversity
- Sensitivity to age and gender differences in the workplace
- The social communication model—improved illustrations
- Writing for multilingual audiences—new example
- Business communication uses of social networks

### Teamwork & Interpersonal

- Communicating effectively in teams—new coverage of collaboration strategies and technologies
- Improving your nonverbal communication skills—new coverage of nonverbal signals as an element of professionalism
- Business etiquette in the workplace, in social settings, and online

### Audience Analysis & Communication Planning

- Audience and context analysis—expanded coverage
- Considerations for choice of media—expanded to include oral, written, visual, and electronic media

### Writing, Style & Tone

- Additional resources for clarity and conciseness—streamlined through use of tables to be more user friendly for students
- Increased emphasis on maintaining professional style and tone
- More discussion of online writing tools and readability in layout and design

## Compositional Modes for Business Communication

- Writing email messages—streamlined
- More emphasis on creating content for social media
- Additional tips for applying the three-part process to blogging, podcasting, and microblogging
- New material on requesting a recommendation, offering condolences, and integrating news releases into social media
- New coverage on rejecting suggestions, proposals, requests for recommendations, or social networking requests such as for LinkedIn
- New cases for social media, negative messages, and persuasive messages, including handling negative commentary in social networking
- More coverage on persuasive appeals

## Report & Proposal Writing

- More emphasis on:
  - evaluation of sources, including use of social media sources, the importance of citation, and Canadian "fair dealing" uses of others' material
  - how to summarize, including an improved example
- New material on infographic reporting, including online resources for making infographics and activities to practise creating them
- Improved readability of this long chapter through the use of tables (five pages shorter without losing sample documents)
- Expanded tips on drafting for websites, wikis, reports, and proposals

## Presentations

- More tips and improved samples on designing effective slides
- Expanded discussion of advantages and disadvantages of structured and free-form slide designs
- More emphasis on presentation practise and on knowing the subject
- Added section on proper use of handouts

## Job Search Techniques

- A new *Communication Notebook* on how to use LinkedIn to further your career
- Additional emphasis *on self-assessment and awareness*, personal brand awareness, professional persona, company research, and audience analysis, and on being *realistic* when applying for jobs
- Social media tools and resources for finding jobs—expanded
- Added writing "the story of you," including a sample "story" showing the value of making a private document for self-assessment to use in the job search
- More emphasis on building networks—both online and in person
- Improved résumé samples
- Expanded discussion on the use of photos, videos, presentations, and infographic or visual résumés—includes a sample infographic résumé of a Canadian digital strategist
- More emphasis and activities on how to use LinkedIn for interview preparation and job searching
- New cases involving applying for jobs on Twitter (using Tweets) and on applying for entry-level jobs that are outside the student's primary field of interest (since many young people don't get to start their careers in a job that perfectly aligns with their professional interests)

# Learning About Business Communication

*Business Communication Essentials'* integrated learning system helps you develop your communication skills so you will be prepared for the workplace. The following features of the text will help you learn and apply the communication skills needed for a successful career:

- **Learning Objectives** are listed on the first page of each chapter and provide a clear overview of the key concepts you are expected to master. Throughout the chapter, margin notes mark the beginning of each objective's discussion. At the end of the chapter, **Learning Objectives: Checking Your Progress** summarizes the main content; these lists are no substitute for reading the chapters, but they can help you quickly review a chapter and verify your grasp of important concepts.
- **Opening Vignettes** introduce each chapter with real-world examples. The related **Tips for Success** give you advice from Canadian business leaders and communication experts on the chapter's topic.
- **The Three-Step Writing Process**, which includes planning, writing, and completing, offers you a practical strategy for writing business messages. This process is applied throughout the text to all business communication tasks.
- **Model Documents** provide a wide selection of documents that you can examine, critique, and revise. In addition, pairs of poor and improved drafts help you recognize the best writing practices.
- **Pointers** appear near many sample documents, giving you a concise list of writing tips. You will also find these pointers handy when you are on the job and need to refresh your memory about effective writing techniques.
- **Marginal Notes** highlight key points in the text and are good tools for reviewing concepts.

# Practising Your Business Communication Skills

Applying what you learn through practise is the best way to develop your confidence and ability as a communicator. Completing the end-of-chapter activities will help you develop and improve your skills. Here are the review and practise activities you will find in each chapter, each tagged by the relevant Learning Objective:

- **Test Your Knowledge** provides questions that review the chapter topics.
- **Apply Your Knowledge** offers exercises to get you thinking about the concepts explained in the chapter.
- **Practise Your Skills** provides you with a wide variety of exercises and activities, allowing you to explore how to handle situations and participate effectively on teams.
- **Cases** at the end of specific chapters offer you a chance to apply the three-step writing process to scenarios from the real world.
- **Business Communication Notebook** centres on one of four themes: ethics, technology, intercultural communication, and workplace skills.

# Student Supplements

MyBCommLab

**MyBCommLab** (www.mybcommlab.ca) combines multimedia, new mini business simulations, tutorials, video, audio, animations, and assessments to engage you in your learning. You can learn at your own pace, completing exercises and having them evaluated for instant feedback.

Select MyBCommLab Blog from the BusComm section of the Resources tab to gain access to blog posts, links to articles, and content updates. The updates include podcasts, PowerPoint presentations, and videos that complement the text's coverage by providing contemporary examples and valuable insights from successful professionals.

MyBCommLab includes a Pearson eText, which gives you access to the text whenever and wherever you have access to the internet. Pearson eText pages look exactly like the printed text and offer powerful new functionality for students and instructors. Users can create notes, highlight text in different colours, create bookmarks, zoom, click hyper-linked words and phrases to view definitions, and read the text either in single-page or two-page view. Pearson eText allows for quick navigation to key parts of the text using both a table of contents or full-text search. The eText may also offer links to associated media files, enabling users to access videos, animations, or other activities as they read the text.

Get started with the personal access code packaged with your new copy of the text. Personal access codes for MyBCommLab can also be purchased separately.

**CourseSmart** goes beyond traditional student expectations—providing instant, online access to the textbooks and course materials you need at significant savings over the price of the printed text. With instant access from any computer and the ability to search your text, you'll find the content you need quickly, no matter where you are. And with online tools like highlighting and note-taking, you can save time and study efficiently. See all the benefits at www.coursesmart.com/students.

# Instructor Supplements

**The moment you know.**

MyBCommLab

Educators know it. Students know it. It's that inspired moment when something that was difficult to understand suddenly makes perfect sense. Our MyLab products have been designed and refined with a single purpose in mind—to help educators create that moment of understanding with their students.

MyBCommLab delivers **proven results** in helping individual students succeed. It provides **engaging experiences** that personalize, stimulate, and measure learning for each student. And, it comes from a **trusted partner** with educational expertise and an eye on the future.

MyBCommLab can be used by itself or linked to any learning management system. To learn more about how MyBCommLab combines proven learning applications with powerful assessment, visit www.mybcommlab.ca.

MyBCommLab—the moment you know.

The following instructor supplements are available for download from a password-protected section of Pearson Education Canada's online catalogue (www.pearsoncanada.ca/highered). Navigate to your book's catalogue page to view a list of those supplements that are available. See your local sales representative for details and access.

- The **Instructor's Manual** provides chapter outlines, suggested solutions to exercises, a pop quiz for each chapter, and fully formatted documents for *every* case in the letter-writing chapters. Additional resources include diagnostic tests of English skills and supplemental grammar exercises.
- The **Test Item File** includes over 1500 multiple choice, true/false, and fill-in-the-blank questions. This test bank is offered in both Microsoft Word format and as a computerized test bank (see below).
- **PowerPoint Presentations** cover the key points in each chapter.

**Computerized Test Bank:** Pearson's computerized test banks allow instructors to filter and select questions to create quizzes, tests, or homework. Instructors can revise questions or add their own, and may be able to choose print or online options. These questions are also available in Microsoft Word format.

Pearson's **Learning Solutions Managers** work with faculty and campus course designers to ensure that Pearson technology products, assessment tools, and online course materials are tailored to meet your specific needs. This highly qualified team is dedicated to helping schools take full advantage of a wide range of educational resources, by assisting in the integration of a variety of instructional materials and media formats. Your local Pearson Education sales representative can provide you with more details on this service program.

**CourseSmart** goes beyond traditional instructor expectations—providing instant, online access to the textbooks and course materials you need at a lower cost for students. And even as students save money, you can save time and hassle with a digital eTextbook that allows you to search for the most relevant content at the very moment you need it. Whether it's evaluating textbooks or creating lecture notes to help students with difficult concepts, CourseSmart can make life a little easier. See how when you visit **www.coursesmart.com/instructors**.

For enrollments of at least 25 students, you can use **Pearson Custom Library** to create your own textbook by choosing the chapters that best suit your own course needs. To begin building your custom text, visit **www.pearsoncustomlibrary.com**. You may also work with a dedicated Pearson Custom editor to create your ideal text—publishing your own original content or mixing and matching Pearson content. Contact your local Pearson Education sales representative to get started.

## Acknowledgments

The dedicated professionals at Pearson Education Canada made working on this book a pleasure. Sponsoring editor Joel Gladstone and developmental editor Jennifer Murray provided excellent advice and support in shaping the fourth Canadian edition. I am also very grateful to project manager Richard di Santo, production editor Rachel Stuckey, and copy editor Caroline Winter for their clarity and attention to detail while preparing the manuscript for production and overseeing the proofreading process. Thanks also to Sonia Tan, media editor, for her assistance in integrating MyBCommLab with this text.

Thank you to my inspiring and supportive colleagues in the communication department at British Columbia Institute of Technology, in particular Gretchen Quiring and Matthew Rockall, for their valuable suggestions, and Linda Matsuba, business librarian, for her knowledge of Canadian business. Special thanks also go to Christopher Wilson at Kwantlen Polytechnic University for his advice, to Kerri Shields of Centennial College for contributing the running cases that appear on MyBCommLab, and to Caroline Jellinck for her employment-related feedback and extensive contacts in Canadian business.

Many educators from across Canada have contributed to the development of this and previous editions of the text. I would like to thank the following instructors who took the time to give me detailed suggestions: Clay Armstrong, Vancouver Island University; Marie Brodie, Nova Scotia Community College School of Business; Patricia Campbell, Red Deer College; Gerta Grieve, JR Shaw School of Business, NAIT; Pamela Ip, Kwantlen Polytechnic University; Condea Krewenki, Nova Scotia Community College School of Business; Alexandra MacLennan, Centre for Liberal and Preparatory Studies, George Brown College; Amy Mitchell, Fanshawe College; Norma-Jean Nielsen, Canadore College; Laura Ricotta, John Abbott College; Matthew Rockall, British Columbia Institute of Technology; Rhonda Sandberg, Centre for Business, George Brown College; and Diana Serafini, Dawson College; Bonnie Benoit, SAIT Polytechnic; Rebecca Book, Keyano College; Sarah Bowers, Langara College; Neil Carter, Sault College; Bill Corcoran, Grande Prairie Regional College; Brent Cotton, Georgian College; Les Hanson, Red River College;

Tanya Haye, Douglas College; Paul Hutchinson, Niagara College of Applied Arts and Technology; Keith Johnson, University of the Fraser Valley; Linda Large, Canadore College; Diana M. Lohnes-Mitchell, Nova Scotia Community College; Alexandra Richmond, Kwantlen Polytechnic University; Heather Thompson, Saint Mary's University; and Bruce Watson, SAIT Polytechnic.

A final thanks goes to my two daughters, Casey and Anna Wilson, for their encouragement.

Jean A. Scribner
Vancouver, B.C.

# business
# communication
# essentials

fourth canadian edition

# Understanding Business Communication in Today's Workplace

**LEARNING OBJECTIVES**

*After studying this chapter, you will be able to*

1 Define *communication*, and explain the importance of effective business communication.

2 Explain what it means to communicate as a professional in a business context.

3 Describe the communication process model and the ways that social media are changing the nature of business communication.

4 Define *ethics*, explain the difference between an ethical dilemma and an ethical lapse, and list six guidelines for making ethical communication choices.

5 Explain how cultural diversity affects business communication and describe the steps you can take to communicate more effectively across cultural boundaries.

6 List four general guidelines for using communication technology effectively.

Copperleaf Technologies provides global consulting services in planning, analysis, and asset management. Though Copperleaf staff use the latest technology to communicate with clients and employees, the leadership team also believes in the power of face-to-face communication. They bring clients from across Canada and around the world to Vancouver for annual user group sessions, including the "Bull Pen," an open forum and conversation they use to build relationships and listen to client needs.

## Understanding Why Communication Matters

**LEARNING OBJECTIVE 1**
Define *communication*, and explain the importance of effective business communication.

Successful professionals such as Hess understand that achieving success in today's workplace is closely tied to the ability of employees and managers to communicate effectively with each other, with people outside the organization, and with people from many cultures. **Communication** is the process of transferring information and meaning between *senders* and *receivers*, using one or more written, oral, visual, or electronic channels. The essence of communication is sharing. As Figure 1.1 indicates, this sharing can happen in a variety of ways, including a simple and successful transfer of information, a negotiation in which the sender and receiver arrive at an agreed-upon meaning, and situations in which the receiver creates a different message than the one the sender intended to convey.

## FIGURE 1.1  Sharing Information

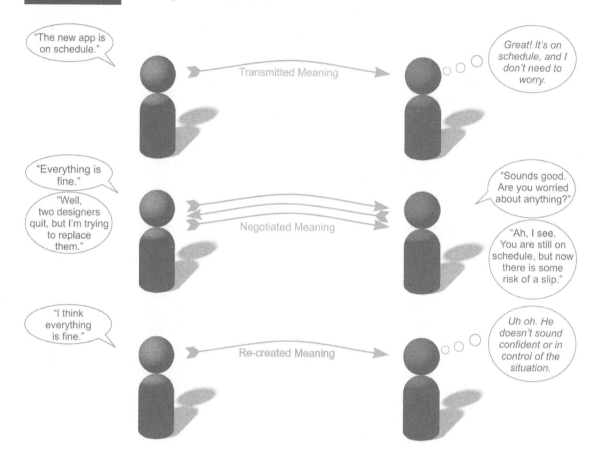

You will invest a lot of time and energy in this course to develop your communication skills, so it's fair to ask whether it will be worthwhile. This section outlines the many ways in which good communication skills are critical for your career and for any company you join.

## Communication Is Important to Your Career

No matter what career path you pursue, communication skills will be essential to your success at every stage. You can have the greatest ideas in the world, but they're no good to your company or your career if you can't express them clearly and persuasively. Some jobs, such as sales and customer support, are primarily about communicating. In fields such as engineering or finance, you often need to share complex ideas with executives, customers, and colleagues, and your ability to connect with people outside your field can be as important as your technical expertise. If you are an entrepreneur, you will need to communicate with a wide range of audiences, from investors, bankers, and government regulators to employees, customers, and business partners. As you take on leadership and management roles, communication becomes even more important.

In fact, improving your communication skills may be the single most important step you can take in your career. The world is full of good marketers, accountants, engineers, and lawyers, but it is not full of good communicators. View this as an opportunity to stand out from your competition in the job market. Communication skills ranked highest on the list of employability skills in the Conference Board of Canada report *Employability Skills 2000+.*[1]

Improving your communication skills could be the single most important thing you do for your career.

Many employers express frustration at the poor communication skills of some employees, particularly recent college graduates who haven't yet learned how to adapt their communication styles to a business environment. If you learn to write well, speak well, listen well, and recognize the appropriate way to communicate in any situation, you'll gain a major advantage that will serve you throughout your career.[2]

This course teaches you how to send and receive information more effectively. It helps you improve your communication skills through practise in an environment that provides honest, constructive criticism. You will discover how to collaborate in teams, listen effectively, master nonverbal communication, and participate in productive meetings. You'll learn about communicating across cultural boundaries. You'll learn a three-step process to help you write effective business messages, and you'll get specific tips for crafting a variety of business messages using a wide range of media, from social networks to blogs to online presentations. Develop these skills, and you'll start your business career with a clear competitive advantage.

## Communication Is Important to Your Company

Aside from the personal benefits, communication should be important to you because it's important to your company. Effective communication helps businesses in numerous ways. It provides[3]

*Effective communication delivers a variety of important benefits.*

- Closer ties with important communities in the marketplace.
- Opportunities to influence conversations, perceptions, and trends.
- Faster problem solving and stronger decision making based on timely, reliable information.
- Increased productivity and steadier work flow.
- Greater employee engagement with their work, leading to higher job satisfaction and lower employee turnover.

## What Makes Business Communication Effective?

Effective communication strengthens the connections between a company and all of its **stakeholders**, those groups affected in some way by the company's actions: customers, employees, shareholders, suppliers, neighbours, the community, the nation, and the world as a whole.[4]

To make your communication efforts as effective as possible, focus on making them practical, factual, concise, clear, and persuasive:

*Effective messages are practical, factual, concise, clear, and persuasive.*

- **Provide practical information.** Give recipients useful information, whether it's to help them perform a desired action or understand a new company policy.
- **Give facts rather than vague impressions.** Use concrete language, specific detail, and information that is clear, convincing, accurate, and ethical. Even when an opinion is called for, present compelling evidence to support your conclusion.
- **Present information in a concise, efficient manner.** Concise messages show respect for people's time, and they increase the chances of a positive response.
- **Clarify expectations and responsibilities.** Craft messages to generate a specific response from a specific audience. When appropriate, clearly state what you expect from audience members or what you can do for them.
- **Offer compelling, persuasive arguments and recommendations.** Show your readers precisely how they will benefit from responding to your message the way you want them to.

Keep these five characteristics in mind as you review Figure 1.2. You might notice that it is more formal and "professional sounding" than many of the messages you send now. Employers expect you to be able to communicate with a similar style.

## FIGURE 1.2 Effective Business Communication

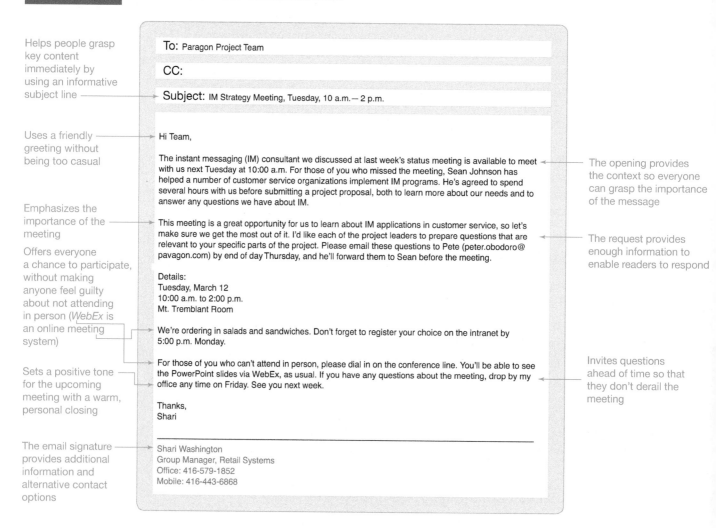

Helps people grasp key content immediately by using an informative subject line

Uses a friendly greeting without being too casual

Emphasizes the importance of the meeting

Offers everyone a chance to participate, without making anyone feel guilty about not attending in person (*WebEx* is an online meeting system)

Sets a positive tone for the upcoming meeting with a warm, personal closing

The email signature provides additional information and alternative contact options

The opening provides the context so everyone can grasp the importance of the message

The request provides enough information to enable readers to respond

Invites questions ahead of time so that they don't derail the meeting

**To:** Paragon Project Team

**CC:**

**Subject:** IM Strategy Meeting, Tuesday, 10 a.m.— 2 p.m.

Hi Team,

The instant messaging (IM) consultant we discussed at last week's status meeting is available to meet with us next Tuesday at 10:00 a.m. For those of you who missed the meeting, Sean Johnson has helped a number of customer service organizations implement IM programs. He's agreed to spend several hours with us before submitting a project proposal, both to learn more about our needs and to answer any questions we have about IM.

This meeting is a great opportunity for us to learn about IM applications in customer service, so let's make sure we get the most out of it. I'd like each of the project leaders to prepare questions that are relevant to your specific parts of the project. Please email these questions to Pete (peter.obodoro@ pavagon.com) by end of day Thursday, and he'll forward them to Sean before the meeting.

Details:
Tuesday, March 12
10:00 a.m. to 2:00 p.m.
Mt. Tremblant Room

We're ordering in salads and sandwiches. Don't forget to register your choice on the intranet by 5:00 p.m. Monday.

For those of you who can't attend in person, please dial in on the conference line. You'll be able to see the PowerPoint slides via WebEx, as usual. If you have any questions about the meeting, drop by my office any time on Friday. See you next week.

Thanks,
Shari

Shari Washington
Group Manager, Retail Systems
Office: 416-579-1852
Mobile: 416-443-6868

---

**LEARNING OBJECTIVE ②**
**Explain what it means to communicate as a professional in a business context.**

Communication is an essential part of being a successful professional.

# Communicating as a Professional

You've been communicating your entire life, of course, but if you don't have a lot of work experience yet, meeting the expectations of a professional environment might require some adjustment. A good place to start is to consider what it means to be a professional. **Professionalism** is the quality of performing at a high level and conducting oneself with purpose and pride. It means doing more than putting in the hours and collecting a paycheque; true professionals go beyond minimum expectations and commit to making meaningful contributions. Professionalism can be broken down into six distinct traits: striving to excel, being dependable and accountable, being a team player, demonstrating a sense of etiquette, making ethical decisions, and maintaining a positive outlook.

Professionalism depends on effective communication. For example, to be a team player, you have to be able to collaborate, resolve conflicts, and interact with a wide variety of personalities. Without strong communication skills, you won't be able to perform to your potential—and others won't recognize you as the professional you'd like to be. See Table 1.1.

This section offers a brief look at the skills that employers will expect you to have, the nature of communication in an organizational environment, and the importance of adopting an audience-centred approach.

| TABLE 1.1 | Elements of Professionalism |
| --- | --- |
| **TRAIT** | **WHAT IT MEANS TO PROFESSIONALS** |
| Strive to excel | Do their best at everything they do. Commit to continuous improvement. |
| Are dependable | Keep promises and meet commitments. Learn from mistakes and take responsibility for their errors. |
| Are team players | Keep the focus on the larger cause. Make others around them better. |
| Are respectful | Show respect for those around them. Understand that respecting others is not only good etiquette, it's good for one's career. |
| Are ethical | Strive to avoid ethical lapses. Weigh their options carefully when facing ethical dilemmas. |
| Are positive | Believe in what they're doing and in themselves. Don't complain about problems; they find them and fix them. |

## Understanding What Employers Expect from You

Given the importance of communication in business, employers expect you to be competent at a wide range of communication tasks:[5]

*Employers expect you to have strong communication skills and you can practise these in this course.*

- Organizing ideas and information logically and completely
- Expressing yourself coherently and persuasively in a variety of media
- Building persuasive arguments to gain acceptance for important ideas
- Evaluating data and information critically to know what you can and cannot trust
- Actively listening to others
- Communicating effectively with people from diverse backgrounds and with diverse experiences
- Using communication technologies effectively and efficiently
- Following accepted standards of grammar, spelling, and other aspects of high-quality writing and speaking
- Adapting your messages and communication styles to specific audiences and situations
- Communicating in a courteous manner that reflects contemporary expectations of business etiquette
- Communicating ethically, even when choices aren't crystal clear
- Respecting the confidentiality of private company information
- Following applicable laws and regulations
- Managing your time wisely and using resources efficiently

### REAL-TIME UPDATES

**Learn More by Reading This Article**

**Will your social media habits kill your career?**

Follow these tips to make sure your social media habits don't keep you from getting a job or derail your career after it has begun. Go to http://real-timeupdates.com/bce6 and click on Learn More. If you are using MyBCommLab, you can access Real-Time Updates within Business Communication Resources.

This is a long list, to be sure, but all these skills can be practised and developed over time. Start by taking advantage of the opportunities you'll have throughout this course, and you'll be well on your way to making a successful transition to the professional environment.

## Communicating in an Organizational Context

In addition to having the proper skills, you need to learn how to apply those skills in the business environment, which can be quite different from the social and scholastic environments you are used to. Every company has a unique communication system that

*You will need to adjust your communication habits to the more formal demands of business and the unique environment of your company.*

connects people within the organization and connects the organization to the outside world. The "system" in this broad sense is a complex combination of communication channels (such as the internet and department meetings), company policies, the organizational structure, and personal relationships.

To succeed in a job, you need to figure out how your company's system operates. For example, one company might rely heavily on instant messaging, social networks, and blogs that are used in an open, conversational way by everyone in the company. In contrast, another company might use a more rigid, formal approach, in which information and instructions are passed down from top managers, and employees are expected to follow the "chain of command" when seeking or distributing information.

## Adopting an Audience-Centred Approach

Focus on the needs of your audiences to make your messages more effective.

Successful business professionals take an **audience-centred approach** to communication, meaning that they focus on understanding and meeting the needs of their audiences (see Figure 1.3). Providing the information your audiences need is obviously an

---

| FIGURE 1.3 | Audience-Centred Communication in a Blog Post |

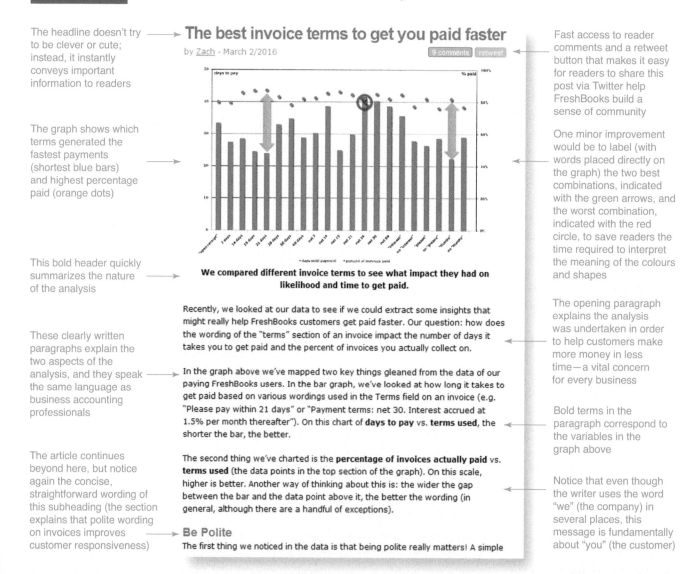

The headline doesn't try to be clever or cute; instead, it instantly conveys important information to readers

The graph shows which terms generated the fastest payments (shortest blue bars) and highest percentage paid (orange dots)

This bold header quickly summarizes the nature of the analysis

These clearly written paragraphs explain the two aspects of the analysis, and they speak the same language as business accounting professionals

The article continues beyond here, but notice again the concise, straightforward wording of this subheading (the section explains that polite wording on invoices improves customer responsiveness)

Fast access to reader comments and a retweet button that makes it easy for readers to share this post via Twitter help FreshBooks build a sense of community

One minor improvement would be to label (with words placed directly on the graph) the two best combinations, indicated with the green arrows, and the worst combination, indicated with the red circle, to save readers the time required to interpret the meaning of the colours and shapes

The opening paragraph explains the analysis was undertaken in order to help customers make more money in less time—a vital concern for every business

Bold terms in the paragraph correspond to the variables in the graph above

Notice that even though the writer uses the word "we" (the company) in several places, this message is fundamentally about "you" (the customer)

### The best invoice terms to get you paid faster
by Zach - March 2/2016

**We compared different invoice terms to see what impact they had on likelihood and time to get paid.**

Recently, we looked at our data to see if we could extract some insights that might really help FreshBooks customers get paid faster. Our question: how does the wording of the "terms" section of an invoice impact the number of days it takes you to get paid and the percent of invoices you actually collect on.

In the graph above we've mapped two key things gleaned from the data of our paying FreshBooks users. In the bar graph, we've looked at how long it takes to get paid based on various wordings used in the Terms field on an invoice (e.g. "Please pay within 21 days" or "Payment terms: net 30. Interest accrued at 1.5% per month thereafter"). On this chart of **days to pay** vs. **terms used**, the shorter the bar, the better.

The second thing we've charted is the **percentage of invoices actually paid** vs. **terms used** (the data points in the top section of the graph). On this scale, higher is better. Another way of thinking about this is: the wider the gap between the bar and the data point above it, the better the wording (in general, although there are a handful of exceptions).

**Be Polite**
The first thing we noticed in the data is that being polite really matters! A simple

important part of this approach, but your ability to listen, your style of writing and speaking, and your ability to maintain positive working relationships are also key. You'll have the chance to explore all these aspects throughout this course.

An important element of audience-centred communication is **etiquette**, the expected norms of behaviour in a particular situation. In today's hectic, competitive world, the notion of etiquette might seem outdated and unimportant. However, the way you conduct yourself can have a profound influence on your company's success and your career. When executives hire and promote you, they expect your behaviour to protect the company's reputation. The more you understand such expectations, the better chance you have of avoiding career-damaging mistakes.

Long lists of etiquette "rules" can be overwhelming, and you'll never be able to memorize all of them. Fortunately, you can count on three principles to get you through just about any situation: respect, courtesy, and common sense. As you encounter new situations, take a few minutes to learn the expectations of the other people involved. Don't be afraid to ask questions, either. People will respect your concern and curiosity. You'll gradually accumulate knowledge, which will help you feel comfortable and be effective in a wide range of business situations. Chapter 2 offers more information about business etiquette.

*Respect, courtesy, and common sense will help you avoid etiquette mistakes.*

# Exploring the Communication Process

**LEARNING OBJECTIVE 3**
Describe the communication process model and the ways that social media are changing the nature of business communication.

Even with the best intentions, communication efforts can fail. Messages can get lost or simply ignored. The receiver of a message can interpret it in ways the sender never imagined. In fact, two people receiving the same information can reach different conclusions about what it means.

Fortunately, by understanding communication as a process with distinct steps, you can improve the odds that your messages will reach their intended audiences and produce their intended effects. This section explores the communication process in two stages: first by following a message from one sender to one receiver in the basic communication model, and then expanding on that with multiple messages and participants in the social communication model.

## The Basic Communication Model

Many variations of the communication process model exist, but these eight steps provide a practical overview (see Figure 1.4):

*The communication process starts with a sender having an idea and then encoding the idea into a message that can be transferred to a receiver.*

1. **The sender has an idea.** Whether a communication effort will ultimately be effective starts right here and depends on the nature of the idea and the motivation for sending it. For example, if your motivation is to offer a solution to a problem, you have a better chance of crafting a meaningful message than if your motivation is merely to complain about a problem.
2. **The sender encodes the idea as a message.** When someone puts an idea into a **message**, he or she is **encoding** it, or expressing it in words or images. Much of the focus of this course is on developing the skills needed to successfully encode your ideas into effective messages.
3. **The sender produces the message in a transmittable medium.** With the appropriate message to express an idea, the sender now needs a **communication medium** to present that message to the intended audience. To update your boss on the status of a project, for instance, you might have a dozen or more media choices, from a phone call to a text message to a slideshow or video presentation.
4. **The sender transmits the message through a channel.** Just as technology continues to increase the number of media options, it also continues to provide **new communication channels** senders can use to transmit their messages. The distinction

FIGURE 1.4 | The Basic Communication Process

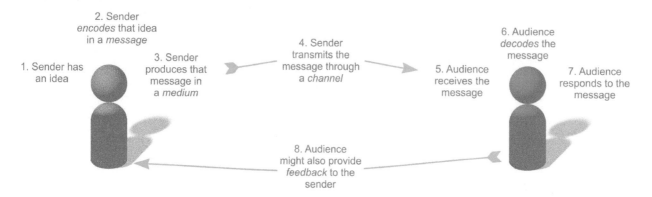

between medium and channel can get a bit murky, but think of the medium as the *form* a message takes (such as a Twitter update) and the channel as the system used to *deliver* the message (such as the internet).

5. **The audience receives the message.** If the channel functions properly, the message reaches its intended audience. However, mere arrival is not enough. For a message to truly be received, the recipient has to *sense* the presence of a message, *select* it from all the other messages clamouring for attention, and *perceive* it as an actual message (as opposed to random noise).[6]

Decoding is a complex process; receivers often extract different meanings from messages than the meanings senders intended.

6. **The receiver decodes the message.** After a message is received, the receiver needs to extract the idea from the message, a step known as **decoding**. Even well-crafted communication efforts can fail at this stage because extracting meaning is a highly personal process that is influenced by culture, experience, learning and thinking styles, hopes, fears, and even temporary moods. Moreover, audiences tend to extract the meaning they expect to get from a message, even if it's the opposite of what the sender intended.[7] In fact, rather than extracting the sender's meaning, it's more accurate to say that receivers re-create their own meanings from the message.

7. **The receiver responds to the message.** In most instances, senders want to accomplish more than simply delivering information. They often want receivers to respond in particular ways, whether it's to invest in a new business venture or to accept an explanation. Whether a receiver responds as the sender hopes depends on the receiver *remembering* the message long enough to act on it, being *able* to act on it, and being *motivated* to respond.

8. **The receiver provides feedback.** If a mechanism is available, receivers can "close the loop" in the communication process by giving the sender **feedback** that helps the sender evaluate the effectiveness of the communication effort. Feedback can be verbal (using written or spoken words), nonverbal (using gestures, facial expressions, or other signals), or both. Just like the original message, however, this feedback also needs to be decoded carefully. A smile, for example, can have many different meanings.

Considering the complexity of this process—and the barriers and distractions that often stand between sender and receiver—it should come as no surprise that communication efforts frequently fail to achieve the sender's objective. Fortunately, the better you understand the process, the more successful you'll be.

## The Social Communication Model

The basic model presented in Figure 1.4 does a good job of illustrating how a single idea moves from one sender to one receiver. In a larger sense, it also helps represent the traditional nature of much business communication, which was primarily defined by a *publishing* or *broadcasting* mindset. Externally, a company issued carefully scripted messages to a mass audience that often had few options for responding to those messages or initiating messages of their own. Customers and other interested parties had few ways to connect with one another to ask questions, share information, or offer support. Internally, communication tended to follow the same "we talk, you listen" model, with upper managers issuing directives to lower-level supervisors and employees.

However, thanks to the efforts of media innovations such as Facebook, a variety of technologies have enabled and inspired a new approach to business communication. In contrast to the publishing mindset, this new **social communication model** is interactive, conversational, and usually open to all who wish to participate. Audience members are no longer passive recipients of messages; now they are active participants in a conversation. Social media have given customers and other stakeholders a voice they did not have in the past, and businesses are listening. One of the most common uses of social media among businesses is monitoring online discussions about a company and its brands.[8]

The social communication model is interactive, conversational, and usually open to all who wish to participate.

Instead of transmitting a fixed message, a sender in a social media environment initiates a conversation by sharing valuable information. This information is often revised and reshaped by the web of participants as they share it and comment on it. People can add to it or take pieces from it, depending on their needs and interests.

Just as **Web 2.0** signifies the second generation of World Wide Web technologies (blogs, wikis, podcasts, and other *social media* tools that you'll read about in Chapter 6), **Business Communication 2.0** is a convenient label for this new approach to business communication. Figure 1.5 lists some of the important differences between traditional business communication and this new approach.

The social communication model offers many advantages, but it has a number of disadvantages as well. Potential problems include information overload (see page 16), fragmented attention, social media fatigue, information security risks, distractions that hurt productivity, and the blurring of the line between personal and professional lives, which can make it difficult for people to feel disconnected from work.[9]

Social media tools present some potential disadvantages that managers and employees need to consider.

---

**FIGURE 1.5**  Business Communication: 1.0 Versus 2.0

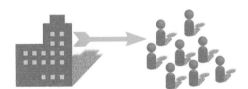

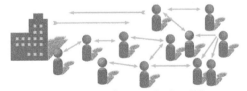

**Business Communication 1.0**
**"We Talk, You Listen"**

**Tendencies**
Publication, broadcast
Lecture
Intrusion
Unidirectional
One to many
Control
Low message frequency
Few channels
Information hoarding
Static
Hierarchical
Structured
Isolated
Planned
Resistive

**Business Communication 2.0**
**"Let's Have a Conversation"**

**Tendencies**
Conversation
Discussion
Permission
Bidirectional, multidirectional
One to one, many to many
Influence
High message frequency
Many channels
Information sharing
Dynamic
Egalitarian
Amorphous
Collaborative
Reactive
Responsive

Of course, no company, no matter how enthusiastically it embraces the social communication model, is going to be run as a club in which everyone has a say in every business matter. Instead, a hybrid approach is emerging in which some communications (such as strategic plans and policy documents) follow the traditional approach, while others (such as project management updates and customer support messages) follow the social model.

You can learn more about business uses of social media in Chapter 6.

**LEARNING OBJECTIVE** ④
Define *ethics*, explain the difference between an ethical dilemma and an ethical lapse, and list six guidelines for making ethical communication choices.

# Committing to Ethical Communication

**Ethics** are the accepted principles of conduct that govern behaviour within a society. Put another way, ethical principles define the boundary between right and wrong. Ethics is "knowing the difference between what you have a right to do and what is the right thing to do."[10] To make the right choices as a business communicator, you have a responsibility to think through not only what you say but also the consequences of saying it.

Ethical communication avoids deception and provides the information audiences need.

Ethical behaviour is a companywide concern, but because communication efforts are the public face of a company, they are subjected to particularly rigorous scrutiny from regulators, legislators, investors, consumer groups, environmental groups, labour organizations, and anyone else affected by business activities.

**Ethical communication** includes all relevant information, is true in every sense, does not violate the rights of others, and is not deceptive. By contrast, examples of unethical communication include the following:[11]

- **Plagiarism.** Plagiarism is using words and ideas you have taken from another source and presenting them as your own without giving credit to the original source. For example, if you were to copy phrasing from a website and include it in your report as if you had written it yourself, without citing the source, you would be plagiarizing. Besides being dishonest, presenting someone else's work as your own could also violate the legal rights of the original author. Theft of intellectual property is protected in Canada by patents and copyright. As a communicator, take care to give credit to the original sources of the material you use. In Chapter 10, you can find methods for proper source citation.
- **Leaving out information that is needed to fully understand a situation or misquoting someone in a way that misrepresents his or her intent.**
- **Misrepresenting numbers.** Statistics and other data can be unethically manipulated by increasing or decreasing numbers, exaggerating, altering statistics, or omitting numeric data.
- **Distorting visuals.** Images can be manipulated in unethical ways, such as making a product seem bigger than it really is or changing the scale of graphs and charts to exaggerate or conceal differences.
- **Failing to respect privacy or information security needs.** Failing to respect the privacy of others or failing to adequately protect information entrusted to your care can also be considered unethical (and is sometimes illegal).

Transparency involves giving audiences access to the information they need in order to make effective decisions.

The widespread use of social media has increased the attention given to the issue of **transparency**, which in this context refers to a sense of openness, of giving all participants in a conversation access to the information they need to accurately process the messages they are receiving. A key aspect of transparency is knowing who is behind the messages one receives. Consider the promotional event Netflix staged in Toronto to announce the launch of its streaming video service in Canada. The outdoor news conference seemed to attract dozens of curious people who were excited about the availability of Netflix. However, many of the people who "spontaneously" showed up were actually paid actors with instructions to "look really excited, particularly if asked by media to do any interviews about the prospect of Netflix in Canada." The company apologized when the stunt was exposed.[12]

Some governments are taking steps to protect consumers from practices they consider unethical. The European Union, for instance, outlaws a number of online marketing tactics, including "fake blogs," in which an employee or a paid agent posing as an independent consumer posts positive stories about a company's products.[13] Aside from the ethical and legal concerns involved, trying to fool the public is simply bad for business.[14]

## Distinguishing Ethical Dilemmas from Ethical Lapses

Some ethical questions are easy to recognize and resolve, but others are not. An ethical dilemma involves choosing among alternatives that aren't clear-cut. Perhaps two conflicting alternatives are both ethical and valid, or perhaps the alternatives lie somewhere in the grey area between clearly right and clearly wrong. Every company has responsibilities to multiple groups of people inside and outside the firm, and those various groups often have competing interests. Unlike a dilemma, an ethical lapse is a clearly unethical (and frequently illegal) choice.

*If you must choose between two ethical alternatives, you are facing an ethical dilemma.*

*If you choose an alternative that is unethical or illegal, you have committed an ethical lapse.*

## Making Ethical Choices

Ensuring ethical business communication requires three elements: ethical individuals, ethical company leadership, and the appropriate policies and structures to support ethical decision making.[15] Many companies establish an explicit ethics policy by using a written **code of ethics** to help employees determine what is acceptable.

*Responsible employers establish clear ethical guidelines for their employees to follow.*

Even the best codes and policies can't address every unique situation, however. If you find yourself in a situation in which the law or a code of ethics can't guide you, answer the following questions:[16]

* Have you defined the situation fairly and accurately?
* What is your intention in communicating this message?
* What impact will this message have on the people who receive it, or who might be affected by it?
* Will the message achieve the greatest possible good while doing the least possible harm?
* Will the assumptions you've made change over time? That is, will a decision that seems ethical now seem unethical in the future?
* Are you comfortable with your decision? Would you be embarrassed if it were printed in tomorrow's newspaper or spread across the internet?

**REAL-TIME UPDATES**

**Learn More by Watching This Presentation**

**Tips for avoiding ethical problems with social media**

New media choices have created a new set of ethical dilemmas and challenges. This presentation will help you recognize and avoid ethical lapses. Go to http://real-timeupdates.com/bce6 and click on Learn More. If you are using MyBCommLab, you can access Real-Time Updates within Business Communication Resources.

*Six questions can act as guidelines for making an ethical choice.*

# Communicating in a World of Diversity

**LEARNING OBJECTIVE ⑤**
**Explain how cultural diversity affects business communication and describe the steps you can take to communicate more effectively across cultural boundaries.**

Throughout your career, you will interact with colleagues from a variety of cultures, people who differ in race, age, gender, sexual orientation, national and regional attitudes and beliefs, family structure, religion, native language, cognitive and physical abilities, life experience, and educational background. This section looks at the advantages and challenges of a diverse workforce from a communication perspective, examines key differences among cultures, and offers advice for communicating across cultures.

## The Advantages and Challenges of a Diverse Workforce

A diverse workforce offers a broader spectrum of viewpoints and ideas, helps companies understand and identify with diverse markets, and enables companies to benefit from a wider range of employee talents. "It just makes good business sense," says Gord Nixon, CEO of Royal Bank of Canada.[17] According to IBM executive Ron Glover, more-diverse teams tend to be more innovative over the long term than teams composed of people from the same culture.[18]

*Diverse workforces offer numerous benefits, but they also pose some important communication challenges.*

Cultural symbols, beliefs, attitudes, values, expectations, and norms for behaviour influence communication.

For all their benefits, diverse workforces and markets do present some communication challenges, and understanding the effect of culture on communication is essential. **Culture** is a shared system of symbols, beliefs, attitudes, values, expectations, and norms for behaviour. Culture is often viewed as a matter of race, but it is much broader in scope. You are a member of several cultures, based on your national origin, religious beliefs, age, and other factors.

Culture influences the way people perceive the world and respond to others, which naturally affects the way they communicate as both senders and receivers. These influences operate on such a fundamental level that people often don't even recognize the influence of culture on their beliefs and behaviours.[19]

This subconscious effect of culture can create friction because it leads people to assume that everybody thinks and feels the way they do. However, differences between cultures can be profound.

The first step to making sure cultural differences don't impede communication is recognizing key factors that distinguish one culture from another. **Cultural competency** is an appreciation for cultural differences that affect communication and the ability to adjust one's communication style to ensure that efforts to send and receive messages across cultural boundaries are successful. It requires a combination of attitude, knowledge, and skills.[20]

## Key Aspects of Cultural Diversity

Improving your cultural sensitivity starts with recognizing the major ways in which cultures differ.

You don't need to become an expert in the details of every culture with which you do business, but you do need to attain a basic level of cultural proficiency to ensure successful communication.[21] You can start by recognizing and accommodating the differences described in the following sections. Be aware that this is an overview only, so some generalizations won't be accurate in every situation. Always consider the unique circumstances of each encounter when making communication decisions.

Cultural context plays a critical role in the communication process. In high-context cultures, communication relies less on the explicit content of a message than on the context of the message.

**CULTURAL CONTEXT**    Every attempt at communication occurs within a **cultural context**: the mixture of traditions, expectations, and unwritten social rules that help convey meaning between members of the same culture. Cultures vary widely in the role that context plays in communication.

In a **high-context culture,** people rely less on verbal communication and more on the context of nonverbal actions and environmental setting to convey meaning. Examples of high-context cultures include Japan, China, and many Middle Eastern and Southern European countries.[22] In such cultures, the rules of everyday life are rarely stated explicitly. Instead, as individuals grow up, they learn how to recognize situational cues (such as gestures and tone of voice) and how to respond as expected.[23] In a high-context culture, the primary role of communication is often building relationships, not exchanging information.[24]

In low-context cultures, communication relies more on the explicit content of a message than on the context of the message.

In a **low-context culture**, people rely more on the explicit content of the message and less on circumstances and cues to convey meaning. In other words, more of the conveyed meaning is encoded into the actual message itself.[25] Canada and many Northern European countries are considered low-context cultures.[26] For example, an English speaker feels responsible for transmitting the meaning of a message and often places sentences in strict chronological sequence to establish a clear cause-and-effect pattern.[27] In a low-context culture, rules and expectations are usually spelled out through explicit statements such as "Please wait until I'm finished."[28] Exchanging information is the primary task of communication in low-context cultures.[29]

The different expectations of low- and high-context cultures can create friction and misunderstanding when people try to communicate across cultural boundaries. The indirect style can be a source of confusion during discussions with people from low-context cultures, who are more accustomed to receiving direct answers. For example, people from a low-context culture might view the high-context emphasis on building relationships as a waste of time. Conversely, people from a high-context culture might view the low-context emphasis on information exchange and task completion as being insensitive to group harmony.[30] Discussing the differences between North American and Chinese business cultures, for instance, a North American executive working in China explained that "in the West, there is such a premium on getting things done quickly, but when you come to work in China, you need to work on listening and being more patient and understanding of local ways of doing business."[31]

Contextual differences are apparent in the way businesspeople approach situations such as decision making, problem solving, negotiating, interaction among levels in the organizational hierarchy, and socializing outside the workplace.[32] For instance, in low-context cultures, businesspeople tend to focus on the results of the decisions they face, a reflection of the cultural emphasis on logic and progress. In comparison, higher-context cultures emphasize the means or the method by which a decision will be made. Building or protecting relationships can be as important as the facts and information used in making the decisions.[33] Consequently, negotiators working on business deals in such cultures may spend most of their time together building relationships rather than hammering out contractual details.

**REAL-TIME UPDATES**

**Learn More by Reading This PDF**

**International etiquette tips**

These quick etiquette tips will smooth the way for working in major business centres around the world. Go to http://real-timeupdates.com/bce6 and click on Learn More. If you are using MyBCommLab, you can access Real-Time Updates within Business Communication Resources.

**LEGAL AND ETHICAL DIFFERENCES** Cultural context influences legal and ethical behaviour, which in turn can affect communication. For example, the meaning of business contracts can vary from culture to culture. While a manager from a North American company would tend to view a signed contract as the end of the negotiating process, with all the details hammered out, his or her counterpart in many Asian cultures might view the signed contract as an agreement to do business—and only then begin to negotiate the details of the deal.[34] As you conduct business with colleagues and customers around the world, you'll find that legal systems and ethical standards differ from culture to culture.

> Members of different cultures sometimes have different views of what is ethical or even legal.

Ethical principles are based to a large extent on cultural values, so trying to make ethical choices across cultures can be complicated. When communicating with people in other cultures, keep your messages ethical by applying four basic principles:[35]

* Actively seek mutual ground.
* Send and receive messages without judgment.
* Send messages that are honest.
* Show respect for cultural differences.

**SOCIAL CUSTOMS** Social behaviour is guided by numerous rules, some of them formal and specifically articulated (table manners are a good example) and others more informal and learned over time (such as the comfortable standing distance between two speakers in an office). The combination of formal and informal rules influences the overall behaviour of everyone in a society in areas such as manners, attitudes toward time, individual versus community values, attitudes toward status and wealth, and respect for authority. Understanding the nuances of social customs takes time and effort, but most businesspeople are happy to explain the habits and expectations of their culture. Plus, they will view your curiosity as a sign of respect.

> Whether formal or informal, the rules governing social customs differ from culture to culture.

**NONVERBAL COMMUNICATION** Nonverbal communication (communicating without words) is a vital part of the communication process. Factors ranging from facial expressions to style of dress can influence the way receivers decode messages, and the interpretation of nonverbal signals can vary widely from culture to culture. Gestures or clothing

> The meanings of gestures and other nonverbal signals can vary widely from culture to culture.

choices that you don't think twice about, for example, might seem inappropriate or even offensive to someone from another culture. You'll learn more about nonverbal communication in Chapter 2.

**AGE DIFFERENCES**   In some cultures, youth is associated with strength, energy, possibilities, and freedom, while age is often associated with declining powers and a loss of respect and authority. In contrast, in cultures that value age and seniority, longevity earns respect and increasing power and freedom.

In addition to cultural values associated with various life stages, multiple generations in the workplace present another dimension of diversity. For the first time in Canadian history, many workplaces employ up to four generations of workers.[36] Each of these generations has been shaped by dramatically different world events, social trends, and technological advances, so it is not surprising that they often have different values, expectations, and communication habits. For instance, Generation Y workers (those born between 1981 and 1995), also known as the Millennials, have a strong preference for communicating via short electronic messages, but baby boomers (born between 1946 and 1964) and Generation X workers (1965 to 1980) sometimes find these brief messages abrupt and impersonal.[37]

Each generation can bring particular strengths to the workplace. For instance, older workers can offer broader experience, the benefits of important business relationships nurtured over many years, and high degrees of "practical intelligence"—the ability to solve complex, poorly defined problems.[38] However, gaining the benefits of having multiple generations in a workplace may require some accommodation on everyone's part because of differing habits and perspectives.

**GENDER**   Gender influences workplace communication in several important ways. First, the perception of men and women in business varies from culture to culture, and gender bias can range from overt discrimination to subtle and even unconscious beliefs.

Second, although the ratio of men and women in entry-level professional positions is roughly equal, the percentage of management roles held by men increases steadily the further one looks up the corporate ladder. This imbalance can significantly affect communication in such areas as mentoring, which is a vital development opportunity for lower and middle managers who want to move into senior positions.

Third, evidence suggests that men and women tend to have somewhat different communication styles. Broadly speaking, men emphasize content and outcomes in their communication efforts, whereas women place a higher premium on relationship maintenance.[39] As one example, men are more likely than women to try to negotiate a pay raise. Changing these perceptions could go a long way toward improving communication and equity in the workplace.[40]

**RELIGIOUS DIFFERENCES**   As one of the most personal and influential aspects of life, religion brings potential for controversy in a work setting.[41] Some employees feel they should be able to express their beliefs in the workplace, but companies try to avoid situations in which openly expressed religious differences cause friction between employees or distract employees.

**ABILITY DIFFERENCES**   People whose hearing, vision, cognitive ability, or physical ability is impaired can be at a significant disadvantage in today's workplace. As with other types of diversity, it is important to show respect for individuals and be sensitive to differences. Employers can also invest in a variety of *assistive technologies* such as speech recognition software, touch screens, or ergonomic equipment to help employees with disabilities. These technologies give employees opportunities to pursue a greater range of career paths and give employers access to a broader base of talent.

Age is an important aspect of culture, both in the way different age groups are treated in a culture and in the cultural differences between age groups.

As with age, perceptions of gender roles differ among cultures.

Assistive technologies and other adaptations can help people with ability differences.

## Advice for Improving Intercultural Communication

In any cross-cultural situation, you can communicate more effectively if you remember the following tips:[42]

- Avoid **ethnocentrism**, the tendency to judge all other groups according to the standards, behaviours, and customs of one's own group. When making such comparisons, people too often decide that their own group is superior.[43]
- Similarly, avoid **stereotyping**, or assigning a wide range of generalized—and often inaccurate—attributes to an individual on the basis of membership in a particular group, without considering the individual's unique characteristics.
- Don't automatically assume that others think, believe, or behave as you do.
- Accept differences in others without judging them.
- Learn how to communicate respect in various cultures.
- Tolerate ambiguity and control your frustration.
- Don't be distracted by superficial factors such as personal appearance.
- Recognize your own cultural biases.
- Be flexible and be prepared to change your habits and attitudes.
- Observe and learn; the more you learn, the more effective you'll be.

Travel guidebooks are a great source of information about norms and customs in other countries. Also, check to see whether your library has online access to the Culture-Gram database or review the country profiles at **www.kwintessential.co.uk** (look for Country Etiquette Guides under Resources).

*Effective intercultural communication starts with efforts to avoid ethnocentrism and stereotyping.*

**WRITING FOR MULTILINGUAL AUDIENCES** Ideally, businesses can communicate with employees, customers, and other stakeholders in their native languages, and many companies invest a lot of time and money in translating print and online communication to achieve this. However, translation isn't always cost effective or possible. To write effectively for people who may not be comfortable using your language, remember these tips (see Figure 1.6):[44]

- **Use plain language.** Use short, precise words that say exactly what you mean.
- **Avoid words with multiple meanings.** For example, "assess" can mean to analyze or to impose a fee.
- **Be clear.** Rely on specific terms and concrete examples to explain your points.
- **Cite numbers carefully.** Use figures (such as 27) instead of spelling numbers out (twenty-seven).
- **Avoid slang and be careful with technical jargon and abbreviations.** Slang and other nonstandard usages can be difficult or impossible for your audience to translate.
- **Be brief.** Construct sentences that are short and simple.
- **Use short paragraphs.** Each paragraph should contain one topic.
- **Use transitions generously.** Help readers follow your train of thought. You'll learn more about transitions in Chapter 4.

*Important tips for improving your intercultural writing include using plain language, avoiding slang, and using short sentences and short paragraphs.*

**SPEAKING WITH MULTILINGUAL AUDIENCES** When speaking to people whose native language is not your own, you may find these tips helpful:

- **Speak clearly, simply, and relatively slowly.** Pronounce words clearly, stop at distinct punctuation points, and make one point at a time.
- **Look for feedback, but interpret it carefully.** Nods and smiles don't necessarily mean understanding.
- **Rephrase if necessary.** If someone doesn't seem to understand you, rephrase using simpler words.
- **Clarify your meaning with repetition and examples.** Use concrete and specific examples to illustrate difficult or vague ideas.

*Important tips for speaking with multilingual audiences include speaking clearly and slowly, looking for feedback, and listening carefully.*

## FIGURE 1.6  Writing for Multilingual Audiences

**Poor**

### Assessing the Office Merger: Bad, Bad, and Not Good

APRIL 22, 2015 BY CYNTHIA MARTIN    LEAVE A COMMENT (EDIT)

When we folded the Brampton office into Toronto headquarters last year, we anticipated some significant challenges during and after the consolidation. Closing a facility and combining two teams into one is never easy, but as I explained at the time, economic pressures—primarily the need to improve our all-important average profit per client metric—forced us to make a difficult decision.

I wish I could say that we hit this one out of the park. If one were to judge from the three most important indicators, we have not yet accomplished our goals. Our performance has actually declined in two of the three. The latest customer satisfaction survey shows a fifteen-percent increase in the number of customers who say they will consider other service providers when their current contracts expire. Employee satisfaction scores have also dropped since the offices were merged. Only seventy-two percent of employees rate their job satisfaction as "high" or "very high," compared to eighty-seven percent before the merger. The only measure of the three that has stayed steady is our average profit per client. While this might sound like good news in comparison to the other two, improving this variable was the primary reason for combining the offices in the first place.

I'll be blunt: This ain't gonna cut it, folks.

FILED UNDER: STRATEGIC PLANNING

The headline tries to be clever regarding the three factors discussed in the post, but the message is not clear.

"Folded" is an example of an English word with multiple meanings; these multiple possibilities make translation more difficult and can lead to confusion.

Complicated sentences are difficult to translate and force readers to follow multiple ideas at once.

The idiomatic phrase "hit one out of the park" might not make sense to readers who aren't familiar with baseball.

Spelling out numbers instead of using numerals creates more work for readers.

Long paragraphs are visually intimidating and more difficult to process.

Nonstandard language ("ain't") and the idiomatic phrase "cut it" will confuse some readers and the tone will be offensive.

**Improved**

The clear, direct headline leaves no question about the content of the message.

Simpler sentence structures are easier to translate and create fewer chances for misunderstanding.

Breaking the long paragraph into a brief introduction and three bullet points simplifies reading and makes it easy to find the key points.

Numerals are easier to read quickly than spelled-out quantities.

Standard English and plain language decrease the potential for confusion.

### We Have Not Met Our Goals for the Office Merger

APRIL 22, 2015 BY CYNTHIA MARTIN    LEAVE A COMMENT (EDIT)

When we merged the Brampton office with Toronto headquarters last year, we knew the move would be challenging. Closing a facility and combining two teams is never easy, but economic pressures forced us to make a difficult decision.

Unfortunately, we have not met the three goals we had for the merger: improving customer satisfaction, improving employee satisfaction, and increasing the average profit per client. In fact, our performance has actually *declined* in two of the three areas:

- The latest customer satisfaction survey shows a 15-percent increase in the number of customers who say they will consider other service providers when their current contracts expire.
- Employee satisfaction has also dropped since the offices were merged. Only 72 percent of employees rate their job satisfaction as "high" or "very high," compared to 87 percent before the merger.
- The only indicator of the three that has remained steady is our average profit per client. While this might sound like good news in comparison to the other two, improving this variable was the primary reason for combining the offices.

Clearly, we need to take a closer look at this situation to see where we went wrong and where we can make improvements.

FILED UNDER: STRATEGIC PLANNING

**Pointers for Writing for Multilingual Audiences**
- Use plain language.
- Be clear.
- Cite numbers carefully.
- Avoid slang and be careful with technical jargon and abbreviations.
- Be brief.
- Use short paragraphs.
- Use transitions generously.

- **Don't talk down to the other person.** Don't blame the listener for not understanding. Say, "Am I going too fast?" rather than "Is this too difficult for you?"
- **Learn important phrases in your audience's language.** Learning common greetings and a few simple phrases simplifies initial contact and shows respect.

- **Listen carefully and respectfully.** If you don't understand a comment, ask the person to repeat it.
- **Adapt your conversation style to the other person's.** For instance, if the other person appears to be direct and straightforward, use that style as well.
- **Check frequently for comprehension.** After you make each point, pause to gauge the other person's comprehension before moving on.
- **Clarify what will happen next.** At the end of a conversation, be sure that you and the other person agree on what has been said and decided.

Finally, remember that oral communication can be more difficult for audiences because it happens in real time and in the presence of other people. In some situations, written communication will be more successful because it gives a reader the opportunity to translate in private and at his or her own pace.

# Using Technology to Improve Communication

LEARNING OBJECTIVE 6
**List four general guidelines for using communication technology effectively.**

Today's businesses rely heavily on technology to facilitate the communication process. In fact, many of the technologies you might use in your personal life, from Facebook to Twitter to video games to virtual worlds, are also used in business (see Figure 1.6).

The benefits of technology are not automatic, of course. To communicate effectively, you need to keep technology in perspective, use technological tools productively, guard against information overload, and disengage from the computer frequently to communicate in person.

## Keeping Technology in Perspective

Don't let technology overwhelm the communication process.

Remember that technology is an aid to communication, not a replacement for it. Technology can't think for you, make up for a lack of essential skills, or ensure that communication really happens. No matter how exciting or popular it may be, a technology has value only if it helps deliver the right information to the right people at the right time.

## Using Tools Productively

You don't have to become an expert to use most communication technologies effectively, but you do need to be familiar with the basic features and functions of the tools your employer expects you to use. For instance, if you don't know the basic functions of your word processing or wiki software, you could spend hours trying to format a document that a skilled user could format in minutes.

## Guarding Against Information Overload

The overuse or misuse of communication technology can lead to **information overload**, in which people receive more information than they can effectively process. Information overload makes it difficult to discriminate between useful and useless information, inhibits the ability to think deeply about complex situations, lowers productivity, and amplifies employee stress both on the job and at home—even to the point of causing health and relationship problems.[45]

Everyone has an important role to play in reducing information overload.

As a sender, make sure every message you intend to send is meaningful and important to your receivers. As a recipient, take steps to control the number and types of messages you receive. Use the filtering features of your communication systems to isolate high-priority messages. Also, be wary of following too many blogs, Twitter accounts, and other sources of recurring messages. Take care when expanding your social networks online so that you don't get buried in too many posts and updates and suffer social media fatigue.[46]

No matter how much technology is involved, communication will always be about people connecting with people.

## Reconnecting with People Frequently

Even the best technologies can hinder communication if they are overused. For instance, a common complaint among employees is that managers rely too heavily on email and don't communicate face-to-face often enough.[47] Speaking with people over the phone or in person can take more time and effort, and can sometimes force you to confront unpleasant situations directly, but it is often essential for solving tough problems and maintaining productive relationships.[48] For example, Cory Edwards, director of social media and company reputation at Dell, regularly organizes gatherings of key customers because, as he says, "in person relationships always trump online relationships."[49]

Even the best communication technologies can't show people who you really are. You might be funny, bright, and helpful, but you're just a voice on the phone or a name on a screen until people can interact with you in person. Remember to step out from behind the technology frequently to learn more about the people you work with, and to let them learn more about you.

# LEARNING OBJECTIVES: Check Your Progress

**1 OBJECTIVE Define *communication*, and explain the importance of effective business communication.**

Communication is the process of transferring information and meaning between senders and receivers, using one or more written, oral, visual, or electronic media. The ability to communicate well will play a key role in your success as a business professional. Communication is essential to every function in business, and poor communication skills will limit your career prospects, no matter how ambitious or skilled you are in other areas. Communication skills also give you an important competitive advantage in the job market.

As an effective communicator, you will be more valuable to your company as well, because good communication skills help companies in many ways: building closer ties with important communities in the marketplace; influencing conversations, perceptions, and trends; increasing productivity and solving problems in less time; attaining better financial results and higher return for investors; enabling earlier warning of potential problems; making better decisions; creating more compelling promotional messages; and improving employee engagement.

To make your communication efforts as effective as possible, focus on making them practical, factual, concise, clear, and persuasive.

**2 OBJECTIVE Explain what it means to communicate as a professional in a business context.**

Communicating as a professional starts with being a professional, which embodies striving to excel, being dependable and accountable, being a team player, demonstrating a sense of etiquette, making ethical decisions, and maintaining a positive outlook.

As a professional, you will be expected to bring a wide range of communication skills, including organizing ideas and information; expressing yourself coherently and persuasively in a variety of media; building persuasive arguments; evaluating data and information critically; actively listening to others; communicating effectively with diverse audiences; using communication technologies; following accepted standards of grammar, spelling, and other aspects of high-quality writing and speaking; adapting your messages and communication styles as needed; demonstrating strong business etiquette; communicating ethically; respecting confidentiality; following applicable laws and regulations; managing your time wisely; and using resources efficiently.

Communicating in an organizational context involves adapting your skills to a professional environment and using the company's communication system (in the broadest sense of the word) to gather and distribute information. An audience-centred approach to communication means focusing on understanding and meeting the needs of all your audience members, rather than focusing on your own needs.

**3 OBJECTIVE Describe the communication process model and the ways that social media are changing the nature of business communication.**

Communication can be modelled as an eight-step process: (1) the sender has an idea, (2) encodes that idea in a message, (3) produces the message in a transmittable medium, and (4) transmits the message through a channel. The audience (5) receives the message, (6) decodes the message, (7) responds to the message, and (8) provides feedback to the sender.

Social media have given customers and other stakeholders a voice they did not have in the past by giving them the tools to gather information from multiple sources, to respond to companies and other organizations, and to initiate conversations in the marketplace. Social media are also changing the nature of messages. A message initiated by one party is often revised and reshaped by the web of participants as they share it and comment on it.

**4 OBJECTIVE Define *ethics*, explain the difference between an ethical dilemma and an ethical lapse, and list six guidelines for making ethical communication choices.**

Ethics are the accepted principles of conduct that govern behaviour within a society; they define the boundary between right and wrong. Ethical communication includes all relevant information, is true in every sense, does not violate the rights of others, and is not deceptive.

An ethical dilemma involves choosing among alternatives that aren't clear-cut; an ethical lapse is a clearly unethical (and frequently illegal) choice. To ensure the decisions you make are ethical, follow these six guidelines: make sure you have defined the situation fairly and accurately, make sure your intentions are honest and fair, understand the impact your messages will have on others, ensure that your messages will achieve the greatest possible good while doing the least possible harm, make sure your underlying assumptions won't change over time, and make sure you are comfortable with your choices.

**5 OBJECTIVE Explain how cultural diversity affects business communication and describe the steps you can take to communicate more effectively across cultural boundaries.**

Cultural diversity affects business communication because culture influences the way people create, send, and interpret messages. Moreover, the influences of culture can be profound, and they are often unrecognized by the people involved. Major aspects of culture that affect communication include cultural context, legal and ethical differences, social customs, nonverbal communication, age differences, gender, religion, and ability.

To communicate effectively across cultures, avoid ethnocentrism and stereotyping, don't make assumptions about others' beliefs and values, avoid judgment, learn to communicate respect, tolerate ambiguity, don't be distracted by superficial elements, recognize your own cultural biases, be flexible, and learn about cultures in which you do business. Also, follow the advice for writing and speaking (page 15) in multilingual environments.

**6 OBJECTIVE List four general guidelines for using communication technology effectively.**

To help avoid the potential drawbacks of using communication technology, (1) keep technology in perspective so that it doesn't overwhelm the communication process, (2) learn to use your tools productively, (3) guard against information overload by sending only those messages of value to your audiences and by protecting yourself from too many low-value incoming messages, and (4) disengage from the computer frequently to communicate in person.

---

## MyBCommLab®

Go to MyBCommLab for everything you need to help you succeed in the job you've always wanted! Tools and resources include the following:
• Writing Activities    • Document Makeovers
• Video Exercises    • Grammar Exercises—and much more!

---

## Practise Your Grammar

Effective business communication starts with strong grammar skills. To improve your grammar skills, go to MyBCommLab, where you'll find exercises and diagnostic tests to help you produce clear, effective communication.

## Test Your Knowledge

To review chapter content related to each question, refer to the indicated Learning Objective.

1. What are the six traits of professionalism? L.O.❷
2. Why should communicators take an audience-centred approach to communication? L.O.❷

3. Define *ethics* and explain what ethical communication involves. L.O.❹
4. How does cultural context affect communication? L.O.❺
5. Why is it important to also connect in person when using technology to communicate? L.O.❻

## Apply Your Knowledge

To review chapter content related to each question, refer to the indicated Learning Objective.

1. Why do you think communication is vital to the success of every business organization? Explain briefly. L.O.❶
2. How does the presence of a reader comments feature on a corporate blog reflect audience-centred communication? L.O.❷
3. Because of your excellent communication skills, your boss always asks you to write his reports for him. But when the CEO compliments him on his logical organization and clear writing style, your boss responds as if he'd written all those reports himself. What kind of ethical choice does this represent? What can you do in this situation? Briefly explain your solution and your reasoning. L.O.❹

4. Your company has relocated to Vancouver, where a Vietnamese subculture is strongly established. Many employees will be from this subculture. As a member of the human resources department, what suggestions could you make to improve communication between management and the Vietnamese Canadians your company is hiring? L.O.❺
5. What kinds of workplace challenges could arise in communications among employees of different generations (for example, between Millennials, Boomers, and Generation X)? How could generational differences influence these employees' choices about methods for communicating? L.O.❻

## Practise Your Skills

### ACTIVITIES

Each activity is labelled according to the primary skill or skills you will need to use. To review relevant chapter content, you can refer to the indicated Learning Objective. In some instances, supporting information will be found in another chapter, as indicated.

1. **Writing: Compositional Modes: Summaries** L.O.❶, **Chapter 3** Write a paragraph introducing yourself to your instructor and your class. Address such areas as your background, interests, achievements, and goals. Submit your paragraph by email, through a blog, or using a social network, as indicated by your instructor.
2. **Media Skills: Microblogging** L.O.❶, **Chapter 6** Write four messages of no more than 140 characters each (short enough to work as Twitter tweets) to persuade other students to take a business communication course. Think of the first message as the "headline" of an advertisement that makes a bold promise about the value this course offers every aspiring business professional. The next three messages should be support points that provide evidence to back up the promise made in the first message.[50]
3. **Fundamentals: Analyzing Communication Effectiveness** L.O.❶ Identify a video clip (on YouTube or another online source) that you believe represents an example of effective communication. It can be in any context, business or otherwise, but make sure it is something appropriate to discuss in class. Post a link to the video on your class blog or discussion forum, along with a brief written summary of why you think this example shows effective communication in action.

4. **Planning: Assessing Audience Needs** L.O.❷, **Chapter 3** Choose a business career that sounds interesting to you and imagine that you are getting ready to apply for jobs in that field. Naturally, you want to create a compelling, audience-focused resumé that answers the key questions a hiring manager is most likely to have. Identify three personal or professional qualities you have that would be important for someone in this career field. Write a brief statement (one or two sentences) about each quality, describing in audience-focused terms how you can contribute to a company. Submit your statements via email or class blog.

5. **Communication Etiquette: Communicating with Sensitivity and Tact** L.O.❷ Potential customers often visit your production facility before making purchase decisions. You and the people who report to you in the sales department have received extensive training in etiquette issues because you frequently deal with high-profile clients. However, the rest of the workforce has not received such training, and you worry that someone might inadvertently say or do something that would offend one of these potential customers. In a two-paragraph email, explain to the general manager why you think anyone who might come in contact with customers should receive basic etiquette training.

6. **Fundamentals: Evaluating Communication Effectiveness** L.O.❸ Use the eight phases of the communication process to analyze a miscommunication you've recently had with a co-worker, supervisor, classmate, instructor, friend, or family member. What idea were you trying to share? How did you encode and transmit it? Did the receiver get the message? Did the receiver decode the message as you had intended? How do you know? Based on your analysis, what do you think prevented your successful communication in this instance? Summarize your conclusions in an email message to your instructor.

7. **Writing: Compositional Modes: Persuasion** L.O.❸, **Chapter 9** Social media use varies widely from company to company. Some firms enthusiastically embrace these new tools and new approaches. Others have taken a more cautious approach, either delaying the adoption of social media or restricting their use. You work for a manufacturing firm that prohibits employees from using social media during work hours. Company management believes that social media offer little or no business value and distract employees from more important duties. In a brief email message to your boss, identify the ways that social media are changing the communication process and relationships between companies and their employees, customers, and communities. Provide at least one example of a real manufacturing company that uses social media.

8. **Communication Ethics: Distinguishing Ethical Dilemmas and Ethical Lapses** L.O.❹ In a report of no more than one page, explain why you think each of the following is or is not ethical:
   a. De-emphasizing negative test results in a report on your product idea
   b. Taking an office computer home to finish a work-related assignment
   c. Telling an associate and close friend that she should pay more attention to her work responsibilities or management will fire her
   d. Recommending the purchase of excess equipment to use up your allocated funds before the end of the fiscal year so that your budget won't be cut next year

9. **Communication Ethics: Protecting Company Resources** L.O.❹ Blogging has become a popular way for employees to communicate with customers and other parties outside the company. In some cases, employee blogs have been quite beneficial for both companies and their customers, providing helpful information and putting a human face on otherwise formal and imposing corporations. However, in some cases, employees have been fired for posting information that their employers said was inappropriate. One particular area of concern is criticism of the company or individual managers. Should employees be allowed to criticize their employers in a public forum such as a blog? In a brief email message, argue for or against company policies that prohibit this type of information in employee blogs. What could companies include in social media policies to prevent problems?

10. **Communication Ethics: Resolving Ethical Dilemmas** L.O.❹ Knowing that you have numerous friends throughout the company, your boss relies on you for feedback concerning employee morale and other issues affecting the staff. She recently approached you and asked you to start reporting any behaviour that might violate company policies, from taking office supplies home to making personal long-distance calls. List the issues you'd like to discuss with her before you respond to her request.

11. **Intercultural Communication: Recognizing Cultural Variations** L.O.❺ Your company represents a Canadian toy company that is negotiating to buy miniature truck wheels from a manufacturer in Osaka, Japan. In the first meeting, your boss explains that your company expects to control the design of the wheels as well as the materials that are used to make them. The manufacturer's representative looks

down and says softly, "Perhaps that will be difficult." Your boss presses for agreement, and to emphasize your company's willingness to buy, he shows the prepared contract he's brought with him. However, the manufacturer seems increasingly vague and uninterested. In an email message to your instructor, identify the cultural differences that may be interfering with effective communication in this situation.

12. **Intercultural Communication: Recognizing Cultural Variations; Collaboration: Solving Problems** L.O.❺, **Chapter 2** Working with two other students, prepare a list of 10 examples of slang (in your own language) that would probably be misinterpreted or misunderstood during a business conversation with someone from another culture. Next to each example, suggest other words you might use to convey the same message. Do the alternatives mean exactly the same as the original slang or idiom? Summarize your findings in an email message or post for a class blog.

13. **Intercultural Communication: Recognizing Cultural Variations** L.O.❺ Choose a specific country or First Nations culture in Canada that you are not familiar with. Research the culture and write a one-page report outlining what a Canadian businessperson would need to know about concepts of personal space and rules of social behaviour in order to conduct business successfully in that culture.

14. **Intercultural Communication: Recognizing Cultural Variations** L.O.❺ Differences in gender, age, and physical and cognitive abilities contribute to the diversity of today's workforce. Working with a classmate, role-play a conversation in which

a. A woman is being interviewed for a job by a male human resources manager.

b. An older person is being interviewed for a job by a younger human resources manager.

c. A person using a wheelchair is being interviewed for a job by a person who can walk.

How did differences between the applicant and the interviewer shape the communication? What can you do to improve communication in such situations? Summarize your findings in an email message or post for a class blog.

15. **Technology: Using Communication Tools** L.O.❻ Find a free online communication service that you have no experience using as a content creator or contributor. Services to consider include blogging (such as Blogger), microblogging (such as Twitter), community Q&A sites (such as Yahoo! Answers), and user-generated content sites (such as Flickr). Perform a basic task such as opening an account or setting up a blog. Was the task easy to perform? Were the instructions clear? Could you find help online if you needed it? Is there anything about the experience that could be improved? Summarize your conclusions in a brief email message to your instructor.

16. **Intercultural Communication: Recognizing Differences, Collaboration** L.O.❺, **Chapter 2**

**Part One** Work in a group of three. Each group member should research one of the following generations: Generation Y/Millennials, Generation X, and Baby Boomers.

Have each group member summarize facts about the generation he or she researched. Cover the following main topics:

a. Range of birth years

b. Age range now

c. Two famous people of this generation

d. Big events that occurred when this generation was between the ages of 5 and 20

e. Common values attributed to the generation

f. Preferences this generation has in receiving information and communicating

Include a list of your sources and bring them, along with your notes, to the next class.

**Part Two** Form a new group with all the classmates who researched the same generation that you did. Compare your notes to gain even more insights about your topic. What points did you find in common?

**Part Three** Return to your original group of three and deliver a two- to three-minute oral presentation on the generation you researched.

**Part Four** Write a reflection in an email message to your instructor summarizing what you learned from the presentations and your own research. Include your own experience of working with others from different generations. How could a business professional use this type of knowledge to be an effective communicator?

# Intercultural Communication

## Test Your Intercultural Knowledge

Never take anything for granted when you're doing business in a foreign country. All sorts of assumptions that are valid in one place can cause you problems elsewhere if you fail to consider that customs may vary. Here are several true stories about businesspeople who blundered by overlooking some simple but important cultural differences. Can you spot the wrong assumptions that led these people astray?

1. You're tired of the discussion and you want to move on to a new topic. You ask your Australian business associate, "Can we table this for a while?" To your dismay, your colleague keeps right on discussing just what you want to put aside. Are Australians that inconsiderate?

2. You finally made the long trip overseas to meet the new German director of your division. Despite slow traffic, you arrive only four minutes late. His door is shut, so you knock on it and walk in. The chair is too far away from the desk, so you pick it up and move it closer. Then you lean over the desk, stick out your hand, and say, "Good morning, Hans, it's nice to meet you." Of course, you're baffled by his chilly reaction. Why?

3. Your meeting went better than you'd ever expected. In fact, you found the Japanese representative for your new advertising agency to be very agreeable; she said yes to just about everything. When you share your enthusiasm with your boss, he doesn't appear very excited. Why?

4. You've finally closed the deal, after exhausting both your patience and your company's travel budget. Now, two weeks later, your Chinese customers are asking for special considerations that change the terms of the agreement. How could they do this? Why are they doing it? And, most important, what should you do?

In each case, the problems have resulted from inaccurate assumptions. Here are explanations of what went wrong:

1. To "table" something in Australia means to bring it forward for discussion. This is the opposite of what North Americans usually mean. The English that's spoken in Australia is closer to British than to North American English. If you are doing business in Australia, become familiar with the local vocabulary. Note the tendency to shorten just about any word whenever possible and adding "ie" to it is a form of familiar slang: for example, *brolly* (umbrella) and *lollie* (candy). And yes, it's true: "G'day" is the standard greeting. Use it.

2. You've just broken four rules of German polite behaviour: punctuality, privacy, personal space, and proper greetings. In time-conscious Germany, you should never arrive even a few minutes late. Also, Germans like their privacy and space, and they adhere to formal greetings of "Frau" and "Herr," even if the business association has lasted for years.

3. The word yes may not always mean "yes" in the Western sense. Japanese people may say yes to confirm they have heard or understood something but not necessarily to indicate that they agree with it. You'll seldom get a direct "no." Some of the ways that Japanese people say no indirectly include "It will be difficult," "I will ask my supervisor," "I'm not sure," "We will think about it," and "I see."

4. For most North American businesspeople, the contract represents the end of the negotiation. For Chinese businesspeople, however, it's just the beginning. Once a deal is made, Chinese negotiators view their counterparts as trustworthy partners who can be relied on for special favours—such as new terms in the contract.

## Applications for Success

Learn how to improve your cultural savvy and gain an international competitive advantage. Visit Cultural Savvy (www.culturalsavvy.com) and read the country reports and cultural tips. Follow the site's links to tips, articles, books, and more.

Answer the following questions:

1. Why should you avoid humour when communicating with people of a different culture?

2. Every culture has its own business protocol. What should you know about a culture's business protocol before you do business within that culture?

3. What are some examples of cultural gift-giving taboos?

# 2

# Mastering Team Skills and Interpersonal Communication

## LEARNING OBJECTIVES

*After studying this chapter, you will be able to*

1. List the advantages and disadvantages of working in teams and describe the characteristics of effective teams.

2. Offer guidelines for collaborative communication, identify major collaboration technologies, and explain how to give constructive feedback.

3. List the key steps needed to ensure productive team meetings and identify the most common meeting technologies.

4. Describe the listening process and explain how good listeners overcome barriers at each stage of the process.

5. Explain the importance of nonverbal communication and identify six major categories of nonverbal expression.

6. Explain the importance of business etiquette and identify three key areas in which good etiquette is essential.

As vice-president responsible for human resources, communication, and corporate affairs for Xerox Canada, Tony Martino relied on effective communication among team members and between teams and upper management. He used meetings to bring people together to solve business problems and help ensure that participants will be committed to the implementation. "To succeed," says Martino, "you need to gather as much input as possible to develop a good business solution. Listening, clarifying, testing understanding, and truly hearing what people are saying makes the difference in teamwork and success."

This chapter focuses on the communication skills you need in order to work well in team settings and on important interpersonal communication skills that will help you on the job: productive meetings, active listening, nonverbal communication, and business etiquette.

## Communicating Effectively in Teams

**Collaboration**—working together to meet complex challenges—has become a core job responsibility for roughly half the workforce.[1] No matter what career path you pursue, it's a virtual guarantee that you will be expected to collaborate in at least some of your work activities. Your communication skills will pay off in these interactions, because the productivity and quality of collaborative efforts depend heavily on communication skills.

A **team** is a unit of two or more people who share a mission and the responsibility for working to achieve their goal.[2] Businesses use a wide variety of teams, from short-term problem-solving teams to permanent committees that sometimes become formal parts of the organization structure. You will participate in teams throughout your career, so developing the skills to communicate successfully in team settings will give you an important advantage. Some teams meet and work together in person, whereas others are virtual teams, whose members work in different locations and interact through one or more electronic channels. Communication skills are particularly important with **virtual teams**, because the physical separation can complicate everything from helping new members get oriented to capturing the knowledge a team accumulates over time.[3]

## Advantages and Disadvantages of Teams

When teams are successful, they can improve productivity, creativity, employee involvement, and even job security.[4] Teams are often at the core of **participative management**, the effort to involve employees in the company's decision making. These are some advantages of successful teamwork:[5]

*Team members have a shared mission and are collectively responsible for the team's performance.*

- **Increased information and knowledge.** By pooling the experience of several individuals, a team has access to more information in the decision-making process.
- **Increased diversity of views.** Bringing a variety of perspectives can improve decision making, provided these diverse viewpoints are guided by a shared goal.[6]
- **Increased acceptance of a solution.** Those who participate in making a decision are more likely to support it and encourage others to accept it.
- **Higher performance levels.** Effective teams can be better than top-performing individuals at solving complex problems.[7]

Although teamwork has many advantages, teams need to be aware of and work to counter the following potential disadvantages:

- **Groupthink.** Like other social structures, business teams can generate tremendous pressures to conform. **Groupthink** occurs when peer pressures cause individual team members to withhold contrary or unpopular opinions and to go along with decisions they don't really believe in. The result can be decisions that are worse than the choices the team members might have made individually.
- **Hidden agendas.** Some team members may have a **hidden agenda**—private, counterproductive motives, such as a desire to take control of the group, to undermine someone else on the team, or to pursue an incompatible goal.
- **Cost.** Aligning schedules, arranging meetings, and coordinating individual parts of a project can take a lot of time and money.

## Characteristics of Effective Teams

Effective teams share a number of traits, including a clear objective, a shared sense of purpose, full engagement from all team members, procedures for reaching decisions by consensus, and the right mix of creative and technical talents for the tasks at hand. While all these traits contribute to team success, however, the single most important factor is how well the team members communicate.[8]

*Effective teams*
- *Understand their purpose*
- *Communicate openly and honestly*
- *Build consensus*
- *Think creatively*
- *Stay focused*
- *Resolve conflict*

In contrast, teams that lack one or more of these attributes can get bogged down in conflict or waste time and resources pursuing unclear goals. Two of the most common reasons cited for unsuccessful teamwork are a lack of trust and poor communication. A lack of trust can result from team members being suspicious of one another's motives or ability to contribute.[9] Another common reason for team failure is poor communication,

*Conflict in team settings isn't necessarily bad, as long as team members can stay focused on the goal.*

particularly when teams operate across cultures, countries, and time zones.[10] Poor communication can also result from basic differences in conversational styles. For example, some people expect conversation to follow an orderly pattern in which team members wait their turn to speak, whereas others might view conversation as more spontaneous and are comfortable with an overlapping, interactive style.[11]

Many teams experience conflict in the course of their work, but conflict isn't necessarily bad. Conflict can be constructive if it forces important issues into the open, increases the involvement of team members, and generates creative ideas for solving a problem. Even teams that have some interpersonal friction can excel if they have effective leadership and team players who are committed to positive outcomes. As teamwork experts Andy Boynton and Bill Fischer put it, "Virtuoso teams are not about getting polite results."[12]

**LEARNING OBJECTIVE 2**
Offer guidelines for collaborative communication, identify major collaboration technologies, and explain how to give constructive feedback.

# Collaborating on Communication Efforts

When a team collaborates on reports, websites, presentations, and other communication projects, the collective energy and expertise of the various members can lead to results that transcend what each individual could do otherwise.[13] However, collaborating on team messages requires special effort; the following section offers a number of helpful guidelines.

## Guidelines for Collaborative Writing

In any collaborative effort, team members coming from different backgrounds may have different work habits or priorities: a technical expert may focus on accuracy and scientific standards; an editor may be more concerned about organization and coherence; and a manager may focus on schedules, cost, and corporate goals. In addition, team members differ in writing styles, work habits, and personality traits.

To collaborate effectively, everyone involved must be flexible and open to other opinions, focusing on team objectives rather than on individual priorities.[14] Most ideas can be expressed in many ways, so avoid the "my way is best" attitude. The following guidelines will help you collaborate more successfully:[15]

*Successful collaboration requires a number of steps, from agreeing on project goals to establishing clear processes.*

- **Allocate roles to best apply the strengths of your team.** Teams work best with people who have a combination of experience, information, skills, and talents needed for the project. Assess the skills of your team, then delegate the graphics to someone with interests and skills in illustration, divide the research tasks according to interests and knowledge, and have the strongest writer assume the role of final editor.
- **Agree on project goals before you start.** Ensure the group understands the assignment and discusses standards for the finished product. In class projects, discuss aspirations about the final grade. In the workplace, clarify what content, length, and format the boss is expecting.
- **Allow time for the team to bond before you begin.** Make sure people get to know each other before being asked to collaborate.
- **Clarify individual responsibilities.** List the tasks ahead and allocate jobs according to team member strengths. Some teams find it helpful to write a "contract" that includes the tasks, deadlines, and people responsible, along with the process that will be used to resolve disputes and the consequences of not contributing.
- **Establish clear processes.** Make sure everyone knows how the work will be managed, including checkpoints and decisions to be made along the way. For example,

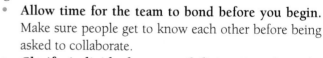

**REAL-TIME UPDATES**

**Learn More by Listening to This Podcast**

**How to keep small battles from escalating into big ones**

Use these insights to manage adversarial relationships in the workplace and keep them from getting destructive. Go to **http://real-timeupdates.com/bce6** and click on Learn More. If you are using MyBCommLab, you can access Real-Time Updates within Business Communication Resources.

have several team deadlines well before the finished product is due so the team goes through the three stages of writing: include dates to discuss the outline or plan, the draft, and the revised draft of the document.

- **Have an open and direct approach for resolving problems.** Sometimes one group member feels that he or she is doing all the work, while the others feel that same person is not sharing information or won't give up control of some aspect of the writing. Or, a group member may not be contributing. Ask questions to find out the reasons for performance issues instead of accusing teammates. Offer extra help to those who may be struggling. If, after review and assistance, the problem persists, the team may need to revert to the consequences outlined in the team contract for not contributing. Regular reviews to evaluate team performance can help avoid problems that can ruin the experience of working in a team. For example, if the team sets aside a little time in each meeting to reflect on performance and approaches it in a positive, supportive way, individuals will get greater satisfaction from participating as well as valuable feedback to strengthen their skills. Consider that your role as writing partner is to help the others on the team improve their writing and team skills. In that supportive spirit, ask how well is each person cooperating, participating, contributing, showing interest in others' ideas and materials, and communicating. If the writing team is large, use a short form to provide feedback on these criteria for each team member.
- **Delegate the writing tasks.** The actual composition is the only part of developing team messages that does not usually benefit from group participation. Brainstorming the wording of short pieces of text, particularly headlines, slogans, and other high-visibility elements, can be an effective way to stimulate creative word choices. However, for longer projects, it is usually more efficient to plan, research, and outline together but assign the task of writing to one person or divide larger projects among multiple writers. If you divide the writing, try to have one person do a final revision pass to ensure a consistent style.
- **Make sure tools and techniques are ready and compatible across the team.** Even minor details such as different versions of software can delay projects.
- **Check to see how things are going along the way.** Don't assume that everything is working just because you don't hear anything negative.

## Technologies for Collaborative Writing

A variety of tools are available to help writers collaborate on everything from short documents to entire websites (see Figure 2.1). The simplest tools are software features such as *commenting* (which lets colleagues write comments in a document without modifying the document text) and *change tracking* (which lets one or more writers propose changes to the text while keeping everyone's edits separate and reversible). The widely used Adobe Acrobat electronic document system (PDF files) also has group review and commenting features, including the option for live collaboration.

Collaborating on website content often involves the use of a **content management system**, which organizes and controls website content and can include features that help team members work together on webpages and other documents. These systems range from simple blogging systems on up to *enterprise* systems that manage web content across an entire corporation. Many systems include *workflow* features that control how pages or documents can be created, edited, and published.

In contrast to the formal controls of a content management system, a **wiki**, from the Hawaiian word for *quick,* is a website that allows anyone with access to add new material and edit existing material. Public wikis (Wikipedia is the best known of these) allow any registered user to edit pages; private wikis are accessible only with permission. A key benefit of wikis is the freedom to post new or revised material without prior approval. Chapter 11 offers guidelines for effective wiki collaboration.

Teams and other work groups can also take advantage of a set of broader technologies often referred to as *groupware* or *collaboration platforms*. These technologies let people

Collaboration tools include group review and commenting features, content management systems, and wikis.

Groupware and shared workspaces give team members instant access to shared resources and information.

| FIGURE 2.1 | Collaboration Technologies |

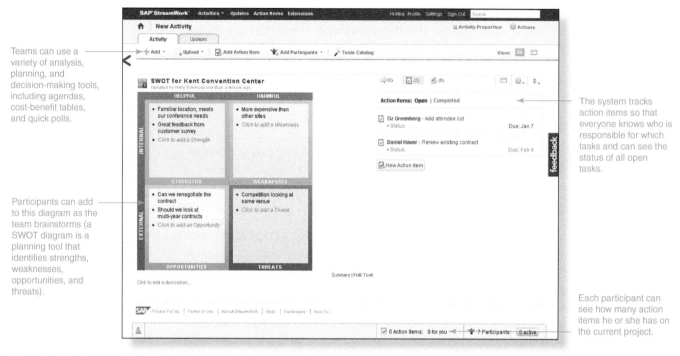

Teams can use a variety of analysis, planning, and decision-making tools, including agendas, cost-benefit tables, and quick polls.

The system tracks action items so that everyone knows who is responsible for which tasks and can see the status of all open tasks.

Participants can add to this diagram as the team brainstorms (a SWOT diagram is a planning tool that identifies strengths, weaknesses, opportunities, and threats).

Each participant can see how many action items he or she has on the current project.

*Source:* Copyright © 2012 by SAP AG. All rights reserved. Reprinted with permission.

communicate, share files, review previous message threads, work on documents simultaneously, and connect using social networking tools. These systems help companies capture and share knowledge from multiple experts, bringing greater insights to bear on tough challenges.[16] Collaboration systems often take advantage of *cloud computing*, a somewhat vague term that refers to "on-demand" capabilities delivered over the internet, rather than through conventional on-site software.[17]

**Shared workspaces** are online "virtual offices" that give everyone on a team access to the same set of resources and information (see Figure 2.2). You may see some of these

| FIGURE 2.2 | Shared Workspaces |

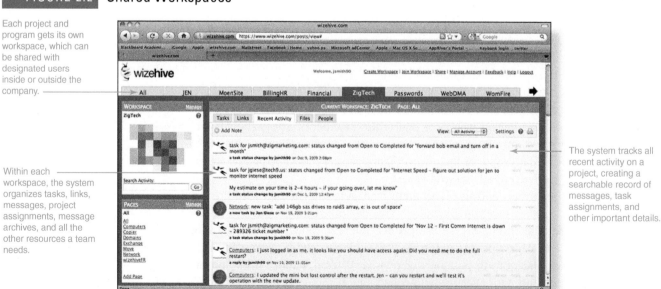

Each project and program gets its own workspace, which can be shared with designated users inside or outside the company.

Within each workspace, the system organizes tasks, links, messages, project assignments, message archives, and all the other resources a team needs.

The system tracks all recent activity on a project, creating a searchable record of messages, task assignments, and other important details.

*Source:* Copyright © 2011 by Wize Hive. Reprinted with permission.

workspaces referred to as *intranets* (restricted-access websites that are open to employees only) or *extranets* (restricted sites that are available to employees and to outside parties by invitation only). Many intranets have now evolved into social networking systems that include a variety of communication and collaboration tools, from microblogging to video clip libraries. Using this technology, such communities also build a repository of organizational knowledge over the long term.[18]

Social networking can also help a company maintain a sense of community even as it grows beyond the size that normally permits a lot of daily interaction. At lululemon athletica, for example, fostering a supportive work environment is a company priority. To encourage the sense of community among its expanding workforce, lululemon uses social networking tools to track employee connections and encourage workers to reach out and build relationships.[19]

## Giving—and Responding to—Constructive Feedback

Aside from processes and tools, collaborative communication often involves giving and receiving feedback about writing efforts. **Constructive feedback**, sometimes called *constructive criticism*, focuses on the process and outcomes of communication, not on the people involved (see Table 2.1). In contrast, **destructive feedback** delivers criticism with no effort to stimulate improvement.[20] For example, "This proposal is a confusing mess, and you failed to convince me of anything" is destructive feedback. Your goal is to be more constructive: "Your proposal could be more effective with a clearer description of the manufacturing process and a well-organized explanation of why the positives outweigh the negatives." When giving feedback, avoid personal attacks and give the person clear guidelines for improvement.

When you receive constructive feedback, resist the understandable urge to defend your work or deny the validity of the feedback. Remaining open to criticism isn't easy when you've poured your heart and soul into a project, but good feedback provides a valuable opportunity to learn and to improve the quality of your work.

> When you give writing feedback, make it constructive by focusing on how the material can be improved.

> When you receive constructive feedback on your writing, keep your emotions in check and view it as an opportunity to improve.

| TABLE 2.1 | Giving Constructive Feedback |
| --- | --- |

| HOW TO BE CONSTRUCTIVE | EXPLANATION |
| --- | --- |
| Think through your suggested changes carefully. | Because many business documents must illustrate complex relationships between ideas and other information, isolated and superficial edits can do more harm than good. |
| Discuss improvements rather than flaws. | Instead of saying "this is confusing," for instance, explain how the writing can be improved to make it clearer. |
| Focus on controllable behaviour. | The writer may not have control over every variable that affected the quality of the message, so focus on those aspects the writer can control. |
| Be specific. | Comments such as "I don't get this" or "Make this clearer" don't give the writer much direction. |
| Keep feedback impersonal. | Focus comments on the message, not on the person who created it. |
| Verify understanding. | If in doubt, ask for confirmation from the recipient to make sure that the person understood your feedback. |
| Time your feedback carefully. | Respond in a timely fashion so that the writer will have sufficient time to implement the changes you suggest. |
| Highlight any limitations your feedback may have. | If you didn't have time to give the document a thorough edit, or if you're not an expert in some aspect of the content, let the writer know so that he or she can handle your comments appropriately. |

**LEARNING OBJECTIVE ❸**
**List the key steps needed to ensure productive team meetings and identify the most common meeting technologies.**

# Making Your Meetings More Productive

Much of your workplace communication will occur in in-person or online meetings, so to a large degree, your ability to contribute to the company—and to be recognized for your contributions—will depend on your meeting skills. Well-run meetings can help companies solve problems, develop ideas, identify opportunities, and promote team building through social networking and interaction.[21] As useful as meetings can be, though, they can be a waste of time if they aren't planned and managed well. Successful meetings start with thoughtful preparation.

## Preparing for Meetings

A single poorly planned or poorly run meeting can waste hundreds or thousands of dollars, so make sure every meeting is necessary and well managed.

The first step in preparing for a meeting is to make sure the meeting is really necessary. Meetings can consume hundreds or thousands of dollars of productive time and take people away from other work, so don't hold a meeting if some other form of communication (such as an email message) can serve the purpose as effectively.[22] If a meeting is truly necessary, proceed with these four planning tasks:

To ensure a successful meeting, clarify your purpose, select the right mix of participants, choose the venue and time carefully, and set a clear agenda.

- **Clarify your purpose.** Most meetings are one of two types: *Informational meetings* involve sharing information and perhaps coordinating action. *Decision-making meetings* involve analysis, problem solving, and in many cases, persuasive communication. Whatever your purpose, make sure it's clear and specific—and clearly communicated to all participants.
- **Select participants for the meeting.** The rule here is simple: Invite everyone who really needs to be involved, and don't invite anyone who doesn't. For decision-making meetings, for example, invite only those people who are in a direct position to help the meeting reach its objective.
- **Choose the venue and the time.** Online meetings are often the best way (and sometimes to the only way) to connect people in multiple locations or to reach large audiences. For onsite meetings, review the facility and the seating arrangements. Are rows of chairs suitable, or do you need a conference table or some other arrangement? Pay attention to room temperature, lighting, ventilation, acoustics, and refreshments; these details can make or break a meeting. If you have control over the timing, morning meetings are often more productive because people are generally more alert and not yet engaged with the work of the day.
- **Set and share the agenda.** People who will be presenting information need to know what is expected of them, nonpresenters need to know what will be presented so they can prepare questions, and everyone needs to know how long the meeting will last. A good agenda lets everyone know what actions or outcomes are needed. For example, will the group *review* or *decide* an issue? In addition, the agenda is an important tool for guiding the progress of the meeting (see Figure 2.3).

## Conducting and Contributing to Efficient Meetings

Everyone in a meeting shares the responsibility for keeping the meeting productive and making it successful. If you are the designated leader of a meeting, however, you have an extra degree of responsibility and accountability. To ensure productive meetings, be sure to do the following:

Everyone shares the responsibility for successful meetings.

- **Keep the meeting on track.** A good meeting draws out the best ideas and information the group has to offer. Good leaders occasionally need to guide, mediate, probe, stimulate, summarize, and redirect discussions that have gotten off track.
- **Follow agreed-upon rules.** The larger the meeting, the more formal you'll need to be to maintain order. Formal meetings often use *parliamentary procedure,* a time-tested method for planning and running effective meetings. The best-known guide to this procedure is *Robert's Rules of Order* (**www.robertsrules.com**).

**FIGURE 2.3** Typical Meeting Agenda

## Agenda: Annual Quality Review
Oct 25, 2016 • 2:00 – 4:00 • Corporate Training Centre, Auditorium

  I.   Review annual goals: 10 min

  II.  Review departmental results

      A.  Manufacturing: 30 min

      B.  Marketing & sales: 15 min

      C.  Procurement & logistics: 20 min

      D.  Human resources: 15 min

  III. Prioritize problem areas: 20 min

  IV. Assign action items: 10 min

- **Encourage participation.** You may discover that some participants are too quiet and others are too talkative. Draw out nonparticipants by asking for their input. For the overly talkative, you can politely say that time is limited and others need to be heard.
- **Participate actively.** Try to contribute to the progress of the meeting and the smooth interaction of the participants. Use your listening skills and powers of observation to size up the interpersonal dynamics of the group, then adapt your behaviour to help the group achieve its goals. Speak up if you have something useful to say, but don't talk or ask questions just to demonstrate how much you know about the subject at hand.
- **Close effectively.** At the conclusion of a meeting, verify that the objectives have been met. If they have not, arrange for follow-up work as needed. Either summarize the decisions reached or list the actions to be taken. Make sure all participants understand and agree on the outcome.

**REAL-TIME UPDATES**

**Learn More by Listening to This Podcast**

How to share your ideas in a meeting

On-site and online meetings can be a great forum for sharing your ideas—if you know how to do so successfully. Go to http://real-timeupdates.com/bce6 and click on Learn More. If you are using MyBCommLab, you can access Real-Time Updates within Business Communication Resources.

For most meetings, particularly formal meetings, it's good practice to appoint one person to record the **minutes**, a summary of the important information presented and the decisions made during a meeting. Figure 2.4 shows the type of information typically included in minutes.

## Using Meeting Technologies

Today's companies use a variety of technologies to enhance or even replace traditional meetings. Replacing in-person meetings with **virtual meetings** can dramatically reduce costs, save resources, reduce wear and tear on employees, and give teams access to a wider pool of expertise. Instant messaging (IM) and teleconferencing are the simplest forms of virtual meetings. Videoconferencing lets participants see and hear each other, demonstrate products, and transmit other visual information. *Telepresence* technologies (see Figure 2.5) enable realistic conferences in which participants thousands of kilometres apart almost seem to be in the same room.[23] The ability to convey nonverbal subtleties such as facial expressions and hand gestures makes these systems particularly good for negotiations, collaborative problem solving, and other complex discussions.[24]

## FIGURE 2.4  Typical Meeting Minutes

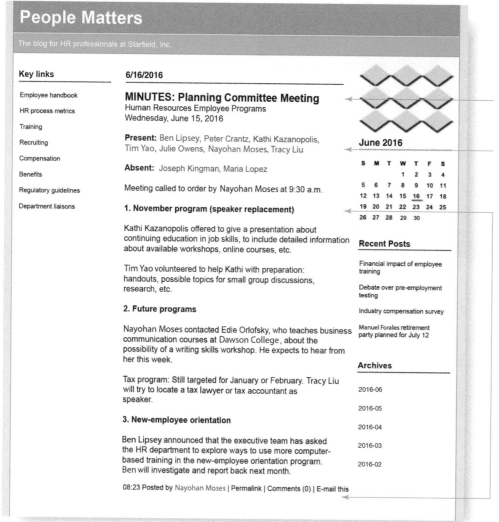

### People Matters

The blog for HR professionals at Starfield, Inc.

**Key links**

Employee handbook

HR process metrics

Training

Recruiting

Compensation

Benefits

Regulatory guidelines

Department liaisons

6/16/2016

**MINUTES: Planning Committee Meeting**
Human Resources Employee Programs
Wednesday, June 15, 2016

**Present:** Ben Lipsey, Peter Crantz, Kathi Kazanopolis, Tim Yao, Julie Owens, Nayohan Moses, Tracy Liu

**Absent:** Joseph Kingman, Maria Lopez

Meeting called to order by Nayohan Moses at 9:30 a.m.

**1. November program (speaker replacement)**

Kathi Kazanopolis offered to give a presentation about continuing education in job skills, to include detailed information about available workshops, online courses, etc.

Tim Yao volunteered to help Kathi with preparation: handouts, possible topics for small group discussions, research, etc.

**2. Future programs**

Nayohan Moses contacted Edie Orlofsky, who teaches business communication courses at Dawson College, about the possibility of a writing skills workshop. He expects to hear from her this week.

Tax program: Still targeted for January or February. Tracy Liu will try to locate a tax lawyer or tax accountant as speaker.

**3. New-employee orientation**

Ben Lipsey announced that the executive team has asked the HR department to explore ways to use more computer-based training in the new-employee orientation program. Ben will investigate and report back next month.

08:23 Posted by Nayohan Moses | Permalink | Comments (0) | E-mail this

**June 2016**

| S | M | T | W | T | F | S |
|---|---|---|---|---|---|---|
| | | | 1 | 2 | 3 | 4 |
| 5 | 6 | 7 | 8 | 9 | 10 | 11 |
| 12 | 13 | 14 | 15 | 16 | 17 | 18 |
| 19 | 20 | 21 | 22 | 23 | 24 | 25 |
| 26 | 27 | 28 | 29 | 30 | | |

**Recent Posts**

Financial impact of employee training

Debate over pre-employment testing

Industry compensation survey

Manuel Forales retirement party planned for July 12

**Archives**

2016-06

2016-05

2016-04

2016-03

2016-02

Clearly indicates which meeting these minutes represent

Lists who did and did not attend the meeting

Summarizes outcomes, not entire discussions:

- Reminds everyone of what took place
- Shows who is responsible for which follow-up tasks
- Summarizes all decisions and suggestions made

*Source:* Based on People Matters—The blog for HR professionals at Starfield, Inc.

## FIGURE 2.5  Telepresence Meeting Technology

The most sophisticated web-based meeting systems combine the best of real-time communication, shared workspaces, and videoconferencing with other tools, such as *virtual whiteboards,* that let teams collaborate in real time. Such systems are used for everything from spontaneous discussions among small groups to carefully planned, formal events such as press conferences, training sessions, sales presentations, and *webinars* (web-based seminars).[25]

Technology continues to create intriguing opportunities for online interaction. For instance, one of the newest virtual tools is online brainstorming, in which a company can conduct "idea campaigns" to generate new ideas from people across the organization. These range from small team meetings to huge events such as IBM's giant Innovation Jam, in which 150 000 IBM employees, family members, and customers from 104 countries were invited to brainstorm online for three days leading to the creation of 10 new lines of business.[26]

Some companies are experimenting with virtual meetings and other communication activities in virtual worlds such as Second Life (**www.secondlife.com**). In much the same way that gamers can create and control characters (often known as *avatars*) in a multiplayer video game, professionals can create online versions of themselves to participate in meetings, training sessions, sales presentations, and even casual conversations with customers they happen to bump into (see Figure 2.6).

Conducting successful meetings over the phone or online requires extra planning before the meeting and more diligence during the meeting. Because virtual meetings offer less visual contact and nonverbal communication than in-person meetings, leaders need to make sure everyone stays engaged and has the opportunity to contribute. Paying attention during online meetings takes greater effort as well. Participants need to stay committed to the meeting and resist the temptation to work on unrelated tasks.[27]

Expect to attend many meetings virtually, using the growing array of online meeting technologies.

Online meetings can save considerable time and money, but they can require extra planning and management steps.

## FIGURE 2.6  Meeting in a Virtual World

LEARNING OBJECTIVE **4**
Describe the listening process and explain how good listeners overcome barriers at each stage of the process.

Listening is one of the most important skills in the workplace, but most people don't do it as well as they assume they do.

To be a good listener, adapt the way you listen to suit the situation.

# Improving Your Listening Skills

Your long-term career prospects are closely tied to your ability to listen effectively. In fact, some 80 percent of top executives say that listening is the most important skill needed to get things done in the workplace.[28] Plus, today's younger employees place a high premium on being heard, so listening is becoming even more vital for managers.[29]

Effective listening strengthens organizational relationships, alerts the organization to opportunities for innovation, and allows the organization to manage growing diversity both in the workforce and in the customers it serves.[30] Companies whose employees and managers listen effectively are able to stay informed, up-to-date, and out of trouble. Conversely, poor listening skills can cost companies millions of dollars per year as a result of lost opportunities, legal mistakes, and other errors. Effective listening is also vital to the process of building trust between organizations and between individuals.[31]

## Recognizing Various Types of Listening

Effective listeners adapt their listening approaches to different situations. The primary goal of **content listening** is to understand and retain the information in the speaker's message. With this type of listening, you ask questions to clarify the material but don't argue or judge. Try to overlook the speaker's style and any limitations in the presentation; just focus on the information.[32] In contrast, the goal of **critical listening** is to understand and evaluate the meaning of the speaker's message on several levels: the logic of the argument, the strength of the evidence, the validity of the conclusions, the implications of the message for you and your organization, the speaker's intentions and motives, and the omission of any important or relevant points. Be on the lookout for bias that might colour the way the information is presented and be careful to separate opinions from facts.[33]

The goal of **empathic listening** is to understand the speaker's feelings, needs, and wants so that you can appreciate his or her point of view, regardless of whether you share that perspective. By listening in an empathic way, you help the individual release emotions that can prevent a calm, clear-headed approach to the subject. Don't jump in with advice unless the person asks for it, and don't judge the speaker's feelings. Instead, let the person know that you appreciate his or her feelings and understand the situation. Once you establish that connection, you can then help the speaker search for a solution.[34]

No matter what mode they are using at any given time, effective listeners try to engage in **active listening**: making a conscious effort to turn off their own filters and biases to truly hear and understand what the other party is saying. They ask questions or summarize the speaker's message to verify key points and encourage the speaker through positive body language and supportive feedback.[35]

## Understanding the Listening Process

Listening seems like a simple procedure. After all, you've been doing it all your life. However, most of us aren't terribly good at it. Most people listen at or below a 25 percent efficiency rate, remember only about half of what's said during a 10-minute conversation, and forget half of that within 48 hours.[36] Furthermore, when questioned about material they've just heard, they're likely to get the facts mixed up.[37]

Why is such a seemingly simple activity so difficult? The reason is that listening is not a simple process by any means. Listening follows the same sequence as the basic communication process model you explored in Chapter 1 (pages 7–8), with the added

**REAL-TIME UPDATES**

**Learn More by Watching This Video**

**Train yourself to listen more effectively**

Learn five ways that you can "retune your ears for conscious listening." Go to http://real-timeupdates.com/bce6 and click on Learn More. If you are using MyBCommLab, you can access Real-Time Updates within Business Communication Resources.

difficulty that it happens in real time. To listen effectively, you need to successfully complete five steps:[38]

1. **Receiving.** Start by physically hearing the message and recognizing it as incoming information.
2. **Decoding.** Assign meaning to sounds, according to your own values, beliefs, ideas, expectations, roles, needs, and personal history.
3. **Remembering.** Store the information for future processing.
4. **Evaluating.** Evaluate the quality of the information.
5. **Responding.** React based on the situation and the nature of the information.

*Listening involves five steps: receiving, decoding, remembering, evaluating, and responding.*

If any one of these steps breaks down, the listening process becomes less effective or even fails entirely. As both a sender and a receiver, you can reduce the failure rate by recognizing and overcoming a variety of physical and mental barriers to effective listening.

## Overcoming Barriers to Effective Listening

*Good listeners actively try to overcome the barriers to successful listening.*

Good listeners look for ways to overcome the many potential barriers to successful listening (see Table 2.2). Some factors you may not be able to control, such as conference room acoustics or poor phone reception. However, you can control other factors, such as not interrupting speakers and not creating distractions that make it difficult for others to pay attention. And don't think that you're not interrupting just because you're not talking. Such actions as texting or checking your watch can interrupt a speaker and lead to communication breakdowns.

**Selective listening** is one of the most common barriers to effective listening. If your mind wanders, you may stay tuned out until you hear a word or phrase that gets your attention once more. But by that time, you'll be unable to recall what the speaker actually said; instead, you'll remember what you think the speaker *probably* said.[39]

| TABLE 2.2 | What Makes an Effective Listener?[40] |
| --- | --- |

| EFFECTIVE LISTENERS | INEFFECTIVE LISTENERS |
| --- | --- |
| Listen actively | Listen passively |
| Take careful and complete notes, when applicable | Take no notes or ineffective notes |
| Make frequent eye contact with the speaker (depends on culture to some extent) | Make little or no eye contact or inappropriate eye contact |
| Stay focused on the speaker and the content | Allow their minds to wander, are easily distracted, work on unrelated tasks |
| Mentally paraphrase key points to maintain attention level and ensure comprehension | Fail to paraphrase |
| Adjust listening style to the situation | Listen with the same style, regardless of the situation |
| Give the speaker nonverbal cues (such as nodding to show agreement or raising eyebrows to show surprise or skepticism) | Fail to give the speaker nonverbal feedback |
| Save questions or points of disagreement until an appropriate time | Interrupt whenever they disagree or don't understand |
| Overlook stylistic differences and focus on the speaker's message | Are distracted by or unduly influenced by stylistic differences; are judgmental |
| Make distinctions between main points and supporting details | Are unable to distinguish main points from details |
| Look for opportunities to learn | Assume they already know everything that's important to know |

*Source:* Based on Madelyn Burley-Allen, *Listening: The Forgotten Skill* (New York: Wiley, 1995), 70–71, 119–120; Judi Brownell, *Listening: Attitudes, Principles, and Skills* (Boston: Allyn & Bacon, 2002), 3, 9, 83, 89, 125; Larry Barker and Kittie Watson, *Listen Up* (New York: St. Martin's, 2000), 8, 9, 64.

One key reason listeners' minds tend to wander is that people think faster than they speak. Most people speak at 120 to 150 words per minute. However, humans can process audio information at up to 500 words per minute or more.[41] Consequently, your brain has a lot of free time whenever you're listening, and, if left unsupervised, it will find a thousand other things to think about. Make a conscious effort to focus on the speaker and use the extra time to analyze and paraphrase what you hear or to take relevant notes.

Overcoming interpretation barriers can be difficult because you may not even be aware of them. **Selective perception** leads listeners to mold messages to fit their own conceptual frameworks. Listeners sometimes make up their minds before fully hearing the speaker's message, or they engage in *defensive listening*—protecting their egos by tuning out anything that doesn't confirm their beliefs or their view of themselves.

Even when your intentions are good, you can still misinterpret incoming messages if you and the speaker don't share enough language or experience. When listening to a speaker whose native language or life experience is different from yours, try to paraphrase that person's ideas. Give the speaker a chance to confirm what you think you heard or to correct any misinterpretation.

LEARNING OBJECTIVE 5
Explain the importance of nonverbal communication and identify six major categories of nonverbal expression.

# Improving Your Nonverbal Communication Skills

**Nonverbal communication** is the process of sending and receiving information, both intentionally and unintentionally, without using written or spoken language. Nonverbal signals play a vital role in communication because they can strengthen a verbal message (when the nonverbal signals match the spoken words), weaken a verbal message (when the nonverbal signals don't match the words), or replace words entirely. For example, you might tell a client that a project is coming along nicely, but your forced smile and nervous glances will send an entirely different message.

Nonverbal communication supplements spoken language.

You've been tuned in to nonverbal communication since your first contact with other human beings. Paying special attention to these signals in the workplace will enhance your ability to communicate successfully. Moreover, as you work with a diverse range of people in the global marketplace, you'll also need to grasp the different meanings of common gestures in various cultures. For instance, the thumbs-up sign and circled index finger and thumb that indicate "OK" are positive gestures in Canada but insulting gestures in some other cultures. Six types of signals are particularly important:

Nonverbal signals include facial expression, gestures and posture, vocal characteristics, personal appearance, touch, and use of time and space.

- **Facial expressions.** Your face is the primary site for expressing your emotions; it reveals both the type and the intensity of your feelings.[42] Your eyes are especially effective for indicating attention and interest, influencing others, regulating interaction, and establishing dominance.[43] As with other areas of nonverbal expressions, however, facial signals can vary widely from culture to culture. For instance, maintaining eye contact is usually viewed as a sign of sincerity and openness in Canada, but it can be viewed as rude in some First Nations cultures and countries such as Japan.[44]
- **Gestures and posture.** Many gestures—a wave of the hand, for example—have a specific and intentional meaning. Other types of body movement are often unintentional and express more general messages. Slouching, leaning forward, fidgeting, and walking briskly are all unconscious signals that can reveal whether you feel confident or nervous, friendly or hostile, assertive or passive, powerful or powerless.

Work to make sure your nonverbal signals match the tone and content of your spoken communication.

- **Vocal characteristics.** Voice carries both intentional and unintentional messages. A speaker can intentionally control pitch, pace, and stress to convey a specific message. For instance, consider the intonation in the question, "*What* are you doing?" versus "What are *you* doing?". Unintentional vocal characteristics can convey happiness, surprise, fear, and other emotions (for example, fear often increases the pitch and the pace of your speaking voice).

What signals does your personal appearance send?

- **Personal appearance.** People respond to others on the basis of their physical appearance, sometimes fairly and other times unfairly. Although an individual's body type and facial features impose limitations, most people are able to control their appearance to some degree. Grooming, clothing, accessories, piercings, tattoos, and hairstyle—you can control all of these. For instance, are you talking like a serious business professional but dressing like you belong in a dance club? If your goal is to make a good impression, adopt the style of the people you want to impress. Many employers also have guidelines concerning attire, body art, and other issues, so make sure you understand and follow them.[45]

**REAL-TIME UPDATES**

**Learn More by Viewing This Infographic**

**Seven common hand gestures that will stir up trouble in other cultures**

Find out what gestures that have positive meanings in North America can have intensively negative meanings in other cultures. Go to http://real-timeupdates.com/bce6 and click on Learn More. If you are using MyBCommLab, you can access Real-Time Updates within Business Communication Resources.

- **Touch.** Touch is an important way to convey warmth, comfort, and reassurance—as well as control. Touch is so powerful, in fact, that it is governed by cultural customs that establish who can touch whom and how in various circumstances. In Canada and Great Britain, for instance, people usually touch less frequently than people in France or Costa Rica do. Even within each culture's norms, however, individual attitudes toward touch vary widely. A manager might be comfortable using hugs to express support or congratulations, but his or her subordinates could interpret those hugs as a show of dominance or sexual interest.[46] Touch is a complex subject. The best advice is when in doubt, don't touch.

- **Time and space.** Like touch, time and space can be used to assert authority, imply intimacy, and send other nonverbal messages. For instance, some people try to demonstrate their own importance or disregard for others by making other people wait; others show respect by being on time. Similarly, taking care not to invade private space, such as standing too close when talking, is a way to show respect for others. Keep in mind that expectations regarding both time and space vary by culture.

When you listen to others, pay attention to nonverbal clues. Do these signals seem to amplify the spoken words or contradict them? Is the speaker intentionally using nonverbal signals to send you a message that he or she can't put into words? Be observant but don't assume that you can "read someone like a book." Nonverbal signals are powerful, but they aren't infallible. For example, contrary to popular belief, avoiding eye contact and covering one's face while talking are not reliable clues that someone is lying. These behaviours may be influenced by culture (in some cultures, sustained eye contact can be interpreted as a sign of disrespect) or might just be ways of coping with stressful situations.[47]

# Developing Your Business Etiquette

You may have noticed a common thread running through the topics of successful teamwork, productive meetings, effective listening, and nonverbal communication: all depend on mutual respect and consideration among all participants. As Chapter 1 notes, etiquette is now considered an essential business skill. Nobody wants to work with someone who is rude to colleagues or an embarrassment to the company. Moreover, shabby treatment of others in the workplace can be a huge drain on morale and productivity.[48] Poor etiquette can drive away customers, investors, and other critical audiences—and it can limit your career potential.

This section addresses some key etiquette points to remember when you're in the workplace, out in public, and online. Long lists of etiquette rules can be difficult to remember, but you can get by in most every situation by remembering to be aware of your effect on others, treating everyone with respect, and keeping in mind that the impressions you leave behind can have a lasting effect on you and your company, so make sure to leave positive impressions wherever you go.

**LEARNING OBJECTIVE 6**

Explain the importance of business etiquette and identify three key areas in which good etiquette is essential.

If you want to appear polished, professional, and confident in business settings, learn the behavioural expectations in your workplace.

## Business Etiquette in the Workplace

Workplace etiquette includes a variety of behaviours, habits, and aspects of nonverbal communication. Although it isn't always thought of as an element of etiquette, your personal appearance in the workplace sends a strong signal to managers, colleagues, and customers. Pay attention to the style of dress where you work and adjust your style to match. Observe others and don't be afraid to ask for advice. If you're not sure, dress modestly and simply—earn a reputation for what you can *do*, not for what you can wear.

Grooming is as important as attire. Pay close attention to cleanliness and avoid using products with powerful scents, such as perfumed soaps, colognes, shampoos, and after-shave. Many people are bothered by these products, and some are allergic to them.

If you work in a conventional office setting, you'll spend as much time with your officemates as you do with family and friends. Personal demeanour is therefore a vital element of workplace harmony. No one expects you to be artificially upbeat and bubbly every second of the day, but a single negative personality can make an entire office miserable and unproductive. Every person in the company has a responsibility to contribute to a positive, energetic work environment.

Meetings require attention to etiquette to ensure a successful outcome and productive use of everyone's time. Start by showing up on time and ready to go. While the meeting is in progress, pay attention and stay engaged. Don't carry on side conversations, and don't multitask on your phone or other device (unless it's expected that you'll be participating in a backchannel conversation—see page 328). If you intend to use your device to take notes during the meeting, let the meeting leader know that's what you're doing.[49]

IM and other text-based tools have taken over many exchanges that used to take place over the phone, but phone skills are still essential. Because phone calls lack the visual richness of face-to-face conversations, you have to rely on your attitude and tone of voice to convey confidence and professionalism. Table 2.3 summarizes helpful tips for placing and receiving phone calls in a confident, professional manner.

Mobile phones are a contentious point of etiquette in today's workplace. They can boost productivity if used mindfully, but they can be a productivity- and morale-draining disruption when used carelessly. Be aware that attitudes about mobile phones vary widely, and don't be surprised if you encounter policies restricting their use in offices or meeting rooms. Nearly half of North American companies already have such policies.[50]

Like every other aspect of communication, your phone habits say a lot about how much respect you have for the people around you. Selecting obnoxious ring tones, talking loudly in open offices or public places, using your phone right next to someone else, making excessive or unnecessary personal calls during work hours, invading someone's privacy by using your camera phone without permission, taking or making calls in restrooms and other inappropriate places, texting while someone is talking to you, allowing incoming calls to interrupt meetings or discussions—these are all disrespectful choices that will reflect negatively on you.[51]

## Business Etiquette in Social Settings

From business lunches to industry conferences, you may be asked to represent your company when you're out in public. Make sure your appearance and actions are appropriate to the situation. Get to know the customs of the culture when you meet new people. For example, in Canada, a firm handshake is expected when two people meet, whereas a respectful bow of the head is more appropriate in Japan. If you are expected to shake hands, be aware that the passive "dead fish" handshake creates an extremely negative impression with most people. If you're physically able, always stand when shaking someone's hand.

When introducing yourself, include a brief description of your role in the company. When introducing two other people, speak their first and last names clearly and then try to offer some information (perhaps a shared professional interest) to help the two people

*Contribute to harmony and productivity in your workplace with a professional, upbeat demeanour.*

*Your telephone skills will be vital to your business success.*

*Poor mobile phone etiquette is a common source of complaints in both the workplace and social settings.*

*You represent your company when you're out in public—or communicating online under your own name—so etiquette continues to be important even after you leave the office.*

| TABLE 2.3 | Quick Tips for Improving Your Phone Skills |

| GENERAL TIPS | PLACING CALLS | RECEIVING CALLS | USING VOICE MAIL |
|---|---|---|---|
| Use frequent verbal responses that show you're listening ("Oh yes," "I see," "That's right"). | Be ready before you call so that you don't waste the other person's time. | Answer promptly and with a smile so that you sound friendly and positive. | When recording your own outgoing message, make it brief and professional. |
| Increase your volume just slightly to convey your confidence. | Minimize the noise level in your environment as much as possible to avoid distracting the other party. | Identify yourself and your company (some companies have specific instructions for what to say when you answer). | If you can, record temporary greetings on days when you are unavailable all day so that callers will know you're gone for the day. |
| Don't speak in a monotone; vary your pitch and inflections so people know you're interested. | Identify yourself and your organization, briefly describe why you're calling, and verify that you've called at a good time. | Establish the needs of your caller by asking, "How may I help you?" If you know the caller's name, use it. | Check your voice mail messages regularly and return all necessary calls within 24 hours. |
| Slow down when conversing with people whose native language isn't the same as yours. | Don't take up too much time. Speak quickly and clearly, and get right to the point of the call. | If you can, answer questions promptly and efficiently; if you can't help, tell them what you can do for them. | Leave simple, short messages with your name, number (don't assume the recipient has caller ID), purpose for calling, and times when you can be reached. |
| Stay focused on the call throughout; others can easily tell when you're not paying attention. | Close in a friendly, positive manner and repeat all vital information such as meeting times and dates. | If you must forward a call or put someone one hold, explain what you are doing first. | State your name and telephone number *slowly* so that the other person can easily write them down; repeat both if the other person doesn't know you. |
| | | If you forward a call to someone else, try to speak with that person first to verify that he or she is available and to introduce the caller. | Be careful what you say; most voice mail systems allow users to forward messages to anyone else in the system. |
| | | If you take a message for someone else, be complete and accurate, including the caller's name, number, and organization. | Replay your message before leaving the system to make sure it is clear and complete. |

*Sources:* "Are You Practicing Proper Social Networking Etiquette?" Forbes, 9 October 2009 [accessed 11 June 2010], www.forbes.com; Pete Babb, "The Ten Commandments of Blog and Wiki Etiquette," InfoWorld, 28 May 2007 [accessed 3 August 2008], www.infoworld.com; Judith Kallos, "Instant Messaging Etiquette," NetM@nners blog [accessed 3 August 2008], www.netmanners.com; Michael S. Hyatt, "E-Mail Etiquette 101," From Where I Sit blog, 1 July 2007 [accessed 3 August 2008], www.michaelhyatt.com.

ease into a conversation.[52] Generally speaking, the lower-ranking person is introduced to the senior-ranking person, without regard to gender.[53]

Business is often conducted over meals, and knowing the basics of dining etiquette will make you more effective and comfortable in these situations.[54] Start by choosing foods that are easy to eat. Avoid alcoholic beverages in most instances, but if drinking one is appropriate, save it for the end of the meal. Leave business documents under your chair until entree plates have been removed; the business aspect of the meal doesn't usually begin until then.

Just as in the office, when you use your mobile phone inappropriately in public, you send the message that people around you aren't as important as your call and that you don't respect your caller's privacy.[55] If it's not a matter of life and death, or at least an urgent request from your boss or a customer, wait until you're back in the office.

Remember that business meals are a forum for business, period. Don't discuss politics, religion, or any other topic that's likely to stir up emotions. Don't complain about work, don't ask deeply personal questions, avoid profanity, and be careful with humour—a joke that entertains some people could easily offend others.

Virtual assistants and other mobile phone voice features can annoy and disrupt the workplace and social settings if not used with respect for others.

Virtual assistants, such as the Siri voice recognition system in Apple iPhones, raise another new etiquette dilemma. From doing simple web searches to dictating entire memos, these systems may be convenient for users, but they can create distractions and annoyances for other people.[56] As with other public behaviours, think about the effect you have on others before using these technologies.

## Business Etiquette Online

Electronic media seem to be a breeding ground for poor etiquette. Learn the basics of professional online behaviour to avoid mistakes that could hurt your company or your career. Here are some guidelines to follow whenever you are representing your company while using electronic media:[57]

When you represent your company online, you must adhere to a high standard of etiquette and respect for others.

- **Avoid personal attacks.** The anonymous and instantaneous nature of online communication can cause even level-headed people to lose their tempers and go after others.
- **Stay focused on the original topic.** If you want to change the subject of an online conversation, start with a new message or thread.
- **Don't present opinions as facts; support facts with evidence.** This guideline applies to all communication, of course, but online venues in particular seem to tempt people into presenting their beliefs and opinions as unassailable truths.
- **Follow basic expectations of spelling, punctuation, and capitalization.** Sending careless, acronym-filled messages that look like you're texting your high school buddies makes you look like an amateur.
  - **Use virus protection and keep it up to date.** Sending or posting a file that contains a computer virus is rude.
  - **Ask if this is a good time for an IM chat.** Don't assume that just because a person is showing as "available" on your IM system that he or she wants to chat with you right this instant.
  - **Watch your language and keep your emotions under control.** A moment of indiscretion could haunt you forever.
  - **Avoid multitasking while using IM or other tools.** You might think you're saving time by doing a dozen things at once, but you're probably making the other person wait while you bounce back and forth between IM and your other tasks.
- **Never assume you have privacy.** Assume that anything you type will be stored forever, could be forwarded to other people, and might be read by your boss or the company's security staff.
- **Don't use "reply all" in email unless everyone can benefit from your reply.** If one or more recipients of an email message don't need the information in your reply, remove their addresses before you send.
- **Don't expect others to instantly reply to your emails or texts.**
- **Don't waste others' time with sloppy, confusing, or incomplete messages.** Doing so is disrespectful.
- **Respect boundaries of time and virtual space.** For instance, don't start using an employee's personal Facebook page for business messages unless you've discussed it beforehand, and don't assume people are available to discuss work matters around the clock, even if you do find them online in the middle of the night.
- **Be careful of online commenting mechanisms.** For example, many blogs and websites now use your Facebook login to let you comment on articles. If your Facebook profile includes your job title and company name, those could show up along with your comment.

### REAL-TIME UPDATES

**Learn More by Reading This Article**

**Why saying "thank you" is good for you, too**

See why "thank you" and other polite expressions benefit the sender, not just the receiver. Go to http://real-timeupdates. com/bce6 and click on Learn More. If you are using MyBCommLab, you can access Real-Time Updates within Business Communication Resources.

Respect personal and professional boundaries when using social networking tools.

**❶ OBJECTIVE** **List the advantages and disadvantages of working in teams and describe the characteristics of effective teams.**

The advantages of successful teamwork include improved productivity, creativity, and employee involvement; increased information and knowledge; greater diversity of views; and increased acceptance of new solutions and ideas. The potential disadvantages of working in teams include groupthink (the tendency to let peer pressure overcome one's better judgment), the pursuit of hidden agendas, and the cost (in money and time) of planning and conducting team activities. The most effective teams have a clear objective and a shared sense of purpose, communicate openly and honestly, reach decisions by consensus, think creatively, stay focused, and know how to resolve conflict.

**❷ OBJECTIVE** **Offer guidelines for collaborative communication, identify major collaboration technologies, and explain how to give constructive feedback.**

To succeed with collaborative writing: (1) select team members carefully to balance talents and viewpoints; (2) agree on project goals; (3) make sure team members have time to get to know one another; (4) make sure that everyone clearly understands individual responsibilities, processes, and tools; (5) generally, avoid writing as a group (assign the writing phase to one person, or assign separate sections to individual writers and have one person edit them all); (6) make sure tools and techniques are compatible; and (7) check in with everyone periodically.

Some of the major collaboration technologies are review and commenting features in document preparation software, wikis, content management systems, groupware, and shared workspaces.

When you are asked to give feedback on someone's writing, focus on how the writing can be improved. Avoid personal attacks and give the person clear and specific advice.

**❸ OBJECTIVE** **List the key steps needed to ensure productive team meetings and identify the most common meeting technologies.**

Meetings are an essential business activity, but they can waste considerable time and money if conducted poorly. Make better use of meetings by preparing carefully, conducting meetings efficiently, and using meeting technologies wisely. Make sure your meetings are necessary, are carefully planned, include only the necessary participants, follow clear agendas, and have minutes that summarize key decisions.

A variety of meeting technologies are available to help teams or groups communicate successfully while not requiring everyone to be in the same place at the same time. The tools range from simple instant messaging sessions and teleconferences to videoconferencing and web-based meetings to specialized capabilities such as online brainstorming systems and virtual worlds.

**❹ OBJECTIVE** **Describe the listening process and explain how good listeners overcome barriers at each stage of the process.**

The listening process involves five steps: receiving, decoding, remembering, evaluating, and responding. Barriers such as prejudgment and selective perception can disrupt the process at any stage, so good listeners practise active listening, avoid disrupting the speaker or other people, work hard to see past superficial differences and distractions, and take care not to let selective perception filter out important information. Effective listeners also adapt their listening approaches to the situation, using content listening, critical listening, or empathic listening as appropriate.

**❺ OBJECTIVE** **Explain the importance of nonverbal communication and identify six major categories of nonverbal expression.**

Nonverbal signals play a vital role in communication because they can strengthen a verbal message (when the nonverbal signals match the spoken words), weaken a verbal message (when nonverbal signals don't match the words), or replace words entirely. The six major categories of nonverbal expression are facial expressions, gestures and posture, vocal characteristics, personal appearance, touch, and use of time and personal space.

**❻ OBJECTIVE** **Explain the importance of business etiquette and identify three key areas in which good etiquette is essential.**

Etiquette is an essential business skill because the impression you make on others and your ability to help others feel comfortable will be major contributors to your career success. Poor etiquette can hinder team efforts, drain morale and productivity, drive away customers and investors, and limit your career potential.

Three key areas that require good business etiquette are the workplace, social settings in which you represent your company, and online venues. Matters of workplace etiquette include personal appearance, grooming, demeanour, and telephone habits. In social settings, make a positive impression by learning how to introduce yourself and others in a professional manner and by conducting yourself gracefully at dinners and other social gatherings. In online settings, learn and follow the standards of acceptable behaviour for each system.

## MyBCommLab®

Go to MyBCommLab for everything you need to help you succeed in the job you've always wanted! Tools and resources include the following:
• Writing Activities    • Document Makeovers
• Video Exercises    • Grammar Exercises—and much more!

## Practise Your Grammar

Effective business communication starts with strong grammar skills. To improve your grammar skills, go to MyBCommLab, where you'll find exercises and diagnostic tests to help you produce clear, effective communication.

## Test Your Knowledge

To review chapter content related to each question, refer to the indicated Learning Objective.

1. What are five characteristics of effective teams? L.O.❶
2. How does an agenda help make a meeting more successful? L.O.❸
3. What activities make up the listening process? L.O.❹
4. What are the six main categories of nonverbal signals? L.O.❺

## Apply Your Knowledge

To review chapter content related to each question, refer to the indicated Learning Objective.

1. You head up the interdepartmental design review team for a manufacturer of high-performance motorcycles, and things are not going well at the moment. The design engineers and marketing strategists keep arguing about which should be a higher priority, performance or aesthetics, and the accountants say both groups are driving the cost of the new model through the roof by adding too many new features. Everyone has valid points to make, but the team is getting bogged down in conflict. Explain how you could go about resolving the stalemate. L.O.❶

2. Whenever your boss asks for feedback, she blasts anyone who offers criticism, so people tend to agree with everything she says. You want to talk to her about it, but what should you say? List some of the points you want to make when you discuss this issue with your boss. L.O.❷

3. One of your teammates never seems to be paying attention during weekly team meetings. He has never contributed to the discussion, and you've never seen him take notes. He says he wants to support the team but that he finds it difficult to focus during routine meetings. List some ideas you could give him that might improve his listening skills. L.O.❹

4. Several members of your sales team are protesting the company's "business casual" dress code, claiming that dressing nicely makes them feel awkward and overly formal in front of customers. You have to admit that most of the company's customers dress like they've just walked in from a picnic or a bike ride, but that doesn't change the fact that you want your company to be seen as conscientious and professional. How will you explain the policy to these employees in a way that will help them understand and accept it? L.O.❻

# Practise Your Skills

## ACTIVITIES

Each activity is labelled according to the primary skill or skills you will need to use. To review relevant chapter content, you can refer to the indicated Learning Objective. In some instances, supporting information will be found in another chapter, as indicated.

1. **Collaboration: Working in Teams** L.O.❶ In teams assigned by your instructor, prepare a 10-minute presentation on the potential advantages or disadvantages of using social media for business communication (choose one). When the presentation is ready, discuss in your team how effective the team was using the following criteria: (1) having a clear objective and a shared sense of purpose, (2) communicating openly and honestly, (3) reaching decisions by consensus, (4) thinking creatively, and (5) knowing how to resolve conflict. Be prepared to discuss your findings with the rest of the class.

2. **Collaboration: Using Collaboration Technologies** L.O.❷ In a team assigned by your instructor, use Zoho (www.zoho.com; free for personal use) or a comparable system to collaborate on a set of directions that out-of-town visitors could use to reach a specific point on your campus, such as the library or a classroom building. The team should choose the location and the mode(s) of transportation involved. Be creative; brainstorm the best ways to guide first-time visitors to the selected location using all the media at your disposal.

3. **Collaboration: Collaborating on Writing Projects; Media Skills: Blogging** L.O.❷ In this project, you will conduct research on your own and then merge your results with those of the rest of your team. Search Twitter for messages on the subject of workplace safety. (You can use Twitter's advanced search page at http://search.twitter.com/advanced or use the "site: twitter.com" qualifier on a regular search engine.)

   Compile at least five general safety tips that apply to any office setting, and then meet with your team to select the five best tips from all those the team has collected. Collaborate on a blog post that lists the team's top five tips.

4. **Collaboration: Planning Meetings; Media Skills: Presentations** L.O.❸ A project leader has made notes about covering the items listed below at the quarterly budget meeting. Prepare an agenda by putting these items into a logical order and rewriting them, where necessary, to give phrases a more consistent sound.

   Create a presentation slide for your agenda (or a blog post, as your instructor indicates).
   - Budget Committee Meeting to be held on December 12, 2014, at 9:30 a.m.
   - I will call the meeting to order.
   - Site director's report: A closer look at cost overruns on Greentree site.
   - The group will review and approve the minutes from last quarter's meeting.
   - I will ask the finance director to report on actual vs. projected quarterly revenues and expenses.
   - I will distribute copies of the overall divisional budget and announce the date of the next budget meeting.
   - Discussion: How can we do a better job of anticipating and preventing cost overruns?
   - Meeting will take place in Conference Room 3.
   - What additional budget issues must be considered during this quarter?

5. **Collaboration: Participating in Meetings** L.O.❸ With a classmate, attend a local community or campus meeting where you can observe group discussion. Take notes individually during the meeting and then work together to answer the following questions. Submit your conclusions in an email message to your instructor.
   a. What is your evaluation of this meeting? In your answer, consider (1) the leader's ability to clearly state the meeting's goals, (2) the leader's ability to engage members in a meaningful discussion, and (3) the group's listening skills.
   b. How well did the individual participants listen? How could you tell?
   c. Compare the notes you took during the meeting with those of your classmate. What differences do you notice? How do you account for these differences?

6. **Collaboration: Participating in Virtual Meetings** L.O.❸ Virtual world culture is an aspect of social networking technology that has applications in business not just for meetings, but also for training and collaboration. To prepare yourself for participating in a 3D virtual meeting, explore what it is like to move around in virtual worlds by creating an avatar in Second Life. You can get training to assist you in making your first visit to a virtual world by visiting www.secondlife.astd.com.

   Write a short summary of your experience in an email to your professor. Include three paragraphs summarizing what happened, the advantages and disadvantages of virtual representation of yourself, and how nonverbal communication is used or affected in the virtual environment.

7. **Interpersonal Communication: Listening Actively** L.O.❹ For the next several days, take notes on your listening performance during at least a half-dozen situations in class, during social activities, and at work, if applicable. Referring to the traits of effective listeners in Table 2.2 on page 35, rate yourself using *always, frequently, occasionally,* or *never* on these positive listening habits. In a report no longer than one page, summarize your analysis and identify specific areas in which you can improve your listening skills.

8. **Interpersonal Communication: Listening to Empathize** L.O.❹ Think back over conversations you have had with friends, family members, co-workers, or classmates in the past week. Select a conversation in which the other person wanted to talk about something that was troubling him or her—a bad situation at work, a scary exam on the horizon, difficulties with a professor, a health problem, financial concerns, or the like. As you replay this conversation in your mind, think about how well you did in terms of empathic listening (see page 34). For example, did you find yourself being critical when the person really just needed someone to listen? Did you let the person know, by your words or actions, that you cared about his or her dilemma, even if you were not able to help in any other way? Analyze your listening performance in a brief email message to your instructor. Be sure not to disclose any private information; you can change the names of the people involved or the circumstances as needed to maintain privacy.

9. **Nonverbal Communication: Analyzing Nonverbal Signals** L.O.❺ Select a piece of mail, from any company, that you received at work or at home. Analyze its appearance. What nonverbal messages does this piece send? Are these messages consistent with the content of the mailing? If not, what could the sender have done to make the nonverbal communication consistent with the verbal communication? Summarize your findings in a post on your class blog or in an email message to your instructor.

10. **Nonverbal Communication: Analyzing Nonverbal Signals** L.O.❺ Describe what the following gestures or postures suggest when someone exhibits them during a conversation. How did you reach your conclusions about each nonverbal signal? How do such signals influence your interpretation of spoken words? Summarize your findings in a post on your class blog or in an email message to your instructor.

a. Shifting one's body continuously while seated
b. Twirling and playing with one's hair
c. Sitting in a sprawled position
d. Rolling one's eyes
e. Extending a weak handshake

11. **Communication Etiquette: Telephone Skills; Media Skills: Scripting a Voice Mail Message** L.O.❻ Late on a Friday afternoon, you learn that the facilities department is going to move you—and your computer, your desk, and all your files—to another office first thing Monday morning. However, you have an important client meeting scheduled in your office for Monday afternoon, and you need to finalize some contract details on Monday morning. You simply can't lose access to your office at that point, and you're more than a little annoyed that your boss didn't ask you before approving the move. He has already left for the day, but you know he usually checks his voice mail over the weekend, so you decide to leave a voice mail message, asking him to cancel the move or at least call you at home as soon as possible. Using the voice mail guidelines listed in Table 2.3 on page 39, plan your message (use an imaginary phone number as your contact number and make up any other details you need for the call). As directed by your instructor, submit either a written script of the message or a recording of the actual message.

12. **Communication Etiquette: Online Etiquette; Media Skills: Writing Blog Posts** L.O.❻ Between the immediate nature of electronic communication and the ability for people to disguise their identity by using screen names, online discussions sometimes get nasty. Posting rude comments or vicious product reviews might help a person release some pent-up anger, but such messages rarely help the situation. The people on the receiving end of these messages are likely to get defensive or ignore the comments entirely, rather than focusing on finding a solution. Find an online review of a product, service, or company that strikes you as rude to the point of being nasty. For your class blog (or other media as assigned by your instructor) write a summary of the situation, explain why the rude comment is ineffective, and write a new version that is more effective (as in, more likely to bring about the change the writer wanted).

13. **Communication Etiquette: Online Etiquette; Media Skills: Using Social Media** L.O.❻ Many celebrities are successful brands managing their careers, and businesses can learn from successful celebrities too, particularly when it comes to building communities online using social media. For instance, social media guru Dan Schawbel cites

Vin Diesel, Ashton Kutcher, and Lady Gaga, as celebrities who have used Facebook to build their personal brands.[58] Locate three celebrities (musicians, actors, authors, or athletes) who have sizable fan bases on Facebook, Twitter, or Instagram and analyze how they use the social network. Using whatever medium your instructor requests, write a brief analysis (no more than one page) of the lessons, positive or negative, that a business could learn from these celebrities. Be sure to cite specific elements from the Facebook, Twitter, or Instagram pages you've chosen, and if you think any of the celebrities have made mistakes in their use of social media, describe those as well. Include a screenshot or image example.

14. **Nonverbal Communication: Self-Assessment** L.O. ⑤ What type of persona do you want to have in the workplace? What nonverbal signals can you send to create this persona? In meetings, others form an impression about your work abilities. How can you ensure that you come across as confident, competent, and easy to get along with? Use the checklist below to assess your nonverbal communication skills.

15. **Collaboration: Using Meeting Technology** L.O. ③ Hold a 10-minute (or longer) conversation with someone you know using Skype or a similar live-video-chat technology. Write a reflection about your experience and send it to your instructor in an email message. In your reflection,
    - Describe the conversation (topics you discussed, the name and role of the person with whom you conversed, the date, time, and locations of the participants).

- Compare the online conversation to the face-to-face conversation you might have had instead.
- Compare the experience to a telephone conversation.
- Identify the advantages and disadvantages of using this particular technology and consider whether these advantages and disadvantages would be similar in a business setting.
- Describe your feelings about using this technology—how did it affect your effectiveness as a communicator?
- Recommend whether a company should use this technology for job interviews and provide your reasons.

16. **Collaboration: Planning Meetings; Media Skills: Email Skills** L.O. ③ You've probably worked as a volunteer on a committee or with team members for class assignments. You know how hard it is to get a diverse group of individuals together for a productive meeting. Maybe you've tried different locations, such as one member's home, or a table at the library. This time you're going to suggest a local coffee shop.

The committee you're leading is a community volunteer group planning a garbage pickup project at a local park. Your meeting goal is to brainstorm ways to encourage public participation in this environmental event, to be held next Earth Day.

Write a short email message telling committee members about the meeting. Include the time, date, duration, and location (choose a place you know). Mention the meeting goal to encourage attendance. Give your instructor a copy of the email.

| Element of Nonverbal Communication | Always | Frequently | Occasionally | Never |
|---|---|---|---|---|
| I stand tall to appear confident. | _____ | _____ | _____ | _____ |
| I walk with purpose. | _____ | _____ | _____ | _____ |
| I greet others when I pass. | _____ | _____ | _____ | _____ |
| I maintain eye contact when speaking with others. | _____ | _____ | _____ | _____ |
| I dress appropriately for the type of workplace. | _____ | _____ | _____ | _____ |
| I avoid provocative clothing. | _____ | _____ | _____ | _____ |
| I avoid controversial slogans on clothing. | _____ | _____ | _____ | _____ |
| I wear appropriate shoes for my workplace. | _____ | _____ | _____ | _____ |
| I maintain personal hygiene. | _____ | _____ | _____ | _____ |
| I take off hats when working inside. | _____ | _____ | _____ | _____ |
| I open doors for others if I get to the door first. | _____ | _____ | _____ | _____ |
| I don't use my electronic devices when in meetings and presentations. | _____ | _____ | _____ | _____ |

## BUSINESS COMMUNICATION NOTEBOOK

# Technology

## What You Should Know About Videoconferencing Versus Face-to-Face Meetings

Ever since AT&T unveiled a videophone at the 1964 World's Fair, two-way TV has been touted as the next revolution in communication. Videoconferencing has always been a good idea, but its high costs and technical complexity had put off widespread acceptance—until now.

Today videoconferencing is better, faster, and more user-friendly. System quality makes participants feel as if they are in the same room. Furthermore, the costs of installing videoconferencing systems have dropped dramatically in the last few years. Software such as WebEx can enable videoconferencing at desktops, and applications for videoconferencing on smartphones enable participation from almost anywhere. In some cases, the time and cost savings from reduced corporate travel could pay for these systems in less than one year.

Spurred by cost savings on corporate travel, the increasing frequency of cancelled flights, and long airport delays, companies are now being pressured by customers and suppliers to install such services. In fact, the hottest first-class seat is no longer on an airplane—instead, it's in front of a videoconferencing camera.

Will videoconferencing make face-to-face meetings obsolete? Probably not. You still need to seal important deals with personal handshakes—especially when conflicts or emotions are involved or when a relationship requires personal interaction to flourish. But videoconferencing will likely change the way people meet. For instance, lower-priority meetings and even details of merger talks could take place without participants leaving their hometown offices.

## Applications for Success

Gather some tips on presenting using the technology at the University of Guelph's Teaching Support Services website at **www.tss.uoguelph.ca/cts/vidcontip.html**. As well, read about WebEx by visiting **www.webex.com**. Follow links for tips on presenting.

Assume you are an assistant to the director of communications at Morris & McWhinney, a law firm with branches in Vancouver, Calgary, and Toronto. The partners have asked your boss to investigate whether the firm should use videoconferencing and purchase any equipment needed. To begin, your boss asks you to examine the general pros and cons.

Do the following:

1. Summarize your own opinion about whether videoconferencing is appropriate for meetings that your firm conducts. Are there any meetings that would not be right for videoconferencing?
2. Make a list of videoconferencing's advantages and disadvantages and how it would be used at Morris & McWhinney.
3. Based on the results of your examination (and assuming that money is no object), make a recommendation to your boss to either purchase or not purchase the equipment.

# Planning Business Messages

**LEARNING OBJECTIVES**

*After studying this chapter, you will be able to*

1. Describe the three-step writing process and explain why it will help you create better messages in less time.
2. Explain what it means to analyze the situation when planning a message.
3. Describe the techniques for gathering information for simple messages and identify three attributes of quality information.
4. Compare the four major classes of media and list the factors to consider when choosing the most appropriate medium for a message.
5. Explain why good organization is important to both you and your audience and explain how to organize any business message.

Google's innovations in web search and advertising have made its website a top internet property and its brand one of the most recognized in the world. Google Canada has offices in Waterloo, Toronto, Montreal, and Ottawa with over 400 'Canooglers' working on teams across engineering, sales, marketing, PR, policy, and HR. Engineers at Google Canada work on many of the company's core products including Chrome, Safe Browsing, and Gmail while the sales teams assist Canadian businesses with their digital advertising strategies.

This chapter is the first of three that explore the three-step writing process, a time-tested method for creating more effective messages in less time. The techniques you'll learn in this chapter will help you plan and organize messages that will capture and keep your audience's attention.

## Understanding the Three-Step Writing Process

No matter what kind of information you need to convey, your goal is to craft a message that has a clear purpose, meets the needs of your audience, and communicates efficiently and effectively. For every message you send, you can reduce the time and energy required to achieve this goal by following a three-step process (see Figure 3.1):

- **Planning business messages.** To plan any message, first *analyze the situation* by defining your purpose and developing a profile of your audience. When you're sure about what you need to accomplish with your message, *gather information*

**LEARNING OBJECTIVE 1**
Describe the three-step writing process and explain why it will help you create better messages in less time.

The three-step writing process consists of *planning, writing,* and *completing* your messages.

## FIGURE 3.1   The Three-Step Writing Process

### ① Planning

**Analyze the Situation**
- Define your purpose and develop an audience profile.

**Gather Information**
- Determine audience needs and obtain the information necessary to satisfy those needs.

**Select the Right Medium**
- Select the best medium for delivering your message.

**Organize the Information**
- Define your main idea, limit your scope, select a direct or an indirect approach, and outline your content.

### ② Writing

**Adapt to Your Audience**
- Be sensitive to audience needs by using a "you" attitude, politeness, positive emphasis, and unbiased language. Build a strong relationship with your audience by establishing your credibility and projecting your company's preferred image. Control your style with a conversational tone, plain English, and appropriate voice.

**Compose the Message**
- Choose strong words that will help you create effective sentences and coherent paragraphs.

### ③ Completing

**Revise the Message**
- Evaluate the content. Edit the message for readability, conciseness, and clarity.

**Produce the Message**
- Use effective design elements and suitable layout for a clean, professional appearance.

**Proofread the Message**
- Review for errors in layout, spelling, and mechanics.

**Distribute the Message**
- Deliver your message using the chosen medium; make sure all documents and all relevant files are distributed successfully.

that will meet your audience's needs. Next, *select the right medium* (oral, written, visual, or electronic) to deliver your message. Then *organize the information* by defining your main idea, limiting your scope, selecting the direct or indirect approach, and outlining your content. Planning messages is the focus of this chapter.

- **Writing business messages.** Once you've planned your message, *adapt your approach to your audience* with sensitivity, relationship skills, and style. Then you're ready to *compose your message* by choosing strong words, creating effective sentences, and developing coherent paragraphs. Writing business messages is discussed in Chapter 4.

- **Completing business messages.** After writing your first draft, *revise your message* to make sure it is clear, concise, and correct. Next, *produce* your message, giving it an attractive, professional appearance. *Proofread* the final product for typos, spelling errors, and other mechanical problems. Finally, *distribute* your message using an appropriate combination of personal and technological tools. Completing business messages is discussed in Chapter 5.

Throughout this book, you'll see the three steps in this process applied to a wide variety of business messages: short messages (Chapters 6 through 9), reports and proposals (Chapters 10 and 11), oral presentations (Chapter 12), and employment messages (Chapters 13 and 14).

*As a starting point, try to allot roughly half your available time for planning, a quarter for writing, and a quarter for completing a message.*

The more you use the three-step process, the easier and faster writing will become for you. You'll also get better at allotting your time for each step. As a general rule, try using roughly half your time for planning, a quarter of your time for writing, and the remaining quarter for completing the project.

Using half your time for planning might seem excessive, but skipping or shortchanging the planning stage often creates extra work later in the process. First, taking the time to understand your audience members helps you find and assemble the information they need. Second, with careful planning, the writing stage is faster, easier, and a lot less stressful. Third, planning can save you from embarrassing blunders that could hurt your company or your career.

Of course, the ideal time allotment varies from project to project. Simpler and shorter messages require less planning than long reports, websites, and other complex projects. However, start with the 50-25-25 split as a guideline, and use your best judgment for each project.

# Analyzing the Situation

**LEARNING OBJECTIVE** ❷
**Explain what it means to analyze the situation when planning a message.**

Every communication effort takes place in a particular situation, meaning you have a specific message to send to a specific audience under a specific set of circumstances. Analyzing the situation gives you the insights necessary to meet your own needs as a communicator while also meeting the information needs of your recipients.

A successful message starts with a clear purpose that connects the sender's needs with the audience's needs. For example, describing your qualifications in an email message to an executive in your own company differs significantly from describing your qualifications in your LinkedIn profile. The email message is likely to be focused on one specific goal, such as explaining why you would be a good choice to head up a major project, and you can focus on the needs of a single, personally identifiable reader. In contrast, your social networking profile could have multiple goals, such as connecting with your peers in other companies and presenting your qualifications to potential employers, and it might be viewed by hundreds or thousands of readers, each with his or her own needs. These two scenarios have different purposes and different audiences, so they require distinctly different messages.

## Defining Your Purpose

All business messages have a **general purpose**: to inform, to persuade, to collaborate, or to initiate a conversation. This purpose helps define the overall approach you'll need to take, from gathering information to organizing your message. Within the scope of that general purpose, each message also has a **specific purpose**, which identifies what you hope to accomplish with your message. To define your specific purpose, consider what action you want the message's recipients to take. One way of developing this **action-based purpose statement** is to complete this sentence with a verb: "I want my reader to. . . ." You need to state your specific purpose as precisely as possible, even identifying which audience members should respond, how they should respond, and when.

*Business messages have both a general and a specific purpose.*

After you have defined your specific purpose, make sure it merits the time and effort required for you to prepare and send the message. Ask these four questions:

- **Will anything change as a result of your message?** Make sure you don't contribute to information overload by sending messages that won't change anything. Complaining about things that you have no influence over is a good example of a message that probably shouldn't be sent.
- **Is your purpose realistic?** If your purpose involves a radical shift in action or attitude, proceed carefully. Consider proposing a first step so that your message acts as the beginning of a learning process.
- **Is the time right?** People who are busy or distracted when they receive your message are less likely to pay attention to it.
- **Is your purpose acceptable to your organization?** Your company's business objectives and policies, and even laws that apply to your particular industry, may dictate whether a given purpose is acceptable.

*After defining your purpose, verify that the message will be worth the time and effort required to create, send, and receive it.*

When you are satisfied that you have a clear and meaningful purpose and that now is a smart time to proceed, your next step is to understand your audience and their needs.

## Developing an Audience Profile

Before audience members will take the time to read or listen to your messages, they need to be interested in what you're saying. They need to see what's in it for them: which of their needs will be met or problems solved by listening to your advice or doing what you ask. The more you know about your audience members, their needs, and their expectations, the more effectively you'll be able to communicate with them. Use a Plan Sheet to help you think through your audience analysis, such as the example in Figure 3.2.

Conducting an audience analysis involves the following steps:

Ask yourself some key questions about your audience:

- Who are they?
- How many people do you need to reach?
- How much do they already know about the subject?
- What is their probable reaction to your message?

If audience members have different levels of understanding of the topic, consider ways to offer choices for more detail.

- **Identify your primary audience.** For some messages, certain audience members might be more important than others. Don't ignore the needs of less influential members, but make sure you address the concerns of the key decision makers.
- **Determine audience size and geographic distribution.** A message aimed at 10 000 people spread around the globe will likely require a different approach than one aimed at a dozen people down the hall.
- **Determine audience composition.** Look for similarities and differences in culture, language, age, education, organizational rank and status, attitudes, experience, motivations, and any other factors that might affect the success of your message. The scenario in Figure 3.3 illustrates how a seemingly positive message about employee benefits could generate a wide range of responses from employees with different concerns and interests.
- **Gauge audience members' level of understanding.** If audience members share your general background, they'll probably understand your material without difficulty. If not, your message will need an element of education, or attachments, glossaries, or links to direct readers to information related to their needs.
- **Understand audience expectations and preferences.** For example, will members of your audience expect complete details or just a summary of the main points? In general, for internal communication, the higher up the organization your message goes, the fewer details people want to see.

---

**FIGURE 3.2**  Audience Analysis Helps You Plan Your Message

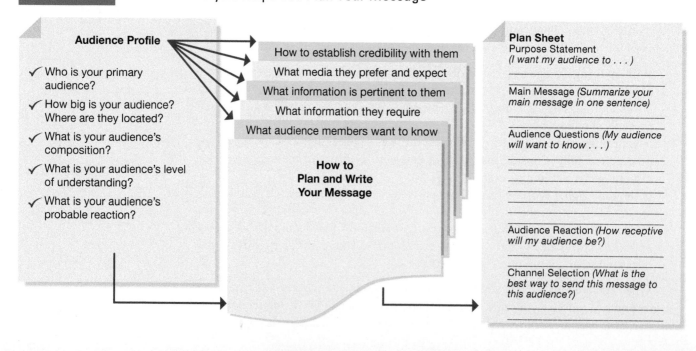

## FIGURE 3.3  Predicting the Effects of Audience Composition

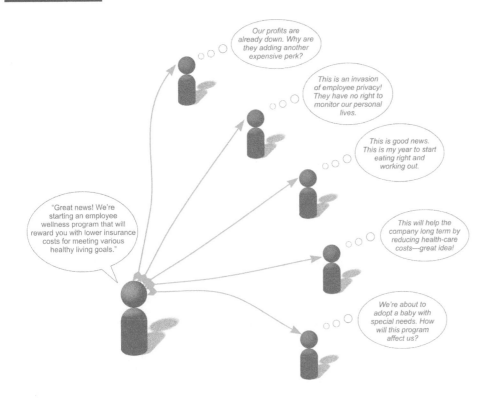

- **Assess the way in which the audience prefers to get information.** While Boomers (those born in the mid-1940s to mid-1960s) often prefer print, Millennials (those born since 1982) often prefer visual and online channels of communication, finding things out by looking on the internet or consulting peers. For example, WorkSafeBC, the Workers' Compensation Board in British Columbia, needed to reach out to young workers between the ages of 18 and 26, since these workers experience a high rate of injury and fatalities. To reach these Millennials, WorkSafeBC produced a series of 60 videos on working safely and posted them on YouTube. In addition, they created a website called Raise Your Hand (www.raiseyourhand.com) in which young people tell their injury stories, peer-to-peer, and pledge to speak up for their safety concerns at work. These choices show excellent audience analysis because the channels of communication matched the age group's style and method of getting information. The messages conveyed emotional content through powerful storytelling—both effective tools in persuasion. The technology also gives the sender a way to track the numbers of people who viewed the material and ensured the messages reached the audience effectively.

- **Forecast probable audience reaction.** As you'll read later in this chapter, the potential reaction from your audience affects the way your message is organized. If you expect a favourable response, you can state conclusions and recommendations up front and offer minimal supporting evidence. If you expect skepticism, you can introduce conclusions gradually and with more proof. Figure 3.4 shows an example of audience analysis.

### REAL-TIME UPDATES

**Learn More by Reading This PDF**

**Dig deep into audience needs with this planning tool**

This in-depth audience analysis tool can help you analyze audiences for even the most complex communication scenarios. Go to http://real-timeupdates.com/bce6 and click on Learn More. If you are using MyBCommLab, you can access Real-Time Updates within Business Communication Resources.

FIGURE 3.4 Using Audience Analysis to Plan a Message

**Audience analysis notes**

**Project:** A report recommending that we close down the on-site exercise facility and subsidize private memberships at local health clubs.

- **Primary audience:** Nicole Perazzo, vice-president of operations, and her supervisory team.

- **Size and geographic distribution:** Nine managers total; Nicole and five of her staff are here on site; three other supervisors are based in Hong Kong. Since the Hong Kong supervisors are not familiar with the facility, I will include a description and usage statistics.

- **Composition:** All have experience in operations management, but several are new to the company so I'll provide statistics and quotes from employees regarding how they benefit from having it on site.

- **Level of understanding:** All will no doubt understand the financial considerations, but the newer managers may not understand the importance of the on-site exercise facility to many of our employees.

- **Expectations and preferences.** They're expecting a firm recommendation, backed up with well-thought-out financial rationale and suggestions for communicating the bad news to employees. For a decision of this magnitude, a formal report is appropriate; email distribution is expected.

- **Probable reaction.** From one-on-one discussions, I know that several of the managers receiving this report are active users of the on-site facility and won't welcome the suggestion that we should shut it down. So, I must emphasize the cost of running it versus the cost of the alternative. However, some nonexercisers generally think it's a luxury the company can't afford. Audience reactions will range from highly positive to highly negative; the report should focus on convincing the people who are likely to have the most negative reactions.

LEARNING OBJECTIVE ③
Describe the techniques for gathering information for simple messages and identify three attributes of quality information.

If a project doesn't require formal research or you need an answer in a hurry, use informal techniques to gather information.

# Gathering Information

When you have a clear picture of your audience, your next step is to assemble the information that you will include in your message. For simple messages, you may already have all the information at hand, but for more complex messages, you may need to do considerable research and analysis before you're ready to begin writing. Chapter 10 explores formal techniques for finding, evaluating, and processing information, but you can often use a variety of informal techniques to gather insights and guide your research efforts:

- **Consider the audience's perspective.** Put yourself in the audience's position: what are these people thinking, feeling, or planning? What information do they need in order to move forward? What questions would they have about your topic? If you are initiating a conversation in a social media context, what information will stimulate discussion in your target communities?
- **Listen to the community.** For almost any subject related to business these days, chances are there is a community of customers, product enthusiasts, or other people who engage in online discussions. Find them and listen to what they have to say.
- **Read reports and other company documents.** Annual reports, financial statements, news releases, blogs and microblogs by industry experts, marketing reports, and customer surveys are just a few of the many potential sources of information. Find out whether your company has a *knowledge-management system*, a centralized database that collects the experiences and insights of employees throughout the organization.

- **Talk with supervisors, colleagues, or customers.** Fellow workers and customers may have information you need, or they may know what your audience will be interested in.
- **Ask your audience for input.** If you're unsure what audience members need from your message, ask them if at all possible. Admitting you don't know but want to meet their needs will impress an audience more than guessing and getting it wrong.

## Uncovering Audience Needs

In many situations, your audience's information needs are readily apparent, such as when a consumer sends an email asking a specific question. In other situations, you may need to do some detective work. For example, if you're asked to suggest steps a company can take to improve employee morale, you'll need to investigate the underlying reasons for low morale. By including this information in your report—even though it wasn't specifically requested— you demonstrate to your audience that you've thoroughly investigated the problem.

## Providing Required Information

In addition to delivering the right *quantity* of required information, you are responsible for verifying the *quality* of that information. Ask yourself these three questions:

- **Is the information accurate and complete?** Inaccuracies and missing information can cause a host of problems, from embarrassment and lost productivity to serious safety and legal issues. Be sure to review any mathematical or financial calculations. Check all dates and schedules. Examine your own assumptions and conclusions to be certain they are valid.
- **Is the information ethical?** By working hard to ensure the accuracy of the information you gather, you'll also avoid many ethical problems in your messages. However, messages can also be unethical if important information is omitted or obscured.
- **Is the information pertinent?** Some points will be more important to your audience than others. Focusing on the information that concerns your audience the most can increase your chances of sending an effective message.

You have a responsibility to make sure the information you provide is accurate, ethical, pertinent, and complete.

# Selecting the Right Medium

LEARNING OBJECTIVE 4
Compare the four major classes of media and list the factors to consider when choosing the most appropriate medium for a message.

As the options continue to multiply, choosing the right medium for each message is becoming an important communication skill in itself. Although media categories have become increasingly blurred in recent years, for the sake of discussion you can think of media as being *oral*, *print*, *visual*, or *electronic* (which often combines several media types).

## Oral Media

Oral media include face-to-face conversations, interviews, speeches, and in-person presentations and meetings: whenever you communicate with someone who is physically in the same place. By giving communicators the ability to see, hear, and react to each other, oral media are useful for encouraging people to ask questions, make comments, and work together to reach a consensus or decision. Face-to-face interaction is particularly helpful in complex, emotionally charged situations in which establishing or fostering a business relationship is important.[1] In particular, experts recommend that managers engage in frequent "walk-arounds," chatting with employees face to face to get input, answer questions, and interpret important business events and trends.[2]

Oral communication is best when you need to encourage interaction, express emotions, or monitor emotional responses.

   The disadvantages of oral media include limited reach (because communication is with only those people who are present at a particular time), reduced control over the message (because people can question, interrupt, or take control of a conversation), and the difficulty of refining your message before transmitting it. Also, the spontaneity of oral communication can be a disadvantage if you don't want a lot of interaction in a particular situation.

However, consider the situation carefully before deciding to limit interaction by changing to another medium. As a manager, you will encounter unpleasant situations (declining an employee's request for a raise, for example) in which sending an electronic message or otherwise avoiding personal contact will seem appealing. In many such cases, though, you owe the other party the opportunity to ask questions or express concerns. Moreover, facing the tough situations in person will earn you a reputation as an honest, caring manager.

## Written Media

Written media increase your control, help you reach dispersed audiences, and minimize distortion.

Written messages (those printed on paper rather than delivered electronically) take many forms, from traditional memos to glossy reports. **Memos** are brief printed documents traditionally used for the routine, day-to-day exchange of information within an organization. In many organizations, electronic media have replaced most paper memos, but you may need to create one from time to time.

**Letters** are brief written messages generally sent to recipients outside the organization. In addition to conveying a particular message, they perform an important public relations function by fostering good working relationships with customers, suppliers, and others. Many organizations save time and money on routine communication with *form letters*, in which a standard message is personalized as needed for each recipient.

**Reports** and **proposals** are usually longer than memos and letters, although both can be created in memo or letter format. These documents come in a variety of lengths, ranging from a few pages to several hundred, and are usually fairly formal in tone. Chapters 10 and 11 discuss reports and proposals in detail. Appendix A includes sample formats for memos, letters, and reports.

## Visual Media

In some situations, a message that is predominantly visual with text used to support the illustration can be more effective than a message that relies primarily on text.

The importance of visual elements in business communication continues to grow. Many business communicators are discovering the power of messages in which the visual element is dominant and supported by small amounts of text. For the purposes of this discussion, you can think of visual media as formats in which one or more visual elements play a central role in conveying the message content.

Messages that combine powerful visuals with supporting text are effective because today's audiences are pressed for time and bombarded with messages, so anything that communicates quickly is appreciated. Visuals are also effective at describing complex ideas and processes with less work on the reader's part. For example, an infographic relies on images to explain a topic, with very little text. Also, in a multilingual business world, diagrams, symbols, and other images can lower communication barriers by requiring less language processing. Finally, visual images can be easier to remember than purely textual descriptions or explanations.

The use of infographics is growing because they convey messages so quickly and are easy to share via social technologies. Many sites offer do-it-yourself templates for constructing infographics, such as **piktochart.com**, **visual.ly**, **infogr.am**, or **easel.ly**.[3]

## Electronic Media

To use many electronic media options successfully, a person must have at least some degree of technical skill.

The range of electronic media is broad and continues to grow, from podcasts and blogs to wikis, email, and text messaging.

The growth of electronic communication options is both a blessing and a curse for business communicators. On the one hand, you have more tools to choose from, with more ways to deliver content. On the other hand, the sheer range of choices can complicate your job because you often need to choose among multiple media, and you need to know how to use each medium successfully.

You'll learn more about using electronic media in business settings throughout this book (and in Chapter 6, in particular); for now, here is a quick overview of the major electronic media used in business today:

- **Electronic versions of oral media.** These media include telephone calls, teleconferencing, voice mail messages, audio recordings such as podcasts (covered in Chapter 6), *voice synthesis* (creating audio signals from computer data), *voice recognition* (converting audio signals to computer data), and even animated online characters with technology borrowed from video games (see Figure 3.5). Some websites now feature talking animated figures (*avatars*) that offer visitors a more engaging experience. On some websites, these are the "face" of automated *bots* that attempt to answer simple questions and direct visitors to specific parts of the website. Even with all the other choices now available, the simple telephone call is still a vital communication link for many organizations, and phone options continue to expand with *internet telephony* services (also known by the technical term VoIP, which stands for *voice over IP*, the internet protocol). Skype, the best known of these, offers voice and video calling on a number of platforms, including computers, mobile phones, and tablets. Wi-Fi phones add a degree of mobility to VoIP as well. Although telephone calls can't convey all the nonverbal signals of an in-person conversation, they can convey quite a few, including tone of voice, pace, laughter, pauses, and so on.

  *Avoid leaving lengthy voice mails.*

- **Electronic versions of written media.** These options range from email and instant messaging (IM) to blogs, websites, social networks, and wikis. These media are in a state of constant change, in terms of both what is available and who tends to use which media. For example, email has been a primary business medium for the past decade or two, but it is being replaced in many cases by IM, blogs, text messaging, and social networks.[4] Many reports and other documents that were once distributed on paper are now easily transferred electronically, often by PDF.

  *Electronic written media have largely replaced printed messages in many companies.*

- **Electronic versions of visual media.** These choices can include electronic presentations (using Microsoft PowerPoint, Apple Keynote, Prezi, and Google Docs and other software), computer animation (using software such as Adobe Flash to create many of the animated sequences you see on websites, for example), and video. Businesses have made extensive use of video (particularly for training, new product promotions, and

---

**FIGURE 3.5** An Example of Electronic Oral Media

executive announcements) for years—first on tape, then on DVD, and now online. Video is also incorporated in podcasting, creating **vidcasts**, and in blogging, creating **video blogs (vlogs)** and **mobile blogs (moblogs)**.[5] **Multimedia** refers to the use of two or more media to craft a single message, typically some combination of audio, video, text, and visual graphics. Multimedia advances continue to create intriguing communication possibilities, such as **augmented reality**, in which computer-generated text, graphics, or sounds are superimposed onto a user's physical reality, either on a device display or directly onto the physical world.[6]

Social visual communication has become an important business communication channel. Technologies such as Instagram and sites such as Pinterest have made it easy to share images, videos, and infographics for business as well as personal uses. For example, within days of Instagram's introduction of 15-second video capability in June 2013, major brands such as Lululemon and Starbucks were using it for marketing.[7]

## Factors to Consider When Choosing Media

You don't always have the option of choosing which medium to use for a particular message. For example, many companies have internal instant messaging (IM) or social networking systems that you are expected to use for certain types of communication, such as project updates. However, when you do have a choice, think carefully about which type of medium will work best for you and your audience. Consider these factors:

- **Media richness.** *Richness* is a medium's ability to: (1) convey a message through more than one informational cue (visual, verbal, or vocal), (2) facilitate feedback, and (3) establish personal focus. The richest medium is face-to-face communication: it's personal, it provides immediate feedback (verbal and nonverbal), and it conveys the emotion behind a message.[8] Multimedia presentations and multimedia webpages are also quite rich, with the ability to present images, animation, text, music, sound effects, and other elements. Many electronic media are also **interactive**, in that they enable audiences to participate in the communication process. At the other extremes are the leanest media such as texting and IM, which communicate in the simplest ways and provide little or no opportunity for audience feedback. In general, use richer media to send nonroutine or complex messages, to humanize your presence throughout the organization, to communicate caring to employees, and to gain employee commitment to company goals. Use leaner media to send routine messages or to transfer information that doesn't require significant explanation.[9] Consider switching media where appropriate; for example, by replying to an email message with a phone call to shorten the response time or clear up confusion, or if several people are copied on the email but your response relates to only one of them.
- **Message formality.** Your media choice is a nonverbal signal that affects the style and tone of your message. For example, a printed memo or letter is likely to be perceived as a more formal gesture than an email message or a blog post.
- **Media limitations.** Every medium has limitations. For instance, IM is perfect for communicating simple, straightforward messages, but it is ineffective for sending complex ones (unless it is incorporated into a larger collaboration system).
- **Urgency.** Some media establish a connection with the audience faster than others. However, be sure to respect audience members' time and workloads. If a message isn't urgent and doesn't require immediate feedback, choose a medium such as email that allows people to respond at their convenience.
- **Cost.** Cost is both a real financial factor and a perceived nonverbal signal. For example, depending on the context, extravagant (and expensive) video or multimedia presentations can send a nonverbal signal of sophistication and professionalism—or careless disregard for company budgets.

Media vary widely in terms of *richness*, which encompasses the number of information cues, feedback mechanisms, and opportunities for personalization.

Face-to-face is the richest media.

Lean media are used for routine messages.

Many types of media offer instant delivery, but take care not to interrupt people unnecessarily (with IM or phone calls, for example) if you don't need an immediate answer.

| TABLE 3.1 | Advantages and Disadvantages of Various Media | |
|---|---|---|

| MEDIA | ADVANTAGES | DISADVANTAGES |
|---|---|---|
| Oral | • Provide opportunity for immediate feedback<br>• Allow a certain ease of interaction<br>• Involve rich nonverbal cues (both physical gesture and vocal inflection)<br>• Allow you to express the emotion behind your message | • Restrict participation to those physically present<br>• Unless recorded, provide no permanent, verifiable record of the communication<br>• Reduce communicator's control over the message<br>• Other than messages that are prewritten and rehearsed, offer no opportunity to revise or edit your spoken words |
| Written | • Allow you to plan and control your message<br>• Reach geographically dispersed audiences<br>• Offer a permanent, verifiable record<br>• Minimize the distortion that can accompany oral messages<br>• Can be used to avoid immediate interactions<br>• De-emphasize any inappropriate emotional components | • Offer limited opportunities for timely feedback<br>• Lack the rich nonverbal cues provided by oral media<br>• Often take more time and more resources to create and distribute<br>• Can require special skills in preparation and production if document is elaborate |
| Visual | • Can convey complex ideas and relationships quickly<br>• Often less intimidating than long blocks of text<br>• Can reduce the burden on the audience to figure out how the pieces of a message or concept fit | • Can require artistic skills to design<br>• Require some technical skills to create<br>• Can require more time to create than equivalent amount of text<br>• Can be more difficult to transmit and store than simple textual messages |
| Electronic | • Deliver messages quickly<br>• Reach geographically dispersed audiences<br>• Offer the persuasive power of multimedia formats<br>• Can increase accessibility and openness in an organization<br>• Can offer a permanent record<br>• Enable audience interaction through social media features | • Enable audience interaction through social media features<br>• Are easy to overuse (sending too many messages to too many recipients)<br>• Create privacy risks and concerns (exposing confidential data; employer monitoring; accidental forwarding)<br>• Entail security risks (viruses; spyware; network breaches)<br>• Create productivity concerns (frequent interruptions; nonbusiness usage) |

- **Audience preferences.** Take into account which medium or media your audience expects or prefers.[10] For instance, businesspeople in Canada and Germany emphasize written messages, whereas in Japan professionals tend to emphasize oral messages—perhaps because Japan's high-context culture carries so much of the message in nonverbal cues and "between-the-lines" interpretation.[11]

*When choosing media, don't forget to consider your audience's expectations.*

Table 3.1 summarizes the advantages and disadvantages of these four categories of media. After you select the best medium for your purpose, situation, and audience, you are ready to start thinking about the organization of your message.

## Organizing Your Message

The ability to organize messages effectively is a skill that helps readers and writers alike. Good organization helps your readers in at least three ways:

- **It helps your audience understand your message.** By making your main idea clear and supporting it with logically presented evidence, you help audiences grasp the essential elements of your message.
- **It helps your audience accept your message.** Careful organization also helps you select and arrange your points in a diplomatic way that can soften the blow of unwelcome news or persuade skeptical readers to see your point of view. In contrast,

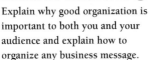

LEARNING OBJECTIVE 5
**Explain why good organization is important to both you and your audience and explain how to organize any business message.**

*Good organization benefits your audiences by helping them understand and accept your message in less time.*

a poorly organized message can trigger negative emotions that prevent people from seeing the value of what you have to say.

Good organization helps you by
reducing the time needed to create
effective messages.

To organize any message,

• Define your main idea

• Limit the scope

• Choose the direct or indirect
  approach

• Outline your information in a
  logical sequence

- **It saves your audience time.** Good organization saves readers time because they don't have to wade through irrelevant information, seek out other sources to fill in missing information, or struggle to follow your train of thought.

In addition to saving time and energy for your readers, good organization saves *you* time and consumes less of your creative energy. Writing proceeds more quickly because you don't waste time putting ideas in the wrong places or composing material that you don't need. You spend far less time rewriting. Good organizational skills are also good for your career because they help you develop a reputation as a clear thinker who cares about your readers and listeners.

But that said, what exactly is good organization? You can think of it as structuring messages in a way that helps recipients get all the information they need while requiring the least amount of time and energy for everyone involved. Good organization starts with a clear definition of your main idea.

## Defining Your Main Idea

The topic is the broad subject; the main idea makes a statement about the topic.

The **topic** of your message is the overall subject, and your **main idea** is a specific statement about that topic.

In longer documents and presentations, you often need to unify a mass of material, so you'll need to define a main idea that encompasses all the individual points you want to make. Sometimes you won't even be sure what your main idea is until you sort through the information. For tough assignments like these, consider a variety of techniques to generate creative ideas:

- **Brainstorming.** Working alone or with others, generate as many ideas and questions as you can, without stopping to criticize or organize. After you capture all these pieces, look for patterns and connections to help identify the main idea and the groups of supporting ideas.
- **Journalistic approach.** The journalistic approach asks *who*, *what*, *when*, *where*, *why*, and *how* questions to distill major thoughts from unorganized information.
- **Question-and-answer chain.** Start with a key question, from the audience's perspective, and work back toward your message. In most cases, you'll find that each answer generates new questions, until you identify the information that needs to be in your message.
- **Storyteller's tour.** Some writers find it best to talk through a communication challenge before trying to write. Record yourself as you describe what you intend to write. Then listen to the playback, identify ways to tighten and clarify the message, and repeat the process until you distill the main idea down to a single, concise message.
- **Mind mapping.** You can generate and organize ideas by using a graphic method called mind mapping. Start with a main idea and then branch out to connect every other related idea that comes to mind. You can find a number of free mind-mapping tools online, including https://bubbl.us.

## Limiting Your Scope

Limit the scope of your message so that you can convey your main idea as briefly as possible.

The **scope** of your message is the range of information you present, the overall length, and the level of detail—all of which need to correspond to your main idea. Some business messages have a length limit, whether from a boss's instructions, the technology you're using, or a time frame such as individual speaker slots during a seminar. Even if you don't have a preset length, limit your scope to the minimum amount of information needed to convey your main idea.

In addition to limiting the scope of your message, limit the number of major supporting points to half a dozen or so—and if you can get your idea across with fewer points, all the better. Listing 20 or 30 supporting points might feel as though you're being thorough, but your audience is likely to view such detail as rambling and mind numbing. Instead, group your supporting points under major headings, such as finance, customers, competitors, employees, or whatever is appropriate for your subject.

The number of words, pages, or minutes you need in order to communicate and support your main idea depends on your topic, your audience members' familiarity with the material and receptivity to your conclusions, and your credibility. You'll need fewer words to present routine information to a knowledgeable audience that already knows and respects you. You'll need more words to build a consensus about a complex and controversial subject, especially if the members of your audience are skeptical or hostile strangers.

## Choosing Between Direct and Indirect Approaches

After you've defined your main idea and supporting points, you're ready to decide on the sequence you will use to present your information. You have two basic options:

- **Direct approach.** When you know your audience will be receptive to your message, use the **direct approach**: start with the main idea (such as a recommendation, conclusion, or request) and follow that with your supporting evidence.
- **Indirect approach.** When your audience will be skeptical about or even resistant to your message, you generally want to use the **indirect approach**: start with the evidence first and build your case before presenting the main idea. Note that taking the indirect approach does not mean avoiding tough issues or talking around in circles. It simply means building up to your main idea in a careful and logical way.

To choose between these two alternatives, analyze your audience's likely reaction to your purpose and message (see Figure 3.6). Bear in mind, however, that each message is

With the direct approach, you open with the main idea of your message and support that with reasoning, evidence, and examples.

With the indirect approach, you withhold the main idea until you have built up to it logically and persuasively with reasoning, evidence, and examples.

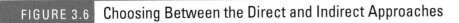

**FIGURE 3.6**   Choosing Between the Direct and Indirect Approaches

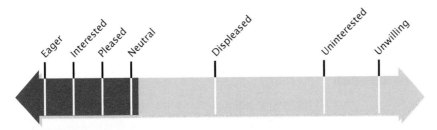

| | **Direct Approach** | **Indirect Approach** | |
|---|---|---|---|
| **Audience Reaction** | Eager/interested/ pleased/neutral | Displeased | Uninterested/unwilling |
| **Message Opening** | Start with the main idea, the request, or the good news. | Start with a neutral statement that acts as a transition to the reasons for the bad news. | Start with a statement or question that captures attention. |
| **Message Body** | Provide necessary details. | Give reasons to justify a negative answer. State or imply the bad news, and make a positive suggestion. | Arouse the audience's interest in the subject. Build the audience's desire to comply. |
| **Message Close** | Close with a cordial comment, a reference to the good news, or a statement about the specific action desired. | Close cordially. | Request action. |

unique. No simple formula will solve all your communication problems. For example, although an indirect approach may be best when you're sending bad news to outsiders, if you're writing a message to an associate, you may want to get directly to the point, even if the information is unpleasant. The direct approach might also be a good choice for long messages, regardless of your audience's attitude, because delaying the main idea could cause confusion and frustration.

The type of message also influences the choice of the direct or indirect approach. In the coming chapters, you'll get specific advice on choosing the best approach for a variety of different communication challenges.

## Outlining Your Content

*Outlining takes some time and effort, but it can often save you considerable time and effort in the composing and revising stages.*

After you have chosen the right approach, it's time to figure out the most logical and effective way to present your major points and supporting details. Get into the habit of creating outlines when you're preparing most business messages. You'll save time, get better results, and do a better job of navigating through complicated business situations. Even if you're just jotting down three or four points on a notepad, making a plan and sticking to it will help you cover the important details.

Basic outline formats identify each point with a number or letter and indent certain points to show their relationships in hierarchy. A good outline divides a topic into at least two parts, restricts each subdivision to one category, and ensures that each subdivision is separate and distinct (see Figure 3.7). It is much easier to rearrange your outline than it is to rearrange your first draft.

### REAL-TIME UPDATES

**Learn More by Watching This Presentation**

**Get helpful tips on creating an outline for any project**

Learn these proven steps for creating robust, practical outlines. Go to http://real-timeupdates.com/bce6 and click on Learn More. If you are using MyBCommLab, you can access Real-Time Updates within Business Communication Resources.

Whichever outlining or organizing scheme you use, start by stating your main idea, then list your major supporting points, and then provide examples and evidence:

- **Start with the main idea.** The main idea helps you establish the goals and general strategy of the message, and it summarizes (1) **what** you want your audience members to do, think, or feel after receiving the message, and (2) **why** it makes sense for them to do so. Everything in your message should either support the main idea or explain its implications. (Remember that

---

**FIGURE 3.7** **A Basic Outline Format**

*The particular message is divided into two major points (I and II)*

I. First major point
　A. First subpoint
　B. Second subpoint
　　1. Examples and evidence
　　2. Examples and evidence
　　　a. Detail
　　　b. Detail
　　3. Examples and evidence
　C. Third subpoint
II. Second major point
　A. First subpoint
　　1. Examples and evidence
　　2. Examples and evidence
　B. Second subpoint

*Subpoint B is supported with three sets of examples and evidence (1, 2, and 3), the second of which is further subdivided with two detail sections*

*The first major point is divided into three subpoints (A, B, and C)*

if you choose the indirect approach, the main idea will appear toward the end of your message, after you've presented your major supporting points.)

- **State the major points.** Support your main idea with the major points that clarify and explain your ideas in more concrete terms. If your purpose is to inform and the material is factual, your major points may be based on something physical or financial, for example—something you can visualize or measure, such as activities to be performed, functional units, spatial or chronological relationships, or parts of a whole.

   When you're describing a process, the major points are usually steps in the process. When you're describing an object, the major points often correspond to the parts of the object. When you're giving a historical account, major points represent events in the chronological chain of events. If your purpose is to persuade or to collaborate, select major points that develop a line of reasoning or a logical argument that proves your central message and motivates your audience to act.

- **Provide examples and evidence.** After you've defined the main idea and identified major supporting points, you're ready to back up those points with examples and evidence that help audience members understand, accept, and remember your message. Choose your examples and evidence carefully. You want to be compelling and complete but also as concise as possible. One strong example or piece of evidence can be more effective than three or four weaker items.

Figure 3.8 illustrates several of the key themes about organizing a message: helping readers get the information they need quickly, defining and conveying the main idea, limiting the scope of the message, choosing the approach, and outlining your information.

*Choose supporting points, evidence, and examples carefully; a few strong points will make your case better than a large collection of weaker points.*

## Building Reader Interest with Storytelling Techniques

Storytelling might seem like an odd subject for a business course, but stories can be an effective way to organize messages in a surprising number of business communication scenarios, from recruiting and training employees to enticing investors and customers. Storytelling is such a vital means of communicating that, in the words of management consultant Steve Tobak, "It's hard to imagine your career going anywhere if you can't tell a story."[12] Fortunately, you've been telling stories all your life, so narrative techniques already come naturally to you; now it's just a matter of adapting those techniques to business situations.

Moreover, you've already been on the receiving end of thousands of business stories—storytelling is one of the most common structures used in television commercials and other advertisements. People love to share stories about themselves and others, too, which makes social media ideal for storytelling.[13]

Career-related stories, such as how someone sought and found the opportunity to work on projects he or she is passionate about, can entice skilled employees to consider joining a firm. Entrepreneurs use stories to help investors see how their new ideas have the potential to affect people's lives (and therefore generate lots of sales). Stories can be cautionary tales as well, dramatizing the consequences of career blunders, ethical mistakes, and strategic missteps.

A key reason storytelling can be so effective is that stories help readers and listeners imagine themselves living through the experience of the person in the story. As a result, people tend to remember and respond to the message in ways that can be difficult to achieve with other forms of communication. In addition, stories can demonstrate cause-and-effect relationships in a compelling fashion.[14] Imagine attending a new employee orientation and listening to the trainer read off a list of ethics rules and guidelines. Now imagine the trainer telling the story of someone who, fresh out of college, and desperate

**REAL-TIME UPDATES**

**Learn More by Visiting This Interactive Website**

**Mine the web to piece together stories on any topic**

Storify is a media curation site that lets you tell or follow a story by linking voices from multiple social media platforms. Go to http://real-timeupdates.com/bce6 and click on Learn More. If you are using MyBCommLab, you can access Real-Time Updates within Business Communication Resources.

*Storytelling is an effective way to organize many business messages because it helps readers personalize the message and understand causes and consequences.*

## FIGURE 3.8 Improving the Organization of a Message

**Poor**

To: bethanycourson@mailsys.com

CC:

Subject: Incorporation

Hi Bethany,

I have to admit, my research had me longing for the simplicity of a sole proprietorship or the security of a traditional corporate job, But we have decided to move forward with this grand adventure, so onward is!

On the question of whether we would be wiser to form a partnership or to incorporate, I came upon this tidbit, which struck me as rather unfair. One of the major disadvantages of partnership is that the general partners have unlimited liability, which means our personal assets would be vulnerable in the event the company gets sued or goes bankrupt. However, people in some professions (but not ours!) are allowed to form the limited liability partnership, which protects them from this unlimited vulnerability.

Anyway, on to the question at hand. Incorporation is clearly the better choice for us. It protects us from unlimited liability, it makes it easier to add or remove managers (since they are simply employees and not partners), and it lets us sell stock to raise capital.

Partnership does have two advantages over incorporation. First, in terms of administration and legal requirements, a partnership is easier to establish and simpler to run. Second, partnerships are subject to only a single layer of taxation on income.

These advantages are compelling, but they are outweighed by unlimited liability, the difficulty of adding or replacing partners, and the lack of any means to sell shares to the public. Corporations are more complicated to set up and run, and income is taxed twice (first on company profits and then on any dividends we might pay out to shareholders). However, these are relatively minor concerns when we consider the powerful advantages and protections that incorporation would give us.

Please let me know your thoughts,
Erik

- This vague subject line offers few clues about the topic of the message.
- Starts off with an irrelevant discussion, doesn't explain what research this refers to, and fails to introduce the topic of the message.
- This paragraph introduces the topic but then shifts to an irrelevant discussion (it makes a good point about unlimited liability, but the point is buried in irrelevant material).
- The main idea, that the pair should incorporate, is buried in the middle of the message.
- By jumping from partnership to incorporation, back to partnership, and then back to incorporation again throughout the course of the message, the writer forces the reader to piece together the comparative evidence herself.

**Improved**

To: bethanycourson@mailsys.com

CC:

Subject: Advantages of Incorporation Over Partnership

Hi Bethany,

After our discussion yesterday about whether we should incorporate or form a partnership, I did some research to compare the advantages and disadvantages of the two structures. In light of our long-range plans for the business, particularly the need to raise funds for expansion, I believe the clear choice for us is incorporation.

Partnership does have two advantages over incorporation. First, in terms of administration and legal requirements, a partnership is easier to establish and simpler to run. Second, partnerships are subject to only a single layer of taxation on income.

These advantages are compelling, but they are outweighed by three disadvantages. First, the general partners in a partnership face unlimited legal liability, which means our personal assets would be vulnerable in the event of a product liability lawsuit or other calamity. Second, growth and succession issues can be tricky, such as if we decide to bring in another partner at some point or one of us wants to leave the company. Third, the inability to sell shares of stock really limits our opportunity to raise capital for expansion.

Incorporation addresses all three disadvantages of partnerships: our personal assets are not vulnerable in the event of lawsuits or company bankruptcy, adding or replacing managers is simpler because we are all employees of the corporation, and—most significantly—we can sell shares of stock to raise capital.

Yes, corporations are more complicated to set up and run, and income is taxed twice (first on company profits and then on any dividends we might pay out to shareholders). However, these are relatively minor concerns when we consider the powerful advantages and protections that incorporation would give us.

Please let me know your thoughts,
Erik

- Uses the email subject line to state the topic (incorporation vs. partnership) and the main idea (incorporation is the better choice).
- Provides context by referring to a previous conversation and then states the main idea.
- These two paragraphs support the main idea by showing how the disadvantages of partnerships outweigh the advantages.
- Continues to provide support by explaining how incorporation overcomes all three key disadvantages of partnerships.
- Completes the comparison by identifying two disadvantages of incorporation but states that these are outweighed by the advantages.

**Pointers for Good Organization**

- Get to the topic of the message quickly; don't make the reader guess what the message is about.
- Start with the main idea and then support it (direct approach) or build up to the main idea at the end (indirect approach).
- Group related ideas and present them in a logical order.
- Include only the information needed to convey and support your main idea.

to hit demanding sales targets, began entering transactions before customers had actually agreed to purchase. He was hoping the sales would eventually come through and no one would be the wiser. However, the scheme was exposed during a routine audit, and the rising star was booted out of the company with an ethical stain that would haunt him for years. You may not remember all the rules and guidelines, but chances are you will remember what happened to that person.

**A classic story has three basic parts.** The beginning of the story presents someone with whom the audience can identify in some way, and who has a dream to pursue or a problem to solve. (Think of how movies and novels often start by introducing a likable character who immediately gets into danger, for example.) The middle of the story shows this character taking action and making decisions as he or she pursues the goal or tries to solve the problem. The storyteller's objective here is to build the audience's interest by increasing the tension: Will the "hero" overcome the obstacles in his or her path and eventually succeed or fail? The end of the story answers that question and usually offers a lesson to be learned about the outcome as well.

Consider adding an element of storytelling whenever your main idea involves the opportunity to inspire, to persuade, to teach, or to warn readers or listeners about the potential outcomes of a particular course of action.

Organize stories in three parts: a beginning that introduces a sympathetic person with a dream or a challenge, a middle that shows the complications to be overcome, and an ending that resolves the situation and shows the moral or message of the story.

# LEARNING OBJECTIVES: Check Your Progress

**❶ OBJECTIVE Describe the three-step writing process and explain why it will help you create better messages in less time.**

The three-step writing process is built around planning, writing, and completing business messages. Planning involves analyzing the situation, gathering the information you will need to meet audience needs, selecting the right medium or combination of media, and organizing your information. The writing step involves adapting to your audience and composing your message. Completing involves the four tasks of revising, proofreading, producing, and distributing the message. The three-step process helps you create more effective messages because it helps you focus on what your audience needs to get from a message, and it saves you time.

**❷ OBJECTIVE Explain what it means to analyze the situation when planning a message.**

Analyzing the situation gives you the insights necessary to meet your own needs as a communicator while also meeting the information needs of your recipients. You can accomplish this goal by defining your purpose in sending the message and by creating a profile of your target audience. The *general purpose* of a message identifies your overall intent—to inform, to persuade, to collaborate, or to initiate a conversation. The *specific purpose* identifies what you hope to accomplish with the message.

Understanding your audience is a vital aspect of planning because the more you know about your audience members, their needs, and their expectations, the more effectively you'll be able to communicate with them. To create an audience profile, identify the primary audience: its size and geographic distribution, its composition (language, education, experience, and so on), its level of understanding, its expectations and preferences, its preferred way of getting information, and its probable reaction to your message.

**❸ OBJECTIVE Describe the techniques for gathering information for simple messages and identify three attributes of quality information.**

Simple messages usually don't require extensive information gathering, but to acquire useful insights: consider the audience's perspective; find and listen to online communities; read reports and other company documents; talk with supervisors, colleagues, or customers; and ask your audience for input if possible. Judge the quality of any information you include by making sure it is accurate, ethical, and pertinent.

**④ OBJECTIVE** Compare the four major classes of media and list the factors to consider when choosing the most appropriate medium for a message.

The four major classes of media are oral (direct conversation between two or more people), print (printed memos, letters, and reports), visual (messages in which visual elements carry the bulk of the message), and electronic (electronic versions of the other three). To choose the most appropriate medium for every message, consider media richness, message formality, media limitations, urgency, cost, and audience preferences.

**⑤ OBJECTIVE** Explain why good organization is important to both you and your audience and explain how to organize any business message.

Good organization helps your audience understand and accept your message with less time and effort. It also saves you time when preparing messages. With a clear path to follow when writing, you'll produce messages faster and spend far less time revising. To organize any message, define your main idea, limit the scope for maximum impact, choose the direct or indirect approach to match the situation, and outline your information in a logical sequence.

## MyBCommLab®

Go to MyBCommLab for everything you need to help you succeed in the job you've always wanted! Tools and resources include the following:
- Writing Activities
- Document Makeovers
- Video Exercises
- Grammar Exercises—and much more!

## Practise Your Grammar

Effective business communication starts with strong grammar skills. To improve your grammar skills, go to MyBCommLab, where you'll find exercises and diagnostic tests to help you produce clear, effective communication.

## Test Your Knowledge

To review chapter content related to each question, refer to the indicated Learning Objective.

1. What are the three steps in the writing process? L.O.❶
2. What two types of purposes do all business messages have? L.O.❷
3. What do you need to know in order to develop an audience profile? L.O.❷
4. What are the three attributes of quality information? L.O.❸
5. What is the difference between the topic of a message and its main idea? L.O.❺

## Apply Your Knowledge

To review chapter content related to each question, refer to the indicated Learning Objective.

1. Some writers argue that planning messages wastes time because they inevitably change their plans as they go along. How would you respond to this argument? Briefly explain. L.O.❶
2. A day after sending an email to all 1800 employees in your company regarding income tax implications of the company's retirement plan, you discover that one of the sources you relied on for your information plagiarized from other sources. You quickly double-check all the information in your message and confirm that it is accurate. However, you are concerned about using plagiarized information, even though you did nothing wrong. How would you handle this situation? L.O.❸
3. As a member of the public relations department, which medium (or media) would you recommend using to inform the local community that your toxic-waste cleanup program has been successful? Justify your choice. L.O.❹

4. Considering how fast, easy, and inexpensive electronic media messages are, should they completely replace meetings and other face-to-face communication in your company? Why or why not? L.O.④

5. Would you use a direct or an indirect approach to ask employees to work overtime to meet an important deadline? Explain. L.O.⑤

## Practise Your Skills

To review chapter content related to each set of exercises, refer to the indicated Learning Objective.

**Specific Purpose** L.O.② For each of the following communication tasks, state a specific purpose (if you have trouble, try beginning with "I want to . . .").

1. A report to your boss, the store manager, about the outdated items in the warehouse
2. A blog posting to customers and the news media about your company's plans to acquire a competitor
3. A letter to a customer who is supposed to make monthly loan payments but hasn't made a payment for three months
4. An email message to employees about the office's high water bills
5. A phone call to a supplier to check on an overdue parts shipment
6. A podcast to new users of the company's online content management system

**Audience Profile** L.O.② For each communication task below, write brief answers to three questions: (1) Who is my audience? (2) What is my audience's general attitude toward my subject? (3) What does my audience need to know?

7. A final-notice collection letter from an appliance manufacturer to an appliance dealer, sent 10 days before initiation of legal collection procedures
8. A promotional message on your company's retailing website, announcing a temporary price reduction on high-definition television sets
9. An advertisement for peanut butter
10. A letter to the property management company responsible for maintaining your office building complaining about persistent problems with the heating and air conditioning
11. A cover letter sent along with your résumé to a potential employer
12. A request (to the seller) for a price adjustment on a piano that incurred $150 in damage during delivery to a banquet room in the hotel you manage

**Media and Purpose** L.O.②, L.O.④ List two messages you have read, viewed, or listened to lately (such as direct-mail promotions, letters, email or instant messages, phone solicitations, blog posts, social network pages, podcasts, or lectures). For each message, determine the general and the specific purposes, then answer the following questions.

13. Message #1:
    General purpose:
    Specific purpose:
    Was the message well timed?
    Did the sender choose an appropriate medium for the message?
    Was the sender's purpose realistic?
14. Message #2:
    General purpose:
    Specific purpose:
    Was the message well timed?
    Did the sender choose an appropriate medium for the message?
    Was the sender's purpose realistic?

**Choosing the Approach** L.O.④ Indicate whether the direct or the indirect approach would be best in each of the following situations.

15. An email message to a car dealer, asking about the availability of a specific make and model of car
16. A letter from a recent college graduate requesting a letter of recommendation from a former instructor
17. A letter turning down a job applicant
18. An internal blog post explaining that because of high air-conditioning costs, the plant temperature will be held at 22 degrees during the summer
19. A final request to settle a delinquent debt
20. A request to your boss to approve your plan for hiring two new people
21. A job application letter
22. A request for a business loan
23. A collection letter for a small amount from a regular customer whose account is slightly past due
24. A collection letter for a large amount from a customer whose account is seriously past due

## ACTIVITIES

Each activity is labelled according to the primary skill or skills you will need to use. To review relevant chapter content, you can refer to the indicated Learning Objective. In some instances, supporting information will be found in another chapter, as indicated.

1. **Planning: Identifying Your Purpose; Media Skills: Email** L.O.❷ Identify three significant communication tasks you'll need to accomplish in the next week or two (for example, a homework assignment, a project at work, a meeting with your academic advisor, or class presentation). In an email message to your instructor, list the general and specific purpose for each communication task.

2. **Planning: Assessing Audience Needs; Media Skills: Blogging; Communication Ethics: Making Ethical Choices** L.O.❸, **Chapter 1** Your supervisor has asked you to withhold important information that you think should be included in a report you are preparing. Obeying her could save the company serious public embarrassment, but it would also violate your personal code of ethics. What should you do? On the basis of the discussion in Chapter 1, would you consider this situation to be an ethical dilemma or an ethical lapse? In a post on your class blog, explain your answer and describe how you would respond in this situation.

3. **Planning: Analyzing the Situation, Selecting Media; Media Skills: Email** L.O.❹, **Chapter 8** You work in public relations for a cruise line that operates out of Vancouver. You are shocked to read a blog post from a disgruntled passenger, complaining about the service and entertainment on a recent cruise. You need to respond to these published criticisms in some way. What audiences will you need to consider in your response? What medium or media should you choose? If the letter had been published in a travel publication widely read by travel agents and cruise travellers, how might your course of action have differed? In an email message to your instructor, explain how you will respond.

4. **Planning: Creating an Audience Profile; Collaboration: Team Projects** L.O.❷, L.O.❸, **Chapter 2** With a team assigned by your instructor, compare the Facebook pages of three companies in the same industry. Analyze the content on all the available tabs. What can you surmise about the intended audience for each company? Which of the three does the best job of presenting the information its target audience is likely to need? Prepare a brief presentation, including slides that show samples of the Facebook content from each company.

5. **Planning: Analyzing the Situation; Choosing an Approach: Selecting Media** L.O.❷ Read the scenario below then answer questions to think through how you would create effective communication strategies for your audience(s), purposes, and messages.

You work at a call centre that has a general manager (in his or her mid-forties), five supervisors (in their thirties), and 100 employees (between the ages of 19 and 58). Staff members are spread over three floors of a downtown office building. You would like to start a composting program for the company—you do it at home, why not in the office? You know that other companies encourage employees to recycle their food wastes. You think it would work well in your offices since you already have a good paper recycling system.

To help you decide how you would communicate your idea, answer the following questions:

- Who has to approve implementing a composting program?
- What would motivate the decision maker to approve your idea?
- Would you choose an indirect or direct pattern of organization to propose the idea? Why?
- What channels of communication or media would work best to propose the idea? Why?
- If your plan is successful, what changes will occur? Who will make them happen?
- Can you assume that all the staff would understand why and how to compost? Why?
- What could motivate staff to participate?
- What channels of communication would work best to promote the program? Why?

Discuss your answers in a group of four and be ready to explain your choices to the class.

6. **Planning: Limiting Your Scope** L.O.❺ Suppose you are preparing to recommend that top management install a new heating system that uses the **cogeneration** process. The following information is in your files. Eliminate topics that aren't essential and then arrange the other topics so that your report will give top managers a clear understanding of the heating system and a balanced, concise justification for installing it. Submit a clear and concise outline to your instructor.

- History of the development of the cogeneration heating process
- Scientific credentials of the developers of the process
- Risks assumed in using this process
- Your plan for installing the equipment in the headquarters building

- Stories about the successful use of cogeneration technology in comparable facilities
- Specifications of the equipment that would be installed
- Plans for disposing of the old heating equipment
- Costs of installing and running the new equipment
- Advantages and disadvantages of using the new process
- Detailed 10-year cost projections
- Estimates of the time needed to phase in the new system
- Alternative systems that management might want to consider

7. **Planning: Using Storytelling Techniques; Collaboration** L.O.⑤ In a group of three, find a nonprofit agency or charity in your community that would benefit from having its story told (perhaps to help with fundraising). Your goal is to come up with a script for a story related to this agency. You could use the script to get the instructor and the agency's approval to produce the story later on. Gather information about the agency's mission, its work, its culture, and the people it helps. Find compelling examples of the good work this agency does and choose one to build a story around. How could you tell this story? Be creative to decide what would be the best way to share it—should you make a short (1 minute) video to post on its website? a couple of (15 second) Instagram videos? a Slide Share presentation? a FaceBook Timeline, or an Infographic? Once you identify the focus of the story, write a script for it, including the type of images you would include and submit it to your instructor.

8. **Planning: Outlining Your Content** L.O.⑤ A writer is working on an insurance information brochure and is having trouble grouping the ideas logically into an outline. Prepare the outline, paying attention to appropriate subordination of ideas. If necessary, rewrite phrases to give them a more consistent sound. Submit a clear and concise outline to your instructor.

**Accident Protection Insurance Plan**

- Coverage is only pennies a day
- Benefit is $100,000 for accidental death on common carrier
- Benefit is $100 a day for hospitalization as result of motor vehicle or common carrier accident
- Benefit is $20,000 for accidental death in motor vehicle accident
- Individual coverage is only $17.85 per quarter; family coverage is just $26.85 per quarter
- No physical exam or health questions
- Convenient payment—billed quarterly
- Guaranteed acceptance for all applicants
- No individual rate increases
- Free, no-obligation examination period
- Cash paid in addition to any other insurance carried
- Covers accidental death when riding as fare-paying passenger on public transportation, including buses, trains, jets, ships, trolleys, subways, or any other common carrier
- Covers accidental death in motor vehicle accidents occurring while driving or riding in or on automobile, truck, camper, motorhome, or nonmotorized bicycle

## BUSINESS COMMUNICATION NOTEBOOK

# Technology

## Caution! Email Can Bite

Gone are the days when memos were dictated, typed, revised, retyped, photocopied, and circulated by inter-office "snail" mail. Today, email messages are created, sent, received, and forwarded in the blink of an eye, and at the stroke of a key. But this quick and efficient method of communication can cause a great deal of trouble for companies.

One of the greatest features—and dangers—of email is that people tend to treat it far more informally than other forms of business communication. They think of email as casual conversation and routinely make unguarded comments. Moreover, they are led to believe that deleting email destroys it permanently. But that's a dangerous misunderstanding of technology.

Even after you delete an email message, it can still exist on the system's hard drive and backup storage devices at both the sender's and the recipient's locations. Deleting files only signals the computer that the space required to store the message is no longer needed. The space is so marked, but the data that occupy that space continue to exist until the computer overwrites it with new data. Thus, deleted messages are recoverable—even though doing so is an involved and expensive process—and can be used as court evidence against you and your company. Embarrassing email has played a big role in corporate battles. In the high-profile Microsoft court battle, for instance, email emerged as the star witness.

So how can companies guard against potential email embarrassment and resulting litigation? Besides restricting the use of email by employees, monitoring employees' email, developing company email policies, and reprimanding or terminating offenders, companies can train their employees to treat email as any other form of written communication. Perhaps one of the best ways to ensure that employee messages won't come back to haunt the company is to teach employees that email messages are at least as permanent as letters and memos—if not more so.

To make sure that you use email effectively, efficiently, and safely, follow these guidelines:

- Don't send large files (including large attachments) without prior notice.
- Proofread every message.
- Respect other people's electronic space by sending messages only when necessary.
- Respond to messages quickly.
- Avoid overusing the label "urgent."
- Be careful about using the "reply all" button.
- Remember that email isn't always private.
- Use the "Save as Draft" feature to give yourself time to consider style and tone for important messages.
- Remember, many people read their emails on smartphones, so keep messages brief and to the point.
- Use complete sentences with proper punctuation and spelling.

## Applications for Success

Improve your email skills by reading "The Art of Writing Email" (www.net-market.com/email.htm). Whether you're working for a company or for yourself, be sure to give your email messages as much consideration as you give more formal types of communication.

Answer the following questions:

1. Why do you think that most people treat email so casually?
2. What kinds of things do you think a company should address in an email policy?
3. Do you think that companies have the right to monitor employees' email? Explain.

# Writing Business Messages

## LEARNING OBJECTIVES

*After studying this chapter, you will be able to*

1.  Identify the four aspects of being sensitive to audience needs when writing business messages.

2.  Explain how establishing your credibility and projecting your company's image are vital aspects of building strong relationships with your audience.

3.  Explain how to achieve a tone that is conversational but businesslike, explain the value of using plain language, and define active and passive voice.

4.  Describe how to select words that are not only correct but also effective.

5.  Define the four types of sentences and explain how sentence style affects emphasis within a message.

6.  Define the three key elements of a paragraph and list five ways to develop coherent paragraphs.

7.  Identify the most common software features that help you craft messages more efficiently.

As a multitalented communication specialist who has succeeded at everything from advertising to professional illustration to scriptwriting, Martin Shovel has had numerous opportunities to see effective communication in action. He knows that the top professionals in every field have worked hard to hone their communication skills, and his years of experience have taught him what it takes to communicate in an engaging and persuasive manner. His number one rule: Keep it simple.[1] This chapter offers practical advice on writing messages that meet audience needs efficiently and effectively. Simplicity is a competitive advantage for Shovel, and you can make it a competitive advantage in your career, too.

## Being Sensitive to Your Audience's Needs

Today, more than ever, writers need the ability to be clear about their intentions, focus on the key points, and form concise messages. The immediate and shorter forms of messaging used for Twitter, email on smartphones, web posts, or online conversations make good writing skills critical. Misinterpreted messages waste time, lead to poor decision making, and shatter business relationships.

**LEARNING OBJECTIVE 1**
Identify the four aspects of being sensitive to audience needs when writing business messages.

Audiences tend to greet incoming messages with a selfish question: "What's in this for me?" If your target readers or listeners don't think a message applies to them, or if they don't think you are being sensitive to their needs, they won't pay attention. You can improve your audience sensitivity by adopting the "you" attitude, maintaining good standards of etiquette, emphasizing the positive, and using bias-free language.

## Adopting the "You" Attitude

You are already becoming familiar with the audience-centred approach: trying to see a subject through your audience's eyes. Now you want to project this approach in your messages by adopting the **"you" attitude**—that is, by speaking and writing in terms of your audience's wishes, interests, hopes, and preferences.

On a simple level, you can adopt the "you" attitude by replacing terms that refer to yourself and your company with terms that refer to your audience. In other words, use *you* and *your* instead of *I, me, mine, we, us,* and *ours*:

| **Instead of** | **Write** |
|---|---|
| Tuesday is the only day that we can promise quick response to purchase order requests; we are swamped the rest of the week. | If you need a quick response, please submit your purchase order requests on Tuesday. |
| We offer MP3 players with 50, 75, or 100 gigabytes of storage capacity. | You can choose an MP3 player with 50, 75, or 100 gigabytes of storage. |

Of course, sometimes it is entirely appropriate to write or speak from your perspective, such as when you are offering your opinions or reporting on something you have seen. However, even in those instances make sure you focus on your readers' needs.

Also, be aware that the "you" attitude is more than simply using particular pronouns; it's a matter of respecting and being genuinely interested in your recipients. You can use *you* 25 times in a single page and still offend your audience or ignore readers' true concerns. If you're writing to a retailer, try to think like a retailer; if you're dealing with a production supervisor, put yourself in that position; if you're writing to a dissatisfied customer, imagine how you would feel at the other end of the transaction.

Keep in mind that on some occasions it's better to avoid using *you*, particularly if doing so will sound overly authoritative or accusing. For instance, instead of saying, "You failed to deliver the customer's order on time," you could avoid the confrontational tone by saying, "The customer didn't receive the order on time," or "Let's figure out a system that will ensure on-time deliveries."

## Maintaining Standards of Etiquette

Good etiquette not only indicates respect for your audience but also helps foster a more successful environment for communication by minimizing negative emotional reaction:

| **Instead of** | **Write** |
|---|---|
| Once again, you've managed to bring down the website through your incompetent programming. | Let's review the last website update so that we can identify potential problems before the next update. |
| You've been sitting on our order for two weeks, and we need it now! | Our production schedules depend on timely delivery of parts and supplies, but we have not yet received the order scheduled for delivery two weeks ago. Please respond today with a firm delivery commitment. |

Readers and listeners are more likely to respond positively when they believe messages address their concerns.

Adopting the "you" attitude means speaking and writing in terms of your audience's wishes, interests, hopes, and preferences.

Avoid using *you* and *your* when doing so

- Makes you sound dictatorial
- Makes someone else feel guilty
- Goes against your organization's style

Although you may be tempted now and then to be brutally frank, try to express the facts in a kind and thoughtful manner.

Use extra tact when communicating with people higher up in the organization or outside the company.

Some situations require more diplomacy than others. If you know your audience well, a less formal approach might be more appropriate. However, when you are communicating with people who outrank you or with people outside your organization, an added measure of courtesy is usually needed.

Written communication and most forms of electronic media generally require more tact than oral communication (see Figure 4.1). When you're speaking, your words are softened by your tone of voice and facial expression. Plus, you can adjust your approach according to the feedback you get. However, if you inadvertently offend someone in writing or in a podcast, for example, you usually don't get the immediate feedback you would need in order to resolve the situation. In fact, you may never know that you offended your audience.

FIGURE 4.1    Fostering a Positive Relationship with an Audience

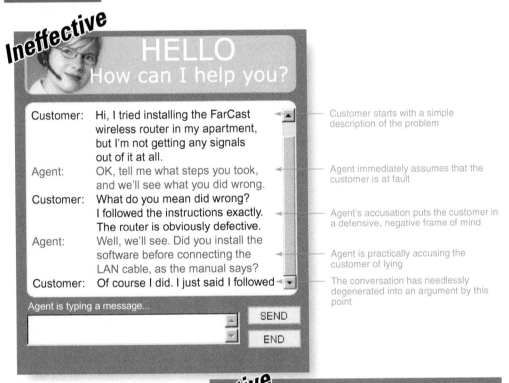

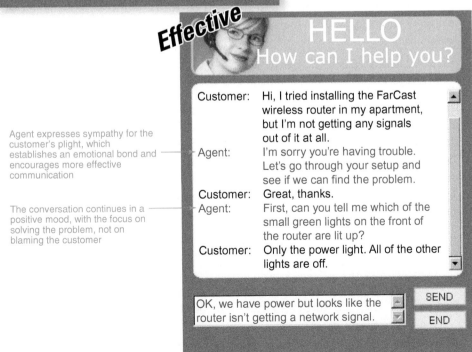

## Emphasizing the Positive

You can communicate negative news without being negative.

You will encounter situations throughout your career in which you need to convey unwanted news. However, sensitive communicators understand the difference between delivering negative news and being negative. Never try to hide the negative news, but do look for positive points that will foster a good relationship with your audience:[2]

| Instead of This | Write This |
|---|---|
| It is impossible to repair your laptop today. | Your computer can be ready by Tuesday. Would you like a loaner until then? |
| We wasted $300,000 advertising in that magazine. | Our $300,000 advertising investment did not pay off; let's analyze the experience and apply the insights to future campaigns. |

Show audience members how they will benefit by responding to your message.

If you're trying to persuade audience members to perform a particular action, point out how doing so will benefit them:

| Instead of This | Write This |
|---|---|
| We will notify all three credit reporting agencies if you do not pay your overdue bill within 10 days. | Paying your overdue bill within 10 days will prevent a negative entry on your credit record. |
| I am tired of seeing so many errors in the customer service blog. | Proofreading your blog postings will help avoid embarrassing mistakes that erode confidence in our brand. |

Euphemisms are milder synonyms that can express an idea while triggering fewer negative connotations.

Look for appropriate opportunities to use **euphemisms**, or milder synonyms, that convey your meaning without carrying negative connotations. For example, when referring to people beyond a certain age, use "senior citizens," rather than "old people." *Senior* conveys respect in a way that *old* doesn't.

However, take care when using euphemisms; it's easy to push the idea too far and wind up sounding ridiculous—or worse yet, obscuring the truth. Speaking to your local community about the disposal of "manufacturing by-products" would be unethical if you're really talking about toxic waste. People respond better to an unpleasant but honest message delivered with integrity than they do to a sugar-coated message that obscures the truth.

## Using Bias-Free Language

Bias-free language avoids words and phrases that unfairly and even unethically categorize or stigmatize people.

**Bias-free language** avoids words and phrases that unfairly and even unethically categorize or stigmatize people in ways related to gender, race, ethnicity, age, or disability. Contrary to what some might think, biased language is not simply about "labels." To a significant degree, language reflects the way people think and what they believe, and biased language may perpetuate the underlying stereotypes and prejudices that it represents.[3] Moreover, because communication is largely about perception, being fair and objective isn't enough; to establish a good relationship with your audience, you must also *appear* to be fair.[4] Good communicators make every effort to change biased language (see Table 4.1). Bias can take a variety of forms:

- **Gender bias.** Avoid sexist language by using the same labels for everyone, regardless of gender. Don't refer to a woman as *chairperson* and then to a man as *chairman*. Use *chair*, *chairperson*, or *chairman* consistently. (Note that it is not uncommon to use *chairman* when referring to a woman who heads a board of directors. Avon's Andrea Jung, Ogilvy & Mather's Shelly Lazarus, and Xerox's Ursula Burns, for example, all refer to themselves as *chairman*.[5]) Reword sentences to use *they* or to use no pronoun

| TABLE 4.1 | Overcoming Bias in Language |
| --- | --- |

| EXAMPLES | UNACCEPTABLE | PREFERABLE |
| --- | --- | --- |
| **Gender Bias** | | |
| Using words containing *man* | Man-made | Artificial, synthetic, manufactured, constructed, human-made |
| | Mankind | Humanity, human beings, human race, people |
| | Manpower | Workers, workforce |
| | Businessman | Executive, manager, businessperson, professional |
| | Salesman | Sales representative, salesperson |
| | Foreman | Supervisor |
| Using female-gender words | Actress, stewardess | Actor, flight attendant |
| Using special designations | Woman doctor, male nurse | Doctor, nurse |
| Using *he* to refer to "everyone" | The average worker . . . he | The average worker . . . he or she *OR* Average workers . . . they |
| Identifying roles with gender | The typical executive spends four hours of his day in meetings. | Most executives spend four hours a day in meetings. |
| | The consumer . . . she | Consumers . . . they |
| | The nurse/teacher . . . she | Nurses/teachers . . . they |
| Identifying women by marital status | Mrs. Norm Lindstrom | Maria Lindstrom *OR* Ms. Maria Lindstrom |
| | Norm Lindstrom and Ms. Drake | Norm Lindstrom and Maria Drake *OR* Mr. Lindstrom and Ms. Drake |
| **Racial and Ethnic Bias** | | |
| Assigning stereotypes | Not surprisingly, Shing-Tung Yau excels in mathematics. | Shing-Tung Yau excels in mathematics. |
| Identifying people by race or ethnicity | Michaelle Jean, Haitian Canadian journalist and former governor general of Canada | Michaelle Jean, journalist and former governor general of Canada |
| **Age Bias** | | |
| Including age when irrelevant | Mary Kirazy, 58, has just joined our trust department. | Mary Kirazy has just joined our trust department. |
| **Disability Bias** | | |
| Putting the disability before the person | Disabled workers face many barriers on the job. | Workers with physical disabilities face many barriers on the job. |
| | An epileptic, Tracy has no trouble doing her job. | Tracy's epilepsy has no effect on her job performance. |

at all rather than refer to all individuals as *he*. Note that the preferred title for women in business is *Ms.* unless the individual asks to be addressed as *Miss* or *Mrs.* or has some other title, such as *Dr.*

- **Racial and ethnic bias.** Avoid identifying people by race or ethnic origin unless such identification is relevant to the matter at hand—and it rarely is.
- **Age bias.** Mention the age of a person only when it is relevant. Moreover, be careful of the context in which you use words that refer to age; such words carry a variety of positive and negative connotations. For example, *young* can imply youthfulness, inexperience, or even immaturity, depending on how it's used.

REAL-TIME UPDATES

**Learn More by Reading This PDF**

**Get detailed advice on using bias-free language**

This in-depth guide offers practical tips for avoiding many types of cultural bias in your writing and speaking. Go to http://real-timeupdates.com/bce6 and click on Learn More. If you are using MyBCommLab, you can access Real-Time Updates within Business Communication Resources.

- **Disability bias.** As with other labels, physical, mental, sensory, or emotional impairments should never be mentioned in business messages unless those conditions are directly relevant to the subject. If you must refer to someone's disability, put the person first and the disability second.[6] For example, by saying "employees with physical disabilities," not "handicapped employees," you focus on the whole person, not the disability. Finally, never use outdated terminology such as *crippled* or *retarded*.

**LEARNING OBJECTIVE 2**
Explain how establishing your credibility and projecting your company's image are vital aspects of building strong relationships with your audience.

# Building Strong Relationships with Your Audience

Successful communication relies on a positive relationship existing between sender and receiver. Establishing your credibility and projecting your company's image are two vital steps in building and fostering positive business relationships.

## Establishing Your Credibility

People are more likely to react positively to your message when they have confidence in you.

Audience responses to your messages depend heavily on your **credibility**, a measure of your believability based on how reliable you are and how much trust you evoke in others. With audiences that don't know and trust you already, you need to establish credibility before they'll accept your messages. On the other hand, when you do establish credibility, communication becomes much easier because you no longer have to spend time and energy convincing people that you are a trustworthy source of information and ideas. To build, maintain, or repair your credibility, emphasize the following characteristics:

To enhance your credibility, emphasize such factors as honesty, objectivity, and awareness of audience needs.

- **Honesty.** Demonstrating honesty and integrity will earn you the respect of your audiences, even if they don't always agree with or welcome your messages.
- **Objectivity.** Show that you can distance yourself from emotional situations and look at all sides of an issue.
- **Awareness of audience needs.** Let your audience members know that you understand what's important to them.
- **Credentials, knowledge, and expertise.** Audiences need to know that you have whatever it takes to back up your message, whether it's education, professional certification, special training, past successes, or simply the fact that you've done your research.

REAL-TIME UPDATES

**Learn More by Reading This Article**

**Building credibility online**

Follow these steps to build your credibility as an online voice. Go to http://real-timeupdates.com/bce6 and click on Learn More. If you are using MyBCommLab, you can access Real-Time Updates within Business Communication Resources.

- **Endorsements.** An *endorsement* is a statement on your behalf by someone who is accepted by your audience as an expert.
- **Performance.** Demonstrating impressive communication skills is not enough; people need to know they can count on you to get the job done.
- **Confidence.** Audiences need to know that you believe in yourself and your message. If you are convinced that your message is sound, you can state your case confidently, without sounding boastful or arrogant.
- **Sincerity.** When you offer praise, don't use *hyperbole*, such as "You are the most fantastic employee I could ever imagine." Instead, point out specific qualities that warrant praise.

Credibility can take days, months, even years to establish—and it can be wiped out in an instant. An occasional mistake or letdown may be forgiven, but major lapses in honesty or integrity can destroy your reputation.

## Projecting Your Company's Image

When you communicate with anyone outside your organization, it is more than a conversation between two individuals. You represent your company and therefore play a vital role in helping the company build and maintain positive relationships with all of its stakeholders. Most successful companies work hard to foster a specific public image, and your external communication efforts need to project that image. As part of this responsibility, the interests and preferred communication style of your company must take precedence over your own views and personal communication style.

Many organizations have specific communication guidelines that show everything from the correct use of the company name to preferred abbreviations and other grammatical details. Specifying a desired style of communication is more difficult, however. Observe more experienced colleagues to see how they communicate and ask for editorial help to make sure you're conveying the appropriate tone. For instance, with clients entrusting thousands or millions of dollars to it, an investment firm communicates in a style quite different from that of a clothing retailer. And a clothing retailer specializing in high-quality business attire communicates in a different style than a store catering to the latest trends in casual wear.

> Your company's interests and reputation take precedence over your personal views and communication style.

# Controlling Your Style and Tone

Your **communication style** involves the choices you make to express yourself: the words you select, the manner in which you use those words in sentences, and the way you build paragraphs from individual sentences. Your style creates a certain **tone**, or overall impression, in your messages. The right tone depends on the nature of your message and your relationship with the reader.

**LEARNING OBJECTIVE** 3
Explain how to achieve a tone that is conversational but businesslike, explain the value of using plain language, and define active and passive voice.

## Creating a Conversational Tone

The tone of your business messages can range from informal to conversational to formal. If you're in a large organization and you're communicating with your superiors or with customers, the right tone will usually be more formal and respectful.[7] However, that same tone might sound distant and cold in a small organization or if used with close colleagues. Part of the challenge of communicating on the job is to read each situation and adopt an appropriate tone.

Compare the three versions of the message in Table 4.2. The first is too formal and stuffy for today's audiences, whereas the third is too casual for any audience other than close associates or friends. The second message demonstrates the **conversational tone** used in most business communication—plain language that sounds businesslike without being stuffy at one extreme or too laid-back and informal at the other extreme. You can achieve a tone that is conversational but still businesslike by following these guidelines:

> Most business messages aim for a conversational style that is warm but businesslike.

- **Understand the difference between texting and writing.** The casual, acronym-filled language friends often use in text messaging, IM, and social networks is not considered professional business writing. Yes, it is an efficient way for friends to communicate—particularly taking into account the limitations of a phone keypad—but if you want to be taken seriously in business, you simply cannot write like this on the job.
- **Avoid obsolete and pompous language.** Most companies now shy away from such dated phrases as "attached please find," "please be advised that," and "do not hesitate to." Similarly, avoid using obscure words, stale or clichéd expressions, and overly complicated sentences to impress others.
- **Avoid preaching and bragging.** Readers tend to get irritated by know-it-alls who like to preach or brag. However, if you need to tell your audience something that should be obvious, phrase it as a reminder.
- **Be careful with intimacy.** Business messages should generally avoid intimacy, such as sharing personal details or adopting a casual, unprofessional tone. However, when

| TABLE 4.2 | Formal, Conversational, and Informal Tones |
|---|---|

| TONE | EXAMPLE |
|---|---|
| **Stuffy:** too formal for today's audiences | Dear Ms. Navarro:<br><br>Enclosed please find the information that was requested during our telephone communication of May 14.<br><br>As was mentioned at that time, Metro Clinic has significantly more doctors of exceptional quality than any other health facility in the province.<br><br>As you were also informed, our organization has quite an impressive network of doctors and other health-care professionals with offices located throughout the province. In the event that you should need a specialist, our professionals will be able to make an appropriate recommendation.<br><br>In the event that you have questions or would like additional information, you may certainly contact me during regular business hours.<br><br>Most sincerely yours,<br><br>Samuel G. Berenz |
| **Conversational:** just right for most business communication | Dear Ms. Navarro:<br><br>Here's the information you requested during our phone conversation on Friday. As I mentioned, Metro Clinic has the highest-rated doctors and more of them than any other clinic in the province.<br><br>In addition, we have a vast network of doctors and other health professionals with offices throughout the province. If you need a specialist, they can refer you to the right one.<br><br>If you would like more information, please call any time between 9:00 and 5:00, Monday through Friday.<br><br>Sincerely,<br><br>Sam. Berenz |
| **Unprofessional:** too casual for business communication | Here's the 411 you requested. IMHO, we have more and better doctors than any other clinic in the province.<br><br>FYI, we also have a large group of doctors and other health professionals w/offices close to U at work/home. If U need a specialist, they'll refer U to the right one<br><br>Any? just ring or msg.<br><br>L8R,<br><br>S |

you have a close relationship with audience members, such as among the members of a close-knit team, a more intimate tone could be expected.

- **Be careful with humour.** Humour can easily backfire and divert attention from your message. If you don't know your audience well or you're not skilled at using humour in a business setting, don't use it at all. Avoid humour in formal messages and when you're communicating across cultural boundaries.

## Using Plain Language

An important aspect of creating a conversational tone is using *plain language*.[8] Plain language presents information in a simple, unadorned style that allows your audience to easily grasp your meaning: language that recipients "can read, understand and act upon the first time they read it."[9] You can see how this definition supports using the "you" attitude and shows respect for your audience. In addition, plain language can make companies more productive and more profitable because everyone spends less time trying to figure out messages that are confusing or aren't written to meet their needs.[10]

*Audiences can understand and act on plain language without reading it over and over.*

| TABLE 4.3 | Choosing Active or Passive Voice |
|---|---|

*In general, avoid passive voice in order to make your writing lively and direct.*

| Dull and Indirect in Passive Voice | Lively and Direct in Active Voice |
|---|---|
| The new procedure was developed by the operations team. | The operations team developed the new procedure. |
| Legal problems are created by this contract. | This contract creates legal problems. |
| Reception preparations have been undertaken by our PR people for the new CEO's arrival. | Our PR people have begun planning a reception for the new CEO. |

*However, passive voice is helpful when you need to be diplomatic or want to focus attention on problems or solutions rather than on people.*

| Accusatory or Self-congratulatory in Active Voice | More Diplomatic in Passive Voice |
|---|---|
| You lost the shipment. | The shipment was lost. |
| I recruited seven engineers last month. | Seven engineers were recruited last month. |
| We are investigating the high rate of failures on the final assembly line. | The high rate of failures on the final assembly line is being investigated. |

## Selecting Active or Passive Voice

Your choice of active or passive voice affects the tone of your message. You are using **active voice** when the subject performs the action and the object receives the action: "Jodi sent the email message." You're using **passive voice** when the subject receives the action: "The email message was sent by Jodi." As you can see, the passive voice combines the helping verb *to be* with a form of the verb that is usually the past tense.

Using the active voice often makes your writing more direct, livelier, and easier to read (see Table 4.3). Passive voice is not wrong grammatically, but it can be cumbersome, lengthy, and vague. In most cases, the active voice is the better choice.[11]

Nevertheless, using the passive voice can help you demonstrate the "you" attitude in some situations.

- When you want to be diplomatic about pointing out a problem or an error
- When you want to point out what's being done without taking or attributing either the credit or the blame
- When you want to avoid personal pronouns (*I* and *we*) in order to create an objective tone

The second half of Table 4.3 illustrates several situations in which the passive voice helps you focus your message on your audience.

Active sentences are usually stronger than passive ones.

Use passive sentences to soften bad news, put yourself in the background, or create an impersonal tone.

## Composing Your Message: Choosing Powerful Words

**LEARNING OBJECTIVE 4**
Describe how to select words that are not only correct but also effective.

After you have decided how to adapt to your audience, you're ready to begin composing your message. As you write your first draft, let your creativity flow. Don't try to draft and edit at the same time or worry about getting everything perfect. Make up words if you can't think of the right word, draw pictures, or talk out loud; do whatever it takes to get the ideas out of your head and onto your computer screen or a piece of paper. If you've planned carefully, you'll have time to revise and refine the material later, before showing it to anyone. In fact, many writers find it helpful to establish a personal rule of never showing a first draft to anyone. By working in this "safe zone," away from the critical eyes of others, your mind will stay free to think clearly and creatively.

You may find it helpful to hone your craft by viewing your writing at three levels: strong words, effective sentences, and coherent paragraphs. Starting at the word level,

Correctness is the first consideration when choosing words.

successful writers pay close attention to the correct use of words.[12] If you make errors of grammar or usage, you lose credibility with your audience, even if your message is otherwise correct. Poor grammar suggests to readers that you're uninformed, and they may choose not to trust an uninformed source. Moreover, poor grammar can imply that you don't respect your audience enough to get things right.

The "rules" of grammar and usage can be a source of worry for writers because some of these rules are complex and some evolve over time. Even professional editors and grammarians occasionally have questions about correct usage, and they sometimes disagree about the answers. For example, the word *data* is the plural form of *datum*, yet some experts now prefer to treat *data* as a singular noun when it's used in nonscientific material to refer to a body of facts or figures. With practice, you'll become more skilled in making correct choices. If you have doubts about what is correct, you have many ways to find the answer. Check MyBCommLab, or consult the many special reference books and resources available in libraries, in bookstores, and on the internet.

In addition to using words correctly, successful writers and speakers take care to use the most effective words and phrases. Selecting and using words effectively is often more challenging than using words correctly because it's a matter of judgment and experience. Careful writers continue to work at their craft to find words that communicate with power (see Figure 4.2).

**REAL-TIME UPDATES**

**Learn More by Visiting This Interactive Website**

**Grammar questions? Click here for help**

This comprehensive online guide can help you out of just about any grammar dilemma. Go to http://real-timeupdates.com/bce6 and click on Learn More. If you are using MyBCommLab, you can access Real-Time Updates within Business Communication Resources.

*Effectiveness is the second consideration when choosing words.*

---

**FIGURE 4.2** Choosing Effective Words

---

To: c.shaw@vteams.biz

CC:

Subject: Re: Next Year's VTCE Show

Dear Ms. Shaw:

Thank you for your interest in next year's Virtual Team Conference & Expo (VTCE). VTCE has quickly become the world's premiere showcase for the latest news in virtual teamwork and online collaboration. This year's event featured more than 600 vendors, from entrepreneurial innovators to established industry leaders. Based on early registrations, we expect to host as many as 800 exhibitors next year.

Participants will benefit from a wide variety of programs and activities:

- Hands-on workshops for training managers and IT specialists
- Networking opportunities with peers from around the world
- Product demonstrations with company experts
- Roundtable discussions on hot topics in virtual collaboration
- Social events and organized sightseeing opportunities

Our website offers in-depth information on all these benefits. You can also find a continuously updated list of vendors who have committed to next year's show.

Individual registrations start at just $195, and group discount packages can reduce the per-employee cost to as low as $110.

We hope to see you and your colleagues in Toronto next year!

## Balancing Abstract and Concrete Words

Words in your business messages can vary dramatically in their degree of abstraction or concreteness. An **abstract word** expresses a concept, quality, or characteristic. Abstractions are usually broad, encompassing a category of ideas, and are often intellectual, academic, or philosophical. *Love, honour, progress, tradition,* and *beauty* are abstractions, as are such important business concepts as *productivity, profits, quality,* and *motivation.* In contrast, a **concrete word** stands for something you can touch, see, or visualize. Most concrete terms are anchored in the tangible, material world. *Chair, table, horse, rose, kick, kiss, red, green,* and *two* are concrete words; they are direct, clear, and exact.

As you can imagine, abstractions tend to cause more trouble for writers and readers than concrete words. Abstractions tend to be "fuzzy" and can be interpreted differently, depending on the audience and the circumstances. The best way to minimize such problems is to blend abstract terms with concrete ones, the general with the specific. State the concept and then pin it down with details expressed in more concrete terms. Save the abstractions for ideas that cannot be expressed any other way. In addition, abstract words such as *small, numerous, sizable, near, soon, good,* and *fine* are imprecise, so try to replace them with terms that are more accurate. Instead of referring to a *sizable loss,* for example, give an exact number.

> The more abstract a word is, the more it is removed from the tangible, objective world of things that can be perceived with the senses.

## Finding Words That Communicate Well

When you compose business messages, look for the most powerful words for each situation (see Table 4.4):

> Try to use words that are powerful and familiar.

- **Choose strong, precise words.** Choose words that express your thoughts clearly, specifically, and strongly. If you find yourself using many adjectives and adverbs, chances are you're trying to compensate for weak nouns and verbs. Saying that *sales plummeted* is stronger and more efficient than saying *sales dropped dramatically* or *sales experienced a dramatic drop.*
- **Choose familiar words.** You'll communicate best with words that are familiar to both you and your readers. Moreover, trying to use unfamiliar words can lead to embarrassing mistakes.

> Avoid clichés, be extremely careful with trendy buzzwords, and use jargon only when your audience is completely familiar with it.

| TABLE 4.4 | Finding Words That Communicate with Power |
|---|---|

| POTENTIALLY WEAKER WORDS AND PHRASES (In Many Situations) | STRONGER ALTERNATIVES (Effective Usage Depends on the Situation) |
|---|---|
| Increase (as a verb) | Accelerate, amplify, augment, enlarge, escalate, expand, extend, magnify, multiply |
| Decrease (as a verb) | Curb, cut back, depreciate, dwindle, shrink, slacken |
| Large, small | (Use a specific number, such as $17 million) |
| Good | Admirable, beneficial, desirable, flawless, pleasant, sound, superior, worthy |
| Bad | Abysmal, corrupt, deficient, flawed, inadequate, inferior, poor, substandard |
| We are committed to providing . . . | We provide . . . |
| It is in our best interest to . . . | We should . . . |
| | |
| UNFAMILIAR WORDS | FAMILIAR WORDS |
| Ascertain | Find out, learn |
| Consummate | Close, bring about |
| Peruse | Read, study |
| Circumvent | Avoid |
| Unequivocal | Certain |

(continued)

| TABLE 4.4 | (Continued) |
| --- | --- |

| CLICHÉS AND BUZZWORDS | PLAIN LANGUAGE |
| --- | --- |
| An uphill battle | A challenge |
| Writing on the wall | Prediction |
| Call the shots | Lead |
| Take by storm | Attack |
| Costs an arm and a leg | Expensive |
| A new ballgame | Fresh start |
| Fall through the cracks | Be overlooked |
| Think outside the box | Be creative |
| Run it up the flagpole | Find out what people think about it |
| Human capital | People, employees, workforce |
| Low-hanging fruit | Tasks that are easy to complete or sales that are easy to close |
| Pushback | Resistance |

- **Avoid clichés and use buzzwords carefully.** Although familiar words are generally the best choice, avoid *clichés*: terms and phrases so common that they have lost some of their power to communicate. *Buzzwords*, newly coined terms often associated with technology, business, or cultural changes, are more difficult to handle than clichés because in small doses and in the right situation, they can be useful. The careful use of a buzzword can signal that you're an insider, someone in the know.[13] However, buzzwords quickly become clichés, and using them too late in their "life cycle" can mark you as an outsider desperately trying to look like an insider. Avoid tired, over-used phrases such as *feel free to*, *do not hesitate to call*, or *your co-operation is appreciated*.
- **Use jargon carefully.** *Jargon*, the specialized language of a particular profession or industry, has a bad reputation, but it's not always bad. Using jargon is usually an efficient way to communicate within the specific groups that understand these terms. After all, that's how jargon develops in the first place, as people with similar interests develop ways to communicate complex ideas quickly.

If you need help finding the right words, try some of the visual dictionaries and thesauruses available online. For example, Visuwords (**www.visuwords.com**) shows words that are similar to or different from a given word and helps you see subtle differences to find the perfect word.[14] See Figure 4.3.

LEARNING OBJECTIVE ⑤
**Define the four types of sentences and explain how sentence style affects emphasis within a message.**

# Composing Your Message: Creating Effective Sentences

Arranging your carefully chosen words in effective sentences is the next step in creating successful messages. Start by selecting the best type of sentence to communicate each point you want to make.

## Varying the Four Types of Sentences

*A simple sentence has one main clause.*

Sentences come in four basic varieties: simple, compound, complex, and compound-complex. A **simple sentence** has one main clause (a single subject and a single predicate), although it may be expanded by nouns and pronouns serving as objects of the

## FIGURE 4.3 Online Tools for Finding Fresh Word Choices

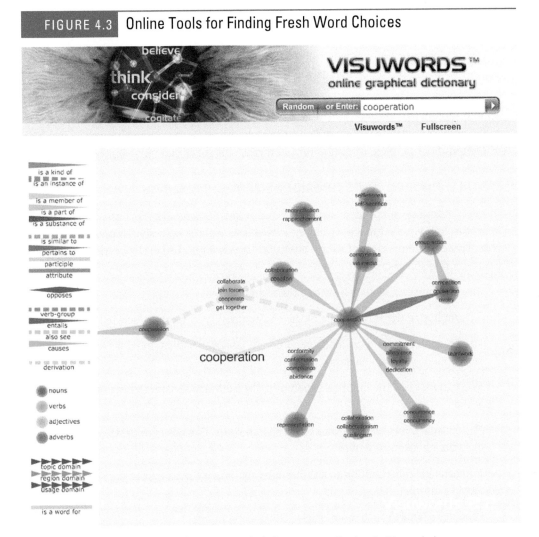

*Source:* Copyright © 2012 by Logical Octopus, www.logicaloctopus.com. Reprinted with permission.

action and by modifying phrases. Consider this example (with the subject underlined once and the predicate verb underlined twice):

Profits increased 35 percent in the past year.

A **compound sentence** has two main clauses that express two or more independent but related thoughts of equal importance, usually joined by *and*, *but*, or *or*. In effect, a compound sentence is a merger of two or more simple sentences (independent clauses) that are related. For example:

Wages declined by 5 percent, and employee turnover has been higher than ever.

The independent clauses in a compound sentence are always separated by a comma and a coordinating conjunction or by a semicolon (in which case the conjunction—*and*, *but*, or *or*—is dropped).

A **complex sentence** expresses one main thought (the independent clause) and one or more subordinate thoughts (dependent clauses) related to it, often separated by a comma. The subordinate thought, which comes first in the following sentence, could not stand alone:

Although you may question Gerald's conclusions, you must admit that his research is thorough.

A compound sentence has two main clauses.

A complex sentence has one main clause and one subordinate clause.

A **compound-complex sentence** has two main clauses, at least one of which contains a subordinate clause:

A compound-complex sentence has two main clauses and at least one dependent clause.

Profits increased 35 percent in the past year, so although the company faces long-term challenges, I agree that its short-term prospects look quite positive.

To make your writing as effective as possible, vary sentence types. If you use too many simple sentences, you won't be able to properly express the relationships among your ideas, and your writing will sound choppy and abrupt. At the other extreme, a long series of compound, complex, or compound-complex sentences can be tiring to read.

## Using Sentence Style to Emphasize Key Thoughts

In every message, some ideas are more important than others. You can emphasize key ideas through your sentence style. One obvious technique is to give important points the most space. When you want to call attention to a thought, use extra words to describe it. Consider this sentence:

Emphasize specific ideas by

- Devoting more words to them
- Putting them at the beginning or at the end of the sentence
- Making them the subject of the sentence

The chairperson called for a vote of the shareholders.

To emphasize the importance of the chairperson, you might describe her more fully:

Having considerable experience in corporate takeover battles, the chairperson called for a vote of the shareholders.

You can increase the emphasis even more by adding a separate, short sentence to augment the first:

The chairperson called for a vote of the shareholders. She has considerable experience in corporate takeover battles.

You can also call attention to a thought by making it the subject of the sentence. In the following example, the emphasis is on the person:

I can write letters much more quickly using a computer.

However, when you change the subject, the computer takes centre stage:

The computer enables me to write letters much more quickly.

Another way to emphasize an idea is to place it either at the beginning or at the end of a sentence.

**Less emphatic:** We are cutting the price to stimulate demand.

**More emphatic:** To stimulate demand, we are cutting the price.

The best placement of the dependent clause depends on the relationship between the ideas in the sentence.

In complex sentences, the ideal placement of the dependent clause depends on the relationship between the ideas expressed. If you want to emphasize the idea expressed in the dependent clause, put that clause at the end of the sentence (the most emphatic position) or at the beginning (the second most emphatic position). If you want to downplay the idea, position the dependent clause within the sentence.

**Most emphatic:** The electronic parts are manufactured in Mexico, which has lower wage rates than Canada.

**Emphatic:** Because wage rates are lower in Mexico than in Canada, the electronic parts are manufactured there.

**Least emphatic:** Mexico, which has lower wage rates than Canada, was selected as the production site for the electronic parts.

Techniques such as these give you a great deal of control over the way your audience interprets what you have to say.

# Composing Your Message: Crafting Coherent Paragraphs

**LEARNING OBJECTIVE 6**
Define the three key elements of a paragraph and list five ways to develop coherent paragraphs.

Paragraphs organize sentences related to the same general topic. Readers expect every paragraph to be *unified*—focusing on a single topic—and *coherent*—presenting ideas in a logically connected way. By carefully arranging the elements of each paragraph, you help your readers grasp the main idea of your document and understand how the specific pieces of support material back up that idea.

## Creating the Elements of a Paragraph

Paragraphs vary widely in length and form, but most contain three basic elements: a topic sentence, support sentences that develop the topic, and transitional words and phrases.

**TOPIC SENTENCE**   An effective paragraph deals with a single topic, and the sentence that introduces that topic is called the **topic sentence.** This sentence, usually the first one in the paragraph, gives readers a summary of the general idea that will be covered in the rest of the paragraph. The following examples show how a topic sentence can introduce the subject and suggest the way the subject will be developed:

> The medical products division has been troubled for many years by public relations problems. [In the rest of the paragraph, readers will learn the details of the problems.]

> To get a refund, please supply us with the following information. [The details of the necessary information will be described in the rest of the paragraph.]

**SUPPORT SENTENCES**   In most paragraphs, the topic sentence needs to be explained, justified, or extended with one or more support sentences. These sentences must be related to the topic and provide examples, evidence, and clarification:

> The medical products division has been troubled for many years by public relations problems. Since 2013 the local newspaper has published 15 articles that portray the division in a negative light. We have been accused of everything from mistreating laboratory animals to polluting the local groundwater. Our facility has been described as a health hazard. Our scientists are referred to as "Frankensteins," and our profits are considered "obscene."

Notice how these support sentences are all more specific than the topic sentence. Each one provides another piece of evidence to demonstrate the general truth of the main thought. Also, each sentence is clearly related to the general idea being developed, which gives the paragraph its **unity**. A paragraph is well developed when it contains enough information to make the topic sentence convincing and interesting and doesn't contain any unneeded or unrelated sentences.

**TRANSITIONS**   **Transitions** connect ideas by showing how one thought is related to another. They also help alert the reader to what lies ahead so that shifts and changes don't cause confusion. In addition to helping readers understand the connections you're trying to make, transitions give your writing a smooth, even flow.

Depending on the specific need within a document, transitional elements can range in length from a single word to an entire paragraph or more (see Table 4.5). You can establish transitions in a variety of ways:

- **Use connecting words.** Use words such as *and, but, or, nevertheless, however,* and *in addition.*
- **Echo a word or phrase from a previous paragraph or sentence.** "A system should be established for monitoring inventory levels. This system will provide . . ."

Most paragraphs consist of

- A topic sentence that reveals the subject of the paragraph
- Related sentences that support and expand the topic
- Transitions that help readers move between sentences and paragraphs

Paragraphs deal with a single topic and its supporting detail.

Every sentence in a paragraph must relate to the topic sentence.

Transitional elements include

- Connecting words (conjunctions)
- Repeated words or phrases
- Pronouns
- Words that are frequently paired

| TABLE 4.5 | Common Transitions |
|---|---|
| Additional detail: | moreover, furthermore, in addition, besides, first, second, third, finally |
| Causal relationship: | therefore, because, accordingly, thus, consequently, hence, as a result, |
| Comparison: | so similarly, here again, likewise, in comparison, still |
| Contrast: | yet, conversely, whereas, nevertheless, on the other hand, however, but, nonetheless |
| Condition: | although, if |
| Illustration: | for example, in particular, in this case, for instance |
| Time sequence: | formerly, after, when, meanwhile, sometimes |
| Intensification: | indeed, in fact, in any event |
| Summary: | in brief, in short, to sum up |
| Repetition: | that is, in other words, as I mentioned earlier |

- **Use a pronoun that refers to a noun used previously.** "Ms. Arthur is the leading candidate for the president's position. She has excellent qualifications."
- **Use words that are frequently paired.** "The machine has a *minimum* output of . . . Its *maximum* output is . . ."

Some transitions serve as mood changers, alerting the reader to a change in mood from the previous material. Some announce a total contrast with what's gone on before, some announce a cause-and-effect relationship, and some signal a change in time.

Consider using a transition whenever readers might need help understanding your ideas and following you from point to point. You can use transitions inside paragraphs to

## FIGURE 4.4 Crafting Unified, Coherent Paragraphs in a Blog Post

Echoing *TwitCause* at the beginning of this paragraph tells readers that this paragraph will continue on the same subject.

The transition *Additionally* signals that the topic in the previous paragraph will be expanded upon in this new paragraph.

*Following suit* functions as a transition from the previous paragraph by linking Pepsi back to the description of Home Depot.

The three sentences in this paragraph start with the broad topic (social media for charities and nonprofits) and narrow down the main idea, which is that TwitCause is a good tool for this purpose. (Note that the third sentence is really a fragment, but Hayes is selectively breaking the rules here to emphasize the suitability of TwitCause.)

*In my opinion* lets readers know she is transitioning from reporting to offering her personal thoughts on the subject at hand.

The second and third sentences in this paragraph provide an example of the observation made in the topic sentence at the beginning of the paragraph.

*Source:* © Copyright 2007–2015 Ignite Social Media.

tie together related points and between paragraphs to ease the shift from one distinct thought to another. In longer reports, a transition that links major sections or chapters is often a complete paragraph that serves as a summary of the ideas presented in the section just ending or as a mini-introduction to the next section.

Figure 4.4 offers several examples of effective transitions and other features of strong paragraphs.

## Developing Paragraphs

You have a variety of options for developing paragraphs, each of which can convey a specific type of idea. Five of the most common approaches are illustration, comparison or contrast, cause and effect, classification, and problem and solution (see Table 4.6).

Five ways to develop paragraphs
- Illustration
- Comparison or contrast
- Cause and effect
- Classification
- Problem and solution

# Using Technology to Compose and Shape Your Messages

Be sure to take advantage of the tools in your word processor or online publishing systems (for websites, blogs, and other documents) to write more efficiently and effectively. The features, functions, and names vary from system to system and version to version, but you'll encounter some combination of the following capabilities:

- **Style sheets, style sets, templates, and themes.** *Style sheets*, *style sets*, *templates*, and *themes* are various ways of ensuring consistency throughout a document and from document to document. These tools also make it easy to redesign an entire document or screen simply by redefining the various styles or selecting a different design theme.

**LEARNING OBJECTIVE 7**
Identify the most common software features that help you craft messages more efficiently.

Take full advantage of your software's formatting capabilities to help produce effective, professional documents in a short time.

| TABLE 4.6 | Methods of Paragraph Development |
| --- | --- |

| TECHNIQUE | EXAMPLE |
| --- | --- |
| Illustration | Some of our most popular products are available through local distributors. For example, Weston carries our frozen soups and entrees. Dandipak carries our complete line of seasonings, as well as the frozen soups. Island Farms, also a major distributor, now carries our new line of frozen desserts. |
| Comparison or Contrast | In previous years, when the company was small, the recruiting function could be handled informally. The need for new employees was limited, and each manager could comfortably screen and hire his or her own staff. Today, however, Norco Performance Bikes must undertake a major recruiting effort. Our successful bid on the Costco contract means that we will be doubling our labour force over the next six months. To hire that many people without disrupting our ongoing activities, we will create a separate recruiting group within the human resources department. |
| Cause and Effect | The heavy-duty fabric of your Wanderer tent probably broke down for one of two reasons: (1) a sharp object punctured the fabric and, without reinforcement, the hole was enlarged by the stress of erecting the tent daily for a week, or (2) the fibres gradually rotted because the tent was folded and stored while still wet. |
| Classification | Successful candidates for our supervisor trainee program generally come from one of several groups. The largest group, by far, consists of recent graduates of accredited data-processing programs. The next largest group comes from within our own company, as we try to promote promising clerical workers to positions of greater responsibility. Finally, we do occasionally accept candidates with outstanding supervisory experience in related industries. |
| Problem and Solution | Selling handmade toys by mail is a challenge because consumers are accustomed to buying heavily advertised toys from major chains. However, if we develop an appealing online catalogue, we can compete on the basis of product novelty and quality. In addition, we can provide craftsmanship at a competitive price: a rocking horse made of birch, with a hand-knit tail and mane; a music box with the child's name painted on the top; a real First Nations teepee, made by Blackfoot artisans. |

Style sheets or sets are collections of formatting choices for words, paragraphs, and other elements. Rather than manually formatting every element, you simply select one of the available styles. Templates usually set overall document parameters such as page size and provide a specific set of styles to use. Templates can be particularly handy if you create a variety of document types, such as letters, calendars, agendas, and so on. Themes tend to address the overall look and feel of the page or screen, including colour palettes and background images.

- **Boilerplate and document components.** A *boilerplate* is a standard block of text that is reused in multiple documents. Two common examples are company descriptions and executive biographies. Some systems offer the means to store these blocks and drop them into a document as needed, which saves time and ensures consistency. Moving beyond simple text blocks, some systems can store fully formatted document components such as cover pages, sidebars, and *pull quotes* (a piece of text copied from the main body of the document and formatted as a large, eye-catching visual element).

- **Autocorrection or autocompletion.** Some programs can automate text entry and correction using a feature called autocompletion, autocorrection, or something similar. In Microsoft Word, for example, the AutoCorrect feature lets you build a library of actions that automatically fill in longer entries based on the first few characters you type or correct common typing errors (such as typing *teh* instead of *the*). Use these features carefully, though. They can make changes you might not want in every instance.

- **File merge and mail merge.** Most word processing software makes it easy to combine files, which is an especially handy feature when several members of a team write different sections of a report. Mail merge lets you personalize form letters by automatically inserting names and addresses from a database.

- **Endnotes, footnotes, indexes, and tables of contents.** Your computer can help you track footnotes and endnotes, renumbering them every time you add or delete references. For a report's indexes and table of contents, you can simply flag the items you want to include, and the software assembles the lists for you.

# LEARNING OBJECTIVES: Check Your Progress

**① OBJECTIVE Identify the four aspects of being sensitive to audience needs when writing business messages.**

First, the "you" attitude refers to speaking and writing in terms of your audience's wishes, interests, hopes, and preferences rather than your own. Writing with this attitude is essential to effective communication because it shows your audience that you have their needs in mind, not yours. Second, good etiquette not only indicates respect for your audience, but also helps foster a more successful environment for communication by minimizing negative emotional reaction. Third, sensitive communicators look for ways to be considerate while delivering negative messages. Fourth, being sensitive includes taking care to avoid biased language that unfairly and even unethically categorizes or stigmatizes people in ways related to gender, race, ethnicity, age, or disability.

**② OBJECTIVE Explain how establishing your credibility and projecting your company's image are vital aspects of building strong relationships with your audience.**

Whether a one-time interaction or a series of exchanges over the course of many months or years, successful communication relies on a positive relationship existing between sender and receiver. Audience responses to your messages depend heavily on your credibility, a measure of your believability, based on how reliable you are and how much trust you evoke in others. Project your company's desired image when communicating with external audiences to help the company build and maintain positive relationships.

**③ OBJECTIVE Explain how to achieve a tone that is conversational but businesslike, explain the value of using plain language, and define active and passive voice.**

To achieve a tone that is conversational but still businesslike, avoid obsolete and pompous language, avoid preaching and bragging, and be careful with intimacy and humour. Plain language is a way of presenting information in a simple, unadorned style so that your audience can easily grasp your meaning. By writing and speaking in plain terms, you demonstrate the "you" attitude and show respect for your audience. In the active voice, the subject performs the action and the object receives the action. In the passive voice, the subject receives the action. The passive voice combines the helping verb *to be* with a form of the verb that is usually in the past tense.

**4 OBJECTIVE** **Describe how to select words that are not only correct but also effective.**

Selecting words that are not only correct but also effective involves balancing abstract and concrete words, choosing powerful and familiar words, and avoiding clichés.

**5 OBJECTIVE** **Define the four types of sentences and explain how sentence style affects emphasis within a message.**

The four types of sentences are *simple* (one main clause), *compound* (two main clauses that express independent but related ideas of equal importance), *complex* (one main clause and one subordinate clause of lesser importance), and *compound-complex* (two main clauses, at least one of which contains a subordinate clause). Sentence style affects emphasis by playing up or playing down specific parts of a sentence. To emphasize a certain point, you can place it at the end of the sentence or make it the subject of the sentence. To de-emphasize a point, put it in the middle of the sentence.

**6 OBJECTIVE** **Define the three key elements of a paragraph and list five ways to develop coherent paragraphs.**

The three key elements of a paragraph are a topic sentence that identifies the subject of the paragraph, support sentences that develop the topic and provide examples and evidence, and transitional words and phrases that help readers connect one thought to the next. Five ways to develop coherent paragraphs are illustration, comparison or contrast, cause and effect, classification, and problem and solution.

**7 OBJECTIVE** **Identify the most common software features that help you craft messages more efficiently.**

Common software features that help you craft messages more efficiently include style sheets, style sets, templates, and themes; features to store and use boilerplate and document components; autocorrection or autocompletion; file merge and mail merge; and endnotes, footnotes, indexes, and tables of contents.

**MyBCommLab®** Go to MyBCommLab for everything you need to help you succeed in the job you've always wanted! Tools and resources include the following:
• Writing Activities   • Document Makeovers
• Video Exercises   • Grammar Exercises—and much more!

## Practise Your Grammar

Effective business communication starts with strong grammar skills. To improve your grammar skills, go to MyBCommLab, where you'll find exercises and diagnostic tests to help you produce clear, effective communication.

## Test Your Knowledge

To review chapter content related to each question, refer to the indicated Learning Objective.

1. What is meant by the term *"you" attitude*? L.O.❶
2. In what three situations should you consider using passive voice? L.O.❸
3. How does an abstract word differ from a concrete word? L.O.❹
4. How can you use sentence style to emphasize key thoughts? L.O.❺
5. What functions do transitions serve? L.O.❻

# Apply Your Knowledge

To review chapter content related to each question, refer to the indicated Learning Objective.

1. How can you create conversational tone? L.O.❸
2. Thousands of people in Canada are allergic to one or more food ingredients. Every year people end up in the emergency room after suffering allergic reactions, and some of them die. Many of these tragic events are tied to poorly written food labels that either fail to identify dangerous allergens or use scientific terms that most consumers don't recognize.[15] Do food manufacturers have a responsibility to ensure that consumers read, understand, and follow warnings on food products? Explain your answer. L.O.❶
3. When composing business messages, how can you communicate with your own voice and project your company's image at the same time? L.O.❷
4. What steps can you take to make abstract concepts such as *opportunity* feel more concrete in your messages? L.O.❹
5. Should you bother using transitions if the logical sequence of your message is already obvious? Why or why not? L.O.❻

# Practise Your Skills

## EXERCISES FOR PERFECTING YOUR WRITING

To review chapter content related to each set of exercises, refer to the indicated Learning Objective.

**The "You" Attitude** Rewrite the following sentences to reflect your audience's viewpoint. L.O.❶

1. We request that you use the order form supplied in the back of our catalogue.
2. We insist that you always bring your credit card to the store.
3. We want to get rid of all our 15-inch monitors to make room in our warehouse for the 19-inch screens. Thus, we are offering a 25 percent discount on all sales this week.
4. I am applying for the position of bookkeeper in your office. I feel that my grades prove that I am bright and capable, and I think I can do a good job for you.
5. As requested, we are sending the refund for $25.

**Emphasizing the Positive** Revise these sentences to be positive rather than negative. L.O.❶

6. To avoid the loss of your credit rating, please remit payment within 10 days.
7. We don't make refunds on returned merchandise that is soiled.
8. Because we are temporarily out of Baby Cry dolls, we won't be able to ship your order for 10 days.
9. You failed to specify the colour of the blouse that you ordered.
10. You should have realized that waterbeds will freeze in unheated houses during winter. Therefore, our guarantee does not cover the valve damage and you must pay the $9.50 valve-replacement fee (plus postage).

**Emphasizing the Positive** Revise the following sentences to replace unflattering terms (in italics) with euphemisms. L.O.❶

11. The new boss is _____ (*stubborn*) when it comes to doing things by the book.
12. When you say we've doubled our profit level, you are _____ (*wrong*).
13. Just be careful not to make any _____ (*stupid*) choices this week.
14. Jim Riley is too _____ (*incompetent*) for that kind of promotion.
15. Glen monopolizes every meeting by being _____ (*a loudmouth*).

**Courteous Communication** Revise the following sentences to make them more courteous. L.O.❶

16. You claim that you mailed your cheque last Thursday, but we have not received it.
17. It is not our policy to exchange sale items, especially after they have been worn.
18. You neglected to sign the enclosed contract.
19. I received your letter, in which you assert that our shipment was three days late.
20. You failed to enclose your instructions for your new will.

**Bias-Free Language** Rewrite each of the following sentences to eliminate bias. LO.❶

21. For an Indian, Maggie certainly is outgoing.
22. He needs a wheelchair, but he doesn't let his handicap affect his job performance.
23. A pilot must have the ability to stay calm under pressure, and then he must be trained to cope with any problem that arises.
24. Candidate Renata Parsons, a wife and the mother of a teenager, will attend the debate.
25. Senior citizen Sam Nugent is still an active salesman.

**Selecting Words** In the following sentences, replace vague phrases (underlined) with concrete phrases. Make up any details you might need. LO.❹

26. We will be opening our new facility sometime this spring.
27. You can now purchase our new Leaf-Away yard and lawn blower at a substantial savings.
28. After the reception, we were surprised that such a large number attended.
29. The new production line has been operating with increased efficiency on every run.
30. Over the holiday, we hired a crew to expand the work area.

**Selecting Words** In the following sentences, replace weak terms (in italics) with words that are stronger. LO.❹

31. The two reporters _____ (ran after) every lead enthusiastically.
32. Even large fashion houses have to match staff size to the normal _____ (seasonal ups and downs).
33. The _____ (bright) colours in that ad are keeping customers from seeing what we have to sell.
34. Health costs _____ (suddenly rise) when management forgets to emphasize safety issues.
35. Once we solved the zoning issue, new business construction _____ (moved forward), and the district has been flourishing ever since.

**Selecting Words** Rewrite these sentences to replace the clichés with fresh, personal expressions. LO.❹

36. Being a jack-of-all-trades, Dave worked well in his new selling job.
37. Don't hesitate to call our office any time.
38. You are our valued customers. Please feel free to send us your questions.
39. Thank you in advance for your co-operation on this matter.
40. It's a dog-eat-dog world out there in the rat race of the asphalt jungle.

**Selecting Words** In the following sentences, replace long, complicated words with short, simple ones. LO.❹

41. Management _____ (inaugurated) the recycling policy six months ago.
42. You can convey the same meaning without _____ (utilizing) the same words.
43. You'll never be promoted unless you _____ (endeavour) to be more patient.
44. I have to wait until payday to _____ (ascertain) whether I got the raise.
45. John will send you a copy once he's inserted all the _____ (alterations) you've requested.
46. Grand Tree _____ (fabricates) office furniture that is both durable and attractive.
47. I understand from your letter that you expect a full refund; _____ (nevertheless), your warranty expired more than a year ago.

**Selecting Words** Rewrite the following sentences, replacing obsolete phrases with up-to-date versions. Write *none* if you think there is no appropriate substitute. LO.❹

48. I have completed the form and returned it to my insurance company, as per your instructions.
49. Attached herewith is a copy of our new contract for your records.
50. Even though it will increase the price of the fence, we have decided to use the redwood in lieu of the cedar.
51. Saunders & Saunders has received your request for the Greenwood file, and in reply I wish to state that we will send you copies of Mr. Greenwood's documents only after Judge Taylor makes her ruling and orders us to do so.
52. Please be advised that your account with National Bank has been compromised, and we advise you to close it as soon as possible.

**Using active and passive voice** Rewrite the following sentences so that they are active rather than passive. LO.❺

53. The raw data are submitted to the data-processing division by the sales representative each Friday.
54. High profits are publicized by management.
55. The policies announced in the directive were implemented by the staff.
56. Our computers are serviced by the Santee Company.
57. The employees were represented by Janet Hogan.

**Transitions** Add transitions to the following sentences to improve the flow of ideas. (Note: You may need to eliminate or add some words to smooth out the sentences.) LO.❻

58. Steve Case saw infinite possibilities for the internet. Steve Case was determined to turn his vision into reality. The techies scoffed at his strategy of building a simple internet service for ordinary people. Case doggedly pursued his dream. He analyzed

other online services. He assessed the needs of his customers. He responded to their desires for an easier way to access information over the internet. In 1992, Steve Case named his company America Online (AOL). Critics predicted the company's demise. By the end of the century, AOL was a profitable powerhouse. AOL grew so big that it was able to merge with the giant traditional media company Time Warner. The merger was widely criticized. The merger did not live up to Case's expectations. He eventually left the company.

59. Facing some of the toughest competitors in the world, Harley-Davidson had to make some changes. The company introduced new products. Harley's management team set out to rebuild the company's production process. New products were coming to market and the company was turning a profit. Harley's quality standards were not on par with those of its foreign competitors. Harley's costs were still among the highest in the industry. Harley made a U-turn and restructured the company's organizational structure. Harley's efforts have paid off.

60. Tim Hortons first opened in 1964 in Hamilton, Ontario. The first Tim Hortons sold only coffee and doughnuts. The chain has more than 3000 restaurants in Canada and more than 500 in the United States. Tim Hortons is growing. The chain plans to add 600 restaurants each year for the next three years. Tim Hortons plans to open 300 more locations in the U.S. The chain enjoys wide popularity with Canadians. Canadians eat three times as many doughnuts per capita as Americans. Canadians consume more doughnuts per capita than any other country in the world. Tim Hortons is the largest chain of fast service restaurants in Canada.[16]

## ACTIVITIES

Each activity is labelled according to the primary skill or skills you will need to use. To review relevant chapter content, you can refer to the indicated Learning Objective. In some instances, supporting information will be found in another chapter, as indicated.

1. **Writing: Creating a Businesslike Tone; Media Skills: Email** L.O.❸ Read the following email message and then (1) analyze the strengths and weaknesses of each sentence, and (2) revise the message so that it follows this chapter's guidelines. The message was written by the marketing manager of an online retailer of baby-related products in the hope of becoming a retail outlet

for Inglesina strollers and high chairs. As a manufacturer of stylish, top-quality products, Inglesina (based in Italy) is extremely selective about the retail outlets through which it allows its products to be sold.[17]

> Our e-tailing company, Best Baby Gear, specializes in only the very best products for parents of newborns, infants, and toddlers. We constantly scour the world looking for products that are good enough and well-built enough and classy enough—good enough that is to take their place alongside the hundreds of other carefully selected products that adorn the pages of our award-winning website, www.bestbabygear.com. We aim for the fences every time we select a product to join this portfolio; we don't want to waste our time with onesey-twosey products that might sell a half dozen units per annum—no, we want every product to be a top-drawer success, selling at least one hundred units per specific model per year in order to justify our expense and hassle factor in adding it to the abovementioned portfolio. After careful consideration, we thusly concluded that your Inglesina lines meet our needs and would therefore like to add it.

2. **Writing: Using Plain Language; Communication Ethics: Making Ethical Choices** L.O.❸, Chapter 1 Your company has been a major employer in the local community for years, but shifts in the global marketplace have forced some changes in the company's long-term direction. In fact, the company plans to reduce local staffing by as much as 50 percent over the next 5 to 10 years, starting with a small layoff next month. The size and timing of future layoffs have not been decided, although there is little doubt that more layoffs will happen at some point. In the first draft of a letter aimed at community leaders, you write, "This first layoff is part of a continuing series of staff reductions anticipated over the next several years." However, your boss is concerned about the vagueness and negative tone of the language and asks you to rewrite that sentence to read, "This staffing adjustment is part of the company's ongoing efforts to continually align its resources with global market conditions." Do you think this suggested wording is ethical, given the company's significant economic presence in the community? Explain your answer in an email message to your instructor.

3. **Writing: Using Plain Language; Media Skills: Blogging** L.O.❸ Download the BC Securities Commission's Plain Language Style Guide at http://professionalcommunications.ca/BCSC_Plain_Language_Style_Guide_2008.pdf. In one or two sentences, summarize what the BCSC means by the phrase *plain English*. Scan a few pages of the Style Guide. Does the information follow the BCSC's plain English guidelines? Cite several examples that support your assessment. Post your analysis on your class blog or submit it as instructed.

4. **Writing: Establishing Your Credibility; Microblogging Skills** L.O.❷, **Chapter 6** Search LinkedIn for the profile of an expert in any industry or profession. Now imagine that you are going to introduce this person as a speaker at a convention. You will make an in-person introduction at the time of the speech, but you decide to introduce him or her the day before on Twitter. Write four tweets: one that introduces the expert and three that cover three key supporting points that will enhance the speaker's credibility in the minds of potential listeners. Make up any information you need to complete this assignment, then email the text of your proposed tweets to your instructor.

5. **Writing: Crafting Unified, Coherent Paragraphs; Media Skills: Email** L.O.❺ Suppose that end-of-term frustrations have produced this email message to Professor Anne Brewer from a student who believes he should have received a B in his accounting class. If this message were recast into three or four clear sentences, the teacher might be more receptive to the student's argument. Rewrite the message to show how you would improve it.

> I think that I was unfairly awarded a C in your accounting class this term, and I am asking you to change the grade to a B. It was a difficult term. I don't get any money from home, and I have to work mornings at the Pancake House (as a cook), so I had to rush to make your class, and those two times that I missed class were because they wouldn't let me off work because of special events at the Pancake House (unlike some other students who just take off when they choose). On the midterm examination, I originally got a 75 percent, but you said in class that there were two different ways to answer the third question and that you would change the grades of students who used the "optimal cost" method and had been counted off 6 points for doing this. I don't think that you took this into account, because I got 80 percent on the final, which is clearly a B. Anyway, whatever you decide, I just want to tell you that I really enjoyed this class, and I thank you for making accounting so interesting.

6. **Writing: Crafting Unified, Coherent Paragraphs; Collaboration: Evaluating the Work of Others** L.O.❻, **Chapter 5** For this exercise, work with four other students. Each of you should choose one of the following five topics and write one paragraph on it. Be sure one student writes a paragraph using the illustration technique, one using the comparison-or-contrast technique, one using a discussion of cause and effect, one using the classification technique, and one using a discussion of problem and solution. Then exchange paragraphs within the team and pick out the main idea and general purpose of the paragraph one of your teammates wrote. Was everyone able to correctly identify the main idea and purpose? If not, suggest how the paragraph might be rewritten for clarity.

   a. Types of cameras (or dogs or automobiles) available for sale
   b. Advantages and disadvantages of eating at fast-food restaurants
   c. Finding that first full-time job
   d. Good qualities of my phone (or house, or apartment, or neighbourhood)
   e. How to make a favourite dessert (or barbecue a steak or make coffee)

7. **Writing: Controlling Tone, Using Passive and Active Voice** L.O.❸ Assume you work for a company that will be holding a BBQ. Make up the details (who can come, where, when, what to bring, etc.). Write a message to invite people using passive voice. Then write the same message using active voice. Trade your two paragraphs with a classmate and discuss which of the two versions is more effective and why. Next, assume it is a few days before the BBQ and not enough people committed to attend it so the manager calls it off. Write the message to cancel the event using passive voice and then again in active. Trade your two messages with a classmate and discuss which is more effective and why.

8. **Writing: Creating Professional Tone** L.O.❸ Write the following message in three ways to create (1) a friendly, informal tone; (2) a neutral tone; and (3) a firm, formal tone. You are an employee in the shipping department of a company of 150 employees. You are setting up a Facebook group for company employees to use for socializing and you want employees to participate in the group. You also want them to use their judgment about the types of things they say and do on the site.

9. **Writing: Using Plain Language, Creating Professional Email** L.O.❸ In a group of three, analyze the style and tone of the following memo. How does the writer come across? What action does the writer want from the reader? Rewrite the email using active voice and "you" attitude to create conversational style and tone. Add headings and other document design features to improve readability.

---

To: Zoe Watts, Personnel Manager

From: William Butterworth, Health and Safety Manager

Date: November 12, 2016

Subject: Application of Ergonomic Principles to Computer Workstations

It is recommended that a copy of the attached booklet entitled *Guide for Computer Workstation Ergonomics* be sent to all senior managers and purchasing agents who may influence the purchase and installation of computer equipment in Bigco over the ensuing years, together with a covering letter from some appropriate upper-level authority in Bigco urging them to pay attention to the selection, purchase, and installation of this type of equipment in the future. Your suggestions as to the most appropriate procedure and list of recipients would be appreciated.

In the course of implementing the Health Services program for monitoring the visual and other health-related complaints of personnel working at computer stations in Bigco, numerous examples of gross violation of ergonomic principles have become evident. Obviously, there cannot be an overnight remedy to these problems as was openly acknowledged by speakers at the National Safety Society conference in Toronto last month. Improvement and conversion of this equipment will cost tens of thousands of dollars at Bigco. And it should be noted that Bigco is by no means unique. Workstation ergonomic problems exist industry wide. But, by the same token, the need for future change is becoming widely recognized and it is important that Bigco keep pace with equipment changes. Much could be done in the interim to improve the currently established workstations and lessen the legitimate health-related complaints of employees, which show a common-sense causal relationship to poor posture, poor lighting arrangements, and so on. It is important that awareness be developed on the part of all those managers, supervisors, and agents who ultimately influence the selection, purchasing, and installation of computer equipment. Any suggestions as to how such awareness could be best cultivated would be appreciated.

---

**BUSINESS COMMUNICATION NOTEBOOK**

# Workplace Skills

## Beating Writer's Block: 10 Workable Ideas to Get Words Flowing

Putting words on a page or on a screen can be a real struggle. Some people get stuck so often that they develop a mental block. If you get writer's block, here are some ways to get those words flowing again:

- **Use positive self-talk.** Stop worrying about how well or easily you write, and stop thinking of writing as difficult, time-consuming, or complicated. Tell yourself that you're capable and that you can do the job. Also, recall past examples of your writing that were successful.

- **Know your purpose.** Be specific about what you want to accomplish. What action do you want to happen as a result of this piece of writing? Without a clear purpose, writing can indeed be impossible.
- **Visualize your audience.** Picture audience backgrounds, interests, subject knowledge, and vocabulary (including the technical jargon they use). Such visualization can help you choose an appropriate style and tone for your writing.
- **Create a productive environment.** Write in a place that's for writing only, and make that place pleasant. Set up "writing appointments." Scheduling a session from nine-thirty to noon is less intimidating

than an indefinite session. Also, keep your mind fresh with scheduled breaks.

- **Make an outline or a list.** Even if you don't create a formal outline, at least jot down a few notes about how your ideas fit together. As you go along, you can revise your notes, so long as you end up with a plan that gives direction and coherence.
- **Just start.** Put aside all worries, fears, and distractions—anything that gives you an excuse to postpone writing. Then start putting down any thoughts you have about your topic. Don't worry about whether these ideas can actually be used; just let your mind range freely.
- **Write the middle first.** Start wherever your interest is greatest and your ideas are most developed. You can follow new directions, but note ideas to revisit later. When you finish one section, choose another without worrying about sequence. Just get your thoughts down.
- **Push obstacles aside.** If you get stuck at some point, don't worry. Move past the thought, sentence, or paragraph, and come back to it later. Try writing or talking about why you're stuck: "I'm stuck because . . ." Also try brainstorming. Before you know it, you'll be writing about your topic.
- **Read a newspaper or magazine.** Try to find an article that uses a style similar to yours. Choose one you'll enjoy so that you'll read it more closely.
- **Work on nontext segments.** Work on a different part of the project, such as formatting or creating graphics or verifying facts and references.

Remember, when deadlines loom, don't freeze in panic. Concentrate on the major ideas first, and save the details for later, after you have something on the page. If you keep things in perspective, you'll succeed.

## Applications for Success

Learn more about beating writer's block. Visit Writer's Block at http://owl.english.purdue.edu/owl/resource/567/01.

1. List the ways you procrastinate, and discuss what you can do to break these habits.
2. Analyze your own writing experiences. What negative self-talk do you use? What might you do to overcome this tendency?

# 5

# Completing Business Messages

## LEARNING OBJECTIVES

*After studying this chapter, you will be able to*

1. Discuss the value of careful revision and describe the tasks involved in evaluating your first drafts and the work of other writers.

2. List four techniques you can use to improve the readability of your messages.

3. Describe the steps you can take to improve the clarity of your writing and give four tips for making your writing more concise.

4. Identify four software tools that can help you revise messages and explain the risks of using them.

5. List four principles of effective design and explain the role of major design elements in document readability.

6. Explain the importance of proofreading and give six tips for successful proofreading.

7. Discuss the most important issues to consider when distributing your messages.

As one of today's most widely read bloggers, Leo Babauta recognizes that the true power of writing often lies in rewriting—revising messages until they are as clear, concise, and effective as possible.[1] Careful revision often means the difference between a rambling, unfocused message and a lively, direct message that gets attention and spurs action. Taking the time to evaluate and improve your messages through revision can also save you from releasing the sort of poorly written messages that can hold back your career and harm your company's reputation.[2]

---

**LEARNING OBJECTIVE 1**
Discuss the value of careful revision and describe the tasks involved in evaluating your first drafts and the work of other writers.

Typing errors and other glitches might seem unimportant, but audiences often equate the quality of your writing with the quality of your thinking.

## Revising Your Message: Evaluating the First Draft

This chapter covers the tasks in the third step of the three-step writing process: revising your message to achieve optimum quality and then producing, proofreading, and distributing it. After you complete your first draft, you may be tempted to breathe a sigh of relief, send the message on its way, and move on to the next project. Resist that temptation. Careful revision improves the effectiveness of your messages and sends a strong signal to your readers that you respect their time and care about their opinions.[3]

The scope of the revision task varies depending on the medium and the nature of your message. For informal messages to internal audiences, particularly when using short-message tools such as IM and email, the revision process is often as simple as quickly looking over your message to correct any mistakes before sending or posting it. However, don't fall into the common trap of thinking that you don't need to worry about grammar, spelling, clarity, and other fundamentals of good writing when you use electronic media. These qualities can be *especially* important in electronic media, particularly if these messages are the only contact your audience has with you. Poor-quality messages create an impression of poor-quality thinking, and even minor errors can cause confusion, frustration, and costly delays. Also remember that your message could be distributed far beyond your original audience.

Whenever possible—particularly with important messages—put your first draft aside for a day or two before you begin the revision process so that you can approach the material with a fresh eye. Then start with the "big picture," making sure that the document accomplishes your overall goals, before moving to finer points such as readability, clarity, and conciseness. Compare the before and after versions of the letter in Figures 5.1 and 5.2 on the following pages for examples of how careful revision makes a message more effective and easier to read.

## Evaluating Your Content, Organization, and Tone

When you begin the revision process, focus on content, organization, and tone. Today's time-pressed readers want messages that convey important content clearly and quickly.[4] To evaluate the content of your message, make sure it's accurate, relevant to the audience's needs, and complete.

When you are satisfied with the basic content of your message, review its organization by asking yourself these questions:

- Are all your points covered in the most logical and convincing order?
- Do the most important ideas receive the most space and greatest emphasis?
- Are any points repeated unnecessarily?
- Are details grouped together logically, or are some still scattered through the document?

Next, consider whether you have achieved the right tone for your audience. Is your writing formal enough to meet the audience's expectations without being too formal or academic? Is it too casual for a serious subject?

Finally, spend a few extra moments on the beginning and end of your message; these sections usually have the greatest impact on the audience. Be sure that the opening of your document is geared to the reader's probable reaction and conveys the subject and purpose of the message. For longer documents, the opening should help readers understand how the material is organized. Review the conclusion to be sure that it summarizes the main idea and leaves the audience with a positive impression.

*The beginning and end of a message usually have the greatest impact on your readers.*

## Evaluating, Editing, and Revising the Work of Other Writers

At many points in your career, you will be asked to evaluate, edit, or revise the work of others. Before you dive into someone else's work, recognize your dual responsibility: first, unless you've specifically been asked to rewrite something in your own style, make sure your input focuses on making the piece more effective, not on making it more like something you would've written. Second, make sure you understand the writer's intent before you begin suggesting or making changes. With those thoughts in mind, ask yourself the following questions as you evaluate someone else's writing:

*When you evaluate, edit, or revise someone else's work, your job is to help that person succeed, not to impose your own style.*

- What is the purpose of this document or message?
- Who is the target audience?
- What information does the audience need?
- Does the document provide this information in a well-organized way?
- Does the writing demonstrate the "you" attitude?
- Is the tone of the writing appropriate for the audience?
- Can the readability be improved?
- Is the writing clear? If not, how can it be improved?

- Is the writing as concise as it could be?
- Does the design support the intended message?

You can read more about using these skills in the context of wiki writing in Chapter 6.

---

**FIGURE 5.1** Improving a Customer Letter Through Careful Revision

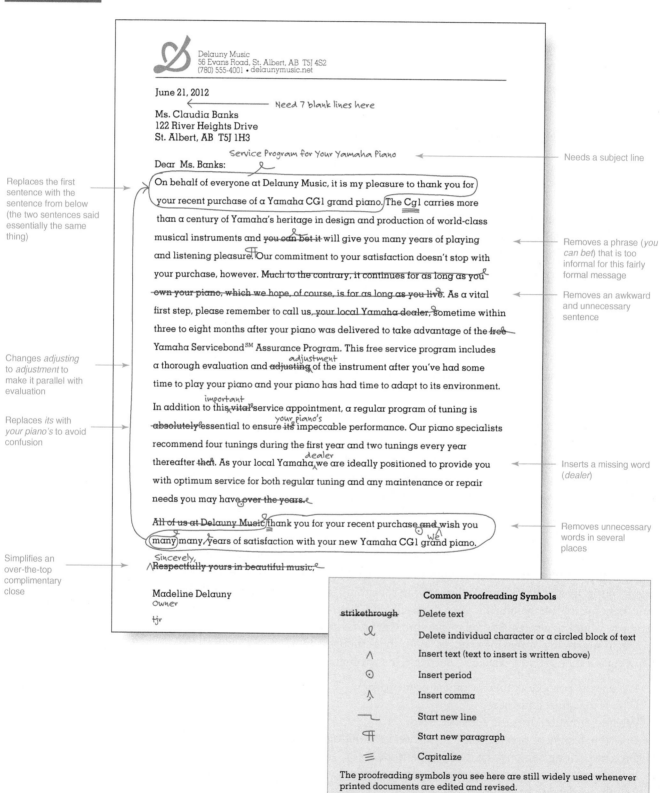

The proofreading symbols you see here are still widely used whenever printed documents are edited and revised.

**FIGURE 5.2** **A Revised Professional Business Letter in Full Block Format**

Delauny Music
56 Evans Road, St. Albert, AB  T5J 4S2
(563) 555-4001 • delaunymusic.net

June 21, 2012

Ms. Claudia Banks
122 River Heights Drive
St. Albert, AB  T5J 1H3

Dear Ms. Banks:

**Service Program for Your Yamaha Piano**

Thank you for your recent purchase. We wish you many years of satisfaction with your new Yamaha CG1 grand piano. The CG1 carries more than a century of Yamaha's heritage in design and production of world-class musical instruments and will give you many years of playing and listening pleasure.

Our commitment to your satisfaction doesn't stop with your purchase, however. As a vital first step, please remember to call us sometime within three to eight months after your piano was delivered to take advantage of the Yamaha Servicebond℠ Assurance Program. This free service program includes a thorough evaluation and adjustment of the instrument after you've had some time to play your piano and your piano has had time to adapt to its environment.

In addition to this important service appointment, a regular program of tuning is essential to ensure your piano's impeccable performance. Our piano specialists recommend four tunings during the first year and two tunings every year thereafter. As your local Yamaha dealer, we are ideally positioned to provide you with optimum service for both regular tuning and any maintenance or repair needs you may have.

Sincerely,

*Madeline Delauny*
Madeline Delauny
Owner

# Revising to Improve Readability

LEARNING OBJECTIVE ❷
**List four techniques you can use to improve the readability of your messages.**

After confirming the content, organization, and tone of your message, make a second pass to improve *readability*. Most professionals are inundated with more reading material than they can ever hope to consume, and they'll appreciate your efforts to make your documents easier to read—and easier to skim for the highlights when they don't have time to read in depth. You'll benefit from this effort, too: if you earn a reputation for creating well-crafted documents that respect the audience's time, people will pay more attention to your work.

Four powerful techniques for improving readability are varying your sentence length, using shorter paragraphs, replacing narrative with lists, and adding effective headings and subheadings.

## Varying Your Sentence Length

Varying sentence length is a good way to maintain reader interest and control the emphasis given to major and minor points. Look for ways to combine a mixture of sentences that are short (up to 15 words or so) or medium (15 to 25 words). Each

To keep readers' interest, look for ways to vary sentence length.

sentence length has advantages. Short sentences can be processed quickly and are easier for non-native speakers and translators to interpret. Medium-length sentences are useful for showing the relationships among ideas. Long sentences are sometimes needed to convey complex ideas, to list a number of related points, or to summarize or preview information.

Of course, each sentence length also has disadvantages. Too many short sentences in a row can make your writing choppy and disconnected. Medium sentences lack the punch of short sentences. Long sentences (more than 25 words) are usually harder to understand than short sentences because they are packed with information; they are also harder to skim when readers are just looking for a few key points in a hurry.

## Keeping Your Paragraphs Short

Short paragraphs are easier to read than long ones.

Large blocks of text can be intimidating, even to the most dedicated reader. Short paragraphs (of 100 words or fewer; this paragraph has 62 words, for example) are easier to read than long ones, and they make your writing look inviting. They also help audiences read more carefully. You can also emphasize an idea by isolating it in a short, forceful paragraph.

However, don't go overboard with short paragraphs at the expense of maintaining a smooth and clear flow of information. In particular, use one-sentence paragraphs only occasionally and only for emphasis. Also, if you need to divide a subject into several pieces in order to keep paragraphs short, use transitions to help your readers keep the ideas connected.

## Using Lists and Bullets to Clarify and Emphasize

Lists are effective tools for highlighting and simplifying material.

In some instances, a list can be more effective than conventional sentences and paragraphs. Lists can show the sequence of your ideas, heighten their impact visually, and increase the likelihood that readers will find your key points. In addition, lists simplify complex subjects, highlight the main point, enable skimming, and give readers a breather. Consider the difference between the following two approaches to the same information:

**Narrative**
Owning your own business has many advantages. One is the opportunity to build a major financial asset. Another advantage is the satisfaction of working for yourself. As a sole proprietor, you also have the advantage of privacy because you do not have to reveal your financial information or plans to anyone.

**List**
Owning your own business has three advantages:
- The opportunity to build a major financial asset
- The satisfaction of working for yourself
- The freedom to keep most of your financial information private

When creating a list, you can separate items with numbers, letters, or bullets (a general term for any kind of graphical element that precedes each item). Bullets are generally preferred over numbers, unless the list is in some logical sequence or ranking, or specific list items will be referred to later on. Make your lists easy to read by making all the items parallel (see "Impose Parallelism" on page 99) and keeping individual items as short as possible.[5] Also, be sure to introduce your lists clearly so that people know what they're about to read.

Lists have a "lead-in," which is an introductory phrase or complete sentence. Lists can be constructed three ways:

1. A lead-in plus a series of complete sentences, punctuated as sentences
2. A complete sentence lead-in plus a series of fragments
3. An introductory phrase lead-in plus a series of parts that complete one sentence

## Adding Headings and Subheadings

A **heading** is a brief title that tells readers about the content of the section that follows. **Subheadings** indicate subsections within a major section; complex documents may have several levels of subheadings. Headings and subheadings help in three important ways: they show readers at a glance how the material is organized, they call attention to important points, and they highlight connections and transitions between ideas.

**Descriptive headings**, such as "Cost Considerations," identify a topic but do little more. **Informative headings**, such as "Redesigning Material Flow to Cut Production Costs," tell your reader about the content. Well-written informative headings are self-contained, which means that readers can skim just the headings and subheadings and understand them without reading the rest of the document. Keep headings brief and grammatically parallel.

The font size of headings should signal the relative importance of information contained under them. For instance, the largest category of information should have the largest font. Make the levels of classification easy to distinguish so that the headings reinforce the organization.

*Use headings to grab the reader's attention and organize material into short sections.*

*Make headings informative.*

# Editing for Clarity and Conciseness

After you've revised your message for readability, your next step is to make sure your message is as clear and as concise as possible.

**LEARNING OBJECTIVE** ❸
**Describe the steps you can take to improve the clarity of your writing and give four tips for making your writing more concise.**

## Editing for Clarity

Make sure every sentence conveys the message you intend and that readers can extract that meaning without reading it more than once. To ensure clarity, look closely at your paragraph organization, sentence structure, and word choices. Can readers make sense of the related sentences in a paragraph? Is the meaning of each sentence easy to grasp? Is every word clear and unambiguous (meaning it doesn't have any risk of being interpreted in more than one way)? See Table 5.1 on the next page for examples of the following tips:

*Clarity is essential to getting your message across accurately and efficiently.*

- **Break up overly long sentences.** If you find yourself stuck in a long sentence, you're probably trying to make the sentence do more than it can reasonably do, such as expressing two dissimilar thoughts or peppering the reader with too many pieces of supporting evidence at once. (Did you notice how difficult this long sentence was to read?)
- **Rewrite hedging sentences.** *Hedging* means pulling back from making an absolutely certain, definitive statement about a topic. Granted, sometimes you have to write *may* or *seems* to avoid stating a judgment as a fact. However, when you hedge too often or without good reason, you come across as being unsure of what you're saying.
- **Impose parallelism.** Making your writing *parallel* means expressing two or more similar ideas using the same grammatical structure. Doing so helps your audience understand that the ideas are related, are of similar importance, and are on the same level of generality. Parallel patterns are also easier to read. You can impose parallelism by repeating a pattern in words, phrases, clauses, or entire sentences.
- **Correct dangling modifiers.** Sometimes a modifier is not just an adjective or an adverb but an entire phrase modifying a noun or a verb. Be careful not to leave this type of modifier *dangling*, with no connection to the subject of the sentence.
- **Reword long noun sequences.** When multiple nouns are strung together as modifiers, the resulting sentence can be hard to read. See if a single well-chosen word will do the job. If the nouns are all necessary, consider moving one or more to a modifying phrase, as shown in Table 5.1.
- **Replace camouflaged verbs.** Watch for words that end in *-ion, -tion, -ing, -ment, -ant, -ent, -ence, -ance,* and *-ency.* These endings often change verbs into nouns and adjectives, requiring you to add a verb to get your point across.

*Hedging is appropriate when you can't be absolutely sure of a statement, but excessive hedging undermines your authority.*

*When you use parallel grammatical patterns to express two or more ideas, you show that they are comparable thoughts.*

| TABLE 5.1 | Revising for Clarity | |
|---|---|---|

| ISSUES TO REVIEW | INEFFECTIVE | EFFECTIVE |
|---|---|---|
| **Overly Long Sentences**<br><br>Stuffing a sentence with too many ideas | The magazine will be published January 1, and I'd better meet the deadline if I want my article included because we want the article to appear before the trade show. | The magazine will be published January 1. I'd better meet the deadline because we want the article to appear before the trade show. |
| **Hedging Sentences**<br><br>Overqualifying sentences | I believe that Mr. Johnson's employment record seems to show that he may be capable of handling the position. | Mr. Johnson's employment record shows that he is capable of handling the position. |
| **Unparallel Sentences**<br><br>Using dissimilar construction for similar ideas | Mr. Simms had been drenched with rain, bombarded with telephone calls, and his boss shouted at him.<br><br>To waste time and missing deadlines are bad habits. | Mr. Sims had been drenched with rain, bombarded with telephone calls, and shouted at by his boss.<br><br>Wasting time and missing deadlines are bad habits. |
| **Dangling Modifiers**<br><br>Creating confusion by placing modifiers close to the wrong nouns and verbs | Walking to the office, a red sports car passed her.<br><br>Reduced by 25 percent, Europe had its lowest semiconductor output in a decade. | A red sports car passed her while she was walking to the office.<br><br>Europe reduced semiconductor output by 25 percent, its lowest level in a decade. |
| **Long Noun Sequences**<br><br>Stringing too many nouns together | The aluminum window sash installation company will give us an estimate on Friday. | The company that installs aluminum window sashes will give us an estimate on Friday. |
| **Camouflaged Verbs**<br><br>Changing verbs and nouns into adjectives | The manager undertook implementation of the rules.<br><br>Verification of the shipments occurs weekly. | The manager implemented the rules.<br><br>We verify shipments weekly. |
| Changing verbs into nouns | reach a conclusion about<br>give consideration to | conclude<br>consider |
| **Sentence Structure**<br><br>Separating subject and predicate | A 10 percent decline in market share, which resulted from quality problems and an aggressive sales campaign by Macleans, the market leader in the Maritimes, was the major problem in 2013. | The major problem in 2013 was a 10 percent loss of market share, which resulted from quality problems and an aggressive sales campaign by Macleans, the market leader in the Maritimes. |
| Placing adjectives, adverbs, or prepositional phrases too far from the words they modify | These ergonomic chairs are ideal for professionals who must spend many hours working at their computers with their adjustable sitting, kneeling, and standing positions. | With their adjustable sitting, kneeling, and standing positions, these ergonomic chairs are ideal for professionals who must spend many hours working at their computers. |
| **Awkward References** | Corporate legal and Alberta field operations recruit the patent lawyers and the sales managers, respectively. | Corporate legal recruits the patent lawyers, and Alberta field operations recruits the sales managers. |

- **Clarify sentence structure.** Keep the subject and predicate of a sentence as close together as possible. Similarly, adjectives, adverbs, and prepositional phrases usually make the most sense when they're placed as close as possible to the words they modify.
- **Clarify awkward references.** Try to avoid vague references such as *the above-mentioned, as mentioned above, the aforementioned, the former, the latter,* and *respectively.* Use a specific pointer such as "as described in the second paragraph on page 10."

> Subject and predicate should be placed as close together as possible, as should modifiers and the words they modify.

## Editing for Conciseness

Many of the changes you make to improve clarity also shorten your message by removing unnecessary words. The next step is to examine the text with the specific goal of reducing the number of words you use. Readers appreciate conciseness and are more likely to read your documents if you have a reputation for efficient writing. See Table 5.2 for examples of the following tips:

> Make your documents tighter by removing unnecessary words, phrases, and sentences.

- **Delete unnecessary words and phrases.** To test whether a word or phrase is essential, try the sentence without it. If the meaning doesn't change, leave it out.
- **Replace long words and phrases.** Short words and phrases are generally more vivid and easier to read than long ones. Also, by using infinitives (the "to" form of a verb) in place of some phrases, you can often shorten sentences while making them more clear.
- **Eliminate redundancies.** In some word combinations, the words say the same thing. For instance, "visible to the eye" is redundant because *visible* is enough without further clarification; "to the eye" adds nothing.
- **Recast "It is/There are" starters.** If you start a sentence with an indefinite pronoun such as *it* or *there*, odds are the sentence could be shorter and more active. For instance, "We believe . . ." is a stronger opening than "It is believed that . . ."

As you make all these improvements, concentrate on how each word contributes to an effective sentence and how each sentence helps to develop a coherent paragraph.

| TABLE 5.2 | Revising for Conciseness | |
|---|---|---|
| ISSUES TO REVIEW | WORDY | CONCISE |
| **Unnecessary Words and Phrases** | | |
| Using wordy phrases | for the sum of | for |
| | in the event that | if |
| | prior to the start of | before |
| | in the near future | soon |
| | at this point in time | now |
| | due to the fact that | because |
| | in view of the fact that | because |
| | until such time as | when |
| | with reference to | about |
| | in order to | to |
| Using too many relative pronouns (*who, that, which*) | Cars that are sold after January will not have a six-month warranty. | Cars sold after January will not have a six-month warranty. |
| | Employees who are driving to the retreat should look for opportunities to carpool. | Employees driving to the retreat should look for opportunities to carpool. |
| Not using enough relative pronouns or putting them in the wrong place (notice how the position of *that* alters the meaning of the sentence) | The project manager told the engineers last week the specifications were changed. | The project manager told the engineers last week that the specifications were changed. *OR* The project manager told the engineers that last week the specifications were changed. |

*(continued)*

| TABLE 5.2 | (Continued) |
| --- | --- |

**Long Words and Phrases**

| | | |
| --- | --- | --- |
| Using overly long words | During the preceding year, the company accelerated operations. | Last year the company sped up operations. |
| | The action was predicated on the assumption that the company was operating at a financial deficit. | The action was based on the belief that the company was losing money. |
| Using wordy phrases rather than infinitives | If you want success as a writer, you must work hard. | To succeed as a writer, you must work hard. |
| | He went to the library for the purpose of studying. | He went to the library to study. |
| | The employer increased salaries so that she could improve morale. | The employer increased salaries to improve morale. |

**Redundancies**

| | | |
| --- | --- | --- |
| Using two words or phrases that essentially say the same thing | absolutely complete | complete |
| | basic fundamentals | fundamentals |
| | follows after | follows |
| | free and clear | free |
| | refer back | refer |
| | repeat again | repeat |
| | collect together | collect |
| | future plans | plans |
| | return back | return |
| | important essentials | essentials |
| | end result | result |
| | actual truth | truth |
| | final outcome | outcome |
| | uniquely unusual | unique |
| | surrounded on all sides | surrounded |
| Using double modifiers | modern, up-to-date equipment | modern equipment |

**Sentences That Start with *It is* or *There are***

| | | |
| --- | --- | --- |
| (Rewriting to eliminate *It is* or *There are* can often shorten a sentence and sometimes clarify its meaning. However, this isn't always the case, so use your best judgment.) | It would be appreciated if you would sign the lease today. | Please sign the lease today. |
| | There are five employees in this division who were late to work today. | Five employees in this division were late to work today. |

**LEARNING OBJECTIVE 4**
Identify four software tools that can help you revise messages and explain the risks of using them.

Spell checkers, thesauruses, grammar checkers, and style checkers can all help with the revision process, but they can't take the place of good writing and editing skills.

# Using Technology to Revise Your Message

When it's time to revise and polish your message, be sure to use the revision features in your software to full advantage. For instance, *revision tracking* (look for a feature called "track changes" or something similar) and *commenting* show proposed editing changes and provide a history of a document's revisions. In Microsoft Word, for example, revisions appear in a different colour, giving you a chance to review changes before accepting or rejecting them. Using revision marks and commenting features is also a great way to keep track of editing changes made by team members. Both Word and Adobe Acrobat let you use different colours for each reviewer, so you can keep everyone's comments separate.

Four other software tools and functions can help you find the best words and use them correctly. First, spell checkers are wonderful for finding typos, but they are no substitute for careful reviewing. For example, if you use *their* when you mean to use *there*, your spell checker won't notice because *their* is spelled correctly.

Second, a grammar checker tries to do for your grammar what a spell checker does for your spelling. Because the program doesn't have a clue about what you're trying to say, it can't tell whether you've said it clearly or completely. However, grammar checkers can highlight items you should consider changing, such as passive voice, long sentences, and words that tend to be misused.

Third, a computer-based thesaurus (either within your software or on a website such as www.thesaurus.com) offers alternatives to a particular word. Use them to find fresh, interesting words when you've been using the same word too many times. Don't use a thesaurus to find impressive-sounding words, however, and don't assume that all the alternatives suggested are correct for each situation.

Fourth, a style checker can monitor your word and sentence choices and suggest alternatives. Style-checking options can help you be consistent such as in the spelling out of numbers and use of contractions.

Use any software tools that you find helpful when revising your documents, but remember that it's unwise to rely on them to do all your revision work, and you are responsible for the final product.

# Producing Your Message

LEARNING OBJECTIVE 5
List three principles of effective design and explain the role of major design elements in document readability.

Now it's time to put your hard work on display. The *production quality* of your message—the total effect of page design, graphical elements, typography, screen presence, and so on—plays an important role in its effectiveness. A polished, inviting design not only makes your document easier to read but also conveys a sense of professionalism and importance.[6]

## Designing for Readability

Design affects readability in two important ways. First, if used carefully, design elements can improve the effectiveness of your message. If used poorly, however, design elements can act as barriers, impeding your communication. Second, the visual design sends a nonverbal message to your readers, influencing their perceptions of the communication before they read a single word (see Figure 5.3).

The quality of your document design, both on paper and onscreen, affects readability and audience perceptions.

To achieve an effective design, pay careful attention to the following design elements:

- **Consistency.** Throughout each message, be consistent in your use of margins, typeface, type size, spacing, colour, lines, and position. Style sheets and themes can be a big help here.
- **Balance.** Balance is an important but sometimes subjective design issue. One document may have a formal, rigid design in which the various elements are placed in a grid pattern, whereas another may have a less formal design in which elements flow more freely across the page—and both could be in balance. Like the tone of your language, visual balance can be too formal, just right, or too informal for a given message. Try to balance the space devoted to text, visuals, and *white space*. For example, many pages of text can be intimidating. Too many visuals could break the text into disjointed chunks.
- **Restraint.** Strive for simplicity. Don't clutter your message with too many design elements, too many colours, or too many decorative touches.
- **Detail.** Pay attention to details that affect your design and thus your message. For instance, extremely wide columns of text can be difficult to read; in many cases, a better solution is to split the text into two narrower columns.

For effective design, pay attention to
- Consistency
- Balance
- Simplicity

Even without special training in graphic design, you can make your printed and electronic messages more effective by understanding the use of white space, margins and line justification, typefaces, and type styles.

**FIGURE 5.3** Designing for Readability—An Example of Restrained Design

White space separates elements in a document and helps guide the reader's eye.

**WHITE SPACE**   Any space free of text or artwork is considered **white space**. (Note that "white space" isn't necessarily white.) These unused areas provide visual contrast and important resting points for your readers. White space includes the open area surrounding headings, margins, paragraph indents, space around images, vertical space between columns, and horizontal space between paragraphs or lines of text. To increase the chance that readers will read your messages, be generous with white space; it makes pages and screens feel less intimidating and easier to read.[7]

Most business documents use a flush left margin and a ragged right margin.

**MARGINS AND JUSTIFICATION**   Margins define the space around text and between text columns. In addition to their width, the look and feel of margins are influenced by the way you arrange lines of text, which can be set in the following ways:

- *Justified,* which means they are *flush,* or aligned vertically, on both the left and the right
- Flush left with a *ragged-right* margin

- Flush right with a *ragged-left* margin
- Centred

The paragraphs in this text are justified, whereas the paragraphs in Figure 5.2 on page 97 are flush left with a ragged-right margin.

Magazines, newspapers, and books often use justified type because it can accommodate more text in a given space. However, justified type creates a denser and more formal look that isn't appropriate for all situations, and can be more difficult to read. It can also produce large gaps between words and excessive hyphenation at the ends of lines. For these reasons, it's best to avoid justified type in most business documents.

In contrast to justified type, flush-left, ragged-right type creates a more open appearance on the page, producing a less formal and more contemporary look.

**TYPEFACES**   **Typeface** refers to the physical design of letters, numbers, and other text characters. (*Font* and *typeface* are often used interchangeably, although strictly speaking, a font is a set of characters in a given typeface.) Typeface influences the tone of your message, making it look authoritative or friendly, businesslike or casual, classic or modern, and so on (see Table 5.3). Choose fonts that are appropriate for your message; many of the fonts on your computer are not appropriate for business use.

**Serif typefaces** have small crosslines (called serifs) at the ends of each letter stroke. Serif faces such as Times Roman are commonly used for body text. They can look busy and cluttered when set in large sizes for headings or other display treatments. **Sans serif typefaces**, in contrast, lack these serifs. The visual simplicity of sans serif typefaces such as Helvetica and Arial makes them ideal for the larger sizes used in headlines. Sans serif typefaces can be difficult to read in long blocks of text, however, unless they are formatted with generous spacing between lines.

For most documents, you shouldn't need more than two typefaces, using one to make captions or other text elements stand out.[8] You can't go wrong with a sans serif typeface (such as Arial) for headings and subheadings and a serif typeface (such as Times Roman) for text and captions. Using more typefaces can clutter a document and look amateurish.

*Serif typefaces are commonly used for body text; sans serif typefaces are commonly used for headings.*

**REAL-TIME UPDATES**

**Learn More by Reading This Article**

**Improve your document designs by learning the fundamentals of typography**

Knowing the basics of type usage will help you create more effective page and screen layouts. Go to http://real-timeup-dates.com/bce6 and click on Learn More. If you are using MyBCommLab, you can access Real-Time Updates within Business Communication Resources.

**TYPE STYLES AND SIZE**   **Type style** refers to any modification that lends contrast or emphasis to type, including boldface, italic, underlining, and colour. For example, you can boldface individual words or phrases to draw more attention to them. Italic type has specific uses as well, such as highlighting quotations and indicating foreign words, irony, humour, book and movie titles, and unconventional usage. Use any type style in moderation. For instance, underlining or using all uppercase letters can interfere with the reader's ability to recognize the shapes of words, improperly placed boldface or italicized type can slow down your reader, and shadowed or outlined type can seriously hinder legibility.

*Avoid using any type style that inhibits your audience's ability to read your messages.*

| TABLE 5.3 | Typeface Personalities: Serious to Casual to Playful | |
|---|---|---|
| **SERIF TYPEFACES** (Best for Text) | **SANS SERIF TYPEFACES** (Best for Headlines; Some Work Well for Text) | **SPECIALTY TYPEFACES** (for Decorative Purposes Only) |
| Bookman Old Style | Arial | Bodoni |
| Courier | **Eras Bold** | *Edwardian* |
| Garamond | Franklin Gothic Book | *LucidaHandwriting* |
| Times Roman | Verdana | **STENCIL** |

For most printed business messages, use a type size of 10 to 12 points for regular text and 12 to 18 points for headings and subheadings. Resist the temptation to reduce the type size to squeeze in text or to enlarge it to fill up space. Type that is too small is hard to read, whereas extra-large type often looks unprofessional.

## Designing Multimedia Documents

A **multimedia document** contains a combination of text, graphics, photographs, audio, animation, video, and interactivity (such as hyperlinks that access webpages or software programs). The document can be a portable, standalone file or part of a website. Most electronic media now support multiple media formats, so you have a variety of options for creating multimedia documents. For example, you can add photos to a word processor file, audio commentary to a PDF, video clips to a blog posting, and animation to webpages.

As rich media, multimedia documents can convey large amounts of information quickly, engage people in multiple ways, express emotions, and allow recipients to personalize the communication process to meet their own needs. However, these documents are more difficult to create than documents that contain only text and static images. To design and create multimedia documents, you need to consider the following factors:

*Multimedia elements can convey large amounts of information quickly, engage audiences, express emotions, and support personalization.*

- **Creative and technical skills.** Depending on what you need to accomplish, creating and integrating multimedia elements can require some creative and technical skills, such as adding photographs or video clips to a webpage. Fortunately, many basic tasks, such as adding photographs or video clips to a webpage, have gotten much easier in recent years. And with the right software, creating animations, videos, and screencasts is within the reach of most business communicators.

- **Tools.** The hardware and software tools needed to create and integrate media elements are now widely available and generally affordable, such as photo and video editing software.

*Multimedia documents can be powerful communication vehicles, but they require more time, tools, and skills to create.*

- **Time and cost.** Creating multimedia documents is easier than ever, but you still need to consider time and cost. You need to exercise good judgment when deciding whether to include multimedia and how much to include.

- **Content.** To include various media elements in a document, you obviously need to create or acquire them. Millions of graphics, photos, video clips, and other elements are available online, but you need to make sure you can legally use each item and give credit to sources. One good option is to search Creative Commons (**www.creativecommons.org**) for multimedia elements available for use at no charge but with various restrictions (such as giving the creator credit).

- **Message structure.** Multimedia documents often lack a rigid linear structure from beginning to end, which means you need to plan for readers to take multiple, individualized paths through the material. In other words, a conventional outline is often inadequate. Chapter 11 discusses the challenge of *information architecture*, the structure and navigational flow of websites and other multimedia documents.

- **Compatibility.** Some multimedia elements require specific software to be installed on the recipient's viewing device. Another challenge is the variety of screen sizes and resolutions, from large, high-resolution computer monitors to tiny, low-resolution phone displays. Make sure you understand the demands your message will place on the audience.

### REAL-TIME UPDATES

**Learn More by Visiting This Website**

**See the newest designs from some of the brightest minds in typography**

Type design is a fascinating and dynamic field; this portfolio shows dozens of innovative new typefaces. Go to http://real-timeupdates.com/bce6 and click on Learn More. If you are using MyBCommLab, you can access Real-Time Updates within Business Communication Resources.

## Using Technology to Produce Your Message

Production tools vary widely, depending on the software and systems you're using. Some systems offer capabilities that rival those of professional publishing software.

For online content, web publishing systems make it easy to produce great-looking webpages quickly. Similarly, blogging systems now simplify the production of blog content. A variety of tools also make it relatively simple to create multimedia presentations, such as screencasts (see Figure 5.4).

No matter what system you're using, become familiar with the basic formatting capabilities. A few hours of exploration on your own or an introductory training course can help you dramatically improve the production quality of your documents. Depending on the types of messages you're creating, you'll benefit from being proficient with the following features:

- **Templates, themes, and style sheets.** As Chapter 4 notes, you can save a tremendous amount of time by using templates, themes, and style sheets.
- **Page setup.** Use page setup to control margins, orientation (*portrait* is vertical; *landscape* is horizontal), and the location of *headers* (text and graphics that repeat at the top of every page) and *footers* (similar to headers but at the bottom of the page).
- **Column formatting.** Most business documents use a single column of text, but multiple columns can be an attractive format for documents such as newsletters. Columns are also handy for formatting long lists.
- **Paragraph formatting.** Take advantage of paragraph formatting controls to enhance the look of your documents. For instance, you can offset quotations by increasing margin width around a single paragraph or subtly compress line spacing to fit a document on a single page.

Learn to use your communication tools effectively so that you can work productively.

Paragraph formatting gives you greater control over the look of your documents.

---

**FIGURE 5.4**  Camtasia, An Example of a Multimedia Tool

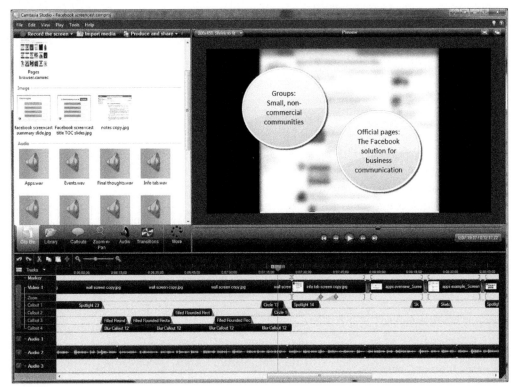

*Source:* Copyright © 2012 by TechSmith Corporation. Reprinted with permission.

- **Numbered and bulleted lists.** Let your software do the work of formatting numbered and bulleted lists.
- **Tables.** Tables are great for displaying any information that lends itself to rows and columns, including calendars, numeric data, comparisons, and multicolumn bulleted lists.
- **Images, text boxes, and objects.** Word processing and desktop publishing software let you insert a wide variety of images (using industry-standard formats such as JPEG and GIF). *Text boxes* are small blocks of text that stand apart from the main text and can be placed anywhere on the page; they are great for captions, callouts, or margin notes. *Objects* can be anything from a spreadsheet to a sound clip to an engineering drawing. Similarly, blogging systems, wikis, and other web development tools let you insert a variety of pictures, audio and video clips, and other multimedia elements.

By improving the appearance of your documents with these tools, you'll improve your readers' impressions of you and your messages.

LEARNING OBJECTIVE ⑥

**Explain the importance of proofreading and give six tips for successful proofreading.**

## Proofreading Your Message

Proofreading is the quality inspection stage for your documents, your last chance to make sure that your document is ready to carry your message—and your reputation—to the intended audience. Even a small mistake can doom your efforts, so take proofreading seriously.

Look for two types of problems: (1) undetected mistakes from the writing, design, and layout stages, and (2) mistakes that crept in during production. For the first category, you can review format and layout guidelines in Appendix A (including standard formats for letters, email, memos, and reports) and brush up on writing basics on MyBCommLab. The second category can include anything from computer glitches such as incorrect typefaces or misaligned page elements to problems with the ink used in printing. Strange things can happen as files move from computer to computer, especially when lots of multimedia elements are involved.

Your credibility is affected by your attention to the details of mechanics and form.

The types of details to look for when proofreading include language errors, missing material, design errors, and typographical errors.

Far from being a casual scan up and down the page or screen, proofreading should be a methodical procedure. Here is some advice from the pros:

- **Make multiple passes.** Go through the document several times, focusing on a different aspect each time. For instance, look for content errors the first time and layout errors the second time.
- **Use perceptual tricks.** To keep from missing errors that are "in plain sight," try reading pages backward, placing your finger under each word and reading it silently, covering everything but the line you're currently reading, or reading the document aloud.
- **Focus on high-priority items.** Double-check names, titles, dates, addresses, and any number that could cause grief if incorrect.
- **Get some distance.** If possible, don't proofread immediately after finishing the document; let your brain wander off to new topics and come back fresh later on.
- **Stay focused and vigilant.** Block out distractions and focus as completely as possible on your proofreading. Avoid reading large amounts of material in one sitting and try not to proofread when you're tired.
- **Take your time.** Quick proofreading is not careful proofreading.

Table 5.4 offers some handy tips to improve your proofreading efforts.

| TABLE 5.4 | Proofreading Tips |
|-----------|-------------------|

**Look for writing and typing errors**

☑ Typographical mistakes

☑ Misspelled words

☑ Grammatical errors

☑ Punctuation mistakes

**Look for design and layout errors**

☑ Violation of company standards

☑ Page or screen layout errors (such as incorrect margins and column formatting)

☑ Clumsy page breaks or line breaks

☑ Inconsistent font usage (such as with headings and subheadings)

☑ Alignment problems (columns, headers, footers, and graphics)

☑ Missing or incorrect page and section numbers

☑ Missing or incorrect page headers or footers

☑ Missing or incorrect URLs, email addresses, or other contact information

☑ Missing or incorrect photos and other graphical elements

☑ Missing or incorrect source notes, copyright notices, or other reference items

**Look for production errors**

☑ Printing problems

☑ Browser compatibility problems

☑ Incorrect or missing tags on blog posts

# Distributing Your Message

LEARNING OBJECTIVE ❼
Discuss the most important issues to consider when distributing your messages.

With the production finished, you're ready to distribute your message. You often have several options for distribution; consider the following factors when making your choice:

- **Cost.** Cost isn't a concern for most messages, but for multiple copies of lengthy reports or multimedia productions, it might well be. Be sure to consider the nonverbal message you send regarding cost as well. Overnight delivery of a printed report could look responsive in one instance and wasteful in another, for example.
- **Convenience.** Make sure your audience can conveniently access the material you send. For instance, sending huge files may be fine on a fast office network, but receiving such files can be a major headache for recipients on slower networks.

Consider cost, convenience, time, and security and privacy when choosing a distribution method.

- **Time.** How soon does the message need to reach the audience? Don't waste money on overnight delivery if the recipient won't read a report for a week.
- **Security and privacy.** The convenience offered by electronic communication needs to be weighed against security and privacy concerns. For the most sensitive messages, your company will probably restrict both the people who can receive the messages and the means you can use to distribute them. In addition, most computer users are wary of opening attachments, particularly word processing files. As an alternative, convert your documents to PDF files using Adobe Acrobat or an equivalent product.

**❶ OBJECTIVE Discuss the value of careful revision and describe the tasks involved in evaluating your first drafts and the work of other writers.**

Revision is an essential aspect of completing messages because it can nearly always make your first drafts tighter, clearer, and more compelling. Revision consists of three main tasks: (1) evaluating content, organization, and tone; (2) reviewing for readability; and (3) editing for clarity and conciseness. After you revise your message, complete it by using design elements effectively, proofreading to ensure quality, and distributing it to your audience.

When asked to evaluate, edit, or revise someone else's work, remember that your job is to help the other writer succeed.

**❷ OBJECTIVE List four techniques you can use to improve the readability of your messages.**

Four techniques that improve readability are varying sentence length, keeping paragraphs short, using lists and bullets, and adding headings and subheadings. Short paragraphs make it easier for readers to consume information in manageable chunks. Lists and bullets are effective devices for delineating sets of items, steps, or other collections of related information. Headings and subheadings organize your message, call attention to important information, and help readers make connections between related pieces of information.

**❸ OBJECTIVE Describe the steps you can take to improve the clarity of your writing and give four tips for making your writing more concise.**

As you work to clarify your messages, (1) break up overly long sentences, (2) rewrite hedging sentences, (3) impose parallelism, (4) correct dangling modifiers, (5) reword long noun sequences, (6) replace camouflaged verbs, (7) clarify sentence structure, and (8) clarify awkward references. To make messages more concise, include only necessary material and write uncluttered sentences by (1) deleting unnecessary words and phrases, (2) shortening overly long words and phrases, (3) eliminating redundancies, and (4) recasting sentences that begin with "It is" and "There are."

**❹ OBJECTIVE Identify four software tools that can help you revise messages and explain the risks of using them.**

Software tools that can help with revision include a spell checker, a thesaurus, a grammar checker, and a style checker. Although these tools can be quite helpful, writers shouldn't count on them without verifying their suggestions.

**❺ OBJECTIVE List four principles of effective design and explain the role of major design elements in document readability.**

Four key principles of effective design are consistency, balance, restraint, and detail. Major design elements for documents include white space, margins and justification, typefaces, and type styles and size. White space provides contrast and balance. Margins define the space around the text and contribute to the amount of white space. Typefaces influence the tone of the message. Type styles—boldface, italics, and underlining—provide contrast or emphasis, and type size affects readability. When selecting and applying design elements, be consistent throughout your document; balance text, art, and white space; show restraint in the number of elements you use; and pay attention to every detail. When designing multimedia documents, consider creative and technical skills, tools, content, time and cost, suitability of multimedia for the message, structure, and compatibility.

**❻ OBJECTIVE Explain the importance of proofreading and give six tips for successful proofreading.**

When proofreading the final version of your document, always keep an eye out for errors in grammar, usage, and punctuation. In addition, watch for spelling errors and typos. Make sure that nothing is missing and no extraneous elements are included. Use the following six tips: (1) make multiple passes, (2) use perceptual tricks, (3) focus on high-priority items, (4) get some distance, (5) stay focused and vigilant, and (6) take your time.

**❼ OBJECTIVE Discuss the most important issues to consider when distributing your messages.**

Consider cost, convenience, time, security, and privacy when choosing the method to distribute your messages. Always consider security and privacy issues before distributing messages that contain sensitive or confidential information.

## Practise Your Grammar

Effective business communication starts with strong grammar skills. To improve your grammar skills, go to MyBCommLab, where you'll find exercises and diagnostic tests to help you produce clear, effective communication.

## Test Your Knowledge

To review chapter content related to each question, refer to the indicated Learning Objective.

1. What are the four main tasks involved in completing a business message? L.O.❶
2. What is parallel construction, and why is it important? L.O.❷
3. How do readers benefit from white space? L.O.❺
4. Why is proofreading an important part of the writing process? L.O.❻
5. What factors should you consider when choosing a method for distributing a message (when you have a choice)? L.O.❼

## Apply Your Knowledge

To review chapter content related to each question, refer to the indicated Learning Objective.

1. Why should you let a first draft "age" for a while before you begin the revision process? L.O.❶
2. Why is it essential to understand the writer's intent before suggesting or making changes to another person's document? L.O.❶
3. What are the ethical implications of murky, complex writing in a document whose goal is to explain how customers can appeal the result of a decision made in the company's favour during a dispute? L.O.❸
4. What nonverbal signals can you send by your choice of distribution methods? L.O.❼

## Practise Your Skills

### EXERCISES FOR PERFECTING YOUR WRITING

To review chapter content related to each set of exercises, refer to the indicated Learning Objective.

**Clarity** Break the following sentences into shorter ones by adding more periods and revising as necessary. L.O.❸

1. The next time you write something, check your average sentence length in a 100-word passage, and if your sentences average more than 16 to 20 words, see whether you can break up some of the sentences.
2. Don't do what the village blacksmith did when he instructed his apprentice as follows: "When I take the shoe out of the fire, I'll lay it on the anvil, and when I nod my head, you hit it with the hammer." The apprentice did just as he was told, and now he's the village blacksmith.
3. Unfortunately, no gadget will produce excellent writing, but using spell checkers and grammar checkers can help by catching common spelling errors and raising grammatical points that writers might want to reconsider, such as suspect sentence structure and problems with noun–verb agreement.
4. Know the flexibility of the written word and its power to convey an idea, and know how to make your words behave so that your readers will understand.

**Conciseness** Cross out unnecessary words in the following sentences. L.O.❸

5. The board cannot act without a consensus of opinion.
6. To surpass our competitors, we need new innovations both in products and in company operations.
7. George McClannahan has wanted to be head of engineering a long period of time, and now he has finally gotten the promotion.
8. Don't pay more than you have to; you can get our new fragrance for a price of just $50.

**Conciseness** Revise the following sentences, using shorter, simpler words. L.O.❸

9. The antiquated calculator is ineffectual for solving sophisticated problems.
10. It is imperative that the pay increments be terminated before an inordinate deficit is accumulated.
11. There was unanimity among the executives that Ms. Jackson's idiosyncrasies were cause for a mandatory meeting with the company's personnel director.
12. The impending liquidation of the company's assets was cause for jubilation among the company's competitors.

**Conciseness** Use infinitives as substitutes for the overly long phrases in the following sentences. L.O.❸

13. For living, I require money.
14. They did not find sufficient evidence for believing in the future.
15. Bringing about the destruction of a dream is tragic.

**Conciseness** Condense the following sentences to as few words as possible; revise as needed to maintain clarity and sense. L.O.❸

16. We are of the conviction that writing is important.
17. In all probability, we're likely to have a price increase.
18. Our goals include making a determination about that in the near future.
19. When all is said and done at the conclusion of this experiment, I'd like to summarize the final windup.

**Modifiers** Remove all the unnecessary modifiers from the following sentences. L.O.❸

20. Tremendously high pay increases were given to the extraordinarily skilled and extremely conscientious employees.
21. The union's proposals were highly inflationary, extremely demanding, and exceptionally bold.

**Hedging** Rewrite the following sentences so that they no longer contain any hedging. L.O.❸

22. It would appear that someone apparently entered illegally.
23. It may be possible that sometime in the near future the situation is likely to improve.
24. Your report seems to suggest that we might be losing money.
25. I believe Nancy apparently has somewhat greater influence over employees in the new accounts department.

**Indefinite Starters** Rewrite the following sentences to eliminate the indefinite starters. L.O.❸

26. There are several examples here to show that Elaine can't hold a position very long.

27. It would be greatly appreciated if every employee would make a generous contribution to Jan Cook's retirement party.
28. It has been learned in Ottawa today from generally reliable sources that an important announcement will be made shortly by the prime minister.
29. There is a rule that states that we cannot work overtime without permission.

**Parallelism** Revise the following sentences to fix the parallelism problems. L.O.❸

30. Mr. Hill is expected to lecture three days a week, to counsel two days a week, and must write for publication in his spare time.
31. She knows not only accounting, but she also reads Latin.
32. Both applicants had families, college degrees, and were in their thirties, with considerable accounting experience but few social connections.
33. This book was exciting, well written, and held my interest.

**Awkward References** Revise the following sentences to delete the awkward references. L.O.❸

34. The vice-president in charge of sales and the production manager are responsible for funding the demo unit program and the loaner unit program, respectively.
35. The demo unit program and the loaner unit program are funded from different budgets, with the former the responsibility of the vice-president in charge of sales and the latter the responsibility of the production manager.
36. The budgets for the demo unit program and the loaner unit program were increased this year, with the aforementioned budgets being increased 10 percent in both cases.
37. A laser printer and an inkjet printer were delivered to John and Megan, respectively.

**Dangling Modifiers** Rewrite the following sentences to clarify the dangling modifiers. L.O.❸

38. Running down the railroad tracks in a cloud of smoke, we watched the countryside glide by.
39. Lying on the shelf, Ruby saw the seashell.
40. Based on the information, I think we should buy the property.
41. Being cluttered and filthy, Sandy took the whole afternoon to clean up her desk.

**Noun Sequences** Rewrite the following sentences to eliminate the long strings of nouns. L.O.❸

42. The focus of the meeting was a discussion of the bank interest rate deregulation issue.

43. Following the government task force report recommendations, we are revising our job applicant evaluation procedures.
44. The production department quality assurance program components include employee training, supplier cooperation, and computerized detection equipment.
45. The supermarket warehouse inventory reduction plan will be implemented next month.

**Sentence Structure** Rearrange each of the following sentences to bring the subjects closer to their verbs. L.O.❸

46. Trudy, when she first saw the bull pawing the ground, ran.
47. It was Terri who, according to Ted, who is probably the worst gossip in the office (Tom excepted), mailed the wrong order.
48. William Oberstreet, in his book *Investment Capital Reconsidered*, writes of the mistakes that bankers through the decades have made.
49. Judy Schimmel, after passing up several sensible investment opportunities, despite the warnings of her friends and family, invested her inheritance in a jojoba plantation.

**Camouflaged Verbs** Rewrite each of the following sentences so that the verbs are no longer camouflaged. L.O.❸

50. Adaptation to the new rules was performed easily by the employees.
51. The assessor will make a determination of the tax due.
52. Verification of the identity of the employees must be made daily.
53. The board of directors made a recommendation that Mr. Ronson be assigned to a new division.

## ACTIVITIES

Each activity is labelled according to the primary skill or skills you will need to use. To review relevant chapter content, you can refer to the indicated Learning Objective. In some instances, supporting information will be found in another chapter, as indicated.

1. **Collaboration: Evaluating the Work of Other Writers** L.O.❶ The email below contains a number of tone problems. Discuss the email with two classmates and identify what causes the tone problems. What type of tone should this email have? Have each person rewrite the email to achieve appropriate tone.

From: Cal Wilson <cpwilson@orgus.net>

To: All Employees

Sent: Friday, September 07, 2016 7:04 PM

Subject: Smoking at Building Entrances

It has come to my attention once again that employees continue to smoke at the entrances to our building.

Not only is this behaviour in contravention of the firm's regulations and the City bylaw, but it is also preventing customers from proper egress into our establishment.

Effective immediately no employees will smoke within five metres of the building entrances.

2. **Revising a Document: Using Collaboration Technology** L.O.❶ In a group of three, select one of your documents written in response to Activity #1, above, and edit it using MS Word's Reviewing feature or using other collaboration software such as Google Docs or Zoho (www.zoho.com), free for personal use.

3. **Communication Ethics: Making Ethical Choices; Media Skills: Blogging** L.O.❸ The time and energy required for careful revision can often benefit you or your company directly, such as by increasing the probability that website visitors will buy your products. But what about situations in which the quality of your writing and revision work really doesn't stand to benefit you directly? For instance, assume that you are putting a notice on your website, informing the local community about some upcoming construction to your manufacturing plant. The work will disrupt traffic for nearly a year and generate a significant amount of noise and air pollution, but knowing the specific dates and times of various construction activities will allow people to adjust their commutes and other activities to minimize the negative impact on their daily lives. However, your company does not sell products in the local area, so the people affected by all this are not potential customers. Moreover, providing accurate information to the surrounding community and updating it as the project progresses will take time away from your other job responsibilities. Do you have an ethical obligation to keep the local community informed with accurate, up-to-date information? Why or why not? In a post on your class blog, explain your position on this question.

4. **Completing: Revising for Readability (Lists)** L.O.❷ Rewrite the following paragraph using a parallel bulleted list and one introductory sentence:

> Our safety consulting expertise gives us the ability to offer a full range of services to help your company be compliant with regulations and meet best industry practices. We have a full range of safety training materials. We also run training sessions on a variety of important safety topics. Another division of our services is accident investigation, including liability assessment. A third area we specialize in is auditing. We can audit your entire safety program to identify where your company is not in compliance or show where best practices could enhance the program. Our fourth area of specialization is safety communication. We can produce a range of documents, posters, newsletter articles, and video podcasts on safety topics based on your company's needs.

5. **Completing: Revising for Readability** L.O.❷ Rewrite the following paragraph to vary the length of the sentences and to shorten the paragraph so it looks more inviting to readers:

> Although major league hockey remains popular, more people are attending minor league hockey games because they can spend less on admission, snacks, and parking and still enjoy the excitement of Canada's favourite game. For example, in the 2012–2013 season almost 500,000 people attended WHL junior hockey games. Saskatchewan has three teams—the Moose Jaw Warriors, Saskatoon Blades, and the Regina Pats—and Manitoba has the Brandon Wheat Kings. These teams play in relatively small rinks, so fans are close enough to see and hear everything, including the sounds of the players hitting the boards or the goalie catching the puck. Best of all, the cost of a family outing to see rising stars play in a local minor league game is just a fraction of what the family would spend to attend a major league game in a much larger, more crowded arena.

6. **Completing: Designing for Readability; Media Skills: Blogging** L.O.❺ Compare the home pages of CBC Business News (www.cbc.ca/news/business) and Globe Investor (www.globeandmail.com/globe-investor/), two websites that cover financial markets. What are your first impressions of these two sites? How do their overall designs compare in terms of information delivery and overall user experience? Choose three pieces of information that a visitor to these sites would be likely to look for, such as a current stock price, news from international markets, and commentary from market experts. Which site makes it easier to find this information? Why? Present your analysis in a post for your class blog.

7. **Completing: Designing for Readability** L.O.❺ Assume you are a supervisor in a large call centre and you have been working with the human resources manager to organize a workshop for staff training. You made notes about the workshop dates and times (see below), but now it is time to email the staff. Select which information is relevant and write the email message. Emphasize important information with document design features. Use headings, lists, layout, boldface, and other document design features. Make the tone friendly—you want the staff to attend even though it is not required.

## YOUR NOTES

> Have to repeat workshop to accommodate everyone. Workshop content—conflict management skills—half day/three hours 9 am–noon. Can't have all staff at same workshop—have to register/signup for desired date—September 5 or Sept. 7. Sept 5—location is Holiday Inn, room 201, Sept. 7 Best Western, Room 102. Time is the same though. Employees can claim for travel (max—$28) and lunch too ($20). Leader is the same too, Dean Olund. Sign up sheet in coffeeroom. Human Resources is paying the reg. fee so no worries about that. Attendance not required but, hey, I don't want to be organizing this for nothing and some people around here could really use a tip or two on getting along with others! What else do they have to do?—have to trade shifts and let me know which date they choose. Have to read workshop manual before attending—can pick up material at my desk. No registrations after deadline (Sept. 1) or catering numbers will be off. Dean Olund trains police and emergency service workers at the Justice Institute.

# Workplace Skills

## Improving Your Writing for the Web

People visit the web because they want to get information efficiently. So you need to grab a reader's attention and make your main points immediately.

Most web users are impatient, and because their time is limited, they tend to scan text rather than read it, moving between sites instead of spending a lot of time on a single webpage. This skim-and-scan style demands extreme brevity. Moreover, reading on a computer screen is more difficult than reading from the printed page, and written information on a webpage can take up multiple screens, forcing readers to scroll through the document. Although most readers move through a printed document in a fairly linear path from beginning to end, web users move about a document and its related screens in any order they please.

Successful web writers help their readers along by breaking information into smaller, screen-sized chunks that may be accessed in any order. *Hyperlinks* are the in-text tags that allow readers to click on a screen element and be instantly transported to information somewhere else.

The following pointers summarize the ways that you can improve your web writing:

1. **Develop a well-organized hyperlink structure:**
   - Plan your navigation first.
   - Make your structure obvious with a hyperlinked site map or a table of contents at the top or bottom of your page.
   - Provide a search engine in your document.

2. **Modify your message style:**
   - Use a lighter, less formal writing style.
   - Avoid clever, humorous, or jargon-filled phrases that could be misunderstood by readers from other cultures.
   - Modify your messages for global audiences, making them "glocal" by localizing material so that it reflects your customers' native language, norms, weights, measures, time, currency, and so on.

3. **Modify your message format:**
   - Break information into independent chunks (self-contained, readable pages of information) and connect the chunks with hyperlinks.
   - Don't repeat information; instead, link your reader to the page where that information already resides.
   - Don't burden others with unwanted detail. Place specific details on subsequent pages.
   - Include a downloadable, printable version of longer documents for offline reading.
   - Adopt an inverted pyramid style so that readers can quickly see your topic, main idea, and conclusion.
   - Put your most important concept in the first 50 words.

4. **Help readers skim text for the information they need:**
   - Write shorter sentences and paragraphs to ease the reading process and to fit in narrow columns.
   - Cut traditional print by about 40 percent and try to keep chunks to 75 words or less.
   - Use lists.
   - Use boldface, colour, and other typographical elements conservatively.
   - Write informative headings that stand on their own and are consistent in their wording.
   - Write concise summaries and descriptions that are informative and clear.

5. **Write effective links and place them strategically:**
   - Use a combination of textual and graphical hyperlinks, but don't overdo graphics, since they slow down document loading time.
   - Avoid self-referential terms such as "click here" or "follow this link."
   - Write informative hyperlinks so that the content of subsequent pages is obvious.
   - Place your links strategically and carefully.

6. **Establish your credibility (important because anyone can post material on a website):**
   - Include your name and the name of your agency (if applicable) on every webpage.
   - Provide contact information (at least an email address) so that readers can get in touch with you or the agency easily.
   - Include posting and revision dates for your information.
   - Make sure your content is error-free.

## Applications for Success

Writing for the Web (www.nngroup.com/topic/writing-web/) offers you a huge amount of information on web writing. Visit this site and access research on how users read on the web and get tips on how to adapt your writing for online readers. Find links to many resources including computer industry style guides for web writing.

Do the following:

1. Select any webpage and critique the headings. Do they make sense on their own? Do they include hyperlinks? Are the hyperlinks placed effectively? Does the author use colour or boldface effectively? What changes, if any, would you recommend?

2. Select any webpage and critique the effectiveness of the written hyperlinks. Does the author use self-referential terms? Is the writing concise? Are linked words embedded in a sentence or paragraph to provide the reader with context?

# Crafting Messages for Electronic Media

**LEARNING OBJECTIVES**

*After studying this chapter, you will be able to*

1. Identify the major electronic media used for brief business messages and describe the nine compositional modes needed for electronic media.

2. Describe the use of social networks in business communication.

3. Explain how companies and business professionals can use information and media sharing websites.

4. Describe the evolving role of email in business communication and explain how to adapt the three-step writing process to email messages.

5. Describe the business benefits of instant messaging (IM) and identify guidelines for effective IM in the workplace.

6. Describe the use of blogging and microblogging in business communication and briefly explain how to adapt the three-step process to blogging.

7. Explain how to adapt the three-step writing process for podcasts.

Mandy Farmer is president of the six-hotel Accent Inns chain based in Vancouver. She knows that monitoring her hotels' online reputation makes smart business. "In the online world, everyone is writing reviews, whether it is in Google Maps, TripAdvisor.com, or Booking.com," says Farmer. Her organization uses social media to listen to customers and improve service.[1]

## Using Electronic Media for Business Communication

The use of social media represents a fundamental shift in business communication. The shift is still taking place, as more consumers adopt social media and businesses experiment with the best ways to integrate these media and to adapt their internal and external communication practices.

**Social media** such as Facebook are electronic media that empower stakeholders as participants in the communication process by allowing them to share content, revise content, respond to content, or contribute new content. Quite a bit of attention gets paid to specific tools and technologies in social and other electronic media, but the most important changes go a lot deeper than the tools themselves. As "The Social Communication Model" in Chapter 1 explains, these technologies have changed the relationships

**LEARNING OBJECTIVE 1**
Identify the major electronic media used for brief business messages and describe the nine compositional modes needed for electronic media.

The range of options for short business messages continues to grow with innovations in electronic and social media.

between companies and their stakeholders, influenced the way companies are managed, and altered the behaviours and expectations of consumers and employees.

Technological advances have changed reader behaviour, forcing changes in the practice of business communication.

For instance, many people now rely heavily on content sharing through social media tools to get information of personal and professional interest. Additionally, many consumers and professionals frequently engage in "content snacking," consuming large numbers of small pieces of information and bypassing larger documents that might require more than a few minutes or even a few seconds to read.[2] Moreover, the amount of content accessed from mobile devices (with the challenges they present in terms of screen size and input mechanisms) continues to rise.[3] Faced with such behaviour, communicators need to be more careful than ever to create audience-focused messages and to consider restructuring messages using more teasers, orientations, and summaries.

With all these changes taking place, the field of business communication is a lot more interesting—but also a lot more complicated—than it was just a few years ago. For example, newer and smaller firms have a better opportunity to compete against big companies with big media budgets, because the quality of the message and the credibility of the sender are supremely important in this new environment. Empowered stakeholders can use the amplifying power of social media to help companies that appear to be acting in their best interests and harm companies that are not. Social media also have the potential to increase transparency, with more eyes and ears to monitor business activities and to use the crowd's voice to demand accountability and change.

Although social media have reduced the amount of control that businesses have over the content and the process of communication,[4] today's smart companies are learning how to adapt their communication efforts to this new media landscape and to welcome customers' participation. Social media are also revolutionizing internal communication, breaking down traditional barriers in the organizational hierarchy, promoting the flow of information and ideas, and enabling networks of individuals and organizations to collaborate on a global scale.[5]

## Media Choices for Brief Messages

Social media are not the only options available for business communication, of course. Individuals and companies have a broad range of options for sending brief messages (from one or two sentences up to several pages long), including the following:

- Social networks
- Information and media sharing sites
- Email
- Instant messaging (IM)
- Text messaging
- Blogging and microblogging
- Podcasting

This chapter covers all of these media, and Chapters 10 and 11 explore two other key electronic media, websites and wikis, which are used for longer messages and documents.

As this list suggests, businesses use many of the same tools you use for personal communication. Generally speaking, companies are quick to jump on any communication platform where consumers are likely to congregate or that promise more efficient internal or external communication (see Figure 6.1).

Businesses continue to experiment with new media; for example, see Figure 6.2. The IBM Business Center in the virtual world Second Life offers customer information along with real-time interaction with IBM product experts.

## FIGURE 6.1 An Infographic on the Rise and Reach of Social Media

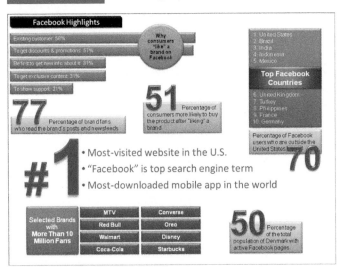

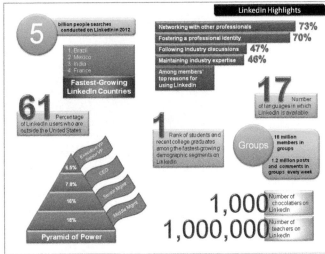

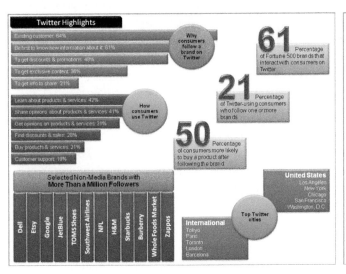

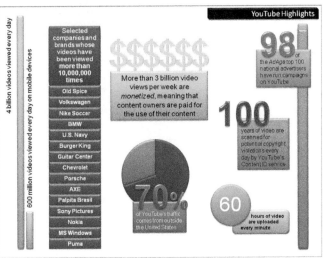

*Source:* Adapted from *2012 CEO, Social Media & Leadership Survey,* Brandfog, www.brandfog.com; "About Us," LinkedIn, accessed 28 May 2012, http://press.linkedin.com/about/; "The Global LinkedIn Audience," LinkedIn, accessed 28 May 2012, http://marketing.linkedin.com; Fan Page List, accessed 28 May 2012, http://fanpagelist.com; Josh Mendelohn, "The Business Impact of Twitter: It's Come a Long Way," Constant Contact, 20 October 2011, http://blogs.constantcontact.com; "10 Facts about Consumer Behavior on Twitter," Social Media Quickstarter, accessed 28 May 2012, www.socialquickstarter.com; "10 Facts about Consumer Behavior on Facebook," Social Media Quickstarter, accessed 28 May 2012, www.socialquickstarter.com; Samantha Murphy, "These Are the Most Engaging Brands on Facebook," Mashable, 15 May 2012, http://mashable.com; "Statistics," YouTube, accessed 28 May 2012, www.youtube.com.

Although most of your business communication is likely to be via electronic means, don't automatically dismiss the benefits of printed messages. Here are several situations in which you should use a printed message over electronic alternatives:

- When you want to make a formal impression
- When you are legally required to provide information in printed form
- When you want to stand out from the flood of electronic messages
- When you need a permanent, unchangeable, or secure record

Obviously, if you can't reach a particular audience electronically, you'll also need to use a printed message. Appendix A offers guidelines on formatting printed memos and letters.

| FIGURE 6.2 | Communication Innovations: Virtual Worlds |

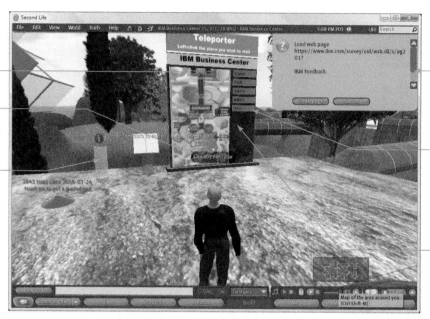

Provides access to IBM's technical library

Site resources include a virtual conference centre and collaboration tools

Offers guided tours of the centre to help visitors interact with IBM's virtual presence

Online survey tools help the company learn more about Second Life visitors and current or potential IBM customers

Offers interaction in a variety of languages to support a global audience; IBM sales staff are available to help visitors explore and choose IBM products

Gives access to a variety of product and technology demonstrations, such as the Green Data Center

## Compositional Modes for Electronic Media

As you practise using electronic media in this course, focus on the principles of social media communication and the fundamentals of planning, writing, and completing messages, rather than on the specific details of any one medium or system.[6] Fortunately, the basic communication skills required usually transfer from one system to another. You can succeed with written communication in virtually all electronic media by using one of nine *compositional modes*:

- **Conversations.** IM is a great example of a written medium that mimics spoken conversation. And just as you wouldn't read a report to someone sitting in your office, don't use conversational modes to exchange large volumes of information.

- **Comments and critiques.** As Mandy Farmer knows, one of the most powerful aspects of social media is the opportunity for interested parties to express opinions and provide feedback, whether it's leaving comments on a blog post or reviewing products on an e-commerce site. Sharing helpful tips and insightful commentary is also a great way to build your personal brand. To be an effective commenter, focus on short chunks of information that a broad spectrum of other site visitors will find helpful. Avoid rants, insults, jokes, and blatant self-promotion.

- **Orientations.** The ability to help people find their way through an unfamiliar system or subject is a valuable writing skill, and a talent that readers greatly appreciate. Unlike summaries (see next list item), orientations don't give away the key points in the collection of information but rather tell readers where to find those points. To write effective orientations step back and view it from the inexperienced perspective of a "newbie."

- **Summaries.** Summaries can serve several purposes. At the beginning of an article or webpage, a summary functions as a miniature version of the document, giving readers all the key points while skipping over details. In some instances, this is all a reader needs. In other instances, the up-front summary helps a reader decide whether to invest the time needed to read the full document. At the end of an article or webpage, a summary functions as a review, reminding readers of the key points they've just read.

- **Reference materials.** One of the greatest benefits of the internet is the access it can provide to vast quantities of reference materials—numerical or textual information

Communicating successfully with electronic media requires a wide range of writing approaches.

that people typically don't read in a linear way but rather search through to find particular data points, trends, or other details. One of the challenges of writing reference material is that you can't always know how readers will want to access it. Making the information accessible via search engines is an important step. However, readers don't always know which search terms will yield the best results, so consider an orientation and organize the material in logical ways with clear headings that promote skimming.

- **Narratives.** The storytelling techniques covered in Chapter 3 (see page 61) can be effective in a wide variety of situations, from company histories to product reviews and demonstrations. Narratives work best when the beginning piques readers' curiosity, the middle moves quickly through the challenges faced, and the ending is inspiring or instructive and gives readers information they can use in their own lives.

- **Teasers.** Teasers intentionally withhold key pieces of information as a way to pull readers or listeners into a story or other document. Teasers are widely used in marketing and sales messages, such as a bit of copy on the outside of an envelope that promises important information on the inside. In electronic media, the space limitations and URL linking capabilities of Twitter and other microblogging systems make them a natural tool for the teaser approach. Figure 6.3 shows how the global accounting and management firm Deloitte uses Twitter to announce and promote resources. The tweet is a teaser inviting the reader to click through for more information. Although they can certainly be effective, teasers need to be used sparingly and with respect for readers' time and intelligence. Be sure that the *payoff*, the information a teaser links to, is valuable and legitimate to avoid losing credibility if readers think they are being tricked.

- **Status updates and announcements.** If you use social media frequently, much of your writing will involve status updates and announcements. However, post only those updates that readers will find useful, and include only the information they need.

With Twitter and other super-short messaging systems, the ability to write a compelling *teaser* is an important skill.

---

**FIGURE 6.3** **Compositional Modes: Using Twitter for Teasers**

Links to an article in a respected business magazine

Links to a seminar invitation on Deloitte's website

Links to an article and information about the firm's consulting services in this market

Links to a video on YouTube

Links to a video on Deloitte's website

Links to an article and information about the firm's consulting services in this market

Links to a report on Deloitte's website

Links to a conference invitation on Deloitte's website

*Source:* Deloitte Global Services Twitter page. Copyright © 2012 Deloitte Global Services Limited. Reprinted with permission.

- **Tutorials.** Given the community nature of social media, the purpose of many messages is to share how-to advice. Becoming known as a reliable expert is a great way to build customer loyalty for your company while enhancing your own personal value.

Of course, many of these modes are also used in print media, but over time you may find yourself using all of them in various electronic and social media contexts. As you approach a new communication task using electronic media, ask yourself what kind of information audience members are likely to need and then choose the appropriate compositional mode.

## Creating Content for Social Media

Writing for social media requires a different approach than writing for traditional media.

No matter what media or compositional mode you are using for a particular message, writing for social media requires a different approach than traditional media. Whether you're writing a blog or posting a product demonstration video to YouTube, consider these tips for creating successful content for social media:[7]

- **Remember that it's a conversation, not a lecture or a sales pitch.** One of the great appeals of social media is the feeling of conversation, of people talking *with* one another instead of one person talking *at* everyone else. For all their technological sophistication, in an important sense social media are really just a new spin on the age-old practice of *word-of-mouth* communication. As more and more people gain a voice in the marketplace, companies that try to maintain the old "we talk, you listen" mindset are likely to be ignored in the social media landscape.
- **Write informally but not carelessly.** Write as a human being with a unique, personal voice. However, don't take this as a license to get sloppy; no one wants to slog through misspelled words and half-baked sentences to find your message.
- **Create concise, specific, and informative headlines.** Given the importance of headlines in the face of content snacking and information overload, headlines are extremely important in social media. Avoid the temptation to engage in clever wordplay when writing headlines and teasers. This advice applies to all forms of business communication, of course, but it is essential for social media. Readers don't want to spend time and energy figuring out what your witty headlines mean. Search engines won't know what they mean, either, so fewer people will find your content.
- **Get involved and stay involved.** Social media make some businesspeople nervous because they don't permit a high level of control over messages. However, don't hide from criticism. Take the opportunity to correct misinformation or explain how mistakes will be fixed.
- **If you need to promote something, do so indirectly.** Just as you wouldn't hit people with a company sales pitch during an informal social gathering, refrain from blatant promotional efforts in social media.
- **Be transparent and honest.** Honesty is always essential, of course, but the social media environment is unforgiving. Attempts to twist the truth, withhold information, or hide behind a virtual barricade only invite attack in the "public square" of social media. Richard Brewer-Hay, who writes the eBay Inc blog (http://blog.ebay.com) for the online auction site, explains that "by demonstrating a willingness to talk openly and transparently about eBay operations and business decisions, the blog is just one way we've ensured trust and confidence in our company."[8]
- **Surrender the illusion of control.** Fear of losing control over their messages and brand images makes some managers leery of adopting or allowing social media in their companies. However, that fear is mostly irrelevant, because whatever control they might have had in the past is more or less gone in this wild new world. The only option is to work with social media, encouraging and shaping conversations, rather than trying to control them.

- **Think before you post!** Because of careless messages, individuals and companies have been sued because of Twitter updates, employees have been fired for Facebook wall postings, vital company secrets have been leaked, and business and personal relationships have been strained. Remember that you share the responsibility of keeping your company's and your customers' data private and secure. Assume that every message you send in any electronic medium will be stored forever and might be read by people far beyond your original audience. Ask yourself two questions: First, "Would I say this to my audience face to face?" And second, "Am I comfortable with this message becoming a permanent part of my personal and professional communication history?"

A momentary lapse of concentration while using social media can cause tremendous career or company damage.

# Social Networks

LEARNING OBJECTIVE ❷
Describe the use of social networks in business communication.

**Social networks**, online services that enable individual and organizational members to form connections and share information, have become a major force in business communication in recent years. In addition to Facebook, a variety of public and private social networks are used by businesses and professionals. They can be grouped into three categories:

- **Public, general-purpose networks.** Facebook is the largest such network, although Google+ is gaining membership rapidly and is attracting many companies and brands. Additionally, regionally focused networks have significant user bases in some countries, such as China's Renren and Kaixin001.[9]
- **Public, specialized networks.** Whereas Facebook and Google+ serve a wide variety of personal and professional needs, other networks focus on a particular function or a particular audience. The most widely known of these is LinkedIn, with its emphasis on career- and sales-related networking. Other networks address the needs of entrepreneurs, small business owners, specific professions, product enthusiasts, and other narrower audiences.
- **Private networks.** Some companies have built private social networks for internal use.

Regardless of the purpose and audience, social networks are most beneficial when all participants give and receive information, advice, support, and introductions—just as in offline social interaction. The following two sections describe how social networks are used in business communication and offer advice on using these platforms successfully.

## Business Communication Uses of Social Networks

With their ability to reach virtually unlimited numbers of people through a variety of electronic formats, social networks are a great fit for many business communication needs. Here are some of the key applications of social networks for internal and external business communication:

- **Integrating company workforces.** Just as public networks can bring friends and family together, internal social networks can help companies grow closer, including helping new employees navigate their way through the organization, finding experts, mentors, and other important contacts; encouraging workforces to "jell" after reorganizations or mergers; and overcoming structural barriers in communication channels, bypassing the formal communication system to deliver information where it is needed in a timely fashion.
- **Fostering collaboration.** Networks can play a major role in collaboration in various ways: by identifying the best people, both inside the company and in other companies, to collaborate on projects; finding pockets of knowledge and expertise within the organization; giving meeting or seminar participants a way to meet before an event and to maintain relationships after an event; accelerating the development of teams by

helping members get to know one another and to identify individual areas of expertise; and sharing information throughout the organization. The information technology company EMC estimates that its internal social network has cut costs by more than $40 million by helping employees use company resources more effectively and reducing the need to hire outside contractors.[10]

- **Building communities.** Social networks are a natural tool for bringing together *communities of practice*, people who engage in similar work, and *communities of interest*, people who share enthusiasm for a particular product or activity. Large and geographically dispersed companies can benefit greatly from communities of practice that connect experts who may work in different divisions or different countries. Communities of interest that form around a specific product are sometimes called **brand communities**, and nurturing these communities can be a vital business communication task. A majority of consumers now trust their peers more than any other source of product information, so formal and informal brand communities are becoming an essential information source in consumer buying decisions.[11] Increasingly, these community building efforts include some aspect of *gamification*, which is the addition of game-playing aspects, such as Foursquare's "check-in" competitions.[12] Foursquare is also an example of *location-based social networking*, which links the virtual world of online social networking with the physical world of retail stores and other locations. As mobile web use in general continues to grow, location-based networking promises to become an important business communication medium because mobile consumers are a significant economic force—through the purchases they make directly and through their ability to influence other consumers.[13]

- **Socializing brands and companies.** According to one recent survey of company executives, *socialization* now accounts for more than half of a company's or brand's global reputation.[14] **Brand socialization** is a measure of how effectively a company engages with its various online stakeholders in a mutually beneficial exchange of information. Social networks and related tools such as Twitter are the primary means of socializing companies and brands. To be successful, the communication on these platforms must be of value to all parties, not just the company. For example, comparing posts from General Motors, Toyota, and Ford suggests that brand socialization plays a significant role in the widely varying degrees of engagement these three companies have on Facebook. Many of Ford's posts focus on its history (including classic Ford cars and the company's efforts to supply the military in past wars) and its involvement in auto racing, topics of likely interest to car enthusiasts. Toyota's posts tend to feature current community-related news and events, such as results from company-sponsored contests (including a video competition for college students). GM's Facebook posts highlight community involvement as well, but tend to emphasize such company-focused items as monthly sales results, new products, and executive profiles. The fact that Toyota has three times as many Facebook fans as General Motors, and Ford has five times more than GM (as of mid-2012) is probably not a coincidence.[15]

- **Understanding target markets.** With hundreds of millions of people expressing themselves via social media, you can be sure that smart companies are listening. When asked about the value of having 33 million Facebook fans, Coca-Cola CEO Muhtar Kent replied, "The value is you can talk with them. They tell you things that are important for your business and brands."[16] In addition, a number of tools now exist to gather market intelligence from social media more or less automatically. For example, *sentiment analysis* is an intriguing research technique in which companies track social networks and other media with automated language-analysis software that tries to take the pulse of public opinion and identify influential opinion makers.[17]

- **Recruiting employees and business partners.** Companies use social networks to find potential employees, short-term contractors, subject-matter experts, product and service suppliers, and business partners. A key advantage here is that these introductions are made via trusted connections in a professional network. On LinkedIn, for example, members can recommend each other based on current or past business relationships, which helps remove the uncertainty of initiating business relationships with complete strangers.

- **Connecting with sales prospects.** Salespeople on networks such as LinkedIn can use their network connections to identify potential buyers and then to ask for introductions through those shared connections. Sales networking can reduce *cold calling*, telephoning potential customers out of the blue—a practice that few people on either end of the conversation find pleasant.

- **Supporting customers.** Customer service is another one of the fundamental areas of business communication that have been revolutionized by social media. *Social customer service* involves using social networks and other social media tools to give customers a more convenient way to get help from the company and to help each other.

- **Extending the organization.** Social networking is also fueling the growth of *networked organizations*, sometimes known as *virtual organizations*, where companies supplement the talents of their employees with services from one or more external partners, such as a design lab, a manufacturing firm, or a sales and distribution company.

**REAL-TIME UPDATES**

**Learn More by Reading This Article**

**Stay on top of new terminology in social media**

The new-media field spins out new buzzwords and technical terms at a rapid pace; this glossary will help you stay on top of things. Go to http://real-timeupdates.com/bce6 and click on Learn More. If you are using MyBCommLab, you can access Real-Time Updates within Business Communication Resources.

## Strategies for Business Communication on Social Networks

Social networks offer lots of business communication potential, but with those opportunities comes a certain degree of complexity. Moreover, the norms and practices of business social networking continue to evolve. Follow these guidelines to make the most of social networks for both personal branding and company communication:[18]

- **Choose the best compositional mode for each message, purpose, and network.** As you visit various social networks, take some time to observe the variety of message types you see in different parts of each website. For example, the informal status update mode works well for Facebook posts but would be less effective for company overviews and mission statements.

- **Offer valuable content to members of your online communities.** People don't join social networks to be sales targets, of course. They join looking for connections and information. *Content marketing* is the practice of providing free information that is valuable to community members; it also helps a company build closer ties with current and potential customers.[19]

- **Join existing conversations.** Search for online conversations that are already taking place. Answer questions, solve problems, and respond to rumours and misinformation.

- **Anchor your online presence in your hub.** Although it's important to join those conversations and be visible where your stakeholders are active, it's equally important to anchor your presence at your own central *hub*—a web presence you own and control. This can be a combination of a conventional website, a blog, and a company-sponsored online community, for example.[20] Use the hub to connect the various pieces of your online "self" (as an individual or a company) to make it easier for people to find and follow you. For example, you can link to your blog from your LinkedIn profile or automatically post your blog entries into the Notes tab on your Facebook page.

- **Facilitate community building.** Make it easy for customers and other audiences to connect with the company and with each other. For example, you can use the group feature on Facebook, LinkedIn, and other social networks to create and foster special-interest groups within your networks. Groups are a great way to connect people who are interested in specific topics, such as owners of a particular product.

Product promotion can be done on social networks, but it needs to be done in a low-key, indirect way.

- **Restrict conventional promotional efforts to the right time and right place.** Persuasive communication efforts are still valid for specific communication tasks, such as regular advertising and the product information pages on a website, but efforts to inject blatant "salespeak" into social networking conversations will usually be rejected by the audience.
- **Maintain a consistent personality.** Each social network is a unique environment with particular norms of communication.[21] For example, as a strictly business-oriented network, LinkedIn has a more formal "vibe" than Facebook and Google+, which cater to both consumers and businesses. However, while adapting to the expectations of each network, be sure to maintain a consistent personality across all the networks in which you are active.[22] The computer giant HP, for instance, uses the same (fairly formal-sounding) company overview on LinkedIn and Facebook, while posting updates on Facebook that are "chattier" and more in keeping with the tone expected by Facebook visitors.[23]

See "Writing Promotional Messages for Social Media" in Chapter 9 (page 213) for more tips on writing messages for social networks and other social media.

**LEARNING OBJECTIVE ③**
Explain how companies and business professionals can use information and media sharing websites.

# Information and Media Sharing Sites

Social networks allow members to share information and media items as part of the networking experience, but a variety of systems have been designed specifically for sharing content. The field is diverse and still evolving, but the possibilities can be divided into user-generated content sites, media curation sites, and community Q&A sites.

## User-Generated Content Sites

YouTube and other user-generated content sites are now important business communication channels.

YouTube, Flickr, Yelp, and other **user-generated content (UGC) sites**, in which users rather than website owners contribute most or all of the content, have become serious business tools. On YouTube, for example, companies post everything from product demonstrations and TV commercials to company profiles and technical support explanations.

Moreover, the business communication value of sites such as YouTube goes beyond the mere ability to deliver content. The social aspects of these sites, including the ability to vote for, comment on, and share material, encourage enthusiasts to spread the word about the companies and products they endorse.[24]

Creating compelling and useful content is the key to leveraging the reach of social networks.

As with other social media, the keys to effective user-generated content are making it valuable and making it easy. First, provide content that people want to see and to share with colleagues. A video clip that explains how to use a product more effectively will be more popular than a clip that talks about how amazing the company behind the product is. Also, keep videos short, generally no longer than three to five minutes, if possible.[25]

Second, make material easy to find, consume, and share. For example, a *branded channel* on YouTube lets a company organize all its videos in one place, making it easy for visitors to browse and subscribe and to share them using their accounts on Twitter, Facebook, and other platforms.

The "voice of the crowd," enabled through social media sites, can dramatically influence the way businesses are managed.

As one example of the way these sites are changing business communication, Yelp (**www.yelp.com**) has become a major influence on consumer behaviour at a local level by aggregating millions of reviews of stores, restaurants, and other businesses in large cities across the country.[26] With the voice of the crowd affecting consumer behaviour, businesses need to (a) focus on performing at a high level so that customers reward them with positive reviews, and (b) get involved on Yelp (the site encourages business owners to tell potential customers about themselves as well). These efforts could pay off much more handsomely than advertising and other conventional communication efforts.

## Media Curation Sites

Newsfeeds from blogs and other online publishers can be a great way to stay on top of developments in any field. However, anyone who has signed up for more than a few RSS feeds has probably experienced the "firehose effect" of getting so many feeds so quickly that it becomes impossible to stay on top of them. Moreover, when a highly active publisher feeds every new article, from the essential to the trivial, the reader is left to sort it all out every day.

An intriguing alternative to newsfeeds is **media curation**, in which someone with expertise or interest in a particular field collects and republishes material on a particular topic. The authors' Business Communication Headline News (http://bchn.businesscommunicationnetwork.com), for instance, was one of the earliest examples of media curation in the field of business communication.

New curation tools, including Pinterest (http://pinterest.com) and Scoop.it (www.scoop.it/), make it easy to assemble attractive online magazines or portfolios on specific topics. Although it raises important issues regarding content ownership and message control,[27] curation has the potential to bring the power of community and shared expertise to a lot of different fields; ultimately, it could reshape audience behaviour and therefore the practice of business communication.

Media curation is the process of collecting and presenting information on a particular topic in a way that makes it convenient for target readers.

### REAL-TIME UPDATES

**Learn More by Reading This Article**

**Putting Pinterest to work in business communication**

Pinterest has been one of the fastest-growing communication platforms in recent years. See how businesses large and small are putting it to work. Go to http://real-timeupdates.com/bce6 and click on Learn More. If you are using MyBCommLab, you can access Real-Time Updates within Business Communication Resources.

## Community Q&A Sites

**Community Q&A sites**, on which visitors answer questions posted by other visitors, are a contemporary twist on the early ethos of computer networking, which was people helping each other. (Groups of like-minded people connected online long before the World Wide Web was even created.) Community Q&A sites include dedicated customer support communities such as those hosted on Get Satisfaction (http://getsatisfaction.com), public sites such as Quora (www.quora.com) and Yahoo! Answers (http://answers.yahoo.com), and member-only sites such as LinkedIn Answers (www.linkedin.com/answers).

Responding to questions on Q&A sites can be a great way to build your personal brand, to demonstrate your company's commitment to customer service, and to counter misinformation about your company and its products. Keep in mind that when you respond to an individual query on a community Q&A site, you are also "responding in advance" to every person in the future who comes to the site with the same question. In other words, you are writing a type of reference material in addition to corresponding with the original questioner, so keep the longer timeframe and wider audience in mind.

Community Q&A sites offer great opportunities for building your personal brand.

# Email

Email has been a primary medium for many companies for years, and in the beginning it offered a huge advantage in speed and efficiency over the media it replaced (printed and faxed messages). Over time, email began to be used for many communication tasks, simply because it was the only widely available electronic medium for written messages and millions of users were comfortable with it. However, newer tools such as instant messaging, blogs, microblogs, social networks, and shared workspaces are taking over specialized tasks for which they are better suited.[28] For example, email is usually not the best choice for brief online conversations (IM is better for this) or project management updates (blogs, wikis, and various purpose-built systems are often better for this).

**LEARNING OBJECTIVE 4**
Describe the evolving role of email in business communication and explain how to adapt the three-step writing process to email messages.

In addition to the widespread availability of better alternatives for many communication purposes, the indiscriminate use of email has lowered its appeal in the eyes of many professionals. In a sense, email is too easy to use—it's too easy to send low-value messages to multiple recipients and to trigger long message chains that become impossible to follow as people chime in along the way. In fact, frustration with email is so high in some companies that managers are making changes to reduce or even eliminate its use for internal communication. The global public relations firm Weber Shandwick recently moved its 3000 employees from email to a custom system described as "equal parts Facebook, work group collaboration software, and employee bulletin board."[29]

*Email is still one of the more important business communication media.*

However, email still has compelling advantages that will keep it in steady use in many companies. First, email is universal. Anybody with an email address can reach anybody else with an email address, no matter which systems the senders and receivers are on. Second, email is still the best medium for many private, short- to medium-length messages, particularly when the exchange is limited to two people. Unlike with microblogs or IM, for instance, midsize messages are easy to compose and easy to read on email. Third, email's noninstantaneous nature is an advantage when used properly. Email allows senders to compose substantial messages in private and on their own schedule, and it allows recipients to read those messages at their leisure.

## Planning Email Messages

*Email gives people time to think through responses.*

The solution to email overload starts in the planning step, by making sure every message has a useful, business-related purpose. Many companies now have formal **email policies** that specify how employees can use email, including restrictions against using company email service for personal messages and sending material that might be deemed objectionable. In addition, many employers now monitor email, either automatically with software programmed to look for sensitive content or manually via security staff actually reading selected email messages. Regardless of formal policies, though, every email user has a responsibility to avoid actions that could cause trouble, from downloading virus-infected software to sending objectionable photographs. *Email hygiene* refers to all the efforts that companies are making to keep email clean and safe—from spam blocking and virus protection to content filtering.[30]

**REAL-TIME UPDATES**

**Learn More by Watching This Video**

**Find out why email starts fights—and how to avoid them**

See why the lean medium of email can lead to misunderstanding when it's used in the wrong situations. See how businesses large and small are putting it to work. Go to http://real-timeupdates.com/bce6 and click on Learn More. If you are using MyBCommLab, you can access Real-Time Updates within Business Communication Resources.

Even with fairly short messages, spend a moment or two on the message planning tasks described in Chapter 3: analyzing the situation, gathering necessary information for your readers, and organizing your message. You'll save time in the long run because you will craft a more effective message on the first attempt. Your readers will get the information they need and won't have to generate follow-up messages asking for clarification or additional information.

## Writing Email Messages

*Business email messages are more formal than the email messages you send to family and friends.*

When you approach email writing on the job, recognize that business email is a more formal medium than you are probably accustomed to with email for personal communication (see Figure 6.4). The expectations of writing quality for business email are higher than for personal email, and the consequences of bad writing or poor judgment can be much more serious. For example, email messages and other electronic documents have the same legal weight as printed documents, and they are often used as evidence in lawsuits and criminal investigations.[31]

## FIGURE 6.4   Email for Business Communication

Burgman includes enough of the original message to remind Williams why she is writing—but doesn't clutter the screen with the entire original message.

By itemizing the steps she wants Williams to follow, she makes it easy for him to respond and helps ensure that the work will be done correctly.

Her email signature includes alternative contact information, making it easy for the recipient to reach her.

**To:** Lawrence Williams <lawrence.williams@hegelassoc.com>

**CC:** Elaine Burgman <elaine.burgman@hegelassoc.com>

**Subject:** re: Shipping the Vancouver Presentation Handouts

At 1/20/2016 11:05 AM, you wrote:
<<Please let me know right away how you want me to send these Handouts to you.>>

Hi Larry,

Your suspicion is correct; sending the handouts overnight is much too expensive. Let's use FedEx Office to print the handouts locally instead. Just upload the file to the FedEx website and specify a branch office. The office will then print and assemble the handouts for us. Even better, they have a location right in the convention center.

Here is all you need to do:

1. Click on www.fedex.com/ca/officeprint/main, then click on "Print to a FedEx Office."
2. Select "Basic Orders," upload the file, then select the appropriate printing options.
3. In the "Recipients & Quantity" screen, select "FedEx Office store locator," then enter V52 2TI in the postal code search. You'll see several dozen locations in Vancouver; please be sure to select "Vancouver Trade and Convention Centre" and enter my name in the "Recipient" field.
4. Verify the order and enter payment information (use the department credit card).

Thanks for all your help!

Elaine

Elaine Burgman
Regional Director
Hegel Associates
www.hegelassoc.com
office: 778-809-2323
mobile: 778-412-1001

She opens with an informal salutation appropriate for communication between colleagues.

She includes the URL of the website she wants Williams to visit, so all he needs to do is click on the link.

The warm complimentary close expresses her appreciation for his efforts.

The **email subject line** is one of the most important parts of an email message because it helps recipients decide which messages to read and when to read them. To capture your audience's attention, make your subject lines informative and compelling. Go beyond simply describing or classifying your message; use the opportunity to build interest with keywords, quotations, directions, or questions.[32]

For example, "July sales results" accurately describes the content of the message, but "July sales results: good news and bad news" is more intriguing. Readers will want to know why some news is good and some is bad.

In addition, many email programs display the first few words or lines of incoming messages, even before the recipient opens them. In the words of social media public relations expert Steve Rubel, you can "tweetify" the opening lines of your email messages to make them stand out. In other words, choose the first few words carefully to grab your reader's attention.[33] Think of the first sentence as an extension of your subject line.

As a lean medium, email can present challenges when you need to express particular emotional nuances, whether positive or negative. For years, users of email (as well as IM and text messaging) have used a variety of *emoticons* to express emotions in casual communication. For example, to express sympathy as a way to take some of the sting out of negative news, one might use a "frowny face," either the character string : ( or a graphical emoticon such as ☹ or one of the colourful and sometimes animated characters available in some systems. Over the years, the use of emoticons was widely regarded as unprofessional and therefore advised against in business communication. Recently, though, an increasing number of professionals seem to be using them, particularly for communication with close colleagues, even as other professionals continue to view them as evidence of lazy or immature writing.[34] In the face of these conflicting perspectives, the best advice is to use caution. Avoid emoticons for all types of external communication and for formal internal communication, and avoid those bright yellow graphical emoticons (and particularly animated emoticons) in all business communication.

A poorly written subject line could lead to a message being deleted or ignored.

Attitudes about emoticons in business communication are changing; you'll have to use your best judgment in every case.

## Completing Email Messages

Particularly for important messages, taking a few moments to revise and proofread might save you hours of headaches and damage control. Also, favour simplicity when it comes to producing your email messages. A clean, easily readable font, in black on a white background, is sufficient for nearly all email messages. Take advantage of your email system's ability to include an **email signature**, a small file that automatically includes such items as your full name, title, company, and contact information at the end of your messages.

When you're ready to distribute your message, pause to verify what you're doing before you click Send. Make sure you've included everyone necessary—and no one else. Did you click Reply All when you meant to click only Reply? The difference could be embarrassing or even career threatening. Don't include people in the Cc (courtesy copy) or Bcc (blind courtesy copy) fields unless you know how these features work. (Everyone who receives the message can see who is on the Cc line but not who is on the Bcc line.) Also, don't set the message priority to "high" or "urgent" unless your message is truly urgent. And if you intend to include an attachment, be sure that it is indeed attached.

Table 6.1 offers a number of helpful tips for effective email messages.

*Think twice before hitting Send; a simple mistake in your content or distribution can cause major headaches.*

| TABLE 6.1 | Tips for Effective Email Messages |
| --- | --- |

| TIP | WHY IT'S IMPORTANT |
| --- | --- |
| When you request information or action, make it clear what you're asking for, why it's important, and how soon you need it; don't make your reader write back for details. | People will be tempted to ignore your messages if they're not clear about what you want or how soon you want it. |
| When responding to a request, either paraphrase the request or include enough of the original message to remind the reader what you're replying to. | Some businesspeople get hundreds of email messages a day and may need reminding what your specific response is about. |
| If possible, avoid sending long, complex messages via email. | Long messages are easier to read as attached reports or web content. Think of the number of people who read email on their smartphones. |
| Adjust the level of formality to the message and the audience. | Overly formal messages to colleagues can be perceived as stuffy and distant; overly informal messages to customers or top executives can be perceived as disrespectful. |
| Activate a signature file, which automatically pastes your contact information into every message you create. | A signature saves you the trouble of retyping vital information and ensures that recipients know how to reach you through other means. However, sometimes signature files get caught in spam filters. |
| Don't let unread messages pile up in your in-basket. | You'll miss important information and create the impression that you're ignoring other people. |
| Never type in all caps. | ALL CAPS ARE INTERPRETED AS SHOUTING. |
| Don't overformat your messages with background colours, multicoloured type, unusual fonts, and so on. | Such messages can be difficult and annoying to read onscreen. |
| Remember that messages can be forwarded anywhere and saved forever. | Don't let a moment of anger or poor judgment haunt you for the rest of your career. |
| Use the "return receipt requested" feature only for the most critical messages. | This feature triggers a message back to you whenever someone receives or opens your message; many consider this an invasion of privacy. |
| Make sure your computer has up-to-date virus protection. | One of the worst breaches of "netiquette" is infecting other computers because you haven't bothered to protect your own system. |
| Pay attention to grammar, spelling, and capitalization. | Some people don't think email needs formal rules, but careless messages make you look unprofessional and can annoy readers. Write in complete sentences. |
| Use acronyms sparingly. | Shorthand such as IMHO (in my humble opinion) and LOL (laughing out loud) can be useful in informal correspondence with colleagues, but avoid using them in more formal messages. |

# Instant Messaging and Text Messaging

Computer-based **instant messaging (IM)**, in which users' messages appear on each other's screens instantly, is used extensively for internal and external communication. IM is available in both stand-alone systems and as a function embedded in online meeting systems, collaboration systems, social networks, and other platforms. For conversational exchanges, it's hard to top the advantages of IM, and the technology is replacing both email and voice mail in many situations.[35] Business-grade IM systems offer a range of capabilities, including basic chat, *presence awareness* (the ability to quickly see which people are at their desks and available to IM), remote display of documents, video capabilities, remote control of other computers, automated newsfeeds from blogs and websites, and automated *bot* (derived from the word *robot*) capabilities in which a computer can carry on simple conversations.[36]

**Text messaging** has a number of applications in business as well, including marketing (alerting customers about new sale prices, for example), customer service (such as airline flight status, package tracking, and appointment reminders), security (for example, authenticating mobile banking transactions), crisis management (such as updating all employees working at a disaster scene), and process monitoring (alerting computer technicians to system failures, for example).[37]

While the following sections focus on IM, many of the benefits, risks, and guidelines that pertain to IM pertain to text messaging as well.

## Understanding the Benefits and Risks of IM

The benefits of IM include its capability for rapid response to urgent messages, lower cost than phone calls and email, ability to mimic conversation more closely than email, and availability on a wide range of devices.[38] In addition, because it more closely resembles one-on-one conversation, IM doesn't get misused as a one-to-many broadcast method as often as email does.[39]

The potential drawbacks of IM include security problems (computer viruses, network infiltration, and the possibility that sensitive messages might be intercepted by outsiders), the need for *user authentication* (making sure that online correspondents are really who they appear to be), the challenge of logging messages for later review and archiving, incompatibility between competing IM systems, and *spim* (unsolicited commercial messages, similar to email spam). Fortunately, with the growth of *enterprise instant messaging (EIM)*, or IM systems designed for large-scale corporate use, many of these problems are being overcome. However, security remains a significant concern for corporate IM systems.[40]

## Adapting the Three-Step Process for Successful IM

Although instant messages are often conceived, written, and sent within a matter of seconds, the principles of the three-step process still apply, particularly when communicating with customers and other important audiences:

- **Planning instant messages.** Except for simple exchanges, take a moment to plan IM "conversations" in much the same way you would plan an important oral conversation. A few seconds of planning can help you deliver information in a coherent, complete way that minimizes the number of individual messages required.
- **Writing instant messages.** As with email, the appropriate writing style for business IM is more formal than the style you may be accustomed to with personal IM or text messaging (see Figure 6.5). Your company might discourage the use of IM acronyms (such as FWIW for "for what it's worth" or HTH for "hope that helps"), particularly for IM with external audiences.
- **Completing instant messages.** Quickly scan it before sending, to make sure you don't have any missing or misspelled words and verify that your message is clear and complete.

To use IM effectively, keep in mind some important behavioural issues when relying on this medium: the potential for constant interruptions, the ease of accidentally mixing

**LEARNING OBJECTIVE 5**
Describe the business benefits of instant messaging (IM) and identify guidelines for effective IM in the workplace.

IM is taking the place of email for routine communication in many companies.

Phone-based text messaging is fast and portable but not as versatile as computer-based IM.

IM offers many benefits:
- Rapid response
- Low cost
- Ability to mimic conversation
- Wide availability

| FIGURE 6.5 | Instant Messaging for Business Communication |
|---|---|

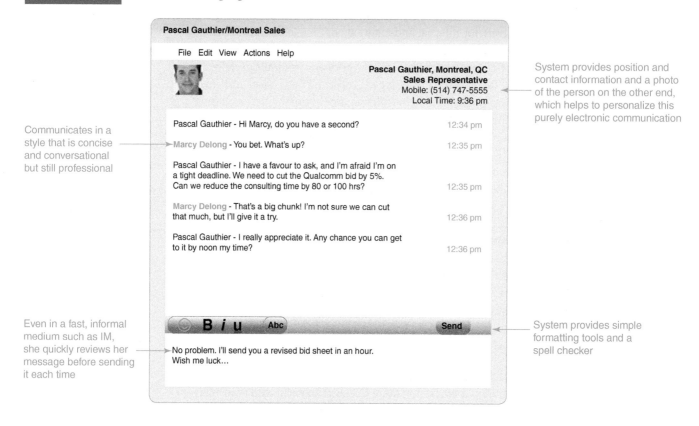

Communicates in a style that is concise and conversational but still professional

Even in a fast, informal medium such as IM, she quickly reviews her message before sending it each time

System provides position and contact information and a photo of the person on the other end, which helps to personalize this purely electronic communication

System provides simple formatting tools and a spell checker

When using IM, be aware of the potential for constant interruptions and wasted time.

personal and business messages, the risk of being out of the loop (if a hot discussion or an impromptu meeting flares up when you're away from your PC or other IM device), and being at the mercy of other people's typing abilities.[41]

Regardless of the system you're using, you can make IM more efficient and effective by heeding these tips:[42]

Understand the guidelines for successful business IM before you begin to use it.

- Be courteous in your use of IM; if you don't need an answer instantly, you can avoid interrupting someone by sending an email or other type of message instead.
- Unless a meeting is scheduled or you're expected to be available for other reasons, make yourself unavailable when you need to focus on other work.
- If you're not on a secure system, don't send confidential information using IM.
- Be extremely careful about sending personal messages—they have a tendency to pop up on other people's computers at embarrassing moments.
- Don't use IM for important but impromptu meetings if you can't verify that everyone concerned will be available.
- Don't use IM for lengthy, complex messages; email is better for those.
- Try to avoid carrying on multiple IM conversations at one time, to minimize the chance of sending messages to the wrong people or making one person wait while you tend to another conversation.
- Follow all security guidelines designed to keep your company's information and systems safe from attack.

**LEARNING OBJECTIVE 6**
Describe the use of blogging and microblogging in business communication and briefly explain how to adapt the three-step process to blogging.

# Creating Effective Business Blogs

**Blogs,** online journals that are easier to personalize and update than conventional websites, have become a major force in business communication. Millions of business-oriented blogs are now in operation, and blogs have become an important source of information for consumers and professionals alike.[43] Good business blogs and micro-blogs pay close attention to several important elements:

- **Communicating with personal style and an authentic voice.** Most business messages designed for large audiences are carefully scripted and written in a "corporate voice" that is impersonal and objective. In contrast, successful business blogs are written by individuals and exhibit their personal style. Audiences relate to this fresh approach and often build closer emotional bonds with the blogger's organization as a result.
- **Delivering new information quickly.** Blogging tools let you post new material as soon as you create it or find it. This feature not only allows you to respond quickly when needed—such as during a corporate crisis—but also lets your audiences know that active communication is taking place. Blogs that don't offer a continuous stream of new and interesting content are quickly ignored in today's online environment.
- **Choosing topics of peak interest to audiences.** Successful blogs cover topics that readers care about.
- **Encouraging audiences to join the conversation.** Not all blogs invite comments, although most do, and many bloggers consider comments to be an essential feature. Blog comments can be a valuable source of news, information, and insights. To guard against comments that are not helpful or appropriate, many bloggers review all comments and post only the most helpful or interesting ones.

Most business blogs invite readers to leave comments.

## Understanding the Business Applications of Blogging

Blogs are a potential solution whenever you have a continuing stream of information to share with an online audience—and particularly when you want the audience to have the opportunity to respond. Here are some of the many ways businesses are using blogs for internal and external communication:[44]

The business applications of blogs include a wide range of internal and external communication tasks.

- **Anchoring the social media presence.** As noted on page 125, the multiple threads of any social media program should be anchored in a central hub the company or individual owns and controls. Blogs make an ideal social media hub.
- **Project management and team communication.** Using blogs is a good way to keep project teams up to date, particularly when team members are geographically dispersed.
- **Company news.** Companies can use blogs to keep employees informed about general business matters, from facility news to benefit updates. Blogs also serve as online community forums, giving everyone in the company a chance to raise questions and voice concerns.
- **Customer support.** Building on the tradition of online customer support forums that have been around since the earliest days of the internet, customer support blogs answer questions, offer tips and advice, and inform customers about new products. Also, many companies monitor the blogosphere (and Twitter), looking for complaints and responding with offers to help dissatisfied customers.[45]
- **Public relations and media relations.** Many company employees and executives now share company news with both the general public and journalists via their blogs.
- **Recruiting.** Using a blog is a great way to let potential employees know more about your company, the people who work there, and the nature of the company culture. Conversely, employers often find and evaluate the blogs and microblogs of prospective employees, making blogging a great way for you to build a name for yourself within your industry or profession.
- **Policy and issue discussions.** Executive blogs in particular provide a public forum for discussing legislation, regulations, and other broad issues of interest to an organization.
- **Crisis communication.** Using blogs is a convenient way to provide up-to-the-minute information during emergencies, correct misinformation, or respond to rumours.

- **Market research.** Blogs can be a clever way to solicit feedback from customers and experts in the marketplace. In addition to using their own blogs to solicit feedback, today's companies should monitor blogs that are likely to discuss them, their executives, and their products.
- **Brainstorming.** Online brainstorming via blogs offers a way for people to toss around ideas and build on each other's contributions.
- **Employee engagement.** Blogs can enhance communication across all levels of a company. For example, as part of a program to align its corporate culture with changes in the global beverage market, Coca-Cola solicited feedback via blog comments from more than 20 000 employees.[46]
- **Customer education.** Blogs are a great way to help current and potential customers understand and use your products and services. This function can improve sales and support productivity as well, by reducing the need for one-on-one communication.
- **Word-of-mouth marketing.** Bloggers often make a point of providing links to other blogs and websites that interest them, giving marketers a great opportunity to have their messages spread by enthusiasts. (Online word-of-mouth marketing is often called *viral marketing,* but viral marketing is not really an accurate metaphor. Biological viruses spread from host to host on their own, whereas these virtual "viruses" are spread *voluntarily* by their "hosts." The distinction is critical, because you need to give people a good reason—good content, in other words—to pass along your message.)[47]
- **Influencing traditional media news coverage.** According to social media consultant Tamar Weinberg, "the more prolific bloggers who provide valuable and consistent content are often considered experts in their subject matter" and are often called upon when journalists need insights into various topics.[48]
- **Community building.** Communities of readers can "grow" around a popular blog, as readers participate in the flow of ideas via comments on various posts.

The uses of blogs are limited only by your creativity, so be on the lookout for new ways you can use them to foster positive relationships with colleagues, customers, and other important audiences (see Figure 6.6).

Blogs are an ideal medium for *word-of-mouth marketing,* the spread of promotional messages from one audience member to another.

**REAL-TIME UPDATES**

**Learn More by Visiting This Website**

**Guidelines for trouble-free blogging**

The free *Legal Guide for Bloggers* can help bloggers steer clear of legal problems, including improper use of intellectual property. Go to http://real-timeupdates.com/bce6 and click on Learn More. If you are using MyBCommLab, you can access Real-Time Updates within Business Communication Resources.

## Adapting the Three-Step Process for Successful Blogging

The three-step writing process is easy to adapt to blogging tasks. The planning step is particularly important when you're launching a blog because you're planning an entire communication channel, not just a single message. Pay close attention to your audience, your purpose, and your scope:

Before you launch a blog, make sure you have a clear understanding of your target audience, the purpose of your blog, and the scope of subjects you plan to cover.

- **Audience.** Except with team blogs and other efforts that have an obvious and well-defined audience, defining the target audience for a blog can be challenging. You want an audience large enough to justify the time you'll be investing but narrow enough that you can provide a clear focus for the blog. For instance, if you work for a firm that develops computer games, would you focus your blog on "hardcore" players, the types who spend thousands of dollars on super-fast PCs optimized for video games, or would you broaden the reach to include all video gamers? The decision often comes down to business strategy.
- **Purpose.** A business blog needs to have a business-related purpose that is important to your company and to your chosen audience. Moreover, the purpose has to be something that can drive the blog's content for months or years, rather than focus on a single event or an issue of only temporary interest. For instance, if you're

| FIGURE 6.6 | A Sample Business Blog |
|---|---|

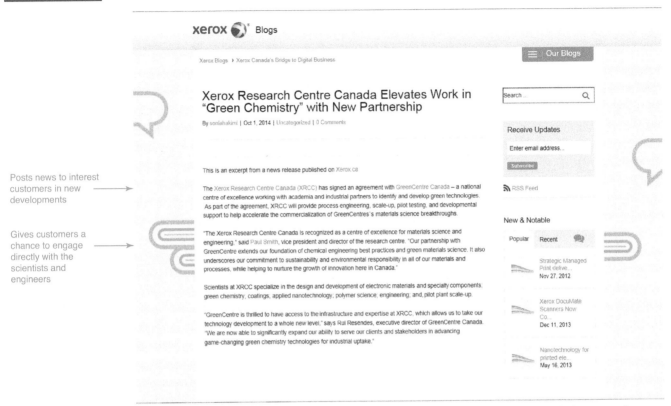

Posts news to interest customers in new developments →

Gives customers a chance to engage directly with the scientists and engineers →

*Source:* Xerox Research Centre Canada Elevates Work in "Green Chemistry" with New Partnership, http://digitalbusiness.blogs.xerox.com/2014/10/01/xerox-research-centre-canada-elevates-work-in-green-chemistry-with-new-partnership/. Xerox Canada Ltd.

a technical expert, you might create a blog to give the audience tips and techniques for using your company's products more effectively—a never-ending subject that's important to both you and your audience. This would be the general purpose of your blog; each posting would have a specific purpose within the context of that general purpose. Finally, if you are not writing an official company blog but rather blogging as an individual employee, make sure you understand your employer's blogging guidelines. As with email and IM, more and more companies are putting policies in place to prevent employee mistakes with blogging.[49]

- **Scope.** Defining the scope of your blog can be a bit tricky. You want to cover a subject area that is broad enough to offer discussion possibilities for months or years but narrow enough to have an identifiable focus.

After you begin writing your blog, the careful planning needs to continue with each message. Unless you're posting to a restricted-access blog, such as an internal blog on a company intranet, you can never be sure who might see your posts. Other bloggers might link to them months or years later.

Use a comfortable, personal writing style. Blog audiences don't want to hear from your company; they want to hear from *you*. Bear in mind, though, that comfortable does not mean careless. Sloppy writing damages your credibility. Successful blog content also needs to be interesting, valuable to readers, and as brief as possible.[50] If you don't have all the information

## REAL-TIME UPDATES

**Learn More by Reading This Article**

**Nine startups that know how to blog**

These growing companies show how to do business blogging effectively. See how businesses large and small are putting blogs to work. Go to http://real-timeupdates.com/bce6 and click on Learn More. If you are using MyBCommLab, you can access Real-Time Updates within Business Communication Resources.

Write blog postings in a comfortable—but not careless— style.

| TABLE 6.2 | Tips for Effective Business Blogging |
|---|---|

| TIP | WHY IT'S IMPORTANT |
|---|---|
| Don't blog without a clear plan. | Without a clear plan, your blog is likely to wander from topic to topic and fail to build a sense of community with your audience. |
| Post frequently; the whole point of a blog is fresh material. | If you won't have a constant supply of new information or new links, create a traditional website instead. |
| Make it about your audience and the issues that are important to them. | Readers want to know how your blog will help them, entertain them, or give them a chance to communicate with others who have similar interests. |
| Write in an authentic voice; never create an artificial character who supposedly writes a blog. | *Flogs*, or fake blogs, violate the spirit of blogging, show disrespect for your audience, and will turn audiences against you as soon as they uncover the truth. Fake blogs used to promote products are now illegal in some countries. |
| Link generously—but carefully. | Providing interesting links to other blogs and websites is a fundamental aspect of blogging, but make sure the links will be of value to your readers and don't point to inappropriate material. |
| Keep it brief. | Most online readers don't have the patience to read lengthy reports. Rather than writing long, report-style posts, write brief posts that link to in-depth reports on your website. |
| Don't post anything you wouldn't want the entire world to see. | Future employers, government regulators, competitors, journalists, and community critics are just a few of the people who might eventually see what you've written. |
| Don't engage in blatant product promotion. | Readers who think they're being advertised to will stop reading. |
| Take time to write compelling, specific headlines for your postings. | Readers usually decide within a couple of seconds whether to read your postings; boring or vague headlines will turn them away instantly. |
| Pay attention to spelling, grammar, and mechanics. | No matter how smart or experienced you are, poor-quality writing undermines your credibility with intelligent audiences. |
| Respond to criticism openly and honestly. | Hiding sends the message that you don't have a valid response to the criticism. If your critics are wrong, patiently explain why you think they're wrong. If they are right, explain how you'll fix the situation. |
| Listen and learn. | If you don't take the time to analyze the comments people leave on your blog or the comments other bloggers make about you, you're missing out on one of the most valuable aspects of blogging. |
| Respect intellectual property. | Improperly using material you don't own is not only unethical but can be illegal as well. |
| Be scrupulously honest and careful with facts. | Honesty is an absolute requirement for every ethical business communicator, of course, but you need to be extra careful online because inaccuracies (both intentional and unintentional) are likely to be discovered quickly and shared widely. If you review products on your blog, disclose any beneficial relationships you have with the companies that make those products. |

yourself, provide links to other blogs and websites that supply relevant information. In fact, *media curation*, selecting content to share in much the same way that museum curators decide which pieces of art to display, is one of the most valuable aspects of blogging.

Completing messages for your blog is usually quite easy. Evaluate the content and readability of your message, proofread to correct any errors, and post using your blogging system's tools, including one or more *newsfeed options* such as RSS, so that your audience can automatically receive headlines and summaries of new blog posts. Whatever blogging system you are using can provide guidance on setting up newsfeeds.

Finally, make your material easier to find by **tagging** it with descriptive words. Your readers can then click on these "content labels" to find additional posts on those topics.

Tags are usually displayed with each post, and they can also be grouped in a *tag cloud* display, which shows all the tags in use on your blog. Visitors to your blog who want to read everything you've written about recruiting just click on that word to see all your posts on that subject. Tagging can also help audiences locate your posts on blog trackers such as Technorati (http://technorati.com) or on **social bookmarking** or social news sites such as Delicious (http://delicious.com) and Digg (www.digg.com).

Table 6.2 summarizes a number of suggestions for successful blogging.

## Microblogging

A **microblog** is a variation on blogging in which messages are sharply restricted to specific character counts. Twitter (http://twitter.com) is the best known of these systems, but many others exist. Some companies have private microblogging systems for internal use only; these systems are sometimes referred to as *enterprise microblogging* or *internal micromessaging*.[51]

Many of the concepts of regular blogging apply to microblogging as well, although the severe length limitations call for a different approach to composition. Microblog messages often involve short summaries or teasers that provide links to more information. In addition, microblogs tend to have a stronger social aspect that makes it easier for writers and readers to forward messages and for communities to form around individual writers.[52]

Like regular blogging, microblogging quickly caught on with business users and is now a mainstream business medium. Microblogs are used for virtually all of the blog applications mentioned on pages 133–134. In addition, microblogs are frequently used for providing company updates, offering coupons and notice of sales, presenting tips on product usage, sharing relevant and interesting information from experts, serving as the backchannel in meetings and presentations, and announcing new blog posts (see Figure 6.7).

Like Facebook and YouTube, Twitter quickly became an important business communication medium.

---

**FIGURE 6.7  Business Applications of Microblogging**

Links to article on one of Deloitte's consulting practice areas

Links to advice on challenges facing businesses

Links to article on Deloitte's website

Links to conference information and invitation on Deloitte's website

Links to article on important business trend in one of Deloitte's areas of expertise

*Source:* Twitter, https://twitter.com/DeloitteCanada

By following top names in your field, you can customize Twitter as your own real-time news source.[53] Customer service is becoming a popular use for Twitter as well, thanks to its ease, speed, and the option to switch between public tweets and private direct messages as the situation warrants.[54] The social networking aspect of Twitter and other microblogs also makes them good for *crowdsourcing* research questions, asking ones' followers for input or advice.[55] Finally, the ease of *retweeting,* the practice of forwarding messages from other Twitter users, is the microblogging equivalent of sharing other content from other bloggers via media curation.

In addition to its usefulness as a stand-alone system, Twitter is also integrated with other social media systems and a variety of publishing and reading tools and services. Many of these systems use the informal Twitter feature known as the *hashtag* (the # symbol followed by a word or phrase), which makes it easy for people to label and search for topics of interest and to monitor ongoing Twitter conversations about particular topics.

Although microblogs are designed to encourage spontaneous communication, when you're using the medium for business communication, don't just tweet out whatever pops into your head. Make sure messages are part of your overall communication strategy. Twitter followers consider tweets that are entertaining, surprising, informative, or engaging (such as asking followers for advice) as the most valuable. In contrast, the least-valuable tweets tend to be complaints, conversations between the Twitter account owner and a specific follower, and relatively pointless messages such as saying "good morning."[56]

<aside>Don't let the speed and simplicity of microblogging lull you into making careless mistakes; every message should support your business communication objectives.</aside>

## Podcasting

<aside>**LEARNING OBJECTIVE 7**

**Explain how to adapt the three-step writing process for podcasts.**</aside>

**Podcasting** is the process of recording audio or video files and distributing them online via RSS subscriptions, in the same way that blog posts are automatically fed to subscribers. Podcasting combines the media richness of voice or visual communication with the convenience of portability. Audiences can listen to or watch podcasts on a blog or website, or they can download them to phones or portable music players to consume on the go. Particularly with audio podcasts, the hands-off, eyes-off aspect makes them great for listening to while driving or exercising.

The most obvious use of podcasting is to replace existing audio and video messages, such as one-way teleconferences in which a speaker provides information without expecting to engage in conversation with the listeners. Training is another good use of podcasting; you may have already taken a college course via podcasts. Podcasting is also a great way to offer free previews of seminars and training classes.[57] Many business writers and consultants use podcasting to build their personal brands and to enhance their other product and service offerings. You can find a wide selection of these on iTunes, many of which are free (go to the Podcasting section and select the Business category).

<aside>Podcasting can be used to deliver a wide range of audio and video messages.</aside>

Although it might not seem obvious at first, the three-step writing process adapts quite nicely to podcasting. First, focus the planning step on analyzing the situation, gathering the information you'll need, and organizing your material. One vital planning step depends on whether you intend to create podcasts for limited use and distribution (such as a weekly audio update to your virtual team) or to create a **podcasting channel** with regular recordings on a consistent theme, designed for a wider public audience. As with planning a blog, if you intend to create a podcasting channel, be sure to think through the range of topics you want to address over time to verify that you have a sustainable purpose. If you bounce from one theme to another, you risk losing your audience.[58] Maintaining a consistent schedule is also important; listeners will stop paying attention if you don't deliver regular updates.[59]

<aside>The three-step process adapts quite well to podcasting.</aside>

As you organize the content for a podcast, pay close attention to previews, transitions, and reviews. These steering devices are especially vital in audio recordings because audio lacks the "street signs" (such as headings) that audiences rely on in print media. Moreover, scanning back and forth to find specific parts of an audio or video message is much more difficult than with textual messages, so you need to do everything possible to make sure your audience successfully receives and interprets your message on the first try.

One of the attractions of podcasting is the conversational, person-to-person feel of the recordings, so unless you need to capture exact wording, speaking from an outline and notes rather than a prepared script is often the best choice. However, no one wants to listen to rambling podcasts that take several minutes to get to the topic or struggle to make a point, so don't try to make up your content on the fly. Effective podcasts, like effective stories, have a clear beginning, middle, and end.

Steering devices such as transitions, previews, and reviews are vital in podcasts.

The completing step is where podcasting differs most dramatically from written communication, for the obvious reason that you are recording and distributing audio or video files. Particularly for more formal podcasts, start by revising your script or thinking through your speaking notes before you begin to record. The closer you can get to recording your podcasts in one take, the more productive you'll be.

Plan your podcast content carefully; editing is more difficult with podcasts than with textual messages.

Most personal computers, smartphones, and other devices now have basic audio recording capability, including built-in microphones, and free editing software is available online (at http://audacity.sourceforge.net, for example). If you need higher production quality or greater flexibility, you'll need additional pieces of hardware and software. These can include an audio processor (to filter out extraneous noise and otherwise improve the audio signal), a mixer (to combine multiple audio or video signals), a better microphone, more sophisticated recording and editing software, and perhaps some physical changes in your recording location to improve the acoustics.

For basic podcasts, your computer and perhaps even your smartphone might have most of the hardware you already need, and you can download recording software.

Podcasts can be distributed in several ways, including through media stores such as iTunes, by dedicated podcast hosting services, or on a blog with content that supports the podcast channel. If you distribute your podcast on a blog, you can provide additional information and use the commenting feature of the blog to encourage feedback from your audience.[60]

# LEARNING OBJECTIVES: Check Your Progress

**1 OBJECTIVE Identify the major electronic media used for brief business messages and describe the nine compositional modes needed for electronic media.**

Electronic media for short business messages include social networking and community participation websites, email, instant messaging (IM), text messaging, blogging and microblogging, podcasting, and online video. The nine compositional modes used in electronic communication are conversations, comments and critiques, orientations, summaries, reference materials, narratives, teasers, status updates and announcements, and tutorials.

**2 OBJECTIVE Describe the use of social networks in business communication.**

Businesses now use a variety of social networks, including well-known public networks such as Facebook, more business-oriented networks such as LinkedIn, as well as a variety of specialized networks, single-company networks for customers, and internal employee-only networks. The business communication applications of social networks are important and diverse; major uses include collaborating, gathering market intelligence, recruiting employees, connecting with business partners, marketing, and fostering brand communities.

**3 OBJECTIVE Explain how companies and business professionals can use information and media sharing websites.**

User-generated content sites such as YouTube allow companies to host media items (such as videos) that customers and other stakeholders can view, comment on, and share. Media curation sites allow professionals and consumers with expertise or interest in a particular field to collect and republish material on a particular topic. Community Q&A sites give individuals the opportunity to build their personal brands by providing expertise, and they give companies the chance to address customer complaints and correct misinformation.

**④ OBJECTIVE** Describe the evolving role of email in business communication and explain how to adapt the three-step writing process to email messages.

As the earliest widely available electronic written medium, email was applied to a broad range of communication tasks—some it was well suited for and some it wasn't. Over time, newer media such as instant messaging, blogs, and social networks have been taking over some of these tasks, but email remains a vital medium that is optimum for many private, short- to medium-length messages.

The three-step process adapts easily to email communication. One of the most important planning decisions in crafting email messages is making sure every message has a valuable purpose. Any key planning decision is to follow the chain of command in your organization; emailing over your boss's head is a good way to stir up resentment. When writing email messages, bear in mind that the expectations of writing quality and formality are higher in business email. Also, pay close attention to the wording of an email message's subject line; it often determines whether and when recipients open and read the message. Effective subject lines are both informative (concisely identifying what the message is about) and compelling (giving readers a reason to read the message). Completing email messages is straightforward. Proof and revise messages (particularly important ones), and make sure you distribute the message to the right people.

**⑤ OBJECTIVE** Describe the business benefits of instant messaging (IM) and identify guidelines for effective IM in the workplace.

The benefits of IM include its capability for rapid response to urgent messages, lower cost than phone calls and email, ability to mimic conversation more closely than email, and availability on a wide range of devices.

As with email, business IM needs to be treated as a professional medium to ensure safe and effective communication. Be courteous in your use of IM to avoid interrupting others unnecessarily. Make yourself unavailable when you need to focus on other work, refrain from sending confidential information if you're not on a secure system, refrain from sending personal messages at work, avoid using IM for lengthy and complex messages, avoid carrying on multiple IM conversations at once, avoid IM slang with anyone other than close colleagues, and follow security guidelines.

**⑥ OBJECTIVE** Describe the use of blogging and microblogging in business communication and briefly explain how to adapt the three-step process to blogging.

Blogs are used in numerous ways in business today, such as for project management and team communication, company news, customer support, public relations and media relations, employee recruiting, policy and issue discussions, crisis communication, market research, brainstorming, employee engagement, viral marketing, influencing traditional media news coverage, and community building. Microblogs such as Twitter are used for many of the same purposes as conventional blogging, along with electronic coupons, sale announcements, one-on-one customer service queries, and customized news channels created by following experts of interest. Microblogs can also serve as the backchannel during meetings and presentations.

The three-step process adapts readily to blogging. In planning, pay particular attention to defining your audience, identifying the overall purpose of your blog and specific purposes of each post, and establishing a scope that is narrow enough to be focused but broad enough to afford a steady supply of topics. Write in a personal, authentic style. Completing involves the usual proofing and revising, along with tasks needed to distribute your posts via newsfeeds.

**⑦ OBJECTIVE** Explain how to adapt the three-step writing process for podcasts.

Although you record audio or video when creating podcasts rather than write messages, the three-step process is an effective approach to develop podcasts as well. Focus the planning step on analyzing the situation, gathering the information you'll need, and organizing your material. If you plan to create a series of podcasts on a given theme, make sure you've identified a range of topics extensive enough to keep you going over time. As you organize and begin to think about the words or images you'll use as content, pay close attention to previews, transitions, and reviews so that audiences don't get lost while listening or watching. Finally, consider the necessary level of production quality; good-quality podcasts usually require some specialized hardware and software.

---

**MyBCommLab®**  Go to MyBCommLab for everything you need to help you succeed in the job you've always wanted! Tools and resources include the following:
- Writing Activities   • Document Makeovers
- Video Exercises    • Grammar Exercises—and much more!

## Practise Your Grammar

Effective business communication starts with strong grammar skills. To improve your grammar skills, go to MyBCommLab, where you'll find exercises and diagnostic tests to help you produce clear, effective communication.

## Test Your Knowledge

To review chapter content related to each question, refer to the indicated Learning Objective.

1. In what situations might a printed memo or letter be preferable to an electronic message? L.O.❶

2. How do the compositional modes of orientations, summaries, and teasers differ? L.O.❷

3. Does the three-step writing process apply to IM? Why or why not? L.O.❺

## Apply Your Knowledge

To review chapter content related to each question, refer to the indicated Learning Objective.

1. Given the strict limits on length, should all your microblogging messages function as teasers that link to more detailed information on a blog or website? Why or why not? L.O.❶

2. Is leveraging your connections on social networks for business purposes ethical? Why or why not? L.O.❸

3. Communication on a major project is suffering because several team members are in the habit of writing cryptic or careless instant messages that often force recipients to engage in several rounds of follow-up messaging to figure out what the sender had in mind. As project leader, you've spoken with these team members about the need to write clearer messages, but they respond that careful planning and writing defeats the whole purpose of *instant* messaging. How should you handle the situation? L.O.❺

4. If one of the benefits of blogging is the personal, intimate style of writing, is it a good idea to limit your creativity by adhering to conventional rules of grammar, spelling, and mechanics? Why or why not? L.O.❻

5. A former classmate reached out to you through LinkedIn and asked for a favour: Would you be willing to review her company's motorcycle accessories on your popular motorsports blog? What information would you need to make this decision, and how could you be sure you are making an ethical choice? L.O.❻

## Practise Your Skills

EXERCISES FOR PERFECTING YOUR WRITING

To review chapter content related to each set of exercises, refer to the indicated Learning Objective.

1. **Planning: Creating an Audience Profile, Selecting Media** L.O.❶, **Chapter 3** You are in charge of public relations for a cruise line that operates out of Vancouver. You are shocked to read a letter in a local newspaper from a disgruntled passenger, complaining about the service and entertainment on a recent cruise. You will have to respond to these publicized criticisms in some way.

   a. What audiences will you need to consider in your response?

   b. For each of these audiences, which medium (or media) should you use to send your message?

2. **Media Skills: Blogging** L.O.❺ The members of the project team you are leading have enthusiastically embraced blogging as a communication medium. Unfortunately, as emotions heat up during the project, some of the blog postings are getting too casual, too personal, and even sloppy. Because your boss and other managers around the company also read this project blog, you don't want the team to look unprofessional in anyone's eyes. Revise the following blog posting so that it communicates in a more businesslike manner while retaining the informal, conversational tone of a blog (be sure to correct any spelling and punctuation mistakes you find as well).

Well, to the profound surprise of absolutely nobody, we are not going to be able meet the June 1 commitment to ship 100 steel tables to Ocean's Cannery. (For those of you who have been living in a cave the past six months, we have been fighting to get our hands on enough high-grade chromium steel to meet our production schedule.) Sure enough, we got news, this morning that we will only get enough for 30 tables. Yes, we look like fools for not being able to follow through on promises we made to the customer, but no, this didn't have to happpen. Six month's ago, purchasing warned us about shrinking supplies and suggested we advance-buy as much as we would need for the next 12 months, or so. We naturally tried to followed their advice, but just as naturally were shot down by the bean counters at corporate who trotted out the policy about never buying more than three months worth of materials in advance. Of course, it'll be us–not the bean counters who'll take the flak when everybody starts asking why revenues are down next quarter and why Ocean's Cannery is talking to our competitors!!! Maybe, some day this company will get its head out of the sand and realize that we need to have some financial flexibility in order to compete.

3. **Collaboration: Working in Teams; Planning: Selecting Media** L.O.❶, **Chapter 2** Working with at least two other students, identify the best medium to use for each of the following messages. For each of these message needs, choose a medium that you think would work effectively and explain your choice. (More than one medium could work in some cases; just be able to support your particular choice.)
   a. A technical support service for people trying to use their digital music players
   b. A message of condolence to the family of an employee who passed away recently
   c. A collection of infographics from a variety of sources on the state of the consumer electronics industry
   d. A series of observations on the state of the consumer electronics industry
   e. A series of messages, questions, and answers surrounding the work of a project team

4. **Media Skills: Writing Email Subject Lines** L.O.❸ Using your imagination to make up whatever details you need, revise the following email subject lines to make them more informative:
   a. New budget figures
   b. Marketing brochure—your opinion
   c. Production schedule

## ACTIVITIES

Each activity is labelled according to the primary skill or skills you will need to use. To review relevant chapter content, you can refer to the indicated Learning Objective. In some instances, supporting information will be found in another chapter, as indicated.

1. **Media Skills: Email** L.O.❸ The following email message contains numerous errors related to what you've learned about planning and writing business messages. First, list the flaws you find in this version. Then use the following steps to plan and write a better memo.

---

TO: Felicia August <b_august@evertrust.com>

SUBJECT: Compliance with new break procedure

Some of you may not like the rules about break times; however, we determined that keeping track of employees while they took breaks at times they determined rather than regular breaks at prescribed times was not working as well as we would have liked it to work. The new rules are not going to be an option. If you do not follow the new rules, you could be docked from your pay for hours when you turned up missing, since your direct supervisor will not be able to tell whether you were on a "break" or not and will assume that you have walked away from your job. We cannot be responsible for any errors that result from your inattentiveness to the new rules. I have already heard complaints from some of you and I hope this memo will end this issue once and for all. The decision has already been made.

Starting Monday, January 2, you will all be required to take a regular 15-minute break in the morning and again in the afternoon, and a regular thirty-minute lunch at the times specified by your supervisor, NOT when you think you need a break or when you "get around to it."

There will be no exceptions to this new rule!

Felicia August

Manager

Billing and accounting

a. Describe the flaws you discovered in this email message.

b. Develop a plan for rewriting the message. Use the following steps to organize your efforts before you begin writing:

   i. Determine the purpose.

   ii. Identify and analyze your audience.

   iii. Define the main idea.

   iv. Outline the major supporting points.

   v. Choose between a direct and an indirect approach.

c. Now rewrite the email message. Don't forget to revise your own work before you turn it in.

2. **Media Skills: Instant Messaging** L.O.④ Review the following IM exchange and explain how the customer service agent could have handled the situation more effectively.

| | |
|---|---|
| **Agent:** | Thanks for contacting Home Exercise Equipment. What's up? |
| **Customer:** | I'm having trouble assembling my home gym. |
| **Agent:** | I hear that a lot! LOL |
| **Customer:** | So is it me or the gym? |
| **Agent:** | Well, let's see ~COLOR~[Green]. Where are you stuck? |
| **Customer:** | The crossbar that connects the vertical pillars doesn't fit. |
| **Agent:** | What do you mean doesn't fit? |
| **Customer:** | It doesn't fit. It's not long enough to reach across the pillars. |
| **Agent:** | Maybe you assembled the pillars in the wrong place. Or maybe we sent the wrong crossbar. |
| **Customer:** | How do I tell? |
| **Agent:** | The parts aren't labelled so could be tough. Do you have a measuring tape? Tell me how long your crossbar is. |

3. **Media Skills: Blogging** L.O.⑤ Identify the numerous errors made by the writer of the following blog posting. List them and then plan and write a better post.

---

[headline]

Get Ready!

[post]

We are hoping to be back at work soon, with everything running smoothly, same production schedule and no late projects or missed deadlines. So you need to clean out your desk,

---

put your stuff in boxes, and clean off the walls. You can put the items you had up on your walls in boxes, also.

We have provided boxes. The move will happen this weekend. We'll be in our new offices when you arrive on Monday.

We will not be responsible for personal belongings during the move.

---

a. Describe the flaws you discovered in this blog post.

b. Develop a plan for rewriting the post. Use the following steps to organize your efforts before you begin writing:

   i. Determine the purpose.

   ii. Identify and analyze your audience.

   iii. Define the main idea.

   iv. Outline the major supporting points.

   v. Choose between direct and indirect approaches.

c. Now rewrite the post. Don't forget to revise your own work before you turn it in.

4. **Media Skills: Podcasting** L.O.⑥ You've recently begun recording a weekly podcast to share information with your large and far-flung staff. After a month, you ask for feedback from several of your subordinates, and you're disappointed to learn that some people stopped listening to the podcast after the first couple of weeks. Someone eventually admits that many staffers feel the recordings are too long and rambling, and the information they contain isn't valuable enough to justify the time it takes to listen. You aren't pleased, but you want to improve. An assistant transcribes the introduction to last week's podcast so you can review it. You immediately see two problems. Revise the introduction based on what you've learned in this chapter.

---

So there I am, having lunch with Selma Gill, who just joined and took over the Atlantic sales region from Jackson Ho. In walks our beloved CEO with Selma's old boss at Uni-Plex; turns out they were finalizing a deal to co-brand our products and theirs and to set up a joint distribution program in all four domestic regions. Pretty funny, huh? Selma left Uni-Plex because she wanted sell our products instead, and now she's back selling her old stuff, too. Anyway, try to chat with her when you can; she knows the biz inside and out and probably can offer insight into just about any sales challenge you might be running up against. We'll post more info on the co-brand deal next week; should be a boost for all of us. Other than those two news items, the other big news this week is the change in commission reporting. I'll go into the details in minute, but when you log onto the intranet, you'll now see your sales results split out by product line and industry sector. Hope this helps you see where you're doing well and where you might beef things up a bit. Oh yeah, I almost forgot the most important bit. Speaking of our beloved CEO, Thomas is going to be our guest of honour, so to speak, at the quarterly sales meeting next week and wants an update on how petroleum prices are affecting customer behaviour. Each district manager should be ready with a brief report. After I go through the commission reporting scheme, I'll outline what you need to prepare.

# CASES

Apply the three-step writing process to the following cases, as assigned by your instructor.

▍ **Social Networking Skills**

**1. Media Skills: Social Networking; Media Skills: Microblogging** L.O.❷, L.O.❺

Foursquare (http://foursquare.com/) is one of the leading providers of location-based social networking services. Millions of people use Foursquare for social engagement and friendly competition, and many business owners are starting to recognize the marketing potential of having people who are on the move in local areas broadcasting their locations and sharing information about stores, restaurants, clubs, and other merchants.

**YOUR TASK** Review the information on Foursquare's Merchant Platform at http://foursquare.com/business/venues. Now write four brief messages, no more than 140 characters long (including spaces). The first should summarize the benefits to stores, restaurants, and other "brick and mortar" businesses of participating in Foursquare, and the next three messages should convey three compelling points that support that overall benefit statement. If your class is set up with private Twitter accounts, use your private account to send your messages. Otherwise, email your four messages to your instructor or post them on your class blog, as your instructor directs.

▍ **Social Networking Skills**

**2. Media Skills: Social Networking; Online Etiquette** L.O.❷, Chapter 2

Employees who take pride in their work are a practically priceless resource for any business. However, pride can sometimes manifest itself in negative ways when employees come under criticism—and public criticism is a fact of life in social media. Imagine that your company has recently experienced a rash of product quality problems, and these problems have generated some unpleasant and occasionally unfair criticism on a variety of social media sites. Someone even set up a Facebook page specifically to give customers a place to vent their frustrations.

You and your public relations team jumped into action, responding to complaints with offers to provide replacement products and help customers who have been affected by the quality problems. Everything seemed to be going as well as could be expected, when you were checking a few industry blogs one evening and discovered that two engineers in your company's product design lab have been responding to complaints on their own. They identified themselves as company employees and defended their product design, blaming the company's production department and even criticizing several customers for lacking the skills needed to use such a sophisticated product. Within a matter of minutes, you see their harsh comments being retweeted and reposted on multiple sites, only fueling the fire of negative feedback against your firm. Needless to say, you are horrified.

**YOUR TASK** You manage to reach the engineers by private message and tell them to stop posting messages, but you realize you have a serious training issue on your hands. Write a post for the internal company blog that advises employees on how to respond appropriately when they are representing the company online. Use your imagination to make up any details you need.

## Social Networking Skills

### 3. Media Skills: Social Networking L.O.❷

Business networking websites such as www.linkedin.com, www.ryze.com, and www.spoke.com have become popular places for professionals to make connections that would be difficult or impossible to make without the internet. An important aspect of business networking is being able to provide a clear description of your professional background and interests. For example, a manufacturing consultant can list the industries in which she has experience, the types of projects she has worked on, and the nature of work she'd like to pursue in the future (such as a full-time position for a company or additional independent projects).

**YOUR TASK** Write a brief statement to introduce yourself, including your educational background, your job history, and the types of connections you'd like to make. You can "fast forward" to your graduation and list your degree, the business specialty you plan to pursue, and any relevant experience. If you have business experience already, use that information instead. Make sure your statement is clear, concise (no more than two sentences), and compelling so that anyone looking for someone like you would want to get in touch with you after reading your introduction.

### 4. Media Skills: Social Networking; Microblogging L.O.❺

You belong to a community group that promotes local and organic producers. One of your big success stories is the summer farmers' markets that started in your neighbourhood but now happen throughout the region. For the last few months, your group has been waiting for a response to an application you submitted for federal funding to stage a community fair that would promote local organic farmers and businesses that have sustainable business practices. The target is to get 50 businesses to participate in a one-day event, so the call you just received from your president, Johanna Prozski, was just what you were waiting to hear. "Good news," she said. "We got our federal grant for the fair!"

This is good news—you now have the rest of the funds needed to get the fair going. "This is exciting! It's going to happen! We need Kira, Puru, and Meghan to begin calling companies to sell them a booth—it'll cost 125 bucks for a booth—which is a good deal," exclaimed Johanna.

"I agree," you replied. "Showcasing your company for that small amount is a good deal."

"Yeah, we'll get somewhere around 800 to 1000 people out, no problem, especially if the surrounding communities get into this event too," offered Johanna.

"What's the timeline for our people to be calling the companies they have been assigned?" you asked.

"It'd be good to know which companies are committed within one month," replied Johanna. "Will you let the group know the news and who needs to do what?"

"Sure, I can do that," you replied. "Remind me of the fair venue details."

"Well—we're in for the Heritage Hall on Main Street on March 30, and I believe we have it from 10 to 4. Make sure everyone knows Dan offered to order the poster printing and Maurice is on for getting the city licence and permit for the event," she instructed. "And Shari agreed to price table rentals. What a great group, hey? Way better than last year when Mark and Matt paid for a bar bill with petty cash and Connor mixed up the table order—way better. Maybe we better meet in two weeks—Tuesday night, let's say 7 to 9 p.m. to iron out all the details," Johanna remarked.

"OK," you agreed. "I'll book the room at Trout Lake Community Centre for that and let everyone know what's going on."

**YOUR TASK** Write a post for the group's Facebook Group page. Select the appropriate information (and add any specific details you think are necessary). Make up your own group name. Update them on the funding and confirm event details and responsibilities. Remember to use document design features to make your post easy to read. Write a Twitter post announcing the event.

## Social Networking Skills: Presentation Skills

### 5. Media Skills: Social Networking; Media Skills: Presentations L.O.❷

Aritzia, a women's fashion retailer, has expanded from its original Vancouver location to stores across Canada and the United States. Aritzia is active in social media, using a variety of social media tools to let customers know about new products and provide information about fashion.

**YOUR TASK** With a team of classmates, study the company's website (www.aritzia.com/) and its social media presence (you can find various social media links on the website). Now identify a business near your college that could benefit from a similar social media strategy. Devise a social media strategy that could help this company expand its customer base and forge stronger links with the local community. Prepare a brief class presentation that describes the business and explains your proposed strategy. (Your instructor may ask you to undertake this as a service project, in which you meet with the company owner and present your proposed social media strategy.)

## Social Networking Skills

### 6. Media Skills: Social Networking L.O.❷

Social media can be a great way to, well, socialize during your college years, but employers are increasingly checking up on the online activities of potential hires to avoid bringing in employees who may reflect poorly on the company.

**YOUR TASK** Team up with another student and review each other's public presence on Facebook, Twitter, Flickr, blogs, and any other website that an employer might check during the interview and recruiting process. Identify any photos, videos, messages, or other material that could raise a red flag when an employer is evaluating a job candidate. Give each other feedback and suggestions. Write a reflection email about what you learned from the exercise and send the reflection to your instructor.

▍ **Email Skills** ▍ **Sustainability**
### 7. Media Skills: Email L.O. ❸

According to a report published by Statistics Canada, in 2008, the proportion of people who purchased or boycotted a product for ethical reasons rose to 27 percent of the population, compared to 20 percent in 2003.[61] Given this growing awareness about the environmental impact of our consumer behaviour, opportunities may exist for your company to make some changes that would broaden the appeal of your product to green consumers. You work for Caneast Foods, a chain of small grocery stores in Ontario. Currently produce is packaged on Styrofoam trays, something you would like to see replaced with a green product. You looked at some products available from Earthcycle Packaging (www.earthcycle.com/sales.html) or Go-Green (http://gogreenpackaging.com) and think your company should consider making the switch to this type of packaging or something similar. As well, you have been looking at ways to use social media to connect with customers and develop customer relationships and loyalty. Your boss is not that familiar with use of social media, so the stores have not capitalized on how to use it to develop customer engagement.

**YOUR TASK** Write an email message to your boss suggesting that the company research the costs and benefits of switching from Styrofoam packaging to an alternative green product. Suggest two different social media channels the store might use to let consumers know about the change, and include a brief description of each media and how the store would benefit from using it.

▍ **Email Skills** ▍ **Sustainability** ▍ **Social Networking Skills**
### 8. Media Skills: Email L.O. ❷

Assume you are a member of a local volunteer group of 15 people interested in nature conservancy. Your group is considering launching a campaign to educate people about an environmental issue affecting your area (select an issue that you care about). The leader of your group

has asked you to find some examples of how other conservation groups use social media to get their message out and to make some recommendations for your group's campaign.

**YOUR TASK** Use Google to find some examples of conservation groups that use social media to promote their cause. Write an email message to your director describing how social media are currently used by one of the groups you found and give your opinion of their effectiveness, as well as the advantages and disadvantages of your group using these media. Include your suggestions.

▍ **Blogging Skills**
### 9. Media Skills: Blogging L.O. ❺

The Quebec Winter Carnival is one of the world's largest winter celebrations, with close to one million people participating in a wide variety of sports, cultural, and entertainment events in January and February each year. Some of its exciting events range from arctic spas to canoe, dog sled, and horse races to an international ice sculpture competition and Bonhomme's Ball.

**YOUR TASK** Assume that you write a pop culture blog and several of the readers of your blog have been asking for your recommendation about visiting the Quebec Winter Carnival next year. Write a two- or three-paragraph posting for your blog that explains what the Quebec Winter Carnival is and what visitors can expect to experience there. Be sure to address your posting to fans of your blog, not insiders who know all about the Carnival. You can learn more at www.carnaval.qc.ca.

▍ **Blogging Skills**
### 10. Media Skills: Blogging; Compositional Modes: Tutorials L.O. ❶, L.O. ❺

Studying abroad for a semester or a year can be a rewarding experience in many ways—improving your language skills, experiencing another culture, making contacts in the international business arena, and building your self-confidence.

**YOUR TASK** Write a post for your class blog that describes your college's study-abroad program and summarizes the steps involved in applying for international study. If your school doesn't offer study-abroad opportunities, base your post on the program offered at another institution in your province.

▍ **Microblogging Skills**
### 11. Media Skills: Microblogging; Compositional Modes: Teasers L.O. ❶, L.O. ❺

Twitter updates are a great way to alert people to helpful articles, videos, and other online resources.

**YOUR TASK** Find an online resource (it can be a website quiz, a YouTube video, a PowerPoint presentation, a newspaper article, or anything else appropriate) that offers some great tips to help college students prepare for job interviews. Write a teaser of no more than 120 characters that hints at the benefits other students can get from this resource. If your class is set up with private Twitter accounts, use your private account to send your message. Otherwise, email it to your instructor. Be sure to include the URL; if you're using a Twitter account, keep within the 140-character limit.

**▌ Microblogging Skills**
**12. Media Skills: Microblogging L.O.⑤**

Assume the boss took your suggestion in the scenario in Case #7. Instead of Styrofoam trays, your store will now be using trays made from palm fibres (www .earthcycle.com).

**YOUR TASK** Write a message to customers about your store's change to green packaging in the produce department. Adapt your message for posting via three different media: Twitter, Facebook, and the blog on the company's website.

**▌ Podcasting Skills Portfolio Builder**
**13. Media Skills: Podcasting L.O.⑥**

With any purchase decision, from a restaurant meal to a college education, recommendations from satisfied customers are often the strongest promotional messages.

**YOUR TASK** Write a script for a one- to two-minute podcast (roughly 150 to 250 words) explaining why your college or university is a good place to get an education. Your audience is high school students. You can choose to craft a general message, something that would be useful to all prospective students, or you can focus on a specific academic discipline, the athletic program, or some other important aspect of your college experience. Either way, make sure your introductory comments clarify whether you are offering a general recommendation or a specific recommendation. If your instructor asks you to do so, record the podcast and submit the file electronically.

**▌ Podcasting Skills Portfolio Builder**
**14. Media Skills: Podcasting L.O.⑥**

What product do you own (or use regularly) that you can't live without? It could be something as seemingly minor as a favourite pen or something as significant as a medical device that you literally can't live without. Now imagine that you're a salesperson for this product; think about how you would sell it to potential buyers. How would you describe it, and how would you explain the benefits of owning it? After you've thought about how you would present the product to others, imagine that you've been promoted to a sales manager position, and it is your job to train other people to sell the product.

**YOUR TASK** Write the script for a brief podcast (200 to 300 words) that summarizes for your sales staff the most important points to convey about the product. Imagine that they'll listen to your podcast while driving to a customer's location or preparing for the day's activity in a retail store (depending on the nature of product). Be sure to give your staffers a concise overview message about the product and several key support points. If your instructor asks you to do so, record the podcast and submit the file electronically.

**▌ Podcasting Skills Portfolio Builder**
**15. Media Skills: Podcasting L.O.⑥**

While writing the many letters and electronic messages that are part of the job search process, you find yourself wishing that you could just talk to some of these companies so your personality could shine through. Well, you've just gotten that opportunity. One of the companies that you've applied to has emailed you back, asking you to submit a two-minute podcast introducing yourself and explaining why you would be a good person to hire.

**YOUR TASK** Identify a company that you'd like to work for after graduation and select a job that would be a good match for your skills and interests. Write a script for a two-minute podcast (about 250 words). Introduce yourself, name the position you're applying for, describe your background, and explain why you think you're a good candidate for the job. Make up any details you need. If your instructor asks you to do so, record the podcast and submit the file electronically.

## BUSINESS COMMUNICATION NOTEBOOK

# Ethics

## Spin Cycle: Deciphering Corporate Doublespeak

If there's one product North American businesses can manufacture in large amounts, it's doublespeak. Doublespeak is language that only pretends to say something but that in reality hides, evades, or misleads. Like most products, doublespeak comes in many forms, from the popular buzzwords that everyone uses but no one really understands—such as *competitive dynamics* and *empowerment*—to words that try to hide meaning, such as *re-engineering, misspeak,* and *restructuring.*

With doublespeak, bribes and kickbacks are called *rebates* or *fees for product testing.* With doublespeak, banks don't have *bad loans* or *bad debts;* they have *nonperforming credits.* And corporations never lose money; they just experience *negative cash flow, deficit enhancement,* or *negative contributions to profits.*

Of course, no one gets fired these days. People high enough in the corporate pecking order *resign for personal reasons.* Those in lower ranks leave as the result of *downsizing, workforce adjustments,* and *headcount reductions.* One automobile company that closed an entire assembly plant and eliminated more than 8000 jobs called the action *a volume-related production schedule adjustment.*

The goal of good writing is to communicate, not to confuse; to be understood, not to hide behind words. Look at this confusing excerpt from an investment document:

> The applicability of the general information and administrative procedures set forth below accordingly will vary depending on the investor and the record-keeping system established for a shareholder's investment in the Fund. Participants in RRSPs and other plans should first consult with the appropriate persons at their employer or refer to the plan materials before following any of the procedures below.

As discussed in Chapter 4, *plain English* is a way of writing and arranging technical materials so that your audience can understand your meaning. Restating our excerpt in plain English reveals one simple thought: "If you are investing through a large retirement plan or other special program, follow the instructions in your program material."

Some companies are concerned that writing documents in plain English will increase their liability, but many companies are finding just the opposite. Documents that are clear and less ambiguous can help reduce liability.

Some lawyers may purposely choose obscure language to profit from people who must then hire them to interpret the difficult language. But many legal professionals strongly endorse the plain-English movement, and as it gains momentum, perhaps confusing language will become obsolete.

## Applications for Success

For more on the subject of doublespeak, visit www.dt.org/html/Doublespeak.html to read William Lutz's article "Life Under the Chief Doublespeak Officer."

Answer the following questions:

1. Isn't corporate doublespeak just another way to emphasize the positive in business situations? Or is it unethical to use business buzzwords and corporate doublespeak to ease negative impressions? Explain your position in an email message to your instructor.

2. The president of one company just learned that some of his employees have been playing a popular game called "buzzword bingo," in which participants ridicule doublespeak by tracking the jargon their bosses use during staff meetings on bingo-like cards. What can managers do to avoid these silly games?

3. Visit the following buzzword bingo website and print out a card or two to identify some typical buzzwords: http://lurkertech.com/buzzword-bingo/.

# Writing Routine and Positive Messages

## LEARNING OBJECTIVES

*After studying this chapter, you will be able to*

1. Outline an effective strategy for writing routine business requests.
2. Describe three common types of routine requests.
3. Outline an effective strategy for writing routine replies and positive messages.
4. Describe six common types of routine replies and positive messages.

Ernst & Young is one of the world's largest providers of professional services, with offices in 670 locations in 140 countries. Ernst & Young Canada operates in 14 Canadian cities, offering accounting, business, and financial consulting services to a variety of industries. As a managing partner, Fred Withers communicates widely with professional staff and clients. "Some people think that accountants only work with numbers," says Withers, "but the key is being able to explain them to people in a clear, professional manner." Whether requesting information from clients or responding to routine inquiries, Withers believes concise, accurate, and open communication can create a positive impression for the business.[1]

Much of your daily business communication will involve routine and positive messages, including routine requests for information or action, replies on routine business matters, and positive messages such as good-news announcements and goodwill messages, from product operation hints and technical support to refunds and ordering glitches. These messages are the focus of this chapter.

## Strategy for Routine Requests

Making requests is a routine part of business. In most cases, your audience will be prepared to comply, as long as you're not being unreasonable or asking people to do work they would expect you to do yourself. By applying a clear strategy and tailoring your approach to each situation, you'll be able to generate effective requests quickly.

Like all other business messages, routine requests have three parts: an opening, a body, and a close. Using the direct approach, open with your main idea, which is a clear statement of your request. Use the body to give details and justify your request, then close by requesting specific action.

## Stating Your Request Up Front

Begin routine requests by placing your initial request first; up front is where it stands out and gets the most attention. Of course, getting right to the point should not be interpreted as licence to be abrupt or tactless:

Take care that your direct approach doesn't come across as abrupt or tactless.

- **Pay attention to tone.** Instead of demanding action ("Send me the latest version of the budget spreadsheet."), soften your request with words such as *please* and *I would appreciate.*
- **Assume that your audience will comply.** You can generally make the assumption that your audience members will comply when they clearly understand the reason for your request. This attitude helps you write in a positive tone.
- **Be specific.** State precisely what you want. For example, if you request the latest market data from your research department, be sure to say whether you want a 1-page summary or 100 pages of raw data.

## Explaining and Justifying Your Request

Use the body of your message to explain your request. Make the explanation a smooth and logical continuation of your opening remarks. If complying with the request could benefit the reader, be sure to mention that. If you have multiple requests or questions, consider these tips:

If you have multiple requests or questions, start with the most important one.

- **Ask the most important questions first.** If cost is your main concern, you might begin with a question such as "How much will it cost to have our new website created by an outside firm?" Then you may want to ask more specific but related questions, such as whether discounts are available for paying early.
- **Deal with only one topic per question.** If you have an unusual or complex request, break it down into specific, individual questions so that the reader can address each one separately. This consideration not only shows respect for your audience's time but also gets you a more accurate answer in less time.

## Requesting Specific Action in a Courteous Close

Close your message with three important elements: (1) a specific request that includes any relevant deadlines, (2) information about how you can be reached (if it isn't obvious), and (3) an expression of appreciation or goodwill. For example: "Please send the figures by April 5 so that I can return first-quarter results to you before the April 15 board meeting. I appreciate your help." Concluding your message with "Thank you" or "Thanks for your help" is fine, but "Thank you in advance" is considered a bit stuffy and presumptuous.

Close request messages with
- A request for some specific action
- Information about how you can be reached
- An expression of appreciation

**LEARNING OBJECTIVE 2**
Describe three common types of routine requests.

# Common Examples of Routine Requests

The most common types of routine messages are asking for information or action, making claims, and requesting adjustments.

## Asking for Information or Action

When you need to know about something, elicit an opinion from someone, or request a simple action, you usually need only ask. In essence, simple requests say:

- What you want to know or what you want readers to do.
- Why you're making the request.
- Why it may be in your readers' interest to help you (if applicable).

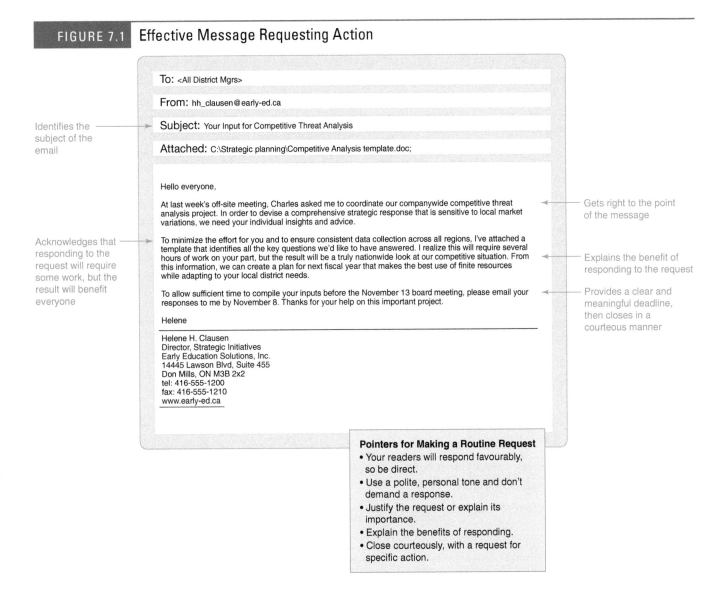

**FIGURE 7.1**  Effective Message Requesting Action

Identifies the subject of the email

To: <All District Mgrs>

From: hh_clausen@early-ed.ca

Subject: Your Input for Competitive Threat Analysis

Attached: C:\Strategic planning\Competitive Analysis template.doc;

Hello everyone,

At last week's off-site meeting, Charles asked me to coordinate our companywide competitive threat analysis project. In order to devise a comprehensive strategic response that is sensitive to local market variations, we need your individual insights and advice.

Gets right to the point of the message

Acknowledges that responding to the request will require some work, but the result will benefit everyone

To minimize the effort for you and to ensure consistent data collection across all regions, I've attached a template that identifies all the key questions we'd like to have answered. I realize this will require several hours of work on your part, but the result will be a truly nationwide look at our competitive situation. From this information, we can create a plan for next fiscal year that makes the best use of finite resources while adapting to your local district needs.

Explains the benefit of responding to the request

To allow sufficient time to compile your inputs before the November 13 board meeting, please email your responses to me by November 8. Thanks for your help on this important project.

Provides a clear and meaningful deadline, then closes in a courteous manner

Helene

Helene H. Clausen
Director, Strategic Initiatives
Early Education Solutions, Inc.
14445 Lawson Blvd, Suite 455
Don Mills, ON M3B 2x2
tel: 416-555-1200
fax: 416-555-1210
www.early-ed.ca

**Pointers for Making a Routine Request**
- Your readers will respond favourably, so be direct.
- Use a polite, personal tone and don't demand a response.
- Justify the request or explain its importance.
- Explain the benefits of responding.
- Close courteously, with a request for specific action.

For simple requests, a straightforward request gets the job done with a minimum of fuss. In more complex situations, you may need to provide more extensive reasons and justification for your request. Naturally, be sure to adapt your request to your audience and the situation (see Figure 7.1).

*Routine requests can be handled with simple, straightforward messages, but more complicated requests can require additional justification and explanation.*

## Asking for Recommendations

The need to inquire about people arises often in business. For example, before extending credit or awarding contracts, jobs, promotions, or scholarships, companies often ask applicants to supply references. Companies ask applicants to list references who can vouch for their ability, skills, integrity, character, and fitness for the job. Before you volunteer someone's name as a reference, ask permission to do so. Some people don't want you to use their names, perhaps because they don't know enough about you to feel comfortable writing a letter or because they or their employers have a policy of not providing recommendations.

*Always ask for permission before using someone as a reference.*

Requests for recommendations and references are routine, so you can organize your inquiry using the direct approach. Open your message by clearly stating why the recommendation is required (if it's not for a job, be sure to explain its purpose) and that you would like your reader to write the letter. If you haven't had contact with the person for

## FIGURE 7.2 Effective Request for a Recommendation

### ① Plan

**Analyze the Situation**

Verify that the purpose is to request a recommendation letter from a college professor.

**Gather Information**

Gather information on classes and dates to help the reader recall you and to clarify the position you seek.

**Select the Right Medium**

The letter format gives this message an appropriate level of formality, although many professors prefer to be contacted by email.

**Organize the Information**

Messages like this are common and expected, so a direct approach is fine.

### ② Write

**Adapt to Your Audience**

Show sensitivity to audience needs with a "you" attitude, politeness, positive emphasis, and bias-free language.

**Compose the Message**

Style is respectful and businesslike, while still using plain language and appropriate voice.

### ③ Complete

**Revise the Message**

Evaluate content and review readability; avoid unnecessary details.

**Produce the Message**

Simple letter format is all the design this message needs.

**Proofread the Message**

Review for errors in layout, spelling, and mechanics.

**Distribute the Message**

Deliver the message via postal mail or email if you have the professor's email address.

---

1181 Ashport Drive
Don Mills, ON M3C 2Y8
March 14, 2016

Professor Linda Kenton
School of Business
Ryerson University
350 Victoria Street
Toronto, ON M5B 2K3

Dear Professor Kenton:

<u>Request for Recommendation</u>

I recently interviewed with Strategic Investments and have been called for a second interview for their Analyst Training Program (ATP). They have requested at least one recommendation from a professor, and I immediately thought of you. May I have a letter of recommendation from you?

As you may recall, I took BUS 485, Financial Analysis, from you in the fall of 2014. I enjoyed the class and finished the term with an "A." Your comments on financial ratio analysis impressed me beyond the scope of the actual course material. In fact, taking your course helped me decide on a future as a financial analyst.

My enclosed résumé includes all my relevant work experience and volunteer activities. I would also like to add that I've handled the financial planning for our family since my father passed away several years ago. Although I initially learned by trial and error, I have increasingly applied my business training in deciding what stocks or bonds to trade. This experience has given me a practical edge over others who may be applying for the same job.

If possible, Ms. Blackmon in Human Resources needs to receive your letter by March 30. For your convenience, I've enclosed a preaddressed, stamped envelope.

I would appreciate your time and effort in writing this letter of recommendation for me. I am looking forward to putting my education to work, and I'll keep you informed of my progress. Thank you for your consideration.

Sincerely,

*Joanne Tucker*

Joanne Tucker

Enclosure

---

*Tucker includes information near the opening to refresh her professor's memory.*

*She provides a deadline for response and includes information about the person who is expecting the recommendation.*

*The opening states the purpose of the letter and makes the request, assuming the reader will want to comply with the request.*

*The body refers to the enclosed résumé and mentions experience that could set the applicant apart from other candidates—information the professor could use in writing the recommendation.*

*The close mentions the preaddressed, stamped envelope to encourage a timely response.*

some time, use the opening to trigger the reader's memory of the relationship you had, the dates of association, and any special events or accomplishments that might bring a clear and favourable picture of you to mind.

Use the body of the request to list all the information the recipient would need to write the recommendation, including the full name and address or email address of the person to whom the recommendation should be sent. Consider including an updated résumé if you've had significant career advancement since your last contact.

Close your message with an expression of appreciation. When asking for an immediate recommendation, you should also mention the deadline. If you are requesting a printed letter, always be sure to enclose a stamped, pre-addressed envelope as a convenience to the other party. Figure 7.2 provides an example of a request that follows these guidelines.

REAL-TIME UPDATES

**Learn More by Reading This PDF**

**The right way to ask for recommendations on LinkedIn**

Follow LinkedIn's etiquette guide for students and recent graduates to increase your response rate and to maintain positive networking connections. Go to http://real-timeupdates.com/bce6 and click on Learn More. If you are using MyBCommLab, you can access Real-Time Updates within Business Communication Resources.

*Refresh the memory of any potential reference you haven't been in touch with for a while.*

## Making Claims and Requesting Adjustments

If you're dissatisfied with a company's product or service, you can opt to make a **claim** (a formal complaint) or request an **adjustment** (a settlement of a claim). In either case, it's important to maintain a professional tone in all your communication, no matter how angry or frustrated you are. Keeping your cool will help you get the situation resolved sooner.

Open with a straightforward statement of the problem along with your request. In the body, give a complete, specific explanation of the details; provide any information the recipient would need to verify your complaint. In your close, politely request specific action or convey a sincere desire to find a solution. And, if appropriate, suggest that the business relationship will continue if the problem is solved satisfactorily. Back up your claim with invoices, sales receipts, cancelled cheques, dated correspondence, and any other relevant documents. Send copies and keep the originals for your files.

If the remedy is obvious, tell your reader exactly what you expect from the company, such as exchanging incorrectly shipped merchandise for the right item or issuing a refund if the item is out of stock. In some cases, you might ask the recipient to resolve a problem. However, if you're uncertain about the precise nature of the trouble, you could ask the company to make an assessment and then advise you on the remedy. Supply your contact information so that the company can discuss the situation with you, if necessary. Compare the ineffective and effective versions in Figure 7.3 for an example of making a claim.

*In a claim letter,*

- *Explain the problem and give details*
- *Provide backup information*
- *Request specific action*

*Be prepared to document any claims you make with a company. Send copies and keep the original documents.*

# Strategy for Routine Replies and Positive Messages

**LEARNING OBJECTIVE 3**
Outline an effective strategy for writing routine replies and positive messages.

Just as you'll make numerous requests for information and action throughout your career, you'll also respond to similar requests from other people. When you are responding positively to a request, sending routine announcements, or sending a positive or goodwill message, you have several goals: to communicate the information or the good news, answer all questions, provide all required details, and leave your reader with a good impression of you and your firm.

Readers receiving routine replies and positive messages will generally be interested in what you have to say, so you'll usually use the direct approach. Place your main idea (the positive reply or the good news) in the opening. Use the body to explain all the relevant details, and close cordially, perhaps highlighting a benefit to your reader.

*Use a direct approach for positive messages.*

**FIGURE 7.3** Poor and Improved Versions of a Claim

### Poor

To: cust_serv@slocity.org

CC:

Subject: Request for Energy Cost Analysis

We have been at our present location only three months, and we don't understand why our December utility bill is $815.00 and our January bill is $817.50. Businesses on both sides of us, in offices just like ours, are paying only and average of $543.50 and $545.67 for the same months. We all have similar computer and office equipments, so something must be wrong. ← *Opens with emotions and details*

Small businesses are helpless against big utility companies. How can we prove that you read the meter wrong or that the November bill from before we even moved in here got added to out December bill? We want someone to check this meter right away. We can't afford to pay these big bills. ← *Uses a defensive tone and blames the meter reader*

This is the first we've complained to you about anything, and I hope you'll agree that we deserve a better deal. ← *Closes with irrelevant information and a weak defence*

Sincerely,

Laura Covington
Proprietor

### Improved

To: cust_serv@slocity.org

CC:

Subject: Request for Energy Cost Analysis

Dear Customer Service Representative:
A comparison of our electricity bills with those of our neighbouring businesses suggests that the utility meter in our store may not be accurate. Please send a technician to check it. ← *Opens by clearly and calmly stating the problem*

*Provides details in the body so that the reader can understand why Covington thinks a problem exists* → The European Connection opened at our current location on December 1, and we have received two monthly bills since then. In both instances the amount of our bill was nearly twice what neighbouring businesses in this building were charged, even though we all have similar storefronts and equipment. We paid $815.00 in December and $817.50 in January. In contrast, the highest bills that neighbouring businesses paid were $543.50 and $545.67 for those two months. ← *Presents details clearly, concisely, and completely*

*Requests specific action in the close and provides contact information to make responding easy* → If your representative would visit our store, he or she could do an analysis of how much energy we are using. I understand that you regularly provide this helpful service to customers, and I would appreciate hearing from you this week. You can reach me by calling (805) 979-7727 during business hours. I look forward to hearing from you.

Sincerely,
Laura Covington
Proprietor

**Pointers for Making a Claim**
- Establish rapport by praising some aspect of the product or explaining why you purchased it.
- Present facts clearly, politely, and honestly.
- Show confidence in the reader's sense of fairness; avoid threats, sarcasm, hostility, or exaggeration.
- Avoid any accusations that you cannot support with facts.
- Close with a request for specific action.

## Starting with the Main Idea

By opening with the main idea or good news, you prepare your audience for the details that follow. Make your opening clear and concise. Although the following introductory statements make the same point, one is cluttered with unnecessary information that buries the purpose, whereas the other is brief and to the point:

With the direct approach, open with a clear and concise expression of the main idea or good news.

| Instead of | Write |
|---|---|
| I am pleased to inform you that after careful consideration of a diverse and talented pool of applicants, each of whom did a thorough job of analyzing Loblaw's training needs, we have selected your bid. | Loblaws has accepted your bid to provide public speaking and presentation training to the sales staff. |

The best way to write a clear opening is to have a clear idea of what you want to say. Before you begin to write, ask yourself, "What is the single most important message I have for the audience?"

## Providing Necessary Details and Explanation

Use the body to explain your point completely so that your audience won't be confused or doubtful about your meaning. As you provide the details, maintain the supportive tone established in the opening. This tone is easy to continue when your message is entirely positive, as in this example:

> Your educational background and internship have impressed us, and we believe you would be a valuable addition to Green Valley Properties. As discussed during your interview, your salary will be $4300 per month, plus benefits. In that regard, you will meet with our benefits manager, Paula Sanchez, at 8 a.m. on Monday, March 21. She will assist you with all the paperwork necessary to tailor our benefit package to your family's needs. She will also arrange various orientation activities to help you acclimate to our company.

However, if your routine message is mixed and must convey mildly disappointing information, put the negative portion of your message into as favourable a context as possible:

Try to embed any negative information in a positive context.

| Instead of | Write |
|---|---|
| No, we no longer carry the Sportsgirl line of sweaters. | The new Olympic line has replaced the Sportsgirl sweaters that you asked about. Olympic features a wider range of colours and sizes and more contemporary styling. |

The more complete description is less negative and emphasizes how the audience can benefit from the change. However, if the negative news is likely to be a shock or particularly unpleasant for the reader, you'll want to use the indirect approach (discussed in Chapter 8).

## Ending with a Courteous Close

Your message is more likely to succeed if it leaves your readers with the feeling that you have their best interests in mind. You can accomplish this by highlighting a benefit to the audience or by expressing appreciation or goodwill. If follow-up action is required, clearly state who will do what next.

Make sure audience members understand what to do next and how that action will benefit them.

# Common Examples of Routine Replies and Positive Messages

LEARNING OBJECTIVE 4
Describe six common types of routine replies and positive messages.

Most routine and positive messages fall into six categories: answers to requests for information and action, grants of claims and requests for adjustment, routine informational messages, good-news announcements, goodwill messages, and procedures.

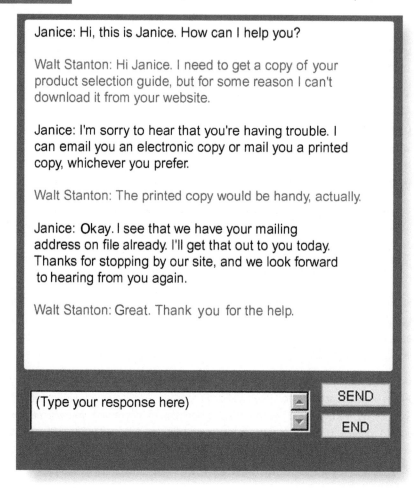

FIGURE 7.4  Effective IM Response to an Information Request

## Answering Requests for Information or Action

Every professional answers requests for information or action from time to time. If the response to a request is a simple "yes" or some other straightforward information, a direct approach is appropriate. A prompt, gracious, and thorough response will positively influence how people think about you and the organization you represent (see Figures 7.4 and 7.5).

## Granting Claims and Requests for Adjustment

Even the best-run companies make mistakes, from billing customers incorrectly to delivering products that fail to perform properly. In other cases, the customer or a third party might be responsible for the mistake, such as misusing a product or damaging it in shipment. Each of these events represents a turning point in your relationship with your customer. If you handle the situation well, your customer will likely be even more loyal than before because you've proven that you're serious about customer satisfaction. However, if a customer believes that you mishandled a complaint, you'll make the situation even worse. Dissatisfied customers often take their business elsewhere and are likely to tell numerous friends and colleagues about the negative experience. A transaction that might be worth only a few dollars by itself could cost you many times that amount in lost business. Consequently, view every mistake as an opportunity to improve a relationship. Your response to the complaint depends on both your company's policies for resolving such issues and your assessment of whether the company, the customer, or some third party is at fault.

**FIGURE 7.5** Personalized Reply to a Request

Uses typical email format

**To:** Julian Zamakis <jzamakis@telus.net>

**From:** Haley Middleton <haley.middleton@hermanmiller.ca>

**CC:**

**Subject:** EMPLOYMENT INFORMATION

Dear Mr. Zamakis:

Refers to previous correspondence

Thank you for your interest in Herman Miller, Inc. Although we currently have no openings matching your qualifications, our needs are continually changing, and we would like to retain a copy of your resumé for one year.

States purpose immediately—that no positions are currently open—but buries the bad news mid-paragraph and balances it with the positive idea that a position may open up

Explains in the body how the company uses résumés that are kept on file

As a leading global manufacturer and marketer of quality furniture systems, products, and services, we are often in need of qualified candidates. When an opening does occur, we review our files to match our needs with candidates' qualifications.

We cultivate a working environment that is conducive to the creative process. Our corporate culture develops and rewards those who acquire new skills and take charge of their careers. Be sure to keep us posted with updates on your progress as you gain experience and skills.

Gives reader a glimpse into the corporate culture and encourages Zamakis to keep in touch

Closes on a warm, positive note

Please check back with us. Our website is continually updated with the most recent employment information. Just follow the links to investigate career opportunities, the variety of benefits we extend to our employees, and the corporate culture at Herman Miller.

Sincerely,

Includes plenty of contact information, in keeping with the friendly audience focus

Haley Middleton
Human Resources
Herman Miller
haley.middleton@hermanmiller.ca
www.hermanmiller.ca
888-443-4357 (Canada and USA only)
Writing at 9:16 A.M. on April 23, 2016

**Pointers for Writing Positive Messages**

*Initial Statement of the Good News or Main Idea*

- Respond promptly.
- If message is mixed, present the good news first.
- Avoid trite, obvious statements.
- Convey an upbeat, courteous, you-oriented tone.

*Middle, Informational Section*

- Imply or express interest in the request.
- Provide details of the good news.
- List all information in an orderly manner.
- If possible, answer all questions in the order posed.
- Adapt replies to the reader's needs.
- Indicate what you have done and what you will do.
- Remind reader of benefits of using your firm.

*Warm, Courteous Close*

- If further action is needed, tell the reader how to proceed and encourage the reader to act promptly.
- Avoid clichés (such as "Please feel free to").
- Offer additional service.
- Express goodwill, or look optimistically to the future.

**RESPONDING TO A CLAIM WHEN YOUR COMPANY IS AT FAULT**   Before you respond when your firm is at fault, make sure you know your company's policies in such cases, which might include specific legal and financial steps to be taken. As a general approch, take the following steps:

- Acknowledge receipt of the customer's claim or complaint.
- Sympathize with the customer's inconvenience or frustration.
- Take (or assign) personal responsibility for setting matters straight.
- Explain precisely how you have resolved, or plan to resolve, the situation.
- Take steps to repair the relationship.
- Follow up to verify that your response was correct.

In addition to these positive steps, maintain professional demeanour by avoiding some key negative steps as well: Don't blame anyone in your organization by name, don't make exaggerated apologies that sound insincere, don't imply that the customer is at fault, and don't promise more than you can deliver.

**RESPONDING TO A CLAIM WHEN THE CUSTOMER IS AT FAULT**  Communication about a claim is a delicate matter when the customer is clearly at fault. If you refuse the claim, you may lose your customer—as well as many of the customer's friends and colleagues, who will hear only one side of the dispute. You must weigh the cost of making the adjustment against the cost of losing future business from one or more customers. Some companies have strict guidelines for responding to such claims, whereas others give individual employees and managers some leeway in making case-by-case decisions.

When granting a claim when the customer is at fault, try to discourage future mistakes without insulting the customer.

If you choose to grant the claim, simply open with that good news. However, the body needs special attention because you need to discourage repeated mistakes without insulting the customer. Close in a courteous manner that expresses your appreciation for the customer's business (see Figure 7.6).

**RESPONDING TO A CLAIM WHEN A THIRD PARTY IS AT FAULT**  Some claims are the result of a mistake by a third party, such as a credit card processing company or a delivery service. Your company may not have made the mistake, but the customer could ask you to resolve the matter anyway.

When a third party is at fault, your response depends on your company's agreements with that organization.

Evaluate each situation carefully and know your company's policies before responding. For instance, an online retailer and the companies that manufacture its merchandise might have an agreement specifying that the manufacturers automatically handle all complaints about product quality. However, regardless of who eventually resolves the problem, if customers contact you, you need to respond with messages that explain how the problem will be solved. Pointing fingers is both unproductive and unprofessional. Resolving the situation is the only issue customers care about.

## Sharing Routine Information

Many messages involve sharing routine information, such as project updates and order status notifications. Use the opening to state the purpose of the message and briefly mention the nature of the information you are providing. Provide the necessary details and end with a courteous close.

When writing informative messages,

• State the purpose at the beginning and briefly mention the nature of the information you are providing
• Provide the necessary details
• End with a courteous close

Most routine communications are neutral. That is, they stimulate neither a positive nor a negative response from readers. For example, when you send departmental meeting announcements and reminder notices, you'll generally receive a neutral response from your readers (unless the purpose of the meeting is unwelcome). Simply present the factual information in the body of the message, and don't worry too much about the reader's attitude toward the information. Some routine informative messages may require additional care. For instance, policy statements or procedural changes may be good news for a company, perhaps because they are saving the company money. However, it may not be obvious to employees that such savings may make available additional employee resources or even pay raises. If the reader may not initially view the information positively, use the body of the message to highlight the potential benefits from the reader's perspective.

## Announcing Good News

To develop and maintain good relationships, smart companies recognize that it's good business to spread the word about positive developments. These developments can include opening new facilities, hiring a new executive, introducing new products or services, or sponsoring community events. Because good news is always welcome, use the direct approach.

Good-news announcements are often communicated in a **news release**, also known as a *press release*, a specialized document used to share relevant information with the news

**FIGURE 7.6** Responding to a Claim When the Customer Is at Fault

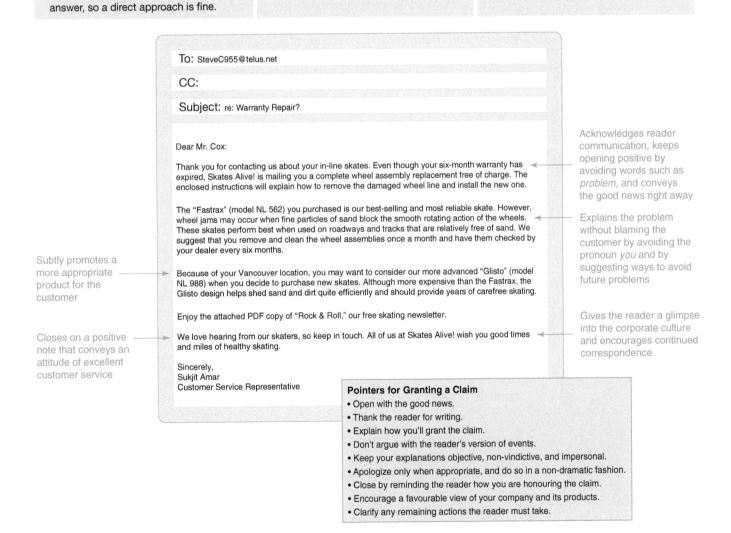

**① Plan**

**Analyze the Situation**
Verify that the purpose is to grant the customer's claim, tactfully educate him, and encourage further business.

**Gather Information**
Gather information on product care, warranties, and resale information.

**Select the Right Medium**
An email message is appropriate in this case because the customer contacted the company via email.

**Organize the Information**
You're responding with a positive answer, so a direct approach is fine.

**② Write**

**Adapt to Your Audience**
Show sensitivity to audience needs with a "you" attitude, politeness, positive emphasis, and bias-free language.

**Compose the Message**
Style is respectful while still managing to educate the customer on product usage and maintenance.

**③ Complete**

**Revise the Message**
Evaluate content and review readability; avoid unnecessary details.

**Produce the Message**
Emphasize a clean, professional appearance.

**Proofread the Message**
Review for errors in layout, spelling, and mechanics.

**Distribute the Message**
Email the reply.

---

To: SteveC955@telus.net

CC:

Subject: re: Warranty Repair?

Dear Mr. Cox:

Thank you for contacting us about your in-line skates. Even though your six-month warranty has expired, Skates Alive! is mailing you a complete wheel assembly replacement free of charge. The enclosed instructions will explain how to remove the damaged wheel line and install the new one.

The "Fastrax" (model NL 562) you purchased is our best-selling and most reliable skate. However, wheel jams may occur when fine particles of sand block the smooth rotating action of the wheels. These skates perform best when used on roadways and tracks that are relatively free of sand. We suggest that you remove and clean the wheel assemblies once a month and have them checked by your dealer every six months.

Because of your Vancouver location, you may want to consider our more advanced "Glisto" (model NL 988) when you decide to purchase new skates. Although more expensive than the Fastrax, the Glisto design helps shed sand and dirt quite efficiently and should provide years of carefree skating.

Enjoy the attached PDF copy of "Rock & Roll," our free skating newsletter.

We love hearing from our skaters, so keep in touch. All of us at Skates Alive! wish you good times and miles of healthy skating.

Sincerely,
Sukjit Amar
Customer Service Representative

*Acknowledges reader communication, keeps opening positive by avoiding words such as problem, and conveys the good news right away*

*Explains the problem without blaming the customer by avoiding the pronoun you and by suggesting ways to avoid future problems*

*Subtly promotes a more appropriate product for the customer*

*Gives the reader a glimpse into the corporate culture and encourages continued correspondence*

*Closes on a positive note that conveys an attitude of excellent customer service*

**Pointers for Granting a Claim**
• Open with the good news.
• Thank the reader for writing.
• Explain how you'll grant the claim.
• Don't argue with the reader's version of events.
• Keep your explanations objective, non-vindictive, and impersonal.
• Apologize only when appropriate, and do so in a non-dramatic fashion.
• Close by reminding the reader how you are honouring the claim.
• Encourage a favourable view of your company and its products.
• Clarify any remaining actions the reader must take.

---

media. (News releases are also used to announce negative news, such as plant closings.) In most companies, news releases are usually prepared or at least supervised by specially trained writers in the public relations department. The content follows the customary pattern for a positive message: good news followed by details and a positive close. However, traditional news releases have a critical difference: you're not writing directly to the ultimate audience (such as the readers of a newspaper); you're trying to interest an editor or a reporter in a story, and that person will then write the material that is eventually read by the larger audience. To write a successful news release, keep the following points in mind:[2]

- Above all else, make sure your information is newsworthy and relevant to the specific publications or websites to which you are sending it.
- Focus on one subject; don't try to pack a single news release with multiple unrelated news items.
- Put your most important idea first. Don't force editors to hunt for the news.
- Be brief; break up long sentences and keep paragraphs short.
- Eliminate clutter, such as redundancy and extraneous facts.
- Be as specific as possible.
- Minimize self-congratulatory adjectives and adverbs. If the content of your message is newsworthy, the media professionals will be interested in the news on its own merits.
- Follow established industry conventions for style, punctuation, and format.

Companies can communicate directly with customers and others with news releases.

Until recently, news releases were crafted in a way to provide information to reporters who would then write their own articles if the subject matter was interesting to their readers. Thanks to the internet and social media, however, the nature of the news release is changing. Many companies now view it as a general-purpose tool for communicating directly with customers and other audiences, creating *direct-to-consumer news releases*. As media expert David Meerman Scott puts it, "Millions of people read press releases directly, unfiltered by the media. You need to be speaking directly to them."[3]

The newest twist on news releases is the **social media release**, which has several advantages over the traditional release. First, the social media release emphasizes bullet-point content that is blog- and Twitter-friendly, making it easy for enthusiasts and others to share key points. Second, as an electronic-only document (a specialized webpage, essentially), the social media release offers the ability to include videos and other multimedia elements. Third, social bookmarking buttons make it easy for people to help publicize the content.[4] Figure 7.7 is an example of a social media news release.

## Fostering Goodwill

*Goodwill is the positive feeling that encourages people to maintain a business relationship.*

All business messages should be written with an eye toward fostering positive relationships with audiences, but some messages are written specifically to build goodwill. You can use these messages to enhance your relationships with customers, colleagues, and other businesspeople by sending friendly, even unexpected, notes with no direct business purpose. The small effort to send a goodwill message can have a positive and lasting effect on the people around you.

*Make sure your compliments are sincere and honest.*

Effective goodwill messages must be sincere and honest. Otherwise, you'll appear to be interested in personal gain rather than in benefiting customers, fellow workers, or your organization. To come across as sincere, avoid exaggerating and support compliments with specific evidence. In addition, readers often regard more restrained praise as being more sincere.

*Taking note of significant events in someone's personal life helps foster the business relationship.*

**SENDING CONGRATULATIONS**   One prime opportunity for sending goodwill messages is to congratulate individuals or companies for significant business achievements—perhaps for being promoted or for attaining product sales milestones (see Figure 7.8). Other reasons for sending congratulations include the highlights in people's personal lives, such as weddings, births, graduations, and success in non-business competitions. You may congratulate business acquaintances on their own achievements or on the accomplishments of a spouse or child. You may also take note of personal events, even if you don't know the reader well. If you're already friendly with the reader, a more personal tone is appropriate.

*An effective message of appreciation documents a person's contributions.*

**SENDING MESSAGES OF APPRECIATION**   An important leadership quality is the ability to recognize the contributions of employees, colleagues, suppliers, and other associates. Your praise does more than just make the person feel good; it encourages further excellence. A message of appreciation may also become an important part of someone's personnel file. So when

## FIGURE 7.7   Social Media News Release

A variety of product photos are available for download and social sharing.

An embedded clip provides a video version of the news release.

The full-text version of the news release message is available for reading and easy sharing.

Additional information is available through these other tabs.

The high-level message is condensed to a single Twitter-friendly "sound bite."

Social media and email buttons make it easy for anyone to share this page.

The full narrative on the left is "bulletized" here on the right, which helps bloggers and others create their own story. Each bullet also has a Twitter button, which lets readers send the bullet point as an individual tweet.

Related links take readers to the company's main website or the specific product webpage.

*Source:* Copyright © 2012 by Noodles and Company. Reprinted with permission.

| Instead of | Write |
|---|---|
| Words cannot express my appreciation for the great job you did. Thanks. No one could have done it better. You're terrific! You've made the whole firm sit up and take notice, and we are ecstatic to have you working here. | Thanks again for taking charge of the meeting in my absence and doing such an excellent job. With just an hour's notice, you pulled the legal and public relations departments together to present a united front in the negotiations. Your dedication and communication abilities have been noted and are truly appreciated. |

you write a message of appreciation, try to specifically mention the person or people you want to praise, as in this example:

Thank you and everyone on your team for the heroic efforts you took to bring our servers back up after last Friday's flood. We were able to restore business right on schedule first thing Monday morning. You went far beyond the level of contractual service in restoring our data centre within 16 hours. The special contribution of networking specialist Julienne Marks, who worked for 12 straight hours to reconnect our internet service, was remarkable. If I can serve as a reference in your future sales activities, please let me know.

### REAL-TIME UPDATES

**Learn More by Reading This Article**

**Simple rules for writing effective thank-you notes**

These tips are easy to adapt to any business or social occasions in which you need to express appreciation. Go to http://real-timeupdates.com/bce6 and click on Learn More. If you are using MyBCommLab, you can access Real-Time Updates within Business Communication Resources.

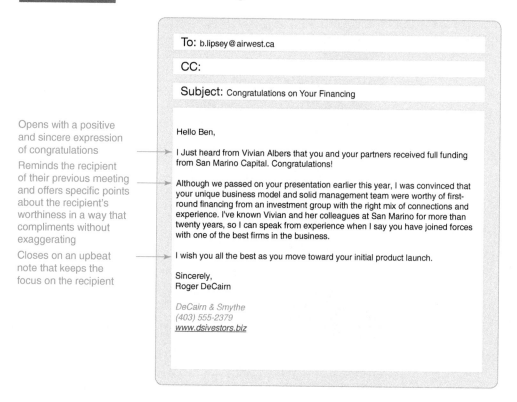

FIGURE 7.8    A Goodwill Message

Opens with a positive and sincere expression of congratulations

Reminds the recipient of their previous meeting and offers specific points about the recipient's worthiness in a way that compliments without exaggerating

Closes on an upbeat note that keeps the focus on the recipient

To: b.lipsey@airwest.ca

CC:

Subject: Congratulations on Your Financing

Hello Ben,

I Just heard from Vivian Albers that you and your partners received full funding from San Marino Capital. Congratulations!

Although we passed on your presentation earlier this year, I was convinced that your unique business model and solid management team were worthy of first-round financing from an investment group with the right mix of connections and experience. I've known Vivian and her colleagues at San Marino for more than twenty years, so I can speak from experience when I say you have joined forces with one of the best firms in the business.

I wish you all the best as you move toward your initial product launch.

Sincerely,
Roger DeCairn

DeCairn & Smythe
(403) 555-2379
www.dsivestors.biz

Hearing a sincere thank you can do wonders for morale.[5] Moreover, in today's electronic media environment, a handwritten thank-you note can be a particularly welcome acknowledgment.[6]

**OFFERING CONDOLENCES**     **Condolence letters** are brief personal messages written to comfort someone after the death of a loved one. You may have occasion to offer condolences to employees or other business associates (when the person has lost a family member) or to the family of an employee or business associate (when that person has died). These messages can feel intimidating to write, but don't let the difficulty of the task keep you from responding promptly.

Timing and media choice are important considerations with condolence letters. The sooner your message is received, the more comforting it will be, so don't delay. And unless circumstances absolutely leave you no choice, do not use electronic media. A brief, handwritten note on quality stationery is the way to go.

Open a condolence message with a brief statement of sympathy, such as "I am deeply sorry to hear of your loss" in the event of a death, for example. In the body, mention the good qualities or the positive contributions made by the deceased. State what the person meant to you or your colleagues. In closing, you can offer your condolences and your best wishes. Here are a few general suggestions for writing condolence messages:

The primary purpose of condolence messages is to let the audience know that you and the organization you represent care about the person's loss.

- **Keep reminiscences brief.** Recount a memory or an anecdote (even a humorous one) but don't dwell on the details of the loss, lest you add to the reader's sadness.
- **Write in your own words.** Write as if you were speaking privately to the person. Don't quote "poetic" passages or use stilted or formal phrases. If the loss is a death, refer to it as such rather than as "passing away" or "departing."
- **Be tactful.** Mention your shock and dismay but remember that bereaved and distressed loved ones take little comfort in lines such as "Richard was too young to die."

- **Take special care.** Be sure to spell names correctly and to be accurate in your review of facts. Try to be prompt.
- **Write about special qualities of the deceased.** You may have to rely on reputation to do this, but let the grieving person know you valued his or her loved one.
- **Consider mentioning special attributes or resources of the bereaved person.** If you know that the bereaved person has attributes or resources that will be a comfort in the time of loss, such as personal resilience, religious faith, or a circle of close friends, mentioning these can make the reader feel more confident about handling the challenges he or she faces.[7]

The following is an example of condolences written by a supervisor to his administrative assistant after learning of the death of her husband:

> My sympathy to you and your children. All your friends at Carter Electric were so very sorry to learn of John's death. Although I never had the opportunity to meet him, I do know how very special he was to you. Your tales of your family's camping trips and his rafting expeditions were always memorable.

Condolence letters are the most personal business messages you may ever have to write, so they require the utmost in care and respect for your reader. By keeping the messages simple, short, and sincere, you will be able to achieve the right tone.

## Writing Procedures

Giving instructions in the workplace is a frequent routine task. Often you have to let clients or co-workers know how to perform an operation. Workplace instructions or procedures lay out the steps to perform the operation or task in an easy-to-follow sequence. Informal, written procedures often are sent in emails, memos, and letters. Longer, more detailed procedures that may be used by many people will be written in a separate document, put online or into a manual, or posted near where the procedures must be followed. Documenting procedures gives employees guidance in performing tasks and helps companies set performance standards.

Examples of procedures include instructions on how to fill out forms, operate machines, follow guidelines for recycling, or carry out office tasks. Just like other communications you prepare, you can apply the three-step process to write an effective procedure.

**PLANNING**    In the planning stage, identify your purpose—to instruct the reader in how to *do* something. The reader will be using the document to perform the steps. Analyze the reader's knowledge about the topic—how much or how little does the reader know and need to know? You may need to include definitions for beginners, or you may be able to skip basic information for readers with advanced knowledge. For example, if your procedures are for chartered accountants, you will not have to define basic terms, but if you are writing procedures for new hires with only one year of accounting experience, more background information may be required.

Organize the steps in chronological order and begin with a general overview that includes:

- What the procedures are about (in general).
- Any definition, background information, or specialized language used.
- A preview of the main stages if the procedure is lengthy.

The introductory information orients the reader to the document and provides a context for the details to follow.

After the overview, list the steps. The procedure may conclude with the last step in the sequence, or it may conclude with troubleshooting suggestions. Figure 7.9 provides a WorkSafeBC sample procedure on how to lock out a piece of industrial equipment to ensure no one will turn on the equipment during maintenance.

**FIGURE 7.9** Sample Safe Work Procedure for Lockout

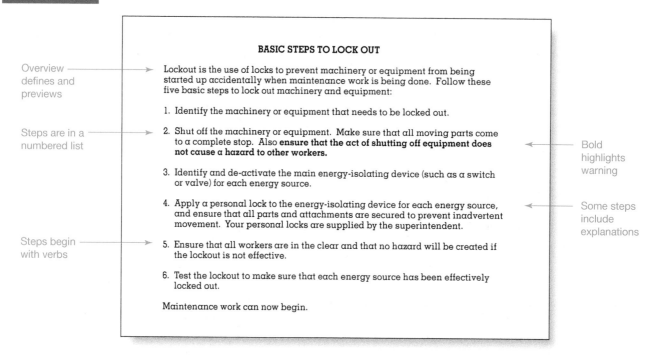

Overview defines and previews

Steps are in a numbered list

Steps begin with verbs

Bold highlights warning

Some steps include explanations

**BASIC STEPS TO LOCK OUT**

Lockout is the use of locks to prevent machinery or equipment from being started up accidentally when maintenance work is being done. Follow these five basic steps to lock out machinery and equipment:

1. Identify the machinery or equipment that needs to be locked out.

2. Shut off the machinery or equipment. Make sure that all moving parts come to a complete stop. Also **ensure that the act of shutting off equipment does not cause a hazard to other workers.**

3. Identify and de-activate the main energy-isolating device (such as a switch or valve) for each energy source.

4. Apply a personal lock to the energy-isolating device for each energy source, and ensure that all parts and attachments are secured to prevent inadvertent movement. Your personal locks are supplied by the superintendent.

5. Ensure that all workers are in the clear and that no hazard will be created if the lockout is not effective.

6. Test the lockout to make sure that each energy source has been effectively locked out.

Maintenance work can now begin.

**WRITING**   Readers will frequently not read the whole procedure before beginning, instead choosing to consult the selected steps while performing the operation. So be sure to make your procedures easy to scan. Here are some tips on how to write effective instructions:

- Use short paragraphs for the overview.
- Put the steps into a list.
- Divide the tasks into a series of action statements.
- Begin each step with a command form verb. By beginning each step with a verb, you emphasize action.
- Number the steps when a sequence must be followed. For instructions that do not have a set order, use bullets for the list instead of numbers.
- Separate explanations from steps so they are easily distinguished.

    One way to separate them is to indent the explanations, thus distinguishing them in alignment from action statements (as is done here).

- **Highlight warnings and precautions.**
- Use active voice and second person—talk directly to the reader.

**Ineffective**

Names and ID numbers are to be filled in on the form in the spaces provided, and the boxes below must be checked to verify your age and policy limit.

**Effective**

1. Fill in your name and ID number in the spaces provided.

2. Check the boxes to verify your age and policy limit.

**COMPLETING**   Ask someone who is typical of the intended audience to use your instructions to complete the task. This will let you know if information is missing or unclear.

Decide what needs emphasis. For example, if a warning is included, is it highlighted with boldface or set apart from the surrounding text? Use document design features such as text boxes, boldface, indentation, and white space to draw attention to key parts, especially for long procedures.

For longer procedures, use headings to show the main organizational divisions. Break up long lists of steps by grouping related steps and providing subheadings. If you have provided headings, readers can more easily find the information they need.

**① OBJECTIVE Outline an effective strategy for writing routine business requests.**

When writing a routine request, open by stating your specific request. In the body, justify your request and explain its importance. Close routine requests by asking for specific action (including a deadline, if appropriate) and expressing goodwill. A courteous close contains three important elements: (1) a specific request, (2) information about how you can be reached (if it isn't obvious), and (3) an expression of appreciation or goodwill.

**② OBJECTIVE Describe three common types of routine requests.**

The most common types of routine requests are asking for information or action, making claims, and requesting adjustments. Requests for information or action should explain what you want to know or what you want readers to do, why you're making the request, and why it may be in your readers' interest to help you (if applicable). To make a claim (a formal complaint about a product or service) or request an adjustment (a settlement of a claim), open with a straightforward statement of the problem, use the body to give a complete explanation of the situation, and close with a polite request to resolve the situation.

**③ OBJECTIVE Outline an effective strategy for writing routine replies and positive messages.**

The direct approach works well for routine replies and positive messages because recipients will generally be interested in what you have to say. Place your main idea (the positive reply or the good news) in the opening. Use the body to explain all the relevant details, and close cordially.

**④ OBJECTIVE Describe six common types of routine replies and positive messages.**

Most routine and positive messages fall into six categories: answers to requests for information and action, grants of claims and requests for adjustment, informative messages, good-news announcements, goodwill messages, and procedures. Answering requests for information or action is a simple task, often assisted with form responses that can be customized as needed. Granting claims and requests for adjustments is more complicated, and the right response depends on whether the company, the customer, or a third party was at fault. Informative messages are often simple and straightforward, but some require extra care if the information affects recipients in a significant way. Good-news announcements are often handled by news releases, which used to be sent exclusively to members of the news media but are now usually made available to the public as well. Goodwill messages, meant to foster positive business relationships, include congratulations, thank-you messages, and messages of condolence. To make goodwill messages effective, make them honest, sincere, and factual. Procedures tell how to carry out workplace tasks. Including an overview and easy-to-scan listed steps will assist the reader.

## MyBCommLab®

Go to MyBCommLab for everything you need to help you succeed in the job you've always wanted! Tools and resources include the following:
- Writing Activities
- Document Makeovers
- Video Exercises
- Grammar Exercises—and much more!

## Practise Your Grammar

Effective business communication starts with strong grammar skills. To improve your grammar skills, go to MyBCommLab, where you'll find exercises and diagnostic tests to help you produce clear, effective communication.

## Test Your Knowledge

To review chapter content related to each question, refer to the indicated Learning Objective.

1. What are three guidelines for asking a series of questions in a routine request? L.O.❶
2. Should you use the direct or indirect approach for most routine messages? Why? L.O.❷
3. If a message contains both positive and negative information, what is the best way to present the negative information? L.O.❸
4. How can you avoid sounding insincere when writing a goodwill message? L.O.❹
5. What are eight tips for writing procedures? L.O.❹

## Apply Your Knowledge

To review chapter content related to each question, refer to the indicated Learning Objective.

1. Every time you send a routine request to one of your co-workers, he fails to comply. His lack of response is beginning to affect your job performance. Should you send him an email message to ask what's wrong? Complain to your supervisor about his uncooperative attitude? Arrange a face-to-face meeting with him? Bring up the problem at the next staff meeting? Explain. L.O.❷

2. Your company's error cost an important business customer a new client; you know it, and your customer knows it. Do you apologize, or do you refer to the incident in a positive light without admitting any responsibility? Briefly explain. L.O.❹
3. You want to put out a news release about your company's latest product. What advantages would you gain by making it a social media release? L.O.❹

## Practise Your Skills

### EXERCISES FOR PERFECTING YOUR WRITING

To review chapter content related to each set of exercises, refer to the indicated Learning Objective. In some instances, supporting information will be found in another chapter, as indicated.

**Revising Messages: Direct Approach** L.O.❶ Revise the following short email messages so that they are more direct and concise. Develop a subject line for each revised message.

1. I'm contacting you about your recent order for a High Country backpack. You didn't tell us which backpack you wanted, and you know we make a lot of different ones. We have the canvas models with the plastic frames and vinyl trim, and we have the canvas models with leather trim, and we have the ones that have more pockets than the other ones. Plus they come in lots of different colours. Also they make the ones that are large for a big-boned person and the smaller versions for little women or kids.

2. Thank you for contacting us about the difficulty you had collecting your luggage at the Pearson airport. We are very sorry for the inconvenience this has caused you. Travelling can create problems of this sort regardless of how careful the airline personnel might be. To receive compensation, please send us a detailed list of the items that you lost and complete the following questionnaire. You can email it back to us.

3. Sorry it took us so long to get back to you. We were flooded with résumés. Anyway, your résumé made the final 10, and after meeting three hours yesterday, we've decided we'd like to meet with you. What is your schedule like for next week? Can you come in for an interview on June 15 at 3:00 p.m.? Please get back to us by the end of this work week and let us know if you will be able to attend. As you can imagine, this is our busy season.

**Revising Messages: Direct Approach** L.O.❶ Rewrite the following sentences so that they are direct and concise.

4. We wanted to invite you to our special 40 percent off by-invitation-only sale. The sale is taking place on November 9.
5. We wanted to let you know that we are giving an iPod with every $100 donation you make to our radio station.

6. The director planned to go to the meeting that will be held on Monday at a little before 11:00 a.m.

7. In today's meeting, we were happy to have the opportunity to welcome Paul Eccelson. He reviewed some of the newest types of order forms. If you have any questions about these new forms, feel free to call him at his office.

**Identifying Strategies: Teamwork** L.O.❶, **Chapter 2** With another student, conduct an audience analysis of the following message topic: a notice to all employees announcing that to avoid layoffs, the company will institute a 10 percent salary reduction for the next six months.

8. If the company is small and all employees work in the same location, which medium would you recommend for communicating this message?

9. If the company is large and employees work in a variety of locations around the world, which medium would you recommend for communicating this message?

10. How is the audience likely to respond to this message?

11. Based on this audience analysis, would you use the direct or the indirect approach for this message? Explain your reasoning.

**Revising Messages: Closing Paragraphs** L.O.❶ Rewrite each of the following closing paragraphs to be concise, courteous, and specific.

12. I need your response sometime soon so I can order the parts in time for your service appointment. Otherwise your air-conditioning system may not be in tip-top condition for the start of the summer season.

13. Thank you in advance for sending me as much information as you can about your products. I look forward to receiving your package in the very near future.

14. To schedule an appointment with one of our knowledgeable mortgage specialists in your area, you can always call our hotline at 1-800-555-8765. This is also the number to call if you have more questions about mortgage rates, closing procedures, or any other aspect of the mortgage process. Remember, we're here to make the home-buying experience as painless as possible.

## ACTIVITIES

Each activity is labelled according to the primary skill or skills you will need to use. To review relevant chapter content, you can refer to the indicated Learning Objective. In some instances, supporting information will be found in another chapter, as indicated.

1. **Message Strategies: Making Routine Requests; Completing: Evaluating Content, Organization, and Tone** L.O.❷, **Chapter 5** Analyze the strengths and weaknesses of this message and then revise it so that it follows this chapter's guidelines for routine requests for information:

> I'm fed up with the mistakes that our current accounting firm makes. I run a small construction company, and I don't have time to double-check every bookkeeping entry and call the accountants a dozen times when they won't return my messages. Please explain how your firm would do a better job than my current accountants. You have a good reputation among homebuilders, but before I consider hiring you to take over my accounting, I need to know that you care about quality work and good customer service.

2. **Message Strategies: Making Routine Requests; Completing: Evaluating Content, Organization, and Tone** L.O.❷, **Chapter 5** Analyze the strengths and weaknesses of this message and then revise it so that it follows this chapter's guidelines for routine requests for information:

> I'm contacting you about your recent email request for technical support on your cable internet service. Part of the problem we have in tech support is trying to figure out exactly what each customer's specific problem is so that we can troubleshoot quickly and get you back in business as quickly as possible. You may have noticed that in the online support request form, there are a number of fields to enter your type of computer, operating system, memory, and so on. While you did tell us you were experiencing slow download speeds during certain times of the day, you didn't tell us which times specifically, nor did you complete all the fields telling us about your computer. Please return to our support website and resubmit your request, being sure to provide all the necessary information; then we'll be able to help you.

3. **Message Strategies: Writing Routine Replies; Completing: Evaluating Content, Organization, and Tone** L.O.❹, **Chapter 5** Analyze the strengths and weaknesses of this message and then revise it so that it follows this chapter's guidelines for responding to requests for adjustments:

We read your letter, requesting your deposit refund. We couldn't figure out why you hadn't received it, so we talked to our maintenance engineer, as you suggested. He said you had left one of the doors off the hinges in your apartment in order to get a large sofa through the door. He also confirmed that you had paid him $5.00 to replace the door since you had to turn in the U-Haul trailer and were in a big hurry.

This entire situation really was caused by a lack of communication between our housekeeping inspector and the maintenance engineer. All we knew was that the door was off the hinges when it was inspected by Sally Tarnley. You know that our policy states that if anything is wrong with the apartment, we keep the deposit. We had no way of knowing that George just hadn't gotten around to replacing the door.

But we have good news. We approved the deposit refund, which will be mailed to you

from our home office in Red Deer, Alberta. I'm not sure how long that will take, however. If you don't receive the cheque by the end of next month, give me a call.

Next time, it's really a good idea to stay with your apartment until it's inspected, as stipulated in your lease agreement. That way, you'll be sure to receive your refund when you expect it. Hope you have a good summer.

4. **Message Strategies: Writing Positive Messages; Media Skills: Microblogging** L.O.❹, **Chapter 6** Locate an online announcement for a new product that you find interesting or useful. Read enough about the product to be able to describe it to someone else in your own words and then write four Twitter tweets: one to introduce the product to your followers and three follow-up tweets that describe three particularly compelling features or benefits of the product.

# CASES

**Apply the three-step writing process to the following cases, as assigned by your instructor.**

### 1. Message Strategies: Requesting a Recommendation L.O.❷

Assume you have completed your educational program and have landed an interview with an employer who has asked you to supply a letter of recommendation from one of your professors or past employers. You are quite excited about the job prospect and carefully consider who to ask for the letter. Be prepared to explain why you are asking this particular person and summarize three or four of your strengths that you could include in your request. Choose a professor or employer who knows your work and who you think would be a strong reference. Make up any details you need and write the letter.

▌**Text Messaging Skills**
### 2. Message Strategies: Writing Positive Messages L.O.❹

You are an assistant manager in a fine restaurant in Toronto and have accompanied your boss to the Vancouver International Wine Festival, a premier event in the wine industry. More than 711 wines and 197 wineries from 14 countries are represented at this year's festival. Trade professionals and collectors join thousands from the general public to taste new products. Your boss is hoping to select several wineries to feature at the restaurant and the two of

you have split up to find specific varietals of particular interest to the restaurant. He is checking out wines from the Alsace and you are concentrating on Pinots—over 160 different Pinots are being poured at the show! You have discovered one that you believe to be exceptional value, but there is not much stock of it. You want to be sure your boss gets to it in time before it's gone. You've picked up quite a bit of buzz about the wine from the people standing around the booth, and no wonder. It tastes like a much more expensive wine than it is. You have noted the price ($35 per bottle), the quantity available (4 cases), the shipping times to Toronto (two months), the Wine Spectator ratings the 2012 vintage scored (92), the winery representative's name (Zara), and the booth number (276 in the Main Hall).

**YOUR TASK**   Compose a text message to your boss alerting him about the wine and asking him to meet you at the booth. Keep in mind that your text messaging service limits messages to 160 characters, including spaces and punctuation.[8]

▌**Email Skills**
### 3. Message Strategies: Making Routine Requests L.O.❷

You head up the corporate marketing department for a nationwide chain of clothing stores. The company has decided to launch a new store-within-a-store concept, in which a small section of each store will showcase "business casual" clothing. To ensure a successful launch of this new strategy, you want to get input from the best retailing minds in the company. You also know it's important to get regional insights from around the country, because a merchandising strategy that works in one area might not succeed in another.

**YOUR TASK**   Write an email message to all 87 store managers, asking them to each nominate one person to serve on an advisory team (managers can nominate themselves if they are local market experts). Explain that you want to find people with at least five years of retailing experience, a good understanding of the local business climate, and thorough knowledge of the local retail competition. In addition, the best candidates will be good team players who are comfortable collaborating long distance, using virtual meeting technologies. Also, explain that while you are asking each of the 87 stores to nominate someone, the team will be limited to no more than eight people. You've met many of the store managers, but not all of them, so be sure to introduce yourself at the beginning of the message.

‖ **Letter Writing Skills**
**4. Message Strategies: Making Routine Requests** L.O.❷

As a consumer, you've probably bought something that didn't work right or paid for a service that didn't turn out the way you expected. Maybe it was a pair of jeans with a rip in a seam that you didn't find until you got home or a watch that broke a week after you bought it. Or maybe your family hired a lawn service to do some yard work, and no one from the company showed up on the day promised. When the crew finally appeared, they did not do what they'd been hired for but did other things that wound up damaging valuable plants. In any of these situations, you'd be wise to write a claim letter asking for a refund, repair, replacement, or other adjustment. You'd need to include all the details of the transaction, plus your contact address and phone number.

**YOUR TASK**   To practise writing claim letters, choose an experience like this from your own background or make up details for these imaginary situations. If your experience is real, you might want to mail the letter. The reply you receive will provide a good test of your claim-writing skills.

‖ **Podcasting Skills**
**5. Message Strategies: Writing Routine Messages** L.O.❹, **Chapter 6**

As a training specialist in the human resources department at Rocky Mountain Cycles, you're always on the lookout for new ways to help employees learn vital job skills. While watching a production worker page through a training manual, learning how to assemble a new bike, you get what seems to be a great idea: record the assembly instructions as audio files that workers can listen to while performing the necessary steps. With audio instructions, they wouldn't need to keep shifting their eyes between the product and the manual—and constantly losing their place. They could focus on the product and listen for each instruction. Plus, the new system wouldn't cost much at all; any computer can record the audio files, and you'd simply make them available on an intranet site for download onto iPods or other digital music players.

**YOUR TASK**   You immediately run your new idea past your boss, who has heard about podcasting but isn't sure it is appropriate for business training. He asks you to prove the viability of the idea by recording a demonstration. Choose a process that you engage in yourself— anything from replacing the strings on a guitar to sewing a quilt to changing the oil in a car—and write a brief (one page or less) description of the process that could be recorded as an audio file. Think carefully about the limitations of the audio format as a replacement for printed text (for instance, do you need to tell people to pause the audio while they perform each task?). If your instructor directs, record your podcast and submit the audio file.

‖ **Email Skills** ‖ **Team Skills**
**6. Message Strategies: Writing Routine Replies; Collaboration: Team Projects** L.O.❹, **Chapter 2**

You are director of customer services at Highway Bytes, which markets a series of small, handlebar-mounted computers for bicyclists. These Cycle Computers do many things, from computing speed and distance travelled to displaying street maps with voice-controlled GPS navigation. Serious cyclists love them, and your company is growing so fast that you can't keep up with all the customer service requests you receive every day. Your boss wants to not only speed up response time but also reduce staffing costs. She also wants to allow your technical experts the time they need to focus on the most difficult and important questions.

You've just been reading about automated response systems, and you quickly review a few articles before discussing the options with your boss. Artificial intelligence researchers have been working for decades to design systems that can actually converse with customers, ask questions, and respond to requests. Some of today's systems have vocabularies of thousands of words and the ability to understand simple sentences. For example, *chatterbots* are automated bots that can mimic human conversation, to a degree.

Unfortunately, even though chatterbots hold a lot of promise, human communication is so complex that a truly automated customer service agent could take years to perfect (and may even prove to be impossible). However, the simplest automated systems, called *autoresponders*, are fast and extremely inexpensive. They have no built-in intelligence, so they do nothing more than send back the same reply to every message they receive.

You explain to your boss that although some of the messages you receive require the attention of your product specialists, many are simply requests for straightforward information. In fact, the customer service staff already answers some 70 percent of email queries with three ready-made attachments:

- **Installing Your Cycle Computer.** Gives customers advice on installing the cycle computer the first time or reinstalling it on a new bike. In most cases, the computer and wheel sensor bolt directly to the bike without modification, but certain bikes require extra work.

- **Troubleshooting Your Cycle Computer.** Provides a step-by-step guide to figuring out what might be wrong with a malfunctioning cycle computer. Most problems are simple, such as dead batteries or loose wires, but others are beyond the capabilities of your typical customer.

- **Upgrading the Software in Your Cycle Computer.** Tells customers how to attach the cycle computer to their computer and download new software from Highway Bytes.

Your boss is enthusiastic when you explain that you can program your current email system to look for specific words in incoming messages and then respond, based on what it finds. For example, if a customer message contains the word *installation*, you can program the system to reply with the *Installing Your Cycle Computer* attachment. This reconfigured system should be able to handle a sizable portion of the hundreds of emails your customer service group gets every month.

**YOUR TASK** With a team assigned by your instructor, first compile a list of key words that you'll want your email system to look for. You'll need to be creative and spend some time with a thesaurus. Identify all the words and word combinations that could identify a message pertaining to one of the three subject areas. For instance, the word *attach* would probably indicate a need for the installation material, whereas *new software* would most likely suggest a need for the upgrade attachment.

Second, draft three short email messages to accompany each ready-made attachment, explaining that the attached document answers the most common questions on a particular subject (installation, troubleshooting, or upgrading). Your messages should invite recipients to write back if the attached document doesn't solve the problem, and don't forget to provide the email address: support2@highwaybytes.com.

Third, draft a fourth message to be sent out whenever your new system is unable to figure out what the customer is asking for. Simply thank the customer for writing and explain that the query will be passed on to a customer service specialist who will respond shortly.

**▌ Blogging Skills**

## 7. Message Strategies: Writing Positive Messages L.O.❹, Chapter 2

You are normally an easygoing manager who gives your employees a lot of leeway in using their own personal communication styles. However, the weekly staff meeting this morning pushed you over the edge. People were interrupting one another, asking questions that had already been answered, sending text messages during presentations, and exhibiting just about every other poor listening habit imaginable.

**YOUR TASK** Review the advice in Chapter 2 on good listening skills, then write a post for the internal company blog. Emphasize the importance of effective listening and list at least five steps your employees can take to become better listeners.

**▌ Blogging Skills ▌ Portfolio Builder**

## 8. Message Strategies: Writing Positive Messages L.O.❹

Mountain Equipment Co-op (MEC) has become known as one of the greenest companies in Canada, adopting a variety of technologies and practices that have reduced its energy usage greatly.

**YOUR TASK** Write a one- or two-paragraph post for an internal blog for MEC, letting employees know how well the company is doing in its efforts to reduce energy usage and thanking employees for the energy-saving ideas they've submitted and the individual efforts they have made to reduce, reuse, and recycle. Learn more about the company's accomplishments by reading their "Sustainability" material at **www.mec.ca**.[9]

**▌ Procedure Writing Skills**

## 9. Message Strategies: Revising a Procedure L.O.❹

Revise the poorly written procedure below. Use the guidelines given in the chapter to identify problems in planning, style, and design, and then reorganize and rewrite the procedures using effective document design. Buy More Industries is an electronics retail operation with a full-time staff of 40 and a part-time staff of 80. The employees are between the ages of 18 and 40. Incorporate these procedures into an email message to all employees from the general manager.

### Evacuations

It is important that all personnel are in compliance with Buy More Industries' Evacuation Procedures in the event of an emergency. An Emergency Team is responsible for shutting down the building but there are some procedures for general staff too. It is imperative that the building be exited and that the staff be congregated with their fellow department staff members in the designated area. The gathering area can be found outside the building by the Pay Station in Parking Lot A. It is advisable that doors must be shut when leaving the area. When the emergency alarm is sounded all staff are to follow the commands of the Emergency Team who have had emergency preparedness training and who will take charge of the removal of all customers from the store. It is incumbent upon all staff to lock any registers and display cabinets that are beside them when the alarm goes off but it is not expected that staff would put themselves in danger to stay in the area or return to the area when the alarm is sounding to go back in to lock up. Don't be alarmed. Panic adds to the problem and is not helpful. It is imperative that staff check in with their supervisors at the gathering area. It is imperative that staff do not go back into the building until the "All Clear" signal has sounded. It is imperative that staff assist any person who is having physical difficulty leaving the building. Emergency Team Captains wear high visibility vests so you can see them in a crowd. Your safety is paramount to Buy More.

### Social Networking Skills

**10. Message Strategies: Writing Positive Messages; Composition Modes: Summarizing L.O.❹**

As energy costs trend ever upward and more people become attuned to the environmental and geopolitical complexities of petroleum-based energy, interest in solar, wind, and other alternative energy sources continues to grow. In locations with high *insolation*, a measure of cumulative sunlight, solar panels can be cost-effective solutions over the long term. However, the upfront costs are still daunting for most homeowners. To help lower the entry barrier, Grasshopper Solar in Ontario finances or sells solar panels to homeowners who then can benefit from the Ontario government's "Feed-in-Tariff" (FIT) Program.[10]

**YOUR TASK**   Visit www.grasshoppersolar.com, click on Residential to read about their program. Next, study Grasshopper Solar's presence on Facebook (www.facebook.com/grasshoppersolar) to get a feel for how the company presents itself in a social networking environment. Now assume that you have been assigned the task of writing a brief summary of the purchase or financing program that will appear on the Notes tab of Grasshopper Solar's Facebook page. In your own words, and in 200 words or less, write an introduction to their program options and email it to your instructor.

### Procedure Writing Skills

**11. Message Strategies: Writing Procedures L.O.❹**

You work at AMC Financial Services, a tax preparation firm with 150 employees. On the way to a human resources meeting this morning, the general manager took you aside to complain about some procedures that were not being followed.

"You've got to let staff know in writing that maintaining confidentiality is crucial in this office," she announced. You're her assistant, but you had no idea what she was talking about so you asked, "What's the problem?"

"Well," she said, "I just walked through the client services department, past two people's desks when they were away getting coffee, and saw that they had left client files open in plain view for anyone to read. That just won't do. Our clients' financial information is in those files. Not only that—I checked to see if the files had been signed out in the log book and they hadn't! As well, the staff with the files were not listed in the log book as having clearance to handle them in the first place. We have rules about this stuff."

You replied, "We have had a lot of turnover in the last few months, and with the tax season in full swing it may be that staff cut a few corners to get the work done in time."

"But the only person who can handle a client file is the representative assigned to it and who has taken the online training and been certified (and given a certification ID) by the human resources department. The certification ID has to be recorded in the log book each time the rep takes a file out of the central filing system. These are the basics and it is clear that staff need a refresher on these procedures. And hey, we never leave files lying around—they have to be locked in a file drawer if not in use by the trained rep. This is basic stuff."

You answered, "OK, I see your point. We have had a good informal system that has worked quite well, but given all the changes in staff we can't rely on people knowing some of these procedures anymore, so you're right, we need to provide some written procedures for handling files. I'll send out an email later today documenting these procedures."

**YOUR TASK** Write an email message to staff documenting procedures for handling client files. Make up any specific details that you feel should be added to the procedures mentioned above. How can you use listing to make the procedures easy to read? How can you introduce the procedures so that staff will be receptive?

▌Email Skills ▌Portfolio Builder

**12. Message Strategies: Using the Direct Approach; Compositional Modes: Comments & Critiques** L.O.❸, **Chapter 6**

As the president of the local Minor Hockey Association, you lead an organization with hundreds of youth players, coaches, officials, and parents. You have to keep up with Hockey Canada policy changes, regulation changes, requirements for screening coaches and certifying officials, and controversies involving the sport. Just this morning, an item in the local newspaper got your attention. A prominent member of the hockey club—a very competitive parent—was quoted saying that the rules prohibiting body checking in Pee Wee Hockey (11- and 12-year-olds) were preventing the kids from learning the skills they would need in the next levels. He claimed that all the concerns about concussion and injury were "baloney" and that in the old days you would just call it "getting your bell rung" if you took a hit to the head. This kind of talk drives you crazy because you know that body checking in this age group causes many injuries and concussions. Lately, you read a couple of studies, one published by the Canadian Medical Association and the other in the *Journal of the*

*American Medical Association.* That study, based on 2451 Pee Wee players in Alberta, where the checking was allowed, and in Quebec, where it was not, concluded that the injury rate was *three times higher* when body checking was permitted. You also know some players who were concussed and have been asked to play again right away rather than take the appropriate time for healing and many who have suffered long-term effects from head injuries. You think many parents, coaches, and players should learn more about concussions.

**YOUR TASK** Write a news release (no more than 300 words) that can be posted on your Minor Hockey Association's Facebook page. Correct the impressions that concussions are not serious and that children as young as 11 and 12 should be learning to body check. If this topic interests you, look up additional facts about concussion rates in youth hockey or soccer, or another sport you are interested in.[11]

▌Media Skills ▌Social Networking Skills

**13. Message Strategies: Writing a News Release** L.O.❹, **Chapter 6**

Assume you are promoting the community fair described in Chapter 6, Case #3, on page 145. Write a news release to post on your group's website to let the public know about the event and encourage them to attend. Make up any details you need and include a photo or a short video clip. If your group had the budget to make the news release a social media release, what features would you add?

# BUSINESS COMMUNICATION NOTEBOOK

# Intercultural Communication

## How Direct Is Too Direct?

Is it possible to be too direct, even if you're simply requesting information? At an event in Mexico, the president of the United States spoke bluntly of political realities, but the president of France spoke more abstractly—his style more grand, his words more beautiful. One man addressed the issues directly; the other was less direct. Which one had greater impact?

Neither speech changed global relationships, but the American president was seen as a product of his outspoken culture, whereas the French president was seen as at least making his listeners feel better for a

while. Countries such as France, Mexico, Japan, Saudi Arabia, Italy, and the Philippines all tend toward high-context cultures (see discussion in Chapter 1). That is, people in those countries depend on shared knowledge and inferred messages to communicate; they gather meaning more from context and less from direct statement. On a continuum of high- to low-context cultures, Canada falls between France, Britain, and the United States, having been influenced by our English and French heritage and by our proximity to the United States. So, although people in the United States believe that being direct is civil, considerate, and honest, people in high-context cultures and mid-context cultures sometimes view that same directness as abrupt, rude, and intrusive. In high-context cultures, don't say outright, "You are wrong." People know when they've made a mistake, but if you put it into words in high-context cultures, you cause them to lose face.

To determine whether your international audience will appreciate a direct or an implied message, consider your audience's attitudes toward four factors: destiny, time, authority, and logic.

- **Destiny.** Do people in this culture believe they can control events themselves? Or are events seen as predetermined and uncontrollable? If you're supervising employees who believe that a construction deadline is controlled by fate, they may not understand your crisp requests to stay on schedule.
- **Time.** Do people in this culture believe that time is exact, precise, and not to be wasted? Or do they view time as relative, relaxed, and necessary for developing interpersonal relationships? If you believe that time is money and you try to get straight to business with your Japanese manager, he may overlook your message because of your lack of relationship skills and disregard for social propriety.
- **Authority.** Do the people in this culture conduct business more autocratically or more democratically? In Mexico, rank and status are highly valued, so when communicating with people who have less authority than you do, you may need to be even more direct than you're used to being in Canada. And when communicating with people who have more authority than you do, you may need to be much less direct than you're used to being in Canada.

- **Logic.** Do the people in this culture pursue logic in a straight line from point A to point B? Or do they communicate in circular or spiral patterns of logic?

You may need to ask not only how direct to be in written messages but also whether to write at all; perhaps a phone call or a visit would be more appropriate. By finding out how much or how little a culture tends toward high-context communication, you can decide whether to be direct or to rely on nuance.

## Applications for Success

For more information on the subject of intercultural communication, go to www.executiveplanet.com.

1. Research a high-context culture such as Japan, Korea, or China, and write a one- or two-paragraph summary of how someone in that culture would go about requesting information.
2. Germany is a low-context culture; by comparison, France and England are more high context. These three translations of the same message were posted on a lawn in Switzerland:

   a. German: "Walking on the grass is forbidden."
   b. English: "Please do not walk on the grass."
   c. French: "Those who respect their environment will avoid walking on the grass."

   How does the language of each sign reflect the way information is conveyed in the cultural context of each nation? Write a brief (two- to three-paragraph) explanation.

# 8

# Writing Negative Messages

## LEARNING OBJECTIVES

*After studying this chapter, you will be able to*

1. Apply the three-step writing process to negative messages.
2. Explain how to use the direct approach effectively when conveying negative news.
3. Explain how to use the indirect approach effectively when conveying negative news and explain how to avoid ethical problems when using this approach.
4. Describe successful strategies for sending negative messages on routine business matters.
5. List the important points to consider when conveying negative organizational news.
6. Describe an effective strategy for responding to negative information in a social media environment.

Communicating during a serious crisis is a challenge that relatively few managers will ever face, but every manager and many employees must convey negative information from time to time. Sharing unwelcome news is never pleasant, but it must be done, and learning how to do it with tact and sensitivity will make the task easier for you as a writer and easier for the recipients of your messages, too.

As Matt Rhodes of the London-based social media agency FreshNetworks suggests, your relationship with the audience is a crucial factor in the delivery of negative messages. For example, social media tools can be effective for communicating negative news and responding to crises and complaints, but they work best when you have already established a meaningful relationship with your stakeholders.[1]

## Using the Three-Step Writing Process for Negative Messages

Delivering negative information is rarely easy and never enjoyable, but with some helpful guidelines, you can craft messages that minimize negative reactions. When you need to deliver bad news, you have five goals: (1) to convey the bad news, (2) to gain acceptance for it, (3) to maintain as much goodwill as possible with your audience, (4) to maintain a good image for your organization, and, (5) if appropriate, to reduce or eliminate the need for future correspondence on the matter. Accomplishing all five goals requires careful attention to planning, writing, and completing your message.

## Step 1: Planning Negative Messages

When you need to convey negative news, you can't avoid the fact that your audience does not want to hear what you have to say. To minimize the damage to business relationships and to encourage the acceptance of your message, plan carefully. With a clear purpose and your audience's needs in mind, gather the information your audience will need in order to understand and accept your message.

Selecting the right medium is critical. For instance, experts advise that bad news for employees always be delivered in person whenever possible, both to show respect for the employees and to give them an opportunity to ask questions. Of course, delivering bad news is never easy, and an increasing number of managers appear to be using email and other electronic media to convey negative messages to employees.[2]

Finally, the organization of a negative message also requires particular care. One of the most critical planning decisions is choosing whether to use the direct or indirect approach (see Figure 8.1). A negative message using the **direct approach** opens with the bad news, proceeds to the reasons for the situation or the decision, and ends with a positive statement aimed at maintaining a good relationship with the audience. In contrast, the **indirect approach** opens with a *buffer* then builds up the reasons behind the bad news before presenting the bad news itself.

To help decide which approach to take in any situation you encounter, ask yourself the following questions:

- **Do you need to get the reader's attention immediately?** If the situation is an emergency, or if someone has ignored repeated messages, the direct approach can help you get attention quickly.
- **Does the recipient prefer a direct style of communication?** Some recipients prefer the direct approach no matter what, so if you know this, go with direct.
- **How important is this news to the reader?** For minor or routine scenarios, the direct approach is nearly always best. However, if the reader has an emotional investment in the situation or the consequences to the reader are considerable, the indirect approach is often better.
- **Will the bad news come as a shock?** The direct approach is fine for many business situations in which people understand the possibility of receiving bad news. However, if the bad news might come as a shock to readers, use the indirect approach to help them prepare for it.

Careful planning is necessary to avoid alienating your readers.

Choose the medium with care when preparing negative messages.

The appropriate organization helps readers accept your negative news.

Use the direct approach when your negative answer or information will have minimal personal impact; consider the indirect approach for more serious matters.

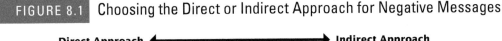

**FIGURE 8.1** Choosing the Direct or Indirect Approach for Negative Messages

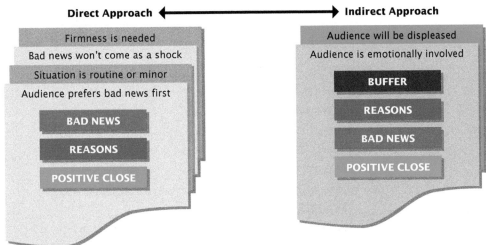

## FIGURE 8.2  Comparing the Direct and Indirect Approaches for Negative Messages

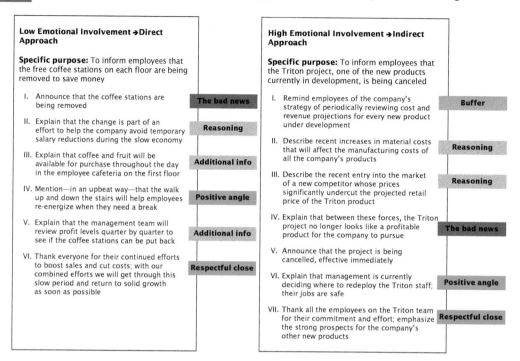

## Step 2: Writing Negative Messages

By writing clearly and sensitively, you can take some of the sting out of bad news and help your reader accept the decision and move on. If your credibility hasn't already been established with an audience, clarify your qualifications so message recipients won't question your authority or ability.

When you use language that conveys respect and avoids an accusing tone, you protect your audience's pride. This kind of communication etiquette is always important, but it demands special care with negative messages. Moreover, you can ease the sense of disappointment by using positive words rather than negative, counterproductive ones (see Table 8.1).

Choose your language carefully; it is possible to deliver negative news without being negative.

## Step 3: Completing Negative Messages

The need for careful attention to detail continues as you complete your message. Revise your content to make sure everything is clear, complete, and concise—even small flaws can be magnified in readers' minds as they react to your negative news. Produce clean,

## TABLE 8.1  Choosing Positive Words

| EXAMPLES OF NEGATIVE PHRASINGS | POSITIVE ALTERNATIVES |
|---|---|
| Your request *doesn't make any sense*. | Please clarify your request. |
| The *damage won't be fixed* for a week. | The item will be repaired next week. |
| Although it wasn't *our fault*, there will be an *unavoidable delay* in your order. | We will process your order as soon as we receive an aluminum shipment from our supplier, which we expect to happen within 10 days. |
| You are clearly *dissatisfied*. | I recognize that the product did not live up to your expectations. |
| I was *shocked* to learn that you're *unhappy*. | Thank you for sharing your concerns about your shopping experience. |
| *Unfortunately*, we haven't received it. | The item hasn't arrived yet. |
| The enclosed statement is *wrong*. | Please verify the enclosed statement and provide a correct copy. |

professional documents and proofread carefully to eliminate mistakes. Careless errors in a negative message can make a bad situation even worse by creating the impression that the sender doesn't care enough about the situation to invest the time and effort it takes to produce a professional-quality message. Finally, be sure to deliver messages promptly; withholding or delaying bad news can be unethical and even illegal.

# Using the Direct Approach for Negative Messages

LEARNING OBJECTIVE ❷
**Explain how to use the direct approach effectively when conveying negative news.**

With the direct approach, you open with a clear statement of the bad news, provide the reasons for the decision or situation, and end with a positive statement aimed at maintaining a good working relationship with the audience (see Figure 8.3). The message may also offer alternatives or a plan of action to fix the situation under discussion.

The primary advantage of the direct approach is efficiency. Direct messages take less time for you to write, and readers need less time to reach the main idea of the message.

## Opening with a Clear Statement of the Bad News

If you've chosen the direct approach to convey bad news, come right out and say it. Maintain a calm, professional tone that keeps the focus on the news and not on individual failures. Also, if necessary, remind the reader why you're writing.

## Providing Reasons and Additional Information

In most cases, follow the direct opening with an explanation of why the news is negative. The extent of your explanation depends on the nature of the news and your relationship with the reader. For example, if you want to preserve a long-standing relationship with an important customer, a detailed explanation could well be worth the extra effort such a message would require.

*The amount of detail you provide depends on your relationship with the audience.*

However, you will encounter some situations in which explaining negative news is neither appropriate nor helpful, such as when the reasons are confidential, excessively complicated, or irrelevant to the reader.

Should you apologize when delivering bad news? The answer isn't quite as simple as one might think. The notion of **apology** is hard to pin down. To some people, it simply

*The decision whether to apologize depends on a number of factors. If you do apologize, be sincere.*

---

| FIGURE 8.3 | Negative Message Using the Direct Approach |

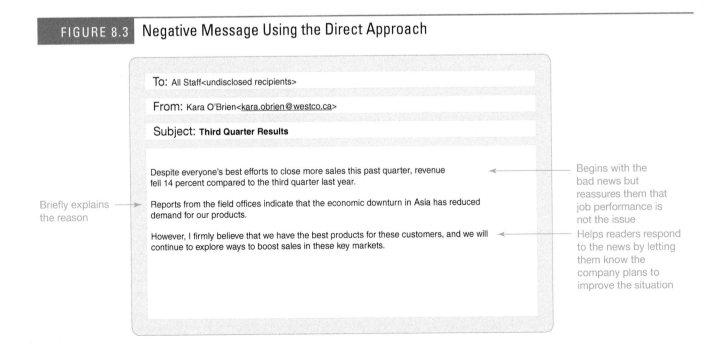

To: All Staff<undisclosed recipients>

From: Kara O'Brien<kara.obrien@westco.ca>

Subject: **Third Quarter Results**

Despite everyone's best efforts to close more sales this past quarter, revenue fell 14 percent compared to the third quarter last year.

Reports from the field offices indicate that the economic downturn in Asia has reduced demand for our products.

However, I firmly believe that we have the best products for these customers, and we will continue to explore ways to boost sales in these key markets.

*Briefly explains the reason*

*Begins with the bad news but reassures them that job performance is not the issue*

*Helps readers respond to the news by letting them know the company plans to improve the situation*

means an expression of sympathy that something negative has happened to another person. At the other extreme, it means admitting fault and taking responsibility for specific compensations or corrections to atone for the mistake.

Some experts have advised that companies never apologize, as apologies might be taken as confessions of guilt that could be used against them in lawsuits. However, six provinces and territories have laws that specifically prevent expressions of sympathy from being used as evidence of legal liability.[3]

The best general advice in the event of a mistake or accident is to immediately and sincerely express sympathy and offer help, if appropriate, without admitting guilt; then seek the advice of your company's lawyers before elaborating. A straightforward, sincere apology can go a long way toward healing wounds and rebuilding relationships. As one recent survey concluded, "The risks of making an apology are low, and the potential reward is high."[4]

If you do apologize, make it a real apology. Don't say "I'm sorry if anyone was offended" by what you did—this statement implies that you're not sorry at all and that it's the other party's fault for being offended.[5]

Note that you can also express sympathy with someone's plight without suggesting that you are to blame. For example, if a business customer damaged a product through misuse and suffered a financial loss as a result of not being able to use the product, you can say something along the lines of "I'm sorry to hear of your difficulties." This demonstrates sensitivity without accepting blame.

## Closing on a Positive Note

Close your message in a positive but respectful tone.

After you've explained the negative news, close the message in a manner that respects the impact the negative news is likely to have on the recipient. If appropriate, consider offering your readers an alternative solution if you can and if doing so is a good use of your time.

In many situations, an important aspect of a positive close is describing the actions being taken to avoid similar mistakes in the future. Offering such explanations can underline the sincerity of an apology because doing so signals that the person or organization is serious about not repeating the error.

# Using the Indirect Approach for Negative Messages

As noted earlier, the indirect approach helps readers prepare for the bad news by outlining the reasons for the situation before presenting the bad news itself. However, the indirect approach is not meant to obscure bad news, delay it, or limit your responsibility. The purpose of this approach is to ease the blow and help readers accept the news. When done poorly, the indirect approach can be disrespectful and even unethical. But when done well, it is a good example of the "you" attitude at work, since the communication is crafted with attention to both ethics and etiquette.

Use the indirect approach when some preparation will help your audience accept your bad news.

A buffer establishes common ground with the reader.

## Opening with a Buffer

A buffer gives you the opportunity to start the communication process without jumping immediately into the bad news.

Messages using the indirect approach open with a **buffer**, a neutral, noncontroversial statement that is closely related to the point of the message but doesn't convey the bad news. Depending on the circumstances, a good buffer can express your appreciation for being considered, assure the reader of your attention to the request, indicate your understanding of the reader's needs, introduce the general subject matter, or simply establish common ground with your readers. A good buffer also needs to be relevant and sincere. In contrast, a poorly written buffer might trivialize the reader's concerns, divert attention from the problem with insincere flattery or irrelevant material, or mislead the reader into thinking your message actually contains good news.

Poorly written buffers mislead or insult the reader.

Consider these possible responses to a manager of the order-fulfillment department who requested some temporary staffing help from your department (a request you won't be able to fulfill):

Our department shares your goal of processing orders quickly and efficiently. ◄——— Establishes common ground with the reader and validates the concerns that prompted the original request, without promising a positive answer

As a result of the last downsizing, every department in the company is running ◄——— shorthanded. Establishes common ground, but in a negative way that downplays the recipient's concerns

Your department is doing a great job over there, and I'd love to be able to help out. ◄——— Potentially misleads the reader into concluding that you will comply with the request

Those new provincial labour regulations are driving me crazy over here; how about in ◄——— your department? Trivializes the reader's concerns by opening with an irrelevant issue

Only the first of these buffers can be considered effective; the other three are likely to damage your relationship with the other manager. Table 8.2 shows several types of effective buffers you can use to tactfully open a negative message.

## Providing Reasons and Additional Information

An effective buffer serves as a transition to the next part of your message, in which you provide explanations and information that will culminate in your negative news. An ideal explanation section leads readers to your conclusion before you come right out and say it. The reader has followed your line of reasoning and is ready for the answer. By giving your reasons effectively, you help maintain focus on the issues at hand and defuse the emotions that always accompany significantly bad news.

*Phrase your reasons to signal the negative news ahead.*

As you lay out your reasons, guide your readers' responses by starting with the most positive points first and moving forward to increasingly negative ones. Provide enough detail for the audience to understand your reasons but be concise. Your reasons need to convince your audience that your decision is justified, fair, and logical.

*Whenever possible, don't use "company policy" as the reason for the bad news.*

| TABLE 8.2 | Types of Buffers | |
|---|---|---|
| BUFFER TYPE | STRATEGY | EXAMPLE |
| Agreement | Find a point on which you and the reader share similar views. | We both know how hard it is to make a profit in this industry. |
| Appreciation | Express sincere thanks for receiving something. | Your cheque for $127.17 arrived yesterday. Thank you. |
| Cooperation | Convey your willingness to help in any way you realistically can. | Employee Services is here to assist all associates with their health insurance, retirement planning, and continuing education needs. |
| Fairness | Assure the reader that you've closely examined and carefully considered the problem, or mention an appropriate action that has already been taken. | For the past week, we have had our bandwidth monitoring tools running around the clock to track your actual upload and download speeds. |
| Good news | Start with the part of your message that is favourable. | We have credited your account $14.95 to cover the cost of return shipping. |
| Praise | Find an attribute or an achievement to compliment. | The Stratford Group clearly has an impressive record of accomplishment in helping clients resolve financial reporting problems. |
| Resale | Favourably discuss the product or company related to the subject of the letter. | With their heavy-duty, full-suspension hardware and fine veneers, the desks and file cabinets in our Montclair line have long been popular with value-conscious professionals. |
| Understanding | Demonstrate that you understand the reader's goals and needs. | So that you can more easily find the printer with the features you need, we are enclosing a brochure that describes all the Epson printers currently available. |

Avoid hiding behind company policy to cushion your bad news. Skilled and sympathetic communicators explain company policy (without referring to it as "policy") so that the audience can try to meet the requirements at a later time. Consider this response to a job applicant:

> Because these management positions are quite challenging, the human resources department has researched the qualifications needed to succeed in them. The findings show that the two most important qualifications are a bachelor's degree in business administration and two years of supervisory experience.

This paragraph does a good job of stating reasons for the refusal because it:

- Provides enough detail to logically support the refusal
- Implies that the applicant is better off avoiding a position in which he or she might fail
- Doesn't apologize for the decision because no one is at fault
- Avoids negative personal statements (such as "You do not meet our requirements")

Even valid, well-thought-out reasons won't convince every reader in every situation, but if you've done a good job of laying out your reasoning, then you've done everything you can to prepare the reader for the main idea, which is the negative news itself.

## Continuing with a Clear Statement of the Bad News

After you've thoughtfully and logically established your reasons and readers are prepared to receive the bad news, you can use three techniques to convey the negative information as clearly and as kindly as possible. First, de-emphasize the bad news:

- Minimize the space or time devoted to the bad news, without trivializing it or withholding any important information. In other words, don't repeat it or belabour it.
- Subordinate bad news within a complex or compound sentence ("My department is already shorthanded, so I'll need all my staff for at least the next two months"). See Figure 8.4 for an example of using the indirect approach with subordination.
- Embed bad news in the middle of a paragraph or use parenthetical expressions ("Our profits, which are down, are only part of the picture").

However, keep in mind that it's possible to abuse this notion of de-emphasizing bad news. For instance, if the primary point of your message is that profits are down, it would be inappropriate to marginalize that news by burying it in the middle of a sentence. State the negative news clearly and then make a smooth transition to any positive news that might balance the story.

Second, use a conditional (*if* or *when*) statement to imply that the audience could have received, or might someday receive, a favourable answer ("When you have more managerial experience, you are welcome to reapply"). Such a statement could motivate the audience.

Third, emphasize what you *can* do or have done rather than what you can't or didn't do. Also, by implying the bad news, you may not need to actually state it, thereby making the bad news less personal ("Our development budget for next year is fully committed to our existing slate of projects"). However, make sure your audience understands the entire message—including the bad news. If an implied message might lead to uncertainty, state your decision in direct terms. Just be sure to avoid overly blunt statements that are likely to cause pain and anger:

| **Instead of This** | **Write This** |
|---|---|
| I *must refuse* your request. | I will be out of town on the day you need me. |
| We *must deny* your application. | The position has been filled. |
| I *am unable* to grant your request. | Contact us again when you have established… |
| We *cannot afford to* continue the program. | The program will conclude on May 1. |
| *Much as I would like to* attend… | Our budget meeting ends too late for me to attend. |
| We *must turn down* your extension request. | Please send in your payment by June 14. |

| FIGURE 8.4 | Refusing a Request Using an Indirect Approach |

**Qualcomm**
Information Services
1692 Bonaventure Avenue
Saint John, NB E2L 3V1
Voice: (506) 658-8219 Fax: (506) 658-8220

April 19, 2016

Mr. Tran Phuoc
774 Rue St. Lambert
Jonquière, QC G7X 7W2

Dear Mr. Phuoc:

**SHARING QUALCOMM INFORMATION**

Qualcomm Corporation appreciates and benefits from the research of companies such as yours. Your study sounds interesting, and the questionnaire is well developed.

Our board requires strict confidentiality of all sales information until quarterly reports are mailed to stockholders. We release press reports at the same time the quarterly reports go out, and we'll be sure to include you in all our future mailings. Although we cannot release projected figures, we are willing to share information that is part of the public record.

I've enclosed several of our past earnings reports for your inspection.

We look forward to seeing the results of your study. Please let us know if we can help in other ways.

Sincerely,

*Francis Newburgh*

Francis Newburgh
Director, Human Resources

Enclosure

*Annotations:*
- Buffer is supportive and appreciative
- Bad news is implied, not stated explicitly
- Body explains reason for decision without falling back on a blanket reference to company policy
- Close is friendly, positive, and helpful
- Bad news is subordinated

## Closing on a Positive Note

As in the direct approach, the close in the indirect approach offers an opportunity to emphasize your respect for your audience, even though you've just delivered unpleasant news. Express best wishes without ending on a falsely upbeat note. Suggest alternative solutions if such information is available. If you've asked readers to decide between alternatives or to take some action, make sure that they know what to do, when to do it, and how to do it. Whatever type of conclusion you use, follow these guidelines:

- **Avoid an uncertain conclusion.** If the situation or decision is final, avoid statements such as "I trust our decision is satisfactory," which imply that the matter is open to discussion or negotiation.
- **Manage future correspondence.** Encourage additional communication *only* if you're willing to discuss your decision further. If you're not, avoid wording such as "If you have further questions, please write."
- **Express optimism, if appropriate.** If the situation might improve in the future, share that with your readers if it's relevant.

A positive close
- Builds goodwill
- Offers a suggestion for action
- Provides a look toward the future
- Is sincere

- **Be sincere.** Steer clear of clichés that are insincere in view of the bad news. If you can't help, don't say, "If we can be of any help, please contact us."

Keep in mind that the close is the last thing audience members have to remember you by. Even though they're disappointed, leave them with the impression that they were treated with respect.

LEARNING OBJECTIVE 4
Describe successful strategies for sending negative messages on routine business matters.

# Sending Negative Messages on Routine Business Matters

Professionals and companies receive a wide variety of requests and cannot respond positively to every single one. In addition, mistakes and unforeseen circumstances can lead to delays and other minor problems that occur in the course of business. Occasionally, companies must send negative messages to suppliers and other parties. Whatever the purpose, crafting routine negative responses and messages quickly and graciously is an important skill for every businessperson.

## Making Negative Announcements on Routine Business Matters

Many negative messages are written in response to requests from an internal or external correspondent, but on occasion managers need to make unexpected announcements of a negative nature. For example, a company might decide to consolidate its materials purchasing with fewer suppliers and thereby need to tell several firms it will no longer be buying from them. Internally, management may need to announce the elimination of an employee benefit or other changes that employees will view negatively.

Although such announcements happen in the normal course of business, they are generally unexpected. Accordingly, except in the case of minor changes, the indirect approach is usually the better choice. Follow the steps outlined for indirect messages: open with a buffer that establishes some mutual ground between you and the reader, advance your reasoning, announce the change, and close with as much positive information and sentiment as appropriate under the circumstances.

## Rejecting Suggestions and Proposals

Rejecting suggestions and proposals, particularly if you asked for input, requires special care and tact because you need to maintain a positive working relationship.

Managers receive a variety of suggestions and proposals, both solicited and unsolicited, from internal and external sources. For an unsolicited proposal from an external source, you may not even need to respond if you don't already have a working relationship with the sender. However, if you need to reject a proposal you solicited, you owe the sender an explanation, and because the news will be unexpected, the indirect approach is better. In general, the closer your working relationship, the more thoughtful and complete you need to be in your response. For example, if you are rejecting a proposal from an employee, explain your reasons fully and carefully so that the employee can understand why the proposal was not accepted and so that you don't damage an important working relationship.

## Refusing Routine Requests

When writing routine negative responses, consider your relationship with the reader.

When you are unable to meet a routine request, your primary communication challenge is to give a clear negative response without generating negative feelings or damaging either your personal reputation or the company's. You often need to deliver negative information while maintaining a positive relationship with the other party.

The direct approach works best for most routine negative responses because it is simpler and more efficient. The indirect approach works best when the stakes are high for you or for the receiver, when you or your company has an established relationship with

**FIGURE 8.5** Effective Letter Declining a Routine Request

418 Glendale Drive, Don Mills, ON  M3B 2X2
Voice: (416) 447-4428    Fax: (416) 447-4429
www.infotech.com

March 5, 2016

Dr. Sandra Wofford, President
Haliburton College
333 Fairley Avenue
Don Mills, ON  M5T 4J6

Dear Dr. Wofford:

**YOUR REQUEST FOR A GRADUATION SITE**

InfoTech has been happy to support Haliburton College in many ways over the years, and we appreciate the opportunities you and your organization provide to students. Thank you for considering our grounds for your graduation ceremony.

Our company-wide sales meetings will be held during the weeks of May 29 and June 5. We will host more than 200 sales representatives and their families, and activities will take place at both our corporate campus and the Ramada Renaissance. As a result, our support staff will be devoting all their time and effort to these events.

My assistant, Roberta Seagers, suggests you contact the Municipal Botanical Gardens as a possible graduation site. She recommends calling Jerry Kane, director of public relations.

We remain firm in our commitment to the college and will continue to be a corporate partner. If we can help in any other way with graduation, please let us know.

Sincerely,

*May Yee Kwan*

May Yee Kwan
Public Relations Director

**Pointers for Writing Buffers and Giving Reasons**

*Buffer*

- Express appreciation, cooperation, fairness, good news, praise, resale, or understanding.
- Introduce a relevant topic.
- Avoid apologies and negative-sounding words *(won't, can't, unable to)*.
- Be brief and to the point.

*Reasons*

- Smooth the transition from the favourable buffer to the reasons.
- Show how the decision benefits your audience.
- Avoid apologies and expressions of sorrow or regret.
- Offer enough detail to show the logic of your position.
- Include only factual information and only business reasons, not personal ones.
- Carefully word the reasons so that readers can anticipate the bad news.

Buffers bad news by demonstrating respect and recapping request

States reason for the bad news explicitly and in detail

Suggests an alternative—showing that Kwan cares about the college and has given the matter some thought

Closes by renewing the corporation's future support

the person making the request, or when you're forced to decline a request that you might have said yes to in the past (see Figure 8.5).

## Handling Bad News About Transactions

Bad news about transactions is always unwelcome and usually unexpected. When you send such messages, you have three goals: (1) to modify the customer's expectations, (2) explain how you plan to resolve the situation, and (3) repair whatever damage might have been done to the business relationship.

The specific content and tone of each message can vary widely, depending on the nature of the transaction and your relationship with the customer. Telling an individual consumer that his new sweater will be arriving a week later than you promised is a much simpler task than telling Toyota that 30 000 transmission parts will be a week late, especially when you know the company will be forced to idle a multimillion-dollar production facility as a result.

Some negative messages regarding transactions carry significant business ramifications.

Your approach to bad news about business transactions depends on the customer's expectations.

If you've failed to meet expectations that you set for the customer, an element of apology should be considered.

If you haven't done anything specific to set the customer's expectations, the message simply needs to inform the customer of the situation, with little or no emphasis on apologies (see Figure 8.6).

If you did set the customer's expectations and now find that you can't meet them, your task is more complicated. In addition to resetting those expectations and explaining how you'll resolve the problem, you may need to include an element of apology. The scope of the apology depends on the magnitude of the mistake. For the customer who ordered the sweater, a simple apology followed by a clear statement of when the sweater will arrive would probably be sufficient. For larger business-to-business transactions, the customer may want an explanation of what went wrong to determine whether you'll be able to perform as you promise in the future.

To help repair the damage to the relationship and encourage repeat business, many companies offer discounts on future purchases, free merchandise, or other considerations. Even modest efforts can go a long way to rebuilding a customer's confidence in your company.

## Refusing Social Networking Recommendation Requests

Making recommendations in a social networking environment is more complicated than with a traditional recommendation letter because the endorsements you give become part of your online profile. On a network such as LinkedIn, others can see whom you've recommended and what you've written about these people. Much more so than with traditional letters, then, the recommendations you make in a social network become part of your personal brand.[6] Moreover, networks make it easy to find people and request recommendations, so chances are you will get more requests than you would have otherwise—and sometimes from people you don't know well.

Social networks have created new challenges in recommendation requests, but they also offer more flexibility in responding to these requests.

Fortunately, social networks give you a bit more flexibility when it comes to responding to these requests. One option is to simply ignore or delete the request. Of

---

**FIGURE 8.6**   **Effective Negative Message Regarding a Transaction**

Conveys the good news first in the buffer

Implies the actual bad news by telling the reader what's being done, not what can't be done

Includes resale information in a simple statement of a consumer benefit

Includes relevant contact information

To: Dr. Elizabeth Fawnworth <bethf@sandnet.net>

From: Suzanne Godfrey <sgodfrey@lazboy.com>

Subject: Order #REC-O-7814 (5 September 2016)

Dear Dr. Fawnworth:

Thank you for your order. The special edition recliner with customized leather trim is being shipped today.

The roll-around ottoman has proved to be one of our most popular items. Even though we've almost doubled production, we're still experiencing some lags. Your matching ottoman will be shipped no later than October 1, to arrive before Thanksgiving.

Your recliner and ottoman carry a lifetime guarantee, as do all La-Z-Boy products. You can check out our latest designs online at www.lazboy.com,

Please email or phone me if you'd like to talk about any of our special fabrics or custom designs. We look forward to serving you again in the future.

Cordially,
Suzanne Godfrey
Manager, Custom Designs
sgodfrey@lazboy.com
(416) 358-2899

States reasons for the delay by indicating that the ottoman is a popular choice

Cushions bad news with a pledge to ship by a definite time

Opens the door to future business in this positive close

course, if you do know a person, ignoring a request could create an uncomfortable situation, so you will need to decide each case based on your relationship with the requester. Another option is to refrain from making recommendations at all, and just letting people know this policy when they ask. Whatever you decide, remember that it is your choice.[7]

If you choose to make recommendations and want to respond to a request, you can write as much or as little information about the person as you are comfortable sharing. Unlike with an offline recommendation, you don't need to write a complete letter. You can write a brief statement, even just a single sentence that focuses on one positive aspect.[8] This flexibility allows you to respond positively in those situations in which you have mixed feelings about a person's overall abilities.

## Refusing Claims and Requests for Adjustment

Customers who make a claim or request an adjustment tend to be emotionally involved, so the indirect approach is usually the better choice. Your job as a writer is to avoid accepting responsibility for the unfortunate situation and yet avoid blaming or accusing the customer. To steer clear of these pitfalls, pay special attention to the tone of your letter. Demonstrate that you understand and have considered the complaint carefully and then rationally explain why you are refusing the request. Close on a respectful and action-oriented note (see Figure 8.7). And be sure to respond quickly. With so many instantaneous media choices at their disposal, some angry consumers

*Use the indirect approach in most cases of refusing a claim.*

---

**FIGURE 8.7   Effective Message Refusing a Claim**

To: rjhensen@mail.com

From: vera.shoemaker@sawshop.ca

Subject: re: Replacement Request -- DynaCut Saw Blade

Dear Mr. Hensen,

We received your request to replace the blade in your DynaCut plunge saw. I'm glad to hear that the saw has been a valuable tool in your flooring business. Thousands of contractors now rely on this saw for fast, precise cuts.

Your message indicated that you inadvertently struck a row of stainless steel fasteners while cutting into an oak floor. The DynaCut warranty covers product failures that result from regular use on wood, composites, and nonferrous metals, but all types of steel fall outside the coverage.

Our sharpening experts would be happy to look at your blade to see if it can sharpened. However, judging from your description, a replacement is probably in order. You can visit our online catalogue at www.sawshop.ca/blades to order a replacement. As a way to say thanks for shopping with us over the years, I've credited your account with a $25 discount coupon that can be applied to either sharpening service or the purchase of a replacement blade.

While you're on the website, you might also want to check out our line of handheld metal detectors. Contractors often find these devices pay for themselves quickly by locating hidden fasteners and hardware that can damage or destroy cutting tools.

Thank you for your business, and we look forward to serving you for many years.

Vera Shoemaker
Customer Service
The Saw Shop
(506) 777-1852
www.sawshop.ca

*Buffers the bad news by starting with a point on which the writer and reader agree*

*States the bad news indirectly while emphasizing the appropriate uses of the product*

*Gives the customer options for the next step, including a helpful link to the company's website*

*Closes on a positive note by thanking the customer and looking to the future*

*Subtly lets the customer know that he made a mistake, but doesn't blame him directly*

*Encourages future purchasing in a way that indicates a desire to help the customer avoid a repeat of this mistake*

**Pointers for Refusing Claims**
• Use the buffer to indicate that you received and understand the request or complaint.
• In the body, provide an accurate, objective account of the transaction.
• Make the refusal clear without being abrupt, insulting, or accusatory.
• Maintain an impersonal tone that doesn't offend the reader.
• Don't apologize for refusing, since your company hasn't done anything wrong.
• If appropriate, offer an alternative solution.
• Emphasize your continued desire for a positive relationship with the customer.
• Close with resale information if appropriate.
• Make any suggested actions easy for the reader to follow.

will take their complaints public if they don't hear back from you within a few days or even a few hours.[9]

Keep in mind that nothing positive can come out of antagonizing a customer, even one who has verbally abused you or your colleagues. Reject the claim or request for adjustment in a professional manner and move on to the next challenge.

LEARNING OBJECTIVE ⑤
List the important points to consider when conveying negative organizational news.

# Sending Negative Organizational News

As a manager you will find yourself in a variety of situations in which you have to convey bad news to individual employees or potential employees. Recipients have an emotional stake in these messages, so taking the indirect approach is usually advised. In addition, use great care in choosing your medium for each situation. For instance, email and other written forms let you control the message and avoid personal confrontation, but one-on-one conversations are often viewed as more sensitive and give both sides the opportunity to ask and answer questions.

When making negative announcements, follow these guidelines:

Negative organizational messages to external audiences often require extensive planning.

Give people as much time as possible to react to negative news.

- **Match your approach to the situation.** For example, in an emergency such as product tampering or a toxic spill, get to the point immediately.
- **Consider the unique needs of each group.** When a company or facility closes, for instance, employees need time to find new jobs, customers may need to find new suppliers, and community leaders may need to be prepared to help people who have lost their jobs.
- **Minimize the element of surprise whenever possible.** Give affected groups as much time as possible to prepare and respond.
- **If possible, give yourself enough time to plan and manage a response.** Make sure you're ready with answers to expected questions.
- **Look for positive angles but don't exude false optimism.** Laying off 10 000 people does not give them "an opportunity to explore new horizons." It's a traumatic event that can affect employees, their families, and their communities for years. The best you may be able to do is thank people for their past support and wish them well in the future.

Ask for legal help and other assistance if you're not sure how to handle a significant negative announcement.

- **Seek expert advice.** Many significant negative announcements have important technical, financial, or legal elements that require the expertise of lawyers, accountants, or other specialists.
- **Use multiple media to reach out to affected audiences.** Provide information through your normal communication network, such as your company website, Facebook page, and Twitter account, but also reach out and participate in conversations that are taking place elsewhere in the social media landscape.[10]
- **Be open and transparent.** During a crisis, companies need to be quick to respond and provide as much information as they can, making company officials available to the people affected by the crisis and to answer media questions. Consider the effect of the Montreal, Maine and Atlantic Railroad's response to the deaths of 50 people and devastation in Lac Megantic from the train disaster in July of 2013. The Chair of the Board arrived after four days and then delivered messages in English to the grieving town of largely French-speaking people.[11]

## REAL-TIME UPDATES

**Learn More by Watching This Video**

**Crisis communication and social media**

Professor Timothy Coombs discusses the role of social media in crisis communication. Go to http://real-timeupdates.com/bce6 and click on Learn More. If you are using MyBCommLab, you can access Real-Time Updates within Business Communication Resources.

Negative situations will test your skills as a communicator and as a business leader. Inspirational leaders try to seize such situations as opportunities to reshape or reinvigorate the organization, and they offer encouragement to those around them (see Figure 8.8).

| FIGURE 8.8 | Effective Internal Message Providing Bad News About Company Operations |

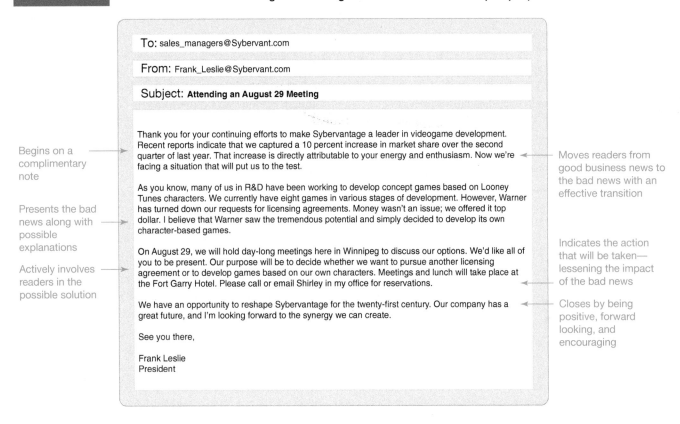

To: sales_managers@Sybervant.com

From: Frank_Leslie@Sybervant.com

Subject: **Attending an August 29 Meeting**

Begins on a complimentary note

Thank you for your continuing efforts to make Sybervantage a leader in videogame development. Recent reports indicate that we captured a 10 percent increase in market share over the second quarter of last year. That increase is directly attributable to your energy and enthusiasm. Now we're facing a situation that will put us to the test.

Moves readers from good business news to the bad news with an effective transition

Presents the bad news along with possible explanations

As you know, many of us in R&D have been working to develop concept games based on Looney Tunes characters. We currently have eight games in various stages of development. However, Warner has turned down our requests for licensing agreements. Money wasn't an issue; we offered it top dollar. I believe that Warner saw the tremendous potential and simply decided to develop its own character-based games.

Actively involves readers in the possible solution

On August 29, we will hold day-long meetings here in Winnipeg to discuss our options. We'd like all of you to be present. Our purpose will be to decide whether we want to pursue another licensing agreement or to develop games based on our own characters. Meetings and lunch will take place at the Fort Garry Hotel. Please call or email Shirley in my office for reservations.

Indicates the action that will be taken—lessening the impact of the bad news

We have an opportunity to reshape Sybervantage for the twenty-first century. Our company has a great future, and I'm looking forward to the synergy we can create.

Closes by being positive, forward looking, and encouraging

See you there,

Frank Leslie
President

# Responding to Negative Information in a Social Media Environment

LEARNING OBJECTIVE ⑥
Describe an effective strategy for responding to negative information in a social media environment.

For all the benefits they bring to business, social media and other communication technologies have created a major new challenge: responding to online rumours, false information, and attacks on a company's reputation. Consumers and other stakeholders can now communicate through blogs, Twitter, YouTube, social networking sites, advocacy sites such as http://makingchangeatwalmart.org, general complaint and feedback websites such as www.epinions.com, company-specific sites such as www.verizonpathetic.com, community Q&A sites such as http://getsatisfaction.com, and numerous e-commerce shopping sites that encourage product reviews.

Customers who feel they have been treated unfairly like these sites because they can use the public exposure as leverage. Many companies appreciate the feedback from these sites, and many actively seek out complaints to improve their products and operations. However, false rumours and unfair criticisms can spread around the world in a matter of minutes. And even when a company is being criticized fairly, it needs to respond with timely information for all affected stakeholders. For example, after a tragic accident involving its Deepwater Horizon oil well in the Gulf of Mexico in 2010, BP set up a special section on its website to provide updates on the progress toward capping the massive oil leak as well as information about how to submit a claim for economic damages that resulted from the spill.[12]

Responding to rumours and countering negative information requires an ongoing effort and case-by-case decisions about which messages require a response. To do this successfully, follow these four steps:[13]

Responding effectively to rumours and negative information requires continual engagement with stakeholders and careful decision making about which messages should get a response.

## REAL-TIME UPDATES

**Learn More by Watching This Video**

**Positive ways to engage when you pick up negative social commentary**

Aetna's Lauren Vargas talks about the challenges of moving a large corporation in a heavily regulated industry (health insurance) into social media, including the best ways to respond to negative comments online. Go to http://real-timeupdates.com/bce6 and click on Learn More. If you are using MyBCommLab, you can access Real-Time Updates within Business Communication Resources.

Respond by providing correct information and genuine efforts to resolve problems.

## REAL-TIME UPDATES

**Learn More by Visiting This Interactive Website**

**Watch the Twitter rumour mill in action**

These fascinating animations show the spread of true and untrue information on Twitter during a public crisis. Go to http://real-timeupdates.com/bce6 and click on Learn More. If you are using MyBCommLab, you can access Real-Time Updates within Business Communication Resources.

1. **Engage early, engage often.** Perhaps the most important step in responding to negative information has to be done *before* the negative information appears, and that is to engage with communities of stakeholders as a long-term strategy. Companies that have active, mutually beneficial relationships with customers and other interested parties are less likely to be attacked unfairly online and more likely to survive such attacks if they do occur. In contrast, companies that ignore constituents or jump into "spin doctoring" mode when a negative situation occurs don't have the same credibility as companies that have done the long, hard work of fostering relationships within their physical and online communities. Some companies set up special websites or sections on their sites to present their perspectives on public issues, either in response to critics or to head off potential criticism.

2. **Monitor the conversation.** If people are interested in what your company does, chances are they are blogging, tweeting, podcasting, posting videos, writing on Facebook Walls, and otherwise sharing their opinions about your company. Use RSS feeds, automated reputation analysis, and other technologies to listen to what people are saying.

3. **Evaluate negative messages.** When you encounter negative messages, resist the urge to fire back immediately. Instead, evaluate the source, the tone, and the content of the message and then choose a response that fits the situation. Try to distinguish between those whose only intent is to stir up conflict, those who are just ranting, those who are misinformed and spreading incorrect information, and those who had a negative experience with your company.

4. **Respond appropriately.** After you have assessed a negative message, make the appropriate response based on an overall public relations plan. For instance, don't respond to ranting. Respond to misguided messages with correct information. In some cases, the best response can be to contact a critic privately (through direct messaging on Twitter), for example, to attempt a resolution away from the public forum.

Whatever you do, keep in mind that positive reputations are an important asset and need to be diligently guarded and defended. Everybody has a voice now, and some of those voices don't care to play by the rules of ethical communication.

## LEARNING OBJECTIVES: Check Your Progress

**❶ OBJECTIVE Apply the three-step writing process to negative messages.**

Because the way you say a negative message can be even more damaging than the fact that you're saying it, planning these messages is crucial. Make sure your purpose is specific and use an appropriate medium to fit the message. Collect all the facts necessary to support your negative decision, adapt your tone to the situation, and choose the optimum approach. Use positive words to construct diplomatic sentences and pay close attention to quality.

**❷ OBJECTIVE Explain how to use the direct approach effectively when conveying negative news.**

The direct approach puts the bad news up front, follows with the reasons, and closes with a positive statement. Even though it is direct, the message should be considerate and polite.

**③ OBJECTIVE** Explain how to use the indirect approach effectively when conveying negative news and explain how to avoid ethical problems when using this approach.

The indirect approach begins with a buffer, explains the reasons, clearly states the negative news, and closes with a positive statement. If the bad news is not unexpected, the direct approach is usually fine, but if the news is shocking or painful, the indirect approach is better. When using the indirect approach, pay careful attention to avoid obscuring the bad news, trivializing the audience's concerns, or even misleading your audience into thinking you're actually delivering good news. Remember that the purpose of the indirect approach is to cushion the blow, not to avoid delivering it.

**④ OBJECTIVE** Describe successful strategies for sending negative messages on routine business matters.

For making negative announcements on routine business matters, the indirect approach is usually preferred, unless the news has minor consequences for the audience. For rejecting suggestions or proposals when you requested input or it came from someone with whom you have an established relationship, the indirect approach is the right choice because it allows you to gently reset the other party's expectations.

For refusing routine requests, the direct approach is usually sufficient, except when the matter is significant, you or your company have an established relationship with the person making the request, or you're forced to decline a request that you might have said yes to in the past.

When conveying bad news about transactions, you need to modify the customer's expectations, explain how you plan to resolve the situation, and repair whatever damage might have been done to the business relationship. Whether or not you should apologize depends in part on the magnitude of the situation and whether you previously established specific expectations about the transaction.

When refusing a claim or a request for adjustment, the indirect approach is usually preferred because the other party is emotionally involved and expects you to respond positively. Demonstrate that you understand and have considered the complaint carefully and then rationally and calmly explain why you are refusing the request.

You have some flexibility when responding to requests for recommendations or endorsements on social networks. You can choose to ignore the request if you don't know the person, you can decline the request as a matter of personal policy, you can write a full recommendation if that matches your assessment of the person, or you can write a limited recommendation on just one or a few aspects of the person's capabilities.

**⑤ OBJECTIVE** List the important points to consider when conveying negative organizational news.

When communicating negative organizational news, (1) match your approach to the situation, (2) consider the unique needs of each group, (3) minimize the element of surprise whenever possible so that affected groups have time to prepare and respond, (4) give yourself as much time as possible to plan and manage a response, (5) make sure you're ready with answers to expected questions, (6) look for positive angles but don't exude false optimism, (7) seek expert advice, and (8) use multiple media to reach out to affected audiences.

**⑥ OBJECTIVE** Describe an effective strategy for responding to negative information in a social media environment.

When responding to negative information in social media, (1) be sure you are engaged with important stakeholders *before* negative situations appear, (2) monitor the conversations taking place about your company and its products, and (3) evaluate negative messages before responding. After evaluating negative messages, take the appropriate response based on an overall public relations plan. Some messages are better ignored, whereas others should be addressed immediately with corrective information.

**MyBCommLab®** Go to MyBCommLab for everything you need to help you succeed in the job you've always wanted! Tools and resources include the following:
• Writing Activities • Document Makeovers
• Video Exercises • Grammar Exercises—and much more!

## Practise Your Grammar

Effective business communication starts with strong grammar skills. To improve your grammar skills, go to MyBCommLab, where you'll find exercises and diagnostic tests to help you produce clear, effective communication.

## Test Your Knowledge

To review chapter content related to each question, refer to the indicated Learning Objective.

1. What are the five general goals when delivering bad news? L.O.❶
2. What questions should you ask yourself when choosing between the direct and indirect approaches? L.O.❶
3. What is the sequence of elements in a negative message organized using the direct approach? L.O.❷
4. What is a buffer, and why might using one be unethical? L.O.❸
5. Why is it important to be engaged with stakeholders before trying to use social media during a crisis or other negative scenario? L.O.❻

## Apply Your Knowledge

To review chapter content related to each question, refer to the indicated Learning Objective.

1. Can you express sympathy with someone's negative situation without apologizing for the circumstances? Explain your answer. L.O.❷
2. Is intentionally de-emphasizing bad news the same as distorting graphs and charts to de-emphasize unfavourable data? Why or why not? L.O.❸
3. What new challenges do social media present to today's companies when it comes to negative information? L.O.❻
4. Why is early and frequent engagement with stakeholder communities so valuable in fending off erroneous rumours and other negative information about your company? L.O.❻

## Practise Your Skills

### EXERCISES FOR PERFECTING YOUR WRITING

To review chapter content related to each set of exercises, refer to the indicated Learning Objective.

**Message Strategies: Writing Negative Messages** L.O.❷, L.O.❸ Select which approach you would use (direct or indirect) for the following negative messages.

1. An email message to your boss, informing her that one of your key clients is taking its business to a different accounting firm
2. An email message to a customer, informing her that one of the books she ordered from your website is temporarily out of stock
3. A letter to a customer, explaining that the DVD burner he ordered for his new custom computer is on back order and that, as a consequence, the shipping of the entire order will be delayed

**Message Strategies: Writing Negative Messages** L.O.❸ Answer the following questions about buffers.

4. You have to tell a local restaurant owner that your plans have changed and you have to cancel the 90-person banquet scheduled for next month. Do you need to use a buffer? Why or why not?
5. Write a buffer for an email declining an invitation to speak at the association's annual fundraising event. Show your appreciation for being asked.
6. Write a buffer for an email rejecting a proposal from an employee on offering fitness incentives for all staff. You like the idea but funding is not available.

Message Strategies: Refusing Routine Requests; Collaboration: Team Projects L.O.❹, Chapter 2 Working alone, revise the following statements to de-emphasize the bad news without hiding it or distorting it. (Hint: Minimize the space devoted to the bad news, subordinate it, embed it, or use the passive voice.) Then team up with a classmate and read each other's revisions. Did you both use the same approach in every case? Which approach seems to be most effective for each of the revised statements?

7. The airline can't refund your money. The "Conditions" section on the back of your ticket states that there are no refunds for missed flights. Sometimes the airline makes exceptions, but only when life and death are involved. Of course, your ticket is still valid and can be used on a flight to the same destination.

8. I'm sorry to tell you that we can't supply the custom decorations you requested. We called every supplier and none of them can do what you want on such short notice. You can, however, get a standard decorative package on the same theme in time. I found a supplier that stocks these. Of course, it won't have quite the flair you originally requested.

9. We can't refund your money for the malfunctioning MP3 player. You shouldn't have immersed the unit in water while swimming; the user's manual clearly states the unit is not designed to be used in adverse environments.

## ACTIVITIES

Each activity is labelled according to the primary skill or skills you will need to use. To review relevant chapter content, you can refer to the indicated Learning Objective. In some instances, supporting information will be found in another chapter, as indicated.

1. **Message Strategies: Making Negative Announcements** L.O.❹ Read the following document and (a) analyze the strengths and weaknesses of each sentence and (b) revise the document so that it follows this chapter's guidelines.

> Your spring party sounds like fun. We're glad you've again chosen us as your caterer. Unfortunately, we have changed a few of our policies, and I wanted you to know about these changes in advance so that we won't have any misunderstandings on the day of the party.
>
> We will arrange the delivery of tables and chairs as usual the evening before the party. However, if you want us to set up, there is now a $100 charge for that service. Of course, you

might want to get some friends to do it, which would save you money. We've also added a small charge for cleanup. This is only $3 per person (you can estimate because I know a lot of people come and go later in the evening).

> Other than that, all the arrangements will be the same. We'll provide the skirt for the band stage, tablecloths, bar setup, and of course, the barbecue. Will you have the tubs of ice with soft drinks again? We can do that for you as well, but there will be a fee.
>
> Please let me know if you have any problems with these changes and we'll try to work them out. I know it's going to be a great party.

2. **Message Strategies: Refusing Routine Requests** L.O.❹ As a customer service supervisor for a mobile phone company, you're in charge of responding to customers' requests for refunds. You've just received an email from a customer who unwittingly ran up a $500 bill for data charges after forgetting to disable his smartphone's WiFi hotspot feature. The customer says it wasn't his fault because he didn't know his roommates were using his phone to get free internet access. However, you've dealt with this situation before and provided a notice to all customers to be careful about excess data charges resulting from the use of the hotspot capability. Draft a short buffer (one or two sentences) for your email reply, sympathizing with the customer's plight but preparing him for the bad news (that company policy specifically prohibits refunds in such cases).

3. **Message Strategies: Refusing Routine Requests** L.O.❹ Read the following document and (a) analyze the strengths and weaknesses of each sentence and (b) revise the message so that it follows this chapter's guidelines.

> I am responding to your letter of about six weeks ago asking for an adjustment on your wireless hub, model WM39Z. We test all our products before they leave the factory; therefore, it could not have been our fault that your hub didn't work.
>
> If you or someone in your office dropped the unit, it might have caused the damage. Or the damage could have been caused by the shipper if he dropped it. If so, you should file a claim with the shipper. At any rate, it wasn't

our fault. The parts are already covered by warranty. However, we will provide labour for the repairs for $50, which is less than our cost, since you are a valued customer.

We will have a booth at the upcoming trade fair there and hope to see you or someone from your office. We have many new models of computing and networking accessories that we're sure you'll want to see. I've enclosed our latest catalogue. Hope to see you there.

4. **Message Strategies: Making Negative Announcements; Communication Ethics: Distinguishing Ethical Dilemmas and Ethical Lapses** L.O.❹, **Chapter 1** The insurance company where you work is planning to raise all premiums for extended health-care coverage. Your boss has asked you to read a draft of her letter to customers announcing the new, higher rates. The first two paragraphs discuss some exciting medical advances and the expanded coverage offered by your company. Only in the final paragraph do customers learn that they will have to pay more for coverage starting next year. What are the ethical implications of this draft? What changes would you suggest?

5. **Message Strategies: Making Negative Announcements** L.O.❹ The following email message about travel budget cutbacks at Black & Decker contains numerous blunders. Using what you've learned in the chapter, read the message carefully and analyze its faults. Then use the questions that follow to outline and write an improved message.

---

From:    M. Juhasz, Travel & Meeting Services <mjuhasz@blackanddecker.com>

To:      [mailing list]

Subject: Travel Budget Cuts Effective Immediately

Dear Travelling Executives:

We need you to start using some of the budget suggestions we are going to issue as a separate memorandum. These include using videoconference equipment instead of travelling to meetings, staying in cheaper hotels, arranging flights for cheaper times, and flying from less-convenient but also less-expensive suburban airports.

The company needs to cut travel expenses by 50 percent, just as we've cut costs in all departments of Black & Decker.

This means you'll no longer be able to stay in fancy hotels and make last-minute, costly changes to your travel plans.

You'll also be expected to avoid hotel phone surcharges. Compose your email offline when you're in the hotel. And never return a rental car with an empty tank! That causes the rental agency to charge us a premium price for the gas they sell when they fill it up upon your return.

You'll be expected to make these changes in your travel habits immediately.

M. Juhasz
Travel & Meeting Services

---

a. Describe the flaws in this bad-news email message about company operations.

b. Develop a plan for rewriting the email to company insiders, using the direct approach. The following steps will help you organize your efforts before you begin writing:

- Create an opening statement of the bad news, using the "you" attitude.
- Decide what explanation is needed to justify the news.
- Determine whether you can use lists effectively.
- Choose some positive suggestions you can include to soften the news.
- Develop an upbeat closing.

c. Now rewrite the email message. Don't forget to revise your work before you turn it in.

6. **Message Strategies: Refusing Routine Requests; Collaboration: Team Projects** L.O.❹, **Chapter 2** The following letter rejecting a faucet manufacturer's product presentation contains many errors in judgment. Working with your classmates in a team effort, you should be able to improve its effectiveness

as a negative message. First, analyze and discuss the letter's flaws. How can it be improved? Use the following points to help guide your discussion and develop an improved version.

a. Describe the problems with this letter, then develop a plan for rewriting the letter using the direct approach.

b. Develop a plan for rewriting the letter, using the indirect approach. Organize your thinking before you begin writing, using the following tactics:

   i. Select a buffer for the opening that uses the "you" attitude.

   ii. Choose the reasons you'll use to explain the rejection.

   iii. Develop a way to soften or embed the bad news.

   iv. Create a conditional (if/then) statement to encourage the recipient to try again.

   v. Find a way to close on a positive, encouraging note.

c. Now rewrite the letter. Don't forget to revise your work before you turn it in.

---

July 15, 2012

Pamela Wilson, Operations Manager
Sterling Manufacturing
133 Industrial Avenue
Richmond, BC V6K 1P4

Dear Ms. Wilson:

We regret to inform you that your presentation at Home Depot's recent product review sessions in St. Petersburg did not meet our expert panelists' expectations. We require new products that will satisfy our customers' high standards. Yours did not match this goal.

Our primary concern is to continue our commitment to product excellence, customer knowledge, and price competitiveness, which has helped make Home Depot a Fortune 500 company with more than a thousand stores nationwide. The panel found flaws in your design and materials. Also, your cost per unit was too high.

The product review sessions occur annually. You are allowed to try again; just apply as you did this year. Again, I'm sorry things didn't work out for you this time.

Sincerely,
Hilary Buchman, Assistant to the Vice-President, Sales

---

# CASES

**Apply the three-step writing process to the following cases, as assigned by your instructor.**

❙ Letter Writing Skills

**1. Message Strategies: Making Negative Announcements** L.O.❹

Your company, PolicyPlan Insurance Services, is a 120-employee insurance claims processor based in Winnipeg. PolicyPlan has engaged Prairie Sparkleen for interior and exterior cleaning for the past five years. Prairie Sparkleen did exemplary work for the first four years, but after a change of ownership last year, the level of service has plummeted. Offices are no longer cleaned thoroughly, you've had to call the company at least six times to remind them to take care of spills and other messes that they're supposed to address routinely, and they've left toxic cleaning chemicals in a public hallway on several occasions. You have spoken with the owner about your concerns twice in the past three months, but his assurances that service would improve have not resulted in any noticeable improvements. When the evening cleaning crew forgot to lock the lobby door last Thursday—leaving your entire facility vulnerable to theft from midnight until 8 a.m. Friday morning—you decided it was time for a change.

**YOUR TASK** Write a letter to Johan Holland, owner of Prairie Sparkleen, 4000 Princess Street, Winnipeg MB, R3H 0J9, telling him that PolicyPlan will not be renewing its annual cleaning contract with Prairie

Sparkleen when the current contract expires at the end of this month. Cite the examples identified above, and keep the tone of your letter professional.

### ▌ Podcasting Skills
### 2. Message Strategies: Making Negative Announcements L.O.❹

Offering an employee concierge seemed like a great idea when you added it as an employee benefit last year. The concierge handles a wide variety of personal chores for employees, everything from dropping off their dry cleaning to ordering event tickets to sending flowers. Employees love the service, and you know that the time they save can be devoted to work or family activities. Unfortunately, profits are way down, and concierge usage is up—up so far that you'll need to add a second concierge to keep up with the demand. As painful as it will be for everyone, you decide that the company needs to stop offering the service.

**YOUR TASK**   Script a brief podcast announcing the decision and explaining why it was necessary. Make up any details you need. If your instructor asks you to do so, record your podcast and submit the file.

### ▌ Email Skills Portfolio Builder
### 3. Message Strategies: Making Negative Announcements L.O.❹

You can certainly sympathize with employees when they complain about having their email and instant messages monitored, but you're implementing a company policy that all employees will be asked to agree to abide by when they join the company. Your firm, Webcor Builders of Calgary, Alberta, is one of the estimated 60 percent of North American companies with such monitoring systems in place. More and more companies are using these systems (which typically operate by scanning messages for key words that suggest confidential, illegal, or otherwise inappropriate content) in an attempt to avoid instances of sexual harassment and other problems.

As the chief information officer, the manager in charge of computer systems in the company, you're often the target when employees complain about being monitored. Consequently, you know you're really going to hear it when employees learn that the monitoring program will be expanded to personal blogs as well.[14]

**YOUR TASK**   Write an email to be distributed to the entire workforce, explaining that the automated monitoring program is about to be expanded to include employees' personal blogs. Explain that although you sympathize with employee concerns regarding privacy and freedom of speech, the management team's responsibility is to protect the company's intellectual property and the value of the company name. Therefore, employees' personal blogs will be added to the monitoring system to ensure that employees don't intentionally or accidentally expose company secrets or criticize management in a way that could harm the company.

### ▌ Email Skills
### 4. Message Strategies: Refusing Routine Requests; Communication Ethics: Resolving Ethical Dilemmas L.O.❹, Chapter 1

A not-so-secret secret is getting more attention than you'd really like after an article in *BusinessWeek* gave the world an inside look at how much money you and other electronics retailers make from extended warranties (sometimes called service contracts). The article explained that typically half of the warranty price goes to the salesperson as a commission and that only 20 percent of the total amount customers pay for warranties eventually goes to product repair.

As a sales consultant in electronics retailing, you also know why extended warranties are such a profitable business. Many electronics products follow a predictable pattern of failure: a high failure rate early in their lives, then a "midlife" period during which failures go way down, and finally an "old age" period when failure rates ramp back up again (engineers refer to the phenomenon as the *bathtub curve* because it looks like a bathtub from the side—high at both ends and low in the middle). Those early failures are usually covered by manufacturers' warranties, and the extended warranties you sell are designed to cover that middle part of the life span. In other words, many extended warranties cover the period of time during which consumers are least likely to need them and offer no coverage when consumers need them most. (Consumers can actually benefit from extended warranties in a few product categories, including laptop computers and plasma TVs. Of course, the more sense the warranty makes for the consumer, the less financial sense it makes for your company.)[15]

**YOUR TASK**   Worried that consumers will start buying fewer extended warranties, your boss has directed you to put together a sales training program that will help cashiers sell the extended warranties even more aggressively. The more you ponder this challenge, though, the more you're convinced that your company should change its strategy so it doesn't rely so much on profits from these warranties. In addition to offering questionable value to the consumer, they risk creating a consumer backlash that could lead to lower sales of all your products. You would prefer to voice your concerns to your boss in person, but both of you are travelling on hectic schedules for the next week. You'll have to write an email instead. Draft a brief message explaining why you think the sales training specifically, and the warranties in general, are both bad ideas.

## ▐ Microblogging Skills
### 5. Message Strategies: Refusing Routine Requests L.O. ❹

WestJet incorporates the Twitter microblogging service into its customer communications, and tens of thousands of flyers and fans now follow the airline's Twittering staff members. Messages include announcements about fare sales (such as limited-time auctions on eBay or special on-site sales at shopping malls), celebrations of company milestones, schedule updates, and even personalized responses to people who Twitter with questions or complaints about the company.[16]

**YOUR TASK**   Write a tweet alerting WestJet customers to the possibility that a huge snowstorm might disrupt flight schedules from January 20 through January 25. Tell them that decisions about delays and cancellations will be made on a city-by-city basis and will be announced on Twitter and the company's website at www.westjet.com. Your message must be no more than 140 characters (including spaces) and must include the 15-character URL.

## ▐ Email Skills
### 6. Message Strategies: Refusing Routine Requests L.O. ❹

Lee Valley Tools (www.leevalley.com) sells high-quality woodworking tools across Canada through its retail stores and around the world through its website and catalogues. Although weekend hobbyists can pick up a mass-produced hand plane (a tool for smoothing wood) for $20 or $30 at the local hardware store, serious woodworkers pay 5 or 10 times that much for one of Lee Valley's precision Veritas planes. For the price, they get top-quality materials, precision manufacturing, and innovative designs that help them do better work in less time.

Lee Valley sells both its own Veritas brand tools as well as 5000 tools made by other manufacturers. One of those companies has just emailed you to ask if Lee Valley would like to carry a new line of midrange hand planes that would cost more than the mass-market, hardware-store models but less than Lee Valley's own Veritas models. Your job is to filter requests such as this, rejecting those that don't meet Lee Valley's criteria and forwarding those that do to the product selection committee for further analysis. After one quick read of this incoming email message, you realize there is no need to send this idea to the committee. Although these planes are certainly of decent quality, they achieve their lower cost through lower-quality steel that won't hold an edge as long, and through thinner irons (the element that holds the cutting edge) that will be more prone to vibrate during use and thus produce a rougher finish. These planes have a market, to be sure, but they're not a good fit for Lee Valley's top-of-the-line product portfolio. Moreover, the planes don't offer any innovations in terms of ease of use or any other product attribute.[17]

**YOUR TASK**   Reply to this email message, explaining that the planes appear to be decent tools, but they don't fit Lee Valley's strategy of offering only the best and most innovative tools. Support your decision with the three criteria described above. Choose the direct or indirect approach carefully, taking into consideration your company's relationship with this other company.

## ▐ Email Skills
### 7. Message Strategies: Refusing a Claim L.O. ❹

You work in human resources for a company called Advertising Inflatables, which designs and builds the huge balloon replicas used for advertising atop retail stores, tire outlets, used-car lots, fast-food outlets, fitness clubs, and so on. Since you started, you've seen balloon re-creations of everything from a 17-metre-tall King Kong to a "small" 3-metre-wide pizza.

Not long ago, company management installed the "cyber-surveillance" software, Silent Watch, to track and record employees' computer usage. At the time, you sent out a memo informing all employees that they should limit their computer use and email to work projects only. You also informed them that their work would be monitored and that Silent Watch would record every keystroke of their work.

As it turned out, Silent Watch caught two of the sales staff spending between 50 percent and 70 percent of their time surfing internet sites unrelated to their jobs. The company docked (withheld) their pay accordingly, without warning. Management sent them a memo notifying them that they were not fired but were on probation. You considered this wise, because when they work, both employees are very good at what they do, and talent is hard to find.

But now salesman Jarod Harkington has sent you a letter demanding reinstatement of his pay and claiming he was "spied on illegally." On the contrary, company lawyers have assured management that the courts almost always side with employers on this issue, particularly after employees receive a warning such as the one you wrote. The computer equipment belongs to Advertising Inflatables, and employees are paid a fair price for their time.

**YOUR TASK**   Write a letter refusing Mr. Harkington's claim. His address is 267 Hale Avenue, Peterborough, ON, K9J 7B1.[18]

## ▐ Text Messaging
### 8. Message Strategies: Refusing Routine Requests L.O. ❹

You are in a meeting, and during one of your only breaks, you get an instant message from one of your employees, marketing rep Arash Param, containing his request to attend a conference on the use of blogging for business, which is being held in Montreal next month. You are quite interested in exploring the use of blogs, but Arash wants your answer within the hour. If he had asked a week ago and included more information, you could have said yes. But no, he has to leave it to the last minute and catch you in this meeting. He'll just have to take no for an answer.

For one thing, you'd need to get budget approval from your group's vice-president because the conference would involve out-of-province travel; to get a green light on travel to attend any conference longer than a day or farther than Calgary (a two-hour drive from your Edmonton office), you've got to get the VP to sign off on it. As well, the high cost of the air travel and hotel for four days would also need a justification, so that should have been part of the request. You'd need a written document explaining how business blogs relate to Arash's marketing position. Not that hard to do, but the fact is, he hasn't done it. Since he waited until one hour before the deadline, none of these issues can be addressed, so you can't possibly say yes! Which is a drag because Arash is a very nice guy and you wish you could send him to the conference. Worse yet, it will have to be an instant message reply that lets him know.

**YOUR TASK** Write a 60- to 75-word instant message to Arash Param declining his request. Decide whether the direct or indirect approach is appropriate.[19]

▌ **Instant Messaging**

**9. Message Strategies: Negative Organizational Messages** L.O.**⑤**

You work as an administrator in the security department at Simon Fraser University on top of Burnaby Mountain, just outside Vancouver. You got to work very early this morning because you knew the drive through the winter storm would be challenging. Although you made it up the mountain, you saw city buses stuck at the side of the road and quite a few vehicles having difficulty making it up the steep hill. Sure enough, as soon as you arrive in the office, your manager, Jesse Sloan, received word from the university's president that classes are to be cancelled. The winter storm has dropped significant snow and now the weather forecast is calling for more snow and freezing rain. These conditions would make the drive up the mountain treacherous—something you just experienced first-hand! The Security Department uses the 3N System (National Notification Network) in emergencies to deliver text messages, instant messages, and emails to all staff and students. These messages can get to students whether they are on campus, at home, or on the way to campus.

**YOUR TASK** Jesse asks you to draft a cancellation alert, staying within the 65-word limit of many instant-messaging programs. The president also authorized the use of the gym for a temporary shelter and sleeping facility if people who are already on campus do not want to head down the hill.[20]

▌ **Email Skills**

**10. Message Strategies: Negative Organizational Messages** L.O.**⑤**

"Company policy states that personnel are not to conduct business using cell phones while driving," David Finch reminds you. He's a partner at the law firm of Wilkes Artis in Toronto, where you work as his administrative assistant.

You nod, waiting for him to explain. He already issued a memo about this rule last year, after a 15-year-old girl was hit and killed by a lawyer from another firm. Driving back from a client meeting, the lawyer was distracted while talking on her cell phone. The girl's family sued the firm and won $30 million, but that's not the point. The point is that cell phones can cause people to be hurt, even killed.

Finch explains, "Yesterday, one of our associates called his secretary while driving his car. We can't allow this. Heck, one province, some of the states, and a few countries have banned the use of hand-held cell phones while driving. From now on, any violation of our cell phone policy will result in suspension without pay, unless the call is a genuine health or traffic emergency."

**YOUR TASK** Finch asks you to write an email message to all employees, announcing the new penalty for violating company policy.[21]

▌ **Email Skills**

**11. Message Strategies: Negative Organizational Messages** L.O.**⑤**

People who live for an adrenaline rush can find a way to go fast from Canada's Bombardier Recreational Products. Bombardier is one of the world's top makers of snowmobiles, personal watercraft, engines for motorboats, and all-terrain vehicles (ATVs)—all designed for fast fun.

Because it sends customers hurtling across snow, water, or land at high speeds, Bombardier takes safety quite seriously. However, problems do arise from time to time, requiring a rapid response with clear communication to the company's customer base. Bombardier recently became aware of a potentially hazardous situation with the "race-ready" version of its Can-Am DS90X ATVs. This model is equipped with a safety device called a tether engine shut-off switch, in which a cord is connected to a special switch that turns off the engine in the event of an emergency. On the affected units, pulling the cord might not shut off the motor, which is particularly dangerous if the rider falls off—the ATV will continue on its own until the engine speed returns to idle.

**YOUR TASK** Write an email message that will be sent to registered owners of 2010 and 2011 DS90X ATVs that include the potentially faulty switch. Analyze the situation carefully as you choose the direct or indirect approach for your message. Explain that the tether engine shut-off switch may not deactivate the engine when it is pulled in an emergency situation. To prevent riders from relying on a safety feature that might not work properly, Bombardier, in cooperation with transportation safety authorities in Canada, is voluntarily recalling these models to have the tether switch removed. Emphasize the serious nature of the situation by explaining that if the rider is ejected and the engine shut-off switch does not work properly, the ATV will run away on its own, potentially resulting in significant injuries or deaths. Owners should stop riding their vehicles immediately and make an appointment with an authorized dealer to have the switch removed. The service will be performed at no charge, and customers will receive a $50 credit voucher for future purchases of Bombardier accessories. Include the following contact information: www.can-am.brp.com and 1-888-555-5397.[22]

**▌Social Networking Skills**

**12. Message Strategies: Responding to Rumours and Public Criticism LO.❼**

The consumer reviews on Yelp (www.yelp.com) can be a promotional boon to any local business—provided the reviews are positive, of course. Negative reviews, fair or not, can affect a company's reputation and drive away potential customers. Fortunately for business owners, sites like Yelp give them the means to respond to reviews, whether they want to apologize for poor service, offer some form of compensation, or correct misinformation in a review.

**YOUR TASK** Search Yelp for a negative review (one or two stars) on any business in any city. Find a review that has some substance to it, not just a simple, angry rant. Now imagine that you are the owner of that business, and write a reply that could be posted via the "Add Owner Comment" feature. Use information you can find on Yelp about the company and fill in any details by using your imagination. Remember that your comment will be visible to everyone who visits Yelp.

---

## BUSINESS COMMUNICATION NOTEBOOK

# Ethics

### Should Employers Use Email to Deliver Negative Messages?

Most people are more comfortable delivering bad news via email than in person or on the phone. But is it appropriate to avoid the dreaded task of explaining layoffs and spending cuts in person by using email to break such bad news? Some think it is.

Few executives advise using email in extremely personal situations such as firing an employee, but some think it's perfectly fine to use email for other uncomfortable scenarios such as job cuts, travel restrictions, hiring freezes, and other significant spending changes. Consider these examples:

- Amazon called an in-person meeting to announce job cuts, but telecommuters who couldn't attend the meeting were informed via email. "I want you to know that this was a very difficult decision for the company to make . . . we know this must be very painful to hear," the email read.
- Discovery Communications used email to alert Discovery workers that staffing changes would take place before announcing layoffs of some of its full-time employees.
- Motorola sent email to employees in its semiconductor sector explaining layoffs and other cost-cutting steps. Workers being let go were told in person, but word of what was happening went out electronically.
- Ameritrade online brokerage notified more than 2000 call-centre workers of layoffs via email.

Employers who use email to deliver bad news claim that it's a quick and effective way to get information to all employees—especially those in remote locations or home offices. With face-to-face or even voice-to-voice communication, people have a tendency to tune out the worst and sugarcoat the bad news. But delivering bad news via email lets people be more honest. Email facilitates straight talk because senders don't see the discomfort of their recipients.

However, critics cry foul when companies break job-related bad news via email. As they see it, email is too impersonal. Email gives management the chance to avoid angry employees, but if you want to maintain good employee relations, job-related bad news should be given in person.

## Applications for Success

For more advice about email and employer/employee communication, go to MyCanadianBusCommLab. In the Composing Space, click on Writer's Toolkit, then on Find Sources to access EBSCO's ContentSelect database. Look up the key words "bad news," "email," and "email etiquette."

a. Do you think employers should deliver negative messages via email? Explain your answer.

b. Why does email facilitate straight talk?

c. If you are sending bad news in an email message, how can you use an indirect approach and still include an informative subject line? Won't the subject line give away your message before you have the chance to explain your reasons? Briefly explain in a one- to two-paragraph memo or email message to your instructor.

# Writing Persuasive Messages

**LEARNING OBJECTIVES**

*After studying this chapter, you will be able to*

1. Apply the three-step writing process to persuasive messages.
2. Describe an effective strategy for developing persuasive business messages.
3. Identify the three most common categories of persuasive business messages.
4. Describe an effective strategy for developing marketing and sales messages, explain how to modify this approach for social media, and identify steps you can take to avoid ethical lapses in marketing and sales messages.

**TIPS FOR SUCCESS**

"Trustworthiness, transparency, credible authority, lots of high-value content, and just plain old decency are your best weapons."

—Sonia Simone,
Co-founder and Chief Marketing
Officer of Copyblogger Media

Sonia Simone was discussing the fear that keeps online shoppers from completing a transaction, but her insight applies to every form of persuasive communication.[1] Whether you're trying to convince people to help fund your new business via Kickstarter, asking your boss for a raise, or promoting a concert, trust is an essential element of persuasion. If people don't believe in you, they won't believe in what you're promoting.

In this chapter, you'll apply what you've learned so far about writing to the unique challenges of persuasive messages. You'll explore two types of persuasive messages: *persuasive business messages* (those that try to convince audiences to approve new projects, enter into business partnerships, and so on) and *marketing and sales messages* (those that try to convince audiences to consider and then purchase products and services).

# Using the Three-Step Writing Process for Persuasive Messages

Whether you're convincing your boss to open a new office in Europe or encouraging potential customers to try your products, you'll use many of the same techniques of **persuasion**—the attempt to change an audience's attitudes, beliefs, or actions.[2] Because persuasive messages ask audiences to give something of value (money in exchange for a product, for example) or take substantial action (such as changing a corporate policy), they are more challenging to write than routine messages. Successful professionals understand that persuasion is not about trickery or getting people to act against their own best interests; it's about letting audiences know they have choices and presenting your offering in the best possible light.[3]

**LEARNING OBJECTIVE** 1
Apply the three-step writing process to persuasive messages.

Persuasion is the attempt to change someone's attitudes, beliefs, or actions.

## Step 1: Planning Persuasive Messages

In today's information-saturated business environment, having a great idea or a great product is no longer enough. Every day, untold numbers of good ideas go unnoticed and good products go unsold simply because the messages meant to promote them aren't compelling enough to be heard above the competitive noise. Creating successful persuasive messages in these challenging situations demands careful attention to all four tasks in the planning step, starting with an insightful analysis of your purpose and your audience.

**ANALYZING THE SITUATION**   In defining your purpose, make sure you're clear about what you really hope to achieve. Suppose you want to persuade company executives to support a particular research project. But what does "support" mean? Do you want them to pat you on the back and wish you well? Or do you want them to give you a staff of five researchers and a $1 million annual budget?

The best persuasive messages are closely connected to your audience's desires and interests.[4] Consider these important questions: Who is my audience? What are my audience members' needs? What do I want them to do? How might they resist? Are there alternative positions I need to examine? What does the decision maker consider to be the most important issue? How might the organization's culture influence my strategy?

To understand and categorize audience needs, you can refer to specific information, such as **demographics** (the age, gender, occupation, income, education, and other quantifiable characteristics of the people you're trying to persuade) and **psychographics** (personality, attitudes, lifestyle, and other psychological characteristics). When analyzing your audiences, take into account their cultural expectations and practices so that you don't undermine your persuasive message by using an inappropriate appeal or by organizing your message in a way that seems unfamiliar or uncomfortable to your readers.

If you aim to change someone's attitudes, beliefs, or actions, it is vital to understand his or her **motivation**—the combination of forces that drive people to satisfy their needs. Table 9.1 lists some of the needs that psychologists have identified or suggested as being important in influencing human motivation. Obviously, the more closely a persuasive message aligns with a recipient's existing motivation, the more effective the message is likely to be. For example, if you try to persuade consumers to purchase a product on the basis of its fashion appeal, that message will connect with consumers who are motivated by a desire to be in fashion but probably won't connect with consumers driven more by functional or financial concerns.

**GATHERING INFORMATION**   Once your situation analysis is complete, you need to gather the information necessary to create a compelling persuasive message. You'll learn more about the types of information to include in persuasive business messages and marketing and sales messages later in the chapter. Chapter 10 presents advice on how to find the information you need.

**SELECTING THE RIGHT MEDIUM**   Media choices are always important, of course, but these decisions are particularly sensitive with persuasive messages because such messages are often unexpected or even unwelcome. For instance, some people don't mind promotional email messages for products they're interested in; others resent every piece of commercial email they receive. *Permission-based marketing*, in which marketers ask permission before sending messages, can help companies avoid antagonizing their target audiences.

**ORGANIZING YOUR INFORMATION**   The most effective main ideas for **persuasive messages** have one thing in common: they are about the receiver, not the sender. For instance, if you're trying to convince others to join you in a business venture, explain how it will help them, not how it will help you.

| TABLE 9.1 | Human Needs That Influence Motivation |
|---|---|

| NEED | IMPLICATIONS FOR COMMUNICATION |
|---|---|
| **Basic physiological requirements:** The needs for food, water, sleep, oxygen, and other essentials | Everyone has these needs, but the degree of attention an individual gives to them often depends on whether the needs are being met; for instance, an advertisement for sleeping pills will have greater appeal to someone suffering from insomnia than to someone who has no problem sleeping. |
| **Safety and security:** The needs for protection from bodily harm, to know that loved ones are safe, and for financial security, protection of personal identity, career security, and other assurances | These needs influence both consumer and business decisions in a wide variety of ways; for instance, advertisements for life insurance often encourage parents to think about the financial security of their children and other loved ones. |
| **Affiliation and belonging:** The needs for companionship, acceptance, love, popularity, etc. | The need to feel loved, accepted, or popular drives a great deal of human behaviour, from the desire to be attractive to potential mates to wearing the clothing style that a particular social group is likely to approve of. |
| **Power and control:** The need to feel in control of situations or to exert authority over others | You can see many examples appealing to this need in advertisements: *Take control of your life, your finances, your future, your career,* and so on. Many people who lack power want to know how to get it, and people who have power often want others to know they have it. |
| **Achievement:** The need to feel a sense of accomplishment—or to be admired by others for accomplishments | This need can involve both *knowing* (when people experience a feeling of accomplishment) and showing (when people are able to show others that they've achieved success); advertising for luxury consumer products frequently appeals to this need. |
| **Adventure and distraction:** The need for excitement or relief from daily routine | People vary widely in their need for adventure; some crave excitement—even danger—whereas others value calmness and predictability. Some needs for adventure and distraction are met *virtually*, such as through horror movies, thriller novels, etc. |
| **Knowledge, exploration, and understanding:** The need to keep learning | For some people, learning is usually a means to an end, a way to fulfill some other need; for others, acquiring new knowledge is the goal. |
| **Aesthetic appreciation:** The desire to experience beauty, order, symmetry, etc. | Although this need may seem "noncommercial" at first glance, advertisers appeal to it frequently, from the pleasing shape of a package to the quality of the gemstones in a piece of jewellery. |
| **Self-actualization:** The need to "be all that one can be," to reach one's full potential as a human being | Psychologists Kurt Goldstein and Abraham Maslow popularized self-actualization as the desire to make the most of one's potential, and Maslow identified it as one of the higher-level needs in his classic hierarchy; even if people met most or all of their other needs, they would still feel the need to self-actualize. |
| **Helping others:** The need to believe that one is making a difference in the lives of other people | This need is the central motivation in fundraising messages and other appeals to charity. |

Because the nature of persuasion is to convince people to change their attitudes, beliefs, or actions, most persuasive messages use the indirect approach. That means you'll want to explain your reasons and build interest before asking for a decision or for action—or perhaps even before revealing your purpose. In contrast, when you have a close relationship with your audience and the message is welcome or at least neutral, the direct approach can be effective.

Most persuasive messages use the indirect approach.

For persuasive business messages, the choice between the direct and indirect approaches is also influenced by the extent of your authority, expertise, or power in an organization. For instance, if you are a highly regarded technical expert with years of experience, you might use the direct approach in a message to top executives. In contrast, if you aren't well known and therefore need to rely more on the strength of your message than the power of your reputation, the indirect approach will probably be more successful.

The choice of approach is influenced by your position (or authority within the organization) relative to your audience's.

## Step 2: Writing Persuasive Messages

Encourage a positive response to your persuasive messages by (1) using positive and polite language, (2) understanding and respecting cultural differences, (3) being sensitive to organizational cultures, and (4) taking steps to establish your credibility.

Positive language usually happens naturally with persuasive messages because you're promoting an idea or a product you believe in. However, take care not to inadvertently insult your readers by implying that they've made poor choices in the past.

Be sure to understand cultural expectations as well. For example, a message that seems forthright and direct in a low-context culture might seem brash and intrusive in a high-context culture.

Just as social culture affects the success of a persuasive message, so too does the culture within various organizations. Some organizations handle disagreement and conflict in an indirect, behind-the-scenes way, whereas others accept and even encourage open discussion and sharing of differing viewpoints.

Finally, when trying to persuade a skeptical or hostile audience, you must convince people that you know what you're talking about and that you're not trying to mislead them. Use these techniques:

- Use simple language to avoid suspicions of fantastic claims and emotional manipulation.
- Provide objective evidence and logical arguments for the claims and promises you make.
- Identify your sources, especially if your audience already respects those sources.
- Establish common ground by emphasizing beliefs, attitudes, and background experiences you share with the audience.
- Be objective and present fair and logical arguments.
- Display your willingness to keep your audience's best interests at heart.
- Persuade with logic, evidence, and compelling narratives, rather than trying to coerce with high-pressure, "hard sell" tactics.
- Whenever possible, try to build your credibility *before* you present a major proposal or ask for a major decision. That way, audiences don't have to evaluate both you and your message at the same time.[5]

## Step 3: Completing Persuasive Messages

Credibility is an essential element of persuasion, so the production quality of your messages is vital. If your message shows signs of carelessness or incompetence, people might think you are careless or incompetent as well.

When you evaluate your content, try to judge your argument objectively and try not to overestimate your credibility. When revising for clarity and conciseness, carefully match the purpose and organization to audience needs. If possible, ask an experienced colleague who knows your audience well to review your draft. Your design elements must complement, not detract from, your argument. In addition, meticulous proofreading will identify any mechanical or spelling errors that would weaken your persuasive potential. Finally, make sure your distribution methods fit your audience's expectations as well as your purpose.

# Developing Persuasive Business Messages

Your success as a businessperson is closely tied to your ability to encourage others to accept new ideas, change old habits, or act on your recommendations. Unless your career takes you into marketing and sales, most of your persuasive messages will consist of *persuasive business messages*, which are any messages designed to elicit a preferred response in a nonsales situation.

Even if you have the power to compel others to do what you want them to do, persuading them is more effective than forcing them. People who are forced into accepting a decision or plan are less motivated to support it and more likely to react negatively than if they're persuaded.[6] Pulling people toward your ideas is more effective than pushing the ideas on them. Within the context of the three-step process, effective persuasion involves four essential strategies: (1) framing your arguments, (2) balancing emotional and logical appeals, (3) reinforcing your position, and (4) anticipating objections.

## Framing Your Arguments

Many persuasive messages follow some variation of the indirect approach. One of the most commonly used variations is called the **AIDA model**, which organizes your presentation into four phases (see Figure 9.1):

- **Attention.** Your first objective is to encourage your audience to want to hear about your problem, idea, or new product—whatever your main idea is. Be sure to find some common ground on which to build your case.
- **Interest.** Provide additional details that prompt audience members to imagine how the solution might benefit them.
- **Desire.** Help audience members embrace your idea by explaining how the change will benefit them and answering potential objections.
- **Action.** Suggest the specific action you want your audience to take. Include a deadline, when applicable.

The AIDA model is tailor-made for using the indirect approach, allowing you to save your main idea for the action phase. However, it can also work with the direct approach, in which case you use your main idea as an attention-getter, build interest with your argument, create desire with your evidence, and emphasize your main idea in the action phase with the specific action you want your audience to take.

When your AIDA message uses the indirect approach and is delivered by memo or email, keep in mind that your subject line usually catches your reader's eye first. Your challenge is to make it interesting and relevant enough to capture reader attention without

*The AIDA model is a useful approach for many persuasive messages:*
- *Attention*
- *Interest*
- *Desire*
- *Action*

*The AIDA model is ideal for the indirect approach.*
*A persuasive email subject line focuses on reader benefit.*

---

**FIGURE 9.1  The AIDA Model for Persuasive Messages**

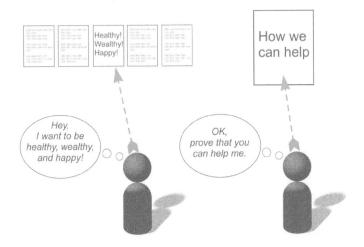

**Attention**
Catch the audience's eyes and ears, then getting people to pay attention to *your* message amid all the other messages clamouring for their attention

**Interest**
Provide concise information points that "pay off" the promise you made to get their attention as you build a case that you can meet their individual needs

**Desire**
Move prospects from "I'm interested" to "I want this" by continuing to show how your solution will benefit them and by removing any doubts

**Action**
Motivate them to take action, whether that is seeking more information, making a decision in your favour, or making a purchase

revealing your main idea. If you put your request in the subject line, you're likely to get a quick "no" before you've had a chance to present your arguments:

| Instead of | Write |
|---|---|
| Request for development budget to add automated IM response system | Reducing the cost of customer support inquiries |

With either the direct or indirect approach, AIDA and similar models do have limitations. First, AIDA is a unidirectional method that essentially talks *at* audiences, not *with* them. Second, AIDA is built around a single event, such as asking an audience for a decision, rather than on building a mutually beneficial, long-term relationship.[7] AIDA is still a valuable tool for the right purposes, but as you'll read later in the chapter, a conversational approach is more compatible with today's social media.

The AIDA approach has limitations:
- It essentially talks *at* audiences, not *with* them
- It focuses on one-time events, not long-term relationships

Emotional appeals attempt to connect with the reader's feelings or sympathies.

## Balancing Emotional and Logical Appeals

Few persuasive appeals are purely logical or purely emotional, and a key skill is finding the right balance for each message (see Figure 9.2). An **emotional appeal** calls on

---

### FIGURE 9.2  Balancing Logical and Emotional Appeals

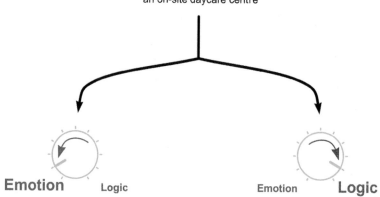

**Specific purpose:**
To persuade management to fund an on-site daycare centre

Emotion / Logic        Emotion / Logic

**Proposal to improve employee satisfaction and work/life balance**

Being separated during the day is stressful for both parents and children.

Many parents are now working more hours and second jobs to make ends meet, so the situation is getting worse.

The extra travel time every morning and evening to put children in daycare adds to the stress and cost of coming to work.

When parents need to leave work to pick up sick children from daycare or stay home with them, this often creates an unfair burden on other employees to pick up the slack.

Knowing that the company cares about them and their children would boost employee morale.

Therefore, the company should provide an on-site daycare facility with a separate infirmary where sick children could stay during the day.

**Proposal to boost productivity and reduce absenteeism**

Analysis of employee time records shows that employees with children under the age of 10 take unscheduled days off three times more often than employees without young children.

Daycare issues are cited as the number one reason for these unscheduled days off.

In the 98 exit interviews conducted last year, 24 departing employees mentioned the need to balance family and work commitments as the primary reason for leaving.

In the last six months, HR has logged 14 complaints from employees who say they have to take on extra work when colleagues leave the office to pick up sick children from daycare.

Research shows that on-site daycare can improve productivity by as much as 20 percent—among parents and nonparents alike.

Therefore, the company should provide an on-site daycare facility with a separate infirmary where sick children could stay during the day.

feelings or audience sympathies. For instance, you can make use of the emotion inspired by words such as *freedom*, *success*, *prestige*, *compassion*, *free*, and *comfort*. Such words put your audience in a certain frame of mind and help people accept your message.

Many marketing and sales messages rely heavily on emotional appeals, but most persuasive business messages rely more on logic. And even if your audience reaches a conclusion based on emotions, they'll look to you to provide logical support as well. A logical appeal uses one of three types of reasoning:

- **Analogy.** With analogy, you reason from specific evidence to specific evidence. For instance, to convince management to buy a more robust firewall to protect your company's computer network, you might use the analogy of "circling the wagons," as when covered wagons crossing the continent gathered in a circle every night to form a safe space within.
- **Induction.** With inductive reasoning, you work from specific evidence to a general conclusion. To convince your boss to change a certain production process, you could point out that every company that has adopted it has increased profits.
- **Deduction.** With deductive reasoning, you work from a generalization to a specific conclusion. To persuade your boss to hire additional customer support staff, you might point to industry surveys that show how crucial customer satisfaction is to corporate profits.

> Logical appeals are based on the reader's notions of reason; these appeals can use analogy, induction, or deduction.

Every method of reasoning is vulnerable to misuse. To avoid faulty logic, practise the following guidelines:[8]

> Using logical appeals carries with it the ethical responsibility to avoid faulty logic.

- **Avoid hasty generalizations.** Make sure you have plenty of evidence before drawing conclusions.
- **Avoid circular reasoning.** Circular reasoning is a logical fallacy in which you try to support your claim by restating it in different words. The statement "we know temporary workers cannot handle this task because temps are unqualified for it" doesn't prove anything because the claim and the supporting evidence are essentially identical.
- **Avoid attacking an opponent.** Attack the argument your opponent is making, not your opponent's character.
- **Avoid oversimplifying a complex issue.** For example, don't reduce a complex situation to a simple "either/or" statement if the situation isn't that simple or clear-cut.
- **Avoid mistaken assumptions of cause and effect.** If you can't isolate the impact of a specific factor, you can't assume that it's the cause of whatever effect you're discussing. You lowered prices, and sales went up. Were lower prices the cause? Maybe, but the sales increase might have been caused by a better advertising campaign or some other factor.
- **Avoid faulty analogies.** Be sure that the two objects or situations being compared are similar enough for the analogy to hold.

## Reinforcing Your Position

After you've worked out the basic elements of your argument, step back and look for ways to bolster the strength of your position. Are all your claims supported by believable evidence? Would a quotation from a recognized expert help make your case?

Next, examine your language. Can you find more powerful words to convey your message? For example, if your company is in serious financial trouble, talking about *fighting for survival* is a more powerful emotional appeal than talking about *ensuring continued operations*. As with any other powerful tool, though, use vivid language and abstractions carefully and honestly.

In addition to examining individual word choices, consider using metaphors and other figures of speech. If you want to describe a quality-control system as being designed to detect every possible product flaw, you might call it a "spider web" to imply that it catches everything that comes its way. Similarly, anecdotes (brief stories) can help your audience grasp the meaning and importance of your arguments. Instead of just listing the number of times the old laptop computers in your department have failed, you could describe how you lost a sale when your computer broke down during a critical sales presentation.

## Anticipating Objections

Even compelling ideas and exciting projects can encounter objections, if only as a consequence of people's natural tendency to resist change. Anticipate as many objections as you can and address them before your audience can bring them up. By doing so, you can remove these potentially negative elements from the conversation and keep the focus on positive communication. Note that you don't need to explicitly mention a particular concern. For instance, if your proposal to switch to lower-cost materials is likely to raise concerns about quality, simply emphasize that the new materials are just as good as existing materials. You'll not only get this issue out of the way sooner, but also demonstrate a broad appreciation of the issue and imply confidence in your message.[9]

If you expect a hostile audience that is biased against your plan, be sure to present all sides of the situation. As you cover each option, explain the pros and cons. You'll gain additional credibility if you present these options before presenting your recommendation or decision.[10] If you can, involve your audience in the design of the solution; people are more likely to support ideas they help create.

## Avoiding Common Mistakes in Persuasive Communication

When you believe in a concept or project you are promoting, it's easy to get caught up in your own confidence and enthusiasm and thereby fail to see things from the audience's perspective. When putting together persuasive arguments, avoid these common mistakes:[11]

- **Using a hard sell.** Don't push. No one likes being pressured into making a decision, and communicators who take this approach can come across as being more concerned with meeting their own goals than with satisfying the needs of their audiences. In contrast, a "soft sell" is more like a comfortable conversation that uses calm, rational persuasion.
- **Resisting compromise.** Successful persuasion is often a process of give-and-take, particularly in the case of persuasive business messages, where you don't always get everything you asked for in terms of budgets, investments, and other commitments.
- **Relying solely on great arguments.** Great arguments are important, but connecting with your audience on the right emotional level and communicating through vivid language are just as vital. Sometimes a well-crafted story can be even more compelling than dry logic.
- **Assuming that persuasion is a one-shot effort.** Persuasion is often a process, not a one-time event. In many cases, you need to move your audience members along one small step at a time rather than try to convince them to say "yes" in one huge step.

Your own character is part of your persuasiveness because, as CTV's vice-president of marketing, Mary Kreuk, says, "Winning someone over generally has a lot to do with past proven performance as well as your ongoing relationship with that individual. If you said you were going to do something, then you better deliver on it."[12] Persuasion is a process. It's a relationship you build with the audience, developing their awareness of the need for action by providing benefits that connect with something that resonates within them, moving them toward the desired action.

# Common Examples of Persuasive Business Messages

**LEARNING OBJECTIVE** 3
Identify the three most common categories of persuasive business messages.

Throughout your career, you'll have numerous opportunities to write persuasive messages within your organization—for example, when suggesting more efficient operating procedures, asking for cooperation from other departments, pitching investors on a new business idea, or requesting adjustments that go beyond a supplier's contractual obligations. In addition, many of the routine requests you studied in Chapter 7 can become persuasive messages if you want a nonroutine result or believe that you haven't received fair treatment. Most of these messages can be divided into persuasive requests for action, persuasive presentation of ideas, and persuasive claims and requests for adjustment.

## Persuasive Requests for Action

The bulk of your persuasive business messages will involve requests for action. In some cases, your request will be anticipated, so the direct approach is fine (see Figure 9.3). In others, you'll need to introduce your intention indirectly, and the AIDA model or a similar approach is ideal for this purpose (see Figure 9.4).

Most persuasive business messages involve a request for action.

---

FIGURE 9.3 **Persuasive Request for Action Using the Direct Approach**

Uses the subject line to announce that the proposal will save money

Grabs attention with the promise of saving money, time, and frustration

Creates more interest with an explanation of how the new plan will work

Creates desire by presenting supporting evidence

Shows audience focus by completing a chore that might have caused the reader to delay

To: <housel@interchange.ubc.ca>

From: "Sandi Sidhu" sidhu@interchange.ubc.ca

Subject: **SAVINGS ON TOLL-FREE NUMBER**

Attached: C:\Temp\NewPhoneMessage.doc

Hello, David:

We can save money, time, and frustration by modifying our toll-free message system. Currently, the bill for our toll-free number at the ticket office runs at least $3000 for August (compared with $493 on average for the other 11 months). Plus, we're so busy fielding calls during August that our other work piles up. In addition, TBirds fans who call in August are frustrated by having to wait on hold at least five minutes and often longer.

**Benefits**
By providing callers with an additional option, we can relieve a lot of the pressure. Under the new system, callers will hear all the same messages and have all the same options as before. But if no operator is available when a caller presses "0" for ticket information, a new message will request the caller's name and phone number so that we can return the call within the next two business days.

This new message system will help us

* Save money on our toll-free line
* Manage our time and stress levels
* Provide better customer service

**Savings**
Reducing the on-hold time should eliminate at least $2000 from our August bill (according to a conversation with Tandy Robertson, our Bell Canada representative). Adding a new message/option costs nothing, and we can implement the plan immediately. We will be able to manage our work more effectively by returning phone calls during quiet times of the day. And, not least important, TBirds fans can avoid the frustration of waiting on hold.

Our staff is enthusiastic about trying this new plan. If we implement it this August, then after hockey season, we could call a random selection of customers to see how they liked the new system.

**Approval**
Attached is a sheet with possible wording for the new message. Please let me know by the end of the month whether you'd like to give this a try.

Thanks,

Sandi

Opens using the direct approach, but still introduces the idea briefly

Uses headings to reinforce key parts of the document

Lists benefits to draw the reader into the meat of the message

Shows audience focus by including a method for measuring customer response

Makes a simple and direct request for action within a specific time frame

---

| FIGURE 9.4 | Persuasive Message Using the AIDA Model |

---

**To:** eleanor.tran@hmservices.com

**Subject: Cost Cutting in Plastics**

**Attached:** 📄 Plastics Cost Analysis.PDF (96 KB)

Eleanor:

**A** → In spite of our recent switch to purchasing plastic product containers in bulk, our costs for these containers are still extremely high. In my January 5 message, I included all the figures showing that we purchase five tons of plastic product containers each year, and the price of polyethylene terephthalate (PET) rises and falls as petroleum costs fluctuate.

*Catches the reader's attention with a blunt statement of a major problem*

**The High Cost of Plastics**

**I** → In January I suggested that we purchase plastic containers in bulk during winter months, when petroleum prices tend to be lower. Because you approved that suggestion, we should realize a 10 percent saving this year. However, our costs are still out of line, around $2 million a year.

*Builds interest in a potential solution to the problem by emphasizing how bad the problem is and highlighting an associated problem*

In addition to the cost in dollars of these plastic containers is the cost in image. We have recently been receiving an increasing number of consumer letters complaining about our lack of a recycling program for PET plastic containers, both on the airplanes and in the airport restaurants.

**D** → **A Recycling Plan**

After conducting some preliminary research, I have come up with the following ideas:
• Provide recycling containers at all Fairmont West airport restaurants
• Offer financial incentives for the airlines to collect and separate PET containers
• Set up a specially designated dumpster at each airport for recycling plastics
• Contract with A-Batt Waste Management for collection

*Increases the recipient's desire or willingness to take action by outlining a solution*

**A** → **Savings**

I've attached a detailed report of the costs involved. As you can see, our net savings the first year should run about $500 000. I've also spoken to Ted Macy in marketing. If we adopt the recycling plan, he wants to build a PR campaign around it.

*Motivates the reader one last time with a specific cost savings figure, then requests a specific action*

**Action**

The PET recycling plan will help build our public image while saving us money. If you agree, let's meet with Ted next week to get things started. Please call me at ext. 2356 if you have any questions.

---

**Pointers for Developing Persuasive Messages**
• Open with a reader benefit, stimulating question, eye-opening fact, or other attention-getter.
• Balance emotional and logical appeals to help the audience accept your message.
• Indicate that you understand the reader's concerns.
• Elaborate on the principal benefits as you continue to stimulate interest and build desire.
• Support your claims with relevant evidence.
• Confidently ask for a decision, stressing the positive results of the action.
• Include pertinent action details such as deadlines.
• Make the desired response simple to understand and easy to accomplish.
• Close with one last reminder of how the audience can benefit.

---

Open with an attention-getting device and show readers that you understand their concerns. Use the interest and desire sections of your message to demonstrate the need or reason for making such a request and to cover the facts, figures, and benefits of taking action and any history or experience that will enhance your appeal. Close with a request for some specific action, and make that course of action as easy to follow as possible to maximize the chances of a positive response.

## Persuasive Presentation of Ideas

*Sometimes the objective of persuasive messages is simply to encourage people to consider a new idea.*

You may encounter situations in which you simply want to change attitudes or beliefs about a particular topic, without asking the audience to decide or do anything—at least not yet. The goal of your first message might be nothing more than convincing your audience to re-examine long-held opinions or admit the possibility of new ways of thinking.

For instance, the World Wide Web Consortium (a global association that defines many of the guidelines and technologies behind the World Wide Web) has launched a campaign called the Web Accessibility Initiative. Although the consortium's ultimate goal is making websites more accessible to people who have disabilities or age-related limitations, a key interim goal is simply making website developers more aware of the need. As part of this effort, the consortium has developed a variety of presentations and documents that highlight the problems many web visitors face.[13]

## Persuasive Claims and Requests for Adjustments

Most claims are routine messages and use the direct approach discussed in Chapter 7. However, both consumers and business professionals sometimes encounter situations in which the claim requires more persuasion.

The key ingredients of a good persuasive claim are a complete and specific review of the facts and a confident and positive tone. Begin persuasive claims by outlining the problem and continue by reviewing what has been done about it so far, if anything. The recipient might be juggling numerous claims and other demands on his or her attention, so be clear, calm, and complete when presenting your case. Be specific about how you would like to see the situation resolved.

Next, give your reader a good reason for granting your claim. Show how the individual or organization is responsible for the problem and appeal to your reader's sense of fair play, goodwill, or moral responsibility. Explain how you feel about the problem but don't get carried away, and don't make threats. People generally respond most favourably to requests that are both calm and reasonable. Close on a positive note that reflects how a successful resolution of the situation will repair or maintain a mutually beneficial working relationship.

**REAL-TIME UPDATES**

**Learn More by Watching This Video**

**Persuasion skills for every business professional**

Persuasion is an essential business skill, no matter what career path you follow. This video offers great tips for understanding, practising, and applying persuasive skills. Go to http://real-timeupdates.com/bce6 and click on Learn More. If you are using MyBCommLab, you can access Real-Time Updates within Business Communication Resources.

# Developing Marketing and Sales Messages

LEARNING OBJECTIVE 4
Describe an effective strategy for developing marketing and sales messages, explain how to modify this approach for social media, and identify steps you can take to avoid ethical lapses in marketing and sales messages.

Marketing and sales messages use the same basic techniques as other persuasive messages, with the added emphasis of encouraging someone to participate in a commercial transaction. Although the terms *marketing message* and *sales message* are often used interchangeably, they are slightly different: **marketing messages** usher potential buyers through the purchasing process without asking them to make an immediate decision. **Sales messages** take over at that point, encouraging potential buyers to make a purchase decision then and there.

Marketing messages focus on such tasks as introducing new brands to the public, providing competitive comparisons, encouraging customers to visit websites for more information, and reminding buyers that a particular product or service is available. In keeping with its interest in healthy lifestyles, for example, lululemon athletica uses a Facebook page to indirectly promote its products by building relationships with potential customers. In contrast, a sales message makes a specific request for people to place an order for a particular product or service.

Most marketing and sales messages, particularly in larger companies, are created and delivered by professionals with specific training in marketing, advertising, sales, or public relations. However, you may be called on to review the work of these specialists or even to write such messages in smaller companies, and having a good understanding of how these messages work will help you be a more effective manager.

## Planning Marketing and Sales Messages

Everything you've learned about planning messages applies in general to marketing and sales messages, but the planning steps for these messages have some particular aspects to consider as well:

- **Assessing audience needs.** As with every other business message, successful marketing and sales messages start with an understanding of audience needs. Depending on the product and the market, these can range from a few functional considerations (such as the size, weight, and finish of office paper) to a complicated mix of emotional and logical issues (all the factors that play into buying a house, for example).

- **Analyzing your competition.** Marketing and sales messages nearly always compete with messages from other companies trying to reach the same audience. When Bell Canada plans a marketing campaign to introduce a new mobile phone plan to current customers, the company knows its audience has also been exposed to messages from Telus, Shaw, and numerous other wireless service providers. Finding a unique message in crowded markets can be quite a challenge.

- **Determining key selling points and benefits.** With some insight into audience needs and the alternatives offered by your competitors, the next step is to decide which features and benefits to highlight. **Selling points** are the most attractive features of a product, whereas **benefits** are the particular advantages purchasers can realize from those features. In other words, selling points focus on what the product does. Benefits focus on what the user experiences or gains. Benefits can be practical, emotional, or a combination of the two. For example, the feature of a thin, flexible sole in a running shoe offers the practical benefit of a more natural feel while running. In contrast, the visual design features of the shoe offer no practical benefits but can offer the emotional benefit of wearing something stylish or unusual (see Table 9.2).

- **Anticipating purchase objections.** Marketing and sales messages usually encounter objections, and, as with persuasive business messages, the best way to handle them is to identify these objections up front and address as many as you can. Objections can range from high price or low quality to a lack of compatibility with existing products or a perceived risk involved with the product. By identifying potential objections up front, you can craft your promotional messages in ways that address those concerns. If price is a likely objection, for instance, you can look for ways to increase the perceived value of the purchase and decrease the perception of high cost. When promoting a home gym, you might say that it costs less than a year's worth of health club dues. Of course, any attempts to minimize perceptions of price or other potential negatives must be done ethically.

| TABLE 9.2 | Features versus Benefits |
| --- | --- |

| PRODUCT OR SERVICE FEATURE | CUSTOMER BENEFIT |
| --- | --- |
| Carrier's Hybrid Heat dual-fuel system combines our Infinity 19 fuel pump with our Infinity 96 furnace. | Carrier's Hybrid Heat dual-fuel system provides the optimum balance of comfort and energy efficiency. |
| Our marketing communication audit accurately measures the impact of your advertising and public relations efforts. | Find out whether your message is reaching the target audience and whether you're spending your marketing budget in the best possible manner. |
| The spools in our fly-fishing reels are machined from solid blocks of aircraft-grade aluminum. | Go fishing with confidence: these lightweight reels will stand up to the toughest conditions. |

## Writing Conventional Marketing and Sales Messages

Conventional marketing and sales messages are often prepared using the AIDA model or some variation of it. (See the next section on crafting messages for social media.) Here are the key points of using the AIDA model for these messages:

- **Getting the reader's attention.** By looking and listening during any given day, you'll notice the many ways advertisers try to get your attention. For example, a headline might offer an exciting product benefit, a piece of interesting news, an appeal to people's emotions or sense of financial value, or a unique solution to a common problem. Of course, words aren't the only attention-getting devices. Depending on the medium, marketers can use evocative images, music, animation, or video. "Cutting through the clutter" to get the audience's attention is one of the biggest challenges with marketing and sales messages.

- **Building interest.** After catching the reader's or viewer's attention, your next step is to build interest in the product, company, or idea you are promoting. A common technique is to "pay off" the promise made in the headline by explaining how you can deliver those benefits. For example, if the headline offers a way to "Get Fit for $2 a Day," the first paragraph could explain that the home gyms your company sells start at less than $700, which works out to less than $2 a day over the course of a year.

- **Increasing desire.** Now that you've given the audience some initial information to start building their interest, the next step is to boost their desire for the product by expanding on your explanation of how it will benefit them. Think carefully about the sequence of support points and use plenty of subheadings, hyperlinks, video demonstrations, and other devices to help people quickly find the information they need. By keeping the focus on potential customers and their practical and emotional needs, you can layer on information that helps convince people that your product really is the best solution for them. For example, the letter in Figure 9.5 focuses on the key benefits of safety and security. You can also use a variety of techniques to address potential objections and minimize doubts, including testimonials from satisfied users, articles written by industry experts, competitive comparisons, offers of product samples or free demonstrations, independent test results, and money-back guarantees.

- **Motivating action.** The final step in the AIDA model is persuading the audience to take action, such as encouraging people to pick up the phone to place an order or visit an online app store to download your software. The keys to a successful *call to action* are making it easy and as risk-free as possible. If the process is confusing or time-consuming, you'll lose potential customers.

If you analyze the advertisements you encounter in any medium, you'll see variations on these techniques used again and again.

*To build interest, expand on and support the promises in your attention-getting opening.*

*Add details and audience benefits to increase desire for the product or service.*

*After you've generated sufficient interest and desire, you're ready to persuade readers to take the preferred action.*

REAL-TIME UPDATES

**Learn More by Reading This Infographic**

**The color of persuasion**

See the powerful influence of colour in marketing and sales messages. Go to http://real-timeupdates.com/bce6 and click on Learn More. If you are using MyBCommLab, you can access Real-Time Updates within Business Communication Resources.

## Writing Promotional Messages for Social Media

*In a social media environment, persuasive efforts require a more conversational, interactive approach.*

The AIDA model and similar approaches have been successful with marketing and sales messages for decades, but in the social media landscape, consumers are more apt to look for product information from other consumers, not the companies marketing those products. Consequently, your emphasis should shift to encouraging and participating in online conversations. Follow these guidelines:[14]

- **Facilitate community building.** Give customers and other audiences an opportunity to connect with you and one another, such as on your Facebook page or through members-only online forums.

**FIGURE 9.5** A Sales Message Using AIDA

**SecureAbel Alarms, Inc.**

5654 Lakemont Drive • Belleville, ON  K0K 3L0 • Voice: (613) 399-4424 • Fax: (613) 399-4422 • http://www.secure.com

October 15, 2016

Mr. Scott MacGregor
St. Lawrence University College
43 King Street
Kingston, ON  K7N 5A6

Dear Mr. MacGregor:

**LOW-COST SECURITY FOR STUDENTS**

How would you feel if you returned to your dorm and discovered that your hard-earned stereo, computer, or microwave had been stolen? Remember, locked doors won't stop a determined thief, and one out of four college students becomes a victim of theft.

**Portable Security for Dorms**
My dorm room was burglarized when I was in university. That's why I've developed a portable security system for your dormitory room. This system works like an auto alarm and can be installed with an ordinary screwdriver. The small activator hooks to your key chain or belt loop. Just press the "lock" key. A "beep" tells you your room is secure, and a blinking red light warns intruders to stay away.

If a thief tries to break in, a loud alarm sounds. Your possessions will be safe. And, even more important, you can activate the system from your bedside, so you're safe while you sleep.

**Low-Cost Relief**
You'd expect this peace of mind to cost a fortune—something most university or college students don't have. But we're offering the SecureAbel Dorm Alarm System for only $75. Here's what you'll receive by return mail:

- The patented alarm unit
- Two battery-operated programmable remote units
- A one-year warranty on all parts
- Complete and easy-to-follow installation instructions

**How to Order**
Order additional alarm boxes to install on your window or bathroom door for only $50. Simply fill out the response card, and mail it along with your choice of payment method in the enclosed envelope. Protect yourself and your belongings by sending in your card today.

Sincerely,

*Dan Abel*

Dan Abel, President

Enclosures

**Annotations (left side):**

Draws the reader into the letter with a provocative question

Seeks to establish a common bond with the reader

Mentions an additional threat (to personal safety), implying another benefit of the security system

Creates the sense of added value

**Annotations (right side):**

Raises reader's awareness of a need

Explains how the product works by comparing it to something familiar—a car alarm

Uses both a logical appeal (protecting possessions) and an emotional appeal (personal safety)

Urges quick action

**Pointers for Writing Sales Letters**
- Get attention with a question, a fact, a solution, an offer/gift, a testimonial, and so on.
- Promise a benefit to the reader.
- Develop the central selling point, vividly relating details to the reader's concerns.
- Describe objective details of the product (size, shape, colour, scent, sound, texture, etc.).
- Anticipate and answer reader questions, and use an appropriate form of evidence.
- Offer a free trial or a guarantee, and refer to samples if they are included.
- Note any enclosures in conjunction with a selling point or a reader benefit.
- Clearly state the action you desire, along with specifics on how to order the product.
- Ease action with reply cards, preaddressed envelopes, phone numbers, and so on.
- Supply a final reader benefit and offer a special inducement to act now.
- In a postscript, convey important donation information or an important sales point.

- **Listen at least as much as you talk.** Listening is just as essential for online conversations as it is for in-person conversations.
- **Initiate and respond to conversations within the community.** Through content on your website, blog postings, social network profiles and messages, newsletters, and other tools, make sure you provide the information customers need in order to

evaluate your products and services. Use an objective, conversational style; people in social networks want useful information, not "advertising speak."

- **Provide information people want.** Whether it's industry-insider news, in-depth technical guides to using your products, or brief answers to questions posted on community Q&A sites, fill the information gaps about your company and its products.
- **Identify and support your champions.** In marketing, *champions* are enthusiastic fans of your company and its products. Champions are so enthusiastic that they help spread your message (through their blogs, for instance), defend you against detractors, and help other customers use your products.
- **Be authentic; be transparent; be real.** Trying to tack social media onto a consumer-hostile business is likely to fail as soon as stakeholders see through the superficial attempt to "be social." In contrast, social media audiences respond positively to companies that are open and conversational about themselves, their products, and subjects of shared interest.
- **Integrate conventional marketing and sales strategies at the right time and in the right places.** AIDA and similar approaches are still valid for specific communication tasks, such as conventional advertising and the product promotion pages on your website.

## Maintaining High Ethical and Legal Standards

The word *persuasion* has negative connotations for some people, especially in a marketing or sales context. However, effective businesspeople view persuasion as a positive force, aligning their own interests with what is best for their audiences. They influence audience members by providing information and aiding understanding, which allows audiences the freedom to choose.[15] To maintain the highest standards of business ethics, always demonstrate the "you" attitude by showing honest concern for your audience's needs and interests.

As marketing and selling grow increasingly complex, so do the legal ramifications of marketing and sales messages. In Canada, the *Competition Act* prohibits misleading advertising. The federal Office of Consumer Affairs provides protection from advertisers that violate federal standards for truthful advertising. Other federal agencies have authority over advertising in specific industries, such as transportation and financial services. In complex situations, marketing and sales people may need clearance from company lawyers before sending messages. In any event, pay close attention to the following legal aspects of marketing and sales communication:[16]

Marketing and sales messages are covered by a wide range of laws and regulations.

- **Marketing and sales messages must be truthful and nondeceptive.** Failing to include important information is also considered deceptive.
- **You must back up your claims with evidence.** You must be able to support your claims with objective evidence such as a survey or scientific study. If you claim that your food product lowers cholesterol, for example, you must have scientific evidence to support that claim.
- **"Bait and switch" advertising is illegal.** Trying to attract buyers by advertising a product that you don't intend to sell—and then trying to sell them another (and usually more expensive) product—is illegal.
- **Marketing messages and websites aimed at children are subject to special rules.** For example, online marketers must obtain consent from parents before collecting personal information about children under age 13.
- **In most cases, you can't use a person's name, photograph, or other identifying information without permission.** Doing so is considered an invasion of privacy. You can use images of people considered to be public figures as long as you don't unfairly imply that they endorse your message.

Before you launch a marketing or sales campaign, make sure you're up to date on the latest regulations affecting spam (or *unsolicited bulk email*, as it's formally known), customer privacy, and data security. The Canada Business website at **www.canadabusiness.ca/ eng/89/903** is a good place to start.

Marketers have a responsibility to stay up to date on laws and regulations that restrict promotional messages.

# LEARNING OBJECTIVES: Check Your Progress

**① OBJECTIVE Apply the three-step writing process to persuasive messages.**

To plan persuasive messages, carefully clarify your purpose to make sure you focus on a single goal. Understand audience needs, demographic and psychographic variables, and motivations. Gathering the right information to convince readers of the benefits of responding is essential. Media choices need to be considered carefully, particularly with marketing and sales messages in a social media landscape. If organizing persuasive messages, you will usually want to choose the indirect approach in order to establish awareness and interest before asking the audience to take action.

When writing persuasive messages, use positive and polite language, understand and respect cultural differences, be sensitive to organizational cultures when writing persuasive business messages, and take steps to establish your credibility. Seven common ways to establish credibility in persuasive messages are using simple language, supporting your claims, identifying your sources, establishing common ground, being objective, displaying good intentions, and avoiding the hard sell.

Accuracy and completeness are especially important because they send signals about your credibility—a crucial element in persuasive messages.

**② OBJECTIVE Describe an effective strategy for developing persuasive business messages.**

Within the context of the three-step process, effective persuasion involves four essential strategies: framing your arguments, balancing emotional and logical appeals, reinforcing your position, and anticipating objections. One of the most commonly used methods for framing a persuasive argument is the AIDA model, in which you open your message by getting the audience's attention; build interest with facts, details, and additional benefits; increase desire by providing more evidence and answering possible objections; and motivate a specific action.

Persuasive business messages combine emotional appeals (which call on feelings and sympathies) and logical appeals (which call on reason, using analogy, induction, or deduction). To reinforce your position, look for ways to add convincing evidence, quotations from experts, or other support material.

By identifying potential objections and addressing them as you craft your message, you can help prevent audience members from gravitating toward negative answers before you have the opportunity to ask them for a positive response.

**③ OBJECTIVE Identify the three most common categories of persuasive business messages.**

The most common types of these messages are (1) persuasive requests for action, in which you ask the recipient to make a decision or engage in some activity; (2) persuasive presentations of ideas, in which you aren't necessarily looking for a decision or action but rather would like the audience to consider a different way of looking at a particular topic; and (3) persuasive claims and requests for adjustments, in which you believe that you have not received fair treatment and would like your case given fresh consideration.

**④ OBJECTIVE Describe an effective strategy for developing marketing and sales messages, explain how to modify this approach for social media, and identify steps you can take to avoid ethical lapses in marketing and sales messages.**

Marketing and sales messages use the same basic techniques as other persuasive messages, with the added emphasis of encouraging someone to participate in a commercial transaction. Marketing messages do this indirectly, whereas sales messages do it directly. The basic strategy for creating these messages includes assessing audience needs; analyzing your competition; determining key selling points and benefits; anticipating purchase objections; applying the AIDA model; adapting your writing to social media, if appropriate; and maintaining high standards of ethical and legal compliance.

To use social media for promotional communication, start by engaging audiences with efforts to build networked communities of potential buyers and other interested parties. Listen to conversations about your company and its products. Initiate and respond to conversations within these communities, being sure to use an objective, conversational style. Provide the information that interested parties want. Identify and support the enthusiastic product champions who want to help spread your message. Be authentic and transparent in all your communication. Speak directly to customers so you don't have to rely on the news media.

Effective and ethical persuasive communicators focus on aligning their interests with the interests of their audiences. They help audiences understand how their proposals will provide benefits to the audience, using language that is persuasive without being manipulative. They choose words that are less likely to be misinterpreted and take care not to distort the truth. Throughout, they maintain a "you" attitude with honest concern for the audience's needs and interests.

## MyBCommLab®

Go to MyBCommLab for everything you need to help you succeed in the job you've always wanted! Tools and resources include the following:
- Writing Activities  • Document Makeovers
- Video Exercises  • Grammar Exercises–and much more!

## Practise Your Grammar

Effective business communication starts with strong grammar skills. To improve your grammar skills, go to MyBCommLab, where you'll find exercises and diagnostic tests to help you produce clear, effective communication.

## Test Your Knowledge

To review chapter content related to each question, refer to the indicated Learning Objective.

1. What are some questions to ask when gauging the audience's needs during the planning of a persuasive message? L.O.❶
2. How do emotional appeals differ from logical appeals? L.O.❷
3. What three types of reasoning can you use in logical appeals? L.O.❷
4. What is the AIDA model, and what are its limitations? L.O.❷

## Apply Your Knowledge

To review chapter content related to each question, refer to the indicated Learning Objective.

1. When writing persuasive messages, why is it so important to give special attention to the analysis of your purpose and audience? L.O.❶
2. Is the "hard sell" approach unethical? Why or why not? L.O.❷
3. What is likely to happen if a promotional message starts immediately with a call to action? L.O.❸
4. Are emotional appeals ethical? Why or why not? L.O.❹

## Practise Your Skills

### EXERCISES FOR PERFECTING YOUR WRITING

To review chapter content related to each set of exercises, refer to the indicated Learning Objective.

**Message Strategies: Persuasive Business Messages; Collaboration: Team Projects** L.O.❷ With another student, analyze the persuasive email message in Figure 9.3 by answering the following questions.

1. What techniques are used to capture the reader's attention?
2. Does the writer use the direct or indirect organizational approach? Why?

3. Is the subject line effective? Why or why not?

4. Does the writer use an emotional appeal or a logical appeal? Why?

5. What reader benefits are included?

6. How does the writer establish credibility?

7. What tools does the writer use to reinforce his position?

## Message Strategies: Persuasive Business Messages

L.O.❷ Compose effective subject lines for the following email messages.

8. A recommendation to your branch manager to install wireless networking throughout the facility. Your primary reason is that management has encouraged more teamwork, and the teams often congregate in meeting rooms, the cafeteria, and other places that lack network access, without which they can't do much of the work they are expected to do.

9. A sales brochure to be sent to area residents, soliciting customers for your new business, "Meals à la Car," a carry-out dining service that delivers from most local restaurants. Diners place orders online, and individual households can order from up to three restaurants at a time to accommodate different tastes. The price is equal to the standard menu prices plus a 10 percent delivery charge.

10. A special request to the company president to allow managers to carry over their unused vacation days to the following year. Apparently, many managers cancelled their fourth-quarter vacation plans to work on the installation of a new company computer system. Under their current contract, vacation days not used by December 31 can't be carried over to the following year.

## Message Strategies: Marketing and Sales Messages

L.O.❹ Determine whether the following sentences focus on features or benefits; rewrite them as necessary to focus on benefits.

11. All-Cook skillets are coated with a durable, patented nonstick surface.

12. You can call anyone and talk as long you like on Saturdays and Sundays with this new mobile phone plan.

13. With 8-millisecond response time, the Westco WC-L2495 48" LCD TV delivers fast video action that is smooth and crisp.

## ACTIVITIES

Each activity is labelled according to the primary skill or skills you will need to use. To review relevant chapter content, you can refer to the indicated Learning Objective. In some instances, supporting information will be found in another chapter, as indicated.

1. **Message Strategies: Persuasive Business Messages; Media Skills: Blogging** L.O.❸, **Chapter 6** Take a look at the information on the RCMP's Internet Safety Resources site for 13- to 16-year-olds at www.rcmp-grc.gc.ca/is-si/index-eng.htm. Keeping in mind the target audience, analyze the effectiveness of this site. Do you think it does a good job of persuading young people to surf the internet safely? Write a blog post that briefly summarizes your analysis, including any recommendations you might have for conveying the message more persuasively.

2. **Message Strategies: Persuasive Business Messages** L.O.❸ Read the following message then (a) analyze the strengths and weaknesses of each sentence and (b) revise the document so that it follows this chapter's guidelines.

> Dear TechStar Computing:
>
> I'm writing to you because of my disappointment with my new multimedia PC display. The display part works all right, but the audio volume is also set too high and the volume knob doesn't turn it down. It's driving us crazy. The volume knob doesn't seem to be connected to anything but simply spins around. I can't believe you would put out a product like this without testing it first.
>
> I depend on my computer to run my small business and want to know what you are going to do about it. This reminds me of every time I buy electronic equipment from what seems like any company. Something is always wrong. I thought quality was supposed to be important, but I guess not.
>
> Anyway, I need this fixed right away. Please tell me what you want me to do.

3. **Message Strategies: Marketing and Sales Messages** L.O.❹ Read the following message then (a) analyze the strengths and weaknesses of each sentence and (b) revise the document so that it follows this chapter's guidelines.

To: Sheila Young, Human Resources Director

From: Shelby Howard, Vice-President

Subject: Recruiting tactics

Date: February 15, 2016

Dear Sheila: I think we should try e-cruiting. I want you to use the huge data banks of resumés now listed on the internet. They provide the software for your searches through these thousands of resumés they receive, so it shouldn't be too difficult. But you will have to define the qualifications you want first. Then they'll supply the resumés that fit.

Eventually, you can develop a website for our company that will post job listings. Then you'll get replies from the kinds of people who might not otherwise post their resumés online. Some of them may be good employees we've been looking for.

Costs breakdowns are: About $1300 apiece per candidate for traditional (newspaper ad) hiring. Plus your time for pre-screening. For e-cruiting, approximately $183 per candidate, with pre-screening supplied by job search databases such as www.monster.ca or www.careerbuilder.com. They will, however, charge us about $100–300 per month to list our jobs, rather than the $1000 the local paper charges us for a Sunday ad. Online job posting word length: unlimited.

You might have to wade through the 30 000 to 100 000 internet sites now devoted to recruiting. Better stick with the names I've already mentioned. You'll be accessing about 150 million internet users in North America, 74 percent of them over the age of 18 looking for jobs.

Right now, our competitors aren't using this method and I can't figure out why. I'm thinking it could be a way to reach talent we might otherwise miss. Maybe they just haven't figured this out yet. You know the ones I mean— the talented individuals we compete for with other construction companies, even though we offer good jobs and benefits.

I read that Bank of Montreal relied on e-cruiting this year. They say they saved $1 million, but we'll have to see how accurate that is with our own trial. Only 2 percent of building industry employers use e-cruiting. Sixty percent of computer companies use it, probably because surfing the internet is no hassle for them. They insist hiring time per candidate is reduced from six weeks to one hour, but I'll have to see that to believe it! Something about not having to wait for snail mail resumés. But then they also don't get to screen candidates by sight first, so maybe it's a toss-up. On the other hand, they can email questions back and forth.

Well, why don't we give it a go anyway?

a. Describe the flaws in approach and execution of this persuasive request for action.

b. Develop a plan for improving the memo. The following questions should help to stimulate your ideas:

- Starting with the subject line, how can you focus on your audience's needs?
- What would be a better opening? Why?
- How can you reorganize the body of the memo to improve the reader's interest and receptivity to the new idea?
- How can you handle facts, statistics, benefits, and appeals more skillfully?
- What should be included in the conclusion to the memo?

c. Now rewrite this persuasive request for action. Don't forget to revise your work.

4. **Message Strategies: Marketing and Sales Messages**
LO.❹ The daily mail often brings a selection of sales messages to your front door. Find a direct-mail package from your mailbox that includes a sales letter. Then answer the following questions to help you analyze and learn from the approach used by the communication professionals who prepare these glossy sales messages. Your instructor might also ask you to share the package and your observations in a class discussion.

a. Who is the intended audience?
b. What are the demographic and psychographic characteristics of the intended audience?

c. What is the purpose of the direct-mail package? Has it been designed to solicit a phone response, make a mail-order sale, obtain a charitable contribution, or do something else?

d. What technique, if any, was used to encourage you to open the envelope?

e. What kind of letter is included? Is it printed with a computer fill-in of certain specific information? For example, is the letter personalized with your name or your family's name? If so, how many times?

f. Did the letter writer follow the AIDA model? If not, explain the letter's organization.

g. What needs does the letter appeal to?

h. What emotional appeals and logical arguments does the letter use?

i. What selling points and consumer benefits does the letter offer?

j. How many and what kinds of enclosures (such as brochures or DVDs) are included for support?

k. Does the letter or package have an unusual format? Does it use eye-catching graphics?

l. Is the message in the letter and on the supporting pieces believable? Would the package sell the product or service to you? Why or why not?

5. **Communication Ethics: Making Ethical Choices** L.O.❻, **Chapter 1** Your boss has asked you to post a message on the company's internal blog, urging everyone in your department to donate money to the company's favourite charity, an organization that operates a summer camp for children with physical challenges. You wind up writing a lengthy posting packed with facts and heartwarming anecdotes about the camp and the children's experiences. When you must work that hard to persuade your audience to take an action such as donating money to a charity, are you being manipulative and unethical? Explain.

# CASES

Apply the three-step writing process to the following cases, as assigned by your instructor.

▌ **Microblogging Skills**

**1. Message Strategies: Persuasive Business Messages** L.O.❸

You've been trying for months to convince your boss, company CEO Will Florence, to start using Twitter. You've told him that top executives in numerous industries now use Twitter as a way to connect with customers and other stakeholders without going through the filters and barriers of formal corporate communications, but he doesn't see the value.

**YOUR TASK** You come up with the brilliant plan to demonstrate Twitter's usefulness using Twitter itself. First, find three executives from three different companies who are on Twitter (choose any companies and executives you find interesting). Second, study their tweets to get a feel for the type of information they share. Third, if you don't already have a Twitter account set up for this class, set one up for the purposes of this exercise (you can deactivate later). Fourth, write four tweets to demonstrate the value of executive microblogging: one that summarizes the value of having a company CEO use Twitter and three support tweets, each one summarizing how your three real-life executive role models use Twitter.

▌ **Email Skills**

**2. Message Strategies: Persuasive Business Messages** L.O.❸

As someone who came of age in the "post-email" world of blogs, wikis, social networks, and other Web 2.0 technologies, you were rather disappointed to find your new employer solidly stuck in the age of email. You use email, of course, but it is only one of the tools in your communication toolbox. From your college years, you have hands-on experience with a wide range of social media tools, having used them to collaborate on school projects, to become involved in your local community, to learn more about various industries and professions, and to research potential employers during your job search. (In fact, without social media, you might never have heard about your current employer in the first place.) Moreover, your use of social media on the job has already paid several important dividends, including finding potential sales contacts at several large companies, connecting with peers in other companies to share ideas for working more efficiently, and learning about some upcoming legislative matters in your province that could profoundly hamper your company's current way of doing business.

You hoped that by setting an example through your own use of social media at work, you would persuade your new colleagues and company management to quickly adopt these tools as well. However, just the opposite has happened. Waiting in your email inbox this morning was a message from the CEO, announcing that the company is now cutting off access to social networking websites and banning the use of any social media at work. The message says that using company time and company computers for socializing is highly inappropriate and might be considered grounds for dismissal in the future if the problem gets out of hand.

**YOUR TASK** You are stunned by the message. You fight the urge to fire off a hotly worded reply to straighten out the CEO's misperceptions. Instead, you wisely decide to send a message to your immediate superior first, explaining why you believe the new policy should be reversed. Using your boss's favourite medium (email, of course!), write a persuasive message, explaining why Facebook, Twitter, and other social networking technologies are valid—and valuable—business tools. Bolster your argument with examples from other companies and advice from communication experts.

▌ **Blogging Skills** ▌ **Team Skills**
### 3. Message Strategies: Persuasive Business Messages L.O.❸

As a strong advocate for the use of social media in business, you are pleased by how quickly people in your company have taken up blogging, wiki writing, and other new-media activities. You are considerably less excited by the style and quality of what you see in the writing of your colleagues. Many seem to have interpreted "authentic and conversational" to mean "anything goes." Several of the Twitter users in the company seem to have abandoned any pretense of grammar and spelling. A few managers have dragged internal disagreements about company strategy out into public view, arguing with each other through comments on various industry-related forums. Production demonstration videos have been posted to the company's YouTube channel virtually unedited, making the whole firm look unpolished and unprofessional. The company CEO has written some blog posts that bash competitors with coarse and even crude language.

You pushed long and hard for greater use of these tools, so you feel a sense of responsibility for this situation. In addition, you are viewed by many in the company as the resident expert on social media, so you have some "expertise authority" on this issue. On the other hand, you are only a first-level manager, with three levels of managers above you, so while you have some "position authority" as well, you can hardly dictate best practices to the managers above you.

**YOUR TASK** Working with two other students, write a post for the company's internal blog (which is not viewable outside the company), outlining your concerns about these communication practices. Use the examples mentioned above, and make up any additional details you need. Emphasize that although social media communication is often less formal and more flexible than traditional business communication, it shouldn't be unprofessional. You are thinking of proposing a social media training program for everyone in the company, but for this message you just want to bring attention to the problem.

▌ **Email Skills**
### 4. Message Strategies: Persuasive Business Messages L.O.❸

Whole Foods Market has grown into a nationwide chain by catering to consumer desires for healthier foods and environmentally sensitive farming methods. Along with selling these products, the company makes a commitment to actively participate in their stores' communities. Whole Foods not only donates 5 percent of after-tax profits to not-for-profit organizations but also financially supports employees who volunteer their time for community service projects. Many Whole Foods stores donate food and household supplies to food banks in their local communities.

You are the manager of the Whole Foods Market on West 8th Avenue in Vancouver, B.C. You developed a program for donating surplus food to local food banks. Because of the success of that program, top executives have asked you to help other Whole Foods stores coordinate this effort into a chainwide food donation program, "Whole Foods for Life." Ideally, by streamlining the process chainwide, the company would be able to increase the number of people it helps and to get more of its employees involved.

You have a limited budget for the program, so the emphasis has to be on using resources already available to the stores and tapping into employees' creativity to come up with locally relevant ideas.[17]

**YOUR TASK** Write a persuasive email message to all managers at Whole Foods Market, explaining the new program and requesting that they help by pooling ideas they've gleaned from their local experience. Even if they don't have food-donation programs currently in place, you want to hear ideas from them and their employees for this charitable project. With their help, you'll choose the best ideas to develop the new Whole Foods for Life program.

▌ **Email Skills**
### 5. Message Strategies: Persuasive Business Messages L.O.❸

Your new company, WorldConnect Language Services, started well and is going strong. However, to expand beyond your Toronto, Ontario, home market, you need a one-time infusion of cash to open branch offices around the country. At the Entrepreneur's Lunch Forum you attended yesterday, you learned about several angels, as they are called in the investment community—private individuals who invest money in small companies in exchange for a share of ownership. One such angel, Melinda Sparks, told the audience that she is looking for investment opportunities outside high technology, where angels often invest their money. She also indicated that she looks for entrepreneurs who know their industries and markets well, who are passionate about the value they bring to the marketplace, who are committed to growing their businesses, and who have a solid plan for how they will spend an investor's money. Fortunately, you meet all of her criteria.

**YOUR TASK**    Draft an email message to Sparks, introducing yourself and your business and asking for a meeting at which you can present your business plan in more detail. Explain that your Toronto office was booked to capacity within two months of opening, thanks to the growing number of international business professionals looking for translators and interpreters. You've researched Canada and identified three other cities that could support language services offices such as yours. Making up whatever other information you need, draft a four-paragraph message following the AIDA model, ending with a request for a meeting within the next four weeks.

▌Email Skills
## 6. Message Strategies: Persuasive Business Messages L.O.❸

Working in human resources at Technology One, you've seen three complaints about repetitive stress injuries (RSIs) already this month. With 50 computer programmers on the payroll, this could develop into a serious problem for the software development company.

The three programmers, along with four from last month, are planning to file worker's compensation claims. They're suffering sharp wrist pains, numbness, and decreased range of motion. Company medical consultants have suggested exercises and wrist splints, but if these don't work, your technical experts could be facing surgery or even permanent disability.

Your boss is Philippe Bonsall, director of human resources. He noticed that these complaints began shortly after the company bought a truckload of new computer equipment at a local merchant's

going-out-of-business sale, and he has hired an outside consultant to check the used equipment. Mary Li, owner of Li and Associates Ergonomic Consulting, reports back that desk and chair heights are fine, but the old-style keyboards and mousing devices are causing the problem. She suggests replacing the keyboards with divided "ergonomic" keyboards, which allow the wrists to stay straight and relieve pressure on the forearm. She also recommends supplying the most advanced form of computer mouse that also reduces hand movement.

Replacing equipment will be expensive, but not nearly as expensive as costs that will arise if more technical workers come in with RSI complaints.

**YOUR TASK**    Bonsall asks you to draft a memo or email he can use to persuade company controller Katherine Wilson to replace the equipment. You must convince her of the urgent need to make the upgrades recommended by Li and Associates Ergonomic Consulting.[18]

▌Blogging Skills ▌Portfolio Builder
## 7. Message Strategies: Persuasive Business Messages L.O.❸

You have a management job in an auto parts manufacturing plant that has 200 employees. Your company has a good recycling program that employees support, but you think the program should be expanded to include composting. In conversation with your boss, you shared some of your ideas and were encouraged to write an email message to the general manager making the suggestion. Read about composting benefits and find some examples of companies that encourage composting in their plants or offices.

**YOUR TASK**
a. Write the email message to the general manager persuading her to approve the idea and provide a small budget to purchase supplies.
b. Assume your email was successful and the general manager has now asked you to write a posting for the company's internal blog, persuading staff to participate. Write the blog post.

▌Email Skills
## 8. Message Strategies: Persuasive Business Messages L.O.❸

You are an administrator in a growing home care services business in metro Vancouver. Your company provides nurses, care aids, companions, and cleaning help for seniors living in the region. Over the past decade, your company has grown from two people to 150 full-time staff. In the last contract with staff, the company opted to provide staff the use of a fleet of 50 Ford Taurus vehicles that were leased locally one year ago. Each vehicle has travelled over 20 000 km on company business. The use of the vehicles has worked out well for staff, especially given the three shifts you run around the clock. But you are concerned about the growing cost of gasoline. Fuel costs run high; you calculate the cost per vehicle at today's gas prices based on each vehicle getting 20 km per litre. You think a hybrid fleet would make much more sense. For one thing, the Toyota Prius gets 44 km to the litre, which would bring a big savings in fuel costs. The cost of the gas is one issue, but you also have some other concerns because your boss isn't really very eco-sensitive. In fact, your boss drives a "honking big SUV" around town and doesn't even use it for sports or off-road activities.

You saw a program on CBC about the "green economy" and did a little research via some links on the CBC website to find CleanTech (www.cleantech.com) and Sustainable Development Technology Canada (www.sdtc.ca). You believe it makes business sense for companies to reduce greenhouse gas emissions. You could not only accomplish this goal but also realize further savings by converting the fleet to a hybrid option. The B.C. government, like California, created a carbon tax, so over the next few years it will become even more costly to run gasoline-based engines in the province. As a result of the tax, the price of gas will go up at least 10 cents per litre within a couple of years. You also read that Sustainable Development Technology Canada has funding available for technology innovations that deliver clean water, clean soil, clean air, and reduced greenhouse emissions. You know other companies are making money by going green—even leading multinationals such as Johnson & Johnson were able to grow business by 300 percent over an eight-year period while reducing greenhouse gas emissions by 7 percent, so you know making this change can be profitable.

**YOUR TASK**   In MyBCommLab, use the Find Sources option in the Writer's Toolkit to research the benefits of reducing greenhouse gas emissions for a business. You want your boss to authorize you to do a feasibility study on the possible savings of switching the company fleet to hybrid technology. As well, you could put together an application for a federal government grant if your boss gives you the OK to look into it. Write a persuasive email message to your boss to get approval of your idea. Who knows? Maybe your idea will result in not just saving your company money but making the air cleaner for a lot of people.[19]

**▍Email Skills**

**9. Message Strategies: Persuasive Business Messages** L.O.❸

You work in the human resources department of an accounting firm that has expanded from 80 employees to over 200 within the last three years. Your offices used to be all on one floor and the atmosphere was friendly and familial. However, two years ago the firm had to expand its office space and moved onto three floors. In the past, conversations around the water cooler used to keep people in touch. Now, the atmosphere has changed and most employees know only a few of their colleagues. Many of the new employees are 23–30 years old.

Your boss, the human resources department manager, recognizes there is a morale problem. You think the morale could be improved by creating a way for people to share positive company experiences. You read that Ernst & Young, an international consulting firm, created an employee contest using video. Each department in a branch of the company was given a video camera and the task of making a short video about what is good about working at Ernst & Young. Creative and entertaining videos were produced and shared on the company's website. Later some of these videos were used for recruitment, and Ernst & Young still uses employee testimonial videos on its Facebook site.[20]

Maybe a video contest for your company's departments would be a good way to get people interacting and would raise morale. You decide to persuade your boss to take this idea to the senior management team, and even though she is not that technology-oriented, she is open to your ideas. You estimate the cost to be $1000 for flip video cameras for 10 departments plus a budget for catering for the grand finale show, and some prizes. You'd hold the finale after work as a social event. Bringing everyone together to see the finished videos would be part of the morale builder. Later, the videos would be posted on the company website.

**YOUR TASK**   Write an email message to your boss persuading her to propose a departmental video contest to senior management.

**▍Microblogging Skills**

**10. Message Strategies: Marketing and Sales Messages; Media Skills: Microblogging** L.O.❹

Effective microblogging messages emphasize clarity and conciseness—and so do effective sales messages.

**YOUR TASK**   Find the website of any product that can be ordered online (any product you find interesting and that is appropriate to use for a class assignment).

Adapt the information on the website, using your own words, and write four tweets to promote the product. The first should get your audience's attention (with an intriguing benefit claim, for example), the second should build audience interest by providing some support for the claim you made in the first message, the third should increase readers' desire to have the product by layering on one or two more buyer benefits, and the fourth should motivate readers to take action to place an order. Your first three tweets can be up to 140 characters, but the fourth should be limited to 120 to accommodate a URL (you don't need to include the URL in your message, however).

If your class is set up with private Twitter accounts, use your private account to send your messages. Otherwise, email your four messages to your instructor or post them on your class blog, as your instructor directs.

**❚ Email Skills**
### 11. Message Strategies: Marketing and Sales Messages L.O.❹

This morning before heading off to your job in the food services department at the Sundown Casino Entertainment Centre in Richmond, B.C., you heard on the news that Canadian Blood Services (CBS) has put out a call for blood. National supplies have fallen dangerously low. Donated blood lasts only 72 hours, and CBS is responsible for more than half the nation's supply of emergency and routine blood and blood products for victims of accidents and diseases. Thousands depend on the CBS for daily transfusions.

You're one of only 5 percent of eligible donors who think of giving blood. However, today, you're going to do more than just roll up your own sleeve. You want Sundown Casino to host the local CBS chapter's bloodmobile for a community blood drive. As soon as you get to work, you quickly persuade other members of the food services staff to help you out. Working together, you'll have all the skills necessary to organize the event. Not only is it the right thing to do, but the event will:

- Improve the casino's community image by demonstrating its interest in the public's welfare.
- Make Sundown's employees and customers feel good about themselves because they are helping others.
- Increase the CBS's blood supply, since Sundown's hundreds of employees and customers are all potential donors.

You also remind your co-workers that the local CBS chapter is part of an international humanitarian organization. As part of its mission to "prevent and alleviate human suffering wherever it may be found," all assistance is given free of charge, made possible by people who donate their time, money, and skills.

**YOUR TASK** With your team of co-workers (classmates), brainstorm additional support for the event. Then work together to write a persuasive letter to the Sundown board of directors, 145 Ocean View Way, Richmond, B.C., V5Y 2S9, convincing readers to host the bloodmobile. Research (or make up) details, such as your team's qualifications to organize the event, anecdotes to add emotional appeal, and so on.

**❚ IM Skills**
### 12. Message Strategies: Marketing and Sales Messages L.O.❹

At WestJet, you are one of the coordinators for the annual Employee Charitable Contributions Campaign. All year, WestJet supports a number of health and human service agencies. These groups include the Canadian National Institute for the Blind (CNIB), Missing Children, Hope Air, The Ontario Hospital for Sick Children, and many other deserving causes. WestJet engages employees in corporate citizenship.

During the winter holidays, WestJet also donates to agencies that cater to the needs of disadvantaged families, women, and children. The prospect of helping children enjoy the holidays, especially children who otherwise might have nothing, usually awakens the spirit of giving in most employees. But some of them wait until the last minute and then forget.

They have until Friday, December 18, to come forth with cash contributions. To make it in time for holiday deliveries, they can also bring in toys, food, and blankets through Tuesday, December 22. They shouldn't have any trouble finding the collection bins; they're everywhere in the corporate office and in all airport staff lounges, and they are marked with big, bright, red banners. But some will want to call you with questions or to make (you hope) credit card donations: 1-800-532-6754, ext. 3342.

**YOUR TASK** It is December 14. Write a 75–100 word instant message encouraging last-minute gifts.[21]

**❚ Social Networking Skills ❚ Teamwork Skills**
### 13. Message Strategies: Marketing and Sales Messages; Media Skills: Social Networking L.O.❹, Chapter 7

You chose your college or university based on certain expectations, and you've been enrolled long enough now to have some idea about whether those expectations have been met. In other words, you are something of an expert about the "consumer benefits" your school can offer prospective students.

**YOUR TASK** In a team of four students, interview six other students who are not taking this business communication course. Try to get a broad demographic and psychographic sample, including students in a variety of majors and programs. Ask these students (1) why they chose this college or university and (2) whether the experience has met their expectations so far. To ensure the privacy of your respondents, do not record their names with their answers. Each member of the team should then answer these same two questions, so that you have responses from a total of 10 students.

After compiling the responses (you might use Google Docs or a similar collaboration tool so that everyone on the team has easy access to the information), analyze them as a team to look for any recurring "benefit themes." Is it the quality of the education? Research opportunities? Location? The camaraderie of school sporting events? The chance to meet and study with fascinating students from a variety of backgrounds? Identify two or three strong benefits that your college or university can promise—and deliver—to prospective students.

Now nominate one member of the team to draft a short marketing message that could be posted on the Notes tab of your school's Facebook page. The message should include a catchy title that makes it clear the message is a student's perspective on why this is a great place to get a college education. When the draft is ready, the other members of the team should review it individually. Finally, meet as a team to complete the message.

## BUSINESS COMMUNICATION NOTEBOOK

# Ethics

## What You May Legally Say in a Sales Letter

As you prepare to write a sales letter, think carefully about your choice of words. False or misleading statements could land you in court, so make sure your language complies with legal and ethical standards. To keep your sales letters within the limits of the law, review the legal considerations of these typical sales phrases:

- **"Our product is the best on the market."** This statement is acceptable for a sales letter because the law permits you to express an opinion about your product. In the process of merchandising a product, statements of opinion are known as "puffery," which is perfectly legal as long as you make no deceptive or fraudulent claims.

- **"Our product will serve you well for many years to come."** This statement from a sales brochure triggered a lawsuit by a disgruntled customer who claimed the manufacturer's product lasted only a few years. The courts ruled that the statement was an acceptable form of puffery because the manufacturer did not promise that the product would last for a specific number of years.

- **"We're so confident you'll enjoy our products that we've enclosed a sample of our most popular line. This sample can be yours for only $5! Please send your payment in the enclosed, prepaid envelope."** If you include a product sample with your sales letter, your readers may keep the merchandise without paying for it. Under the law, consumers may consider unordered goods as gifts. They are not obligated to return the items to you or submit payments for unsolicited merchandise.

- **"Thousands of high school students—just like you—are already enjoying this fantastic CD collection! Order before March 1 and save!"** If your sales letter appeals to minors, you are legally obligated to honour their contracts. At the same time, however, the law permits minors to cancel their contracts and return the merchandise to you. Sellers are legally obligated to accept contracts voided by minors and any goods returned by them. Legal adult status is defined differently from province to province, ranging from age 18 to 21.

- **"You'll find hundreds of bargains at our annual 'scratch and dent' sale! All sales are final on merchandise marked 'as is.'"** When you use the term *as is* in your sales letter, you are not misleading customers about the quality of your products. By warning consumers that the condition of sale items is less than perfect, you are not legally obligated to issue refunds to customers who complain about defects later on.

## Applications for Success

1. You probably receive sales letters through the mail or via email all the time. Review two of these sales letters for content. List the "puffery" statements in each letter.

2. Note any statements in these sales letters that appear questionable to you. Rewrite one of the statements, carefully choosing words that won't be misleading to consumers.

3. What do you think? Are these sales letters convincing? How have they persuaded you? If you don't believe they are convincing, explain how they have failed to persuade you.

# Understanding and Planning Reports and Proposals

**LEARNING OBJECTIVES**

*After studying this chapter, you will be able to*

1 Adapt the three-step writing process to reports and proposals.

2 Describe an effective process for conducting business research, explain how to evaluate the credibility of an information source, and identify the five ways to use research results.

3 Explain the role of secondary research and describe the two major categories of online research tools.

4 Explain the role of primary research and identify the two most common forms of primary research for business communication purposes.

5 Explain how to plan informational reports and website content.

6 Identify the three most common ways to organize analytical reports.

7 Explain how to plan proposals.

The Inualiut Regional Corporation (IRC) was established in 1984 to manage the affairs of the first Aboriginal Canadians from the Northwest Territories to negotiate a comprehensive land claim settlement with the Government of Canada. Today, IRC's principal business subsidiaries and interests include the land, the investment or heritage fund, and diverse industries such as environmental services, property management, hospitality, construction, transportation, manufacturing, and oil and gas. Reports are designed to speak to many audiences; Gerry Roy writes reports that facilitate decision making among the boards of directors in this unique business setting. "Conveying an understanding of what we do and where we do it with such a diverse audience," says Roy, "requires careful message planning." Decision makers depend on well-planned reports to summarize carefully researched data, define problems, discuss pertinent issues, and analyze information.

## Applying the Three-Step Writing Process to Reports and Proposals

**LEARNING OBJECTIVE 1**
Adapt the three-step writing process to reports and proposals.

Like Gerry Roy, most managers make decisions and solve problems based on the information and analyses they receive in reports, written factual accounts that objectively communicate information about some aspect of business.

Business reports help companies make decisions and solve business problems.

In previous chapters, you learned to use the three-step writing process when developing shorter business messages; now it's time to apply those skills to longer messages such as business plans. Reports fall into three basic categories (see Figure 10.1):

Reports can be classified as informational reports, analytical reports, or proposals.

Reports can be a lot of work, but they also give you the opportunity to demonstrate your grasp of important business issues.

- **Informational reports** offer data, facts, feedback, and other types of information, without analysis or recommendations.
- **Analytical reports** offer both information and analysis and can also include recommendations.
- **Proposals** present persuasive recommendations to internal or external audiences, often involving investments or purchases.

Try to view every business report as an opportunity to demonstrate your understanding of your audience's challenges and your ability to contribute to your organization's success.

The three-step process is easily adapted to reports and, in fact, makes these larger projects easier to produce by ensuring a methodical, efficient approach to planning, writing, and completing.

---

**FIGURE 10.1  Common Types of Business Reports and Proposals**

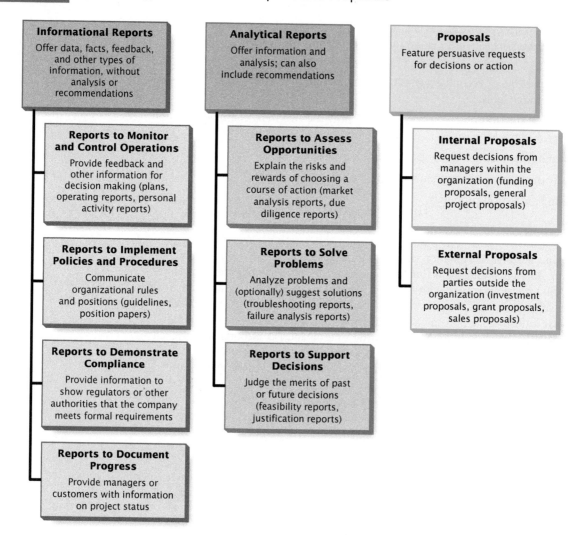

**Informational Reports**
Offer data, facts, feedback, and other types of information, without analysis or recommendations

- **Reports to Monitor and Control Operations**
  Provide feedback and other information for decision making (plans, operating reports, personal activity reports)

- **Reports to Implement Policies and Procedures**
  Communicate organizational rules and positions (guidelines, position papers)

- **Reports to Demonstrate Compliance**
  Provide information to show regulators or other authorities that the company meets formal requirements

- **Reports to Document Progress**
  Provide managers or customers with information on project status

**Analytical Reports**
Offer information and analysis; can also include recommendations

- **Reports to Assess Opportunities**
  Explain the risks and rewards of choosing a course of action (market analysis reports, due diligence reports)

- **Reports to Solve Problems**
  Analyze problems and (optionally) suggest solutions (troubleshooting reports, failure analysis reports)

- **Reports to Support Decisions**
  Judge the merits of past or future decisions (feasibility reports, justification reports)

**Proposals**
Feature persuasive requests for decisions or action

- **Internal Proposals**
  Request decisions from managers within the organization (funding proposals, general project proposals)

- **External Proposals**
  Request decisions from parties outside the organization (investment proposals, grant proposals, sales proposals)

---

## Analyzing the Situation

Define your purpose clearly so you don't waste time with unnecessary rework.

Reports can be complex, time-consuming projects, so be sure to analyze the situation carefully before you begin to write. Pay special attention to your **statement of purpose**, which explains *why* you are preparing the report and *what* you plan to deliver.

The most useful way to phrase your purpose statement is to begin with an infinitive phrase (*to* plus a verb), which helps pin down your general goal (*to inform, to identify, to analyze*, and so on). For instance, in an informational report, your statement of purpose can be as simple as one of these:

* To identify potential markets for our new phone-based video games.
* To update the board of directors on the progress of the research project.
* To submit required information to the Toronto Stock Exchange.

The statement of purpose for an analytical report often needs to be more comprehensive. For example, if you were asked to find ways of reducing employee travel and entertainment (T&E) costs, you might phrase the statement of purpose like this:

> To analyze the T&E budget, evaluate the impact of recent changes in airfares and hotel costs, and suggest ways to tighten management's control over T&E expenses.

A proposal must also be guided by a clear statement of purpose to help you focus on crafting a persuasive message. Here are several examples:

* To secure funding in next year's budget for new conveyor systems in the warehouse.
* To get management approval to reorganize the western Canadian sales force.
* To secure $2 million from outside investors to start production of the new titanium mountain bike.

In addition to considering your purpose carefully, you will want to prepare a **work plan** for most reports and proposals in order to make the best use of your time. For simpler reports, the work plan can be an informal list of tasks and a simple schedule. However, if you're preparing a lengthy report, particularly when you're collaborating with others, you'll want to develop a more detailed work plan (see Figure 10.2).

*The statement of purpose for a proposal should help guide you in developing a persuasive message.*

*A detailed work plan saves time and often produces more effective reports.*

## Gathering Information

Obtaining the information needed for many reports and proposals requires careful planning, and you may even need to do a separate research project just to acquire the data and information you need. To stay on schedule and on budget, be sure to review both your statement of purpose and your audience's needs so that you can prioritize your information needs and focus on the most important questions.

*Some reports require formal research projects in order to gather all the necessary information.*

## Selecting the Right Medium

In addition to the general media selection criteria discussed in Chapter 3, consider several points for reports and proposals. First, for many reports and proposals, audiences have specific media requirements, and you might not have a choice. For instance, executives in many corporations now expect to review many reports via their in-house intranets, sometimes in conjunction with an **executive dashboard** (see Figure 10.3), a customized graphical presentation of key performance parameters. The latest generation of software makes it easy to customize screens to show each manager the specific summaries he or she needs to see. Second, consider how your audience members want to provide feedback on your report or proposal. Do they prefer to write comments on a printed document or edit a wiki article? Third, will people need to search through your document electronically or update it in the future? Fourth, bear in mind that your choice of medium sends a message. For instance, a routine sales report dressed up in expensive multimedia will look like a waste of valuable company resources.

*The best medium for any given report might be anything from a professionally printed and bound document to an online executive dashboard that displays nothing but report highlights.*

## Organizing Your Information

The direct approach is often used for reports because it is efficient and easy to follow (see Figure 10.4). When your audience is likely to be receptive or at least open-minded, use

*The direct approach is popular with reports, but some situations call for the indirect approach.*

| FIGURE 10.2 | Work Plan for a Report |

Clearly and succinctly defines the problem

**STATEMENT OF THE PROBLEM**
The rapid growth of our company over the past five years has reduced the sense of community among our staff. People no longer feel like they are part of an intimate organization that values teamwork.

**PURPOSE AND SCOPE OF WORK**
The purpose of this study is to determine whether social networking technology such as Facebook and Socialtext would help rebuild a sense of community within the workforce and whether encouraging the use of such tools in the workplace will have any negative consequences. The study will attempt to assess the impact of social networks in other companies in terms of community-building, morale, project communication, and overall productivity.

Identifies exactly what will be covered by the research and in the final report

Explains how the researchers will find the data and information they need

**SOURCES AND METHODS OF DATA COLLECTION**
Data collection will start with secondary research, including a review of recently published articles and studies on the use of social networking in business and a review of product information published by technology vendors. Primary research will focus on an employee and management survey to uncover attitudes about social networking tools. We will also collect anecdotal evidence from bloggers and others with experience using networks in the workplace.

**PRELIMINARY OUTLINE**
The preliminary outline for this study is as follows:
  I. What experiences have other companies had with social networks in the workplace?
      A. Do social networks have a demonstrable business benefit?
      B. How do employees benefit from using these tools?
      C. Has network security and information confidentiality been an issue?
  II. Is social networking an appropriate solution for our community-building needs?
      A. Is social networking better than other tools and methods for community building?
      B. Are employees already using social networking tools on the job?
      C. Will a company-endorsed system distract employees from essential duties?
      D. Will a company system add to managerial workloads in any way?
  III. If we move ahead, should we use a "business-class" network such as Socialtext or a consumer tool such as Facebook?
      A. How do the initial and ongoing costs compare?
      B. Do the additional capabilities of a business-class network justify the higher costs?
  IV. How should we implement a social network?
      A. Should we let it grow "organically," with employees choosing their own tools and groups?
      B. Should we make a variety of tools available and let employees improvise on their own?
      C. Should we designate one system as the official company social network and make it a permanent, supported element of the information technology infrastructure?
  V. How can we evaluate the success of a new social network?
      A. What are the criteria of success or failure?
      B. What is the best way to measure these criteria?

Offers a preliminary outline with sufficient detail to guide the research and set reader expectations

Clearly lists responsibilities and due dates

**TASK ASSIGNMENTS AND SCHEDULE**
Each phase of this study will be completed by the following dates:

| | |
|---|---|
| Secondary research: Rob Waters | September 14, 2016 |
| Employee and management survey: Julienne Cho | September 21, 2016 |
| Analysis and synthesis of research: Rob Waters/Julienne Cho | October 5, 2016 |
| Comparison of business and consumer solutions: Julienne Cho | October 12, 2016 |
| Comparison of implementation strategies: Rob Waters | October 12, 2016 |
| Final report: Rob Waters | October 19, 2016 |

the direct approach: Lead with a summary of your key findings, conclusions, recommendations, or proposal, whichever is relevant. This "up-front" arrangement saves time and makes the rest of the report easier to follow. For those readers who have questions or want more information, later parts of the report provide complete findings and supporting details.

However, if the audience is unsure about your credibility or is not ready to accept your main idea without first seeing some reasoning or evidence, the indirect approach is a better choice because it gives you a chance to prove your points and gradually overcome audience reservations. To enable the use of AIDA-style persuasion, unsolicited proposals in particular often use the indirect approach. Bear in mind, though, that the longer the document, the less effective the indirect approach is likely to be.

## FIGURE 10.3  Executive Dashboards

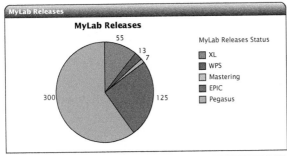

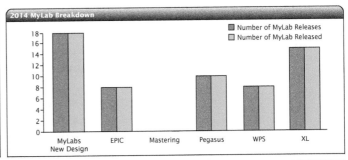

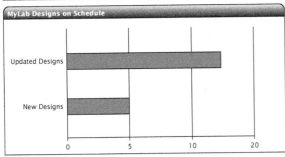

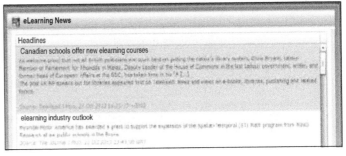

*Source:* Based on Pearson Education MyLab dashboard.

## FIGURE 10.4  Direct Approach Versus Indirect Approach in an Introduction

**DIRECT APPROACH**

Since the company's founding 25 years ago, we have provided regular repair service for all our electric appliances. This service has been an important selling point as well as a source of pride for our employees. However, rising labour costs have made it impossible to maintain profitability while offering competitive service rates. Last year, we lost $500 000 on our repair business.

— Summarizes the situation

Because of your concern over these losses, you asked me to study whether we should discontinue our repair service. After analyzing the situation in depth, I have concluded that the repair service is an expensive, impractical tradition, and I recommend that the service be discontinued.

— Reminds the audience why the report was prepared

— Immediately introduces one of the report's major conclusions and presents the report's key recommendation, that the repair service should be discontinued

By withdrawing from the electric appliance repair business, we can substantially improve our financial performance without damaging our reputation with customers. This conclusion is based on three basic points that are covered in the following pages:

— Emphasizes the benefits of acting on the recommendation and addresses any fears about possible negative consequences

• It is highly unlikely that we will ever be able to make a profit in the repair business.

• We can refer customers to a variety of qualified repair firms without significantly reducing customer satisfaction.

• Closing down the service operation will create few internal problems.

— Lists three important conclusions that led to the recommendation to end the service (notice how the indirect approach that follows presents these same three points as questions to be considered)

Summarizes the situation ——

Reminds the audience why the report was prepared ——

Indicates that conclusions and recommendations will be presented later in the report ——

Introduces the three points that will eventually lead to the conclusions and ultimately to the recommendation ——

**INDIRECT APPROACH**

→ Since the company's founding 25 years ago, we have provided regular repair service for all our electric appliances. This service has been an important selling point as well as a source of pride for our employees. However, rising labour costs have made it impossible to maintain profitability while offering competitive service rates.

→ Because of your concern over these losses, you have asked me to study whether we should discontinue our repair service. I have analyzed the situation in depth, and the following pages present my findings and recommendations for your review. The analysis addressed three basic questions:

• What is the extent of our losses, and what can we do to turn the business around?

• Would withdrawal hurt our sales of electrical appliances?

→ • What would be the internal repercussions of closing down the repair business?

**LEARNING OBJECTIVE 2**
Describe an effective process for conducting business research, explain how to evaluate the credibility of an information source, and identify the five ways to use research results.

# Supporting Your Messages with Reliable Information

Effective research involves a lot more than simply typing a few terms into a search engine. Save time and get better results by using a clear process:

1. **Plan your research.** Planning is the most important step of any research project; a solid plan yields better results in less time.
2. **Locate the data and information you need.** Your next step is to figure out *where* the data and information are and *how* to access them.
3. **Process the data and information you located.** The data and information you find probably won't be in a form you can use immediately and may require statistical analysis or other processing.
4. **Apply your findings.** You can apply your research findings in three ways: summarizing information, drawing conclusions, and developing recommendations.
5. **Manage information efficiently.** Many companies are trying to maximize the return on the time and money invested in business research by collecting and sharing research results in a variety of computer-based systems, known generally as **knowledge management systems**.

> Researching without a plan wastes time and usually produces unsatisfactory results.

## Planning Your Research

> The problem statement guides your research by focusing on the decision you need to make or the conclusion you need to reach.

Start by developing a **problem statement** that defines the purpose of your research—the decision you need to make or the conclusion you need to reach at the end of the process. Next, identify the information you need in order to make that decision or reach that conclusion. You can then begin to generate the questions that will constitute your research. Chances are you will have more questions than you have time or money to answer, so prioritize your information needs.

Before beginning any research project, remember that research carries some significant ethical responsibilities. Your research tactics affect the people from whom you gather data and information, the people who read your results, and the people who are affected by the way you present those results. To avoid ethical lapses, follow these guidelines:

- Keep an open mind so that you don't skew the research toward answers you want or expect to see.
- Respect the privacy of your research participants, and don't mislead people about the purposes of your research.[1]
- Document sources and give appropriate credit.
- Respect your sources' *intellectual property rights* (the ownership of unique ideas that have commercial value in the marketplace).[2]
- Don't distort information from your sources.
- Don't misrepresent who you are or what you intend to do with the research results.

In addition to ethics, research etiquette deserves careful attention. For example, respect the time of anyone who agrees to be interviewed or to be a research participant and maintain courtesy throughout the interview or research process.

## Locating Data and Information

> Primary research contains information that you gather specifically for a new research project; secondary research contains information that others have gathered (and published, in many cases).

The range of sources available to business researchers today can be overwhelming. The good news is that if you have a question about an industry, a company, a market, a new technology, or a financial topic, somebody else has probably already researched the subject. Research done previously for another purpose is considered **secondary research**; sources for such research information include magazines, newspapers, public websites, books, and other reports. Don't let the name *secondary* fool you, though. You want to start with secondary research because it can save you considerable time and money for many projects. In contrast, **primary research** involves the collection of new data, through surveys, interviews, and other techniques.

## Evaluating Information Sources

No matter where you're searching, it is your responsibility to separate quality information from unreliable junk, so you don't taint your results or damage your reputation. Social media tools have complicated this challenge by making many new sources of information available. On the positive side, independent sources communicating through blogs, Twitter and other microblogging sites, wikis, user-generated content sites, and podcasting channels can provide valuable and unique insights, often from experts whose voices might never be heard otherwise. On the negative side, these nontraditional information sources often lack the editorial boards and fact checkers commonly used in traditional publishing. You cannot assume that the information you find in blogs and other sources is accurate, objective, and current. Answer the following questions about each piece of material:

Evaluate your sources carefully to avoid embarrassing and potentially damaging mistakes.

- **Does the source have a reputation for honesty and reliability?** For example, try to find out how the source accepts articles and whether it has an editorial board, conducts peer reviews, or follows fact-checking procedures.
- **Is the source potentially biased?** To interpret an organization's information, you need to know its point of view.
- **What is the purpose of the material?** For instance, was the material designed to inform others of new research, to advance a political position, or to promote a product?
- **Is the author credible?** Is the author a professional journalist or merely someone with an opinion?
- **Where did the source get its information?** Try to find out who collected the data and the methods used.
- **Can you verify the material independently?** Verification is particularly important when the information goes beyond simple facts to include projections, interpretations, and estimates.
- **Is the material current and complete?** Make sure you are using the most current information available. Have you accessed the entire document or only a selection from it?
- **Does the information make sense?** Step back and determine whether the information stands up to logical scrutiny.

You probably won't have time to conduct a thorough background check on all your sources, so focus your efforts on the most important or most suspicious pieces of information. And if you can't verify critical facts or figures, be sure to let your readers know that.

## Using Your Research Results

After you've collected your data and information, the next step is to transform this raw material into the specific content you need. This step can involve quoting, paraphrasing, or summarizing textual material; drawing conclusions; and making recommendations.

After you collect data and information, the next step is converting it into usable content.

**QUOTING, PARAPHRASING, AND SUMMARIZING INFORMATION** You can use textual information from secondary sources in three ways. *Quoting* a source means you reproduce the material exactly as you found it (giving full credit to the source, of course). Use direct quotations when the original language will enhance your argument or when rewording the passage would reduce its impact. However, be careful with direct quotes: using too many creates a choppy patchwork of varying styles and gives the impression that all you've done is piece together the work of other people. When quoting sources, set off shorter passages with quotation marks and set off longer passages (generally five lines or more) as separate, indented paragraphs.

Quoting a source means reproducing the content exactly and indicating who created the information originally.

Paraphrasing is expressing someone else's ideas in your own words.

You can often maximize the impact of secondary material in your own writing by *paraphrasing* it: restating it in your own words and with your own sentence structures.[3] Paraphrasing helps you maintain consistent tone while using vocabulary that's familiar to your audience. Of course, you still need to credit the originator of the information (by citing the source), but you don't need quotation marks or indented paragraphs.

Summarizing is similar to paraphrasing but distills the content into fewer words.

*Summarizing* is similar to paraphrasing but presents the gist of the material in fewer words than the original by leaving out details, examples, and less important information (see Figure 10.5). Like quotations and paraphrases, summaries also require complete documentation of sources. Summarizing is not always a simple task, and your audience will judge your ability to separate significant issues from less significant details.

Of course, all three approaches require careful attention to ethics. When quoting directly, take care not to distort the original intent of the material by quoting selectively or out of context. And never resort to **plagiarism**—presenting someone else's words as your own, such as copying material from an online source and dropping it into a report without giving proper credit.

In Canada, copyright law includes the concept of "fair dealing," which allows the use of other's material for certain purposes specified in the *Copyright Act*—provided credit is given to the original source and that the use is fair. Five Supreme Court of Canada decisions in 2012 defined these purposes as: education, research, private study, criticism, and review or news reporting. Uncertainties in the law still exist as to what constitutes "fair" use, especially if the borrowed material is circulated widely.[4]

**DRAWING CONCLUSIONS**   A **conclusion** is a logical interpretation of facts and other information. Your conclusion often answers the question posed by your purpose statement. In addition to being logically sound, a conclusion should be based only on the information provided or at least referred to in the report. Reaching good conclusions is one of the most important skills you can develop in your business career. In fact, the ability to see patterns and possibilities that others can't see is one of the hallmarks of innovative business leaders.

**MAKING RECOMMENDATIONS**   Whereas a conclusion interprets information, a **recommendation** suggests what to do about the information. The following example shows the difference between a conclusion and a recommendation:

---

**FIGURE 10.5**   Summarizing Effectively

**Original: 116 words**

Our facilities costs spiraled out of control last year. The 23 percent jump was far ahead of every other cost category in the company and many times higher than the 4 percent average rise for commercial real estate in the Portland metropolitan area. The rise can be attributed to many factors, but the major factors include repairs (mostly electrical and structural problems at the downtown office), energy (most of our offices are heated by electricity, the price of which has been increasing much faster than for oil or gas), and last but not least, the loss of two sublease tenants whose rent payments made a substantial dent in our cost profile for the past five years.

**Analyze the text to find main idea, major supporting points, and details**

*Main idea* → Our facilities costs spiraled out of control last year. The 23 percent jump was far ahead of every other cost category in the company and many times higher than the 4 percent average rise for commercial real estate in the Portland metropolitan area.

*Major support points* → The rise can be attributed to many factors, but the major factors include repairs (mostly electrical and structural problems at the downtown office),

*Details* → energy (most of our offices are heated by electricity, the price of which has been increasing much faster than for oil or gas), and last but not least, the loss of two sublease tenants whose rent payments made a substantial dent in our cost profile for the past five years.

**45-word summary**

Our facilities costs jumped 23 percent last year, far ahead of every other cost category in the company and many times higher than the 4 percent local average. The major factors contributing to the increase are repairs, energy, and the loss of two sublease tenants.

**22-word summary**

Our facilities costs jumped 23 percent last year, due mainly to rising repair and energy costs and the loss of sublease income.

**Conclusion**

On the basis of its track record and current price, I believe that this company is an attractive buy.

**Recommendation**

I recommend that we offer to buy the company at a 10 percent premium over the current market value of its stock.

To be credible, recommendations must be practical and based on sound logical analysis. Also, when making a recommendation, be certain that you have adequately described the recommended course of action so that readers aren't left wondering what happens next.

Since recommendations are often the most important information in a report, decide how you can design the document to make the recommendations easily accessible to the reader. Consider using a heading and putting recommendations in a list to emphasize them. Depending on your authority, you may emphasize action and strengthen the tone of your recommendations if you write them in second person, active command form. If you also put them in a numbered list, you will assign priority and make them very accessible. On the other hand, if you have not been authorized to be so direct, you can still emphasize action but soften the tone by changing the verb form as shown in the following example.

**Recommendations**

To increase business, WestJet can:

1. Offer a special business traveller's pass.
2. Increase the number of flights that leave in the evening.

**Recommendations**

WestJet can increase business by:

1. Offering a special business traveller's pass.
2. Increasing the number of flights leaving in the evening.

# Conducting Secondary Research

**LEARNING OBJECTIVE 3**

Explain the role of secondary research and describe the two major categories of online research tools.

Even if you intend to eventually conduct primary research, start with a review of any available secondary research. Inside your company, you might be able to find a variety of reports and other documents that could help. Outside the company, business researchers can choose from a wide range of print and online resources, both in libraries and online.

You'll want to start most projects by conducting secondary research first.

## Finding Information at a Library

Public, corporate, and university libraries offer printed sources with information that is not available online and online sources that are available only by subscription. Libraries are also where you'll find one of your most important resources: librarians. Reference librarians are trained in research techniques and can often help you find obscure information you can't find on your own. They can also direct you to the typical library's many sources of business information:

Even in the internet age, libraries offer information and resources you can't find anywhere else—including experienced research librarians.

- **Newspapers and periodicals.** Libraries offer access to a wide variety of popular magazines, general business magazines, *trade journals* (which provide information about specific professions and industries), and *academic journals* (which provide research-oriented articles from researchers and educators).
- **Business books.** Although less timely than newspapers, periodicals, and online sources, business books provide in-depth coverage and analysis that often can't be found anywhere else.
- **Directories.** Thousands of directories are published in print and electronic formats, and many include membership information for all kinds of professions, industries, and special-interest groups. To find specific company information, consult *The Globe and Mail*'s Annual Report Service. Go to http://globeinvestor.ar.wilink.com/ to find the link to order free copies of companies' annual reports. Information about Canadian

companies, markets, and economic trends can be found on Site-By-Site! International Investment Portal & Research Center (**www.site-by-site.com**). Also, check the company's website (if it maintains one). You can also obtain news releases and general company news from news release sites such as Canada NewsWire (**www.newswire.ca**). This site offers free databases of news releases from companies subscribing to their services. News release sites are also good places to look for webcasts, podcasts, announcements of new products, management changes, earnings, dividends, mergers, acquisitions, and other company information. Company sites generally include detailed information about the firm's products, services, history, mission, strategy, financial performance, and employment needs. Many sites provide links to related company information, such as news releases, and more.

Local, provincial, and federal government agencies publish a huge array of information that is helpful to business researchers.

- **Almanacs and statistical resources.** Almanacs are handy guides to factual and statistical information about countries, politics, the labour force, and so on. One of the most extensive is *Statistics Canada* (available at **www.statcan.gc.ca**).
- **Government publications.** Information on laws, court decisions, tax questions, regulatory issues, and other governmental concerns can often be found in collections of government documents.
- **Electronic databases.** Databases offer vast collections of computer-searchable information, often in specific areas such as business, law, science, technology, and education. Some of these are available only by institutional subscription, so the library can be your only way to gain access to them. Some libraries offer remote online access to some or all databases; for others, you'll need to visit in person.

## Finding Information Online

Internet research tools fall into two basic categories: search tools and monitoring tools.

The internet can be a tremendous source of business information, provided that you know where to look and how to use the tools available. Roughly speaking, the tools fall into two categories: those you can use to actively *search* for existing information and those you can use to *monitor* selected sources for new information. (Some tools can perform both functions.)

General-purpose search engines are tremendously powerful tools, but they do have several shortcomings that you need to consider.

**ONLINE SEARCH TOOLS** The most familiar search tools are general-purpose **search engines**, such as Google and Bing, which scan millions of websites to identify individual webpages that contain a specific word or phrase and then attempt to rank the results from most useful to least useful. Website owners use *search engine optimization* techniques to help boost their rankings in the results, but the ranking algorithms are kept secret to prevent unfair manipulation of the results.

For all their ease and power, conventional search engines have three primary shortcomings: (1) no human editors are involved to evaluate the quality or ranking of the search results; (2) various engines use different search techniques, so they often find different material; and (3) search engines can't reach all the content on some websites (this part of the internet is sometimes called the *hidden internet* or the *deep internet*).

"Human-powered search engines" and web directories rely on human editors to evaluate and select content.

A variety of tools are available to overcome the three main weaknesses of general-purpose search engines, and you should consider one or more of them in your business research. First, **web directories**, such as the Open Directory Project at **www.dmoz.org**, use human editors to categorize and evaluate websites. A variety of other directories focus on specific media types, such as blogs or podcasts.

Second, *metacrawlers* or *metasearch engines* (such as Bovée and Thill's Web Search, at **http://businesscommunicationblog.com/websearch**) help overcome the differences among search engines by formatting your search request for multiple search engines, making it easy to find a broader range of results. With a few clicks, you can compare results from multiple search engines to make sure you are getting a broad view of the material.

Third, **online databases** help address the challenge of the hidden internet by offering access to newspapers, magazines, journals, electronic copies of books, and other resources often not available with standard search engines. Check whether your library has access to these:

- **Canadian Business & Current Affairs**—indexes more than 600 Canadian periodicals and newspapers, making 150 of these available to subscribers in full-text form. The most comprehensive source of business current events information in Canada.
- **SEDAR (System for Electronic Document Analysis and Retrieval)**—lists all companies on stock exchanges in Canada.
- **CanCorp Financials**—provides financial and management information from 13 000 Canadian companies.
- **EBSCOhost**—includes a number of databases and full-text products, including Business Source Premier and Business Wire news.[5]

*Online databases and specialty search engines can help you access parts of the hidden internet.*

**ONLINE MONITORING TOOLS**   One of the most powerful aspects of online research is the ability to automatically monitor selected sources for new information. The possibilities include subscribing to newsfeeds from blogs and websites, following people on Twitter and other microblogs, and setting up alerts on search engines and online databases.

*Online monitoring tools help you track industry trends, consumer sentiment, and other information.*

**SEARCH TIPS**   Search engines, web directories, and databases work in different ways, so make sure you understand how to optimize your search and interpret the results for each tool you're using. With a *keyword search*, the engine or database attempts to find items that include all the words you enter. A *Boolean search* lets you define a query with greater precision, using such operators as *and* (the search must include two terms linked by *and*), *or* (it can include either or both words), or *not* (the search ignores items with whatever word comes after *not*). *Natural language searches* let you ask questions in everyday English. *Forms-based searches* help you create powerful queries by simply filling out an online form.[6]

**REAL-TIME UPDATES**

**Learn More by Visiting This Website**

**Learn to use Google more effectively**

Google's Inside Search offers the tips and techniques you need to get the best research results in the least amount of time. Go to http://real-timeupdates.com/bce6 and click on Learn More. If you are using MyBCommLab, you can access Real-Time Updates within Business Communication Resources.

To make the best use of any search tool, keep the following points in mind:

- Think before you search. The neatly organized results you get from a search engine can create the illusion that the internet is an orderly warehouse of all the information in the universe, but the reality is far different. The internet is an incomplete, unorganized hodge-podge of millions of independent websites with information that ranges in value from priceless to utter rubbish. After you have identified what you need to know, spend a few moments thinking about where that information might be found, how it might be structured, and what terms various websites might use to describe it.
- Read the instructions and pay attention to the details. A few minutes of learning can save hours of inefficient search time.
- Review the search and display options carefully so you don't misinterpret the results; some of these settings can make a huge difference in the results you see.
- Try variations of your terms, such as *adolescent* and *teenager* or *management* and *managerial*.
- User fewer search terms to find more results; use more search terms to find fewer results.
- Look beyond the first page of results. Don't assume that the highest-ranking results are the best sources for you. For example, materials that haven't been optimized for search engines won't rank as highly (meaning they won't show up in the first few pages of results), but they may be far better for your purposes. The algorithm used to rank the results might not reflect your priorities, so the first few hits might not be the best for your project.

Search technologies continue to evolve rapidly, so look for new ways to find the information you need. Some new tools search specific areas of information (such as Twitter) in better ways, whereas others approach searches in new ways. For instance, Yolink (www.yolink.com) finds webpages like a regular search engine does but then also searches through documents and webpages that are linked to those first-level results.[7]

Other powerful search tools include *desktop search engines* that search all the files on your personal computer, *enterprise search engines* that search all the computers on a company's network, *research and content managers* such as the free Zotero browser extension (www.zotero.org), and *social tagging* or *bookmarking sites* such as Reddit (www.reddit.com), Digg (http://digg.com), and Delicious (http://delicious.com) and media curation sites such as Pinterest (www.pinterest.com).

## Documenting Your Sources

Proper documentation of the sources you use is both ethical and an important resource for your readers.

Documenting your sources serves three important functions. It:

- Properly and ethically credits the person who created the original material.
- Shows your audience that you have sufficient support for your message.
- Helps readers explore your topic in more detail if they choose. Be sure to take advantage of the source documentation tools in your software, such as automatic endnote or footnote tracking.

Appendix B discusses the common methods of documenting sources. Whatever method you choose, documentation is necessary for website material, books, articles, tables, charts, diagrams, song lyrics, scripted dialogue, letters, speeches—anything that you take from someone else, including ideas and information that you've re-expressed through paraphrasing or summarizing. However, you do not have to cite a source for knowledge that's generally known among your readers, such as the fact that First Nations have treaty rights or that computers are pervasive in business today.

LEARNING OBJECTIVE ❹
**Explain the role of primary research and identify the two most common forms of primary research for business communication purposes.**

# Conducting Primary Research

If secondary research can't provide the information and insights you need, your next choice is to gather the information yourself with primary research. Primary research encompasses a variety of methods, from observations to experiments such as test marketing, but the two tools most commonly used for business research are surveys and interviews.

## Conducting Surveys

Surveys and interviews are the most common primary techniques for business research.

Surveys need to be reliable, valid, and representative in order to be useful.

Surveys can provide invaluable insights, but only if they are *reliable* (would produce identical results if repeated) and *valid* (actually measure what they are designed to measure). To conduct a survey that generates reliable and valid results, you need to choose research participants carefully and develop an effective set of questions. For important surveys, consider hiring a research specialist to avoid errors in design and implementation. To develop an effective survey questionnaire, follow these tips:[8]

Provide clear instructions to prevent mistaken answers.

- Provide clear instructions to make sure people can answer every question correctly.
- Don't ask for information that people can't be expected to remember, such as how many times they went grocery shopping in the past year.
- Keep the questionnaire short and easy to answer; don't expect people to give you more than 10 or 15 minutes of their time.
- Whenever possible, formulate questions to provide answers that are easy to analyze; for example, questions that have a Yes/No answer. Numbers and facts are easier to summarize than opinions.

- Avoid *leading questions* that could bias your survey. If you ask, "Do you prefer that we stay open in the evenings for customer convenience?" you'll no doubt get a "yes." Instead, ask, "What time of day do you normally do your shopping?"
- Avoid ambiguous descriptors such as "often" or "frequently." Such terms mean different things to different people.
- Avoid compound questions such as "Do you read books and magazines?"

When selecting people to participate in a survey, the most critical task is getting a *representative sample* of the entire population in question. For instance, if you want to know how consumers feel about something, you can't just survey a few hundred people in a shopping mall. Different types of consumers shop at different times of the day and different days of the week, and many consumers rarely, if ever, shop at malls. The online surveys you see on many websites potentially suffer from the same *sampling bias:* They capture only the opinions of people who visit the sites and who want to participate, which might not be a representative sample of the population. A good handbook on survey research will help you select the right people for your survey, including selecting enough people to have a statistically valid survey.[9]

## Conducting Interviews

Getting in-depth information straight from an expert, customer, or other interested party can be a great method for collecting primary information. Interviews can take a variety of formats, from email exchanges to group discussions. For example, the British supermarket chain Tesco invites thousands of customers to visit its stores every year for meetings known as Customer Question Time, when it asks customers how the company can serve them better.[10]

Like surveys, interviews require careful planning to get the best results. The answers you receive are influenced by the types of questions you ask and the way you ask them. Ask **open-ended questions** to invite an expert to offer opinions, insights, and information, such as "Why do you believe that South America represents a better opportunity than Europe for this product line?" Ask **closed questions** to elicit a specific answer, such as yes or no. These can be helpful for certain topics, but including too many closed questions in an interview makes the experience feel more like a simple survey and doesn't take full advantage of the interactive interview setting.

Think carefully about the sequence of your questions and the potential answers so you can arrange them in an order that helps uncover layers of information. Also consider providing each subject with a list of questions at least a day or two before the interviews, especially if you'd like to quote your subjects in writing or if your questions might require people to conduct research or think extensively about the answers. If you want to record interviews, ask ahead of time; never record without permission.

> Interviews can take place online, over the phone, or in person, and they can involve individuals or groups.

> Open-ended questions, which can't be answered with a simple yes or no, can provide deeper insights, opinions, and information.

> Arrange the sequence of questions to help uncover layers of information.

## Planning Informational Reports

Informational reports provide the feedback that employees, managers, and others need in order to make decisions, take action, and respond to changes. As Figure 10.1 indicates, informational reports can be grouped into four general categories:

- **Reports to monitor and control operations.** Managers rely on a wide range of reports to see how well their companies are functioning. *Plans* establish expectations and guidelines to direct future action. Among the most important of these are *business plans*, which summarize a proposed business venture and describe the company's goals and plans for each major functional area. *Operating reports* provide feedback on a wide variety of an organization's functions, including sales, inventories, expenses, shipments, and so on. *Personal activity* reports provide information regarding an individual's experiences during sales calls, industry conferences, and other activities.

LEARNING OBJECTIVE 5
Explain how to plan informational reports and website content.

> Informational reports are used to monitor and control operations, to implement policies and procedures, to demonstrate compliance, and to document progress.

- **Reports to implement policies and procedures.** *Policy reports* range from brief descriptions of business procedures to manuals that run dozens or hundreds of pages. *Position papers*, sometimes called *white papers* or *backgrounders*, outline an organization's official position on issues that affect the company's success.
- **Reports to demonstrate compliance.** Businesses are required to submit a variety of *compliance reports*, from tax returns to reports describing the proper handling of hazardous materials.
- **Reports to document progress.** Supervisors, investors, and customers frequently expect to be informed of the progress of projects and other activities. *Progress reports* range from simple updates in memo form to comprehensive status reports.

## Organizing Informational Reports

The messages conveyed by informational reports can range from extremely positive to extremely negative, so the approach you take warrants careful consideration.

In most cases, the direct approach is the best choice for informational reports because you are simply conveying information. However, if the information is disappointing, such as a project being behind schedule or over budget, you might consider using the indirect approach to build up to the bad news. Most informational reports use a **topical organization**, arranging material in one of the following ways:

- **Comparison.** Showing similarities and differences (or advantages and disadvantages) between two or more entities (see Figure 10.6).

---

**FIGURE 10.6** **Effective Informational Report**

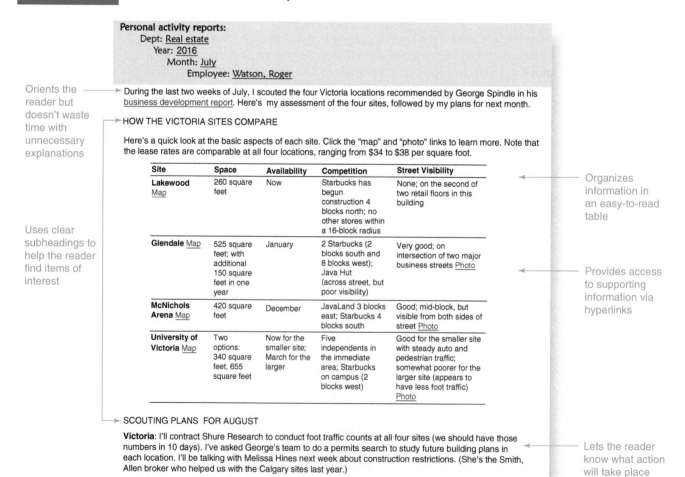

- **Importance.** Building up from the least important item to the most important (or from most important to the least, if you don't think your audience will read the entire report).
- **Sequence.** Organizing the steps or stages in a process or procedure.
- **Chronology.** Organizing a chain of events in order from oldest to newest or vice versa.
- **Geography.** Organizing by region, city, province or territory, country, or other geographic unit.
- **Category.** Grouping by topical category, such as sales, profit, cost, or investment.

## Organizing Infographic Reports

A growing number of organizations rely on infographics to present data and explain ideas. Infographics communicate through pictures, graphs, and limited amounts of text and since they are largely visual, readers process them rapidly. Use of infographics is increasing for at least two reasons. First, the overload of text and information that we are exposed to every day is affecting how people read, leading some to claim that many readers are in a state of "continuous partial attention."[11] Brain research has shown that people process pictures must faster than the coding and decoding process of reading text.[12] In a TED talk, writer David McCandless describes visual information as having a "magical" quality, because to process a visual, is "effortless. It literally pours in. If you are navigating a dense information jungle, coming across a beautiful graphic or lovely data visualization is a relief. It is like coming across a clearing in the jungle."[13] Choosing a visual medium to report your information could help you get attention and keep it. Second, infographics are easy to share and social technology has created a thirst for "shareable" forms of communication. It is easy to embed sharing tools in an infographic and people are more likely to share infographics than long articles or reports.[14]

Infographics can be used for both external and internal communication. Consider using an infographic style of reporting if the message:

- Has to reach a wide audience.
- Is difficult to explain in words or could be communicated more clearly with visuals.
- Has data, especially significant data that you want to emphasize.
- Is significant enough to warrant the extra time for design and production.
- Is intended for distribution on social media.

The three-step process applies well to making an infographic. The planning stage involves identifying your purpose, thinking carefully about audience, and taking time to select appropriate images, symbols, or analogies that can convey your message. Consult sites such as The Noun Project (http://thenounproject.com) that curate hundreds of searchable symbols and icons, which can help you visualize your concept. Whether you create the document yourself or hire a designer, carefully defining your purpose and audience will ensure your message is clearly focused, suited to this medium, and worth the extra time it will take to plan, write, design, and produce. Even using free, online templates found on such sites as Visualy.ly (http://visual.ly) requires extra time, which may not be justifiable for basic and routine reporting. However, if your message needs to capture the attention of a wide audience, the time invested in making an infographic may pay off.

Follow the direct pattern for organizing, beginning with a bold title that gets attention, putting a summary statement of the main message below it in a prominent place. Then, using lots of white space, organize the information in distinct segments with clear headings. Limit text to brief explanations or interpretations of the graphs, charts, or images. Rely mainly on images to tell your story. Find free images in the Open Clipart Library (http://openclipart.org), and use online free tools such as Chartle (http://chartle.net) or draw.io (www.draw.io) to create appropriate graphics for your purpose.

For example, are you explaining a process or reporting statistical information? Once you have completed the content and layout, cite all your sources and include them in your infographic.[15]

## Organizing Website Content

When planning online reports or other website content, remember that the online reading experience differs from offline reading in several important ways.

Most of what you've already learned about informational reports applies to website writing, but the online environment requires some special considerations:

* **Web readers are demanding.** If they can't find what they're looking for in a few minutes, most site visitors will click away to another site.[16]
* **Reading online can be difficult.** Studies show that reading speeds are about 25 percent slower on a monitor than on paper.[17] Reading from computer screens can also be exhausting and a source of physical discomfort.[18]
* **The web is a nonlinear, multidimensional medium.** Readers of online material move around in any order they please; often there is no beginning, middle, or end.

In addition, many websites have to perform more than one communication function and therefore have more than one purpose. Each of these individual purposes needs to be carefully defined and then integrated into an overall statement of purpose for the entire website.[19]

The information architecture of a website is the equivalent of the outline for a paper report, but it tends to be much more complicated than a simple linear outline.

Moreover, many websites also have multiple target audiences, such as potential employees, customers, investors, and the news media. You need to analyze each group's unique information needs and find a logical way to organize all that material. Website designers use the term **information architecture** to describe the structure and navigational flow of all the parts of a website. As you develop the site architecture, you can begin to simulate how various audiences will enter and explore the site. Accommodating multiple entry points is one of the most difficult tasks in site design.[20]

To organize your site effectively, keep the following advice in mind:

* Plan your site structure and navigation before you write.[21]
* Let your readers be in control by creating links and pathways that let them explore on their own.
* Help online readers scan and absorb information by breaking it into self-contained, easily readable chunks that are linked together logically. Use lots of headings.

**LEARNING OBJECTIVE 6**
**Identify the three most common ways to organize analytical reports.**

## Planning Analytical Reports

The purpose of analytical reports is to analyze, to understand, or to explain—to think through a problem or an opportunity and explain how it affects an organization and how the organization should respond. As you also saw in Figure 10.1, analytical reports fall into three basic categories:

Analytical reports are used to assess opportunities, to solve problems, and to support decisions.

* **Reports to assess opportunities.** Every business opportunity carries some degree of risk and requires a variety of decisions and actions in order to capitalize on the opportunity. You can use analytical reports to assess both risk and required decisions and actions. For instance, *market analysis reports* are used to judge the likelihood of success for new products or sales. *Policy analysis reports* assess how new policy or legislation affects business operations (see Figure 10.7). *Due diligence* reports examine the financial aspects of a proposed decision, such as acquiring another company.
* **Reports to solve problems.** Managers often assign *troubleshooting reports* when they need to understand why something isn't working properly and how to fix it. A variation,

the *failure analysis report*, studies events that happened in the past, with the hope of learning how to avoid similar failures in the future.

- **Reports to support decisions.** *Feasibility reports* explore the potential ramifications of a decision that managers are considering, and *justification reports* explain a decision that has already been made.

Writing analytical reports presents a greater challenge than writing informational reports for three reasons. First, you're doing more than simply delivering information—you're also analyzing a situation and presenting your conclusions. Second, when your analysis is complete, you need to present your thinking in a compelling and persuasive manner. Third, analytical reports often convince other people to make significant financial

---

**FIGURE 10.7** Sample Policy Report in Semiformal Format

**HIGHLAND TENNIS CLUB EMAIL**

**TO:** Cal Smith, General Manager <csmith@highland.ca>
**FROM:** Sue North, Accounting Supervisor <snorth@highland.ca>
**DATE:** November 19, 2016 9:52 AM
**SUBJECT:** Effect of New Recommendations from the CICA on our Pension Accounting Policy

*Covering email includes the main conclusion*

Here is the analysis you requested regarding whether accounting practice changes are needed as a result of the newly released recommendations from the Canadian Institute of Chartered Accountants. We will have to adjust our pension accounting methods but may wait until next fiscal year.

**EFFECT OF NEW RECOMMENDATIONS FROM THE CANADIAN INSTITUTE OF CHARTERED ACCOUNTANTS**

*Title, author, and date*

Submitted by the Accounting Department
November 19, 2016

**Summary**

*The direct approach opening summarizes key points of the report*

The Board of Directors asked the Accounting Department to comment on how the Canadian Institute of Chartered Accountants' (CICA's) new recommendations on current accounting practices and new reporting requirements for employee pension plans will affect the Club. We secured a copy of the September 2015 CICA recommendations, studied the new requirements, and have summarized the details in this report.

A few procedural changes in how we report our pension plan savings will be required to comply. Overall, we suggest that we adopt the CICA recommendations but wait to implement the changes until our next actuarial report time.

**New CICA Pension Recommendations**

The new CICA Pension recommendations present a complex technical restructuring of how pension costs and obligations are accounted and reported.

*Interprets*

The main purposes behind these changes are to
- avoid management manipulating the company's profit and thereby losing results by over- or underfunding the pension plan.
- provide more accurate, comparative income statements within the company (from year to year), and outside the company (from one firm to another).

(Continued)

**FIGURE 10.7** (Continued)

2

**Impact on Highland Tennis Club**
Public companies must comply with these recommendations by the fiscal year
beginning December 1, 2016. For a private organization such as ours, the
changes in accounting method would not be mandatory until the fiscal year
beginning December 1, 2017. The detailed changes are included in Attachment 1.

**Cost of Implementation**
To commission a new actuarial valuation to implement the recommendations will
cost the Club approximately $4500. Since we paid for an updated valuation earlier
this year, the next report is not due until January 2017. For a private organization,
the changes in accounting method are minor and do not justify the cost of
implementing the new practices immediately.

**Timing**
Although earlier adoption of the recommendations has been suggested, the
immediate changes in accounting method would not be significant enough to
warrant the extra expense. The best time for us to implement the new
recommendations would be the new fiscal year beginning 2017. This means that
a valuation would take place in January 2017. Since we would require a valuation
at that time under our old system, we could implement the changes at no extra cost.

**Our Interim Position**
We have up to three years to implement the new CICA ruling. I have reviewed an
interim position with respect to the Club's pension investments and valuation
method. We also checked with Sterling Investments, our pension consulting firm.
They have verified a conservative approach was taken in preparing our last
actuarial report. Our pension fund is currently vested with Mutual Life Assurance
and has generated an average 7 percent return during the last three years.
Therefore, the risk of being underfunded is minimal.

**Conclusion and Recommendation**
In conclusion, while the new rules do require us to change some procedures, there
is no compelling reason to implement the CICA recommendations immediately.

We recommend deferring implementation of the new rules until the fiscal year
beginning 2017.

Attachment 1: Pension Accounting Changes Required by CICA September 2015 Recommendations

*Subheadings provide easy access to topic divisions*

*Attachment is used for the technical detail*

and personnel decisions, and these reports carry the added responsibility of the consequences of such decisions.

## Focusing on Conclusions

*Focusing on conclusions is often the best approach when you're addressing a receptive audience.*

When planning reports for audiences that are likely to accept your conclusions—
either because they've asked you to perform an analysis or they trust your judgment—
consider using the direct approach, focusing immediately on your conclusions. This
structure communicates the main idea quickly, but it does present some risks. Even if
audiences trust your judgment, they may have questions about your data or the methods you used. Moreover, starting with a conclusion may create the impression that you
have oversimplified the situation. To give readers the opportunity to explore the

**FIGURE 10.8** Preliminary Outline of a Research Report Focusing on Conclusions

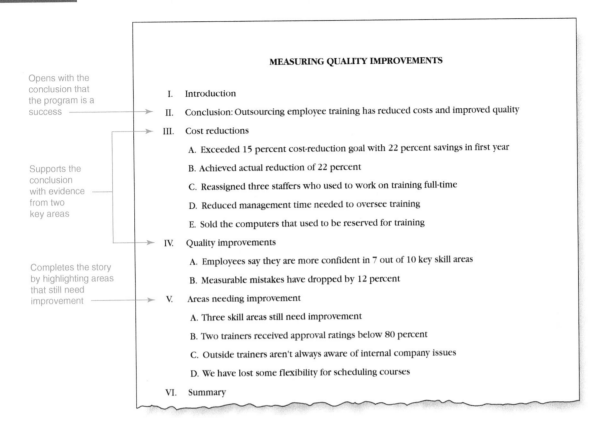

Opens with the conclusion that the program is a success

Supports the conclusion with evidence from two key areas

Completes the story by highlighting areas that still need improvement

**MEASURING QUALITY IMPROVEMENTS**

I.   Introduction

II.  Conclusion: Outsourcing employee training has reduced costs and improved quality

III. Cost reductions

    A. Exceeded 15 percent cost-reduction goal with 22 percent savings in first year

    B. Achieved actual reduction of 22 percent

    C. Reassigned three staffers who used to work on training full-time

    D. Reduced management time needed to oversee training

    E. Sold the computers that used to be reserved for training

IV.  Quality improvements

    A. Employees say they are more confident in 7 out of 10 key skill areas

    B. Measurable mistakes have dropped by 12 percent

V.   Areas needing improvement

    A. Three skill areas still need improvement

    B. Two trainers received approval ratings below 80 percent

    C. Outside trainers aren't always aware of internal company issues

    D. We have lost some flexibility for scheduling courses

VI.  Summary

thinking behind your conclusion, support that conclusion with solid reasoning and evidence. In Figure 10.8, you can see an outline prepared by a human resource officer of a bank. Her company decided to have an outside firm handle its employee training, and a year after the outsourcing arrangement was established, she was asked to evaluate the results. Her analysis shows that the outsourcing experiment was a success, and she opens with that conclusion but supports it with clear evidence. Readers who accept the conclusion can stop reading, and those who desire more information can continue.

## Focusing on Recommendations

A slightly different approach is useful when your readers want to know what they ought to do in a given situation (as opposed to what they ought to conclude). The actions you want your readers to take become the main subdivisions of your report.

*When readers want to know what you think they should do, organize your report to focus on recommendations.*

When structuring a report around recommendations, use the direct approach, as you would for a report that focuses on conclusions. Then unfold your recommendations using a series of five steps:

1. Establish the need for action in the introduction by briefly describing the problem or opportunity.
2. Introduce the benefit(s) that can be achieved if the recommendation is adopted, along with any potential risks.
3. List the steps (recommendations) required to achieve the benefit, using action verbs for emphasis.

4. Explain each step more fully, giving details on procedures, costs, and benefits. If necessary, also explain how risks can be minimized.

5. Summarize your recommendations.

## Focusing on Logical Arguments

Logical arguments can follow two basic approaches: 2 + 2 = 4 (adding everything up) and the yardstick method (comparing ideas against a predetermined set of standards).

When readers are potentially skeptical or hostile, consider using the indirect approach to logically build toward your conclusion or recommendation. If you guide readers along a rational path toward the answer, they are more likely to accept it when they encounter it. The two most common logical approaches are known as the *2 + 2 = 4 approach*, in which you convince readers by demonstrating that everything adds up to your conclusion, and the *yardstick approach*, in which you use a number of criteria to decide which option to select from two or more possibilities (see Figure 10.9).

---

**FIGURE 10.9** | Analytical Report Focusing on Logical Arguments

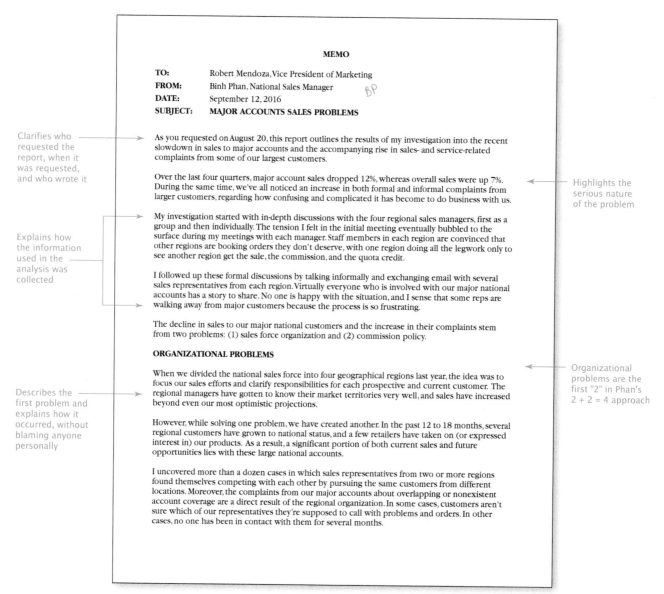

Clarifies who requested the report, when it was requested, and who wrote it

Explains how the information used in the analysis was collected

Describes the first problem and explains how it occurred, without blaming anyone personally

Highlights the serious nature of the problem

Organizational problems are the first "2" in Phan's 2 + 2 = 4 approach

**MEMO**

TO:        Robert Mendoza, Vice President of Marketing
FROM:      Binh Phan, National Sales Manager    BP
DATE:      September 12, 2016
SUBJECT:   **MAJOR ACCOUNTS SALES PROBLEMS**

As you requested on August 20, this report outlines the results of my investigation into the recent slowdown in sales to major accounts and the accompanying rise in sales- and service-related complaints from some of our largest customers.

Over the last four quarters, major account sales dropped 12%, whereas overall sales were up 7%. During the same time, we've all noticed an increase in both formal and informal complaints from larger customers, regarding how confusing and complicated it has become to do business with us.

My investigation started with in-depth discussions with the four regional sales managers, first as a group and then individually. The tension I felt in the initial meeting eventually bubbled to the surface during my meetings with each manager. Staff members in each region are convinced that other regions are booking orders they don't deserve, with one region doing all the legwork only to see another region get the sale, the commission, and the quota credit.

I followed up these formal discussions by talking informally and exchanging email with several sales representatives from each region. Virtually everyone who is involved with our major national accounts has a story to share. No one is happy with the situation, and I sense that some reps are walking away from major customers because the process is so frustrating.

The decline in sales to our major national customers and the increase in their complaints stem from two problems: (1) sales force organization and (2) commission policy.

**ORGANIZATIONAL PROBLEMS**

When we divided the national sales force into four geographical regions last year, the idea was to focus our sales efforts and clarify responsibilities for each prospective and current customer. The regional managers have gotten to know their market territories very well, and sales have increased beyond even our most optimistic projections.

However, while solving one problem, we have created another. In the past 12 to 18 months, several regional customers have grown to national status, and a few retailers have taken on (or expressed interest in) our products. As a result, a significant portion of both current sales and future opportunities lies with these large national accounts.

I uncovered more than a dozen cases in which sales representatives from two or more regions found themselves competing with each other by pursuing the same customers from different locations. Moreover, the complaints from our major accounts about overlapping or nonexistent account coverage are a direct result of the regional organization. In some cases, customers aren't sure which of our representatives they're supposed to call with problems and orders. In other cases, no one has been in contact with them for several months.

(Continued)

**FIGURE 10.9** (Continued)

Major Accounts Sales Problem          2          September 12, 2016

Brings the first problem to life by complementing the general description with a specific example

For example, having retail outlets across the country, HBC received pitches from reps out of our Western, Prairie, and Atlantic regions. Because our regional offices have a lot of negotiating freedom, the three were offering different prices. But all HBC buying decisions were made at the Winnipeg headquarters, so all we did was confuse the customer. The irony of the current organization is that we're often giving our weakest selling and support efforts to the largest customers in the country.

**COMMISSION PROBLEMS**

Commission problems are the second "2" in Phan's 2 + 2 = 4 approach

The regional organization problems are compounded by the way we assign commissions and quota credit. Salespeople in one region can invest a lot of time in pursuing a sale, only to have the customer place the order in another region. So some sales rep in the second region ends up with the commission on a sale that was partly or even entirely earned by someone in the first region. Therefore, sales reps sometimes don't pursue leads in their regions, thinking that a rep in another region will get the commission.

Simplifies the reader's task by maintaining a parallel structure for the discussion of the second problem: a general description followed by a specific example

For example, Sport Chek, with outlets in 10 provinces spread across all four regions, finally got so frustrated with us that the company president called our headquarters. Sport Chek has been trying to place a large order for tennis and golf accessories, but none of our local reps seem interested in paying attention. I spoke with the rep responsible for Toronto, where the company is headquartered, and asked her why she wasn't working the account more actively. Her explanation was that last time she got involved with Sport Chek, the order was actually placed from their Vancouver regional office, and she didn't get any commission after more than two weeks of selling time.

**CONCLUSIONS & RECOMMENDATIONS**

Phan concludes the 2 + 2 = 4 approach: organizational problems + commission problems = the need for a new sales structure

Our sales organization should reflect the nature of our customer base. To accomplish that goal, we need a group of reps who are free to pursue accounts across regional borders—and who are compensated fairly for their work. The most sensible answer is to establish a national account group. Any customers whose operations place them in more than one region would automatically be assigned to the national group.

Explains how the new organizational structure will solve both problems

In addition to solving the problem of competing sales efforts, the new structure will also largely eliminate the commission-splitting problem because regional reps will no longer invest time in prospects assigned to the national accounts team. However, we will need to find a fair way to compensate regional reps who are losing long-term customers to the national team. Some of these reps have invested years in developing customer relationships that will continue to yield sales well into the future, and everyone I talked to agrees that reps in these cases should receive some sort of compensation. Such a "transition commission" would also motivate the regional reps to help ensure a smooth transition from one sales group to the other. The exact nature of this compensation would need to be worked out with the various sales managers.

Acknowledges that the recommended solution does create a temporary compensation problem, but expresses confidence that a solution to that can be worked out

Major Accounts Sales Problem          3          September 12, 2016

**SUMMARY**

Used the indirect approach because his topic was controversial

The regional sales organization is effective at the regional and local levels but not at the national level. We should establish a national accounts group to handle sales that cross regional boundaries. Then we'll have one set of reps who are focused on the local and regional levels and another set who are pursuing national accounts.

Neatly summarizes both the problem and the recommended solution

To compensate regional reps who lose accounts to the national team, we will need to devise some sort of payment to reward them for the years of work invested in such accounts. This can be discussed with the sales managers once the new structure is in place.

# Planning Proposals

Proposals can be grouped into two general categories. *Internal proposals* (see Figure 10.10) request decisions from managers within the organization. *External proposals* request decisions from parties outside the organization. For example, *investment proposals* request funding from outside investors, *grant proposals* request funds from government agencies and other sponsoring organizations, and *sales proposals* present solutions for potential customers and request purchase decisions.

The best strategy for a proposal depends on whether it is unsolicited or solicited.

The most significant factor in planning a proposal is whether the recipient has asked you to submit a proposal. *Solicited proposals* are generally prepared at the request of external parties that require a product or a service, but they may also be requested by such

---

**FIGURE 10.10** Internal Proposal—Analytical (Unsolicited)

**MEMO**

TO: Jamie Engle
FROM: Shandel Cohen
DATE: July 9, 2016
SUBJECT: **SAVING $145K/YEAR WITH AUTOMATED EMAIL RESPONSE**

*Subject line focuses on main benefit to capture attention*

**THE PROBLEM: SLOW RESPONSE TO CUSTOMER REQUESTS FOR INFORMATION**

Our new product line has been very well received, and orders have surpassed our projections. This very success, however, has created a shortage of printed catalogues and data sheets, as well as considerable overtime for people in the customer response centre. As we introduce upgrades and new options, our printed materials quickly become outdated. If we continue to rely on printed materials for customer information, we have two choices: Distribute existing materials (even though they are incomplete or inaccurate) or discard existing materials and print new ones.

*Describes the current situation and explains why a new system is needed*

**THE SOLUTION: AN AUTOMATED MAIL-RESPONSE SYSTEM**

With minor modifications to our current email system, we can set up an automated system to respond to customer requests for information. This system can save us time and money and can keep our distributed information current.

*The "solution" explains what should happen in enough detail to be convincing without burdening the reader with too many details*

**BENEFITS**

Automated mail-response systems have been tested and proven effective. Companies such as Sunco Systems and Freshpac already use this method to respond to customer information requests, so we won't have to worry about relying on untested technology. Using the system is easy, too: Customers simply send a blank email message to a specific address, and the system responds by sending an electronic copy of the requested brochure.

*1. Always-Current Information*
Rather than discard and print new materials, we would need to update only the electronic files. We would be able to provide customers and our field sales organization with up-to-date, correct information as soon as the upgrades or options are available.

*Listing a number of compelling benefits as subheadings builds reader interest in the proposed solution*

*2. Instantaneous Delivery*
Almost immediately after requesting information, customers would have that information in hand. Electronic delivery would be especially advantageous for our northern and international customers. Regular mail to remote locations sometimes takes a week to arrive, by which time the information may already be out of date. Both customers and field salespeople will appreciate the automatic mail-response system.

*3. Minimized Waste*
With our current method of sending printed information, we discard tonnes of obsolete catalogues, data sheets, and other materials.

(Continued)

**FIGURE 10.10** (Continued)

Automated Email Response        2        July 9, 2016

**BENEFITS (cont'd)**

By maintaining and distributing the information electronically, we would eliminate this waste. We would also free up 10 square metres of floor space and shelving that is required for storing printed materials.

*[Acknowledges one potential shortcoming but provides a convincing solution to that as well]*

Of course, some of our customers may still prefer to receive printed materials, or they may not have access to electronic mail. For these customers, we could simply print copies of the files when we receive requests.

**4. *Lower Overtime Costs***
Besides savings in paper and space, we would also realize $20 000 savings in wages. Because of the increased interest in our new products, we have been working overtime or hiring new people to meet the demand. An automatic mail-response system would eliminate this need, allowing us to deal with fluctuating interest without a fluctuating workforce.

**COST ANALYSIS**

The necessary equipment and software costs approximately $15 000. System maintenance and upgrades are estimated at $5000 per year. However, those costs are offset many times over by the predicted annual savings:

| | |
|---|---|
| Printing | $100 000 |
| Storage | 25 000 |
| Postage | 5 000 |
| Wages | 20 000 |
| **Total** | **$150 000** |

*[Justifies the cost by detailing projected annual savings and supports $145K claim in subject line]*

Based on these figures, the system would save $130 000 the first year and $145 000 every year after that.

**CONCLUSION**

*[Summarizes the benefits and invites further discussions]*

An automated mail-response system would yield benefits in both customer satisfaction and operating costs. If you approve, we can have it installed and running in six weeks. Please give me a call if you have any questions.

---

internal sources as management or the board of directors. Some organizations prepare a formal invitation to bid on their contracts, called a **request for proposals (RFP)**, which includes instructions that specify exactly the type of work to be performed or products to be delivered, along with budgets, deadlines, and other requirements. Other companies then respond by preparing proposals that show how they would meet those needs. In most cases, organizations that issue RFPs also provide strict guidelines on what the proposals should include, and you need to follow these guidelines carefully in order to be considered.

*Unsolicited proposals* offer more flexibility but a completely different sort of challenge because recipients aren't expecting to receive them. In fact, your audience may not be aware of the problem or opportunity you are addressing, so before you can propose a solution, you might first need to convince your readers that a problem or an opportunity exists. Consequently, the indirect approach is often the wise choice for unsolicited proposals.

Regardless of its format and structure, a good proposal explains what a project or course of action will involve, how much it will cost, and how the recipient and his or her organization will benefit.

# LEARNING OBJECTIVES: Check Your Progress

**❶ OBJECTIVE** **Adapt the three-step writing process to reports and proposals.**

To adapt the three-step process to reports and proposals, apply what you learned in Chapters 3 through 5, with particular emphasis on clearly identifying your purpose, preparing a work plan, determining whether a separate research project might be needed, choosing the medium, and selecting the best approach for the specific type of report.

**❷ OBJECTIVE** **Describe an effective process for conducting business research, explain how to evaluate the credibility of an information source, and identify the five ways to use research results.**

Begin the research process with careful planning to make sure you focus on the most important questions. Then locate the data and information, using primary and secondary research as needed. Process the results of your research and apply your findings by summarizing information, drawing conclusions, and in some cases, developing recommendations. Finally, manage information effectively so that you and others can retrieve it later and reuse it in other projects.

Evaluating the credibility of an information source can involve eight questions. (1) Does the source have a reputation for honesty and reliability? (2) Is the source potentially biased? (3) What is the purpose of the material? (4) Is the author credible? (5) Where did the source get *its* information? (6) Can you verify the material independently? (7) Is the material current and complete? (8) Does the information make sense?

Five ways to use research results are quoting, paraphrasing, or summarizing textual material; drawing conclusions; and making recommendations. All sources used must be cited using accepted documentation practices shown in Appendix B.

**❸ OBJECTIVE** **Explain the role of secondary research and describe the two major categories of online research tools.**

Secondary research is generally used first, both to save time in case someone else has already gathered the information needed and to offer additional insights into your research questions. The two major categories of online research tools are tools used for searching (including various types of search engines, web directories, and online databases) and tools used for automatically monitoring for new information.

**❹ OBJECTIVE** **Explain the role of primary research and identify the two most common forms of**

primary research for business communication purposes.

Primary research involves the collection of new data, and it is conducted when the information required is not available through secondary research. The two most common primary research methods for business communication purposes are surveys and interviews.

**❺ OBJECTIVE** **Explain how to plan informational reports and website content.**

Informational reports focus on the delivery of facts, figures, and other types of information. The four general categories are reports that monitor and control operations, implement policies and procedures, demonstrate compliance, and document progress. Most informational reports use a topical organization, arranging material by comparison, importance, sequence, chronology, geography, or category.

When developing online reports and websites in general, start by planning the structure and navigation paths before writing the content. Next, make sure you let readers be in control by giving them navigational flexibility. Finally, break your information into chunks and include lots of headings so the report can be scanned and absorbed quickly.

**❻ OBJECTIVE** **Identify the three most common ways to organize analytical reports.**

Analytical reports assess a situation or problem and recommend a course of action in response. The three most common ways to organize analytical reports are by focusing on conclusions, focusing on recommendations, and focusing on logical arguments.

**❼ OBJECTIVE** **Explain how to plan proposals.**

The most significant factor in planning a proposal is whether the proposal is solicited or unsolicited. Solicited proposals are obviously expected and welcomed by the recipient, but they often must follow a specific organization, particularly when they are submitted in response to a request for proposals (RFP). For unsolicited proposals, the writer has flexibility in choosing the most effective organization, format, and content. However, because unsolicited proposals are unexpected, the writer often needs to explain why the solution offered in the proposal is even necessary for the reader to consider. Because of this, the indirect approach is usually preferred for unsolicited proposals.

## MyBCommLab®

Go to MyBCommLab for everything you need to help you succeed in the job you've always wanted! Tools and resources include the following:
- Writing Activities
- Document Makeovers
- Video Exercises
- Grammar Exercises—and much more!

## Practise Your Grammar

Effective business communication starts with strong grammar skills. To improve your grammar skills, go to MyBCommLab, where you'll find exercises and diagnostic tests to help you produce clear, effective communication.

## Test Your Knowledge

To review chapter content related to each question, refer to the indicated Learning Objective.

1. What are the three basic categories of reports? L0.①
2. What is typically covered in the work plan for a report? L0.①
3. How does a conclusion differ from a recommendation? L0.②
4. Should you use primary research before or after secondary research? L0.④
5. How do proposal writers use an RFP? L0.⑦

## Apply Your Knowledge

To review chapter content related to each question, refer to the indicated Learning Objective.

1. Why must you be careful when using information from the internet in a business report? L0.②
2. Companies occasionally make mistakes that expose confidential information, such as when employees lose laptop computers containing sensitive data files or webmasters forget to protect confidential webpages from search engine indexes. If you conducted an online search that turned up competitive information on webpages that were clearly intended to be private, what would you do? Explain your answer. L0.③
3. Can you use the same approach for planning website content as you use for planning printed reports? Why or why not? L0.⑤
4. If you were writing a recommendation report for an audience that didn't know you, would you use the direct approach, focusing on the recommendation, or the indirect approach, focusing on logic? Why? L0.⑤
5. Why are unsolicited proposals more challenging to write than solicited proposals? L0.⑦

## Practise Your Skills

### ACTIVITIES

Each activity is labelled according to the primary skill or skills you will need to use. To review relevant chapter content, you can refer to the indicated Learning Objective. In some instances, supporting information will be found in another chapter, as indicated.

1. **Planning: Analyzing the Situation, Drafting a Work Plan** L0.① You are the assistant to the human resources manager at Tandem Industries. The atmosphere in your company has been deteriorating over the last year since the company merged with another firm. You've noticed employees

complaining more about each other, tempers seem a little short, and stress is on the rise. You know that employee engagement is one of the keys to a successful business, and you are not sure the company is doing enough to keep its employees loyal and happy at work. You want to prepare a formal study of the current state of employee satisfaction. Your report will include conclusions and recommendations for your boss's consideration. Draft a work plan, including the problem statement, purpose statement, scope of topics you will include, a description of what will result from your investigation, the sources and methods of data collection, and a preliminary outline for the report.

2. **Research: Documenting Sources** L.O.❷ Select five business articles from a combination of print and online sources. Develop a resource list, using Appendix B as a guideline. Your instructor will specify which documentation style to use.

3. **Research: Conducting Secondary Research** L.O.❸ Using online, database, or printed sources, find the following information. Be sure to properly cite your sources, using APA format discussed in Appendix B.

   a. Contact information for the Canadian Marketing Association
   b. Median weekly earnings of men and women by occupation
   c. Current market share for Maudite beer
   d. Percentage of Canadians who own cell phones
   e. Annual stock performance for Bombardier
   f. Number of franchise outlets in Canada
   g. Composition of the Canadian workforce by profession

4. **Research: Conducting Secondary Research** L.O.❸ Select any public company and find the following information.

   a. Names of the company's current officers
   b. List of the company's products or services (or, if the company has a large number of products, the product lines or divisions)
   c. Some important current issues in the company's industry
   d. The outlook for the company's industry as a whole

5. **Research: Conducting Primary Research** L.O.❹ You work for a movie studio in Toronto that is producing a young director's first motion picture, the story of a group of unknown musicians finding work and making a reputation in a competitive industry. Unfortunately, some of your friends leave the screening saying that the 182-minute movie is simply too long. Others say they can't imagine any sequences to cut out. Your boss wants to test the movie on a typical audience and ask viewers to complete a questionnaire that will help the director decide whether edits are needed and, if so, where. Design a questionnaire that you can use to solicit valid answers for a report to the director about how to handle the audience's reaction to the movie.

6. **Research: Conducting Primary Research** L.O.❹ You're conducting an information interview with a manager in another division of your company. Partway through the interview, the manager shows clear signs of impatience. How should you respond? What might you do differently to prevent this from happening in the future? Explain your answers.

7. **Avoiding Plagiarism: Practising Paraphrasing** L.O.❷

   a. Extracting key details and putting them into your own words takes practice. Visit MyBCommLab and, in the Resources area, click on, in sequence, "Research," "Avoiding Plagiarism," and "APA" to find "Paraphrase." Read over the samples, then complete the first two practice exercises on paraphrasing sources. Print out your results and bring them to class to exchange with another student. How closely does your paraphrasing match with your classmate's? Have you both cited the source properly?
   b. Use EBSCO (in your library or in the Writer's Toolkit on MyBCommLab) to find a two-page article and bring it to class to share with another student. Read each other's articles and summarize five key points the articles make. Exchange your summaries and identify which parts of the summary should be cited. Insert proper citations and write out your entry to be included in the reference list.

8. **Research: Summarizing** L.O.❷ Business associates are expected to be socially confident. In every office, those who are comfortable interacting with others and who know how to act in social situations gain more opportunities for advancement.

   Build your knowledge of polite interaction by exploring a book on the art of conversation—for example, *How to Win Friends and Influence People*, by Dale Carnegie. Practise your summarizing skills by selecting key points from two to three chapters of the book and putting the advice you find into your own words. Based on your reading of two or three chapters, would you recommend the book to classmates? Write your summary in three short paragraphs. Then write a shorter summary (140 characters or less) that you could post on Twitter.[22]

9. **Message Strategies: Informational Reports** L.O.❺ You're an administrator for an Ontario fast-food chain. In the aftermath of a major snowstorm, you're drafting a report on the emergency procedures to be followed by personnel in each restaurant

when extreme storm warnings are in effect. Answer who, what, when, where, why, and how, and then prepare a one-page outline of your report. Make up any details you need.

10. **Message Strategies: Informational Reports** L.O.**5** From your college library, company websites, or an online service such as **www.annualreportservice.com**, find the annual reports recently released by two corporations in the same industry. Analyze each report and be prepared to discuss the following questions in class.

    a. What organizational differences, if any, do you see in the way each corporation discusses its annual performance? Are the data presented clearly so that shareholders can draw conclusions about how well the company performed?

    b. What goals, challenges, and plans do top managers emphasize in their discussion of results?

    c. How do the format and organization of each report enhance or detract from the information being presented?

11. **Message Strategies: Informational Reports; Collaboration: Team Projects** L.O.**5**, **Chapter 2** You and a classmate are helping Linda Moreno prepare her report on Electrovision's travel and entertainment costs (see pages 277–290). This time, however, the report is to be informational rather than analytical, so it will not include recommendations. Review the existing report and determine what changes would be needed to make it an informational report. Be as specific as possible. For example, if your team decides the report needs a new title, what title would you use? Draft a transmittal email for Moreno to use in conveying this informational report to Dennis McWilliams, Electrovision's vice-president of operations.

12. **Message Strategies: Informational Reports** L.O.**5** Assume that your college president has received many student complaints about campus parking problems. You are appointed to chair a student committee organized to investigate the problems and recommend solutions. The president gives you a file labelled "Parking: Complaints from Students," and you jot down the essence of the complaints as you inspect the contents. Your notes look like this:

- Inadequate student spaces at critical hours
- Poor night lighting near the computer centre
- Inadequate attempts to keep resident neighbours from occupying spaces
- Dim marking lines
- Motorcycles taking up full spaces
- Discourteous security officers
- Spaces (often empty) reserved for college officials
- Relatively high parking fees
- Full fees charged to night students even though they use the lots only during low-demand periods
- Vandalism to cars and a sense of personal danger
- Inadequate total space
- Harassment of students parking on residential streets in front of neighbouring houses

Now prepare an outline for an informational report to be submitted to committee members. Use a topical organization for your report that categorizes this information.

13. **Message Strategies: Analytical Reports** L.O.**6** Of the organizational approaches introduced in the chapter, which is best suited for writing a report that answers the following questions? Briefly explain why.

    a. Which social media strategies should our accounting firm use to build its business?

    b. Should Major Manufacturing, Inc., close down operations of its antiquated Quesnel, B.C., plant despite the adverse economic impact on the town (that grew up around the plant)?

    c. Should you and your partner adopt a new accounting method to make your financial statements look better to potential investors?

14. **Message Strategies: Proposals** L.O.**7** Read the step-by-step hints and examples for writing a funding proposal at **www.learnerassociates.net/proposal**. Review the entire sample proposal online. What details did the writer decide to include in the appendixes? Why was this material placed in the appendixes and not the main body of the report? According to the writer's tips, when is the best time to prepare a project overview?

15. **Message Strategies: Proposals; Collaboration: Team Projects** L.O.**7**, **Chapter 2** Break into small groups and identify an operational problem occurring at your campus—perhaps involving registration, university housing, food services, parking, study space, or library services. Then develop a workable solution to that problem. Finally, develop a list of pertinent facts that your team will need to gather to convince readers that the problem exists and that your solution will work.

# CASES

Apply the three-step writing process to the following cases, as assigned by your instructor.

## ▌ Informational Reports

### 1. Message Strategies: Informational Reports L.O. ⑤

Assume an instructor or supervisor of a project you are working on has asked you to document what you have completed so far, what problems you have encountered and solved, and what work is remaining on the project. If you do not have a current project, assume you are halfway through one you have completed in the past. If your course work does not require any projects, assume you have a scholarship to attend school. As part of your scholarship requirements, you must submit a report each term that summarizes the work you have completed and what you will be taking next.

**YOUR TASK** Plan and write a progress report. What format would best suit your audience?

### 2. Message Strategies: Informational Reports L.O. ⑤

Assume you work for the Canadian Alliance of Student Associations (**www.casa-acae.com/**), a nonprofit group that works on behalf of post secondary students across the country. The Alliance is monitoring tuition costs. Your supervisor has asked you to research tuition increases for the last four years in your school and one other in the nearby area. Are tuition costs going up, down, or remaining the same? For each school, once you have determined the costs for each year, calculate the percentage change in tuition costs from year to year and between first and fourth year.

**YOUR TASK** Using memo format, plan an informal report presenting your findings and conclusions to your supervisor. Plan to include graphics that explain your findings and support your conclusions.

### 3. Message Strategies: Informational Reports L.O. ⑤

If you're like many other college students, your first year was more than you expected: more difficult, more fun, more frustrating, more expensive, more exhausting, more rewarding—more of everything, positive and negative. Oh, the things you know now that you didn't know then!

**YOUR TASK** With several other students, identify five or six things you wish you would've realized or understood better before you started your first year of college. These can relate to your school life (such as "I didn't realize how much work I would have for my classes" or "I should've asked for help as soon as I got stuck") and your personal and social life ("I wish I would've been more open to meeting people"). Use these items as the foundation of a brief informational report that you could post on a blog that is read by high school students and their families. Your goal with this report is to help the next generation of students make a successful and rewarding transition to college.

## ▌ Analytical Reports

### 4. Message Strategies: Analytical Reports L.O. ⑥

No doubt you have learned the importance of time management in trying to complete your studies and perhaps work part time. It is not easy to juggle classes, work obligations, and family or personal commitments and still have time for health and exercise. You have found it so challenging, in fact, that you signed up for some free counselling sessions on time management. The counsellor has asked you to keep a record of how you use your time over the course of one week. "Design a table that you can use to record your time," she said. "Record what you do in 15-minute increments for 7 days (24-hour periods); then at the end of the week, you can analyze your use of time." At first you thought it would be tedious, but soon you get into it and record everything you do in a week.

**YOUR TASK** Design the table and record your time use for one week. At the end of the week, analyze your use of time. What categories can you use to describe the different ways you use time? How effective is your use of time? Can you see any ways to improve your use of time? What graphics could you use to show your use of time?

Write a short report to the counsellor that describes what you did and what you found out, and provides conclusions and some recommendations. Include at least two graphics. Assume the counsellor has asked you to submit your report before your next session with her. Decide what type of format would best suit this audience and subject.

### 5. Message Strategies: Analytical Reports L.O. ⑥

Visit any restaurant, possibly your school cafeteria. The workers and fellow customers will assume that you are an ordinary customer, but you are really a secret shopper (spy) for the owner.

**YOUR TASK** After your visit, write a short letter to the owner explaining (a) what you did and what you observed, (b) any possible violations of policy that you observed, and (c) your recommendations for improvement. The first part of your report (what you did and what you observed) will be the longest. Include a description of the premises, inside and out. Tell how long it took for each step of ordering and receiving your meal. Describe the service and food thoroughly. You are interested in both the good and bad aspects of the establishment's decor, service, and food. For the second section (violations of policy), use some common sense: if all the servers but one have their hair covered, you may assume that policy requires hair to be covered; a dirty window or restroom obviously violates policy. The last section (recommendations for improvement) involves professional judgment. What management actions will improve the restaurant?

### 6. Message Strategies: Analytical Reports L.O.6

You work at Tandem Industries as a human resource officer. You are meeting later in the week with the managers of four departments to review employee attendance records. They have asked you to write a short report to document employee attendance for the first period of this fiscal year and to make recommendations if needed. Below are employee records from this year's first reporting period and from the same period last year.

**YOUR TASK**  Meet in a group of two to discuss the data and draw conclusions. Make up any other information you would gather in "real life." Then, as a team, write a short report to the senior management. Include conclusions and recommendations and at least one graphic to illustrate (or dramatize) a key point.

### 2016 Attendance Records Tandem Industries
First Reporting Period
Total Number of Work Days = 80
Sept. 1–Dec. 31

#### Operations Department

| Employee Surname | Number of Absences | Number of Times Late |
|---|---|---|
| Adams | 3 | 0 |
| Brown | 0 | 0 |
| Chan | 2 | 0 |
| Dhillon | 3 | 1 |
| Eng | 6 | 6 |

#### Production Department

| Employee Surname | Number of Absences | Number of Times Late |
|---|---|---|
| Fabiano | 2 | 0 |
| Gill | 4 | 1 |
| Hablano | 2 | 1 |
| Ilianivich | 2 | 0 |
| Jang | 2 | 0 |
| Kwong | 1 | 0 |
| Laslo | 6 | 1 |

#### Quality Control

| Employee Surname | Number of Absences | Number of Times Late |
|---|---|---|
| Monahan | 1 | 2 |
| Nardolefsky | 2 | 0 |
| Olafson | 1 | 0 |

#### Packaging

| Employee Surname | Number of Absences | Number of Times Late |
|---|---|---|
| Petrie | 0 | 0 |
| Quincy | 3 | 0 |
| Rastafarian | 0 | 0 |
| Singh | 3 | 1 |
| Tyler | 3 | 3 |
| Ustinov | 0 | 0 |
| Valdy | 6 | 4 |

### 2015 Attendance Records Tandem Industries
First Reporting Period
Total Number of Work Days = 80
Sept. 1–Dec. 31

#### Operations Department

| Employee Surname | Number of Absences | Number of Times Late |
|---|---|---|
| Adams | 0 | 0 |
| Brown | 0 | 0 |
| Chan | 0 | 0 |
| Dhillon | 0 | 1 |
| Eng | 4 | 5 |

#### Production Department

| Employee Surname | Number of Absences | Number of Times Late |
|---|---|---|
| Fabiano | 0 | 0 |
| Gill | 2 | 1 |
| Hablano | 0 | 1 |
| Ilianivich | 0 | 0 |
| Jang | 0 | 0 |
| Kwong | 0 | 0 |
| Laslo | 5 | 1 |

#### Quality Control

| Employee Surname | Number of Absences | Number of Times Late |
|---|---|---|
| Monahan | 1 | 2 |
| Nardolefsky | 2 | 0 |
| Olafson | 1 | 0 |

## Packaging

| Employee Surname | Number of Absences | Number of Times Late |
|---|---|---|
| Petrie | 0 | 0 |
| Quincy | 3 | 0 |
| Rastafarian | 0 | 0 |
| Singh | 1 | 1 |
| Tyler | 2 | 2 |
| Ustinov | 0 | 0 |
| Valdy | 5 | 6 |

### 7. Message Strategies: Analytical Reports L.O.⑥

Spurred in part by the success of numerous do-it-yourself (DIY) TV shows, homeowners across the country are redecorating, remodelling, and rebuilding. Many people are content with superficial changes, such as new paint or new accessories, but some are more ambitious. These homeowners want to move walls, add rooms, redesign kitchens, convert garages to home theatres—the big stuff.

Publishers try to create magazines that appeal to carefully identified groups of potential readers and the advertisers who'd like to reach them. The DIY market is already served by numerous magazines, but you see an opportunity in the homeowners who tackle the heavy-duty projects. Case Tables 10.1, 10.2, and 10.3 summarize the results of some preliminary research you asked your company's research staff to conduct.

**YOUR TASK** You think the data show a real opportunity for a "big projects" DIY magazine, although you'll need more extensive research to confirm the size of the market and refine the editorial direction of the magazine. Prepare a brief analytical report that presents the data you have, identifies the opportunity or opportunities you've found (suggest your own ideas, based on the data in the tables), and requests funding from the editorial board to pursue further research.

| CASE TABLE 10.1 | Rooms Most Frequently Remodelled by DIYers |
|---|---|

| ROOM | PERCENTAGE OF HOMEOWNERS SURVEYED WHO HAVE TACKLED OR PLAN TO TACKLE AT LEAST A PARTIAL REMODEL |
|---|---|
| Kitchen | 60 |
| Bathroom | 48 |
| Home office/study | 44 |
| Bedroom | 38 |
| Media room/home theatre | 31 |
| Den/recreation room | 28 |
| Living room | 27 |
| Dining room | 12 |
| Sun room/solarium | 8 |

| CASE TABLE 10.2 | Average Amount Spent on Remodelling Projects |
|---|---|

| ESTIMATED AMOUNT | PERCENTAGE OF SURVEYED HOMEOWNERS |
|---|---|
| Under $5K | 5 |
| $5K–$10K | 21 |
| $10K–$20K | 39 |
| $20K–$50K | 22 |
| More than $50K | 13 |

| CASE TABLE 10.3 | Tasks Performed by Homeowner on a Typical Remodelling Project |
|---|---|

| TASK | PERCENTAGE OF SURVEYED HOMEOWNERS WHO PERFORM OR PLAN TO PERFORM MOST OR ALL OF THIS TASK THEMSELVES |
|---|---|
| Conceptual design | 90 |
| Technical design/architecture | 34 |
| Demolition | 98 |
| Foundation work | 62 |
| Framing | 88 |
| Plumbing | 91 |
| Electrical | 55 |
| Heating/cooling | 22 |
| Finish carpentry | 85 |
| Tile work | 90 |
| Painting | 100 |
| Interior design | 52 |

### 8. Message Strategies: Infographics L.O.⑤

Look at sample infographics on Column Five (www.ColumnFive.com), Cool Infographics (http://coolinfographics.com), or Fast Company (http://fastcodesign.com/section/infographic-of-the-day), or search them on Pinterest (www.pinterest.com). Select one you think does an excellent job of explaining a complex process or concept. Bring it to your next class and be prepared to present it and explain why you chose it.

### 9. Message Strategies: Infographics L.O. ⑤

Use the data provided in Case # 7 to plan an infographic that conveys your main persuasive message about the do-it-yourself market for the magazine publishing company. Explore online templates available for making an infographic at www.infogr.am/ or http://create.visual.ly/ or other free online resources. Then, sketch your design and content. If your instructor directs, produce your infographic and post it on the class blog or print a copy and submit it to your instructor.

**▌ Proposals**

### 10. Message Strategies: Proposals L.O. ⓐ

Think of a course you would love to see added to the curriculum at your school. Conversely, if you would like to see a course offered as an elective rather than being required, write your email report accordingly. Construct a sequence of logical reasons to support your choice. (This is the 2 + 2 = 4 approach mentioned in the chapter.)

**YOUR TASK**   Plan and draft a short email proposal to be submitted to the academic dean by email. Be sure to include all the reasons supporting your idea.

### 11. Message Strategies: Recommendation Report L.O. ⓐ

Assume you work for a small manufacturing firm that has an office staff of three. Your supervisor has asked you to recommend new accounting software for the company to purchase. "It has to be easy to use," she said. "None of us is really what you would call a techie," she warned. Evaluate several types of office software that do the same kind of job—for example, ACCPAC and Simply Accounting. Read reviews of the software and identify which one you would recommend to your boss.

**YOUR TASK**   Write a short report recommending the product to your boss. Decide what type of format would best suit your audience and subject.

### 12. Message Strategies: Proposals L.O. ⓐ

How can a firm be thorough yet efficient when considering dozens of applicants for each position? One tool that may help is IntelliView, a 10-minute question-and-answer session conducted by touch-tone telephone. The company recruiter dials up the IntelliView computer and then leaves the room. The candidate punches in answers to roughly 100 questions about work attitudes and other issues. In a few minutes, the recruiter can call Pinkerton (the company offering the service) and find out the results. On the basis of what the IntelliView interview reveals, the recruiter can delve more deeply into certain areas and, ultimately, have more information on which to base the hiring decision.

**YOUR TASK**   As assistant recruiter for Canadian Tire, you think that IntelliView might help your firm. Plan a brief email to Paula Wolski, director of human resources, in which you propose a test of the IntelliView system. Your memo should tell your boss why you believe your firm should test the system before making a long-term commitment.[23]

### 13. Message Strategies: Proposals L.O. ⓐ

You are a sales manager for GPS Tracking Canada, and one of your responsibilities is writing sales proposals for potential buyers of your company's GPS tracking system. The system uses the global positioning system (GPS) to track the location of vehicles and other assets. For example, the dispatcher for a trucking company can simply click a map display on a computer screen to find out where all the company's trucks are at that instant. GPS Tracking Canada lists the following as benefits of the system:

- Making sure vehicles follow prescribed routes, with minimal loitering time
- "Geofencing," in which dispatchers are alerted if vehicles leave assigned routes or designated service areas
- Route optimization, in which fleet managers can analyze routes and destinations to find the most time- and fuel-efficient path for each vehicle
- Comparisons between scheduled and actual travel
- Enhanced security, protecting both drivers and cargos

**YOUR TASK**   Write a brief (unsolicited) proposal to Matt Harding, fleet manager for Prairie Express, 338 6th Avenue SW, Calgary AB, T1K 1L6. Introduce your company, explain the benefits of the GPS Tracking Canada system, and propose a trial deployment in which you would equip five Express trucks. For the purposes of this assignment, you don't need to worry about the cost or technical details of the system; focus on promoting the benefits and asking for a decision regarding the test project. (You can learn more about the system at **www.gpstrackingcanada.com**.)[24]

---

## BUSINESS COMMUNICATION NOTEBOOK

# Technology

The internet helps businesses make closer connections with other organizations and customers all over the planet. Businesses use the internet to:

- Share text, photos, slides, videos, and other data within the organization

- Permit employees to telecommute, or work away from a conventional office, whether at home, on the road, or across the country
- Participate in meetings through webcasting and virtual world technology

- Recruit employees cost-effectively
- Locate information from external sources
- Find new business partners and attract new customers
- Locate and buy parts and materials from domestic and international suppliers
- Promote and sell goods and services to customers in any location
- Provide customers with service, technical support, and product information
- Collaborate with local, national, and international business partners
- Inform investors, industry analysts, and government regulators about business developments

In addition, companies can set up special employee-only websites using an *intranet*, a private internal corporate network. Intranets use the same technology as the internet but restrict the information and access to members of the organization (regardless of a member's actual location). Once a company has an intranet, it can add an *extranet* that allows people to communicate and exchange data within a secure network of qualified people outside the organization—such as suppliers, contractors, and customers who use a password to access the system.

## Online Reporting

Thanks to the internet, more and more companies are using online reports to keep employees, managers, investors, and other stakeholders informed. For example, companies with many branches and operations can have staff enter data into the computer system by following report formats on the screen. These reports are sent electronically to headquarters, where corporate managers can track sales, adjust resources, and resolve potential problems much more quickly than if they had to wait for printed reports.

Well-known package-shipper FedEx lets customers access electronic reports to monitor the status of their shipments at any time. This reporting system not only helps FedEx serve its customers better but also puts valuable information in the hands of customers. And like many companies, FedEx posts its annual report and other corporate informational reports on its website for interested customers and investors.

## Applications for Success

Answer the following questions:

1. Do you think companies should monitor their employees' use of the internet and email? Explain your answer.
2. What kinds of electronic reports might a company want to post on its website?
3. What advantages and disadvantages do you see in asking managers to go beyond their informational operations reports and start filing electronic problem-solving reports on the company's intranet?

# Writing and Completing Reports and Proposals

## LEARNING OBJECTIVES

*After studying this chapter, you will be able to*

1. List the topics commonly covered in the introduction, body, and close of informational reports, analytical reports, and proposals.

2. Identify six guidelines for drafting effective website content, and offer guidelines for becoming a valuable wiki contributor.

3. Discuss six principles of graphic design that can improve the quality of your visuals and identify the major types of business visuals.

4. Summarize the four tasks involved in completing business reports and proposals.

The Vancity Community Foundation in Vancouver provides grants and lending advice to nonprofit organizations proposing initiatives to improve communities through community economic development. Sidney Sawyer is part of a team that assesses these proposals, evaluating many of them each year. "Proposal writers," says Sawyer, "create positive impressions by providing clear answers, using plain language, and providing facts to support the proposal." Proposals should be concise but contain enough detail to convince the audience that the idea is valuable, practical, and desirable. Proposals must contain a compelling argument—the key to a successful report.[1]

# Writing Reports and Proposals

This chapter focuses on writing and completing reports, along with creating content for websites, collaborating on wikis, and creating graphical elements to illustrate messages of all kinds.

All the writing concepts and techniques you learned in Chapter 4 apply to the longer format of business reports. However, the length and complexity of reports call for special attention to several issues, starting with adapting to your audience.

## Adapting to Your Audience

Reports and proposals can put heavy demands on your readers, so the "you" attitude is especially important with these long messages. In general, try to strike a balance between overly informal (which can be perceived as trivializing important issues) and overly formal (which can put too much distance between writer and reader). If you know your readers reasonably well and your report is likely to meet with their approval, you can generally adopt an informal tone. To make your tone less formal, speak to readers in the

**LEARNING OBJECTIVE 1**
List the topics commonly covered in the introduction, body, and close of informational reports, analytical reports, and proposals.

The "you" attitude is especially important with long or complex reports because they demand a lot from readers.

first person: refer to them as *you*, and refer to yourself as *I* (or *we* if there are multiple report authors) (see Figure 11.1).

To make your tone more formal, use the impersonal journalism style: emphasize objectivity, avoid personal opinions, and build your argument on provable facts. Eliminate all personal pronouns (including *I*, *you*, *we*, *us*, and *our*). Avoid humour, and be careful with your use of similes, metaphors, and particularly colourful adjectives or adverbs. However, don't go so far as to make the writing monotonous. For example, you can still create interest by varying the types of sentences you use to create a pleasing rhythm.

Take into account that communicating with people in other cultures often calls for more formality in reports, both to respect cultural preferences and to reduce the risk of miscommunication. Informal elements such as humour and casual language tend to translate poorly from one culture to another.

## FIGURE 11.1  Effective Problem-Solving Report Focusing on Recommendations

**MEMO**

**TO:**     Board of Directors, Executive Committee members
**FROM:**   Alycia Jenn, Business Development Manager
**DATE:**   July 6, 2016
**SUBJECT: WEBSITE EXPANSION**

*Reminds readers of the origin and purpose of the report*

In response to your request, my staff and I investigated the potential for expanding our website from its current "brochureware" status (in which we promote our company and its products but don't provide any way to place orders online) to full e-commerce capability (including placing orders and checking on order delivery status). After analyzing the behaviour of our customers and major competitors and studying the overall development of electronic retailing, we have three recommendations. We should

1. Expand our online presence from "brochureware" to e-commerce capability within the next 6 months.

2. Engage a firm that specializes in online retailing to design and develop the new e-commerce capabilities.

3. Integrate online retailing with our store-based and mail-order operations.

*Clarifies the recommendation by listing the necessary actions in clear, direct language*

**1. EXPANDING THE WEBSITE TO FULL E-COMMERCE CAPABILITY**

*Presents logical reasons for recommending that the firm expand its website to include e-commerce*

First, does e-commerce capability make sense today for a small company that sells luxury housewares? Even though books and many other products are now commonly sold online, in most cases, this enterprise involves simple, low-cost products that don't require a lot of hands-on inspection before purchasing. As we've observed in our stores, shoppers like to interact with our products before purchasing them. However, a growing number of websites do sell specialty products, using "virtual product tours" (in which shoppers can interactively view a product in three dimensions, rather than simply looking at a static photograph) and generous return policies (to reduce the perceived risk of buying products online).

Second, do we need to establish a presence now in order to remain competitive in the future? The answer is an overwhelming "yes." The initial steps taken by our competitors are already placing us at a disadvantage among those already comfortable buying online, and every trend indicates our minor competitive weakness today will turn into a major weakness in the next few years:

• Several of our top competitors are implementing full e-commerce, including virtual product tours. Our research suggests that their online sales are growing.

• Younger consumers who grew up with the internet will soon be reaching their peak earning years (ages 35–54). This demographic segment expects e-commerce in nearly every product category, and we'll lose them to the competition if we don't offer it.

• The web has erased geographical shopping limits, presenting both a threat and an opportunity. Even though our customers can now shop websites anywhere in the world (so that we have thousands of competitors instead of a dozen), we can now target customers anywhere in the world.

*Supports the reasoning with evidence*

(Continued)

**FIGURE 11.1** (Continued)

Website expansion                              2                              July 6, 2016

**2. ENGAGING A CONSULTANT TO IMPLEMENT THE SITE**

Implementing a competitive retailing site can take anywhere from 1000 to 1500 hours of design and programming time. We have some of the expertise needed in-house, but the marketing and information systems departments have only 300 person-hours available in the next 6 months. I recommend that we engage a web design firm to help us with the design and to do all the programming.

**3. INTEGRATING THE WEBSITE INTO EXISTING OPERATIONS**

The studies we reviewed showed that the most successful web retailers are careful to integrate their online retailing with their store- and mail-based retailing. Companies that don't integrate carefully find themselves with higher costs, confused customers, and websites that don't generate much business. Before we begin designing our website, we should develop a plan for integrating the web into our existing marketing, accounting, and production systems. The online site could affect every department in the company, so it's vital that everyone has a chance to review the plans before we proceed.

**SUMMARY**

1. Begin working immediately to expand our website to include full e-commerce capability. Even though the financial returns might be minimal in the near term, every sign indicates they will grow in the future. Moreover, we will start to lose customers to other e-commerce sites if we don't expand.

2. Use the services of a web designer because we don't have enough person-hours available in-house.

3. Integrate the website with existing operations, particularly in marketing, accounting, and production.

*Goes beyond the basic recommendation of what to do by suggesting how to do it*

*Addresses some important concerns that must be dealt with if the recommended action is taken*

*Concludes with a concise summary of the recommended action*

## Drafting Report Content

You can simplify report writing by breaking the job into three main sections: an introduction (or opening), a body, and a close. Table 11.1 summarizes the goals of each section and lists elements to consider including in each as well. You can use this table as a handy reference whenever you need to write a report in school or on the job.

At a minimum, an effective *introduction*:

- Helps the reader understand the context of the report by tying it to a problem or an assignment.
- Introduces the subject matter and indicates why it is important.
- Previews the main idea (if you're using the direct approach).
- Establishes the tone and the writer's relationship with the audience.

The *body* presents, analyzes, and interprets the information gathered during your investigation and supports your recommendations or conclusions. The length and content of the body can vary widely based on the subject matter.

The *close* has three important functions:

- It summarizes your key points.
- It emphasizes the benefits to the reader if the document suggests a change or some other course of action.
- It brings all the action items together in one place.

To serve the needs of your readers and build your reputation as a careful and insightful professional, make sure your content in every section is accurate, complete, balanced, clear, and logical. As always, be sure to properly document all your sources (see Appendix B).

*The introduction needs to put the report in context for the reader, introduce the subject, preview main ideas, and establish the tone of the document.*

*The body of your report presents, analyzes, and interprets the information you gathered during your investigation.*

*Your close is often the last opportunity to get your message across, so make it clear and compelling.*

| TABLE 11.1 | Content Elements to Consider for Reports and Proposals |
| --- | --- |

**REPORTS**

**Introduction:**

Establish the context, identify the subject, preview main ideas (if using the direct approach), and establish tone and reader relationship.

- **Authorization.** Reiterate who authorized the report, if applicable.
- **Problem/purpose.** Explain the reason for the report's existence and what the report will achieve.
- **Scope.** Describe what will and won't be covered in the report.
- **Background.** Review historical conditions or factors that led up to the report.
- **Sources and methods.** Discuss the primary and secondary sources consulted and methods used.
- **Definitions.** List terms and their definitions, including any terms that might be misinterpreted. Terms may also be defined in the body, explanatory notes, or glossary.
- **Limitations.** Discuss factors beyond your control that affect report quality (but do not use this as an excuse for poor research or a poorly written report).
- **Report organization.** Identify the topics to be covered and in what order.

**Body:**

Present relevant information and support your recommendations or conclusions.

- **Explanations.** Give complete details of the problem, project, or idea.
- **Facts, statistical evidence, and trends.** Lay out the results of studies or investigations.
- **Analysis of action.** Discuss potential courses of action.
- **Pros and cons.** Explain advantages, disadvantages, costs, and benefits of a particular course of action.
- **Procedures.** Outline steps for a process.
- **Methods and approaches.** Discuss how you've studied a problem (or gathered evidence) and arrived at your solution (or collected your data).
- **Criteria.** Describe the benchmarks for evaluating options and alternatives.
- **Conclusions and recommendations.** Discuss what you believe the evidence reveals and what you propose should be done about it.
- **Support.** Give the reasons behind your conclusions or recommendations.

**Close:**

Summarize key points, emphasize benefits of any recommendations, list action items; label as "Summary" or "Conclusions and Recommendations."

- **For direct approach.** Summarize key points (except in short reports), listing them in the order in which they appear in the body. Briefly restate your conclusions or recommendations, if appropriate.
- **For indirect approach.** If you haven't done so at the end of the body, present your conclusions or recommendations.
- **For motivating action.** Spell out exactly what should happen next and provide a schedule with specific task assignments.

**PROPOSALS**

**Introduction:**

Identify the problem you intend to solve or the opportunity you want to pursue.

- **Background or statement of the problem.** Briefly review the situation at hand, establish a need for action, and explain how things could be better. In unsolicited proposals, convince readers that a problem or an opportunity exists.
- **Solution.** Briefly describe the change you propose, highlighting your key selling points and their benefits to show how your proposal will solve the reader's problem.
- **Scope.** State the boundaries of the proposal—what you will and will not do.
- **Report organization.** Orient the reader to the remainder of the proposal and call attention to the major divisions of thought.

**Body:**

Give complete details on the proposed solution and describe anticipated results.

- **Facts and evidence to support your conclusions.** Provide explanations, specific examples, and concrete details to back up your main points.
- **Proposed approach.** Describe your concept, product, or service. Stress reader benefits and emphasize any advantages you have over your competitors.
- **Work plan.** Describe how you'll accomplish what must be done (unless you're providing a standard, off-the-shelf item). Explain the steps you'll take, their timing, the methods or resources you'll use, and the person(s) responsible. State when work will begin, how it will be divided into stages, when you'll finish, and whether follow-up will be needed.
- **Statement of qualifications.** Describe your organization's experience, personnel, and facilities—relating it all to readers' needs. Include a list of client references.
- **Costs.** Prove that your costs are realistic—break them down so that readers can see the costs of labour, materials, transportation, travel, training, and other categories.

**Close:**

Summarize key points, emphasize the benefits and advantages of your proposed solution, ask for a decision from the reader.

- **Review of argument.** Briefly summarize the key points.
- **Review of reader benefits.** Briefly summarize how your proposal will help the reader.
- **Review of the merits of your approach.** Briefly summarize why your approach will be more effective than alternatives.
- **Restatement of qualifications.** For external proposals, briefly reemphasize why you and your firm should do the work.
- **Request.** Ask for a decision from the reader.

**HELPING READERS FIND THEIR WAY**   To help today's time-pressed readers find what they're looking for and stay on track as they navigate through your documents, learn to make good use of headings or links, smooth transitions, and previews and reviews:

- **Headings or links.** Readers should be able to follow the structure of your document and pick up the key points of your message from the headings and subheadings (see Figure 11.3). For online reports, make generous use of hyperlinks to help your readers navigate the reports and access additional information.

- **Transitions.** Chapter 4 defines transitions as words or phrases that tie together ideas and show how one thought is related to another. In addition, in a long report, an entire paragraph might be used to highlight transitions from one major section to the next.

Help your readers find what they want and stay on track with headings or links, transitions, previews, and reviews.

---

**FIGURE 11.2   A Solicited Proposal**

**JWR Remodelling Solutions**

3240 Richard Road SW • Calgary, AB  T3E 6R2
(403) 240-8845 • Fax: (403) 240-8846 • Email: jwr@telus.net

October 29, 2016

Mr. Daniel Yurgren
Data Dimensions
15 Foothills Lane
Calgary, AB  T4M 1X2

Dear Mr. Yurgren:

**PROPOSAL FOR HOME OFFICE CONSTRUCTION**

**Timing**
JWR Remodelling Solutions would be happy to convert your existing living room area into a home office according to the specifications discussed during our October 15 meeting. We can schedule the project for the week beginning November 12, 2016 (two weeks from today). The project will take roughly three weeks to complete.

**Benefits**
Our construction approach is unique. We provide a full staff of licensed trades people and schedule our projects so that when one trade finishes, the next trade is ready to begin. To expedite this project, as you requested, we have agreed to overlap several trades whose work can be done concurrently.

**Services Provided**
JWR Remodelling Solutions will provide the following work:

- Remove baseboard, door casing, fluted casing, and sheetrock to prepare for construction of new partition wall at north end of living room.
- Partition and finish walls to create two separate storage closets at north end of living room with access through two 3'0" six-panel door units. Replace all disturbed sheetrock.
- Hang and trim new door units and replace all disturbed baseboards and door casings.
- Install 5'0" double French door unit in location of current cased opening at the SW entrance to living room adjacent to foyer. Trim appropriately.
- Provide all rough and finished electrical using recessed lighting in the ceiling and appropriate single pole switches and duplex outlets.
- Move cold air return from west wall to east wall of living room.
- Paint or finish all surfaces/trim to match specs used throughout house.

**Exceptions**
The work does *not* include custom office cabinetry, carpeting, or phone or cable wiring. We would be happy to bid on these projects in the future.

*Annotations (left):*
Acknowledges scope of project

Specifies exactly what contractor will and won't do

*Annotations (right):*
Uses introduction to grab the reader's attention with expedited completion date—a key selling point

Uses body to explain how company will expedite schedule, outline approach, provide work plan, and (on the next page) list qualifications and state costs

(Continued)

**FIGURE 11.2** (Continued)

Mr. Daniel Yurgren                 October 29, 2016                    Page 2

**Qualifications**
JWR Remodelling Solutions has been in business in the Calgary area for more than 17 years. We have a strong reputation for being a quality builder. We take great pride in our work and we treat all projects with the same high-level attention, regardless of their size or scope. Our trades people are all licensed, insured professionals with years of experience in their respective crafts. Enclosed is a copy of our company brochure discussing our qualifications in greater detail, along with a current client list. Please contact any of the names on this list for references.

*Increases desire by highlighting qualifications*

**Costs**
The total cost for this project is $6800, broken down as follows:

*Justifies cost by providing detail*

| Materials and supplies | $3300 |
|---|---|
| Labour | 2700 |
| Overhead | 800 |
| Total | $6800 |

An initial payment of $3800 is due upon acceptance of this proposal. The remaining $3000 is due upon completion of the work.

**Hiring JWR**
If you would like to have JWR Remodelling Solutions complete this work, please sign this letter and return it to us with your deposit in the enclosed envelope. We currently anticipate no construction delays, since the materials needed for your job are in stock and our staff of qualified workers is available during the period mentioned. If you have any questions regarding the terms of this proposal, please call me at (403) 946-8845.

*Uses brief closing to emphasize fast turnaround and immediate call for action*

Sincerely,

*[signature]*

Jordan W. Spurrier
President

Enclosures

Accepted by:

*Makes letter a binding contract, if signed*

_____
Daniel Yurgren

---

**Pointers for Developing Proposals**
- Carefully review and follow all requirements listed in the RFP (if applicable).
- Define the scope of work you intend to complete.
- Determine the methods and procedures to be used.
- Carefully estimate requirements for time, personnel, and costs.
- Write, format, and deliver the proposal exactly as the RFP specifies.
- Open by stating the purpose of the proposal, defining the scope of work, presenting helpful background information, and explaining any relevant restrictions or limitations.
- In the body, provide details and specify anticipated results, including methods, schedule, facilities, quantities, equipment, personnel, and costs.
- Close by summarizing key selling points and benefits, then ask for a decision from the audience.

---

- **Previews and reviews.** *Preview sections* introduce important topics by helping readers get ready for new information. *Review sections* come after a body of material and summarize the information for your readers, helping them absorb details.

Creating lengthy reports and proposals can be a huge task, so take advantage of all available productivity tools. For example, the size and complexity of many reports make templates and style sheets particularly helpful. If you include graphics, spreadsheets, or database records produced in other programs, make sure you know how your writing software handles the file connection. You might have the choice to maintain a "live" connection with these included files, so that any changes in the original automatically show up in your report. And be sure to explore your multimedia options with electronic documents.

*Look for ways to use technology to reduce the mechanical work involved in writing long reports.*

**FIGURE 11.3** Heading Format for Reports and Proposals

**TITLE**

The title is centred at the top of the page in all-capital letters, usually bold-faced, often in a large font (for example, 14 point), and often using a sans serif typeface. When the title runs to more than one line, the lines are usually arranged as an inverted pyramid (longer line on the top).

**FIRST-LEVEL HEADING**

A first-level heading indicates what the following section is about, perhaps by describing the subdivisions. All first-level headings are grammatically parallel, with the possible exception of such headings as "Introduction," "Conclusions," and "Recommendations." Some text appears between every two headings, regardless of their levels. Still boldfaced and sans serif, the font may be smaller than that used in the title but larger than the typeface used in the text (for example, 12 point) and still in all-capital letters.

*Headings allow readers to scan a report and choose which sections to read*

**Second-Level Heading**

Like first-level headings, second-level headings indicate what the following material is about. All second-level headings within a section are grammatically parallel. Still boldfaced and sans serif, the font may either remain the same or shrink to the size used in the text, and the style is now initial capitals with lower case. Never use only one second-level heading under a first-level heading. (The same is true for every other level of heading.)

*Headings and subheadings show the content at a glance*

**Third-Level Heading**

A third-level heading is worded to reflect the content of the material that follows. All third-level headings beneath a second-level heading should be grammatically parallel.

**Fourth-Level Heading.** Like all the other levels of headings, fourth-level headings reflect the subject that will be developed. All fourth-level headings within a subsection are parallel.

*Subheading levels are distinguished by font size and style and by alignment*

**Fifth-level headings** are generally the lowest level of heading used. However, you can indicate further breakdowns in your ideas by using a list:

1. *The first item in a list.* You may indent the entire item in block format to set it off visually. Numbers are optional.
2. *The second item in a list.* All lists have at least two items. An introductory phrase or sentence may be italicized for emphasis, as shown here.

Video clips, animation, presentation slides, *screencasts* (recordings of on-screen activity), and other media elements can enhance the communication and persuasion powers of the written word.

## Drafting Proposal Content

All of the guidelines for writing reports apply to proposals as well, but these persuasive messages also have some unique considerations. As Chapter 10 notes, the most important factor is whether the proposal is solicited or unsolicited, because this can affect your organization, content, and tone.

The general purpose of any proposal is to persuade readers to do something, so your writing approach is similar to that used for persuasive messages, perhaps including the use of the AIDA model or something similar to gain attention, build interest, create desire, and motivate action. To convince your reader to accept your proposal, you will need to:

- Know your product's features.
- Identify how those features can benefit the readers and relate exactly to their needs.

*Approach proposals the same way you approach persuasive messages.*

- Provide concrete facts and examples.
- Show how your proposal favourably compares to the competition.
- Prove that your proposal is feasible.

Moreover, make sure your proposal is error-free, inviting, and readable. Readers will prejudge the quality of your products, services, or capabilities by the quality of the proposal you submit. Errors, omissions, and inconsistencies will work against you—and might even cost you important career and business opportunities.

In addition to the productivity tools listed on page 262, consider using proposal-writing software if you and your company need to submit proposals as a routine part of doing business. These programs can automatically personalize proposals, ensure proper structure (making sure you don't forget any sections, for instance), organize storage of all your boilerplate text, integrate contact information from sales databases, scan RFPs to identify questions (and even assign them to content experts), and fill in preliminary answers to common questions from a centralized knowledge base.[2]

See Table 11.1 for a summary of the content to include in reports and proposals.

# Writing for Websites and Wikis

In addition to standalone reports and proposals, you may be asked to write in-depth content for websites or to collaborate on a wiki. The basic principles of report writing apply to both formats, but each has some unique considerations as well.

## Drafting Website Content

Major sections on websites, particularly those that are fairly static (unlike, say, a blog) function in much the same way as reports. The skills you've developed for report writing adapt easily to this environment, as long as you keep a few points in mind:

- Take special care to **build trust** with your intended audiences, because careful readers can be skeptical of online content. Make sure your content is accurate, current, complete, and authoritative.
- As much as possible, **adapt your content for a global audience**. Translating content is expensive, so some companies compromise by *localizing* the homepage while keeping the deeper, more detailed content in its original language.
- In an environment that presents many reading challenges, **compelling, reader-oriented content is key** to success.[3] Wherever you can, use the *inverted pyramid* style, in which you cover the most important information briefly at first and then gradually reveal successive layers of detail—letting readers choose to see those additional layers if they want to.
- Present your information in a **concise, skimmable format**. Most online readers won't dig for buried information. If they can't find the right information quickly, they will move on to another page or site.[4] Effective websites use a variety of means to help readers skim pages quickly, including lists, careful use of colour and boldface, informative headings, and helpful summaries that give readers a choice of learning more if they want to.
- Write **effective headings and links** that serve for both site navigation and content skimming. Above all, clearly identify where each link will take readers, and don't force them to click through and try to figure out where they're going.
- **Make your website a "living" document** by regularly adding fresh content and deleting content that is out of date or no longer relevant to your target audience. Over time, websites can accumulate many pages of outdated information that get in the way and send a negative message about the company's efforts to stay on top of user needs.[5]

# Collaborating on Wikis

Effective collaboration on wikis requires a unique approach to writing.

As Chapter 2 points out, using a wiki is a great way for teams and other groups to collaborate on writing projects, from brief articles to long reports and reference works. Although wikis have many benefits, they do require a unique approach to writing. To be a valuable wiki contributor, keep these points in mind:[6]

- Let go of traditional expectations of authorship, including individual recognition and control. The value of a wiki stems from the collective insight of all its contributors.
- Encourage all team members to edit and improve each other's work.
- Use page templates and other formatting options to ensure that your content matches the rest of the wiki.
- Use the separate editing and discussion capabilities appropriately.
- Take advantage of the *sandbox*, if available; this is a "safe," nonpublished section of the wiki where team members can practise editing and writing.

Wikis usually have guidelines to help new contributors integrate their work into the group's ongoing effort. Be sure to read and understand these guidelines, and don't be afraid to ask for help.

Before you add new pages to a wiki, figure out how the material fits with the existing content.

If you are creating a new wiki, think through your long-term purpose carefully, just as you would with a new blog or podcast channel. Will the wiki be a one-time project (creating a report, for example) or an ongoing effort (such as maintaining "help" files for a software program)? Who will be allowed to add or modify content? Will you or someone else serve as editor, reviewing all additions and changes? What rules and guidelines will you establish to guide the growth of the wiki? What security measures might be required?

If you are adding a page or an article to an existing wiki, figure out how this new material fits in with the existing structure of the wiki and learn the wiki's preferred style for handling incomplete articles. For example, on the wiki that contains the user documentation for the popular WordPress blogging software, contributors are discouraged from adding new pages until the content is "fairly complete and accurate."[7]

If you are revising or updating an existing wiki article, use the checklist on pages 95–96 in Chapter 5 to evaluate the content before you make changes. If you don't agree with published content and plan to revise it, you can use the wiki's discussion facility to share your concerns with other contributors. The wiki environment should encourage discussions and even robust disagreements, as long as everyone remains civil and respectful.

# Illustrating Your Reports with Effective Visuals

LEARNING OBJECTIVE 3
Discuss six principles of graphic design that can improve the quality of your visuals and identify the major types of business visuals.

Well-designed visual elements can enhance the communication power of textual messages and, in some instances, even replace textual messages. Generally speaking, in a given amount of time, well-designed images can convey much more information than text.[8] Using pictures is also an effective way to communicate with multilingual audiences.

Visual literacy is the ability to create effective images and to interpret images correctly.

Given the importance of visuals in today's business environment, **visual literacy**—the ability (as a sender) to create effective images and (as a receiver) to correctly interpret visual messages—has become a key business skill.[9] Even without any formal training in design, being aware of the following six principles will help you be a more effective visual communicator:

Pay close attention to consistency, contrast, balance, emphasis, convention, and simplicity.

- **Consistency.** Think of consistency as *visual parallelism*, similar to textual parallelism that helps audiences understand and compare a series of ideas.[10] You can achieve visual parallelism through the consistent use of colour, shape, size, texture, position, scale, or typeface.

- **Contrast.** To emphasize differences, depict items in contrasting colours, such as red and blue or black and white. To emphasize similarities, make colour differences more subtle.
- **Balance.** Visual balance can be either *formal*, in which the elements in the images are arranged symmetrically around a central point or axis, or *informal*, in which elements are not distributed evenly, but stronger and weaker elements are arranged in a way that achieves an overall effect of balance.[11] Generally speaking, formal balance is calming and serious, whereas informal balance tends to feel dynamic and engaging (which is why most advertising uses this approach, for example).
- **Emphasis.** Audiences usually assume that the dominant element in a design is the most important, so make sure that the visually dominant element really does represent the most important information.
- **Convention.** Just as written communication is guided by spelling, grammar, punctuation, and usage conventions, visual communication is guided by generally accepted rules or conventions that dictate virtually every aspect of design.[12] In any given culture, for example, certain colours and shapes have specific meanings.
- **Simplicity.** When you're designing graphics for your documents, limit the number of colours and design elements and take care to avoid *chartjunk*—decorative elements that clutter documents without adding any relevant information.[13] Think carefully about using some of the chart features available in your software, too. Many of these features can actually get in the way of effective visual communication.[14] For example, three-dimensional bar charts, cones, and pyramids can look appealing, but the third dimension usually adds no additional information and can be visually deceiving as well.[15]

**REAL-TIME UPDATES**

**Learn More by Watching This Video**

**The beauty of data visualization**

Information designer David McCandless discusses the power of data visualization tools and techniques. Go to http://real-timeupdates.com/bce6 and click on Learn More. If you are using MyBCommLab, you can access Real-Time Updates within Business Communication Resources.

## Choosing the Right Visual for the Job

After you've identified which points would benefit most from visual presentation, your next decision is to choose what types of visuals to use. As you can see in Figure 11.4, you have many choices for business graphics. (Note that *chart* and *graph* are used interchangeably for most of the display formats discussed here.)

**TABLES** When you need to present detailed, specific information, choose a **table**, a systematic arrangement of data in columns and rows. Tables are ideal when your audience needs information that would be either difficult or tedious to handle in the main text. Most tables contain the standard parts illustrated in Figure 11.5. Follow these guidelines to create clear, effective tables:

*Printed tables can display extensive amounts of data, but tables for online display and electronic presentations need to be simpler.*

- Use common, understandable units and clearly identify them: dollars, percentages, price per tonne, and so on.
- Express all items in a column in the same unit and round off for simplicity.
- Label column headings clearly, and use subheads if necessary.
- Separate columns or rows with lines or extra space to make the table easy to follow. Make sure the intended reading direction—down the columns or across the rows—is obvious.
- Don't cram too much information into a table so that it becomes difficult to read.
- Keep online tables small enough to read comfortably onscreen.
- Document the source of data using the same format as a text footnote (see Appendix B).

FIGURE 11.4   Selecting the Best Visual

| Communication Challenge | Effective Visual Choice |
| --- | --- |

**Presenting Data**

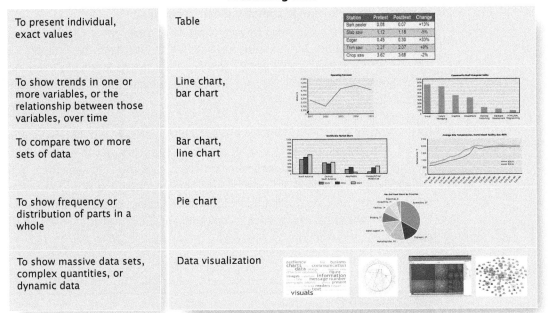

| To present individual, exact values | Table |
| To show trends in one or more variables, or the relationship between those variables, over time | Line chart, bar chart |
| To compare two or more sets of data | Bar chart, line chart |
| To show frequency or distribution of parts in a whole | Pie chart |
| To show massive data sets, complex quantities, or dynamic data | Data visualization |

**Presenting Information, Concepts, and Ideas**

| To illustrate processes or procedures | Flowchart, diagram |
| To show conceptual or spatial relationships (simplified) | Drawing |
| To tell data-driven story visually | Infograph |
| To show spatial relationships (realistic) | Photograph |
| To show processes, transformations, and so on, in action | Animation, video |

FIGURE 11.5   Parts of a Table

| | Multicolumn Heading | | | Single-Column Heading |
| --- | --- | --- | --- | --- |
| | Column Subheading | Column Subheading | Column Subheading | |
| Row Heading | xxx | xxx | xxx | xxx |
| Row Heading | xxx | xxx | xxx | xxx |
| *Row Subheading* | xxx | xxx | xxx | xxx |
| *Row Subheading* | xxx | xxx | xxx | xxx |
| Row Heading | xxx | xxx | xxx | xxx |
| Row Heading | xxx | xxx | xxx | xxx |
| TOTALS | xxx | xxx | xxx | xxx |

**LINE CHARTS AND SURFACE CHARTS**    A **line chart** (see Figure 11.6) illustrates trends over time or plots the relationship of two variables. In line charts that show trends, the vertical, or *y*, axis shows the amount, and the horizontal, or *x*, axis shows the time or other quantity against which the amount is being measured. You can plot just a single line or overlay multiple lines to compare different entities.

A **surface chart**, also called an **area chart**, is a form of line chart that shows a cumulative effect; all the lines add up to the top line, which represents the total (see Figure 11.7). This type of chart helps you illustrate changes in the composition of something over time. When preparing a surface chart, put the most significant line at the bottom and move up toward the least significant.

**BAR CHARTS AND PIE CHARTS**    A **bar chart** portrays numbers with the height or length of its rectangular bars, making a series of numbers easy to grasp quickly. Bars can be oriented horizontally or vertically (in which case they are sometimes referred to as *column charts*). Bar charts are particularly valuable when you want to show or compare quantities over time. As the charts in Figure 11.8 suggest, bar charts can appear in various forms. Specialized bar charts such as *timelines* and *Gantt charts* are used often in project management, for example.

**FIGURE 11.6** Line Chart

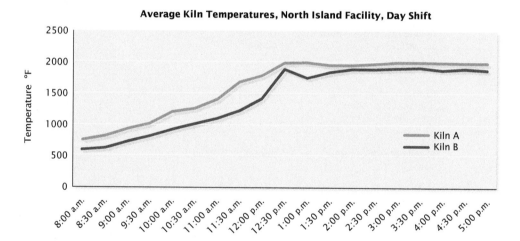

**FIGURE 11.7** Surface Chart

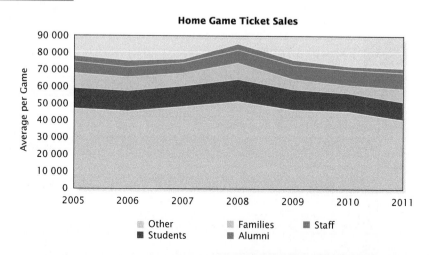

## FIGURE 11.8 Four Kinds of Bar Charts

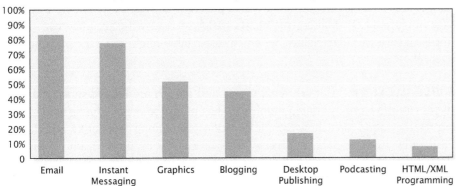

**(a) CommuniCo Staff Computer Skills (Singular bars)**

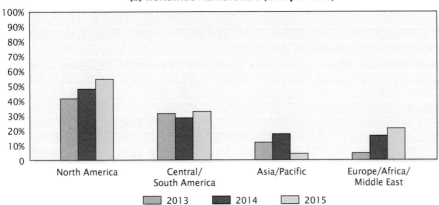

**(b) Worldwide Market Share (Grouped bars)**

2013    2014    2015

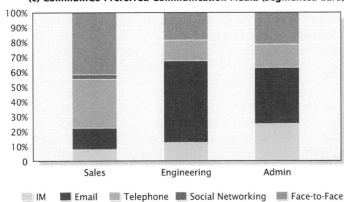

**(c) CommuniCo Preferred Communication Media (Segmented bars)**

IM    Email    Telephone    Social Networking    Face-to-Face

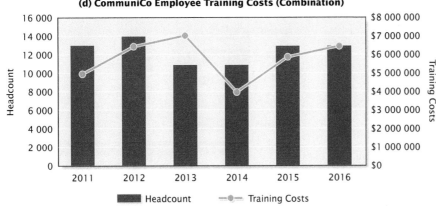

**(d) CommuniCo Employee Training Costs (Combination)**

Headcount    Training Costs

A **pie chart** is a commonly used tool for showing how the parts of a whole are distributed. Although pie charts are popular and can quickly highlight the dominant parts of a whole, they are often not as effective as bar charts or tables. For example, comparing percentages accurately is often difficult with a pie chart but can be fairly easy with a bar chart (see Figure 11.9). Making pie charts easier to read with accuracy can require labelling each slice with data values, in which case a table might serve the purpose more effectively.[16]

**DATA VISUALIZATION**    Conventional charts and graphs are limited in several ways: most types can show only a limited number of data points before becoming too cluttered to interpret, they often can't show complex relationships among data points, and they can represent only numeric data. A diverse class of display capabilities known as **data visualization** works to overcome all these drawbacks.

Data visualization is about extracting broad meaning from giant masses of data or putting the data in context.[17] For instance, the Facebook "friend wheel" in Figure 11.10a offers a visual sense of this particular Facebook user's network by showing which of his friends are friends of each other and thereby indicating "clustering" within the network (work friends, social friends, and so on). The diagram doesn't attempt to show quantities but rather the overall nature of the network.

In addition to displaying large data sets and linkages within data sets, other kinds of visualization tools combine data with textual information to communicate complex or dynamic data much faster than conventional presentations can. For example, a *tag cloud* shows the relative frequency of terms, or tags (user-applied content labels), in an article, a blog, a website, survey data, or another collection of text.[18] Figure 11.10 shows a few of the many data visualization tools now available.

Many of these tools are also interactive. Like all tools, however, they can be used to good effect or misused to bad effect. Visualizations that might look dazzling at first can actually have little or no practical communication value. In fact, some data visualizations are intended to be works of art more than practical tools.

Unlike conventional charts, data visualization tools are more about uncovering broad meaning and finding hidden connections.

## REAL-TIME UPDATES

**Learn More by Visiting This Website**

**Data visualization and infographics gateway: A comprehensive collection for business communicators**

This unique web resource offers links to a vast array of data visualization and infographics techniques and examples. Go to http://real-timeupdates.com/bce6 and click on Learn More. If you are using MyBCommLab, you can access Real-Time Updates within Business Communication Resources.

---

**FIGURE 11.9**  **Pie Charts Versus Bar Charts**

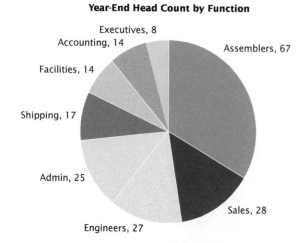

**Year-End Head Count by Function**

Executives, 8
Accounting, 14
Facilities, 14
Shipping, 17
Admin, 25
Engineers, 27
Sales, 28
Assemblers, 67

**Year-End Head Count by Function**

|  |  |
|----------|-------|
| Executives | 8 |
| Accounting | 14 |
| Facilities | 14 |
| Shipping | 17 |
| Admin | 25 |
| Engineers | 27 |
| Sales | 28 |
| Assemblers | 67 |

## FIGURE 11.10 Data Visualization and Infographics

(a) Facebook "friend wheel" showing how the connections of one Facebook user are connected with one another

(c) Infographic that uses a calendar motif to suggest differences in browser security vulnerabilities

(b) A tag cloud showing the relative frequency of the 50 most-used words in this chapter (other than common words such as *and*, *or*, and *the*)

(d) How to satisfy your social media fix in one hour

**FLOWCHARTS AND ORGANIZATION CHARTS** A **flowchart** (see Figure 11.11) illustrates a sequence of events from start to finish; it is indispensable when illustrating processes, procedures, and sequential relationships. For general business purposes, you don't need to be too concerned about the specific shapes on a flowchart; just be sure to use them consistently. However, you should be aware that there is a formal flowchart "language," in which each shape has a specific meaning (diamonds are decision points, rectangles are process steps, and so on). If you're communicating with computer programmers and others who are accustomed to formal flowcharting, make sure you look up the correct symbols in each case to avoid confusion.

Be aware that there is a formal symbolic "language" in flowcharting; each shape has a specific meaning.

As the name implies, an **organization chart** illustrates the positions, units, or functions in an organization and the ways they interrelate (see Figure 11.12). Organization charts can be used to portray almost any hierarchy, in fact, including the topics, subtopics, and supporting points you need to organize for a report.

**MAPS, DRAWINGS, DIAGRAMS, INFOGRAPHICS, AND PHOTOGRAPHS** Maps are useful for showing territories, routes, and locations. Simple maps are available via clip art libraries, but more powerful uses (such as automatically generating colour-coded maps

Use maps to represent statistics by geographic area and to show spatial relationships.

FIGURE 11.11 Flowchart

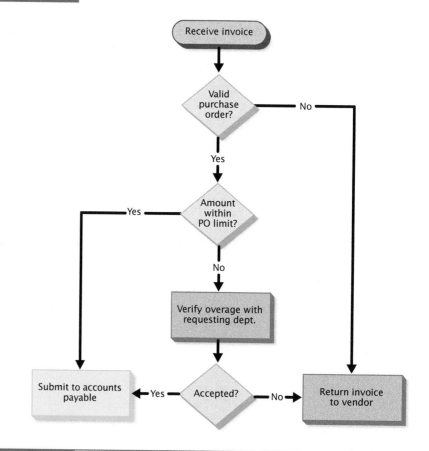

FIGURE 11.12 Organization Chart

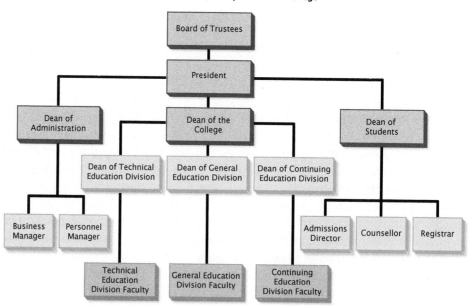

based on data inputs) usually require the specialized capabilities of *geographic information systems (GIS)*. You may also want to explore online resources such as Google Earth (**www .google.com/earth**) and Bing Maps (**www.bing.com/maps**), which offer a variety of mapping and aerial photography features.

Drawings can show an endless variety of business concepts, such as the network of suppliers in an industry, the flow of funds through a company, or the process for completing payroll each week. More complex diagrams can convey technical topics such as the operation of a machine or repair procedures. As you learned in Chapter 10, diagrams that contain enough visual and textual information to function as independent documents are called **infographics** (see Figure 11.13). Infographics have become extremely popular on websites and blogs, partly because their eye-catching appeal attracts visitors, click-throughs, and social sharing. The best use of an infographic is to help readers make connections between fragmented pieces of information, rather than simply dressing up basic data charts with design elements that might be attractive but add little to understanding.[19] Be sure to cite sources of information used in infographics.

Photographs offer both functional and decorative value, and nothing can top a photograph when you need to show exact appearances. However, in some situations, a photograph can show too much detail, which is one reason repair manuals frequently use drawings instead of photos, for instance. Because audiences expect photographs to show literal visual truths, you must take care when using image-processing tools such as Adobe Photoshop.

**ANIMATION AND VIDEO**   Computer animation and video are among the most specialized forms of business visuals; when they are appropriate and done well, they offer unparalleled visual impact. At a simple level, you can animate shapes and text within electronic presentations (see Chapter 12). At a more sophisticated level, software such as Adobe Flash enables creation of multimedia files that include computer animation, digital video, and other elements.

The combination of low-cost digital video cameras and video-sharing websites such as YouTube has spurred a revolution in business video applications in recent years. Product demonstrations, company overviews, promotional presentations, and training seminars are among the most popular applications of business video. *Branded channels* on YouTube allow companies to present their videos as an integrated collection in a customized user interface.

## Designing Effective Visuals

Computers make it easy to create visuals, but they also make it easy to create ineffective visuals. However, by following the design principles discussed on page 265, you can create basic visuals that are attractive and effective. If possible, have a professional designer set up a *template* for the various types of visuals you and your colleagues need to create. By specifying colour palettes, font selections, slide layouts, and other choices, design templates have three important benefits: they help ensure better designs, they promote consistency across the organization, and they save everyone time by eliminating repetitive decision making.

Remember that the style and quality of your visuals communicate a subtle message about your relationship with the audience. A simple sketch might be fine for a working meeting but inappropriate for a formal presentation or report. On the other hand, elaborate, full-colour visuals may be viewed as extravagant for an informal report but may be entirely appropriate for a message to top management or influential outsiders.

## Integrating Visuals with Text

In addition to being well designed, visuals need to be well integrated with text:

- Position your visuals so that your audience won't have to flip back and forth (in printed documents) or scroll (onscreen) between visuals and the text that discusses them.

REAL-TIME UPDATES

**Learn More by Visiting This Website**

**Ten tips for effective infographics**

Use these techniques to create infographics that out from the crowd. Go to http://real-timeupdates.com/bce6 and click on Learn More. If you are using MyBCommLab, you can access Real-Time Updates within Business Communication Resources.

Drawings are sometimes better than photographs because they let you focus on the most important details.

Use photographs for visual appeal and to show exact appearances.

To tie visuals to the text, introduce them in the text and place them near the points they illustrate.

**FIGURE 11.13** Sample Infographic

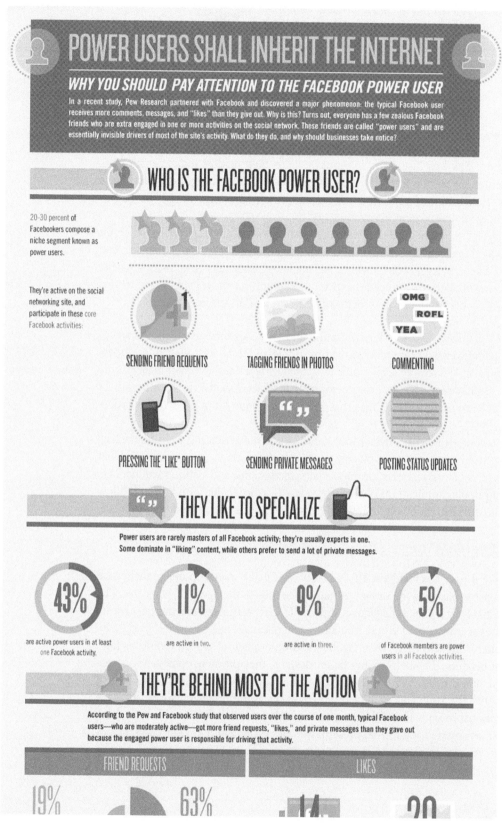

Well-designed infographics tell a story by showing readers how the various pieces of a picture fit together. To see this entire infographic, visit http://real-timeupdates.com/bce6 and click on Learn More.

*Source:* "Power Users Shall Inherit the Internet." Copyright © Demandforce, Inc. in partnership with Column Five Media. Reprinted with permission.

- Refer to visuals by number in the text of your report and help your readers understand the significance of visuals by referring to them *before* readers encounter them in the document or onscreen.
- Write effective *titles*, *captions*, and *legends*. A **title** provides a short description that identifies the content and purpose of the visual. A **caption** usually offers additional discussion of the visual's content. A **legend** helps readers "decode" the visual by explaining what various colours, symbols, or other design choices mean.

## Proofreading for Accuracy and Ethics

Review your visuals carefully for accuracy. Check for mistakes such as typographical errors, inconsistent colour treatment, confusing or undocumented symbols, and misaligned elements. Make sure that your computer hasn't done something unexpected, such as arranging chart bars in an order you don't want or plotting line charts in unusual colours. Make sure your visuals are properly documented by citing sources. Most important, make sure your visuals are honest—that they don't intentionally or unintentionally distort the truth. To avoid ethical lapses in your visuals, consider all possible interpretations, provide enough background information for readers to interpret your visuals correctly, and don't hide or minimize visual information that readers need in order to make informed judgments.[20]

*Proof visuals as carefully as you proof text.*

# Completing Reports and Proposals

LEARNING OBJECTIVE ④
Summarize the four tasks involved in completing business reports and proposals.

As with shorter messages (Chapter 5), when you have finished your first draft, you need to perform four tasks to complete your document: revise, produce, proofread, and distribute.

## Revising Reports and Proposals

The revision process is essentially the same for reports as for other business messages, although it may take considerably longer, depending on the length of your document. Evaluate your organization, style, and tone to make sure that your content is clear, logical, and reader oriented. Then work to improve the report's readability by varying sentence length, keeping paragraphs short, using lists and bullets, and adding headings and subheadings. Keep revising the content until it is clear, concise, and compelling. Remember that even minor mistakes can affect your credibility.

*The revision process for long reports can take considerable time, so be sure to plan ahead.*

Tight, efficient writing that is easy to skim is always a plus, but it's especially important for impatient online audiences.[21] Review online content carefully; strip out all information that doesn't meet audience needs and condense everything else as much as possible. Audiences will gladly return to sites that deliver quality information quickly—and they'll avoid sites that don't.

*The revision process for long reports can take considerable time, so be sure to plan ahead.*

After assembling your report or proposal in its final form, review it thoroughly one last time, looking for inconsistencies, errors, and missing components. Don't forget to proof your visuals thoroughly and make sure they are positioned correctly. For online reports, make sure all links work as expected and all necessary files are active and available. If you need specific tips on proofreading documents, look back at Chapter 5.

## Producing Formal Reports and Proposals

Formal reports and proposals can include a variety of features beyond the text and visuals (see Table 11.2). Most of these provide additional information; a few are more decorative and add a degree of formality.

*The number and variety of parts you include in a report depend on the type of report, audience requirements, organizational expectations, and report length.*

| TABLE 11.2 | Production Elements to Consider for Formal Reports and Proposals |
| --- | --- |

**REPORTS**

**Prefatory elements**
(before the introduction)

- **Cover.** Include a concise title that gives readers the information they need to grasp the purpose and scope of the report. For a formal printed report, choose heavy, high-quality *cover stock.*
- **Title fly.** Some formal reports open with a plain sheet of paper that has only the title of the report on it, although this is certainly not necessary.
- **Title page.** Typically includes the report title, name(s) and title(s) of the writer(s), and date of submission; this information can be put on the cover instead.
- **Letter of authorization.** If you received written authorization to prepare the report, you may want to include that letter or memo in your report.
- **Letter of transmittal.** "Cover letter" that introduces the report and can include scope, methods, limitations, highlights of the report; offers to provide follow-on information or assistance; and acknowledges help received while preparing the report.
- **Table of contents.** List all section headings and major subheadings to show the location and hierarchy of the information in the report.
- **List of illustrations.** Consider including this list if the illustrations are particularly important and you want to call attention to them.
- **Synopsis or executive summary.** See discussion in the text.

**PROPOSALS**

**Prefatory elements**
(before the introduction)

- **Cover, title fly, title page.** Same uses as with reports; be sure to follow any instructions in the RFP, if relevant.
- **Copy of or reference to the RFP.** Instead of having a letter of authorization, a solicited proposal should follow the instructions in the RFP. Some will instruct you to include the entire RFP in your proposal; others may want you to simply identify it by a name and tracking number.
- **Synopsis or executive summary.** These components are less common in formal proposals than in reports. However, a brief overview of a solicited proposal's key points provides a succinct guide to the content.
- **Letter of transmittal.** If the proposal is solicited, treat the transmittal letter as a positive message, highlighting those aspects of your proposal that may give you a competitive advantage. If the proposal is unsolicited, the transmittal letter should follow the advice for persuasive messages (see Chapter 9)—the letter must persuade the reader that you have something worthwhile to offer that justifies reading the proposal.

**Supplementary elements**
(after the close)

- **Appendixes.** Additional information related to the report but not included in the main text because it is too lengthy or lacks direct relevance. List appendixes in your table of contents and refer to them as appropriate in the text.
- **Bibliography.** List the secondary sources you consulted; see Appendix B.
- **Index.** List names, places, and subjects mentioned in the report, along with the pages on which they occur.

**Supplementary elements**
(after the close)

- **Appendixes.** Same uses as with reports; be sure to follow any instructions in the RFP, if relevant.
- **Résumés of key players.** For external proposals, résumés can convince readers that you have the talent to achieve the proposal's objectives.

One of the most important elements to consider is an introductory feature that helps time-pressed readers either get a sense of what's in the document or even get all the key points without reading the document. A **synopsis**, sometimes called an **abstract** or a **summary**, is a brief overview (one page or less) of a report's most important points. The phrasing of a synopsis can be *informative* (presenting the main points in the order in which they appear in the text) if you're using the direct approach, or *descriptive* (simply describing what the report is about, without "giving away the ending") if you're using the indirect approach. As an alternative to a synopsis or an abstract, a longer report may include an **executive summary**, a fully developed "mini" version of the report, for readers who lack the time to read the entire document.

For an illustration of how the various parts fit together in a report, see Figure 11.14. This report was prepared by Linda Moreno, manager of the cost accounting department

A synopsis is a brief overview of a report's key points; an executive summary is a fully developed "mini" version of the report.

at Electrovision, a company whose main product is equipment for optical character recognition. Moreno's job is to help analyze the company's costs. She has used the direct approach and organized her report based on conclusions and recommendations.

---

**FIGURE 11.14** Analyzing an Effective Formal Report

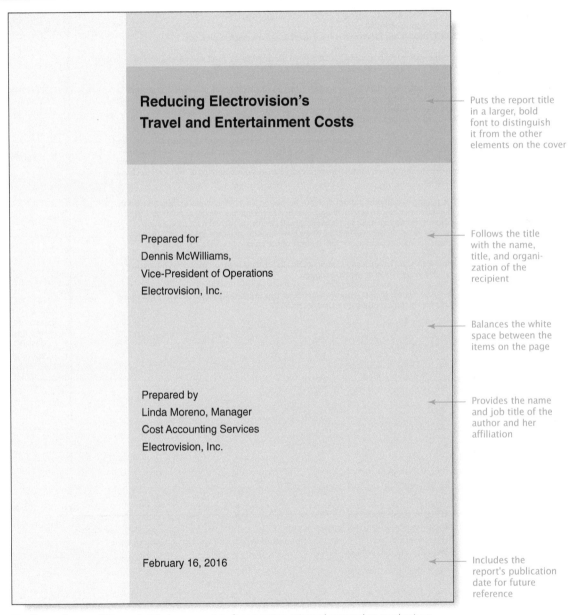

**Reducing Electrovision's Travel and Entertainment Costs** ← Puts the report title in a larger, bold font to distinguish it from the other elements on the cover

Prepared for
Dennis McWilliams,
Vice-President of Operations
Electrovision, Inc.
← Follows the title with the name, title, and organization of the recipient

← Balances the white space between the items on the page

Prepared by
Linda Moreno, Manager
Cost Accounting Services
Electrovision, Inc.
← Provides the name and job title of the author and her affiliation

February 16, 2016 ← Includes the report's publication date for future reference

The "how-to" tone of Moreno's title is appropriate for an action-oriented report that emphasizes recommendations. A more neutral title, such as "An Analysis of Electrovision's Travel and Entertainment Costs," would be more suitable for an informational report.

(Continued)

**FIGURE 11.14** (Continued)

Uses memo format for transmitting this internal report; otherwise, letter format would be used for transmitting external reports

Uses a conversational style

Acknowledges help that has been received

---

**MEMORANDUM**

TO: Dennis McWilliams, Vice-President of Operations
FROM: Linda Moreno, Manager of Cost Accounting Services  *LM*
DATE: February 16, 2016
SUBJECT: **Reducing Electrovision's Travel and Entertainment Costs**

Here is the report you requested January 28 on Electrovision's travel and entertainment costs.

Your suspicions were right. We are spending far too much on business travel. Our unwritten policy has been "anything goes," leaving us with no real control over T&E expenses. Although this hands-off approach may have been understandable when Electrovision's profits were high, we can no longer afford the luxury.

To solve the problem we need to have someone with centralized responsibility for travel and entertainment costs, a clear statement of policy, an effective control system, and a business-oriented travel service that can optimize our travel arrangements. We should also investigate alternatives to travel, such as videoconferencing. Perhaps more important, we need to change our attitude.

Getting people to economize is not going to be easy. In the course of researching this issue, I've found that our employees are deeply attached to their generous travel privileges. We'll need a lot of top management involvement to sell people on the need for moderation. One thing is clear: People will be very bitter if we create a two-class system in which top executives get special privileges while the rest of the employees make the sacrifices.

I'm grateful to Mary Lehman and Connie McIllvain for their help in collecting and sorting through five years' worth of expense reports.

Thanks for giving me the opportunity to work on this assignment. If you have any questions about the report, please give me a call at local 6977.

Presents the main conclusion right away (because Moreno expects a positive response)

Closes with thanks and an offer to discuss results (when appropriate, you could also include an offer to help with future projects)

In this report, Moreno decided to write a brief memo of transmittal and include a separate executive summary. Short reports (fewer than 10 pages) often combine the synopsis or executive summary with the memo or letter of transmittal.

(Continued)

**FIGURE 11.14** (Continued)

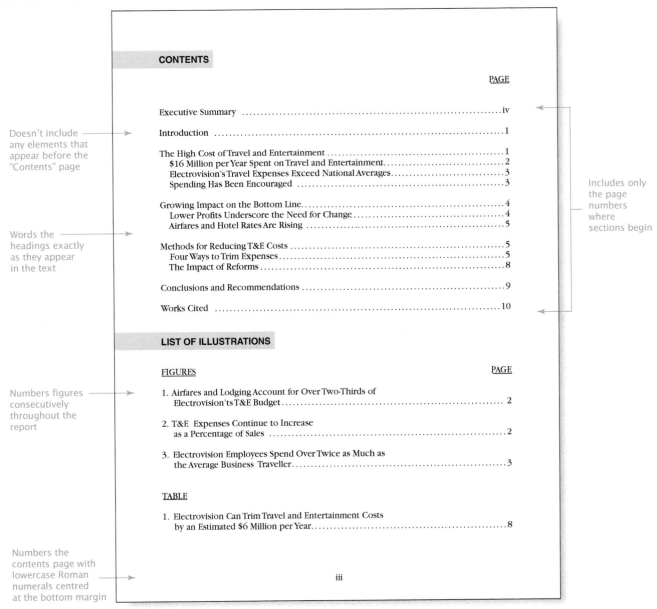

**CONTENTS**

**LIST OF ILLUSTRATIONS**

iii

Moreno included only first- and second-level headings in her table of contents, even though the report contains third-level headings. She prefers a shorter table of contents that focuses attention on the main divisions of thought. She used informative titles, which are appropriate for a report to a receptive audience.

(Continued)

FIGURE 11.14 (Continued)

Begins by stating the purpose of the report

**EXECUTIVE SUMMARY**

This report analyzes Electrovision's travel and entertainment (T&E) costs and presents recommendations for reducing those costs.

Presents the points in the executive summary in the same order as they appear in the report, using subheadings that summarize the content of the main sections of the report

**Travel and Entertainment Costs Are Too High**

Travel and entertainment is a large and growing expense category for Electrovision. The company spends over $16 million per year on business travel, and these costs have been increasing by 12 percent annually. Company employees make roughly 3390 trips each year at an average cost per trip of $4720. Airfares are the biggest expense, followed by hotels, meals, and rental cars.

The nature of Electrovision's business does require extensive travel, but the company's costs are excessive: Our employees spend more than twice the national average on travel and entertainment. Although the location of the company's facilities may partly explain this discrepancy, the main reason for our high costs is that monitoring travel expenses has not been a management priority.

**Cuts Are Essential**

Electrovision management now recognizes the need to gain more control over this element of costs. The company is currently entering a period of declining profits, prompting management to look for every opportunity to reduce spending. At the same time, rising airfares and hotel rates are making T&E expenses more significant.

Her audience is receptive, so the tone in the executive summary is forceful; a more neutral approach would be better for hostile or skeptical readers

**Electrovision Can Save $6 Million per Year**

Fortunately, Electrovision has a number of excellent opportunities for reducing T&E costs. Savings of up to $6 million per year should be achievable, judging by the experience of other companies. A sensible travel-management program can save companies as much as 35 percent a year (Gilligan 39–40), and we should be able to save even more, since we purchase many more business-class tickets than the average. Four steps will help us cut costs:

1. Hire a director of travel and entertainment to assume overall responsibility for T&E spending, policies, and technologies, including the hiring and management of a national travel agency.
2. Educate employees on the need for cost containment, both in avoiding unnecessary travel and reducing costs when travel is necessary.
3. Negotiate preferential rates with travel providers.
4. Implement technological alternatives to travel, such as virtual meetings.

As necessary as these changes are, they will likely hurt morale, at least in the short term. Management will need to make a determined effort to explain the rationale for reduced spending. By exercising moderation in their own travel arrangements, Electrovision executives can set a good example and help other employees accept the changes. On the plus side, using travel alternatives such as web conferencing will reduce the travel burden on many employees and help them balance their business and personal lives.

Executive summary uses the same font and paragraph treatment as the text of the report

Continues numbering the executive summary pages with lowercase Roman numerals

iv

Moreno decided to include an executive summary because her report is aimed at a mixed audience, some of whom are interested in the details of her report and others who just want the "big picture." The executive summary is aimed at the second group, giving them enough information to make a decision without burdening them with the task of reading the entire report.

Her writing style matches the serious nature of the content without sounding distant or stiff. Moreno chose the formal approach because several members of her audience are considerably higher up in the organization, and she did not want to sound too familiar. In addition, her company prefers the impersonal style for formal reports.

(Continued)

**FIGURE 11.14** (Continued)

Uses a colour bar to highlight the report title and the first-level headings; a variety of other design treatments are possible as well.

## REDUCING ELECTROVISION'S TRAVEL AND ENTERTAINMENT COSTS

### INTRODUCTION

Electrovision has always encouraged a significant amount of business travel. To compensate employees for the stress and inconvenience of frequent trips, management has authorized generous travel and entertainment (T&E) allowances. This philosophy has been good for morale, but last year Electrovision spent $16 million on travel and entertainment—$7 million more than it spent on research and development.

This year's T&E costs will affect profits even more, due to increases in airline fares and hotel rates. Also, the company anticipates that profits will be relatively weak for a variety of other reasons. Therefore, Dennis McWilliams, Vice-President of Operations, has asked the accounting department to explore ways to reduce the T&E budget.

The purpose of this report is to analyze T&E expenses, evaluate the effect of recent hotel and airfare increases, and suggest ways to tighten control over T&E costs. The report outlines several steps that could reduce Electrovision's expenses, but the precise financial impact of these measures is difficult to project. The estimates presented here provide a "best guess" view of what Electrovision can expect to save.

In preparing this report, the accounting department analyzed internal expense reports for the past five years to determine how much Electrovision spends on travel and entertainment. These figures were then compared with average statistics compiled by RBC Dominion Securities as reported in the *Report on Business* Travel Index. We also analyzed trends and suggestions published in a variety of business journal articles to see how other companies are coping with the high cost of business travel.

### THE HIGH COST OF TRAVEL AND ENTERTAINMENT

Although many companies view travel and entertainment as an incidental cost of doing business, the dollars add up. At Electrovision the bill for airfares, hotels, rental cars, meals, and entertainment totalled $16 million last year. Our T&E budget has increased by 12 percent per year for the past five years. Compared to the average Canadian business traveller, Electrovision's expenditures are high, largely because of management's generous policy on travel benefits.

Opens by establishing the need for action

Mentions sources and methods to increase credibility and to give readers a complete picture of the study's background

Uses a *running footer* that contains the report title and the page number

In her brief introduction, Moreno counts on topic sentences and transitions to indicate that she is discussing the purpose, scope, and limitations of the study.

(Continued)

**FIGURE 11.14** (Continued)

### $16 Million per Year Spent on Travel and Entertainment

Electrovision's annual budget for travel and entertainment is only 8 percent of sales. Because this is a relatively small expense category compared with such things as salaries and commissions, it is tempting to dismiss T&E costs as insignificant. However, T&E is Electrovision's third-largest controllable expense, directly behind salaries and information systems.

Last year Electrovision personnel made about 3390 trips at an average cost per trip of $4720. The typical trip involved a round-trip flight of 3000 kilometres, meals, and hotel accommodations for two or three days, and a rental car. Roughly 80 percent of trips were made by 20 percent of the staff—top management and sales personnel travelled most, averaging 18 trips per year.

Figure 1 illustrates how the T&E budget is spent. The largest categories are airfares and lodging, which together account for $7 out of $10 that employees spend on travel and entertainment. This spending breakdown has been relatively steady for the past five years and is consistent with the distribution of expenses experienced by other companies.

**Figure 1**
Airfares and Lodging Account for Over
Two-Thirds of Electrovision's T&E Budget

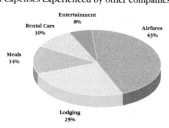

Although the composition of the T&E budget has been consistent, its size has not. As mentioned earlier, these expenditures have increased by about 12 percent per year for the past five years, roughly twice the rate of the company's sales growth (see Figure 2). This rate of growth makes T&E Electrovision's fastest-growing expense item.

**Figure 2**
T&E Expenses Continue to Increase as a
Percentage of Sales

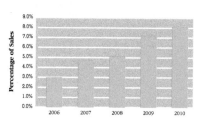

*Reducing Electrovision's Travel and Entertainment Costs*     P a g e  **2**

Places the visual as close as possible to the point it illustrates

Gives each visual a title that clearly indicates what it's about; titles are consistently placed to the left of each visual

Moreno opens the first main section of the body with a topic sentence that introduces an important fact about the subject of the section. Then she orients the reader to the three major points developed in the section.

(Continued)

**FIGURE 11.14** (Continued)

### Electrovision's Travel Expenses Exceed National Averages

Much of our travel budget is justified. Two major factors contribute to Electrovision's high T&E budget:

- With our headquarters on the West Coast and our major customer on the East Coast, we naturally spend a lot of money on cross-country flights.

- A great deal of travel takes place between our headquarters here on the West Coast and the manufacturing operations in Winnipeg, Windsor, and Halifax. Corporate managers and division personnel make frequent trips to coordinate these disparate operations.

However, even though a good portion of Electrovision's travel budget is justifiable, the company spends considerably more on T&E than the average business traveller (see Figure 3).

*[Annotation: Introduces visuals before they appear and indicates what readers should notice about the data]*

**Figure 3**
Electrovision Employees Spend Over Twice as Much as the Average Business Traveller

Source: *Globe & Mail Report on Business* and company records

*[Annotation: Numbers the visuals consecutively and refers to them in the text by their numbers]*

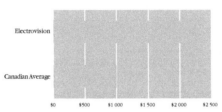

**Dollars Spent per Day**

The *Report on Business* Travel Index calculates the average cost per day of business travel in Canada, based on average airfare, hotel rates, and rental car rates. The average fluctuates weekly as travel companies change their rates, but it has been running at about $1000 per day for the last year or so. In contrast, Electrovision's average daily expense over the past year has been $2250—a hefty 125 percent higher than average. This figure is based on the average trip cost of $4720 listed earlier and an average trip length of 2.1 days.

### Spending Has Been Encouraged

Although a variety of factors may contribute to this differential, Electrovision's relatively high T&E costs are at least partially attributable to the company's philosophy and management style. Since many employees do not enjoy business travel, management has tried to make the trips more pleasant by authorizing business-class airfare, luxury hotel accommodations, and full-size rental cars. The sales staff is encouraged to entertain clients at top restaurants and to invite them to cultural and sporting events.

*Reducing Electrovision's Travel and Entertainment Costs*  Page **3**

The chart in Figure 3 is simple but effective; Moreno includes just enough data to make her point. Notice how she is as careful about the appearance of her report as she is about the quality of its content.

(Continued)

**FIGURE 11.14** (Continued)

Uses a bulleted list to make it easy for readers to identify and distinguish related points

The cost of these privileges is easy to overlook, given the weakness of Electrovision's system for keeping track of T&E expenses:

- The monthly financial records do not contain a separate category for travel and entertainment; the information is buried under Cost of Goods Sold and under Selling, General, and Administrative Expenses.

- Each department head is given authority to approve any expense report, regardless of how large it may be.

- Receipts are not required for expenditures of less than $100.

- Individuals are allowed to make their own travel arrangements.

- No one is charged with the responsibility for controlling the company's total spending on travel and entertainment.

### GROWING IMPACT ON THE BOTTOM LINE

Uses informative headings to focus reader attention on the main points (such headings are appropriate when a report uses direct order and is intended for a receptive audience; however, descriptive headings are more effective when a report is in indirect order and readers are less receptive)

During the past three years, the company's healthy profits have resulted in relatively little pressure to push for tighter controls over all aspects of the business. However, as we all know, the situation is changing. We're projecting flat to declining profits for the next two years, a situation that has prompted all of us to search for ways to cut costs. At the same time, rising airfares and hotel rates have increased the impact of T&E expenses on the company's financial results.

#### Lower Profits Underscore the Need for Change

The next two years promise to be difficult for Electrovision. After several years of steady increases in spending, Canada Post is tightening procurement policies for automated mail-handling equipment. Funding for the A-12 optical character reader has been cancelled. As a consequence, the marketing department expects sales to drop by 15 percent. Although Electrovision is negotiating several other promising R&D contracts, the marketing department does not foresee any major procurements for the next two to three years.

At the same time, Electrovision is facing cost increases on several fronts. As we have known for several months, the new production facility now under construction in Winnipeg is behind schedule and over budget. Labour contracts in Windsor and Halifax will expire within the next six months, and plant managers there anticipate that significant salary and benefits concessions may be necessary to avoid strikes.

Moreover, marketing and advertising costs are expected to increase as we attempt to strengthen these activities to better cope with competitive pressures. Given the expected decline in revenues and increase in costs, the Executive Committee's prediction that profits will fall by 12 percent in the coming fiscal year does not seem overly pessimistic.

*Reducing Electrovision's Travel and Entertainment Costs*                    Page **4**

Moreno designed her report to include plenty of white space so even those pages that lack visuals are still attractive and easy to read.

(Continued)

**FIGURE 11.14** (Continued)

**Airfares and Hotel Rates Are Rising**

Business traveller have grown accustomed to frequent fare wars and discounting in the travel industry in recent years. Excess capacity and aggressive price competition, particularly in the airline business, made travel a relative bargain.

However, that situation has changed with rising fuel costs and as weaker competitors have been forced out and the remaining players have grown stronger and smarter. Airlines and hotels are better at managing inventory and keeping occupancy rates high, which translates into higher costs for Electrovision. Last year saw some of the steepest rate hikes in years. Business airfares (tickets most likely to be purchased by business travellers) jumped more than 40 percent in many markets. The trend is expected to continue, with rates increasing another 5 to 10 percent overall (Phillips 331; "Travel Costs Under Pressure" 30; Dahl B6).

Given the fact that air and hotel costs account for almost 70 percent of our T&E budget, the trend toward higher prices in these two categories will have serious consequences, unless management takes action to control these costs.

**METHODS FOR REDUCING T&E COSTS**

By implementing a number of reforms, management can expect to reduce Electrovision's T&E budget by as much as 40 percent. This estimate is based on the general assessment made by American Express (Gilligan 39) and on the fact that we have an opportunity to significantly reduce air travel costs by eliminating business-class travel. However, these measures are likely to be unpopular with employees. To gain acceptance for such changes, management will need to sell employees on the need for moderation in T&E allowances.

**Four Ways to Trim Expenses**

By researching what other companies are doing to curb T&E expenses, the accounting department has identified four prominent opportunities that should enable Electrovision to save about $6 million annually in travel-related costs.

**Institute Tighter Spending Controls**

A single individual should be appointed director of travel and entertainment to spearhead the effort to gain control of the T&E budget. More than a third of all Canadian companies now employ travel managers ("Businesses Use Savvy Managers" 4). The director should be familiar with the travel industry and should be well versed in both accounting and information technology. The director should also report to the vice-president of operations. The director's first priorities should be to establish a written T&E policy and a cost-control system.

Electrovision currently has no written policy on travel and entertainment, a step that is widely recommended by air travel experts (Smith D4). Creating a policy would clarify management's position and serve as a vehicle for communicating the need for moderation.

*Reducing Electrovision's Travel and Entertainment Costs*　　　　　　　　Page **5**

*Documents the facts to add weight to Moreno's argument*

*Gives recommendations an objective flavour by pointing out both the benefits and the risks of taking action*

Moreno creates a forceful tone by using action verbs in the third-level subheadings of this section. This approach is appropriate to the nature of the study and the attitude of the audience. However, in a status-conscious organization, the imperative verbs might sound a bit too presumptuous coming from a junior member of the staff.

(Continued)

**FIGURE 11.14** (Continued)

At a minimum, the policy should include the following:

- All travel and entertainment should be strictly related to business and should be approved in advance.

- Except under special circumstances to be approved on a case-by-case basis, employees should travel by coach and stay in mid-range business hotels.

- The T&E policy should apply equally to employees at all levels.

To implement the new policy, Electrovision will need to create a system for controlling T&E expenses. Each department should prepare an annual T&E budget as part of its operating plan. These budgets should be presented in detail so that management can evaluate how T&E dollars will be spent and can recommend appropriate cuts. To help management monitor performance relative to these budgets, the director of travel should prepare monthly financial statements showing actual T&E expenditures by department.

The director of travel should also be responsible for retaining a business-oriented travel service that will schedule all employee business trips and look for the best travel deals, particularly in airfares. In addition to centralizing Electrovision's reservation and ticketing activities, the agency will negotiate reduced group rates with hotels and rental car firms. The agency selected should have offices nationwide so that all Electrovision facilities can channel their reservations through the same company. This is particularly important in light of the dizzying array of often wildly different airfares available between some cities. It's common to find dozens of fares along frequently travelled routes (Rowe 30). In addition, the director can help coordinate travel across the company to secure group discounts whenever possible (Barker 31; Miller B6).

**Reduce Unnecessary Travel and Entertainment**

One of the easiest ways to reduce expenses is to reduce the amount of travelling and entertaining that occurs. An analysis of last year's expenditures suggests that as much as 30 percent of Electrovision's travel and entertainment is discretionary. The professional staff spent $2.8 million attending seminars and conferences last year. Although these gatherings are undoubtedly beneficial, the company could save money by sending fewer representatives to each function and perhaps by eliminating some of the less valuable seminars.

Similarly, Electrovision could economize on trips between headquarters and divisions by reducing the frequency of such visits and by sending fewer people on each trip. Although there is often no substitute for face-to-face meetings, management could try to resolve more internal issues through telephone, electronic, and written communication.

Electrovision can also reduce spending by urging employees to economize. Instead of flying business class, employees can fly coach class or take advantage of discount fares. Rather than ordering a $50 bottle of wine, employees can select a less expensive bottle or dispense with

*Breaks up text with bulleted lists, which not only call attention to important points but also add visual interest*

*Specifies the steps required to implement recommendations*

Moreno takes care not to overstep the boundaries of her analysis. For instance, she doesn't analyze the value of the seminars that employees attend every year, so she avoids any absolute statements about reducing travel to seminars.

(Continued)

FIGURE 11.14 (Continued)

alcohol entirely. People can book rooms at moderately priced hotels and drive smaller rental cars.

**Obtain Lowest Rates from Travel Providers**

Apart from urging employees to economize, Electrovision can also save money by searching for the lowest available airfares, hotel rates, and rental car fees. Currently, few employees have the time or knowledge to seek out travel bargains. When they need to travel, they make the most convenient and comfortable arrangements. A professional travel service will be able to obtain lower rates from travel providers.

Judging by the experience of other companies, Electrovision may be able to trim as much as 30 to 40 percent from the travel budget simply by looking for bargains in airfares and negotiating group rates with hotels and rental car companies. Electrovision should be able to achieve these economies by analyzing its travel patterns, identifying frequently visited locations, and selecting a few hotels that are willing to reduce rates in exchange for guaranteed business. At the same time, the company should be able to save up to 40 percent on rental car charges by negotiating a corporate rate.

The possibilities for economizing are promising; however, making the best travel arrangements often requires trade-offs such as the following:

- The best fares might not always be the lowest. Indirect flights are usually cheaper, but they take longer and may end up costing more in lost work time.

- The cheapest tickets often require booking 14 or even 30 days in advance, which is often impossible for us.

- Discount tickets are usually nonrefundable, which is a serious drawback when a trip needs to be cancelled at the last minute.

**Replace Travel with Technological Alternatives**

Less-expensive travel options promise significant savings, but the biggest cost reductions over the long term might come from replacing travel with virtual meeting technology. Both analysts and corporate users say that the early kinks that hampered online meetings have largely been worked out, and the latest systems are fast, easy to learn, and easy to use (Solheim 26). For example, Webex (a leading provider of webconferencing services) offers everything from simple, impromptu team meetings to major online events with up to 3000 participants ("Online Meeting Solutions").

One of the first responsibilities of the new travel director should be an evaluation of these technologies and a recommendation for integrating them throughout Electrovision's operations.

*Reducing Electrovision's Travel and Entertainment Costs*  Page **7**

Points out possible difficulties to show that all angles have been considered and to build confidence in her judgment

Note how Moreno makes the transition from section to section. The first sentence under the second heading on this page refers to the subject of the previous paragraph and signals a shift in thought.

(Continued)

FIGURE 11.14 (Continued)

### The Impact of Reforms

By implementing tighter controls, reducing unnecessary expenses, negotiating more favourable rates, and exploring alternatives to travel, Electrovision should be able to reduce its T&E budget significantly. As Table 1 illustrates, the combined savings should be in the neighbourhood of $6 million, although the precise figures are somewhat difficult to project.

**Table 1**
Electrovision Can Trim Travel and Entertainment Costs
by an Estimated $6 Million per Year

| SOURCE OF SAVINGS | ESTIMATED SAVINGS |
|---|---|
| Switching from business-class to coach airfare | $2 300 000 |
| Negotiating preferred hotel rates | 940 000 |
| Negotiating preferred rental car rates | 460 000 |
| Systematically searching for lower airfares | 375 000 |
| Reducing interdivisional travel | 675 000 |
| Reducing seminar and conference attendance | 1 250 000 |
| **TOTAL POTENTIAL SAVINGS** | **$6 000 000** |

To achieve the economies outlined in the table, Electrovision will incur expenses for hiring a director of travel and for implementing a T&E cost-control system. These costs are projected at $115 000: $105 000 per year in salary and benefits for the new employee and a one-time expense of $10 000 for the cost-control system. The cost of retaining a full-service travel agency is negligible, even with the service fees that many are now passing along from airlines and other service providers.

The measures required to achieve these savings are likely to be unpopular with employees. Electrovision personnel are accustomed to generous T&E allowances, and they are likely to resent having these privileges curtailed. To alleviate their disappointment

- Management should make a determined effort to explain why the changes are necessary.

- The director of corporate communication should be asked to develop a multifaceted campaign that will communicate the importance of curtailing T&E costs.

- Management should set a positive example by adhering strictly to the new policies.

- The limitations should apply equally to employees at all levels in the organization.

*Reducing Electrovision's Travel and Entertainment Costs*          Page **8**

---

**Uses informative title in the table, which is consistent with the way headings are handled in this report and is appropriate for a report to a receptive audience**

**Uses complete sentences to help readers focus immediately on the point of the table**

**Includes financial estimates to help management envision the impact of the suggestions, even though estimated savings are difficult to project**

Note how Moreno calls attention in the first paragraph to items in the following table, without repeating the information in the table.

(Continued)

**FIGURE 11.14** (Continued)

Uses a descriptive heading for the last section of the text (in informational reports, this section is often called "Summary"; in analytical reports, it is called "Conclusions" or "Conclusions and Recommendations")

Summarizes conclusions in the first two paragraphs—a good approach because Moreno organized her report around conclusions and recommendations, so readers have already been introduced to them

### CONCLUSIONS AND RECOMMENDATIONS

Electrovision is currently spending $16 million per year on travel and entertainment. Although much of this spending is justified, the company's costs are high relative to competitors' costs, mainly because Electrovision has been generous with its travel benefits.

Electrovision's liberal approach to travel and entertainment was understandable during years of high profitability; however, the company is facing the prospect of declining profits for the next several years. Management is therefore motivated to cut costs in all areas of the business. Reducing T&E spending is particularly important because the bottom-line impact of these costs will increase as airline fares increase.

Electrovision should be able to reduce T&E costs by as much as 40 percent by taking four important steps:

1. *Institute tighter spending controls.* Management should hire a director of travel and entertainment who will assume overall responsibility for T&E activities. Within the next six months, this director should develop a written travel policy, institute a T&E budget and a cost-control system, and retain a professional, business-oriented travel agency that will optimize arrangements with travel providers.

2. *Reduce unnecessary travel and entertainment.* Electrovision should encourage employees to economize on T&E spending. Management can accomplish this by authorizing fewer trips and by urging employees to be more conservative in their spending.

3. *Obtain lowest rates from travel providers.* Electrovision should also focus on obtaining the best rates on airline tickets, hotel rooms, and rental cars. By channelling all arrangements through a professional travel agency, the company can optimize its choices and gain clout in negotiating preferred rates.

4. *Replace travel with technological alternatives.* With the number of computers already installed in our facilities, it seems likely that we could take advantage of desktop videoconferencing and other distance-meeting tools. Technological alternatives won't be quite as feasible with customer sites, since these systems require compatible equipment at both ends of a connection, but such systems are certainly a possibility for communication with Electrovision's own sites.

Because these measures may be unpopular with employees, management should make a concerted effort to explain the importance of reducing travel costs. The director of corporate communication should be given responsibility for developing a plan to communicate the need for employee cooperation.

Emphasizes the recommendations by presenting them in list format

*Reducing Electrovision's Travel and Entertainment Costs*　　　　　Page **9**

Moreno doesn't introduce any new facts in this section. In a longer report she might have divided this section into subsections, labelled "Conclusions" and "Recommendations," to distinguish between the two.

(Continued)

**FIGURE 11.14** (Continued)

**WORKS CITED**

Barker, Julie. "How to Rein in Group Travel Costs." *Successful Meetings* Feb. 2011: 31. Print.

"Businesses Use Savvy Managers to Keep Travel Costs Down." *Christian Science Monitor* 17 July 2008: 4. Print.

Dahl, Jonathan. "2000: The Year Travel Costs Took Off." *Globe & Mail Report on Business* 29 Dec. 2007: B6. Print.

Gilligan, Edward P. "Trimming Your T&E Is Easier Than You Think." *Managing Office Technology* Nov. 2013: 39–40. Print.

Miller, Lisa. "Attention, Airline Ticket Shoppers." *Wall Street Journal* 7 July 2011: B6. Print.

Phillips, Edward H. "Airlines Post Record Traffic." *Aviation Week & Space Technology* 8 Jan. 2013: 331. Print.

"Product Overview: Cisco WebEx Meeting Center," *Webex.com*. 2011. WebEx, n.d. 2 Feb. 2014. Web.

Rowe, Irene Vlitos. "Global Solution for Cutting Travel Costs." *European Business* 12 Oct. 2014: 30. Print.

Smith, Carol. "Rising, Erratic Airfares Make Company Policy Vital." *Los Angeles Times* 2 Nov. 2012: D4. Print.

Solheim, Shelley. "Web Conferencing Made Easy." *eWeek* 22 Aug. 2010: 26. Web.

"Travel Costs Under Pressure." *Purchasing* 15 Feb. 2012: 30. Print.

Lists references alphabetically by the author's last name, and when the author is unknown, by the title of the reference (see Appendix B for additional details on preparing reference lists)

Moreno's list of references follows the style recommended in *The MLA Style Manual*. The box below shows how these sources would be cited following APA style.

**REFERENCES**

Barker, J. (2011, February). How to rein in group travel costs. *Successful Meetings*, 31.

Businesses use savvy managers to keep travel costs down. (2008, July 17). *Christian Science Monitor*, 4.

Dahl, J. (2007, December 29). 2000: The year travel costs took off. *Globe & Mail Report on Business*, B6.

Gilligan, E. (2013, November). Trimming your T&E is easier than you think. *Managing Office Technology*, 39–40.

Miller, L. (2011, July 7). Attention, airline ticket shoppers. *Wall Street Journal*, B6.

Phillips, E. (2013, January 8). Airlines post record traffic. *Aviation Week & Space Technology*, 331.

Rowe, I. (2014, October 12). Global solution for cutting travel costs. *European*, 30.

Smith, C. (2012, November 2). Rising, erratic airfares make company policy vital. *Los Angeles Times*, D4.

Solheim, S. (2010, August 22). Web conferencing made easy. *eWeek*, 26.

Travel costs under pressure. (2012, February 15). *Purchasing*, 30.

WebEx.com. (2011). *Product Overview: Cisco WebEx Meeting Center*. Retrieved 2 February 2011, from http://www.webex.com/product-overview/index.html.

Just as with reports, the text of a proposal includes an introduction, a body, and a close. The introduction presents and summarizes the problem you intend to solve and your solution. It highlights the benefits the reader will receive from the solution. The body explains the complete details of the solution: how the job will be done; how it will be broken into tasks; what method will be used to do it (including the required equipment, material, and personnel); when the work will begin and end; how much the entire job will cost (including a detailed breakdown); and why your company is qualified. The close emphasizes the benefits readers will realize from your solution and ends with a persuasive *call to action* (see Figure 11.15).

*The introduction of a proposal summarizes the problem or opportunity that your proposal intends to address.*

---

**FIGURE 11.15** **External Solicited Proposal**

**O'Donnell & Associates, Inc.**

1793 East Westerfield Road, Montreal, QC J4P 2X1
(819) 441-1148 Fax: (819) 441-1149 Email: dod@inter.net

July 28, 2015

Ms. Joyce Colton, P.E.
AGI Builders, Inc.
1280 Spring Lake Drive
Montreal, QC  J7R 8T2

Dear Ms. Colton:

PROPOSAL NO. F-0087 FOR AGI BUILDERS, SAINT-BRUNO MANUFACTURING PLANT

*(Uses opening paragraph in place of an introduction)*

O'Donnell & Associates is pleased to submit the following proposal to provide construction testing services for the mass grading operations and utility work at the Saint-Bruno Manufacturing Plant, 1230 Parent Street, Saint-Bruno, Quebec. Our company has been providing construction-testing services in the Montreal area since 1972 and has performed more than 100 geotechnical investigations at airports within Ontario and Quebec—including Pearson International Airport, Dorval, and Mirabel.

*(Grabs reader's attention by highlighting company qualifications)*

*(Uses headings to divide proposal into logical segments for easy reading)*

**Background**
It is our understanding that the work consists of two projects: (1) the mass grading operations will require approximately six months, and (2) the utility work will require approximately three months. The two operations are scheduled as follows:

Mass Grading Operations    September 2015–February 2016
Utility Work               March 2016–May 2016

*(Acknowledges the two projects and their required time lines)*

**Proposed Approach and Work Plan**
O'Donnell & Associates will perform observation and testing services during both the mass grading operations and the excavation and backfilling of the underground utilities. Specifically, we will
- perform field density tests on the compacted material as required by the job specifications using a nuclear moisture/density gauge
- conduct appropriate laboratory tests such as ASTM D-1557 Modified Proctors
- prepare detailed reports summarizing the results of our field and laboratory testing

*(Describes scope of project and outlines specific tests the company will perform)*

Fill materials to be placed at the site may consist of natural granular materials (sand), processed materials (crushed stone, crushed concrete, slag), or clay soils.

(Continued)

**FIGURE 11.15** (Continued)

Ms. Joyce Colton, AGI Builders          July 28, 2015          Page 2

Explains who will be responsible for the various tasks →

**Staffing**
O'Donnell & Associates will provide qualified personnel to perform the necessary testing. Kevin Patel will be the lead field technician responsible for the project. A copy of Mr. Patel's resumé is included with this proposal for your review. Kevin will coordinate field activities with your job site superintendent and make sure that appropriate personnel are assigned to the job site. Overall project management will be the responsibility of Joseph Proesel. Project engineering services will be performed under the direction of Dixon O'Donnell, P.E. All field personnel assigned to the site will be familiar with and abide by the Project Site Health and Safety Plan prepared by Carlson Environmental, Inc., dated April 2015.

← Encloses resumé rather than listing qualifications in the document

**Qualifications**
O'Donnell & Associates has been providing quality professional services since 1972 in
- Geotechnical engineering
- Materials testing and inspection
- Pavement evaluation
- Environmental services
- Engineering and technical support (CADD) services

Grabs attention by mentioning distinguishing qualifications →

The company provides Phase I and Phase II environmental site assessments, preparation of LUST site closure reports, installation of groundwater monitoring wells, and testing of soil/groundwater samples for environmental contaminants. Geotechnical services include all phases of soil mechanics and foundation engineering, including foundation and lateral load analysis, slope stability analysis, site preparation recommendations, seepage analysis, pavement design, and settlement analysis.

O'Donnell & Associates' materials testing laboratory is certified by AASHTO Accreditation Program for the testing of Soils, Aggregate, Hot Mix Asphalt, and Portland Cement Concrete. A copy of our laboratory certification is included with this proposal. In addition to in-house training, field and laboratory technicians participate in a variety of certification programs, including those sponsored by the American Concrete Institute (ACI), Quebec Chapter.

← Gains credibility by describing certifications

(Continued)

**FIGURE 11.15** (Continued)

Ms. Joyce Colton, AGI Builders                 July 28, 2015                 Page 3

**Costs**
On the basis of our understanding of the scope of the work, we estimate the
total cost of the two projects to be $100 260.00, as shown in the table.

Builds
interest by
describing
all services
provided by
the company

Itemizes
costs by
project and
gives
supporting
detail

**Table of Cost Estimates**

| Cost Estimate: Mass Grading | Units | Rate ($) | Total Cost ($) |
|---|---|---|---|
| *Field Inspection* | | | |
| Labour | 1320 hours | $38.50 | $ 50 820.00 |
| Nuclear Moisture Density Meter | 132 days | 35.00 | 4 620.00 |
| Vehicle Expense | 132 days | 45.00 | 5 940.00 |
| *Laboratory Testing* | | | |
| Proctor Density Tests (ASTM D-1557) | 4 tests | 130.00 | 520.00 |
| *Engineering/Project Management* | | | |
| Principal Engineer | 16 hours | 110.00 | 1 760.00 |
| Project Manager | 20 hours | 80.00 | 1 600.00 |
| Administrative Assistant | 12 hours | 50.00 | 600.00 |
| *Subtotal* | | | ***$ 65 860.00*** |

| Cost Estimate: Utility Work | Units | Rate ($) | Total Cost ($) |
|---|---|---|---|
| *Field Inspection* | | | |
| Labour | 660 hours | $ 38.50 | $ 25 410.00 |
| Nuclear Moisture Density Meter | 66 days | 35.00 | 2 310.00 |
| Vehicle Expense | 66 days | 45.00 | 2 970.00 |
| *Laboratory Testing* | | | |
| Proctor Density Tests (ASTM D-1557) | 2 tests | 130.00 | 260.00 |
| *Engineering/Project Management* | | | |
| Principal Engineer | 10 hours | 110.00 | 1 100.00 |
| Project Manager | 20 hours | 80.00 | 1 600.00 |
| Administrative Assistant | 15 hours | 50.00 | 750.00 |
| *Subtotal* | | | ***$ 34 400.00*** |

| **Total Project Costs** | | | **$100 260.00** |
|---|---|---|---|

This estimate assumes full-time inspection services. However, our services
may also be performed on an as-requested basis, and actual charges will
reflect time associated with the project. We have attached our standard fee
schedule for your review. Overtime rates are for hours in excess of 8.0 hours
per day, before 7:00 a.m., after 5:00 p.m., and on holidays and weekends.

Provides
alternative
option in
case full-time
service costs
exceed client's
budget

(Continued)

**FIGURE 11.15** (Continued)

Ms. Joyce Colton, AGI Builders          July 28, 2015          Page 4

**Authorization**

With a staff of more than 30 personnel, including registered professional engineers, resident engineers, geologists, construction inspectors, laboratory technicians, and drillers, we are confident that O'Donnell & Associates is capable of providing the services required for a project of this magnitude.

If you would like our firm to provide the services as outlined in this proposal, please sign this letter and return it to us along with a certified cheque for $10 000 (our retainer) by August 15, 2015. Please call me if you have any questions regarding the terms of this proposal or our approach.

Sincerely,

*Dixon O'Donnell*

Dixon O'Donnell
Vice-President

Enclosures

Accepted for AGI BUILDERS, INC.

By_____     Date _____

*Uses brief closing to emphasize qualifications and ask for client decision*

*Provides deadline and makes response easy*

*Makes letter a binding contract, if signed*

## Distributing Your Reports and Proposals

For physical distribution of important printed reports or proposals, consider spending the extra money for a professional courier or package delivery service. Doing so can help you stand out in a crowd, and it lets you verify receipt. Alternatively, if you've prepared the document for a single person or small group in your office or the local area, delivering it in person will give you the chance to personally "introduce" the report and remind readers why they're receiving it.

For electronic distribution, unless your audience specifically requests a word processor file, provide documents as portable document format (PDF) files. Using Adobe Acrobat or similar products, you can quickly convert reports and proposals to PDF files that are easy to share electronically. PDFs are generally considered safer than word processor files, but they can also be used to transmit computer viruses.[22] For information on protecting yourself and your readers when using PDF files, visit www.adobe.com/security.

If your company or client expects you to distribute your reports via a web-based content management system, a shared workspace, or some other online location, double-check that you've uploaded the correct file(s) to the correct location. Verify the onscreen display of your reports after you've posted them, making sure graphics, charts, links, and other elements are in place and operational.

Many businesses use the Adobe Portable Document Format (PDF) to distribute reports electronically.

# LEARNING OBJECTIVES: Check Your Progress

❶ **OBJECTIVE** **List the topics commonly covered in the introduction, body, and close of informational reports, analytical reports, and proposals.**

The introduction of a report highlights who authorized the report, its purpose and scope, the sources or methods used to gather information, important definitions, any limitations, and the order in which the various topics are covered. The body provides enough information to support its conclusion and recommendations, which can range from explanations of problems or opportunities to facts and trends to results of studies or investigations. The close summarizes key points, restates conclusions and recommendations if appropriate, and lists action items.

The content of proposals is influenced by whether the proposal is solicited or unsolicited. Proposals submitted in response to an RFP should always follow the instructions it contains. The introduction commonly includes a background or statement of the problem, an overview of the proposed solution (or, for indirect proposals, a statement that a solution is about to be presented), the scope of the proposals, and a description of how the proposal is organized. The body usually includes a description of the proposed solution, the benefits of your solution, a work plan that outlines how and when the work will be accomplished, a statement of qualifications of the individual or organization presenting the proposal, and a discussion of costs. The close summarizes the key points, emphasizes benefits, restates why your firm is a good choice, and asks for a decision from the reader.

❷ **OBJECTIVE** **Identify six guidelines for drafting effective website content, and offer guidelines for becoming an effective wiki contributor.**

Follow these six guidelines to draft effective online content: (1) Build trust by being accurate, current, complete, and authoritative; (2) adapt content to global audiences; (3) write web-friendly content that is compact and efficient; (4) present information in a concise, skimmable format; (5) make effective use of links; and (6) make the website a "living" document by adding fresh content and deleting content that is out of date.

To become a valuable wiki contributor, let go of traditional expectations of authorship, including individual recognition and control; don't be afraid to edit and improve existing content; use page templates and other formatting options to make sure your content is consistent; keep edits and comments separate by using the "talk page" to discuss content; learn how to use the wiki's writing and editing tools; and understand and follow the wiki's contributor guidelines.

❸ **OBJECTIVE** **Discuss six principles of graphic design that can improve the quality of your visuals and identify the major types of business visuals.**

When preparing visuals, (1) use elements of design consistently; (2) use colour and other elements to show contrast effectively; (3) strive for visual balance, either formal or informal, that creates a feel that is appropriate for your overall message; (4) use design choices to draw attention to key elements; (5) understand and follow design conventions; and (6) strive for simplicity in your visuals.

The major types of business visuals include tables; line charts and surface charts; bar charts and pie charts; data visualization; flowcharts and organization charts; maps, drawings, diagrams, infographics, and photographs; and animation and video.

❹ **OBJECTIVE** **Summarize the four tasks involved in completing business reports and proposals.**

The four completion tasks of revising, producing, proofreading, and distributing all need to be accomplished with care, given the size and complexity of many reports. The production stage for a formal report or proposal can involve creating a number of elements not found in most other business documents. Possible prefatory parts (those coming before the main text of the report or proposal) include a cover, a title page, a letter of authorization, a letter of transmittal, a table of contents, a list of illustrations, and a synopsis (a brief overview of the report) or an executive summary (a miniature version of the report). Possible supplemental parts (those coming after the main text of the report or proposal) include one or more appendixes, a bibliography, and an index.

## MyBCommLab®

Go to MyBCommLab for everything you need to help you succeed in the job you've always wanted! Tools and resources include the following:
- Writing Activities
- Document Makeovers
- Video Exercises
- Grammar Exercises—and much more!

## Practise Your Grammar

Effective business communication starts with strong grammar skills. To improve your grammar skills, go to MyBCommLab, where you'll find exercises and diagnostic tests to help you produce clear, effective communication.

## Test Your Knowledge

To review chapter content related to each question, refer to the indicated Learning Objective.

1. Why must the introduction of an unsolicited proposal include a statement of the problem or opportunity that the proposal addresses? L.O.❶
2. What navigational elements can you use to help readers follow the structure and flow of information in a long report? L.O.❶
3. How can you use the inverted pyramid style of writing to craft effective online content? L.O.❷
4. What is the purpose of a "sandbox" on a wiki? L.O.❷
5. How does an executive summary differ from a synopsis? L.O.❹

## Apply Your Knowledge

To review chapter content related to each question, refer to the indicated Learning Objective.

1. Why is it important to write clear, descriptive headings and link titles with online content, as opposed to clever, wordplay headings? L.O.❷
2. Should the most experienced member of a department have final approval of the content for the department's wiki? Why or why not? L.O.❷
3. For providing illustration in a report or proposal, when is a diagram a better choice than a photograph? L.O.❸
4. If you wanted to compare average monthly absenteeism for five divisions in your company over the course of a year, which type of visual would you use? Explain your choice. L.O.❸
5. If a company receives a solicited formal proposal outlining the solution to a particular problem, is it ethical for the company to adopt the proposal's recommendations without hiring the firm that submitted the proposal? Why or why not? L.O.❹

# Practise Your Skills

## ACTIVITIES

Each activity is labelled according to the primary skill or skills you will need to use. To review relevant chapter content, you can refer to the indicated Learning Objective. In some instances, supporting information will be found in another chapter, as indicated.

1. **Message Strategies: Informational Reports** L.O.❶ You and a classmate are helping Linda Moreno prepare her report on Electrovision's travel and entertainment costs (see Figure 11.14). This time, however, the report is to be informational rather than analytical, so it will not include recommendations. Review the existing report and determine what changes would be needed to make it an informational report. Be as specific as possible. For example, if your team decides the report needs a new title, what title would you use? Draft a transmittal memo for Moreno to use in conveying this informational report to Dennis McWilliams, Electrovision's vice-president of operations.

2. **Media Skills: Wiki Collaboration** L.O.❷ Assume you work in a human resources (HR) department, and you want members of your department to be able to collaborate online to develop various human resources policies and procedures. You form a small subcommittee of four to set up a wiki and write guidelines for the HR staff who will be using it.

   **YOUR TASK**  Using http://pbwiki.com or a similar free wiki host, follow the instructions to set up the wiki and have your subcommittee use it to develop guidelines for contributors, which will instruct the whole department when they begin to use the wiki to write and revise departmental policies. In your subcommittee, decide the following:

   * Who will be allowed to add or modify content?
   * Who will serve as editor, reviewing all changes and additions?
   * What rules and guidelines will you establish to guide the growth of the wiki?
   * What security measures will be required?
   * Will incomplete pages be encouraged or should people wait until their material is "fairly complete and accurate?"

   Include a comment on what to do if a writer does not agree with published content and wants to discuss it with others working on the wiki. Write your guidelines on the wiki and send an invitation to your instructor to comment on the guidelines.

3. **Visual Communication: Choosing the Best Visual** L.O.❸ You're preparing the annual report for FretCo Guitar Corporation. For each of the following types of information, select the appropriate chart or visual to illustrate the text. Explain your choices.
   a. Data on annual sales for the past 20 years
   b. Comparison of FretCo sales, product by product (electric guitars, bass guitars, amplifiers, acoustic guitars), for this year and last year
   c. Explanation of how a FretCo acoustic guitar is manufactured
   d. Explanation of how the FretCo Guitar Corporation markets its guitars
   e. Data on sales of FretCo products in each of 12 countries
   f. Comparison of FretCo sales figures with sales figures for three competing guitar makers over the past 10 years

4. **Visual Communication: Creating Visuals** L.O.❹ You work for C&S Holdings, a company that operates coin-activated, self-service car washes. Research shows that the farther customers live from a car wash, the less likely they are to visit. You know that 50 percent of customers at each of your car washes live within a 6 km radius of the location, 65 percent live within 10 km, 80 percent live within 15 km, and 90 percent live within 20 km. C&S's owner wants to open two new car washes in your city and has asked you to prepare a report recommending locations. Using a map of your city from an online or printed source, choose two possible locations for car washes and create a visual that depicts the customer base surrounding each location (make up whatever population data you need or, if your instructor directs, find actual demographics using Statistics Canada's database).

5. **Visual Communication: Creating Visuals** L.O.❸ As directed by your instructor, team up with other students, making sure that at least one of you has a digital camera or camera phone capable of downloading images to your word processing software. Find a busy location on campus or in the surrounding neighbourhood, someplace with lots of signs, storefronts, pedestrians, and traffic. Scout out two

different photo opportunities, one that maximizes the visual impression of crowding and clutter, and one that minimizes this impression. For the first, assume that you are someone who advocates reducing the crowding and clutter, so you want to show how bad it is. For the second, assume that you are a real estate agent or someone else who is motivated to show people that even though the location offers lots of shopping, entertainment, and other attractions, it's actually a rather calm and quiet neighbourhood.

Insert the two images in a word processing document and write a caption for each that emphasizes the two opposite messages just described. Finally, write a brief paragraph, discussing the ethical implications of what you've just done. Have you distorted reality or just presented it in ways that work to your advantage? Have you prevented audiences from gaining the information they would need to make informed decisions?

6. **Message Strategies: Informational Reports** L.O.❶ Review a long business article in a journal or newspaper. Highlight examples of how the article uses headings, transitions, previews, and reviews to help the readers find their way.

7. **Message Strategies: Analytical Reports; Communication Ethics: Resolving Ethical Dilemmas** L.O.❶, **Chapter 1** Your boss has asked you to prepare a feasibility report to determine whether the company should advertise its custom-crafted cabinetry in the weekly neighbourhood newspaper. Based on your primary research, you think it should. As you draft the introduction to your report, however, you discover that the survey administered to the neighbourhood newspaper subscribers was flawed. Several of the questions were poorly written and misleading. You used the survey results, among other findings, to justify your recommendation. The report is due in three days. What actions might you want to take, if any, before you complete your report?

8. **Completing: Producing Formal Reports** L.O.❹ You are president of the Friends of the Library, a not-for-profit group that raises funds and provides volunteers to support your local library. Every February, you send a report of the previous year's activities and accomplishments to the County Arts Council, which provides an annual grant of $1000 toward your group's summer reading festival. Now it's February 6, and you've completed your formal report. Here are the highlights:

- Back-to-school book sale raised $2000.
- Holiday craft fair raised $1100.
- Promotion and prizes for summer reading festival cost $1450.
- Materials for children's program featuring local author cost $125.
- New reference databases for library's career centre cost $850.
- Bookmarks promoting library's website cost $200.
- Attendance at the reading festival events was 1200, up 120 from last year.

Write a letter of transmittal to Erica Maki, the council's director. Because she is expecting this report, you can use the direct approach. Be sure to express gratitude for the council's ongoing financial support.

# CASES

Apply the three-step writing process to the following cases, as assigned by your instructor.

## ‖ Short Reports

### 1. Message Strategies: Informational Reports L.O.❶, L.O.❹

You've been in your new job as human resources director for only a week, and already you have a major personnel crisis on your hands. Some employees in the marketing department got their hands on a confidential salary report and learned that, on average, marketing employees earn less than engineering employees. In addition, several top performers in the engineering group make significantly more than anybody in marketing. The report was instantly passed around the company by email, and now everyone is discussing the situation. You'll deal with the data security issue later; for now, you need to address the dissatisfaction in the marketing group.

Case Table 11.1 lists the salary and employment data you were able to pull from the employee database. You also had the opportunity to interview the engineering and marketing directors to get their opinions on the pay situation; their answers are listed in Case Table 11.2.

## CASE TABLE 11.1  Selected Employment Data for Engineers and Marketing Staff

| EMPLOYMENT STATISTIC | ENGINEERING DEPARTMENT | MARKETING DEPARTMENT |
| --- | --- | --- |
| Average number of years of work experience | 18.2 | 16.3 |
| Average number of years of experience in current profession | 17.8 | 8.6 |
| Average number of years with company | 12.4 | 7.9 |
| Average number of years of college education | 6.9 | 4.8 |
| Average number of years between promotions | 6.7 | 4.3 |
| Salary range | $58–165K | $45–85K |
| Median salary | $77K | $62K |

## CASE TABLE 11.2  Summary Statements from Department Director Interviews

| QUESTION | ENGINEERING DIRECTOR | MARKETING DIRECTOR |
| --- | --- | --- |
| 1. Should engineering and marketing professionals receive roughly similar pay? | In general, yes, but we need to make allowances for the special nature of the engineering profession. In some cases, it's entirely appropriate for an engineer to earn more than a marketing person. | Yes. |
| 2. Why or why not? | Several reasons: (1) Top engineers are extremely hard to find, and we need to offer competitive salaries; (2) the structure of the engineering department doesn't provide as many promotional opportunities, so we can't use promotions as a motivator the way marketing can; (3) many of our engineers have advanced degrees, and nearly all pursue continuous education to stay on top of the technology. | Without marketing, the products the engineers create wouldn't reach customers, and the company wouldn't have any revenue. The two teams make equal contributions to the company's success. |
| 3. If we decide to balance pay between the two departments, how should we do it? | If we do anything to cap or reduce engineering salaries, we'll lose key people to the competition. | If we can't increase payroll immediately to raise marketing salaries, the only fair thing to do is freeze raises in engineering and gradually raise marketing salaries over the next few years. |

**YOUR TASK**   The CEO has asked for a short report, summarizing whatever data and information you have on engineering and marketing salaries. Offer your own interpretation of the situation as well (make up any information you need), but keep in mind that because you are a new manager with almost no experience in the company, your opinion might not have a lot of influence.

▌**Portfolio Builder**
**2. Message Strategies: Analytical Reports** L.O.❶, L.O.❹

Like any other endeavour that combines hard-nosed factual analysis and creative freethinking, the task of writing business plans generates a range of opinions.

**YOUR TASK**   Find at least six sources of advice on writing successful business plans (focus on start-up businesses that are likely to seek outside investors). Use at least two books, two magazine or journal articles, and two websites, blogs, or other online resources. Analyze the advice you find and identify points where most or all the experts agree and points where they don't agree. Wherever you find points of significant disagreement, identify which opinion you find most convincing and explain why. Summarize your findings in a brief formal report. Include a list of references.

**▮ Portfolio Builder ▮ Team Skills**

### 3. Message Strategies: Analytical Reports L.O.❶, L.O.❹

You work as an administrator for Westport Innovations, a high-tech firm that makes bus engines that run on hydrogen and compressed natural gas. Your high-tech environment is exciting to work in and the field has been expanding rapidly, with sales in South America, China, India, and Europe. Many of the employees working at Westport are engineers and designers. Your company needs to attract the brightest talent and is looking for ways to expand recruitment and move away from traditional campus recruitment. You have been asked to research how companies are using Facebook and other social technologies to recruit employees.

**YOUR TASK**  Summarize your findings in a report to the human resources department manager. Consult at least 10 sources, including three business journal articles. Provide a list of references in APA style.

**▮ Portfolio Builder**

### 4. Message Strategies: Informational Reports L.O.❶, L.O.❹

After 15 years in the corporate world, you're ready to strike out on your own. Rather than building a business from the ground up, however, you think that buying a franchise is a better idea. Unfortunately, some of the most lucrative franchise opportunities, such as the major fast-food chains, require significant start-up costs—some more than half a million dollars. Fortunately, you've met several potential investors who seem willing to help you get started in exchange for a share of ownership. Between your own savings and these investors, you estimate that you can raise from $350 000 to $600 000, depending on how much ownership share you want to concede to the investors.

You've worked in several functional areas already, including sales and manufacturing, so you have a fairly well-rounded business resumé. You're open to just about any type of business, too, as long as it provides the opportunity to grow; you don't want to be so tied down to the first operation that you can't turn it over to a hired manager and expand into another market.

**YOUR TASK**  To convene a formal meeting with the investor group, you need to first draft a report that outlines the types of franchise opportunities you'd like to pursue. Write a brief report, identifying five franchises that you would like to explore further. (Choose five based on your own personal interests and the criteria identified above.) For each possibility, identify the nature of the business, the financial requirements, the level of support the company provides, and a brief statement of why you could run such a business

successfully (make up any details you need). Be sure to carefully review the information you find about each franchise company to make sure you can qualify for it. For instance, McDonald's doesn't allow investment partnerships to buy franchises, so you won't be able to start up a McDonald's outlet until you have enough money to do it on your own.

For a quick introduction to franchising, see How Stuff Works (**www.howstuffworks.com/franchising**). You can learn more about the business of franchising at **www.franchising.com** and search for specific franchise opportunities at Francorp Connect (**www.francorpconnect.com**). In addition, many companies that sell franchises, such as Subway, offer additional information on their websites.

**▮ Long Reports**

### 5. Message Strategies: Informational Reports L.O.❶, L.O.❹

Your company is the largest private employer in your metropolitan area, and the 43 500 employees in your workforce have a tremendous impact on local traffic. A group of city and county transportation officials recently approached your CEO with a request to explore ways to reduce this impact. The CEO has assigned you the task of analyzing the workforce's transportation habits and attitudes as a first step toward identifying potential solutions. He's willing to consider anything from subsidized bus passes to company-owned shuttle buses to telecommuting, but the decision requires a thorough understanding of employee transportation needs. Case Tables 11.3 through 11.7 summarize data you collected in an employee survey.

---

**CASE TABLE 11.3  Employee Carpool Habits**

| FREQUENCY OF USE: CARPOOLING | PORTION OF WORKFORCE |
|---|---|
| Every day, every week | 10 138 (23%) |
| Certain days, every week | 4361 (10%) |
| Randomly | 983 (2%) |
| Never | 28 018 (64%) |

---

**CASE TABLE 11.4  Use of Public Transportation**

| FREQUENCY OF USE: PUBLIC TRANSPORTATION | PORTION OF WORKFORCE |
|---|---|
| Every day, every week | 23 556 (54%) |
| Certain days, every week | 2029 (5%) |
| Randomly | 5862 (13%) |
| Never | 12 053 (28%) |

## CASE TABLE 11.5 — Effect of Potential Improvements to Public Transportation

| WHICH OF THE FOLLOWING WOULD ENCOURAGE YOU TO USE PUBLIC TRANSPORTATION MORE FREQUENTLY? (CHECK ALL THAT APPLY) | PORTION OF RESPONDENTS |
|---|---|
| Increased perception of safety | 4932 (28%) |
| Improved cleanliness | 852 (5%) |
| Reduced commute times | 7285 (41%) |
| Greater convenience: fewer transfers | 3278 (18%) |
| Greater convenience: more stops | 1155 (6%) |
| Lower (or subsidized) fares | 5634 (31%) |
| Nothing could encourage me to take public transportation | 8294 (46%) |

Note: This question was asked of respondents who use public transportation randomly or never, a subgroup that represents 17 915 employees, or 41 percent of the workforce.

## CASE TABLE 11.6 — Distance Travelled to/from Work

| DISTANCE YOU TRAVEL TO WORK (ONE WAY) | PORTION OF WORKFORCE |
|---|---|
| Less than 5 km | 531 (1%) |
| 6–10 km | 6874 (16%) |
| 11–20 km | 22 951 (53%) |
| 21–30 km | 10 605 (24%) |
| More than 30 km | 2539 (6%) |

## CASE TABLE 11.7 — Is Telecommuting an Option?

| DOES THE NATURE OF YOUR WORK MAKE TELECOMMUTING A REALISTIC OPTION? | PORTION OF WORKFORCE |
|---|---|
| Yes, every day | 3460 (8%) |
| Yes, several days a week | 8521 (20%) |
| Yes, random days | 12 918 (30%) |
| No | 18 601 (43%) |

**YOUR TASK** Present the results of your survey in an informational report, using the data provided in the tables.

**Team Skills Portfolio Builder**

### 6. Message Strategies: Informational Reports L.O.❶, L.O.❹

As a researcher in your province's consumer protection agency, you're frequently called on to investigate consumer topics and write reports for the agency's website. Thousands of consumers have arranged the purchase of cars online, and millions more do at least some of their research online before heading to a dealership. Some want to save time and money, some want to be armed with as much information as possible before talking to a dealer, and others want to completely avoid the often uncomfortable experience of negotiating prices with car salespeople. In response, a variety of online services have emerged to meet these consumer needs. Some let you compare information on various car models, some connect you to local dealers to complete the transaction, and some complete nearly all the transaction details for you, including negotiating the price. Some search the inventory of thousands of dealers, whereas others search only a single dealership or a network of affiliated dealers. In other words, a slew of new tools are available for car buyers, but it's not always easy to figure out where to go and what to expect. That's where your report will help.

By visiting a variety of car-related websites and reading magazine and newspaper articles on the car-buying process, you've compiled a variety of notes related to the subject:

- **Process overview.** The process is relatively straightforward and fairly similar to other online shopping experiences, with two key differences. In general, a consumer identifies the make and model of car he or she wants, and then the online car-buying service searches the inventories of car dealers nationwide and presents the available choices. The consumer chooses a particular car from that list, and then the service handles the communication and purchase details with the dealer. When the paperwork is finished, the consumer visits the dealership and picks up the car.

- **Information you can find online** (not all information is available at all sites). You can find information on makes, models, colours, options, option packages (often, specific options are available only as part of a package; you need to know these constraints before you select your options), photos, specifications (everything from engine size to interior space), fuel efficiency estimates, performance data, safety information, predicted resale value, reviews, comparable models, insurance costs, consumer ratings, repair and reliability histories, available buyer incentives and rebates, true ownership costs (including costs for fuel, maintenance, repair, and so on), warranty, loan and lease payments, and maintenance requirements.

- **Advantages of shopping online.** Advantages of shopping online include shopping from the comfort and convenience of home, none of the dreaded negotiating at the dealership (in many cases), the ability to search far and wide for a specific car (even nationwide, on many sites), rapid access to considerable amounts of data and information, and reviews from both professional automotive journalists and other consumers. In general, online auto shopping reduces a key advantage that auto dealers used to have, which was control of most of the information in the purchase transaction. Now consumers can find out how reliable each model is, how quickly it will depreciate, how often it is likely to need repairs, what other drivers think of it, how much the dealer paid the manufacturer for it, and so on.

- **Changing nature of the business.** The relationship between dealers and third-party websites (such as **www.carsdirect.com**) continues to evolve. At first, the relationship was more antagonistic, as some third-party sites and dealers frequently competed for the same customers, and each side made bold proclamations about driving the other out of business. However, the relationship is more collaborative in many cases now, with dealers realizing that some third-party sites already have wide brand awareness and nationwide audiences. As the percentage of new car sales that originate via the internet continues to increase, dealers are more receptive to working with third-party sites.

- **Comparing information from multiple sources.** Consumers shouldn't rely solely on information from a single website. Each site has its own way of organizing information, and many sites have their own ways of evaluating car models and connecting buyers with sellers.

- **Understanding what each site is doing.** Some sites search thousands of dealers, regardless of ownership connections. Others, such as AutoNation, search only affiliated dealers. A search for a specific model might yield only a half dozen cars on one site but dozens of cars on another site. Find out who owns the site and what their business objectives are, if you can; this will help you assess the information you receive.

- **Leading websites.** Consumers can check out a wide variety of websites, some of which are full-service operations, offering everything from research to negotiation; others provide more specific and limited services. For instance, CarsDirect (**www.carsdirect.com**) provides a full range of services, whereas Carfax (**www.carfax.com**) specializes in uncovering the repair histories of individual used cars. Case Table 11.8 lists some of the leading car-related websites.

| CASE TABLE 11.8 | Leading Automotive Websites |
| --- | --- |

| SITE | URL |
| --- | --- |
| autoadvice | www.autoadvice.com |
| Autos.ca | www.autos.ca |
| Autotrader | www.autotrader.ca |
| AutoVantage | www.autovantage.com |
| Autoweb | www.autoweb.com |
| CanadianCarPrices.Com | www.canadiancarprices.com |
| CarBargains | www.carbargains.com |
| Carfax | www.carfax.com |
| CarPrices.com | www.carprices.com |
| Cars.com | www.cars.com |
| CarsDirect | www.carsdirect.com |
| Car$mart | www.carsmart.ca |
| Consumer Reports | www.consumerreports.org |
| eBay Motors | www.ebay.com/motors |
| edmunds.com | www.edmunds.com |
| IntelliChoice | www.intellichoice.com |
| InvoiceDealers | www.invoicedealers.com |
| JDPower | www.jdpower.com |
| Kelly Blue Book | www.kbb.com |
| MonsterAuto.ca | www.monsterauto.ca |
| PickupTrucks.com | www.pickuptrucks.com |
| The Car Connection | www.thecarconnection.com |
| Yahoo! Autos | http://autos.yahoo.com |

**YOUR TASK** With a team assigned by your instructor, write an informational report based on your research notes. The purpose of the report is to introduce consumers to the basic concepts of integrating the internet into their car-buying activities and to educate them about important issues.[23]

**Portfolio Builder**

**7. Message Strategies: Analytical Reports** L.O.❶, L.O.❹

As a college student and an active consumer, you may have considered one or more of the following questions at some point in the past few years:

- What criteria distinguish the top-rated MBA programs in Canada? How well do these criteria correspond to the needs and expectations of business? Are the criteria fair for students, employers, and business schools?
- Which of three companies you might like to work for has the strongest sustainability policies?
- Which industries and job categories are forecast to experience the greatest growth—and therefore the greatest demand for workers—in the next 10 years?
- What has been the impact of Starbucks's aggressive growth on small, independent coffee shops?
- How much have minor league sports—hockey, soccer, lacrosse, volleyball, or football—grown in small- and medium-market cities? What is the local economic impact when these municipalities build stadiums and arenas?

**YOUR TASK** Answer one of the preceding questions using secondary research sources for information. Be sure to document your sources, using the format your instructor indicates. Give conclusions and offer recommendations where appropriate.

**‖ Proposals Portfolio Builder**
**8. Message Strategies: Proposals L.O.❶, L.O.❹**

Presentations can make—or break—both careers and businesses. A good presentation can bring in millions of dollars in new sales or fresh investment capital. A bad presentation might cause any number of troubles, from turning away potential customers to upsetting fellow employees to derailing key projects. To help business professionals plan, create, and deliver more effective presentations, you offer a three-day workshop that covers the essentials of good presentations:

- Understanding your audience's needs and expectations
- Formulating your presentation objectives
- Choosing an organizational approach
- Writing openings that catch your audience's attention
- Creating effective graphics and slides
- Practising and delivering your presentation
- Leaving a positive impression on your audience
- Avoiding common mistakes with electronic slides
- Making presentations online using webcasting tools
- Handling questions and arguments from the audience
- Overcoming the top 10 worries of public speaking (including How can I overcome stage fright? and I'm not the performing type; can I still give an effective presentation?)

**Workshop benefits:** Students will learn how to prepare better presentations in less time and deliver them more effectively.

**Who should attend:** Executives, project managers, employment recruiters, sales professionals, and anyone else who gives important presentations to internal or external audiences.

**Your qualifications:** 18 years of business experience, including 14 years in sales and 12 years of public speaking. Experience speaking to audiences as large as 5000 people. More than a dozen speech-related articles published in professional journals. Have conducted successful workshops for nearly 100 companies.

**Workshop details:** Three-day workshop (9 a.m. to 3:30 p.m.) that combines lectures, practice presentations, and both individual and group feedback. Minimum number of students: 6. Maximum number of students per workshop: 12.

**Pricing:** The cost is $3500, plus $100 per participant; 10 percent discount for additional workshops.

**Other information:** Each attendee will have the opportunity to give three practice presentations that will last from three to five minutes. Everyone is encouraged to bring PowerPoint files containing slides from actual business presentations. Each attendee will also receive a workbook and a digital video recording of his or her final class presentation on DVD. You'll also be available for phone or email coaching for six months after the workshop.

**YOUR TASK** Identify a company in your local area that might be a good candidate for your services. Learn more about the company by visiting its website so you can personalize your proposal. Using the information listed above, prepare a sales proposal that explains the benefits of your training and what students can expect during the workshop.

**9. Message Strategies: Proposals L.O.❶, L.O.❹**

Look around your campus or local community for a problem you are interested in. Maybe it is related to campus parking, food services, or a neighbourhood playground that is run down. Maybe the lack of training given to workers at your part-time job is causing poor sales.

What types of solutions may be possible? What information and facts would you need to have to present a solution to this problem? What types of primary research could you do to gather information for your proposal? Is it practical to survey a representative sample of people who use the service or whose opinion would be helpful to include in the proposal? Would interviews with a representative sample of those affected by the proposal be useful? Work with your professor to define the scope of your proposal and to identify suitable kinds of primary research you will do for the assignment. Identify a real audience for your proposal and design your research methods. Here are a few examples of proposal scenarios and audiences:

- A community association to fund a playground renovation
- A college board of governors to light the student parking area
- A college board of governors and student association to provide an evening "safe walk" program
- The city government to fund an arts or cultural event
- The city government or a private foundation to fund restoration of a stream in your area
- Your part-time employer to request funding for staff training on avoiding harassment or fostering multicultural communication

The best topic would be a problem that you would like to solve in real life.

### YOUR TASK

a. Define your topic, audience, and purpose and get your topic approved by your instructor.
b. Identify what sources of information you will need to research.
c. Find articles or technical material about your subject. What were the experiences of other companies or agencies that implemented a similar idea? Keep a list of references to include with the proposal.
d. Research the cost of implementing your idea.
e. What support exists for your proposal? Prepare questions for interviews and a survey and bring them to class for feedback. Are you asking the right questions to get appropriate evidence for your proposal? Are your questions unbiased? What is a representative sample of people to interview or survey?
f. Conduct your surveys/interviews and summarize the results.
g. Write your proposal draft and bring it to class for feedback.
h. Submit the final copy of the proposal with a list of references. Include an envelope containing all copies of your completed surveys/interview summaries.

### 10. Message Strategies: Proposals L.O.❶, L.O.❹

Assume you work as an office manager (a position that includes hiring responsibilities) for Undergo, a small but growing construction company that specializes in the installation of underground services, including water, sewer, and electrical piping. In the past year the staff has grown from 20 to 80; the company has multiple worksites and projects and 45 new male employees between the ages of 17 and 25.

Since no one else on staff is assigned responsibility for safety, you have handled some of the safety duties in the office, such as checking the vocational certifications of all new staff, filing accident investigation and inspection reports, and keeping training records. You also get notices from the provincial workers' compensation board, and recently they sent a bulletin stating that the injury rate for young (especially male) workers is much higher than for other workers. You learned that every day, 30 young workers are injured, and every week 5 are permanently disabled in workplace injuries.[24] Since you are in the "young worker" age bracket yourself, these statistics troubled you and motivated you to take some action at Undergo.

You know your company's supervisors do a great job in giving new hires training on the job and in covering hazard avoidance, but nothing is written down about what is covered, and without records, if a serious accident occurred, the company would be in a very bad legal position. As well, without some sort of checklist or guide, the topics covered are not necessarily the same for each new hire. Now that the company has grown, you believe the company needs to have a formal safety orientation program. Further, you think written records about this training should be kept. You decide to research what material might be available for developing a safety orientation program for young workers. You also think that some of the training material your company has is outdated—it mostly consists of print materials in dusty binders in the site trailers. You intend to see if any web-based materials are available on some general safety topics (such as ladder safety, using fall-arrest equipment, housekeeping on construction sites, wearing personal protective clothing, and so on). Each of your company's worksites has a trailer and a laptop, so you might be able to get some material on YouTube that could help motivate young workers to work safely.

**YOUR TASK** Write a proposal to the company's owner to establish an orientation program for all new hires. You decide the orientation would take about two hours and be run in a site office by each supervisor gaining the new employee(s).

If your proposal is approved, you will put together the program and train the supervisors on how to give a safety orientation. Begin your research by going online to look into your province's workers' compensation board resources. Your proposal should describe the topics to be covered in the orientation, the costs (including your time to put together the session, train the supervisors in how to run it, and design some forms to guide and record the training), the reasons why the company should have such a program (benefits), and some of the resources you would like to have for the program.

### 11. Message Strategies: Proposals L.O.❶, L.O.❹

You work for Tim Hortons in the human resources department in the Halifax regional office. Your job is to coordinate training material for the more than 30 store managers and their 400 employees in the region. You update the company's training manuals and send out product updates that are put into product knowledge binders for the employees to read. Recently one of the managers, Mark Harding, commented to you that it was difficult to get the employees to read the product update manual. "Even when the traffic slows down, and employees have time to read, they just don't seem to want to and the environment isn't really set up for reading either. It's a real hassle nagging them, but when they don't know about the products we lose sales," he complained. "This week alone, five employees didn't know the new process for making a new popular drink and had to have a supervisor spend 30 minutes with each of the five on different shifts. That's how poor employee knowledge costs us money. And it is not just the starting wage employee time; it's also the supervisory time that is wasted. So, I keep nagging them."

You replied, "I've heard this complaint from other store managers and maybe it is time to try something that may be more appealing to the age group of your employees. What do you think of using podcasts for this kind of employee training? Starbucks has used podcasts to tell staff about new products. They play the podcasts when staff members are in the store without customers, like at opening and closing."

"Sounds like it would be more interesting than a manual, but what about if you forget something and want to look it up?" asked Mark.

"The podcasts would be in addition to the print training materials—the podcasts just provide a different way to get the information," you say.

Mark added, "But surely we don't want our employees to be plugged into MP3 players while they are in the store—that would not improve employee communication."

"True enough, what we would do is play the audio files on the in-store system, and if employees want to download files to review after work hours, they could," you reply.

You decide to persuade your boss, the manager of human resources (Martin Law), to experiment with podcasting for employee communication. He may be a tough sell. He is 55, has been with the company for the last 10 years, and is not that oriented to social technologies. While not a bean counter, he is very interested in

the business's bottom line. He'll need to know the costs and benefits. He'd want to know that other businesses are using this technology to some advantage. A little research would be helpful on that.

You are not too worried about the cost of producing the podcasts. You would write the scripts and hire a local freelance broadcaster ($200/hour) to record 10-minute programs that can be played in the stores during opening and closing. You figure there would be enough material to make a weekly podcast, but to get it going, you decide starting small is best, so you want to propose making five podcasts that would be released every two weeks during the fall promotion period. As well, you'll start off with just one voice making the recordings, and if it is popular, work into using sound effects, music, and more than one voice recording. Who knows, if the idea works in this region, maybe it could be used nationally. How will you evaluate its success?

You find out the department could buy some recording and editing software called RecordForAll for approximately $70, but you also want to purchase a high-quality recorder such as an R-09HR Edirol MP3 Recorder ($600) to produce the podcasts. It would take you four hours to learn how to use the editing software, two to three hours to write the script for each podcast, and two to three hours to edit each program. The finished programs would be available as MP3 files to be used in the store or downloaded by employees and listened to on nonwork time. You figure the number of employees who would be reached would make the effort worthwhile.

**YOUR TASK** Write a proposal to Martin Law. Include a description of your idea, how it would work, what it would cost, and of course, what benefits would be gained. Tip: use your math skills to estimate savings so that you can be persuasive with your audience.

### 12. Message Strategies: Proposals L.O.❶, L.O.❹

Pick a company you are interested in and research a social networking strategy that you think would be useful for the company. Determine the advantages and disadvantages for the marketing department of the company. The company's goal would be to create opportunities for relationship building and interactivity with customers online. What social technology would you recommend?

What would be involved in getting the strategy implemented and what success has it had in other businesses? How costly is the strategy to implement? What types of resources do you need and what is the ongoing cost of monitoring or maintaining the online presence?

For example, you might propose that the marketing department produce product knowledge podcasts to use in company branches. Or, you may investigate and propose the use of a Facebook event to promote the product. Or, perhaps you'd like to investigate the best uses of wikis—maybe the department could use a wiki to develop marketing literature for a new product. How can the company build relationships either with customers or employees online?

**YOUR TASK**  Write a proposal to the company's Operations Manager suggesting the adoption of your strategy.

### 13. Message Strategies: Proposals L.O.❹

You think the energy use on campus could be improved by changing the lighting and introducing other energy saving measures. One example of a town that improved its sustainability is the Town of Orillia, Ontario, which saved energy and money by rewiring the lighting switches in its city-run buildings so that they could be more easily turned off when not in use (www.amo.on.ca). The B.C. Institute of Technology in Burnaby, B.C., adopted a "Lightsavers" program to better monitor lighting costs, which resulted in significant hydro savings. Look around your college and identify ways to make the college campus more sustainable. For example, are lights left on in unused areas? Are there adequate recycling programs? A composting program? Ways to use wind, water, or other energy sources? What would it cost to implement the change? Who would have to act to implement the change? How would it happen? What would be saved? What other benefits would result?

**YOUR TASK**  Choose one initiative that would improve sustainability at your school. Get the facts on related energy costs, research the impact of the initiative, and write a proposal to the administration proposing its adoption.

---

## BUSINESS COMMUNICATION NOTEBOOK

# Ethics

### Top Tips for Writing Reports That Tell the Truth

Put nothing in writing that you're unwilling to say in public, and write nothing that may embarrass or jeopardize your employer. Does this mean you should cover up problems? Of course not. However, when you're dealing with sensitive information, be discreet. Present the information in such a way that it will help readers solve a problem. Avoid personal gripes, criticisms, alibis, attempts to blame other people, sugar-coated data, and unsolicited opinions.

To be useful, the information must be accurate, complete, and honest. But remember, being honest is not always a simple matter. Everyone sees reality a little differently, and individuals describe what they see in their own way. To restrict the distortions introduced by differences in perception, follow these guidelines:

- **Describe facts or events in concrete terms.** Indicate quantities whenever you can. Say, "Sales have increased 17 percent," or "Sales have increased from $40 000 to $43 000 in the past two months." Don't say, "Sales have skyrocketed."

- **Report all relevant facts.** Regardless of whether these facts support your theories or please your readers, they must be included. Omitting the details that undermine your position may be convenient, but it is misleading and inaccurate.

- **Put the facts in perspective.** Taken out of context, the most concrete facts are misleading. If you say, "Stock values have doubled in three weeks," you offer an incomplete picture. Instead, say, "Stock values have doubled in three weeks, rising from $2 to $4 per share."

- **Give plenty of evidence for your conclusions.** Statements such as "We have to reorganize the sales force or we'll lose market share" may or may not be true. Readers have no way of knowing unless you provide enough data to support your claim.

- **Present only verifiable conclusions.** Check facts, and use reliable sources. Don't draw conclusions too quickly (one rep may say that customers are unhappy, but that doesn't mean they all are). And don't assume that one event caused another (sales may have dipped right after you switched ad agencies, but that doesn't mean the new agency is at fault—the general state of the economy may be responsible).

- **Keep your personal biases in check.** Even if you feel strongly about your topic, keep those feelings from influencing your choice of words. Don't say, "Locating a plant in Kingston is a terrible idea because the people there are mostly students who would rather play than work and who don't have the ability to operate our machines." Such language not only offends but also obscures the facts and provokes emotional responses.

## Applications for Success

1. When would you use vague language instead of concrete detail? Would this action be unethical or merely one form of emphasizing the positive?

2. Recent budget cuts have endangered the daycare program at your local branch of a national company. You're writing a report for headquarters about the grave impact on employees. Describe the situation in a single sentence that reveals nothing about your personal feelings but that clearly shows your position.

3. When writing an unsolicited proposal to a potential client, you need to persuade your audience to consider hiring your firm or purchasing your product. How can you be persuasive and completely truthful at the same time?

# 12

# Developing Oral and Online Presentations

**LEARNING OBJECTIVES**

*After studying this chapter, you will be able to*

1. Highlight the importance of presentations in your business career and explain how to adapt the planning step of the three-step process to presentations.

2. Describe the tasks involved in developing a presentation.

3. Describe the six major writing and design tasks required to enhance your presentation with effective visuals.

4. Outline three special tasks involved in completing a presentation.

5. Describe four important aspects of delivering a presentation in today's social media environment.

With more than 30 years of experience in public speaking, teaching, and training, Marc Friedman has witnessed many technological changes that have transformed oral presentations. Although the right tools used in the right way can help a speaker build a strong connection with the audience, too often the technology gets in the way. Friedman says holding an audience's attention is challenging enough in the best of circumstances, so any kind of communication barrier—from poorly designed slides to distracting laser pointers to excessive reliance on visual aids—makes the challenge that much greater. By all means, use the latest presentation tools whenever they can help, but don't let them interfere with the conversation you want to have with your audience.[1]

**LEARNING OBJECTIVE** ❶
Highlight the importance of presentations in your business career and explain how to adapt the planning step of the three-step process to presentations.

## Planning a Presentation

Like Marc Friedman, chances are you'll have an opportunity to deliver a number of oral presentations throughout your career. Oral presentations, delivered in person or online, offer important opportunities to put all your communication skills on display, including research, planning, writing, visual design, and interpersonal and nonverbal communication. Presentations also let you demonstrate your ability to think on your feet, grasp complex business issues, and handle challenging situations—all attributes that executives look for when searching for talented employees to promote.

Planning oral presentations is much like planning other business messages: you analyze the situation, gather information, select the right medium, and organize the information (see Figure 12.1). Gathering information for oral presentations is essentially the same as it is for written communication projects. The other three planning tasks have some special applications when it comes to oral presentations; they are covered in the following sections.

## FIGURE 12.1 The Three-Step Process for Developing Oral and Online Presentations

### ① Plan

**Analyze the Situation**

Define your purpose and develop a profile of your audience, including their likely emotional states and language preferences.

**Gather Information**

Determine audience needs and obtain the information necessary to satisfy those needs.

**Select the Right Medium**

Choose the best medium or combination of media for delivering your presentation, including handouts and other support materials.

**Organize the Information**

Define your main idea, limit your scope and verify timing, select the direct or indirect approach, and outline your content.

### ② Write

**Adapt to Your Audience**

Adapt your content, presentation style, and room setup to the audience and the specific situation. Be sensitive to audience needs and expectations with a "you" attitude, politeness, positive emphasis, and bias-free language. Plan to establish your credibility as required.

**Compose Your Presentation**

Outline an attention-getting introduction, body, and close. Prepare supporting visuals and speaking notes.

### ③ Complete

**Revise the Message**

Evaluate your content and speaking notes.

**Master Your Delivery**

Choose your delivery mode and practise your presentation.

**Prepare to speak**

Verify facilities and equipment, including online connections and software setups. Hire an interpreter if necessary.

**Overcome Anxiety**

Take steps to feel more confident and appear more confident on stage.

Preparing a professional-quality business presentation can take a considerable amount of time. Nancy Duarte, whose design firm has years of experience creating presentations for corporations, offers this rule of thumb: for a one-hour presentation that uses 30 slides, allow 36 to 90 hours to research, conceive, create, and practise.[2] Not every one-hour presentation justifies a week or two of preparation, of course, but the important presentations that can make your career or your company certainly can.

*The three-step writing process can help you create more effective presentations and turn your public speaking anxiety into positive energy.*

## Analyzing the Situation

As with written communications, analyzing the situation involves defining your purpose and developing an audience profile (see Table 12.1). The purpose of most of your presentations will be to inform or to persuade, although you may occasionally need to make a collaborative presentation, such as when you're leading a problem-solving or brainstorming session.

In addition to following the audience analysis advice in Chapter 3, try to anticipate the likely emotional state of your audience members. Figure 12.2 offers tips for dealing with a variety of audience mindsets.

As you analyze the situation, also consider the circumstances. Is the audience in the room or online? How many people will be present, and how will they be seated? Can you control the environment to minimize distractions? What equipment will you need? Such variables can influence not only the style of your presentation but the content itself.

*Try to learn as much as you can about the setting and circumstances of your presentation.*

## Selecting the Right Medium

The task of selecting the right medium might seem obvious. After all, you are speaking, so it's an oral medium. However, you have an array of choices these days, ranging from live, in-person presentations to *webcasts* (online presentations that people either view live

*Innovations in social media continue to reshape the nature of presentations.*

| TABLE 12.1 | Analyzing Audiences for Oral Presentations |
|---|---|

| TASK | ACTIONS |
|---|---|
| To determine audience size and composition | • Estimate how many people will attend.<br>• Identify what they have in common and how they differ.<br>• Analyze the mix of men and women, age ranges, socioeconomic and ethnic groups, occupations, and geographic regions represented. |
| To predict the audience's probable reaction | • Analyze why audience members are attending the presentation.<br>• Determine the audience's general attitude toward the topic: interested, moderately interested, unconcerned, open-minded, or hostile.<br>• Analyze the mood that people will be in when you speak to them.<br>• Find out what kind of backup information will most impress the audience: technical data, historical information, financial data, demonstrations, samples, and so on.<br>• Consider whether the audience has any biases that might work against you.<br>• Anticipate possible objections or questions. |
| To gauge the audience's experience | • Analyze whether everybody has the same background and level of understanding.<br>• Determine what the audience already knows about the subject.<br>• Decide what background information the audience will need to better understand the subject.<br>• Consider whether the audience is familiar with the vocabulary you intend to use.<br>• Analyze what the audience expects from you.<br>• Think about the mix of general concepts and specific details you will need to present. |

| FIGURE 12.2 | Planning for Various Audience Mindsets |
|---|---|

**Supportive:** Reward their goodwill with a presentation that is clear, concise, and upbeat; speak in a relaxed, confident manner.

**Interested but neutral:** Build your credibility as you present compelling reasons to accept your message; address potential objections as you move forward; show confidence but a willingness to answer questions and concerns.

**Uninterested:** Use the techniques described in this chapter to get their attention and work hard to hold it throughout; find ways to connect your message with their personal or professional interests; be well organized and concise.

**Worried:** Don't dismiss their fears or tell them they are mistaken for feeling that way; if your message will calm their fears, use the direct approach; if your message will confirm their fears, consider the indirect approach to build acceptance.

**Hostile:** Recognize that angry audiences care deeply but might not be open to listening; consider the indirect approach to find common ground and to diffuse anger before sharing your message; work to keep your own emotions under control.

or download later from your website), *screencasts* (recordings of activity on computer displays with audio voiceover), or *twebinars* (the use of Twitter as a *backchannel*—see page 328—for real-time conversation during a web-based seminar[3]).

## Organizing Your Presentation

Organizing a presentation involves the same tasks as organizing a written message: define your main idea, limit your scope, select the direct or indirect approach, and outline your content. Keep in mind that when people read written reports, they can skip back and forth if they're confused or don't need certain information. However, in an oral presentation, audiences are more or less trapped in your time frame and sequence. For some presentations, you should plan to be flexible and respond to audience feedback, such as skipping over sections the audience doesn't need to hear and going into more detail in other sections.

**REAL-TIME UPDATES**

**Learn More by Watching This Video**

**Dealing with the difficult four**

Get advice on dealing with four difficult audience members: the Resister, the Expert, the Dominator, and the Rambler. Go to http://real-timeupdates.com/bce6 and click on Learn More. If you are using MyBCommLab, you can access Real-Time Updates within Business Communication Resources.

**DEFINING YOUR MAIN IDEA**   If you've ever heard a speaker struggle to get his or her main point across ("What I really mean to say is . . . "), you know how frustrating such an experience can be for an audience. To avoid that struggle, figure out the one key message you want audience members to walk away with. Then compose a one-sentence summary that links your subject and purpose to your audience's frame of reference. Here are some examples:

> Convince management that reorganizing the technical support department will improve customer service and reduce employee turnover.

> Convince the board of directors that we should build a new plant in Mississauga to eliminate manufacturing bottlenecks and improve production quality.

> Address employee concerns regarding a new health care plan by showing how the plan will reduce costs and improve the quality of their care.

Each of these statements puts a particular slant on the subject, one that directly relates to the audience's interests. By focusing on your audience's needs and using the "you" attitude, you help keep their attention and convince them that your points are relevant.

*If you can't express your main idea in a single sentence, you probably haven't defined it clearly enough.*

**LIMITING YOUR SCOPE**   Limiting your scope is important with any message, but it's particularly vital with presentations, for two reasons. First, for most presentations, you must work within strict time limits. Second, the longer you speak, the more difficult it is to hold the audience's attention levels, and the more difficult it is for your listeners to retain your key points.[4]

The only sure way to know how much material you can cover in a given time is to practise your presentation after you complete it. As an alternative, if you're using conventional structured slides (see page 318) you can figure on three or four minutes per slide as a rough guide.[5] Of course, be sure to factor in time for introductions, coffee breaks, demonstrations, question-and-answer sessions, and anything else that takes away from your speaking time.

If you're having trouble meeting a time limit or just want to keep your presentation as short as possible, consider a hybrid approach in which you present your key points in summary form and give people printed handouts with additional detail.[6] Limitations can force you to focus on the most essential message points that are important to your audience.[7] (See Case 1 on page 333 for the special twist on time-constrained presentations known as *pecha-kucha*.)

*Limiting your scope ensures that your presentation fits the allotted time and your content meets audience needs and expectations.*

*The only sure way to measure the length of your presentation is to complete a practice run.*

Use the direct approach for routine or positive messages and indirect if the subject is bad news or persuasion.

**CHOOSING YOUR APPROACH**   With a well-defined main idea to guide you and a clear idea about the scope of your presentation, you can begin to arrange your message. If you have 10 minutes or less, organize your presentation much as you would a letter or other brief message: Use the direct approach if the subject involves routine information or good news and use the indirect approach if the subject involves bad news or persuasion. Plan your introduction to arouse interest and to give a preview of what's to come. For the body of the presentation, be prepared to explain the who, what, when, where, why, and how of your subject. In the final section, review the points you've made and close with a statement that will help your audience remember the subject of your speech (see Figure 12.3).

Longer presentations are organized more like reports. If the purpose is to motivate or inform, you'll typically use the direct approach and a structure imposed naturally by the subject: comparison, importance, sequence, chronology, geography, or category (as discussed in Chapter 10). If your purpose is to analyze, persuade, or collaborate, organize your material around conclusions and recommendations or around a logical argument. Use the direct approach if the audience is receptive and the indirect approach if you expect resistance.

Using a storytelling model can be a great way to catch and hold the audience's attention.

No matter what the length, look for opportunities to integrate storytelling (see page 315) into the structure of your presentation. The dramatic tension (not knowing what will happen to the "hero") at the heart of effective storytelling is a great way to capture and keep the audience's attention.

In addition to planning your speech, a presentation outline helps you plan your speaking notes.

**PREPARING YOUR OUTLINE**   A presentation outline helps you organize your message, and it serves as the foundation for delivering your speech. Prepare your outline in several stages:[8]

• State your purpose and main idea and then use these elements to guide the rest of your planning.

---

**FIGURE 12.3**   Effective Outline for a 10-Minute Presentation

**Progress Update: August 2015**

**Purpose:** To update the Executive Committee on our product development schedule.

I.   Review goals and progress.
   A. Mechanical design:
      1. Goal: 100%
      2. Actual: 80%
      3. Reason for delay: Unanticipated problems with case durability
   B. Software development:
      1. Goal: 50%
      2. Actual: 60%
   C. Material sourcing:
      1. Goal: 100%
      2. Actual: 45% (and materials identified are at 140% of anticipated costs)
      3. Reason for delay: Purchasing is understaffed and hasn't been able to research sources adequately.
II.   Discuss schedule options.
   A. Option 1: Reschedule product launch date.
   B. Option 2: Launch on schedule with more expensive materials.
III.   Suggest goals for next month.
IV.   Q&A

- Organize your major points and subpoints in logical order, expressing each major point as a single, complete sentence.
- Identify major points in the body first, then outline the introduction and close.
- Identify transitions between major points or sections, then write these transitions in full-sentence form.
- Prepare your bibliography or source notes; highlight those sources you want to identify by name during your talk.
- Choose a compelling title. Make it brief, action-oriented, and focused on what you can do for the audience.[9]

You may find it helpful to create a simpler speaking outline from your planning outline.

Many speakers like to prepare both a detailed *planning outline* (see Figure 12.4) and a simpler *speaking outline* for the presentation that provides all the cues and reminders they

## FIGURE 12.4 Effective Outline for a 30-Minute Presentation

**OUR TRAVEL AND ENTERTAINMENT COSTS ARE OUT OF CONTROL**

*Includes the statement of purpose* →

**Purpose:** To explain why Electrovision's travel and entertainment (T&E) costs are so high and to propose a series of changes to bring them under control.

**INTRODUCTION**

I. Our T&E costs are way above average, and they pose a threat to the company's financial health; fortunately, we can fix the problem in four straightforward steps that could save as much as $6 million a year. ← *Highlights the purpose in the introduction*

II. How we approached the investigation
  A. We analyzed internal expense reports. ← *Explains the investigation process*
  B. We compared our cost data with nationwide averages.
  C. We analyzed published information on trends and cost-control suggestions.

(Transition: This presentation reviews Electrovision's spending patterns, analyzes the impact on company profits, and recommends four steps for reducing the budget.)

**BODY**

I. Analysis of spending patterns
  A. The amount we've been spending on T&E:
    1. Airfares, hotels, rental cars, restaurants, and entertainment totalled $16 million last year.
    2. T&E budget increased by 12 percent per year for the past five years.
  B. Where the money goes:
    1. We took 3390 trips last year at an average cost per trip of $4725.
    2. Airfares and lodging represent 70 percent of T&E expenses.
  C. How our spending compares with national averages:
    1. Facilities and customers spread from coast to coast force us to spend a lot on travel.
    2. However, we spend 125 percent more than the national average for every day of travel. (Source: *Globe & Mail*)
  D. Why do we spend so much?
    1. First-class travel has been viewed as compensation for the demands of extensive travel.
    2. The sales staff is encouraged to entertain clients.
    3. T&E costs are hard for managers to view and study.
    4. No one has central responsibility for controlling costs.

*Uses a logical and simple organization*

*Explains why the problem exists*

(Transition: We need to control spending for two reasons: (1) profits are projected to be flat or declining over the next two years, and (2) hotel rates and airfares continue to rise sharply.)

(Continued)

**FIGURE 12.4** (Continued)

II. Impact on profits

    A. T&E costs continue to rise, as do other company costs.
    B. Revenue is projected to decline in coming years.
    C. Bottom line: We're headed for trouble.

*Explains why T&E costs are a problem*

(Transition: By implementing a number of reforms, management can expect to reduce Electrovision's T&E budget by as much as 40 percent. We can cut expenses in four ways.)

III. Solution

    A. We should institute tighter spending controls:
        1. Hire a travel manager to control costs and negotiate group discounts.
        2. Develop a formal, written policy to contain costs.
        3. Give departmental managers the data they need to make smarter decisions.
    B. We can reduce unnecessary travel and entertainment costs:
        1. Cut down on discretionary trips (seminars, etc.).
        2. Reduce the number of intracompany trips and employees sent on each trip.
        3. Encourage employees to economize.
    C. We can find lower travel rates:
        1. Negotiate corporate discounts.
        2. Plan trips more carefully to take advantage of lower fares.
    D. We can replace some travel with technological alternatives:
        1. Conference calls
        2. Videoconferences
        3. Other possibilities
    E. Potential impact of all these changes: As much as $6 million in reduced costs (Source: American Express)

*Maintains the logical organization throughout*

*Provides the four-step solution mentioned in the introduction, then makes a recommendation for implementing the steps*

(Transition: This presentation reviews Electrovision's spending patterns, analyzes the impact on company profits, and recommends four steps for reducing the budget.)

**CLOSE**

I. We spend more on T&E than we should
II. Four fairly obvious steps will yield significant cost savings

    A. Establish tighter controls
    B. Rein in unnecessary T&E costs
    C. Find lower travel rates
    D. Reduce travel by using technological alternatives

*Restates the four recommended steps*

need in order to present their material. To prepare an effective speaking outline, follow these steps:[10]

- Start with the planning outline and then strip away anything you don't plan to say directly to your audience.
- Condense points and transitions to key words or phrases.
- Add delivery cues, such as places where you plan to pause for emphasis or use visuals.
- Arrange your notes on numbered cards or use the notes capability in your presentation software.

**LEARNING OBJECTIVE 2**
Describe the tasks involved in developing a presentation.

## Developing a Presentation

Although you usually don't write out a presentation word for word, you still engage in the writing process—developing your ideas, structuring support points, phrasing your transitions, and so on. Depending on the situation and your personal style, the eventual presentation might follow your initial words closely, or you might express your thoughts in fresh, spontaneous language.

## Adapting to Your Audience

Your audience's size, the venue (in person or online), your subject, your purpose, your budget, and the time available for preparation all influence the style of your presentation. If you're speaking to a small group, particularly people you already know, you can use a casual style that encourages audience participation. A small conference room, with your audience seated around a table, may be appropriate. Use simple visuals and invite your audience to interject comments. Deliver your remarks in a conversational tone, using notes to jog your memory if necessary.

If you're addressing a large audience or if the event is important, establish a more formal atmosphere. During formal presentations, speakers are often on a stage or platform, standing behind a lectern and using a microphone so that their remarks can be heard throughout the room or captured for broadcasting or webcasting.

*Adapting to your audience involves a number of issues, from speaking style to technology choices.*

### REAL-TIME UPDATES

**Learn More by Watching This Video**

**How to establish an emotional connection with any audience**

Entertainment executive Peter Guber talks about the art of purposeful storytelling. Go to http://real-timeupdates.com/bce6 and click on Learn More. If you are using MyBCommLab, you can access Real-Time Updates within Business Communication Resources.

## Composing Your Presentation

Like written documents, oral presentations are composed of distinct elements: the introduction, the body, and the close.

**PRESENTATION INTRODUCTION**  A good introduction arouses the audience's interest in your topic, establishes your credibility, and prepares the audience for what will follow. That's a lot to accomplish in the first few minutes, so give yourself plenty of time to develop the words and visuals you'll use to get your presentation off to a great start.

*An effective introduction arouses interest in your topic, establishes your credibility, and prepares the audience for the body of your presentation.*

Getting Your Audience's Attention  Some subjects are naturally more interesting to some audiences than others. If your presentation involves the health, wealth, or happiness of your listeners, most people will be interested, regardless of how you begin. All you really have to do is announce your topic, and you'll have their attention. Other subjects call for more imagination. Here are six ways to arouse audience interest:[11]

*Capture the audience's attention and interest with your opening remarks.*

- Unite the audience around a common goal.
- Tell a compelling story that illustrates an important and relevant point. If your entire presentation is structured as a story, of course, you'll want to keep the interest high by not giving away the ending yet.
- Pass around an example or otherwise appeal to listeners' senses.
- Ask a question that will get your audience thinking about your message.
- Share an intriguing, unexpected, or shocking detail.
- Open with an amusing observation about yourself, the subject matter of the presentation, or the circumstances surrounding the presentation—but make sure any humorous remarks are relevant, appropriate, and not offensive to anyone in the audience.

Regardless of which technique you choose, make sure you can give audience members a reason to care and to believe that the time they're about to spend listening to you will be worth their while.[12]

Building Your Credibility  Audiences tend to decide within a few minutes whether you're worth listening to, so establishing your credibility quickly is vital.[13] If you're not a well-known expert or haven't already earned your audience's trust in other situations, you'll need to build credibility in your introduction. If someone else will introduce you, he or she can present your credentials. If you will be introducing yourself, tell them briefly who you are, why you're there, and how they'll benefit from listening to you. You might say something like this:

*If someone else will be introducing you, ask this person to present your credentials.*

I'm Karen Whitney, a market research analyst with Information Resources Corporation. For the past five years, I've specialized in studying high-technology markets. Your director of engineering, John LaBarre, asked me to talk about recent trends in computer-aided design so that you'll have a better idea of how to direct your research efforts.

This speaker establishes credibility by tying her credentials to the purpose of her presentation. By mentioning her company's name, her specialization and position, and the name of the audience's boss, she lets her listeners know immediately that she is qualified to tell them something they need to know.

**Previewing Your Message**    In addition to getting the audience's attention and establishing your credibility, a good introduction gives your audience a preview of what's ahead. Your preview should summarize the main idea of your presentation, identify major supporting points, and indicate the order in which you'll develop those points. Of course, if you're using the indirect approach, you'll have to decide how much information to review in your introduction.

> Offer a preview to help your audience understand the importance, the structure, and the content of your message.

**PRESENTATION BODY**    The bulk of your presentation is a discussion of the main points in your outline. No matter what organizational pattern you're using, your goals are to make sure that the organization of your presentation is clear and that your presentation holds the audience's attention.

**Connecting Your Ideas**    In written documents, you can show how ideas are related with a variety of design clues: headings, paragraph indentions, white space, and lists. However, with oral communication—particularly when you aren't using visuals for support—you have to rely primarily on spoken words to link various parts and ideas.

> Use transitions to repeat key ideas, particularly in longer presentations.

For the links between sentences and paragraphs, use one or two transitional words: *therefore, because, in addition, in contrast, moreover, for example, consequently, nevertheless,* or *finally*. To link major sections of a presentation, use complete sentences or paragraphs, such as "Now that we've reviewed the problem, let's take a look at some solutions." Every time you shift topics, be sure to stress the connection between ideas by summarizing what's been said and previewing what's to come. The longer your presentation, the more important your transitions. Your listeners need clear transitions to guide them to the most important points. Furthermore, they'll appreciate brief interim summaries to pick up any ideas they may have missed.

**Holding Your Audience's Attention**    A successful introduction will have grabbed your audience's attention; now the body of your presentation needs to hold that attention. Here are a few helpful tips for keeping the audience tuned into your message:

> Hold an audience's attention by showing how your message relates to their individual needs and concerns.

- Keep relating your subject to your audience's needs.
- Anticipate—and answer—your audience's questions as you move along so people don't get confused or distracted.
- Use clear, vivid language and throw in some variety; repeating the same words and phrases over and over puts people to sleep.
- Show how your subject is related to ideas that audience members already understand, and give people a way to categorize and remember your points.[14]
- If appropriate, encourage participation by asking for comments or questions.
- Illustrate your ideas with visuals, which enliven your message, help you connect with audience members, and help them remember your message more effectively (see "Enhancing Your Presentation with Effective Visuals," page 317).

**PRESENTATION CLOSE**    The close of a speech or presentation has two critical jobs to accomplish: making sure your listeners leave with the key points from your talk clear in their minds and putting your audience in the appropriate emotional state. For example, if the purpose of your presentation is to warn managers that their out-of-control spending threatens the company's survival, you want them to leave with that message ringing in their ears—and with enough concern for the problem to stimulate changes in their behaviour.

**Restating Your Main Points** Use the close to succinctly restate your main points, repeat your main idea, emphasizing what you want your listeners to do or to think. For example, to close a presentation on your company's executive compensation program, you could repeat your specific recommendations and then conclude with a memorable statement to motivate your audience to take action:

> We can all be proud of the way our company has grown. However, if we want to continue that growth, we need to take four steps to ensure that our best people don't start looking for opportunities elsewhere:
>
> * First, increase the overall level of compensation.
> * Second, establish a cash bonus program.
> * Third, offer a variety of stock-based incentives.
> * Fourth, improve our health insurance and pension benefits.
>
> By taking these steps, we can ensure that our company retains the management talent it needs to face our industry's largest competitors.

Repetition of key ideas, as long as you don't overdo it, greatly improves the chance that your audience will hear your message in the way you intended.

**Ending with Clarity and Confidence** If you've been successful with the introduction and body of your presentation, your listeners now have the information they need, and they're in the right frame of mind to put that information to good use. End on a strong note that confirms expectations about any actions or decisions that will follow the presentation—and to bolster the audience's confidence in you and your message one final time.

Some presentations require the audience to reach a decision or agree to take specific action, in which case the close provides a clear wrap-up. If the audience reached agreement on an issue covered in the presentation, briefly review the consensus. If they didn't agree, make the lack of consensus clear by saying something like, "We seem to have some fundamental disagreement on this question." Then be ready to suggest a method of resolving the differences.

If you expect any action to occur as a result of your speech, be sure to explain who is responsible for doing what. List the action items and, if possible within the time available, establish due dates and assign responsibility for each task.

Make sure your final remarks are memorable and expressed in a tone that is appropriate to the situation. For example, if your presentation is a persuasive request for project funding, you might emphasize the importance of this project and your team's ability to complete it on schedule and within budget. Expressing confident optimism will send the message that you believe in your ability to perform.

Whatever final message is appropriate, think through your closing remarks carefully before stepping in front of the audience. You don't want to wind up on stage with nothing to say but "Well, I guess that's it."

# Enhancing Your Presentation with Effective Visuals

Slides and other visuals can improve the quality and impact of your oral presentation by creating interest, illustrating points that are difficult to explain in words alone, adding variety, and increasing the audience's ability to absorb and remember information.

You can select from a variety of visuals to enhance oral presentations. Don't overlook "old-school" technologies such as overhead transparencies, chalkboards, whiteboards, and flipcharts—they can all have value in the right circumstances. However, the medium of choice for most business presentations is an electronic presentation using Microsoft PowerPoint, Apple Keynote, Google Documents, Prezi, or similar software. Electronic

When you repeat your main idea in the close, emphasize what you want your audience to do or to think.

Plan your final statement carefully so you can end on a strong, positive note.

Make sure your final remarks are memorable and have the right emotional tone.

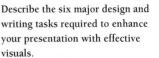
**LEARNING OBJECTIVE ❸**
Describe the six major design and writing tasks required to enhance your presentation with effective visuals.

Thoughtfully designed visuals create interest, illustrate complex points in your message, add variety, and help the audience absorb and remember information.

presentations are easy to edit and update; you can add sound, photos, video, and animation; they can be incorporated into online meetings, webcasts, and *webinars* (a common term for web-based seminars); and you can record self-running presentations for trade shows, websites, and other uses.

Electronic presentations are practically universal in business today, but their widespread use is not always welcome. You may have already heard the expression "death by PowerPoint," which refers to the agonizing experience of sitting through too many poorly conceived and poorly delivered presentations. In the words of presentation expert and author Garr Reynolds, "Most presentations remain mind-numbingly dull, something to be endured by presenter and audience alike."[15]

That's the bad news. The good news is that presentations can be an effective communication medium and an experience that is satisfying, and sometimes even enjoyable, for presenter and audience alike. Start with the mindset of *simplicity* (clear ideas presented clearly) and *authenticity* (talking *with* your audience about things they care about, rather than talking at them or trying to be a "performer"), and you'll be well on your way to becoming an effective presenter.

> Focusing on making your presentations simple and authentic will help you avoid "death by PowerPoint."

## Choosing Structured or Free-Form Slides

> Structured slides are usually based on templates and usually involve a lot of bullet points; free-form slides are much less rigid and emphasize visual appeal.

Perhaps the most important design choice you face when creating slides is whether to use conventional, bullet-point–intensive *structured slides* or the looser, visually oriented *free-form slides* that many presentation specialists now advocate. Compare the two rows of slides in Figure 12.5. The structured slides in the top row follow the same basic format

---

**FIGURE 12.5** Structured Versus Free-Form Slide Design

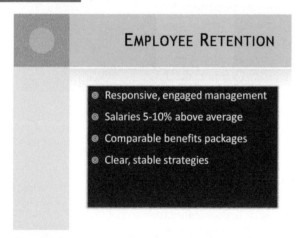

Figure 12.5a

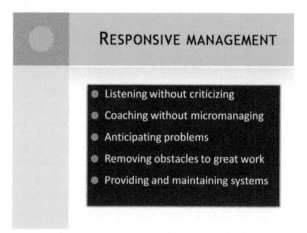

Figure 12.5b

Figure 12.5c

Figure 12.5d

throughout the presentation. In fact, they're based directly on the templates built into PowerPoint, which tend to feature lots and lots of bullet points.

The free-form slides in the bottom row don't follow a rigid structure. However, free-form designs should not change randomly from one slide to the next. Effectively designed slides should still be unified by design elements such as colour and font selections, as can be seen in Figures 12.5c and 12.5d. Also, note how Figure 12.5d combines visual and textual messages to convey the point about listening without criticizing. This complementary approach of pictures and words is a highlight of free-form design.

**ADVANTAGES AND DISADVANTAGES OF STRUCTURED SLIDES**  Structured slides have the advantage of being easy to create; you simply choose an overall design scheme for the presentation, select a template for a new slide, and start typing. If you're in a schedule crunch, going the structured route might save the day because at least you'll have *something* ready to show. Given the speed and ease of creating them, structured slides can be a more practical choice for routine presentations such as project status updates.

*Structured slides are often the best choice for project updates and other routine information presentations, particularly if the slides are intended to be used only once.*

Also, because more information can usually be packed on each slide, carefully designed structured slides can be more effective at conveying complex ideas or sets of interrelated data to the right audiences. For example, if you are talking to a group of executives who must decide where to make budget cuts across the company's eight divisions, at some point in the presentation they probably will want to see summary data for all eight divisions on a single slide for easy comparison. Such a slide would be overcrowded by the usual definition, but this might be the only practical way to get a "big picture" view of the situation. (The best solution is probably some high-level, summary slides supported by a detailed handout, as "Creating Effective Handouts" on page 324 explains.)

The primary disadvantage of structured design is that mind-numbing effect Garr Reynolds describes, caused by text-heavy slides that all look alike. Slide after slide of dense, highly structured bullet points with no visual relief can put an audience to sleep.

**ADVANTAGES AND DISADVANTAGES OF FREE-FORM SLIDES**  Free-form slide designs can overcome the drawbacks of text-heavy structured design, Such slides can fulfill three criteria researchers have identified as important for successful presentations: (1) providing complementary information through both textual and visual means, (2) limiting the amount of information delivered at any one time to prevent cognitive overload, and (3) helping viewers process information by identifying priorities and connections, such as by highlighting the most important data points in a graph.[16] (Of course, well-designed structured slides can also meet these criteria, but the constraints of prebuilt templates make doing so more of a challenge.)

*Well-designed free-form slides help viewers understand, process, and remember the speaker's message.*

With appropriate imagery, free-form designs can also create a more dynamic and engaging experience for the audience. Given their ability to excite and engage, free-form designs are particularly good for motivational, educational, and persuasive presentations—particularly when the slides will be used multiple times and therefore compensate for the extra time and effort required to create them.

Free-form slides have several potential disadvantages, however. First, effectively designing slides with both visual and textual elements is more creatively demanding and more time consuming than simply typing text into preformatted templates. The emphasis on visual content also requires more images, which take time to find.

*Free-form slides can require more skill and time to create, and they put more demands on the speaker during the presentation.*

Second, because far less textual information tends to be displayed on screen, the speaker is responsible for conveying more of the content. Ideally, of course, this is how a presentation *should* work, but presenters sometimes find themselves in less than ideal circumstances, such as being asked to fill in for a colleague on short notice.

Third, if not handled carefully, the division of information into smaller chunks can make it difficult to present complex subjects in a cohesive, integrated manner. For instance, if you're discussing a business problem that has five interrelated causes, it might be helpful to insert a conventional bullet-point slide as a summary and reminder after discussing each problem on its own.

## Designing Effective Slides

Use presentation software wisely to avoid the "death by PowerPoint" stigma that presentations have in the mind of many professionals.

Despite complaints about "death by PowerPoint," the problem is not with that software itself (or with Apple Keynote or any other presentation program). It is just a tool and, like other tools, can be used well or poorly. Unfortunately, lack of design awareness, inadequate training, schedule pressures, and the instinctive response of doing things the way they've always been done can lead to ineffective slides and lost opportunities to really connect with audiences.

"Slideuments" are hybrids that try to function as both presentation slides and readable documents—and usually fail at both tasks.

Another reason for ineffective slides is the practice of treating slide sets as standalone documents that can be read on their own, without a presenter. (The emergence of websites such as SlideShare, www.slideshare.net, might be contributing to this, too, by making it so easy to share slide sets.) These "slideument" hybrids that try to function as both presentation visuals and printed documents don't work well as either: They often have too much information to be effective visuals and too little to be effective reports (in addition to being clumsy to read).

Rather than packing your slides with enough information to make them readable as standalone documents, complement well-designed slides with printed handouts.

As "Creating Effective Handouts" on page 324 explains, the ideal solution is to create an effective slide set and a separate handout document that provides additional details and supporting information. This way, you can optimize each piece to do the job it is really meant to do. An alternative is to use the notes field in your presentation software to include your speaking notes for each slide. Anyone who gets a copy of your slides can at least follow along by reading your notes, although you will probably need to edit and embellish them to make them understandable by others.

However, if creating sliduments is your only option for some reason, be sure to emphasize clarity and simplicity. If you have to add more slides to avoid packing individual slides with too much text, by all means do so. Having a larger number of simpler slides is a better compromise all around than a smaller number of jam-packed slides. Remember that the primary purpose of the slides is supporting your presentation, so make sure your slides work well for that purpose.

Organizing a slide around a key visual can help the audience quickly grasp how ideas are related.

**DESIGNING SLIDES AROUND A KEY VISUAL** With both structured and free-form design strategies, it is often helpful to structure specific slides around a key visual that helps organize and explain the points you are trying to make. For example, a pyramid suggests a hierarchical relationship, and a circular flow diagram emphasizes that the final stage in a process loops back to the beginning of the process. Figure 12.6 shows six of the many types of visual designs you can use to organize information on a slide.

**WRITING READABLE CONTENT** One of the most common mistakes beginners make—and one of the chief criticisms levelled at structured slide designs in general—is stuffing slides with too much text. Doing so creates several problems: it overloads the audience with too much information too fast; it takes attention away from the speaker by forcing people to read more; and it requires the presenter to use smaller type, which in turn makes the slides even harder to read.

Effective text slides supplement your words and help the audience follow the flow of ideas (see Figure 12.7). Use them to highlight key points, summarize and preview your message, signal major shifts in thought, illustrate concepts, or help create interest in your spoken message.

| FIGURE 12.6 | Using a Key Visual to Organize Points on a Slide |

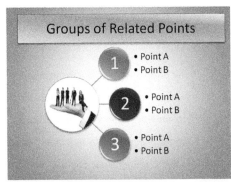

Figure 12.6a

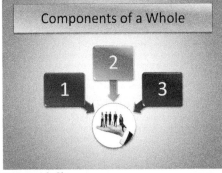

Figure 12.6b

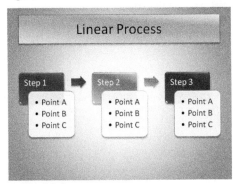

Figure 12.6c

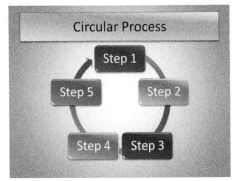

Figure 12.6d

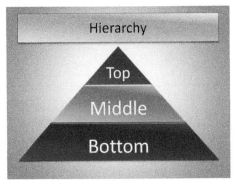

Figure 12.6e

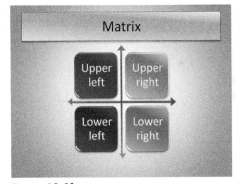

Figure 12.6f

**CREATING CHARTS AND TABLES FOR SLIDES**   Charts and tables for presentations need to be simpler than visuals for printed documents. Detailed images that look fine on the printed page can be too dense and too complicated for presentations. Remember that your audience members will view your visuals from across the room—not from a foot or two away, as you do while you create them. Keep the level of detail at an absolute minimum, eliminating anything that is not absolutely essential. If necessary, break information into more than one illustration.

*Visuals for presentations need to be simpler than visuals for printed documents.*

**SELECTING DESIGN ELEMENTS**   As you create slides, pay close attention to the interaction of colour, background and foreground designs, artwork, fonts, and type styles.

- **Colour.** Colour is a critical design element that can grab attention, emphasize important ideas, create contrast, and stimulate various emotions (see Table 12.2). Research shows that colour visuals can account for 60 percent of an audience's acceptance or rejection of an idea. Colour can increase willingness to read by up to 80 percent, and

*Colours have meanings based on both cultural experience and the relationships that you established between the colours in your designs.*

---

**FIGURE 12.7** Writing Text for Slides

### Writing Readable Content

To choose effective words and phrases, think of the text on your slides as guides to the content, not the content itself. In a sense, slide text serves as the headings and subheadings for your presentation. Accordingly, choose words and short phrases that help your audience follow the flow of ideas, without forcing people to read in depth. You primarily want your audience to *listen*, not to *read*. Highlight key points, summarize and preview your message, signal major shifts in thought, illustrate concepts, or help create interest in your spoken message.

Figure 12.7a

### Writing Readable Content

❖ Think of **text** as a guide to your content

❖ Use **text** like headings and subheadings

❖ Help audience follow the flow of ideas

❖ Encourage audience to *listen*, not *read*

❖ Highlight, summarize, preview, illustrate

Figure 12.7b

Use enough text to help your audience follow the flow of ideas— and not a single word more.

Figure 12.7c

Just enough

Figure 12.7d

---

**TABLE 12.2** Colour and Emotion

| COLOUR | EMOTIONAL ASSOCIATIONS | BEST USES |
|---|---|---|
| Blue | Peaceful, soothing, tranquil, cool, trusting | Background for electronic business presentations (usually dark blue); safe and conservative |
| White | Neutral, innocent, pure, wise | Font colour of choice for most electronic business presentations with a dark background |
| Yellow | Warm, bright, cheerful, enthusiastic | Text bullets and subheadings with a dark background |
| Red | Passionate, dangerous, active, painful | For promoting action or stimulating the audience; seldom used as a background ("in the red" specifically refers to financial losses) |
| Green | Assertive, prosperous, envious, relaxed | Highlight and accent colour |

---

it can enhance learning and improve retention by more than 75 percent.[17] Colour is powerful, so use it carefully.

- **Background designs and artwork.** All visuals have two layers of design: the *background* and the *foreground*. The background is the equivalent of paper in a printed report and "should be open, spacious, and simple," says design expert Nancy Duarte.[18] Be aware that many of the template designs in presentation software have backgrounds that are too distracting.

Make sure the background of your slides stays in the background; it should never get in the way of the informational elements in the foreground.

- **Foreground designs and artwork.** The foreground contains the unique text and graphic elements that make up each individual slide. Foreground elements can be either functional or decorative. *Functional artwork* includes photos, technical drawings, charts, and other visual elements containing information that's part of your message. In contrast, *decorative artwork* simply enhances the look of your slides and should be used sparingly, if at all.

- **Fonts and type styles.** Type is harder to read onscreen than on the printed page because projectors have lower resolution (the ability to display fine details) than typical office printers. Consequently, choose sans serif fonts because they are usually easier to read than serif fonts. Use both uppercase and lowercase letters, with extra white space between lines of text, and limit the number of fonts to one or two per slide. Create high contrast between font colour and background colour—for example, a dark font on light background. Choose font sizes that are easy to read from anywhere in the room, usually between 28 and 36 points, and test them in the room if possible.

> Use upper and lower case and a sans serif font.

Maintaining design consistency is critical because audiences start to assign meaning to visual elements beginning with the first slide. For instance, if yellow is used to call attention to the first major point in your presentation, viewers will expect the next occurrence of yellow to also signal an important point. The *slide master* feature makes consistency easy to achieve because it applies design choices to every slide in a presentation.

> Keep the design consistent.

**ADDING ANIMATION AND MULTIMEDIA**   Today's presentation software offers many options for livening up your slides, including sound, animation, video clips, transition effects, and hyperlinks. Think about the impact that all these effects will have on your audience and use only those special effects that support your message.[19]

> Make sure an animation has a purpose.

*Functional animation* involves motion that is directly related to your message, such as a highlight arrow that moves around the screen to emphasize specific points in a technical diagram. In contrast, *decorative animation* (such as having a block of text cartwheel in from offscreen) can easily distract audiences.

**Transitions** control how one slide replaces another, such as having the current slide gently fade out before the next slide fades in. Subtle transitions like this can ease your viewers' gaze from one slide to the next, but many of the transition effects now available are little more than distractions and are best avoided. **Builds** control the release of text, graphics, and other elements on individual slides. With builds, you can make key points appear one at a time rather than having all of them appear on a slide at once, thereby making it easier for you and the audience to focus on each new message point.

> If you use transitions between slides, make sure they are subtle.

A **hyperlink** instructs your computer to jump to another slide in your presentation, to a website, or to another program entirely. Using hyperlinks is also a great way to build flexibility into your presentations so that you can instantly change the flow of your presentation in response to audience feedback.

> Hyperlinks let you build flexibility into your presentations.

*Multimedia elements* offer the ultimate in active presentations. Using audio and video clips can be a great way to complement your textual message. Just be sure to keep these elements brief and relevant, as supporting points for your presentation, not as replacements for it.

## Completing a Presentation

> **LEARNING OBJECTIVE 4**
> Outline three special tasks involved in completing a presentation.

The completion step for presentations involves a wider range of tasks than most printed documents require. Make sure you allow enough time to test your presentation slides, verify equipment operation, practise your speech, and create handout materials. With a first draft of your presentation in hand, revise your slides to make sure they are readable, concise, consistent, and fully operational (including transitions, builds, animation, and multimedia). Complete your production efforts by finalizing your slides and support materials, choosing your presentation method, and practising your delivery.

## Finalizing Your Slides

Electronic presentation software can help you throughout the editing and revision process. For example, the *slide sorter* view (different programs have different names for this feature) lets you see some or all of the slides in your presentation on a single screen. Use this view to add and delete slides, reposition slides, check slides for design consistency, and verify the operation of any effects. Moreover, the slide sorter is a great way to review the flow of your story.[20]

In addition to using content slides, you can help your audience follow the flow of your presentation by creating slides for your title, agenda and program details, and navigation:

Navigation slides help your audience keep track of what you've covered already and what you plan to cover next.

- **Title slide(s).** You can make a good first impression with one or two title slides, the equivalent of a report's cover and title page.
- **Agenda and program details.** These slides communicate the agenda for your presentation and any additional information the audience might need (see Figure 12.8).
- **Navigation slides.** To tell your audience where you're going and where you've been, you can use a series of **navigation slides** based on your outline or agenda. A simple way to do this is to repeat your agenda slide at the beginning of each major section in your presentation, with the upcoming section highlighted in some way. (The two navigation slides in Figure 12.8 show a more stylized way of showing the audience where you are in the presentation.)

Figure 12.8 illustrates some of the many options you have for presenting various types of information. Note that although these slides don't follow a rigid structure of text-heavy bullet points, they are unified by the colour scheme (silver background and bold colour accents) and typeface selections.

## Creating Effective Handouts

*Handouts*—any printed materials you give the audience to supplement your talk—should be considered an integral part of your presentation strategy. Handouts can include detailed charts and tables, case studies, research results, magazine articles, and anything else that supports the main idea of your presentation.

Use handout materials to support the points made in your presentation and to offer the audience additional information on your topic.

Plan your handouts as you develop your presentation so that you use each medium as effectively as possible. Your presentation should paint the big picture, convey and connect major ideas, set the emotional tone, and rouse the audience to action (if that is relevant to your talk). Your handouts can then carry the rest of the information load, providing the supporting details that audience members can consume at their own speed, on their own time. You won't need to worry about stuffing every detail into your slides because you have the more appropriate medium of printed documents to do that. As Garr Reynolds puts it, "Handouts can set you free."[21]

### REAL-TIME UPDATES

**Learn More by Watching This Video**

**Five easy tips to add a professional finish to your slides**

Learn some simple techniques pros use to create and edit high-quality images for PowerPoint presentations. Go to http://real-timeupdates.com/bce6 and click on Learn More. If you are using MyBCommLab, you can access Real-Time Updates within Business Communication Resources.

## Choosing Your Presentation Method

With all your materials ready, your next step is to decide which method of speaking you want to use. In nearly all situations, the best choice is speaking from notes, rather than reciting from memory or reading a prepared statement word for word. Even if you can memorize your entire speech, your presentation will sound stiff and overly formal because you are "delivering lines," rather than talking to your audience. Worse yet, you might forget your lines. However, memorizing a quotation, an opening statement, or a few concluding remarks can bolster your confidence and strengthen your delivery.

FIGURE 12.8  Designing Effective Visuals: Selected Slides

*Left*: This introductory slide is a blunt attention-getter, something that would have to be used with caution and only in special circumstances.

*Right*: This simple math equation gets the point across about how expensive high employee turnover is.

*Left*: This stylized bar graph sends a stark visual message about how bad the company's turnover really is.

*Right*: This slide is essentially a bullet list, with three groups of two bullets each. Repeating the photo element from the introductory slide emphasizes the message about employee turnover.

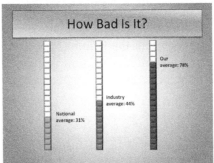

These two *navigation slides* show one way to introduce each of the four subtopics in this particular section. As the highlight moves around the central circle, the audience is reminded of which subtopics have been covered and which subtopic is going to be covered next. And each time it is shown, the message is repeated that all these problems are the "true cost of chaos" in the company's employment practices.

*Left*: This slide introduces three key points the speaker wants to emphasize in this particular section.

*Right*: This slide shows a linear flow of ideas, each with bulleted subpoints. This slide could be revealed one section at a time to help the speaker keep the audience's attention focused on a single topic.

*Left*: This flowchart packs a lot of information onto one slide, but seeing the sequence of events in one place is essential.

*Right*: This simple visual highlights the presenter's spoken message about being careful to choose the right tasks to focus on and them completing them quickly.

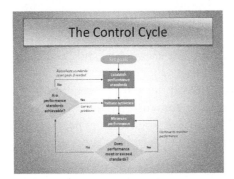

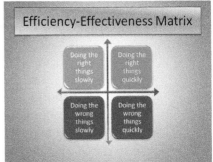

Reading your speech is necessary in rare circumstances, such as when delivering legal information, policy statements, or other messages that must be conveyed in an exact manner. However, for all other business presentations, reading is a poor choice because it limits your interaction with the audience and lacks the fresh, dynamic feel of natural talking. If you must read a prepared speech, practise enough so that you can still maintain eye contact with your audience. Print your speech with triple-spaced lines, wide margins, and large type.

Speaking from notes, with the help of an outline, note cards, or visuals, is usually the most effective and easiest delivery mode. This approach gives you something to refer to and still allows for plenty of eye contact, interaction with the audience, and improvisation in response to audience feedback.

Another important decision at this point is preparing the venue where you will speak. In many instances, you won't have much of a choice, such as when presenting at a conference or when visiting a client's offices. However, if you do have some control over the environment, think carefully about the seating for the audience, your position in the room, and the lighting. For instance, dimming the lights is common practice for many presenters, but dimming the lights too far can hamper the nonverbal communication between you and your audience and therefore limit opportunities for interaction.[22]

## Practising Your Delivery

Practising your presentation is essential. Practise boosts your confidence, gives you a more professional demeanour, helps ensure that you appear polished, and lets you verify the operation of visuals and equipment. A test audience can tell you if your slides are understandable and whether your delivery is effective. A day or two before you're ready to step on stage for an important talk, make sure you and your presentation are ready:

- Can you present your material naturally, without reading your slides?
- Could you still make a compelling and complete presentation if you experience an equipment failure and have to proceed without using your slides at all?
- Is the equipment working, and do you know how to work it?
- Is your timing on track?
- Can you easily pronounce all the words you plan to use?
- Have you anticipated likely questions and objections?

With experience, you'll get a feel for how much practise is enough in any given situation. Practising helps keep you on track, helps you maintain a conversational tone with your audience, and boosts your confidence and composure. As you practise, try to be aware of the nonverbal signals you're transmitting. Regardless of how you feel inside, your effectiveness greatly depends on how you look and sound. Your posture is important in projecting confidence. Stand tall, with your weight on both feet and your shoulders back. Use your hands to emphasize your remarks with appropriate gestures. Meanwhile, vary your facial expressions to make the message more dynamic. Practise speaking in a normal, conversational tone but with enough volume for everyone to hear you and varying your pitch and speaking rate to add emphasis. Use silence instead of meaningless filler words such as *um*, *you know*, *okay*, and *like*. Silence adds dramatic punch and gives the audience time to think about the message.

When you deliver an oral presentation to people from other cultures, you may need to adapt the content of your presentation. It is also important to take into account any cultural differences in appearance, mannerisms, and other customs. Your interpreter or host will be able to suggest appropriate changes for a specific audience or occasion.

# Delivering a Presentation

**LEARNING OBJECTIVE** 5
Describe four important aspects of delivering a presentation in today's social media environment.

It's showtime. This section offers practical advice for four important aspects of delivery: overcoming anxiety, handling questions responsively, embracing the backchannel, and giving presentations online.

## Overcoming Anxiety

Keep in mind that nervousness is an indication that you care about your audience, your topic, and the occasion. These techniques will help you convert anxiety into positive energy:[23]

- **Stop worrying about being perfect.** Everyone makes mistakes, whether it's tripping over a hard-to-pronounce word or literally tripping while on stage. Successful speakers focus on making an authentic connection with their listeners, rather than on trying to deliver a note-perfect presentation.
- **Know your subject.** The more familiar you are with your material, the less panic you'll feel.
- **Practise, practise, practise.** The more you rehearse, the more confident you will feel.
- **Visualize your success.** Visualize mental images of yourself in front of the audience, feeling confident, prepared, and able to handle any situation that might arise.[24] Remember that your audience wants you to succeed, too.
- **Remember to breathe.** Tension can lead people to breathe in a rapid and shallow fashion, which can create a lightheaded feeling. Breathe slowly and deeply to maintain a sense of calm and confidence.
- **Be ready with your opening line.** Have your first sentence memorized and on the tip of your tongue.
- **Be comfortable.** Dress appropriately but as comfortably as possible. Drink plenty of water ahead of time to hydrate your voice (bring a bottle of water with you, too).
- **Take a three-second break.** If you sense that you're starting to race, pause and arrange your notes or perform some other small task while taking several deep breaths. Then start again at your normal pace. If you feel that you're losing your audience, try to pull them back by asking for comments or questions.
- **Concentrate on your message and your audience, not on yourself.** When you're busy thinking about your subject and observing your audience's response, you tend to forget your fears.
- **Maintain eye contact with friendly audience members.** Eye contact not only makes you appear sincere, confident, and trustworthy but can give you positive feedback as well.
- **Keep going.** Things usually get better as you move along, with each successful minute giving you more and more confidence.

Preparation is the best antidote for anxiety.

## Handling Questions Responsively

Don't leave the question-and-answer period to chance: anticipate potential questions and think through your answers.

Whether you take them during a formal question-and-answer (Q&A) period or as they come up during your presentation, questions are often one of the most important parts of an presentation. They give you a chance to obtain important information, to emphasize your main idea and supporting points, and to build enthusiasm for your point of view. When you're speaking to high-ranking executives in your company, the Q&A period will often consume most of the time allotted for your presentation.[25]

Whether or not you can establish ground rules for Q&A depends on the audience and the situation. If you're presenting to a small group of upper managers or potential investors, for example, you will probably have no say in the matter: audience members will likely ask as many questions as they want, whenever they want, to get the information they need. On the other hand, if you are presenting to your peers or a large public audience, establish some guidelines, such as the overall time limit for questions.

Don't assume that you can handle whatever comes up without some preparation.[26] Learn enough about your audience members to get an idea of their concerns and think through answers to potential questions.

When people ask questions, pay attention to nonverbal signals to help determine what each person really means. Repeat the question to confirm your understanding and to ensure that the entire audience has heard it. If the question is vague or confusing, ask for clarification; then give a simple, direct answer.

If you don't have the complete answer to an important question, offer to provide it after the presentation.

If you are asked a difficult or complex question, avoid the temptation to sidestep it. Offer to meet with the questioner afterward if the issue isn't relevant to the rest of the audience or if giving an adequate answer would take too long. If you don't know the answer, don't pretend that you do. Instead, offer to get a complete answer as soon as possible.

Be on guard for audience members who use questions to make impromptu speeches or to take control of your presentation. Without offending anyone, find a way to stay in control. You might admit that you and the questioner have differing opinions and offer to get back to the questioner after you've done more research.[27]

If you ever face hostile questions, respond honestly and directly while keeping your cool.

If a question ever puts you on the hot seat, respond honestly but keep your cool. Look the person in the eye, answer the question as well as you can, and keep your emotions under control. Defuse hostility by paraphrasing the question and asking the questioner to confirm that you've understood it correctly. Maintain a businesslike tone of voice and a pleasant expression.[28]

When the time allotted for your presentation is almost up, prepare the audience for the end by saying something like, "Our time is almost up. Let's have one more question." After you reply to that last question, summarize the main idea of the presentation and thank people for their attention. Conclude with the same confident demeanour you've had from the beginning.

## Embracing the Backchannel

Many business presentations these days involve more than just the spoken conversation between the speaker and his or her audience. Using Twitter and other electronic media, audience members often carry on their own parallel communication during a presentation via the **backchannel**, which presentation expert Cliff Atkinson defines as "a line of communication created by people in an audience to connect with others inside or outside the room, with or without the knowledge of the speaker."[29] Chances are you've participated in a backchannel already, such as when texting with your classmates or live-blogging during a lecture.

Twitter and other social media are dramatically changing business presentations by making it easy for all audience members to participate in the *backchannel*.

The backchannel presents both risks and rewards for business presenters. On the negative side, for example, listeners can research your claims the instant you make them and spread the word quickly if they think your information is shaky. The backchannel also gives contrary audience members more leverage, which can lead to presentations spinning out of control. On the plus side, listeners who are excited about your message can build support for it, expand on it, and spread it to a much larger audience in a matter of seconds. You can also get valuable feedback during and after presentations.[30]

Resist the urge to ignore or fight the backchannel; instead, learn how to use it to your advantage.

By embracing the backchannel, rather than trying to fight it or ignore it, presenters can use this powerful force to their advantage. Follow these tips to make the backchannel work for you:[31]

- **Integrate social media into the presentation process.** For example, you can set up a formal backchannel yourself, create a website for the presentation so that people can access relevant resources during or after the presentation, create a Twitter hashtag that everyone can use when sending tweets, or display the Twitterstream during Q&A so that everyone can see the questions and comments on the backchannel.

- **Monitor and ask for feedback.** Using a free service such as TweetDeck, which organizes tweets by hashtag and other variables, you can monitor in real time what the people in the audience are writing about. To avoid trying to monitor the backchannel while speaking, you can schedule "Twitter breaks," during which you review comments and respond as needed.

- **Review comments point by point to improve your presentation.** After a presentation is over, review comments on audience members' Twitter accounts and blogs to see which parts confused them, which parts excited them, and which parts seemed to have little effect (based on few or no comments).

- **Automatically tweet key points from your presentation while you speak.** Add-ons for presentation software can send out prewritten tweets as you show specific slides during a presentation. By making your key points readily available, you make it easy for listeners to retweet and comment on your presentation.

- **Establish expectations with the audience.** Explain that you welcome audience participation, but to ensure a positive experience for everyone, comments should be civil, relevant, and productive.

## Giving Presentations Online

Online presentations offer many benefits, including the opportunity to communicate with a geographically dispersed audience at a fraction of the cost of travel and the ability for a project team or an entire organization to meet at a moment's notice. However, this format also presents some challenges for presenters, thanks to that layer of technology between you and your audience. Many of those "human moments" that guide and encourage you through an in-person presentation won't travel across the digital divide. For instance, it's often difficult to tell whether audience members are bored or confused because your view of them is usually confined to small video images (and sometimes not even that).

Online presentations give you a way to reach more people in less time, but they require special preparation and skills.

To ensure successful online presentations, keep the following advice in mind:

- **Consider sending preview study materials ahead of time.** Doing so allows audience members to familiarize themselves with any important background information. Also, by using a free service such as SlideShare (**www.slideshare.net**), you can distribute your presentation slides to either public or private audiences, and you can record audio narrative to make your presentations function on their own.[32] Some presenters advise against giving out your slides ahead of time, however, because doing so gives away the ending of your presentation.

- **Keep your presentation as simple as possible.** Break complicated slides down into multiple slides if necessary, and keep the direction of your discussion clear so that no one gets lost.

- **Ask for feedback frequently.** You won't have as much of the visual feedback that alerts you when audience members are confused, and many online viewers will be reluctant to call attention to themselves by interrupting you to ask for clarification. Setting up a backchannel via Twitter or as part of your online meeting system will help in this regard.

- **Consider the viewing experience from the audience members' point of view.** Will they be able to see what you think they can see? For instance, webcast video is typically displayed in a small window onscreen, so viewers may miss important details.

- **Allow plenty of time for everyone to get connected and familiar with the screen they're viewing.** Build extra time into your schedule to ensure that everyone is connected and ready to start.

Last but not least, don't get lost in the technology. Use these tools whenever they'll help but remember that the most important aspect of any presentation is getting the audience to receive, understand, and embrace your message.

**❶ OBJECTIVE** **Highlight the importance of presentations in your business career and explain how to adapt the planning step of the three-step process to presentations.**

Oral and online presentations give the opportunity to use all your communication skills. The tasks in planning oral presentations are generally the same as with any other business message, but three tasks require special consideration. First, anticipate the likely emotional states of your listeners during the presentation. Second, although some presentations consist only of the purely oral medium of spoken communication, presentations increasingly involve integration with a variety of electronic media. Third, organizing your presentation takes on special importance because audience members can't flip or click back and forth as they can with printed or electronic media. Limiting the scope is particularly vital, because many presentations must fit strict time limits.

**❷ OBJECTIVE** **Describe the tasks involved in developing a presentation.**

Although you usually don't write out a presentation word for word, you still engage in the writing process—developing your ideas, structuring support points, phrasing your transitions, and so on. To compose a presentation, break it down into three essential parts: an introduction that arouses the audience's interest in your topic, establishes your credibility, and prepares the audience for what will follow; a body that conveys your information in a way that maintains audience interest and makes it easy to connect one idea to the next; and a close that restates your main points and ends with confidence.

**❸ OBJECTIVE** **Describe the six major design and writing tasks required to enhance your presentation with effective visuals.**

First, choose between structured and free-form slides. Structured slides follow the same design plan for most or all the slides in a presentation, are often created by using the templates provided with presentation software, and tend to convey most of their information through bullet points. In contrast, visually oriented free-form slides do not follow any set design scheme from slide to slide, although they should have a unified sense of colour, font selection, and other design elements. Second, look for opportunities to design slides around a key visual that unites and explains important points. Third, for any slides that have textual content, be sure to strictly limit the word count and keep the font size large enough to read easily. Fourth, make sure any graphic elements are simple and clear enough to be easily grasped from anywhere in the room. Fifth, choose and use design elements—colour, background and foreground designs, artwork, typefaces, and type styles—in a way that enhances, not obscures, your message. Sixth, add animation and multimedia elements if they will help build audience interest and understanding.

**❹ OBJECTIVE** **Outline three special tasks involved in completing a presentation.**

The completion stage for presentations involves a wider range of tasks than printed documents require. First, finalize your slides and support materials using the slide sorter to get a big picture view of your presentation and creating title slide(s), agenda and program detail slides, and navigation slides. Second, choose your presentation method: speaking from notes is the best choice for most presentations. Third, practise your delivery to ensure a smooth presentation, and boost your confidence.

**❺ OBJECTIVE** **Describe four important aspects of delivering a presentation in today's social media environment.**

First, take steps to reduce your anxiety, which include not trying to be perfect, preparing more material than is necessary, and practising extensively. Second, handle questions responsively. Prepare answers to potential questions. Pay attention to nonverbal signals and be sure to respond to all questions. Finally, alert the audience when the Q&A period is almost over. Third, embrace the backchannel, the parallel conversation that might be going on among audience members on Twitter and other media. To take advantage of the backchannel, you can integrate social media into your presentation, monitor and ask for feedback, review point-by-point comments to improve your presentation, automatically tweet key points from your presentation while you speak, and establish expectations with the audience. Fourth, to ensure a successful online presentation, consider sending preview materials ahead of time, keep your content and presentation as simple as possible, ask for feedback frequently, consider the viewing experience from the audience's side, and give participants time to get connected.

MyBCommLab®  Go to MyBCommLab for everything you need to help you succeed in the job you've always wanted! Tools and resources include the following:
- Writing Activities
- Document Makeovers
- Video Exercises
- Grammar Exercises—and much more!

## Practise Your Grammar

Effective business communication starts with strong grammar skills. To improve your grammar skills, go to MyBCommLab, where you'll find exercises and diagnostic tests to help you produce clear, effective communication.

## Test Your Knowledge

To review chapter content related to each question, refer to the indicated Learning Objective.

1. What skills do presentations give you the opportunity to practise and demonstrate? L.O.❶
2. What three goals should you accomplish during the introduction of a presentation? L.O.❷
3. What techniques can you use to get an audience's attention during your introduction? L.O.❷
4. What three tasks should you accomplish in the close of your presentation? L.O.❷
5. What steps can you take to ensure success with online presentations? L.O.❺

## Apply Your Knowledge

To review chapter content related to each question, refer to the indicated Learning Objective.

1. Why is it important to limit the scope of presentations? L.O.❶
2. How can visually oriented free-form slides help keep an audience engaged in a presentation? L.O.❸
3. Is it ethical to use design elements and special effects to persuade an audience? Why or why not? L.O.❸
4. Why is speaking from notes usually the best method of delivery? L.O.❹
5. How does embracing the backchannel reflect the "you" attitude? L.O.❺

## Practise Your Skills

### ACTIVITIES

Each activity is labelled according to the primary skill or skills you will need to use. To review relevant chapter content, you can refer to the indicated Learning Objective. In some instances, supporting information will be found in another chapter, as indicated.

1. **Presentations: Planning a Presentation** L.O.❶
   Select one of the following topics:
   Inform classmates or management trainees about
   a. How to dress for success
   b. How to work with the other gender in the workplace
   c. Nonverbal communication and your persona at work
   d. The etiquette for a business lunch
   e. Business culture practices in a specific country—choose one of the following:
   - Japan
   - India
   - South Korea
   - Iran
   - Saudi Arabia
   - France
   - Germany

- England
- Australia
- Canada
- United States
- Philippines

f. Interview dos and don'ts
g. Employee incentive programs
h. Building an effective exhibit for a trade show
i. Environmental best practices for the office

Persuade management that the company should

j. Purchase and display Canadian art in the workplace
k. Start a composting program
l. Sponsor a young worker safety program
m. Organize and hold a fundraiser for charity
n. Offer fitness incentives for employees

Research your topic as needed and prepare a brief presentation (5–10 minutes) to be given to your class.

2. **Presentations: Developing a Presentation; Collaboration: Team Projects** L.O.❷, **Chapter 2** You've been asked to give an informative 10-minute talk on vacation opportunities in your home province. Draft your introduction, which should last no more than two minutes. Then pair off with a classmate and analyze each other's introductions. How well do these two introductions arouse the audience's interest, build credibility, and preview the presentation? Suggest how these introductions might be improved.

3. **Presentations: Developing a Presentation** L.O.❷ Locate the transcript of a speech, either online or through your school library. Good sources include Yahoo's directory of commencement speeches (http://dir.yahoo.com/Education/Graduation/Speeches) and the publication *Vital Speeches of the Day*. (Recent years of *Vital Speeches of the Day* are available in the ProQuest database; ask at your library.) Many corporate websites also have archives of executives' speeches; look in the "investor relations" section. Examine both the introduction and the close of the speech you've chosen and then analyze how these two sections work together to emphasize the main idea. What action does the speaker want the audience to take? Next, identify the transitional sentences or phrases that clarify the speech's structure for the listener, especially those that help the speaker shift between supporting points. Using these transitions as clues, list the main message and supporting points; then indicate how each transitional phrase links the current supporting point to the succeeding one. Prepare a two- to three-minute presentation summarizing your analysis for your class.

4. **Presentations: Designing Presentation Visuals** L.O.❹ Look through recent issues (print or online) of *Maclean's*, *The Globe & Mail Report on Business*, or other business publications for articles discussing challenges that a specific company or industry is facing. Using the articles and the guidelines discussed in this chapter, create three to five slides summarizing these issues. Include citations and sources for any material you quote directly.

5. **Presentations: Designing Presentation Visuals** L.O.❹ Find a business-related slide presentation on SlideShare (www.slideshare.net) and analyze the design. Do you consider it structured or free form? Does the design help the audience understand and remember the message? Why or why not? What improvements would you suggest to the design? Select two slides (one free form and one structured) that you think are effective and bring them to class.

6. **Presentations: Mastering Delivery; Nonverbal Communication: Analyzing Nonverbal Signals** L.O.❺, **Chapter 2** Observe and analyze the delivery of a speaker in a school, work, or other setting, or watch a TED talk online (www.ted.com). What type of delivery did the speaker use? Was this delivery appropriate for the occasion? What nonverbal signals did the speaker use to emphasize key points? Were these signals effective? Which nonverbal signals would you suggest to further enhance the delivery of this oral presentation? Why?

7. **Presentations: Delivering a Presentation; Communication Ethics: Making Ethical Choices** L.O.❺, **Chapter 1** Think again about the oral presentation you observed and analyzed in the previous activity. How could the speaker have used nonverbal signals to unethically manipulate the audience's attitudes or actions?

8. **Presentations: Delivering a Presentation; Collaboration: Team Projects; Media Skills: Microblogging** L.O.❺, **Chapter 2, Chapter 6** In a team of six students, develop a 10-minute slide presentation on any topic that interests you. Nominate one person to give the presentation; the other five will participate via a Twitter backchannel. Create a webpage that holds at least one downloadable file that will be discussed during the presentation, and set up a backchannel. Practise using the backchannel, including using a hashtag for the meeting and having the presenter ask for audience feedback during a "Twitter break." Be ready to discuss your experience with the entire class.

9. **Presentations: Mastering Delivery, Introducing a Classmate** L.O.❺ Work in groups of two. Interview each other to find out enough information to

introduce each other to the group. Ask questions such as these:

- What did the person do before this course?
- What kind of work and educational experience does he or she have?
- What activities does the person enjoy in his or her spare time?
- What are the person's strengths? What is the person's career goal?

Prepare a one-minute introduction of your classmate. Your instructor will invite you to present to the class or to a small group of five.

10. **Presentations: Mastering Delivery, Presenting a Personal View** L.O.⑤ Take a few minutes to develop three to five points about one of the following topics to prepare for a practice oral presentation. Most of the topics can be developed by thinking of the following questions: What is it? Why is it enjoyable or worthwhile? When/where can you do it? Add a brief introduction and a summary and you have a short presentation!

a. A sport you enjoy
b. A book you'd recommend
c. A movie you think everyone should see
d. A website you'd recommend
e. Software you'd recommend
f. An online retail site you like
g. A television program worth watching
h. A hobby you enjoy
i. A course you would recommend
j. A life skill that's important to have
k. Tips for getting along with others
l. Tips for studying
m. Tips for getting good marks on assignments
n. Tips for having a balanced life as a student
o. Tips for how to stay healthy at school
   Prepare a three- to five-minute oral presentation on one of the topics. Your instructor will invite you to present to the class or to a small group of five students.

# CASES

**Apply the three-step writing process to the following cases, as assigned by your instructor.**

▌ Presentation Skills ▌ Portfolio Builder
## 1. Presentations: Planning a Presentation L.O.❶

Pecha-kucha (Japanese for "chit-chat") is a style of presentation that might be the ultimate in creative constraint: the speaker is limited to 20 slides, each of which is displayed for exactly 20 seconds before automatically advancing. Pecha-kucha Nights, which are open to the public, are now put on in cities all over the world. Visit **www.pechakucha.org** for more information on these events or to view some archived presentations.

**YOUR TASK** Select one of the subjects from Activity 1 on pages 331–332, and develop a pecha-kucha–style presentation with 20 slides, each designed to be displayed for 20 seconds. Use the slide-timing capabilities in your presentation software to control the timing. Make sure you practise before presenting to your class so that you can hit the precise timing requirements.[33]

▌ Presentation Skills ▌ Social Networking Skills
## 2. Presentations: Planning a Presentation L.O.❶

You know those times when you're craving Thai food or the perfect fruit smoothie, but you don't know where

to go? Or when you're out shopping or clubbing and want to let your friends know where you are? Foursquare's location-based services connect you with friends and companies that offer products and services of interest.

**YOUR TASK** Create a brief presentation explaining the Foursquare concept and its features and benefits. List two Foursquare competitors and give a brief assessment of which of the three you would recommend to your classmates.[34]

▌ Presentation Skills ▌ Team Skills
## 3. Presentations: Planning a Presentation L.O.❶

In your job as a business development researcher for a major corporation, you're asked to gather and process information on a wide variety of subjects. Management has gained confidence in your research and analysis skills and would now like you to begin making regular presentations at management retreats and other functions. Topics are likely to include the following:

- Offshoring of Canadian jobs
- Foreign ownership of Canadian firms
- Employment issues involving workers from other countries

- Tax breaks offered by local and provincial or territorial governments to attract new businesses
- Economic impact of environmental regulations

**YOUR TASK** With a team assigned by your instructor, choose one of the topics from the list and conduct enough research to familiarize yourself with the topic. Identify at least three important issues that anyone involved with this topic should know about. Prepare a 10-minute presentation that introduces the topic, comments on its importance to the Canadian economy, and discusses the issues you've identified. Assume that your audience is a cross-section of business managers who don't have any particular experience in the topic you've chosen.

**❚ Presentation Skills ❚ Portfolio Builder**
**4. Presentations: Designing Presentation Visuals** L.O.❹

Depending on the sequence your instructor chose for this course, you've probably covered several chapters at this point and learned or improved many valuable skills. Think through your progress and identify five business communication skills that you've either learned for the first time or developed during this course.

**YOUR TASK** Create a six-slide presentation, with a title slide and five slides that describe each of the five skills you've identified. Be sure to explain how each skill could help you in your career. Use any visual style that you feel is appropriate for the assignment.

---

## BUSINESS COMMUNICATION NOTEBOOK

# Workplace Skills

## Nerves: The Secret Weapon of Polished Presenters

What do Barbra Streisand, Liza Minnelli, and Donny Osmond have in common? These professional performers and many others admit to being nervous about public speaking. If the pros can feel fear, it's no wonder beginners are sometimes scared speechless. Survey after survey has confirmed that public speaking is the number one fear in Canada and the United States—so if you're anxious about stepping in front of an audience, you're not alone.

Nervousness might make your hands tremble, your knees knock, your mouth feel dry, or your stomach churn. As bad as these symptoms can be, remember that nerves are a good indicator of your concern for the occasion, your subject, and your audience. If you didn't care, you wouldn't be anxious. A speaker who cares is more likely to seek out every method of communicating with the audience.

Remember also that you'll feel a little less nervous with every oral presentation. Once you see how the audience responds to your first attempt, you'll realize that you did better than you feared you would. People in the audience want you to succeed; they're interested in learning from you or being inspired by your words, not in straining to hear the sound of your knees knocking together.

You can harness your nerves by focusing on what you want to accomplish. In the words of actress Carol Channing, "I don't call it nervousness—I prefer to call it concentration." Like Channing, you can concentrate your efforts on making that all-important connection with your audience. But don't make the mistake of expecting perfection. Put that nervous energy into planning, preparing, and practising. Turn your negative fears into positive energy, and you'll be better equipped to face your audience the first time and every time.

You might start by listing statements that describe each of your fears: the *behaviour* that will show your fear, the *effect* this behaviour will have, and the *action* you can take to change the behaviour and get rid of the fear. For example, if you're afraid that you won't be as good as you would like to be, you might say, "I'll leave out parts of my speech or act nervous (behaviour), so I won't impress the audience or get my message across (effect)." The solution is to make the speech your own before addressing your audience (action). Practise, practise, practise. Record your speech or videotape yourself and look for strengths and weaknesses. Practise out loud until you've mastered the speech and it's yours. If you like your speech, your audience will like it, and you'll get your message across.

Or perhaps you're saying something like "I'll look scared (behaviour), and the audience will sense my nervousness and will snicker and make fun of me (effect)." The solution is to act confident—even if you don't feel it (action). Listeners want you to succeed, and they can't see what's happening inside you. Don't apologize for anything. If you make a mistake, don't start over; just keep going. Then enjoy the applause—your moment in the spotlight.

## Applications for Success

Learn how to overcome your fear of public speaking by visiting **www.pe2000.com/pho-speaking.htm**.

Answer the following questions:

1. Think of any lectures or presentations you've recently attended. Have you ever noticed a speaker's level of anxiety? Did any speakers succeed in overcoming this fear? Describe the ways a particular speaker visibly conquered his or her nervousness. If that speaker failed, what techniques might have helped?

2. As a member of the audience, what can you do to help a speaker overcome his or her nervousness? Briefly explain.

3. Using the behaviour-effect-action strategy, list one of your fears and show how you plan to counter it in your next presentation.

# 13

## Building Careers and Writing Résumés

## LEARNING OBJECTIVES

*After studying this chapter, you will be able to*

1. List eight key steps to finding the ideal opportunity in today's job market.
2. Explain the process of planning your résumé, including how to choose the best résumé organization.
3. Describe the tasks involved in writing your résumé and list the sections to consider including in your résumé.
4. Characterize the completing step for résumés, including the six most common formats in which you can produce a résumé.

Stephanie Sykes—a former human resources practise leader at BCE, now running her own HR services company in London, Ontario—provides recruitment and human resource planning to attract and retain talented employees. Bell Canada receives more than 60 000 applications each year. "What stands out in an application," says Sykes, "is clarity and simplicity. Tell me why you want to work for the company and what you will bring to it. Technical skills show through easily but remember that most companies are also looking for people with leadership skills or potential."

---

**LEARNING OBJECTIVE 1**
List eight key steps to finding the ideal opportunity in today's job market.

# Building Careers

As Stephanie Sykes will tell you, getting the job that's right for you takes more than sending out a few résumés and application letters. Before entering the workplace, you need to learn as much as you can about your capabilities, what employers seek, and the job marketplace.

## Understanding Today's Dynamic Workplace

The workplace today is changing constantly.[1] The attitudes and expectations of both employers and employees are being affected not only by globalization, technology, diversity, and teams but also by deregulation, shareholder activism, corporate downsizing, mergers and acquisitions, outsourcing, and entrepreneurialism (people starting their own business or buying a franchise).[2] These factors affect the following aspects of the workplace:

Numerous forces are changing today's workplace.

- **How often people look for work.** Rather than looking for lifelong employees, many employers now hire temporary workers and consultants on a project-by-project basis. Likewise, rather than staying with one employer for their entire career, growing numbers of employees are moving from company to company.

- **Where people find work.** Fewer jobs are being created by large companies. One expert predicts that soon 80 percent of the labour force will be working for firms employing fewer than 200 people. Moreover, self-employment seems to be an increasingly attractive option for many former employees.[3]
- **The type of people who find work.** Employers today are looking for people who are able and willing to adapt to diverse situations and who continue to learn throughout their careers.

What do all these forces mean to you? First, take charge of your career—and stay in charge of it. Understand your options, have a plan, and don't count on others to watch out for your future. Second, understanding your audience is key to successful communication, so it is essential for you to understand how employers view today's job market.

**WHAT EMPLOYERS LOOK FOR IN JOB APPLICANTS**   Given the complex forces in the contemporary workplace and the unrelenting pressure of global competition, what are employers looking for in the candidates they hire? The short answer: a lot. Specific expectations vary by profession and position, of course, but virtually all employers look for the following general skills and attributes:[4]

- **Communication skills.** This item isn't listed first because you're reading a business communication textbook. Communication is listed first because it is far and away the most commonly mentioned skill set when employers are asked about what they look for in employees. Business leader Iain Black, CEO of the Vancouver Board of Trade, says effective communication skills give applicants a "sustainable competitive advantage."[5] Tools and technology change or become obsolete, but the skills of being able to write clearly and present effectively last for a lifetime. Improving your communication skills will help in every aspect of your professional life.
- **Interpersonal and team skills.** You will have many individual responsibilities on the job, but chances are you won't work all alone very often. Learn to work with others—and help them succeed as you succeed.
- **Intercultural and international awareness and sensitivity.** Successful employers tend to be responsive to diverse workforces, markets, and communities, and they look for employees with the same outlook.
- **Data collection, analysis, and decision-making skills.** Employers want people who know how to identify information needs, find the necessary data, convert the data into useful knowledge, and make sound decisions.
- **Computer and electronic media skills.** Today's workers need to know how to use common office software and to communicate using a wide range of electronic media.
- **Time and resource management.** If you've had to juggle multiple priorities during college, consider that great training for the business world. Your ability to plan projects and manage the time and resources available to you will make a big difference on the job.
- **Flexibility and adaptability.** Stuff happens, as they say. Employees who can roll with the punches and adapt to changing business priorities and circumstances will go further (and be happier) than employees who resist change.
- **Professionalism.** Professionalism is the quality of performing at the highest possible level. True professionals strive to excel, continue to hone their skills and build their knowledge, are dependable and accountable, demonstrate a sense of business etiquette, make ethical decisions, show loyalty and commitment, don't give up when things get tough, and maintain a positive outlook.

A great way to get inside the heads of corporate recruiters is to "listen in" on their professional conversations by reading periodicals such as *Workforce Magazine* (www.workforce.com) and blogs such as Fistful of Talent (www.fistfuloftalent.com) and The HR Capitalist (www.hrcapitalist.com).

Follow the online conversations of professional recruiters to learn what their hot-button issues are.

## Adapting to Today's Job Market

Before you limit your employment search to a particular industry or job, do some advance preparation. Analyze what you want to do, what you have to offer, and how you can make yourself more valuable to potential employers. This preliminary analysis will help you identify employers who are likely to want you and vice versa.

**WHAT DO YOU WANT TO DO?**   Economic necessities and changes in the marketplace will influence much of what happens in your career, of course; nevertheless, it's wise to start your employment search by examining your values and interests. Identify what you want to do first, then see whether you can find a position that satisfies you at a personal level while also meeting your financial needs. Consider these questions:

*Examine your values and interests.*

- **What would you like to do every day?** Research occupations that interest you. Talk to people in various occupations about their typical workday. You might consult relatives, local businesses, and former graduates or contacts.
- **How would you like to work?** Consider how much independence you want on the job, how much variety you like, and whether you prefer to work with products, machines, people, ideas, figures, or some combination of them all.
- **How do your financial goals fit with your other priorities?** For instance, many high-paying jobs involve a lot of stress, sacrifices of time with family and friends, and frequent travel or relocation. If location, lifestyle, or other factors are more important to you, are you willing to sacrifice some level of pay to achieve them?
- **Have you established some general career goals?** For example, do you want to pursue a career specialty such as finance or manufacturing, or do you want to gain experience in multiple areas with an eye toward upper management?
- **What sort of corporate culture are you most comfortable with?** Would you be happy in a formal hierarchy with clear reporting relationships? Or do you prefer less structure? Teamwork or individualism? Do you like a competitive environment?

You might need some time in the workforce to figure out what you really want to do or to work your way into the job you really want, but it's never too early to start thinking about where you want to be.

**WHAT DO YOU HAVE TO OFFER?**   When seeking employment, you must tell people about who you are. So you need to know what talents and skills you have, and you'll need to explain how these skills will benefit potential employers. Follow these guidelines:

*To determine what you have to offer, carefully examine your skills, education, experience, and personality traits.*

- **Jot down 10 achievements you're proud of.** Think about what skills these achievements demanded (leadership skills, speaking ability, and artistic talent may have helped you produce a successful presentation). You'll begin to recognize a pattern of skills. Which of them might be valuable to potential employers?
- **Look at your educational preparation, work experience, and extracurricular activities.** What do your knowledge and experience qualify you to do? What have you learned from volunteer work or class projects that could benefit you on the job? Have you held any offices, won any awards or scholarships, or mastered a second language?
- **Take stock of your personal characteristics.** Are you aggressive, a born leader? Or would you rather follow? Are you outgoing, articulate, and great with people? Or do you prefer working alone? Make a list of what you believe are your four or five most important qualities. Ask a relative or friend to rate your traits as well.

**HOW CAN YOU MAKE YOURSELF MORE VALUABLE TO EMPLOYERS?**   While you're figuring out what you want from a job and what you can offer an employer, you can take positive steps now toward building your career. First, look for volunteer projects, temporary jobs, freelance work, or internships that will help expand your experience base and skill set.[6] You can look for freelance projects on Craigslist (**www.craigslist.org**) and numerous other websites; some of these jobs have only nominal pay, but they do provide an opportunity for you to display your skills.

Also consider applying your talents to *crowdsourcing* projects, in which companies and nonprofit organizations invite the public to contribute solutions to various challenges. For example, crowdsourcing.org (**www.crowdsourcing.org**) posts articles and projects involving crowd funding, cloud labour, community building, open innovation, and crowdsourcing sites.[7]

These opportunities help you gain valuable experience and relevant contacts, provide you with important references and work samples for your *employment portfolio*, and help you establish your *personal brand* (see the following sections).

Second, learn more about the industry or industries in which you want to work, and stay on top of new developments. Join networks of professional colleagues and friends who can help you keep up with trends and events. Many professional societies have student chapters or offer students discounted memberships. Take courses and pursue other educational or life experiences that would be difficult while working full time.

For more ideas and advice on planning your career, check out the resources listed in Table 13.1.

Make yourself valuable to employers by keeping samples, broadening your experience, and constantly improving your skills.

## Building an Employment Portfolio

Employers want proof that you have the skills to succeed on the job, but even if you don't have much relevant work experience, you can use your college classes to assemble that proof. Simply create and maintain an *employment portfolio*, which is a collection of projects that demonstrate your skills and knowledge. You can create a *print portfolio* and an *e-portfolio*; both can help with your career effort. A print portfolio gives you something tangible to bring to interviews, and it lets you collect project results that might not be easy to show online, such as a handsomely bound report.

An e-portfolio is a multimedia presentation of your skills and experiences.[8] Think of it as a website that contains your résumé, work samples, letters of recommendation, relevant videos or podcasts you have recorded, blog posts and articles you may have written, and other information about you and your skills. Be creative. For example, a student who was pursuing a degree in meteorology added a video clip of himself delivering a weather forecast.[9] The portfolio can be burned on a CD or DVD for physical distribution or, more commonly, it can be posted online—whether it's a personal website, your college's site (if student pages are available), a specialized portfolio hosting site such as Behance (**www.behance.com**), or a résumé hosting site such as VisualCV (**www.visualcv.com**) that offers multimedia résumés.

As you assemble your portfolio, collect anything that shows your ability to perform, whether it's in school, on the job, or in other venues. However, you *must* check with

Collect samples of your work in a portfolio.

| TABLE 13.1 | Career Planning Resources |
| --- | --- |

| RESOURCE | URL |
| --- | --- |
| Career Rocketeer | www.careerrocketeer.com |
| The Creative Career | http://thecreativecareer.com |
| Brazen Careerist | www.brazencareerist.com |
| The Career Key Blog | http://careerkey.blogspot.com |
| RiseSmart | www.risesmart.com/blog |
| The Career Doctor Blog | www.careerdoctor.org/career-doctor-blog |

Ensure you have permission for portfolio contents.

employers before including any items that you created while you were an employee and check with clients before including any *work products* (anything you wrote, designed, programmed, and so on) they purchased from you. Many business documents contain confidential information that companies don't want distributed to outside audiences.

For each item you add to your portfolio, write a brief description that helps other people understand the meaning and significance of the project. Include such items as these:

- **Background.** Why did you undertake this project? Was it a school project, a work assignment, or something you did on your own initiative?
- **Project objectives.** Explain the project's goals, if relevant.
- **Collaborators.** If you worked with others, be sure to mention that.
- **Constraints.** Sometimes the most impressive thing about a project is the time or budget constraints under which it was created.
- **Outcomes.** If the project's goals were measurable, what was the result? For example, if you wrote a letter soliciting donations for a charitable cause, how much money did you raise?
- **Learning experience.** If appropriate, describe what you learned during the course of the project.

Remove anything that might be embarrassing on social networking sites.

Keep in mind that the portfolio itself is a communication project too, so be sure to apply everything you'll learn in this course about effective communication and good design. Also, if you have anything embarrassing on Facebook, Twitter, or any other social networking site, remove it immediately.

To get started, first check with the career centre at your college; many schools now offer e-portfolio systems for their students. (Some schools now require e-portfolios, so you may already be building one.) You can also find plenty of advice online; search for "e-portfolio," "student portfolio," or "professional portfolio."

## Building Your Personal Brand

Products and companies have brands that represent collections of certain attributes, such as the safety emphasis of Volvo cars or the performance emphasis of BMW. Similarly, when people who know you think about you, they have a particular set of qualities in mind based on your professionalism, your priorities, the various skills and attributes you have developed over the years, and how you do things. Perhaps without even being conscious of it, you have created a **personal brand** for yourself.

As you plan the next stage of your career, start managing your personal brand deliberately. Branding specialist Mohammed Al-Taee defines personal branding succinctly as "a way of clarifying and communicating what makes you different and unique."[10]

You can learn more about personal branding from the sources listed in Table 13.2. To get you started, here are the basics of a successful personal branding strategy:[11]

What's your story? Thinking about where you've been and where you want to go will help focus your job search.

- **Write the "story of you."** Simply put, where have you been in life, and where are you going? Whether you're about to begin your career or are already well into it, writing or updating your résumé is a great opportunity to step back and think about where you've been and where you'd like to go. Do you like the path you're on, or is it time for a change? Are you focused on a particular field, or do you need some time to explore?

  You might find it helpful to think about the "story of you": the things you are passionate about, your skills, your ability to help an organization reach its goals, the path you've been on so far, and the path you want to follow in the future (see Figure 13.1). Think in terms of an image or a theme you'd like to project. Are you academically gifted? An effective leader? A well-rounded professional with wide-ranging talents? A creative problem solver? A technical guru? Writing your story is a valuable planning exercise that helps you think about where you want to go and how to present yourself to target employers.

| TABLE 13.2 | Personal Branding Resources |
| --- | --- |

| RESOURCE | URL |
| --- | --- |
| Personal Branding Blog | www.personalbrandingblog.com |
| Mohammed Al-Taee | http://altaeeblog.com |
| Brand Yourself | http://blog.brand-yourself.com |
| Cube Rules | http://cuberules.com |
| Jibber Jobber | www.jibberjobber.com/blog |
| The Engaging Brand | http://theengagingbrand.typepad.com |
| Brand-Yourself | http://blog.brand-yourself.com |

- **Clarify your professional theme.** Volvos, BMWs, and Volkswagens can all get you from Point A to Point B in safety, comfort, and style—but each brand emphasizes some attributes more than others to create a specific image in the minds of potential

| FIGURE 13.1 | Writing the Story of You: A Private Document to Help You Clarify Your Thoughts |
| --- | --- |

**My Story**

**Where I Have Been**

- Honour student and all around big shot in high school (but discovered that college is full of big shots!)
- Have worked several part-time jobs; only thing that really appealed to me in any of them was making improvements, making things work better

*What experiences from your past give you insight into where you would like to go in the future?*

**Where I Am Now**

- Third year University; on track to graduate in 2016
- Enjoy designing creative solutions to challenging problems
- Not a high-end techie in an engineering sense, but I figure most things out eventually
- Not afraid to work hard, whatever it takes to get the job done
- I can tolerate some routine, as long as I have the opportunity to make improvements if needed
- Tend to lead quietly by example, rather than by visibly and vocally taking charge
- Knowing that I do good work is more important than getting approval from others
- I tend not to follow fads and crowds; sometimes I'm ahead of the curve, sometimes I'm behind the curve

*Where do you stand now in terms of your education and career, and what do you know about yourself?*

**Where I Want to Be**

- Get an advanced degree; not sure what subject area yet, though
- Haven't really settled on one industry or profession yet; working with systems of any kind is more appealing than any particular profession that I've learned about so far
- Develop my leadership and communication skills to become a more "obvious" leader
- Collaborate with others while still having the freedom to work independently (may be become an independent contractor or consultant at some point?)
- Have the opportunity to work internationally, at least for a few years
- I like the big bucks that corporate executives earn, but I don't want to live in the public eye like that or have to "play the game" to get ahead
- Believe I would be a good manager, but not sure I want to spend all my time just managing people
- Want to be known as an independent thinker and creative problem solver, as somebody who can analyse tough situations and figure out solutions that others might not consider
- Are there jobs where I could focus on troubleshooting, improving processes, or designing new systems?

*What would you like your future to be? What do you like and dislike? What would you like to explore? If you haven't figured everything out yet, that's fine—as long as you've started to think about the future.*

buyers. Similarly, you want to be seen as something more than just an accountant, a supervisor, a salesperson. What will your theme be? (What do you want to be known by?) Dependable hard worker? Strategist? Get-it-done tactician? Technical guru? Problem solver? Customer service specialist? Inspirational leader?

- **Network.** Major corporations spread the word about their brands with multimillion-dollar advertising campaigns. You can promote your brand for free or close to it. The key is networking (see pages later in this chapter). Build your brand by connecting with like-minded people, sharing information, demonstrating skills and knowledge, and helping others succeed.

- **Deliver on your brand's promise—every time, all the time.** When you deliver quality results time after time, your talents and your professionalism will speak for you.

# Finding the Ideal Opportunity in Today's Job Market

Finding and landing the ideal job can be a complex process, with lots of stress and frustration along the way. The good news is that it is all about communication, so the skills you're developing in this course will give you a competitive advantage. This section offers a general job search strategy with advice that applies to just about any career path you might want to pursue. Once you have analyzed your goals and what you have to offer, you'll need to begin by finding out where the job opportunities are, which industries are strong, which parts of the country are booming, and which specific job categories offer the best prospects for the future. From there you can investigate individual organizations, doing your best to learn as much about them as possible.

Stay abreast of business and financial news. Subscribe to a major newspaper (print or online) and scan the business pages every day. Watch television programs that focus on business. Consult the *National Occupational Classification* (Human Resources Development Canada, in print and online at **www5.hrsdc.gc.ca/NOC-CNP**). View forecasts about various job titles to develop ideas for a career. Check to see if your province has a Work Futures site. For example, WorkBC (**www.workbc.ca**) lists employment opportunities in the province.

## Researching Industries and Companies of Interest

Learning more about professions, industries, and individual companies is easy to do with the library and online resources available to you. Don't limit your research to easily available sources, however. Companies are likely to be impressed by creative research, such as interviewing their customers to learn more about how the firm does business. "Detailed research, including talking to our customers, is so rare it will almost guarantee you get hired," explains the recruiting manager at Alcon Laboratories.[12]

Table 13.3 lists some of the many websites where you can learn more about companies and find job openings.

To learn more about contemporary business topics, peruse some of these leading business periodicals and newspapers with significant business sections (in some cases, you may need to go through your library's online databases in order to access back issues):

- *The Globe & Mail*
- *Canadian Business*
- *Report on Business*
- *Business 2.0* (http://money.cnn.com/magazines/business2)
- *Fast Company* (www.fastcompany.com)
- *Fortune* (http://money.cnn.com/magazines/fortune)

In addition, thousands of bloggers, microbloggers, and podcasters offer news and commentary on the business world. For example, The Toronto Public Library Career

*Employers expect you to be familiar with important developments in their industries, so stay on top of business news.*

| TABLE 13.3 | Selected Job Search Websites |
|---|---|

| WEBSITE* | URL | HIGHLIGHTS |
|---|---|---|
| The Riley Guide | www.rileyguide.com | Vast collection of links to both general and specialized job sites for every career imaginable. Don't miss this one—it could save you hours of searching. |
| TwitJobSearch | www.twitjobsearch.com | A job search engine for Twitter; create an account and receive tweets about industry postings. |
| CollegeRecruiter.com | www.collegerecruiter.com | Focused on opportunities for graduates with less than three years of work experience. Some Canadian listings. |
| Monster | http://home.monster.ca | One of the most popular job sites with hundreds of thousands of openings, many from hard-to-find small companies; extensive collection of advice on the job search process. |
| CareerBuilder | www.careerbuilder.ca | One of the largest job boards; affiliated with more than 150 newspapers around the country. |
| Jobster | www.jobster.com | Uses social networking to link employers with job seekers. |
| Careers in the Federal Public Service | www.jobs.gc.ca | The official job search site for the Canadian government. |
| Eluta | www.eluta.ca | Searches company career pages and by postal codes. |
| Service Canada Job Bank | www.jobbank.gc.ca | Free job posting for employers; good service for entry-level and service jobs. |
| Net-Temps | www.net-temps.ca | Popular site for contractors and freelancers looking for short-term assignments. |
| Workopolis | www.workopolis.ca | Canada's largest job-related site; includes site for students. |
| Simply Hired and Indeed | www.simplyhired.ca www.indeed.ca | Specialized search engines that look for job postings on hundreds of websites worldwide; they find many postings that aren't listed on job board sites such as Monster. |
| Dice | www.dice.com | Good source for technology jobs. |

*Note: This list represents only a small fraction of the hundreds of job-posting sites and other resources available online; be sure to check with your college's career centre for the latest information.

& Job Search Help Blog (www.torontopubliclibrary.ca/job-help/) provides excellent links to employment search engines and job-posting sites. To identify some that you might find helpful, start with directories such as Technorati (http://technorati.com) for blogs or Podcast Alley (www.podcastalley.com; select the "Business" genre) for podcasts. Alltop (http://alltop.com) is another good resource for finding people who write about topics that interest you. In addition to learning more about professions and opportunities, this research will help you identify essential *keywords* currently in use in a particular field. You can also explore applications for smartphones such as LinkUp Canada, which brings search engines to your phone, or Jobfinder, which aggregates jobs from multiple job sites. Hire Android links together three major job search engines: LinkUp, Indeed, and Simply Hired.

## Translating Your General Potential into a Specific Solution for Each Employer

Customizing your résumé to each job opening is an important step in showing employers that you will be a good fit. From your initial contact all the way through the interviewing process, in fact, you will have opportunities to impress recruiters by explaining how your general potential translates to the specific needs of the position.

An essential task in your job search is presenting your skills and accomplishments in a way that is relevant to the employer's business challenges.

## Taking the Initiative to Find Opportunities

When it comes to finding the right opportunities for you, the easiest ways are not always the most productive ways. The major job boards such as Monster and classified services such as Craigslist might have thousands of openings, but thousands of job seekers are looking at and applying for these same openings. Moreover, posting job openings on these sites is often a company's last resort, after it has exhausted other possibilities.

Instead of searching through the same job openings as everyone else, take the initiative and go find opportunities. Identify the companies you want to work for and focus your efforts on them. Get in touch with their human resources departments (or individual managers if possible), describe what you can offer the company, and ask to be considered if any opportunities come up.[13] Your message might appear right when a company is busy looking for someone but hasn't yet advertised the opening to the outside world.

## Building Your Network

Start thinking like a networker now; your classmates could turn out to be some of your most important business contacts.

**Networking** is the process of making informal connections with mutually beneficial business contacts. Networking takes place wherever and whenever people talk: at industry functions, at social gatherings, at alumni reunions—and all over the internet, from LinkedIn to Facebook to Twitter. Networking is more essential than ever, because the vast majority of job openings are never advertised to the general public. To avoid the time and expense of sifting through thousands of applications and the risk of hiring complete strangers, most companies prefer to ask their employees for recommendations first.[14] The more people who know you, the better chance you have of being recommended for one of these hidden job openings.

Put your network in place before you need it.

Start building your network now, before you need it. Your classmates could end up being some of your most valuable contacts, if not right away then possibly later in your career. Then branch out by identifying people with similar interests in your target professions, industries, and companies. Read news sites, blogs, and other online sources. Follow industry leaders on Twitter. You can also follow individual executives at your target companies to learn about their interests and concerns.[15] Connect with people on LinkedIn and Facebook, particularly in groups dedicated to particular career interests. You can introduce yourself via private messages, as long as you are respectful of people and don't take up much of their time.[16] Participate in student business organizations, especially those with ties to professional organizations. Visit *trade shows* to learn about various industries and meet people who work in those industries.[17] Consider volunteering; you not only meet people but also demonstrate your ability to solve problems, manage projects, and lead others.

Remember that networking is about people helping each other, not just about other people helping you. Pay close attention to networking etiquette: try to learn something about the people you want to connect with, don't overwhelm others with too many messages or requests, be succinct in all your communication efforts, don't give out other people's names and contact information without their permission to do so, never email your résumé to complete strangers, and remember to say thank you every time someone helps you.[18]

Networking is a mutually beneficial activity, so look for opportunities to help others in some way.

To become a valued network member, you need to be able to help others in some way. You may not have any influential contacts yet, but because you're actively researching a number of industries and trends in your own job search, you probably have valuable information you can share via your social networks, blog, or Twitter account. Or you might simply be able to connect one person with another who can help. The more you network, the more valuable you become in your network—and the more valuable your network becomes to you.

Finally, be aware that your online network reflects on who you are in the eyes of potential employers, so exercise some judgment in making connections. Also, some employers are beginning to contact people in a candidate's network for background information, even if the candidate doesn't list those people as references.[19]

## Seeking Career Counselling

Your college's career centre probably offers a wide variety of services, including individual counselling, job fairs, on-campus interviews, and job listings. Counsellors can give you advice on career planning and provide workshops on job search techniques, résumé preparation, job readiness training, interview techniques, self-marketing, and more.[20] You can also find career planning advice online. Many of the websites listed in Table 13.1 offer articles and online tests to help you choose a career path, identify essential skills, and prepare to enter the job market.

*Don't overlook the many resources available through your college's career centre.*

## Avoiding Mistakes

While you're making all these positive moves to show employers you will be a quality hire, take care to avoid the simple blunders that can torpedo a job search—not catching mistakes in your résumé, misspelling the name of a manager you're writing to, showing up late for an interview, tweeting something unprofessional, failing to complete application forms correctly, asking for information that you can easily find yourself on a company's website, or making any other error that could flag you as someone who is careless or disrespectful. Assume that every employer will conduct an online search on you. Busy recruiters will seize on these errors as a way to narrow the list of candidates they need to spend time on, so don't give them a reason to toss out your résumé.

*Don't let a silly mistake knock you out of contention for a great job.*

**REAL-TIME UPDATES**

**Learn More by Visiting This Website**

**Follow these people to a new career**

Alison Doyle maintains a great list of career experts to follow on Twitter. Go to http://real-timeupdates.com/bce6 and click on Learn More. If you are using MyBCommLab, you can access Real-Time Updates within Business Communication Resources.

# Planning Your Résumé

**LEARNING OBJECTIVE 2**
**Explain the process of planning your résumé, including how to choose the best résumé organization.**

Although you will create many messages during your career search, your résumé will be the most important document in this process. You will be able to use it directly in many instances, adapt it to a variety of uses such as an e-portfolio or a social media résumé, and reuse pieces of it in social networking profiles and online application forms.

Developing a résumé is one of those projects that really benefits from multiple planning, writing, and completing sessions spread out over several days or weeks. You are trying to summarize a complex subject (yourself!) and present a compelling story to complete strangers in a brief document. Follow the three-step writing process (see Figure 13.2) and give yourself plenty of time.

Before you dive into your résumé, be aware that you will find a wide range of opinions about résumés, regarding everything from appropriate length, content, design, distribution methods, and acceptable degrees of creativity to whether it even makes sense to write a traditional résumé in this age of online applications. You may run across examples of effective résumés that were produced as infographics, interactive videos, simulated search engine results, puzzles, games, or graphic novels—you name it, somebody has probably tried it.

When you hear conflicting advice or see trendy concepts that you might be tempted to try, remember the most important question in business communication: What is the most effective way to adapt your message to the individual needs of each member of your audience? An approach that is wildly successful with one company or in one industry could be a complete disaster in another industry. A design that says "clever and creative" to one recruiter can shout "amateurish gimmick!" to another. Your infographic résumé might look awesome but get rejected by an automated résumé scanner that can't make sense of it. Your best approach will be to try to think the way they think—then apply the principles of effective communication you are learning in this course.

*You will see lots of ideas and even some conflicting advice about résumés; use what you know about effective business communication to decide what is right for your résumé.*

---

## FIGURE 13.2 Three-Step Writing Process for Résumés

### ① Plan

**Analyze the Situation**

Recognize that the purpose of your résumé is to get an interview, not to get a job.

**Gather Information**

Research target industries and companies so that you know what they're looking for in new hires; learn about various jobs and what to expect; learn about the hiring manager, if possible.

**Select the Right Medium**

Start with a traditional paper résumé and develop scannable, electronic plain-text, PDF, and online versions, as needed. Consider using PowerPoint and video for your e-portfolio.

**Organize the Information**

Choose an organizational model that highlights your strengths and downplays your shortcomings; use the chronological approach unless you have a strong reason not to.

### ② Write

**Adapt to Your Audience**

Plan your wording carefully so that you can catch a recruiter's eye within seconds; translate your education and experience into attributes that target what employers find valuable.

**Compose the Message**

Write clearly and succinctly, using active, powerful language that is appropriate to the industries and companies you're targeting; use a professional tone in all communications, including email.

### ③ Complete

**Revise the Message**

Evaluate content and review readability, and then edit and rewrite for conciseness and clarity.

**Produce the Message**

Use effective design elements and suitable layout for a clean, professional appearance; seamlessly combine text and graphical elements. When printing, use quality paper and a good printer.

**Proofread the Message**

Review for errors in layout, spelling, and mechanics; mistakes can cost you interview opportunities.

**Distribute the Message**

Deliver your résumé, following the specific instructions of each employer or job board website.

## Analyzing Your Purpose and Audience

*Once you view your résumé as a persuasive business message, it's easier to decide what should and shouldn't be in it.*

A **résumé** is a structured, written summary of a person's education, employment background, and job qualifications. Before you begin writing a résumé, make sure you understand its true function—as a brief, persuasive business message intended to stimulate an employer's interest in meeting you and learning more about you (see Table 13.4). In other words, the purpose of a résumé is not to get you a job but rather to get you an interview.[21]

---

## TABLE 13.4 Fallacies and Facts About Résumés

| FALLACY | FACT |
|---|---|
| The purpose of a résumé is to list all your skills and abilities. | The purpose of a résumé is to kindle employer interest and generate an interview. |
| A good résumé will get you the job you want. | All a résumé can do is get you in the door. |
| Your résumé will always be read carefully and thoroughly. | In most cases, your résumé needs to make a positive impression within 30 or 45 seconds; only then will someone read it in detail. Moreover, it will likely be screened by a computer looking for keywords first, and if it doesn't contain the right keywords, a human being may never see it. |
| The more good information you present about yourself in your résumé, the better, so stuff your résumé with every positive detail you can think of. | Recruiters don't need that much information about you at the initial screening stage, and they probably won't read it. |
| If you want a really good résumé, have it prepared by a résumé service. | You can certainly seek out formal or informal help, but if you have succeeded in this course, you have the skills needed to prepare an effective résumé yourself. |

As you conduct your research on various professions, industries, companies, and individual managers, you will have a better perspective on your target readers and their information needs. Learn as much as you can about the individuals who may be reading your résumé. Many professionals and managers are bloggers, Twitter users, and LinkedIn members, for example, so you can learn more about them online even if you've never met them. Any bit of information can help you craft a more effective message.

By the way, if employers ask to see your "CV," they're referring to your *curriculum vitae*, the term used instead of *résumé* in academic professions and in many countries outside Canada. Résumés and CVs are essentially the same, although CVs can be much more detailed. If you need to adapt a Canadian-style résumé to CV format, or vice versa, career expert Alison Doyle offers advice on her website, **www.alisondoyle.com**.

Thanks to Twitter, LinkedIn, and other social media, you can often learn valuable details about individual managers in your target employers.

## Gathering Pertinent Information

If you haven't been building an employment portfolio thus far, you may need to do some research on yourself at this point. Gather all the pertinent personal history you can think of, including all the specific dates, duties, and accomplishments from any previous jobs you've held, as well as educational experiences—formal degrees, skills certificates, academic awards, or scholarships. Also, gather information about school or volunteer activities that might be relevant to your job search, including offices you have held in any club or professional organization, presentations given, and online or print publications. You probably won't use every piece of information you come up with, but you'll want to have it at your fingertips before you begin composing your résumé.

## Selecting the Best Medium

You should expect to produce your résumé in several media and formats. "Producing Your Résumé" on page 360 explores the various options.

## Organizing Your Résumé Around Your Strengths

Although you will see a number of ways to organize a résumé, most are some variation of chronological, functional, or a combination of the two. The right choice depends on your background and your goals.

**THE CHRONOLOGICAL RÉSUMÉ** In a **chronological résumé**, the work experience section dominates and is placed immediately after your contact information and introductory statement (see Figure 13.4). The chronological approach is the most common way to organize a résumé, and many employers prefer this format because it presents your professional history in a clear, easy-to-follow arrangement.[22] If you're just graduating from college and have limited professional experience, you can vary this chronological approach by putting your educational qualifications before your experience.

The chronological résumé is the most common approach, but it might not be right for you at this stage in your career.

Develop your work experience section by listing your jobs in **reverse chronological order, beginning with the most recent position**. For each job, start by listing your official job title, the employer's name and location, and the dates you held the position (write "to present" if you are still in your most recent position). Next, in a short block of text, ideally in a list, highlight your accomplishments in a way that is relevant to your readers. This may require "translating" the terminology used in a particular industry or profession into terms that are more meaningful to your target readers. If the general responsibilities of the position are not obvious from the job title, provide a little background to help readers understand what you did. See Figures 13.3 and 13.4 for examples of ineffective and effective approaches.

**FIGURE 13.3   Ineffective Chronological Résumé**

Fails to combine accounting expertise with international experience in the minds of employers by stating it in an overall objective

Uses bulleted lists ineffectively:

- Lacks parallelism

- Lacks logical organization

- Often highlights wrong information

- Uses the word "I" too often

- Uses too many unnecessary words (such as "I was responsible for")

- Fails to highlight important skills by breaking them out into a separate list

Includes too many words in educational information and lacks parallelism

---

**Lareine Chan**

5687 Crosswoods Drive, Richmond, BC  V5S 2T1
Home: (604) 273-0086    Office: (604) 273-6624

I have been staff accountant/financial analyst at Inter-Asian Imports in Vancouver, B.C., from March 2012 to present.

- I have negotiated with major suppliers.

- I speak both Cantonese and Mandarin fluently, and I was recently encouraged to implement an electronic funds transfer for vendor disbursements.

- In my current position, I am responsible for preparing accounting reports.

- I have audited financial transactions.

- I have also been involved in the design of a computerized model to adjust accounts for fluctuations in currency exchange rates.

- I am skilled in the use of Excel, Access, HTML, and Visual Basic.

Was staff accountant with Monsanto Agricultural Chemicals in Shanghai, China (October 2008 to March 2012).

- While with Monsanto in Shanghai, I was responsible for budgeting and billing.

- I was responsible for credit-processing functions.

- I was also responsible for auditing the travel and entertainment expenses for the sales department.

- I launched an online computer system to automate all accounting functions.

- Also during this time, I was able to travel extensively in Asia.

I have my Master's of Business Administration with emphasis on international business, which I earned while attending University of British Columbia in Vancouver, B.C., from 2006 to 2008.

Bachelor of Business Administration (2001–2006), earned while attending Memorial University in St. John's, Newfoundland and Labrador.

---

Organizes information chronologically but hides that fact with awkward format

Fails to draw reader's attention to important points

- Fails to provide the sort of specific information on duties and accomplishments that catches an employer's eye

- Fails to use concise, active language consistently to describe duties

Lacks informative headings throughout, making it difficult for potential employers to find work-related, educational, or skills information easily

---

The functional résumé is often considered by people with limited or spotty employment history, but many employers are suspicious of this format.

A combination résumé is a hybrid of the chronological and functional résumés.

If you don't have a lot of work history to show, consider a combination résumé to highlight your skills while still providing a chronological history of your employment.

**THE FUNCTIONAL RÉSUMÉ**   A **functional résumé**, sometimes called a *skills résumé*, emphasizes your skills and capabilities, identifying employers and academic experience in subordinate sections. This arrangement stresses individual areas of competence rather than job history. The functional approach also has three advantages: without having to read through job descriptions, employers can see what you can do for them, you can emphasize earlier job experience, and you can de-emphasize any lengthy unemployment or lack of career progress. However, you should be aware that because the functional résumé can obscure your work history, many employment professionals are suspicious of it.[23] If you don't believe the chronological format will work for you, consider the combination résumé instead.

**THE COMBINATION RÉSUMÉ**   A **combination résumé** meshes the skills focus of the functional format with the job history focus of the chronological format (see Figure 13.5). The chief advantage of this format is that it allows you to focus attention on your

## FIGURE 13.4 Effective Chronological Résumé

Combines accounting expertise with international experience in the minds of employers by stating it in a summary of qualifications →

Organizes information chronologically and emphasizes that organization with format →

Makes each description concise, easy to read, and informative:

• Avoids the word "I" throughout

• Uses no unnecessary words

**LAREINE R. CHAN**
5687 Crosswoods Drive
Richmond, BC  V5S 2T1
lchan@telus.net

Home: (604) 273-0086                                                                 @LaraineChan

### SUMMARY OF QUALIFICATIONS

• Master of Business Administration, International Business
• Seven years of experience in accounting for international trade
• Fluent in Mandarin, Cantonese, and skilled in use of accounting software

### EXPERIENCE

**Financial Analyst,** INTER-ASIAN IMPORTS (Vancouver, BC)
March 2012–present

• Preparing accounting reports for wholesale giftware importer ($15 million annual sales)
• Auditing financial transactions with suppliers in 12 Asian countries
• Creating a computerized model to adjust accounts for fluctuations in currency exchange rates
• Negotiating joint-venture agreements with major suppliers in China and Japan
• Implementing electronic funds transfer for vendor disbursements, improving cash flow, and eliminating payables clerk position

**Staff Accountant,** Monsanto Agricultural Chemicals (Shanghai, China)
October 2008–March 2012

• Handled budgeting, billing, and credit-processing functions for the Shanghai branch of an agricultural chemicals manufacturer
• Audited travel and entertainment expenses for the sales department
• Assisted in launching an online system to automate all accounting functions

Draws reader's attention to important points:

• Provides the sort of specific information on duties and accomplishments that catches an employer's eye

• Highlights duties and work achievements in bulleted lists

• Uses active language to describe duties

### EDUCATION

**Master of Business Administration,** International Business, University of British Columbia, Vancouver, British Columbia, 2006–2008

**Bachelor of Business Administration,** Accounting, Memorial University, St. John's, Newfoundland and Labrador, 2001–2006

Highlights important skills by breaking them out into a list in a separate section →

### SKILLS AND INTERESTS

Fluent in Cantonese and Mandarin            CPR, Industrial First Aid, Level C
Travelled extensively in Asia               Reading, Tennis, Skiing
Excel, Access, HTML, Visual Basic           Volunteer, Big Sisters of Canada

← Includes informative headings throughout, making it easy for potential employers to find work-related, educational, or skills information

### REFERENCES

Meghan McCandless
Manager
Accounting Division
Inter-Asian Imports
4312 Pender Street
Vancouver, BC  V5J 2T4
604 669 1276
mmccandless@interasian.com

Dr. Anna Wilson
Professor
International Business
University of British Columbia
1200 Westbrook Mall
Vancouver, BC  V6T 1B4
604 222 8943
awilson@interchange.ubc.ca

| FIGURE 13.5 | Combination Résumé |

**Erica Vorkamp**

993 Church Street, Mission, BC  V5R 1P8
(604) 885-2153
evor@shaw.ca

**OBJECTIVE**  To obtain a position as a special events coordinator

**SKILLS AND CAPABILITIES**

- Plan and coordinate large-scale public events
- Develop community support for concerts, festivals, and the arts
- Manage publicity for major events
- Coordinate activities of diverse community groups
- Establish and maintain financial controls for public events
- Negotiate contracts with performers, carpenters, electricians, and suppliers

**SPECIAL EVENT EXPERIENCE**

- Arranged 2015's week-long Arts and Entertainment Festival for the Public Library, involving performances by 25 musicians, dancers, actors, magicians, and artists

- Coordinated a 2014 Parent Association Carnival, an all-day festival with game booths, live bands, contests, and food service that raised $7600 for a local school

- Organized the 2013 Western Convention for 800 members of the Canadian Figure Skating Officials, which extended over a three-day period and required arrangements for hotels, meals, speakers, and special tours

- Served as chairperson for the 2012 to 2014 Children's Helpline Show, a luncheon for 450 that raised $5000–$6700 for children at risk

**EDUCATION**

- **Diploma, Marketing Management,** British Columbia Institute of Technology (Burnaby, BC), 2013

**EMPLOYMENT HISTORY**

- **ScotiaBank** (Langley, BC), 2013–2016, Operations Processor; tracked cheques with a lost/stolen status, contacted customers by phone, registered payment amounts, verified receipt reports, researched cheque authenticity, managed orientation program for entry-level trainees

- **BCIT Marketing Department** (Burnaby, BC), 2011–2013, part-time Administrative Assistant

**ACTIVITIES & INTERESTS**

- Volunteer, Mission Public Library (two years)—Prepared podcast readings for CNIB
- Slow pitch softball—player on community team (three years)
- Fitness and yoga enthusiast

**AWARDS & ACHIEVEMENTS**

- BCIT Marketing Department Award for Best Proposal (2013)
- Second in BC Provincial Figure Skating Championships (2010)
- Employee of the Month, ScotiaBank (May 2015)

*Annotations (left margin):* Relates all capabilities and experience to the specific job objective, giving a selective picture of the candidate's abilities

*Annotation (left margin):* Includes work history (even though it has little bearing on job target) because Vorkamp believes recruiters want to see evidence that she's held a paying position

*Annotation (right margin):* Includes event attendance statistics and fundraising results to quantify accomplishments

capabilities when you don't have a long or steady employment history, without raising concerns that you might be hiding something about your past.

When Erica Vorkamp developed her résumé, she chose not to use a chronological pattern, which would focus attention on her lack of recent work experience. As Figure 13.5 shows, she used a combination approach to emphasize her abilities, skills, and accomplishments while also including a complete job history.

As you look at a number of sample résumés, you'll probably notice many variations on the three basic formats presented here. Study these other options in light of the effective communication principles you've learned in this course and the unique circumstances of your job search. If you find one that seems like the best fit for your unique situation, by all means use it.

## Addressing Areas of Concern

Many people have gaps in their careers or other issues that could be a concern for employers. Here are some common issues and suggestions for handling them in a résumé:[24]

Frequent job changes and gaps in your work history are two of the more common issues that employers may perceive as weaknesses.

- **Frequent job changes.** If you've had a number of short-term jobs of a similar type, such as independent contracting and temporary assignments, try to group them under a single heading. Also, if past job positions were eliminated as a result of layoffs or mergers, find a subtle way to convey that information (if not in your résumé, then in your cover letter). Reasonable employers understand that many professionals have been forced to job hop by circumstances beyond their control.
- **Gaps in work history.** Mention relevant experience and education you gained during employment gaps, such as volunteer or community work.
- **Inexperience.** Mention related volunteer work and membership in professional groups. List relevant course work and internships.
- **Overqualification.** Tone down your résumé, focusing exclusively on the experience and skills that relate to the position.
- **Long-term employment with one company.** Itemize each position held at the firm to show growth within the organization and increasing responsibilities along the way.
- **Job termination for cause.** Be honest with interviewers and address their concerns with proof, such as recommendations and examples of completed projects.

# Writing Your Résumé

**LEARNING OBJECTIVE ③**
Describe the tasks involved in writing your résumé and list the sections to consider including in your résumé.

With the necessary information and a good plan in hand, you're ready to begin writing. If you feel uncomfortable writing about yourself, you're not alone. Many people, even accomplished writers, can find it difficult to write their own résumés. If you get stuck, imagine you are somebody else, writing a résumé for this person called you. By "being your own client" in this sense, you might find the words and idea flow more easily. You can also find a classmate or friend who is writing a résumé and swap projects for a while. Working on each other's résumés might speed up the process for both of you.

## Keeping Your Résumé Honest

Estimates vary, but one comprehensive study uncovered lies about work history in more than 40 percent of the résumés tested.[25] And dishonest applicants are getting bolder all the time—going so far as to buy fake diplomas online, pay a computer hacker to insert their names into prestigious universities' graduation records, and sign up for services that offer phony employment verification.[26]

Applicants with integrity know they don't need to stoop to lying. If you are tempted to stretch the truth, bear in mind that professional recruiters have seen every trick in the book, and frustrated employers are working aggressively to uncover the truth. Nearly all employers do some form of background checking, from contacting references and verifying employment to checking criminal records and sending résumés through verification services.[27] Employers are also beginning to craft certain interview questions specifically to uncover dishonest résumé entries.[28]

**REAL-TIME UPDATES**

**Learn More by Watching This Video**

**Learn to use LinkedIn's résumé builder**

See how to build and customize a résumé on Linked In and then use it on other social networking sites. Go to http://realtimeupdates.com/bce6 and click on Learn More. If you are using MyBCommLab, you can access Real-Time Updates within Business Communication Resources.

Résumé fraud has reached epidemic proportions, but employers are fighting back with more rigorous screening techniques.

More than 90 percent of companies that find lies on résumés refuse to hire the offending applicants, even if that means withdrawing formal job offers.[29] And if you do sneak past these filters and get hired, you'll probably be exposed on the job when you can't live up to your own résumé. Given the networked nature of today's job market, lying on a résumé could haunt you for years—and you could be forced to keep lying throughout your career to hide the original misrepresentations on your résumé.[30]

## Adapting Your Résumé to Your Audience

Translate your past accomplishments into a compelling picture of what you can do for employers in the future.

The importance of adapting your résumé to your target readers' needs and interests cannot be overstated. In a competitive job market, the more you look like a good fit, the better your chances will be of securing interviews. Address your readers' business concerns by showing how your capabilities meet the demands and expectations of the position and the organization as a whole.

Adapting to your readers can mean customizing your résumé, sometimes for each job opening. However, the effort can pay off with more interviewing opportunities. Use what you've learned about your target readers to express your experience in the terminology of the hiring organization. For example, if you are applying for business positions after military experience, "translate" your experience into the language of your civilian employers.

## Composing Your Résumé

Draft your résumé using short, crisp phrases built around strong verbs and nouns.

Write your résumé using a simple and direct style. Use short, crisp phrases instead of whole sentences and focus on what your reader needs to know. Avoid using the word *I*, which can sound both self-involved and repetitive by the time you outline all your skills and accomplishments. Instead, start your phrases with strong action verbs such as these:[31]

| | | | | |
|---|---|---|---|---|
| accomplished | coordinated | initiated | participated | set up |
| achieved | created | installed | performed | simplified |
| administered | demonstrated | introduced | planned | sparked |
| approved | developed | investigated | presented | streamlined |
| arranged | directed | launched | proposed | strengthened |
| assisted | established | maintained | raised | succeeded |
| assumed | explored | managed | recommended | supervised |
| budgeted | forecasted | motivated | reduced | systematized |
| chaired | generated | negotiated | reorganized | targeted |
| changed | identified | operated | resolved | trained |
| compiled | implemented | organized | saved | transformed |
| completed | improved | oversaw | served | upgraded |

REAL-TIME UPDATES

**Learn More by Reading This Infographic**

**See how an applicant tracking system handles your résumé**

Once you see how the system works, you'll understand why it's so crucial to customize the wording on your résumé for every job opening. Go to http://real-timeupdates.com/bce6 and click on Learn More. If you are using MyBCommLab, you can access Real-Time Updates within Business Communication Resources.

For instance, you might say, "Created a campus organization for students interested in entrepreneurship" or "Managed a fast-food restaurant and four employees." Whenever you can, quantify the results. Don't just say you're a team player or detail oriented—show you are by offering concrete proof.[32] Here are some examples of phrasing accomplishments using active statements that show results:

| Instead of | Write Active Statements that Show Results |
|---|---|
| Responsible for developing a new filing system | Developed a new filing system that reduced paperwork by 50 percent |
| I was in charge of customer complaints and all ordering problems | Handled all customer complaints and resolved product order discrepancies |
| I won a trip to Europe for opening the most new customer accounts in my department | Generated the highest number of new customer accounts in my department |
| Member of special campus task force to resolve student problems with existing cafeteria assignments | Assisted in implementing new campus dining program that balances student wishes with cafeteria capacity |

Providing specific supporting evidence is vital, but make sure you don't go overboard with small details.[33]

In addition to clear writing with specific examples, the particular words and phrases you use throughout your résumé are critically important. The majority of résumés are now subjected to *keyword searches* in an applicant tracking system or other database, in which a recruiter searches for résumés most likely to match the requirements of a particular job. Résumés that don't match the requirements closely may never be seen by a human reader, so it is essential to use the words and phrases that a recruiter is most likely to search on. (Although most experts used to advise including a separate *keyword summary* as a standalone list, the trend nowadays is to incorporate your keywords into your introductory statement and other sections of your résumé.[34])

Identifying these keywords requires some research, but you can uncover many of them while you are researching various industries and companies. Study job descriptions carefully to understand your target audience's needs. In contrast to the action verbs that catch a human reader's attention, keywords that catch a computer's attention are usually nouns that describe the specific skills, attributes, and experiences an employer is looking for in a candidate. Keywords can include the business and technical terms associated with a specific profession, industry-specific jargon, names or types of products or systems used in a profession, job titles, and university or college degrees and diplomas.[35] For example, here are some sample keywords you might include if you were in accounting:

Accountant, Receivables, Payables, Inventory, Cash Flow, Financial Analysis, Payroll Experience, Reconciliations, Corporate Taxes, Activity-Based Budgeting, Problem-Solving, Computer Skills, Excel, Access, Quick Books, Bachelor's Degree in Accounting, CPA, Articulate, Teamwork, Flexible, Willing to Travel, Computer Skills, Networks, HTML, HMML, Simply Accounting

**NAME AND CONTACT INFORMATION**   Your name and contact information constitute the heading of your résumé, so include the following:

- Name
- Physical address (both permanent and temporary, if you're likely to move during the job search process; however, if you're posting a résumé in an unsecured location online, leave off your physical address for security purposes)
- Email address
- Phone number(s)
- The URL of your personal webpage, e-portfolio, or social media résumé (if you have one)
- Your Twitter handle

Include relevant *keywords* in your introductory statement, work history, and education sections.

Be sure to provide complete and accurate contact information; mistakes in this section of the résumé are surprisingly common.

If the only email address you have is through your current employer, get a free personal email address from one of the many services that offer them. Using company resources for a job search is not fair to your current employer, and it sends a bad signal to potential employers. Also, if your personal email address is anything like **precious .princess@something.com** or **PsychoDawg@something.com**, get a new email address for your business correspondence.

You can choose to open with a career objective or a qualifications summary.

Use a summary of qualifications instead of an objective if you have several key qualifications to highlight.

**INTRODUCTORY STATEMENT** Of all the parts of a résumé, the brief introductory statement that follows your name and contact information probably generates the most disagreement. You can put one of three things here:[36] You can choose to open with a career objective, a qualifications summary, or a career summary. Whichever option you choose, make sure it includes many of the essential keywords you identified in your research—and adapt these words and phrases to each job opportunity as needed.

Career Objective A career objective identifies either a specific job you want to land or a general career track you would like to pursue. Some experts advise against including a career objective because it can categorize you so narrowly that you miss out on interesting opportunities, and it is essentially about fulfilling your desires, not about meeting the employer's needs. In the past, most résumés included a career objective, but in recent years more job seekers are using a qualifications summary. However, if you have little or no work experience in your target profession, a career objective might be your best option. If you do opt for an objective, word it in a way that relates your qualifications to employer needs (see Figure 13.5).

**REAL-TIME UPDATES**

**Learn More by Visiting This Website**

**Find the keywords that will light up your résumé**

This list of tips and tools will help you find the right keywords to customize your résumé for every opportunity. Go to **http:// real-timeupdates.com/bce6** and click on Learn More. If you are using MyBCommLab, you can access Real-Time Updates within Business Communication Resources.

Summary of Qualifications Instead of stating your objective, you might summarize your qualifications in a brief statement that highlights your strongest points, particularly if you have had a good deal of varied experience. Use a short, simple phrase:

Summary of qualifications: Ten years of experience in commission selling with record of generating new customer leads through social media and community leadership positions

Or, you could put a heading at the beginning of your résumé, "Summary of Qualifications," and under it list three or four points summarizing the main reasons that the company should hire you. You may want to add together the months of experience you have had in short, part-time jobs to get a total and express how that experience is transferable to the professional environment you are entering. For example, if you had a number of part-time jobs in restaurants and retail, each lasting several months, you might say "three years of experience in hospitality and retail" and highlight it in the summary as follows:

## SUMMARY OF QUALIFICATIONS

- Bachelor of Commerce, University of British Columbia
- Three years of experience in customer service in retail and hospitality
- Bilingual (French/English)
- Skilled in office and accounting software

The career objective or summary may be the only section read fully by the employer, so if you include either one, make it strong, concise, and convincing. Make sure it includes many of the essential keywords you identified in your research.

In Figure 13.6, Charlene Tang has used a "Highlights of Qualifications" section in her résumé to emphasize the combination of her education and experience. Since she is an applicant with both post-secondary education and several years of job experience, she combines these key qualifications in the opening segment. In addition, since Charlene immigrated to Canada recently, she wants to show she has improved her English through English language training and through studying business once in Canada. These qualifications are less significant than her professional designation, but they show she has made the transition to work culture in Canada. She also chose an English language instructor for her reference to show that her language skills are strong.

Career Summary   A career summary offers a brief recap of your career with the goal of presenting increasing levels of responsibility and performance. A career summary can be particularly useful for managers who have demonstrated the ability to manage increasingly larger and more complicated business operations—a key consideration when companies look to hire upper-level executives.

**EDUCATION**   If you're still in school, education is probably your strongest selling point, so present your educational background in depth, choosing facts that match the position you are seeking. Give this section a heading such as "Education" or "Professional Training." Then, starting with the school you most recently attended, list the name and location of each one, the term of your enrolment (in months and years), your major and minor fields of study, significant skills and abilities you've developed in your course work, and the degrees, diplomas, or certificates you've earned. If you're working on an uncompleted degree or diploma, include in parentheses the expected date of completion. Showcase your qualifications by listing skills courses that have directly equipped you for the job you are seeking, and indicate any scholarships, awards, or academic honours you've received.

> If education is your strongest selling point, discuss it thoroughly and highlight it visually.

The education section also includes off-campus training sponsored by business or government. Include any relevant seminars or workshops you've attended, as well as the certificates or other documents you've received. Whether you list your grades depends on the job you want and the quality of your grades. If you choose to show a grade-point average, be sure to mention the scale, especially if a five-point scale is used instead of a four-point scale.

Education is usually given less emphasis in a résumé after you've worked in your chosen field for a year or more. If work experience is your strongest qualification, save the section on education for later in the résumé and provide less detail.

In Figure 13.7, Alex Warren's résumé devotes most of the space to education and related activities since Alex is just entering the workforce and does not have a lot of work experience. If you must rely mostly on your education at this stage in your job-hunting career, don't worry. Young workers have other advantages for employers, often bringing enthusiasm and energy into the workplace. Notice that Alex conveys skills from his past jobs that are transferable into an accounting job. He also keeps the main elements of his résumé to one page, suitable for a young applicant.

**WORK EXPERIENCE, SKILLS, AND ACCOMPLISHMENTS**   Like the education section, the work-experience section focuses on your overall theme. Tailor your description to highlight the relationship between your previous responsibilities and your target field. Call attention to skills you've developed and your progression from jobs of lesser to greater responsibility.

> In the work experience section, include
> - Name and location of employer
> - What the organization does (if not clear from its name)
> - Your job title
> - How long you worked there
> - Your duties and responsibilities

When describing your work experience, list your jobs in reverse chronological order, with the current or last one first. Include any part-time, summer, or intern positions, even if unrelated to your current career objective. Employers will see that you have the ability to get and hold a job—an important qualification in itself. If you have worked your way through school, say so. Employers interpret this behaviour as a sign of character.

Each listing includes the name and location of the employer. If readers are unlikely to recognize the organization, briefly describe what it does. When you want to keep the name of your current employer confidential, identify the firm by industry only ("a large

**FIGURE 13.6** Résumé of Charlene Tang

# Charlene Tang

#412, 692 High Street
Sherbrooke, QC  J1H 5N1
819-561-6740
chartang@gmail.com

## HIGHLIGHTS OF QUALIFICATIONS

- Ten years' experience in office administration, including one year in leasing
- Diploma in Business Administration plus Master of Economics
- Computer skills in MS Office and Simply Accounting
- Languages include Mandarin and basic French

## WORK EXPERIENCE

**Lease Administrator/Sales Coordinator**                          2015–2016
Atticus Financial Group, Sherbrooke, QC
- Prepare quotes and contracts
- Process and submit credit applications
- Follow up with customers and vendors via phone, fax, and email
- Report to management on application/funding status

**Office Administrator**                                          2001–2011
Tianjin Tax Bureau, Tianjin, China
- Managed and coordinated a high volume of financial documents
- Assigned work schedules and maintained department records
- Liaised with budgeting, accounting, and collections departments

## EDUCATION

**Diploma of Technology** (Business Administration)               2014–2015
British Columbia Institute of Technology, Burnaby, BC. Graduated with Honours

- Accounting                          - Microsoft Applications
- Business Law                        - Business Communication

**English Language College Preparation Program**                 2012–2014
Vancouver Community College, Vancouver, BC

**Master of Economics**                                          2003–2005

**Bachelor of Economics**                                        1997–2001
Tianjin Finance & Economics University, Tianjin, China

## ACTIVITIES

Volunteering
- French Cultural Centre, Vancouver                              2013–2015
- Tutor in Economics, Burnaby                                    2014–2015
- *Run for the Cure*, Vancouver & Sherbrooke                     2014–2015

Jogging, reading, and watching movies with friends

## REFERENCES

Gretchen Quiring                          Rob Svetic
Communication Instructor                  Accounts Manager
B.C. Institute of Technology              Atticus Financial
3700 Willingdon Avenue                    823 Main Street
Burnaby, BC V5G 5H2                       Sherbrooke, QC
G.Quiring@bcit.ca                         Rob.Svetic@atticus.com
(604) 434-5734                            (819) 689-4319

**FIGURE 13.7** Résumé of a Young Applicant

## Alex Warren

952 Oxford Street
Winnipeg, MB R3H 0S9

(204) 737-2954
alex_warren@gmail.com

### EDUCATION

Completed first year of **Accounting Diploma, Red River College,** Winnipeg, Manitoba, September 2015–present.

Skills include
- Journalizing accounting entries, accounts receivable and payable
- Preparing financial statements and bank reconciliations
- Producing end-of-period reports and statements
- Using Word, Excel, Simply Accounting, Quick Books, and PowerPoint

Graduated, Kelvin Secondary School, Winnipeg, Manitoba, June 2015

### WORK EXPERIENCE

**Server, Salisbury House Restaurant,** Winnipeg, Weekends
June 2013–present
- Serve up to 500 customers per shift accurately and efficiently and support others on work team
- Handle cash of approximately $5000 per shift

**Cleaner, Manitoba Historical Society,** Winnipeg, Summers
2013–2014
- Cleaned museum five evenings per week
- Took care with valuable exhibits and worked with no supervision

### SKILLS AND ACTIVITIES

- Organized, disciplined, hardworking
- Skilled in accounting software and spreadsheets
- Active in hockey and cross-country running

### ACCOMPLISHMENTS

- Kelvin School Physical Education Award 2014
- Most Valuable Player—Western Canada High School Hockey Championships 2014
- Canadian Hockey Referee Certification Level 3, 2013

### VOLUNTEER EXPERIENCE

- Hockey Coach for Grade 5 & 6 team at Grosvenor Elementary, 2013–2014
- Hockey Referee, River Heights Hockey Club, 2014–2015
- *River Run* water booth assistant, 2011–2014

### REFERENCES

Johanna Vik, Manager
Salisbury House
Winnipeg, MB
(204) 488-1630
jvik@gmail.com

Mr. Paul Black, Counsellor
Kelvin Secondary School
Winnipeg, MB
(204) 488-7815
pblack@sympatico.ca

video game developer") or use the name but request confidentiality in the application letter or in an underlined note ("Résumé submitted in confidence") at the top or bottom of the résumé. If an organization's name or location has since changed, state the current name and location and then "formerly. . . ."

Before each job listing, state your functional title, such as "salesperson." If you were a dishwasher, say so. Don't try to make your role seem more important by glamorizing your job title, functions, or achievements. Employers are checking on candidates' backgrounds more than they used to, so inaccuracies are likely to be exposed sooner or later. Also state how long you worked on each job, from month/year to month/year. Use the phrase "to present" to denote current employment. If a job was part time, say so.

Devote the most space to the jobs that are related to your target position. If you were personally responsible for something significant, be sure to mention it; for example, "Devised a new collection system that accelerated payment of overdue receivables." Facts about your skills and accomplishments are the most important information you can give a prospective employer, so quantify them whenever possible:

*Quantify your accomplishments whenever possible.*

Designed a new ad that increased sales by 9 percent

Raised $2500 in 15 days for cancer research

*Draw attention to key qualifications by making them section titles; for example, "Language Skills."*

You may also include a section describing other aspects of your background that pertain to your career objective. If you were applying for a position with a multinational organization, you would mention your command of another language or your travel experience. Other skills you might mention include computer skills, and specialized software or relevant equipment. You might title a special section "Computer Skills" or "Language Skills" and place it near your "Education" or "Work Experience" section. If samples of your work might increase your chances of getting the job, insert a line at the end of your résumé offering to supply a portfolio of them on request.

## REAL-TIME UPDATES

**Learn More by Listening to This Podcast**

**Résumé advice from a PR insider**

Public relations executive Jessica Bernot offers her thoughts on how students can create effective résumés. Go to http://real-timeupdates.com/bce6 and click on Learn More. If you are using MyBCommLab, you can access Real-Time Updates within Business Communication Resources.

**ACTIVITIES, INTERESTS, AND ACHIEVEMENTS** Many employers are involved in their local communities and would look positively on candidates who are active in their communities as well. Your résumé should also describe any volunteer activities that demonstrate your abilities. Include the category "Volunteer Experience." List projects that require leadership, organization, teamwork, and cooperation. Emphasize career-related activities, such as "member of the Student Marketing Association." List skills you learned in these activities, and explain how these skills are related to the job you're applying for. Include speaking,

*Nonpaid activities may provide evidence of work-related skills.*

writing, or tutoring experience; participation in athletics or creative projects; fundraising or community-service activities; and offices held in academic or professional organizations. (However, mention of political or religious organizations may be a red flag to someone with differing views, so use your judgment.)

Including interests can enhance the employer's understanding of how you would fit in the company.[37] For instance, candidates applying to Mountain Equipment Co-op may want to list outdoor activities. Such information helps show how a candidate will fit in with the organization's culture.

*Provide only the personal data that will help you get the job.*

Some information is best excluded from your résumé. Federal human rights laws prohibit employers from discriminating on the basis of gender, marital or family status, age, race, religion, national origin, and physical or mental disability. So be sure to exclude any items that could encourage discrimination. If you want to highlight skills developed with a political or religious organization, you could refer to it as a "not-for-profit organization."

Finally, if you have little or no job experience and not much to discuss outside of your education, indicating involvement in athletics or other organized student activities lets employers know that you don't spend all your free time hanging around your apartment playing video games (which might be a plus if you are applying for a game developer position). Also consider mentioning publications, projects, and other accomplishments that required relevant business skills.

Note any awards you've received. Again, quantify your achievements whenever possible. Instead of saying that you addressed various student groups, state how many and the approximate audience sizes. If your activities have been extensive, you may want to group them into divisions such as "College Activities," "Community Service," "Professional Associations," "Seminars and Workshops," and "Speaking Activities." An alternative is to divide them into two categories: "Service Activities" and "Achievements, Awards, and Honours."

**REFERENCES** Experts debate the value of putting references in a résumé. Some say that putting them in is unnecessary and takes up valuable space since they are not used until after the interview. In this case, bring reference information from past employment and education to the interview. Ensure that you have the reference's name, job title, company name and address, telephone number, and email address. Also have the person's permission. Talk to references about what they will say about you.

Others say that having references in the résumé shows you are organized and it may make it easy for the recruiter to call references without any further communication with you. Also, it may be possible to create a positive impression of the applicant if the reference named is impressive. If you do decide to put references in, since you are limited in space, consider putting in two: one from work and one from education. Personal references are not as persuasive.

# Completing Your Résumé

LEARNING OBJECTIVE 4
Characterize the completing step for résumés, including the six most common formats in which you can produce a résumé.

Completing your résumé involves revising it for optimum quality, producing it in the various forms and media you'll need, and proofreading it for any errors before distributing it or publishing it online. Be prepared to produce several versions of your résumé, in multiple formats and multiple media. These are discussed later in this section.

## Revising Your Résumé

Ask professional recruiters to list the most common mistakes they see on résumés, and you'll hear the same things over and over again. Take care to avoid these flaws:

* Too long or too wordy
* Too short or sketchy
* Difficult to read
* Poorly written
* Displaying weak understanding of the business world in general or of a particular industry or company
* Poor-quality printing or cheap paper
* Full of spelling and grammar errors
* Boastful
* Gimmicky design

Avoid the common errors that will get your résumé excluded from consideration.

The ideal length of your résumé depends on the depth of your experience and the level of the positions for which you are applying. As a general guideline, if you have fewer than 10 years of professional experience, try to keep your conventional résumé to one page. For online résumé formats, you can always provide links to additional information. If you have more experience and are applying for a higher-level position, you may need to prepare a somewhat longer résumé, but aim for a maximum of two pages.[38]

If your employment history is brief, keep your résumé to one page.

## Producing Your Résumé

Effective résumé designs are simple, clean, and professional—not gaudy, clever, or cute.

No matter how many media and formats you eventually choose for producing your résumé, a clean, professional-looking design is a must. Recruiters and hiring managers want to skim your essential information in a matter of seconds, and anything that distracts or delays them will work against you.

Fortunately, good résumé design is not difficult to achieve. As you can see in Figures 13.6 and 13.7, good designs feature simplicity, order, effective use of white space, and clear typefaces. Make subheadings easy to find and easy to read, placing them either above each section or in the left margin. Use lists to itemize your most important qualifications. Colour is not necessary by any means, but if you add colour, make it subtle and sophisticated, such as for a thin horizontal line under your name and address. The most common way to get into trouble with résumé design is going overboard.

Be prepared to produce several versions of your résumé in multiple media.

Depending on the companies you apply to, you might want to produce your résumé in as many as six formats (all are explained in the following sections):

- Printed traditional résumé
- Printed scannable résumé
- Electronic plain-text file
- Microsoft Word file
- PDF file
- Online résumé, also called a multimedia or social media résumé

Unfortunately, no single format or medium works for all the situations you will encounter, and employer expectations continue to change as technology evolves. Find out what each employer or job posting website expects, and provide your résumé in that specific format.

Do not include or enclose a photo in résumés that you send to employers or post on job websites.

**CONSIDERING PHOTOS, VIDEOS, PRESENTATIONS, AND INFOGRAPHICS**  As you produce your résumé in various formats, you will encounter the question of whether to include a photograph of yourself on or with your résumé. For print or electronic documents that you will be submitting to employers or job websites, the safest advice is to avoid photos. Seeing visual cues of the age, ethnicity, and gender of candidates early in the selection process exposes employers to complaints of discriminatory hiring practices. In fact, some employers won't even look at résumés that include photos, and some applicant tracking systems automatically discard résumés with any kind of extra files.[39] However, photographs are acceptable for social media résumés and other online formats where you are not actually submitting a résumé to an employer.

In addition to these six main formats, some applicants create PowerPoint presentations, videos, or infographics to supplement a conventional résumé. Two key advantages of a PowerPoint supplement are flexibility and multimedia capabilities. For instance, you can present a menu of choices on the opening screen and allow viewers to click through to sections of interest. (Note that most of the things you can accomplish with PowerPoint can be done with an online résumé, which is probably more convenient for most readers.)

A video résumé can be a compelling supplement as well, but be aware that some employment law experts advise employers not to view videos, at least not until after candidates have been evaluated solely on their credentials. The reason for this caution is the same as with photographs. In addition, videos are more cumbersome to evaluate than paper or electronic résumés, and some recruiters refuse to watch them.[40] However, not all companies share this concern over videos, so you'll have to research their individual preferences.

An infographic résumé attempts to convey a person's career development and skill set graphically through a visual metaphor such as a timeline or subway map or as a poster with an array of individual elements (see Figure 13.8). A well-designed infographic could

| FIGURE 13.8 | An Infographic Résumé |
|---|---|

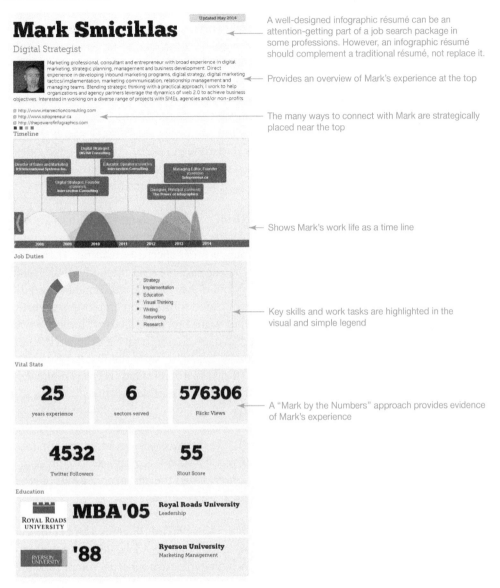

A well-designed infographic résumé can be an attention-getting part of a job search package in some professions. However, an infographic résumé should complement a traditional résumé, not replace it.

Provides an overview of Mark's experience at the top

The many ways to connect with Mark are strategically placed near the top

Shows Mark's work life as a time line

Key skills and work tasks are highlighted in the visual and simple legend

A "Mark by the Numbers" approach provides evidence of Mark's experience

*Source:* Used by permission of Mark Smiciklas.

be an intriguing element of the job-search package for candidates in certain situations and professions because it can definitely stand out from traditional résumés and can show a high level of skill in visual communication. However, infographics are likely to be incompatible with most applicant tracking systems and with the screening habits of most recruiters, so while you might stand out with an infographic, you might also get tossed out if you try to use an infographic in place of a conventional résumé. In virtually every situation, an infographic should complement a conventional résumé, not replace it. In addition, successful infographics require skills in graphic design, and if you lack those skills, you'll need to hire a designer (see Chapter 11 for infographic tools and tips).

**PRODUCING A TRADITIONAL PRINTED RÉSUMÉ** Even though most of your application activity will take place online, having a copy of a conventional printed résumé is important for bringing to job fairs, interviews, and other events. Many interviewers expect you to bring a printed résumé to the interview, even if you applied online. The résumé can serve as a note-taking form or discussion guide, and it is tangible evidence of your attention to professionalism and detail.[41] When printing a résumé, choose a heavier, higher-quality

Use high-quality paper when printing your résumé.

paper designed specifically for résumés and other important documents. White or slightly off-white is the best colour choice. Avoid papers with borders or backgrounds.

Some employers still prefer résumés in scannable format, but most now want electronic submissions.

**PRINTING A SCANNABLE RÉSUMÉ** You might encounter a company that prefers *scannable résumés*, a type of printed résumé that is specially formatted to be compatible with optical scanning systems that convert printed documents to electronic text. These systems were quite common just a few years ago, but their use appears to be declining rapidly as more employers prefer email delivery or website application forms.[42] A scannable résumé differs from the traditional format in two major ways: it should always include a keyword summary (employers search on these terms to find promising candidates), and it should be formatted in a simpler fashion that avoids underlining, special characters, and other elements that can confuse the scanning system. If you need to produce a scannable résumé, search online for "formatting a scannable résumé" to get detailed instructions.

A plain-text version of your résumé is simply a computer file without any of the formatting that you typically apply using a word processor.

**CREATING A PLAIN-TEXT FILE OF YOUR RÉSUMÉ** A *plain-text file* (sometimes known as an ASCII text file) is an electronic version of your résumé that has no font formatting, no bullet symbols, no colours, no lines or boxes, or other special formatting. The plain-text version can be used in two ways. First, you can include it in the body of an email message, for employers who want email delivery but don't want file attachments. Second, you can copy and paste the sections into the application forms on an employer's website.

Make sure you verify the plain-text file that you create with your word processor; it might need a few manual adjustments using a text editor such as Notepad.

A plain-text version is easy to create with your word processor. Start with the file you used to create your scannable résumé, use the "Save As" choice to save it as "plain text" or whichever similarly labelled option your software has, and verify the result by using a basic text editor (such as Microsoft Notepad). If necessary, reformat the page manually, moving text and inserting space as needed. For simplicity's sake, left-justify all your headings rather than trying to centre them manually.

Many employers and websites want your résumé in Microsoft Word or PDF format.

**CREATING A WORD FILE OF YOUR RÉSUMÉ** In many cases, an employer or job-posting website will want you to upload a Microsoft Word file or attach it to an email message. This method of transferring information preserves the design and layout of your résumé and saves you the trouble of creating a plain-text version.

**CREATING A PDF VERSION OF YOUR RÉSUMÉ** Creating a PDF file is a simple procedure, but you need the right software. Adobe Acrobat (not the free Adobe Reader) is the best-known program, but many others are available, including some free versions. You can also use Adobe's online service, at **http://createpdf.adobe.com**, to create PDFs without buying software.

You have many options for creating an online résumé, from college-hosted e-portfolios to multimedia résumés on commercial websites.

**CREATING AN ONLINE RÉSUMÉ** A variety of terms are used to describe online résumés, including *personal webpage*, *e-portfolio*, *social media résumé*, and *multimedia résumé*. Whatever the terminology used on a particular site, all these formats provide the opportunity to expand on the information contained in your basic résumé with links to projects, publications, screencasts, online videos, course lists, social networking profiles, and other elements that give employers a more complete picture of who you are and what you can offer (see Figure 13.8).

A good place to start is your college's career centre. Ask whether the career centre (or perhaps the information technology department) hosts online résumés or e-portfolios for students.

Many employers check Facebook to find out about the character of applicants.

A commercial hosting service is another good possibility for an online résumé. For instance, the free service VisualCV (**www.visualcv.com**) lets you build an online résumé with video clips and other multimedia elements. This site is a good place to see numerous examples, from students just about to enter the workforce full time all the way up to corporate CEOs.[43] Another important way to reach employers is to build a profile in a social networking site such as LinkedIn (**www.linkedin.com**). LinkedIn is quickly becoming the most important place to have an online presence. The Notebook at the end of this chapter provides tips on ways to use LinkedIn in your job search and career.

Regardless of the approach you take to creating an online résumé, keep these helpful tips in mind:

- **Remember that your online presence is a career-management tool.** The way you are portrayed online can work for you or against you, and it's up to you to create a positive impression. Most employers now conduct online searches to learn more about promising candidates, and 70 percent of those who do have rejected applicants because of information they dug up online.[44] Images from Facebook can also help applicants, however. Consider the example of a recruiter looking for a financial officer for a music industry position. Concerned about how the financial applicant would fit with a company in the creative business, the recruiter found pictures of the applicant playing his electric guitar on Facebook and saw that the applicant had a genuine interest in music.
- **Take advantage of social networking.** Use whatever tools are available to direct people to your online résumé, such as including your URL on Twitter, LinkedIn, and the "Info" tab on your Facebook page.
- **During the application process, don't expect or ask employers to retrieve a résumé from your website.** Submit your résumé using whatever method and medium each employer prefers. If employers then want to know more about you, they will likely do a web search on you and find your site, or you can refer them to your site in your résumé or application materials.

## Proofreading Your Résumé

Employers view your résumé as a concrete example of your attention to quality and detail. Your résumé doesn't need to be good or pretty good—it needs to be *perfect*. Although it may not seem fair, just one or two errors in a job application package are enough to doom a candidate's chances.[45]

Your résumé is one of the most important documents you'll ever write, so don't rush or cut corners when it comes to proofreading. Check all headings and lists for clarity and parallelism and be sure that your grammar, spelling, and punctuation are correct. Ask at least three other people to read it, too. As the creator of the material, you could stare at a mistake for weeks and not see it.

*Your résumé can't be "pretty good" or "almost perfect"—it needs to be perfect, so proofread it thoroughly and ask several other people to verify it, too.*

## Distributing Your Résumé

How you distribute your résumé depends on the number of employers you target and their preferences for receiving résumés. Employers usually list their requirements on their websites, so verify this information and follow it carefully. Beyond that, here are some general distribution tips:

*When distributing your résumé, pay close attention to the specific instructions provided by every employer, job website, or other recipient.*

- **Mailing printed résumés.** Take some care with the packaging. Spend a few extra cents to mail these documents in a flat 9-by-12 envelope, or better yet, use a Priority Mail flat-rate envelope, which gives you a sturdy cardboard mailer and faster delivery for just a few more dollars.
- **Emailing your résumé.** Some employers want applicants to include the text of their résumés in the body of an email message; others prefer an attached Microsoft Word or PDF file. If you have a reference number or a job ad number, include it in the subject line of your email message.
- **Submitting your résumé to an employer's website.** Many employers, including most large companies, now prefer or require applicants to submit their résumés online. In some instances, you will be asked to upload a complete file. In others, you will need to copy and paste sections of your résumé into individual boxes in an online application form.
- **Posting your résumé on job websites.** You can post your résumé on general-purpose job websites such as Monster (www.monster.ca) and CareerBuilder (www.careerbuilder.com), on more specialized websites such as Jobster (www.jobster.com) or Jobfox

*Don't post a resume on any public website unless you understand its privacy and security policies.*

(www.jobfox.com), or with staffing services such as Volt (http://jobs.volt.com). Before you upload your résumé to any site, however, learn about its confidentiality protection. Some sites allow you to specify levels of confidentiality, such as letting employers search your qualifications without seeing your personal contact information or preventing your current employer from seeing your résumé. Don't post your résumé to any website that doesn't give you the option of restricting the display of your contact information. (Only employers that are registered clients of the service should be able to see your contact information.)[46]

# LEARNING OBJECTIVES: Check Your Progress

**① OBJECTIVE List eight key steps to finding the ideal opportunity in today's job market.**

The eight steps discussed in the chapter are (1) figuring out the story of you, which involves describing your career so far and your future goals; (2) learning to think like an employer; (3) researching industries and companies to identify opportunities; (4) translating your general potential into a specific solution for each employer so that you show you are a good fit for each opening; (5) taking the initiative to approach companies; (6) building your network so you and your connections can help each other in the job search process; (7) seeking career counselling if appropriate; and (8) avoiding mistakes that can ruin your chances of getting a job.

**② OBJECTIVE Explain the process of planning your résumé, including how to choose the best résumé organization.**

Planning a résumé starts with recognizing what it is: a persuasive message designed to get you job interviews. Gathering the necessary information involves learning about target industries, professions, companies, and specific positions, and collecting information about yourself. Choosing the best résumé organization depends on your background. A chronological résumé helps employers easily locate necessary information, highlights your professional growth and career progress, and emphasizes continuity and stability. Chronological format is the approach employers tend to prefer. A functional résumé helps employers easily see what you can do for them, allows you to emphasize earlier job experience, and lets you downplay any lengthy periods of unemployment or a lack of career progress. However, many employers are suspicious of functional résumés. The combination approach uses the best features of the other two and is often the best choice for recent graduates.

**③ OBJECTIVE Describe the tasks involved in writing your résumé and list the sections to consider including in your résumé.**

Adapting to the audience is crucial, because readers are looking to see how well you understand their businesses and whether you can present a solution to their talent needs. The major sections to consider including in your résumé are (1) your name and contact information; (2) an introductory statement, which can be a career objective, a qualifications summary, or a career summary; (3) your education; (4) your work experience; and (5) activities, interests, and achievements that are professionally relevant.

**④ OBJECTIVE Characterize the completing step for résumés, including the six most common formats in which you can produce a résumé.**

Quality is paramount with résumés, so the tasks of revising and proofing are particularly important. The six common résumé formats are traditional printed résumé, scannable résumé, electronic plain-text file, Microsoft Word file, PDF, and online résumé (which might be called a personal webpage, an e-portfolio, or a social media résumé).

MyBCommLab®  Go to MyBCommLab for everything you need to help you succeed in the job you've always wanted! Tools and resources include the following:
• Writing Activities   • Document Makeovers
• Video Exercises   • Grammar Exercises—and much more!

## Practise Your Grammar

Effective business communication starts with strong grammar skills. To improve your grammar skills, go to MyBCommLab, where you'll find exercises and diagnostic tests to help you produce clear, effective communication.

## Test Your Knowledge

To review chapter content related to each question, refer to the indicated Learning Objective.

1. Why is networking an essential part of your lifelong career planning? L.O.❶

2. How can you make yourself more valuable to employers? L.O.❷

3. Why do most employers prefer chronological résumés over functional résumés? L.O.❷

4. Why is it important to find and use relevant keywords in your résumé? L.O.❸

5. What are the advantages of a social media résumé? L.O.❹

## Apply Your Knowledge

To review chapter content related to each question, refer to the indicated Learning Objective.

1. Some people don't have a clear career path when they enter the job market. If you're in this situation, how would your uncertainty affect the way you write your résumé? L.O.❶

2. How should you present a past job that is unrelated to your current career plans? L.O.❸

3. Can you use a qualifications summary if you don't yet have extensive professional experience in your desired career? Why or why not? L.O.❸

4. Between your second and third years, you quit school for a year to earn the money to finish college. You worked as a loan-processing assistant in a finance company, checking references on loan applications, word processing, and filing. Your manager made a lot of the fact that he had never attended college. He seemed to resent you for pursuing your education, but he never criticized your work, so you thought you were doing okay. After you'd been working there for six months, he fired you, saying that you had failed to be thorough enough in your credit checks. You were actually glad to leave, and you found another job right away, at a bank doing similar duties and earning positive reviews. Now that you've graduated from college, you're writing your résumé. Will you include the finance company job in your work history? Explain. L.O.❸

5. You've completed an attractive, professional-quality online résumé but haven't created a conventional résumé yet. You run across an intriguing job opportunity for which the hiring manager asks interested applicants to email résumés as Microsoft Word attachments. You don't want to let this opportunity slip by. Should you email the manager a link to your online résumé and explain that you haven't had time to create a conventional résumé yet? Why or why not? L.O.❹

## Practise Your Skills

### ACTIVITIES

Each activity is labelled according to the primary skill or skills you will need to use. To review relevant chapter content, you can refer to the indicated Learning Objective. In some instances, supporting information will be found in another chapter, as indicated.

1. **Career Management: Work-Related Preferences, Self-Assessment** L.O.❶ What work-related activities and situations do you prefer? Evaluate your preferences in each of the areas listed in the table below. Use the results as a good start for guiding your job search.

| Activity or Situation | Strongly Agree | Agree | Disagree | No Preference |
|---|---|---|---|---|
| a. I want to work independently. | _____ | _____ | _____ | _____ |
| b. I want variety in my work. | _____ | _____ | _____ | _____ |
| c. I want to work with people. | _____ | _____ | _____ | _____ |
| d. I want to work with products or machines. | _____ | _____ | _____ | _____ |
| e. I want physical work. | _____ | _____ | _____ | _____ |
| f. I want mental work. | _____ | _____ | _____ | _____ |
| g. I want to work for a large organization. | _____ | _____ | _____ | _____ |
| h. I want to work for a nonprofit organization. | _____ | _____ | _____ | _____ |
| i. I want to work for a small family business. | _____ | _____ | _____ | _____ |
| j. I want to work for a service business. | _____ | _____ | _____ | _____ |
| k. I want regular, predictable work hours. | _____ | _____ | _____ | _____ |
| l. I want to work in a city location. | _____ | _____ | _____ | _____ |
| m. I want to work in a small town or suburb. | _____ | _____ | _____ | _____ |
| n. I want to work in another country. | _____ | _____ | _____ | _____ |
| o. I want to work outdoors. | _____ | _____ | _____ | _____ |
| p. I want to work in a structured environment. | _____ | _____ | _____ | _____ |

2. **Career Management: Researching Career Opportunities** L.O.❶ Based on the preferences you identified in the self-assessment in Activity 1 and the academic, professional, and personal qualities you have to offer, perform an online search for a career opportunity that matches your interests and qualifications (starting with any of the websites listed in Table 13.3). Draft a one-page report indicating how the career you select and the job openings you find match your strengths and preferences.

3. **Message Strategies: Planning a Résumé** L.O.❷ Identify a position in an interesting career field that you could potentially be qualified for upon graduation. Using at least three different sources, including the description in an online job posting, create a list of ten keywords that should be included in a résumé customized for this position.

4. **Message Strategies: Writing a Résumé** L.O.❸ Rewrite this résumé so that it follows the guidelines presented in this chapter.

Sylvia Manchester
765 Belle Fleur Blvd.
St-Laurent, QC H8L 3X9
(514) 312-9504
smanchester@bce.net

PERSONAL: Single, excellent health, 5'7", 136 lbs.; hobbies include cooking, dancing, and reading.

JOB OBJECTIVE: To obtain a responsible position in marketing or sales with a good company.

Education: BSc degree in biology, Dalhousie University, 2006. Graduated with a 3.0 average. Member of the varsity volleyball team. President of Dalhousie chess club.

WORK EXPERIENCE

Fisher Scientific Instruments, 2013 to now, field sales representative. Responsible for calling on customers and explaining the features of Fisher's line of laboratory instruments. Also responsible for writing sales letters, attending trade shows, and preparing weekly sales reports.

Fisher Scientific Instruments, 2010–2012, customer service representative. Was responsible for handling incoming phone calls from customers who had questions about delivery, quality, or operation of Fisher's line of laboratory instruments. Also handled miscellaneous correspondence with customers.

Medical Electronics, Inc., 2007–2010, administrative assistant to the vice president of marketing. In addition to handling typical administrative chores for the vice-president of marketing, I was in charge of compiling the monthly sales reports, using figures provided by members of the field sales force. I also was given responsibility for doing various market research activities.

Halifax Convention and Visitors Bureau, 2004–2006, summers, tour guide. During the summers of my university years, I led tours of Halifax for tourists visiting the city. My duties included greeting conventioneers and their spouses at hotels, explaining the history and features of the city during an all-day sightseeing tour, and answering questions about Halifax and its attractions. During my fourth summer with the bureau, I was asked to help train the new tour guides. I prepared a handbook that provided interesting facts about the various tourist attractions, as well as answers to the most commonly asked tourist questions. The Bureau was so impressed with the handbook they had it printed up so that it could be given as a gift to visitors.

Dalhousie University, 2004–2007, part-time clerk in admissions office. While I was a student in universities, I worked 15 hours a week in the admissions office. My duties included filing, processing applications, and handling correspondence with high school students and administrators.

5. **Message Strategies: Writing a Résumé; Collaboration: Team Projects** L.O.❸, **Chapter 2** Working with another student, change the following statements to make them more effective for a résumé by using action verbs, concrete keywords, and parallel construction.
   a. Have some experience with database design
   b. Assigned to a project to analyze the cost accounting methods for a large manufacturer
   c. I was part of a team that developed a new inventory control system
   d. Am responsible for preparing the quarterly department budget

e. Was a manager of a department with seven employees working for me
f. Was responsible for developing a spreadsheet to analyze monthly sales by department
g. Put in place a new program for ordering supplies

6. **Message Strategies: Writing a Résumé** L.O.❸ Using your partner's answers to Activity 5, make the statements stronger by quantifying them (make up any numbers you need).

7. **Message Strategies: Writing a Résumé; Communication Ethics: Resolving Ethical Dilemmas** L.O.❸, **Chapter 1** Assume that you achieved all the tasks shown in Activity 5 not as an individual employee but as part of a work team. In your résumé, must you mention other team members? Explain your answer.

8. **Career Management: Use of Facebook to Check the Character of Applicants** L.O.❶ Many recruiters and managers are using Facebook, LinkedIn, and other online spaces to find out more about applicants. Do you think this is an ethical practice? Discuss in groups of four and be ready to share your views with the class. What should applicants do in response to this practice? How can applicants manage their "online personas"? In your group, prepare a list of suggestions.

   After your class discussion, write a short reflection on your online persona. What can employers learn about you online? How can you manage your presence? Do you have a professional profile online?

9. **Message Strategies: Writing a Résumé** L.O.❸ Develop a LinkedIn profile for yourself at **www.linkedin.com**.

10. **Career Management: Writing the Story of You** L.O.❶ Using the example in Figure 13.1, think about what you have done so far and what you hope to do next. Write "the story of you" as a private document you can use to help you start a career plan. Write an email to your instructor sharing your story.

# CASES

Apply the three-step writing process to the following cases, as assigned by your instructor.

## 1. Career Management: Researching Career Opportunities L.O.❶

Chances are you won't be able to land your dream job right out of college, but that doesn't mean you shouldn't start planning right now to make that dream come true.

**YOUR TASK** Using online job search tools, find a job that sounds just about perfect for you, even if you're not yet qualified for it. It might even be something that would take 10 or 20 years to reach. Don't settle for something that's

not quite right; find a job that is so "you" and so exciting that you would jump out of bed every morning, eager to go to work (such jobs really do exist!). Start with the job description you found online and then supplement it with additional research so that you get a good picture of what this job and career path are all about. Compile a list of all the qualifications you would need to have a reasonable chance of landing such a job. Now compare this list with your current résumé. Write a brief email message to your instructor that identifies all the areas in which you would need to improve your skills, work experience, education, and other qualifications in order to land your dream job.

### 2. Message Strategies: Planning a Résumé L.O.❷

Think about yourself. What are some things that come easily to you? What do you enjoy doing? In what part of the country would you like to live? Do you like to work indoors? Outdoors? A combination of the two? How much do you like to travel? Would you like to spend considerable time on the road? Do you like to work closely with others or more independently? What conditions make a job unpleasant? Do you delegate responsibility easily, or do you like to do things yourself? Are you better with words or numbers? Better at speaking or writing? Do you like to work under fixed deadlines? How important is job security to you? Do you want your supervisor to state clearly what is expected of you, or do you like having the freedom to make many of your own decisions?

**YOUR TASK** After answering these questions, gather information about possible jobs that suit your current qualifications by consulting reference materials (from your college library, or placement centre) and by searching online. Next, choose a location, a company, and a job that interest you. Write a résumé that matches your qualifications and the job description; use whatever format and media your instructor specifies.

### 3. Message Strategies: Completing a Résumé L.O.❹

Creating presentations and other multimedia supplements can be a great way to expand on the brief overview that a résumé provides.

**YOUR TASK** Starting with any version of a résumé that you've created for yourself, create an electronic presentation that expands on your résumé information to give potential employers a more complete picture of what you can contribute. Include samples of your work, testimonials from current or past employers and colleagues, videos of speeches you've made, and anything else that tells the story of the professional "you." If you have a specific job or type of job in mind, focus on that. Otherwise, present a more general picture that shows why you would be a great employee for any company to consider. Be sure to review the information from Chapter 12 about creating professional-quality presentations.

### 4. Career Management: Researching the Use of Twitter for Job Search L.O.❶

With two classmates, have each person look up "Twitter Résumés" to find out how Twitter might be used by job seekers and employers. Look on sites such as **www.TweetMyJobs.com** or other similar sites that you can find. Report back in your group to describe what each of these sites offers. Discuss the advantages and disadvantages of using Twitter to find jobs. What should a person know before subscribing to a site that will tweet his or her résumé?

**YOUR TASK** Write a one-page report to your instructor about what you learned about tweeting résumés, including your suggestions to fellow classmates about Twitter résumés.

# Tips for Using LinkedIn to Further Your Career

LinkedIn and other social job search sites are revolutionizing recruiting practices.[47] Frequently, employers are bypassing job boards such as Monster and using LinkedIn and technologies such as Entelo and TalentBin to sift through social data to find talent.[48] In 2010 LinkedIn had 90 million members but by January 2014 had grown to 259 million, adding members at a rate of two per second. You can't afford not to be on LinkedIn. Staying connected on the site even when you are *not* job hunting can help you build your network and make you a "passive candidate" for those companies seeking talent in the "hidden job market" by searching for skill sets using social technologies.[49]

As you plan the next stage of your career, make the most of LinkedIn. Here are the basics:

- Embed in your profile keywords that employers in your field would be searching. For example, if your experience is in logistics, *supply chain management, asset management, capital budget, change management, and continuous improvement* are just a few of the words you should include.

- Join groups related to your field, especially professional and alumni associations. Once in the group, ask and answer questions and post resources to build your reputation and make connections.

- Use the "Follow" function to keep tabs on companies and people of interest. You can follow anyone in a group that you belong to, or a company that is mentioned in your contact's profiles. Or, use the "Company Follow" icon to receive updates and alerts.
- Ask for "endorsements" and recommendations from co-workers or influential people who can vouch for your expertise.[50]
- Take time to read the "Track the Jobs" section, and if you see a job suited to someone you know, forward it. If you receive notifications of someone getting a job, send congratulatory notes to stay connected.[51]
- Use "Advanced People Search" to look up someone who has your dream job. Read their profile to see how they got to that position—a kind of reverse engineering for your own career path.

- If you have a blog, Twitter account, a website or samples of your work, link them to your profile.
- Once on the job, use LinkedIn to research people before going to meetings or calling on clients.
- Ask your first-level connections to introduce you to a second-level contact—write polite notes to request the introductions.

## Applications for Success

1. LinkedIn provides users the ability to hide endorsements that others have given them. Why might this be an important feature from an ethical point of view?

2. How can you combine your use of LinkedIn with face-to-face networking and what advantage would it bring?

## 14

# Applying and Interviewing for Employment

**LEARNING OBJECTIVES**

*After studying this chapter, you will be able to*

1. Explain the purposes of application letters and describe how to apply the AIDA organizational approach to them.
2. Describe the typical sequence of job interviews, the major types of interviews, and what employers look for during an interview.
3. List six tasks you need to complete to prepare for a successful job interview.
4. Explain how to succeed in all three stages of an interview.
5. Identify the most common employment messages that follow an interview and explain when you would use each one.

In her career, and now with Korn Ferry, the world's largest global executive search firm, Caroline Jellinck has interviewed hundreds of people. When evaluating candidates, she looks for people who are confident without being arrogant and who can be specific yet succinct in their replies. "The only way to judge if someone is going to be successful in the future," says Jellinck, "is to know where they have been successful in the past. Realistic, honest stories about past achievements can give interviewers a picture of future potential."

An interview should be approached as a business conversation in which both parties get to know each other better. Don't view it as a test in which you try to guess the "right" answers or as an interrogation in which you have to defend your background and skills. Treat interviews as opportunities to share information. After all, you need to determine which company is the right employer for you, just as companies need to determine whether you are the right employee for them. You'll learn more this way, and you'll lower the stress level, too.

This chapter will give you a foundation for successful interviewing, along with tips on writing effective application letters and other important employment-related messages.

**LEARNING OBJECTIVE 1**
Explain the purposes of application letters and describe how to apply the AIDA organizational approach to them.

Always accompany your résumé with an application message (letter or email) that motivates the recipient to read the résumé.

## Submitting Your Résumé and Application Letter

Your résumé (see Chapter 13) is the centrepiece of your job search package, but it needs support from several other employment messages, including application letters, job-inquiry letters, application forms, and follow-up notes.

### Writing Application Letters

Whenever you mail, email, hand-deliver, or upload your résumé, you should include an **application letter**, also known as a *cover letter*, to let readers know what you're sending, why you're sending it, and how they can benefit from reading it. (Even though this message is often not a printed letter anymore, many professionals still refer to it as a letter.) Take the same care with your application letter that you took with your résumé. A poorly written application letter can prompt employers to skip over your résumé, even if you are a good fit for a job.[1] Staffing specialist Abby Kohut calls the application letter "a writing-skills evaluation in disguise" and emphasizes that even a single error can get you bounced from contention.[2]

The best approach for an application letter depends on whether you are applying for an identified job opening or are *prospecting*—taking the initiative to write to companies even though they haven't announced a job opening that is right for you.[3] In many ways, the difference between the two is like the difference between solicited and unsolicited proposals (see pages 246–247). Figure 14.1 shows a **solicited application letter** written in response to a posted job opening. The writer knows exactly what qualifications the organization is seeking and can "echo" those attributes back in his letter.

Writing a **prospecting letter** is more challenging because you don't have the clear target you have with a solicited letter. You will need to do more research to identify the qualities that a company would probably seek for the position you hope to occupy (see Figure 14.2). Also, search for news items that involve the company, its customers, the profession, or the individual manager to whom you are writing. Using this information in

Resist the temptation to stand out with gimmicky application letters; impress with knowledge and professionalism instead.

## FIGURE 14.1 Solicited Application Letter

2893 Jack Pine Road
Hamilton, ON L2H 8Y7

February 3, 2015

Ms. Angela Clair
Director of Administration
Cummings and Welbane, Inc.
770 Campus Point Drive
Hamilton, ON L8N 3T2

Dear Ms. Clair:

**JOINING YOUR FIRM AS AN OFFICE ASSISTANT**

States the reason for writing and links the writer's experience to stated qualifications →

Please consider me for the office assistant position you advertised on LinkedIn. In addition to experience in a variety of office settings, I am trained in the software used in your office.

I recently completed a three-course sequence at Hamilton College on Microsoft Office. I learned how to use Word and Excel to speed up report-writing tasks and manage databases. Workshops on using Adobe, Illustrator, and PowerPoint gave me practical experience, enabling me to quickly and competently compose and format financial reports, presentation slides, and a variety of graphics.

← Discusses how specific skills apply to the job sought, showing that Caruso understands the job's responsibilities

Explains an achievement mentioned in the résumé and refers the reader to the enclosure →

These skills have been invaluable to me as assistant to the chief nutritionist at Cara Food Services (please refer to my résumé). The order-confirmation system I designed has sharply reduced late shipments and improved inventory levels.

I would appreciate an interview with you. Please telephone me any afternoon at (905) 220-6139 to let me know the day and time most convenient for you.

← Asks for an interview and facilitates action

Sincerely,

*Nick Caruso*

Nick Caruso

Enclosure: Résumé

**FIGURE 14.2**  Unsolicited Application Letter

1254 Main Street
Summerside, PE  C1N 3C4

gjohns@telus.net

June 16, 2015

Ms. Patricia Downings
Store Manager
Hudson's Bay
840 South Oak
Charlottetown, PE  C2R 5H6

Dear Ms. Downings:

**APPLICATION FOR MANAGERIAL POSITION**

*Gains attention in the first paragraph* →

It is rare to get a chance to work for a company that is 345 years old yet in 2015 leads the pack in marketing and managing department stores. Please consider me for your next management trainee position. I would love to use my marketing diploma and my two years of retail experience to contribute to the Hudson Bay's continuing success.

Working as a clerk and then as an assistant manager at Canadian Tire has taught me how to anticipate problems and deliver the kind of customer service that keeps customers coming back. I stocked shelves, answered customer enquiries, built displays and gained experience in nine different departments, often working extra shifts and evenings. Patience with customer questions helped me develop good listening skills and identify opportunities for new products. Recognizing that many customers can go online instead of coming into the store, I built relationships whenever I could to help encourage return visits. Completing team projects during my marketing program at Ryerson helped me lead, listen, encourage others' ideas, and speak up tactfully when needed. The interpersonal skills developed in these projects will be useful in serving your customers and in becoming the kind of manager that others will trust.

← *Makes a claim then backs it up with supporting details and examples*

In addition to customer service skills, I bring strong administrative skills. During my diploma program, I added knowledge of marketing and experience in solving problems by analyzing spreadsheets. I have used databases at Canadian Tire for stock-taking, ordering, and producing month-end merchandising reports. I also studied international sourcing during my special projects course and learned about many of your company's best practices. The reach of Hudson's Bay's purchasing is exciting. Please look over my résumé, to see other skills I can bring to the job.

← *Mentions examples that relate to needs of the position*

*Interests reader with knowledge of the company's policy toward promotion* →

I understand that Hudson's Bay prefers to promote its managers from within the company, so am seeking an entry-level position. I will telephone you early next Wednesday to arrange a meeting to discuss my qualifications, or please call me at (204) 733-5981.

Sincerely,

*Glenda Johns*

Glenda Johns

Enclosure: Résumé

your application letter helps you establish common ground with your reader—and it shows that you are tuned in to what is going on in the industry.

For either type of letter, follow these tips to be more effective:[4]

- If the name of an individual manager is at all findable, address your letter to that person, rather than something generic such as "Dear Hiring Manager." Search LinkedIn, the company's website, industry directories, Twitter, and anything else you can think of to find an appropriate name. Ask the people in your network if they know a name. If another applicant finds a name and you don't, you're at a disadvantage.

- Clearly identify the opportunity you are applying for or expressing interest in.
- Show that you understand the company and its marketplace.
- Never volunteer salary history or requirements unless an employer has asked for this information.
- Keep it short—no more than one page. Keep in mind that all you are trying to do at this point is move the conversation forward one step.
- Show some personality, while maintaining a business-appropriate tone. The letter gives you the opportunity to balance the facts-only tone of your résumé.
- Project confidence without being arrogant.
- Convey your reasons for wanting the job.

Because application letters are persuasive messages, the AIDA approach you learned in Chapter 9 is ideal, as the following sections explain.

**GETTING ATTENTION** The opening paragraph of your application letter must accomplish two essential tasks: (1) explain why you are writing and (2) give the recipient a reason to keep reading by demonstrating that you have some immediate potential for meeting the company's needs. Consider this opening:

> With the recent slowdown in corporate purchasing, I can certainly appreciate the challenge of new fleet sales in this business environment. With my high energy level and 16 months of new-car sales experience, I believe I can produce the results you listed as vital in the job posting on your website.

This applicant does a smooth job of mirroring the company's stated needs while highlighting his personal qualifications and providing evidence that he understands the broader market. He balances his relative lack of experience with enthusiasm and knowledge of the industry. Table 14.1 suggests some other ways that you can spark interest and grab attention in your opening paragraph.

*The opening paragraph of your application letter needs to clearly convey the reason you're writing and give the recipient a compelling reason to keep reading.*

| TABLE 14.1 | Tips for Getting Attention in Application Letters |
|---|---|

| TIP | EXAMPLE |
|---|---|
| **Unsolicited Application Letters** | |
| Show how your strongest skills will benefit the organization. | If you need a regional sales specialist who consistently meets sales targets while fostering strong customer relationships, please consider my qualifications. |
| Describe your understanding of the job's requirements and show how well your qualifications fit them. | Your annual report stated that improving manufacturing efficiency is one of the company's top priorities for next year. Through my research in systems engineering and consulting work for several companies in the industry, I've developed reliable methods for quickly identifying ways to cut production time while reducing resource use. |
| Mention the name of a person known to and highly regarded by the reader. | When Janice McHugh of your franchise sales division spoke to our business communication class last week, she said you often need promising new marketing graduates at this time of year. |
| Refer to publicized company activities, achievements, changes, or new procedures. | Today's issue of the *Globe* reports that you may need the expertise of computer programmers versed in robotics when your London tire plant automates this spring. |
| Use an opening that addresses a current issue faced by the company. | Social networking technologies enable people to connect, share their stories, and build friendships. My skills in using these technologies could help build strong relationships with customers and employees that can result in your company benefiting from the stories customers have to tell about your products. |
| **Solicited Application Letters** | |
| Identify where you discovered the job opening; describe what you have to offer. | Your ad in the April issue of *Travel & Leisure* for a cruise-line social director sounds like an exciting opportunity. My eight years of experience as an event planner would allow me to serve your new cruise division well. |

Use the middle section of your application letter to expand on your opening and present a more complete picture of your strengths.

**BUILDING INTEREST AND INCREASING DESIRE**   The middle section of your letter presents your strongest selling points in terms of their potential benefit to the organization, thereby building interest in you and creating a desire to interview you. Be specific and back up your assertions with convincing evidence:

> **Poor:** I completed three college courses in business communication, earning an A in each course, and have worked for the past year at Imperial Construction.
> **Improved:** Using the skills gained from three semesters of college training in business communication, I developed a collection system for Imperial Construction that reduced annual bad-debt losses by 25 percent.

When writing a solicited letter, be sure to discuss each requirement listed in the job posting. If you are deficient in any of these requirements, stress other solid selling points to help strengthen your overall presentation. Don't restrict your message to just core job duties, either. Also highlight personal characteristics that apply to the targeted position, such as your ability to work hard or handle responsibility:

> While attending university full time, I worked part-time during the school year and up to 60 hours a week each summer in order to be totally self-supporting. I can offer your organization the same level of effort and perseverance.

Toward the end of this section, refer the reader to your résumé by citing a specific fact or general point covered there:

> As you can see in the attached résumé, I've been working part-time with a local publisher since my second year of university. During that time, I've used client interactions as an opportunity to build strong customer service skills.

If you have an online portfolio that showcases your work that is relevant to the position, consider including its web address or inserting a QR code at the bottom of your letter to provide the reader quick access to your online material.

In the final paragraph of your application letter, respectfully ask for specific action and make it easy for the reader to respond.

**MOTIVATING ACTION**   The final paragraph of your application letter has two important functions: (1) to ask the reader for a specific action (usually an interview) and (2) to facilitate a reply. Offer to come to the employer's office at a convenient time or, if the firm is some distance away, to meet with its nearest representative or arrange a telephone or Skype interview. Include your email address and phone number, as well as the best time to reach you. Alternatively, you can take the initiative and say that you will follow up with a phone call. Refer again to your strongest selling point and, if desired, your date of availability:

> After you have reviewed my qualifications, could we discuss the possibility of putting my marketing skills to work for your company? I am available at (604) 555-7845 from 2 PM to 10 PM Monday to Friday or by email at rashid.amoni@gmail.com.

## Following Up After Submitting a Résumé

Think creatively about a follow-up letter; show that you've continued to add to your skills or that you've learned more about the company or the industry.

Deciding if, when, and how to follow up after submitting your résumé and application letter is one of the trickiest parts of a job search. First keep in mind that employers continue to evaluate your communication efforts and professionalism during this phase, so don't say or do anything to leave a negative impression. Second, adhere to whatever instructions the employer has provided. If a job posting says "no calls," for example, don't call. Third, if the job posting lists a *close date*, don't call or write before then, because the company is still collecting applications and will not have made a decision about inviting people for interviews. Wait a week or so after the close date. If no close date is given and you have no other information to suggest a timeline, you can generally contact the company starting a week or two after submitting your résumé.[5]

When you follow up by email or telephone, you can share an additional piece of information that links your qualifications to the position (keep an eye out for late-breaking news about the company, too) and ask a question about the hiring process as a way to gather some information about your status. Good questions to ask include:[6]

- Has a hiring decision been made yet?
- Can you tell me what to expect next in terms of the hiring process?
- What is the company's time frame for filling this position?
- Could I follow up in another week if you haven't had the chance to contact me yet?
- Can I provide any additional information regarding my qualifications for the position?

Whatever the circumstances, a follow-up message can demonstrate that you're sincerely interested in working for the organization, persistent in pursuing your goals, and committed to upgrading your skills.

If you don't land a job at your dream company on the first attempt, don't give up. You can apply again if a new opening appears, or you can send an updated résumé with a new unsolicited application letter that describes how you have gained additional experience, taken a relevant course, or otherwise improved your skill set. Many leading employers take note of applicants who came close but didn't quite make it and may extend offers when positions open up in the future.[7]

# Understanding the Interviewing Process

**LEARNING OBJECTIVE** ②
**Describe the typical sequence of job interviews, the major types of interviews, and what employers look for during an interview.**

An **employment interview** is a formal meeting during which both you and the prospective employer ask questions and exchange information. The employer's objective is to find the best talent to fill available job openings, and your objective is to find the right match for your goals and capabilities.

As you get ready to begin interviewing, keep two vital points in mind. First, recognize that the process takes time. Start your preparation and research early; the best job offers usually go to the best-prepared candidates. Second, don't limit your options by looking at only a few companies. Exploring a wide range of firms and positions might uncover great opportunities.

Start preparing early for your interviews—and be sure to consider a wide range of options.

## The Typical Sequence of Interviews

Most employers interview an applicant multiple times before deciding to make a job offer. At the most selective companies, you might have a dozen or more individual interviews across several stages.[8] Depending on the company and the position, the process may stretch out over many weeks, or it may be completed in a matter of days.[9]

Employers start with the **screening stage**, in which they filter out applicants who are unqualified or otherwise not a good fit for the position. Screening can take place on your school's campus, at company offices, via telephone (including Skype or another internet-based phone service), or through a computer-based screening system. Time is limited in screening interviews, so keep your answers short while providing a few key points about your strongest attributes. If your screening interview will take place by phone, try to schedule it for a time when you can be focused and free from interruptions.[10]

During the screening stage of interviews, use the limited time available to mention your key strengths.

The next stage of interviews, the **selection stage**, helps the organization identify the top candidates from all those who qualify. During these interviews, show keen interest in the job, relate your skills and experience to the organization's needs, listen attentively, and ask insightful questions that show you've done your research.

During the selection stage, continue to show how your skills and attributes can help the company.

If the interviewers agree that you're a good candidate, you may receive a job offer, either on the spot or a few days later by phone, mail, or email. In other instances, you may be invited back for a final evaluation, often by a higher-ranking executive. The objective of the **final stage** is often to sell you on the advantages of joining the organization.

During the final stage, the interviewer may try to sell you on working for the firm.

## Common Types of Interviews

Employers can use a variety of interviewing methods, and you need to recognize the different types and be prepared for each one. These methods can be distinguished by the way they are structured, the number of people involved, and the purpose of the interview.

**STRUCTURED VERSUS UNSTRUCTURED INTERVIEWS**   In a **structured interview**, the interviewer (or a computer program) asks a series of questions in a predetermined order. Structured interviews help employers identify candidates who don't meet basic job criteria, and they allow the interview team to compare answers from multiple candidates.[11]

> A structured interview follows a set sequence of questions.

In contrast, in an **open-ended interview**, the interviewer adapts his or her line of questioning based on the answers you give and any questions you ask. Even though it may feel like a conversation, remember that it's still an interview, so keep your answers focused and professional.

> In an open-ended interview, the interviewer adapts the line of questioning based on your responses.

**PANEL AND GROUP INTERVIEWS**   Although one-on-one interviews are the most common format, some employers use panel or group interviews as well. In a **panel interview**, you meet with several interviewers at once.[12] Try to make a connection with each person on the panel and keep in mind that each person has a different perspective, so tailor your responses accordingly.[13] For example, an upper-level manager is likely to be interested in your overall business sense and strategic perspective, whereas a potential colleague might be more interested in your technical skills and ability to work in a team. In a **group interview**, one or more interviewers meet with several candidates simultaneously. A key purpose of a group interview is to observe how the candidates interact.[14]

> In a panel interview, you meet with several interviewers at once; in a group interview, you and several other candidates meet with one or more interviewers at once.

**BEHAVIOURAL, SITUATIONAL, WORKING, AND STRESS INTERVIEWS**   Perhaps the most common type of interview these days is the **behavioural interview**, in which you are asked to relate specific incidents and experiences from your past.[15] Generic interview questions can often be answered with "canned" responses, but behavioural questions require candidates to use their own experiences and attributes to craft answers. Studies show that behavioural interviewing is a much better predictor of success on the job than traditional interview questions.[16] To prepare for a behavioural interview, review your work or university experiences to recall several instances in which you demonstrated an important job-related attribute or dealt with a challenge such as uncooperative team members or heavy workloads. Get ready with responses that quickly summarize the situation, the actions you took, and the outcome of those actions.[17] Table 14.2 lists other

> In a behavioural interview, you are asked to describe how you handled situations from your past.

| TABLE 14.2 | Sample Behavioural Questions |
| --- | --- |

1. Describe a situation where you had to persuade someone to do things your way.
2. Give an example of when you communicated well with someone even though that person may not have liked you or you didn't like the person.
3. In your work experience, have you had to handle a problem when your manager was not available?
4. Give an example of a difficult situation you have faced and how you handled it.
5. If you were in the store by yourself and a customer began to act in a loud and threatening manner, how would you react?
6. If you observed a fellow employee acting in an unsafe manner, what would you do?
7. If you were in training, and the supervisor training you criticized you in front of a customer, how would you react?
8. Think of a past supervisor or instructor whom you have worked with closely and whom you respect. What would that supervisor say are your strengths?
9. What would your supervisor say that you could improve?

samples of behavioural questions. In management interviews, expect a majority of the questions to be behavioural.

In your answers to these kinds of questions, follow a four-part approach:

1. Describe a specific situation.
2. Tell what your role was.
3. Tell what action you took.
4. Describe the positive result of your actions.

Find specific examples from your past (work, education, extracurricular activities, or volunteer experiences) for each question you anticipate.

A **situational interview** is similar to a behavioural interview except that the questions focus on how you would handle various hypothetical situations on the job. The situations will likely relate to the job you're applying for, so the more you know about the position, the better prepared you'll be.

A **working interview** is the most realistic type of interview: you actually perform a job-related activity during the interview. You may be asked to lead a brainstorming session, solve a business problem, engage in role-playing, or even make a presentation.[18]

The most unnerving type of interview is the **stress interview**, during which you might be asked questions designed to unsettle you or might be subjected to long periods of silence, criticism, interruptions, and even hostile reactions by the interviewer. The theory behind this approach is that you'll reveal how well you handle stressful situations, although some experts find the technique of dubious value.[19] If you find yourself in a stress interview, recognize what is happening and collect your thoughts for a few seconds before you respond.

## Interview Media

Expect to be interviewed through a variety of media. Employers trying to cut travel costs and the demands on staff time now interview candidates via telephone, email, instant messaging, virtual online systems, and videoconferencing, in addition to traditional face-to-face meetings.

To succeed at a **telephone interview**, make sure you treat it as seriously as an in-person interview. Be prepared with a copy of all the materials you have sent to the employer, including your résumé and any correspondence. In addition, prepare some note cards with key message points you'd like to make and questions you'd like to ask. If possible, arrange to speak on a landline so you don't have to worry about mobile phone reception problems. And remember that you won't be able to use a pleasant smile, a firm handshake, and other nonverbal signals to create a good impression. A positive, alert tone of voice is therefore vital.[20]

Email and IM are also sometimes used in the screening stage. Although you have almost no opportunity to send and receive nonverbal signals with these formats, you do have the major advantage of being able to review and edit each response before you send it. Maintain a professional style in your responses, and be sure to ask questions that demonstrate your knowledge of the company and the position.[21]

Many employers use video technology for both live and recorded interviews.[22] With **recorded video interviews**, an online system asks a set of questions and records the respondent's answers. Recruiters then watch the videos as part of the screening process.[23] Prepare for a video interview as you would for an in-person interview—including dressing and grooming—and take the extra steps needed to become familiar with the equipment and the process. If you're interviewing from home, arrange your space so that the webcam doesn't pick up anything distracting or embarrassing in the background. During any video interview, remember to sit up straight and focus on the camera.

**Online interviews** can range from simple structured questionnaires and tests to sophisticated job simulations that are similar to working interviews (see Figure 14.3).

In situational interviews, you're asked to explain how you would handle various hypothetical situations.

In a working interview, you actually perform work-related tasks.

Stress interviews help recruiters see how you handle yourself under pressure.

Expect to use a variety of media when you interview, from in-person conversations to virtual meetings.

Treat a telephone interview as seriously as you would an in-person interview.

When interviewing via email or IM, be sure to take a moment to review your responses before sending them.

In a video interview, speak to the camera as though you are addressing the interviewer in person.

Computer-based virtual interviews range from simple structured interviews to realistic job simulations to meetings in virtual worlds.

## FIGURE 14.3 Job Task Simulations

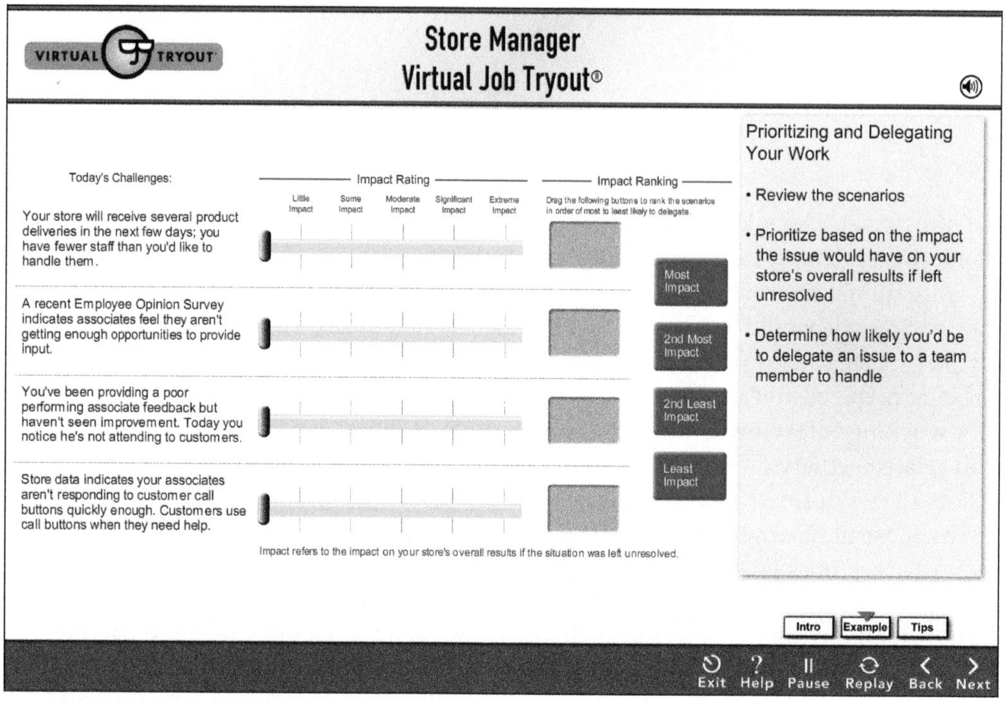

*Source:* Shaker Consulting Group website.

Computer-based job simulations are an increasingly popular approach to testing job-related skills in decision-making scenarios. These simulations help identify good candidates, give applicants an idea of what the job is like, and reduce the risk of employment discrimination lawsuits because they closely mimic actual job skills.[24]

## What Employers Look For in an Interview

Suitability for a specific job is judged on the basis of such factors as

- Academic preparation
- Work experience
- Job-related personality traits

Interviews give employers the chance to get to know you and to answer two essential questions. The first is whether you can handle the responsibilities of the position. Naturally, the more you know about the demands of the position, and the more you've thought about how your skills match those demands, the better you'll be able to respond.

The second essential question is whether you will be a good fit with the organization and the position based on your overall personality and approach to work. All good employers want people who are confident, dedicated, positive, curious, courteous, ethical, and willing to commit to something larger than their own individual goals.

Compatibility with an organization and a position is judged on the basis of personal background, attitudes, and style.

They also want a fit with the particular company and position. Just like people, companies have different "personalities." Some are intense; others are more laid back. Some emphasize teamwork; others expect employees to forge their own way and even to compete with one another. Expectations also vary from job to job within a company and from industry to industry. An outgoing personality is essential for sales but less so for research, for instance.

## Pre-employment Testing and Background Checks

Pre-employment tests attempt to provide objective, quantitative information about a candidate's skills, attitudes, and habits.

In an effort to improve the predictability of the selection process, many employers now conduct a variety of pre-employment evaluations and investigations. Here are types of assessments you are likely to encounter during your job search:[25]

- **Integrity tests.** Integrity tests attempt to measure how truthful and trustworthy a candidate is likely to be.
- **Personality tests.** Personality tests are designed to gauge such aspects as attitudes toward work, interests, managerial potential, dependability, commitment, and motivation.

- **Cognitive tests.** Cognitive tests measure a variety of attributes involved in acquiring, processing, analyzing, using, and remembering information. Typical tests involve reading comprehension, mathematics, problem solving, and decision making.
- **Job knowledge and job skills tests.** These assessments measure the knowledge and skills required to succeed in a particular position. An accounting candidate, for example, might be tested on accounting principles and legal matters (knowledge) and asked to create a simple balance sheet or income statement (skills).
- **Substance tests.** Some companies perform drug and alcohol testing. Many employers believe such testing is necessary to maintain workplace safety, ensure productivity, and protect companies from lawsuits, but others view it as an invasion of employee privacy.
- **Background checks.** In addition to testing, most companies conduct some sort of background check, including reviewing your credit record, checking to see whether you have a criminal history, and verifying your education. Moreover, you should assume that every employer will conduct a general online search on you. To help prevent a background check from tripping you up, verify that your college transcripts are current, look for any mistakes or outdated information in your credit record, plug your name into multiple search engines to see whether anything embarrassing shows up, and scour your social network profiles and connections for potential problems.

Pre-employment assessments are a complex and controversial aspect of workforce recruiting. For instance, even though personality testing is widely used, some research suggests that current tests are not a reliable predictor of job success.[26] However, expect to see more innovation in this area and greater use of testing in general in the future as companies try to reduce the risks and costs of poor hiring decisions.

# Preparing for a Job Interview

**LEARNING OBJECTIVE ③**
**List six tasks you need to complete to prepare for a successful job interview.**

Now that you're armed with insights into the interviewing and assessment process, you're ready to begin preparing for your interviews. Preparation will help you feel more confident and perform better under pressure, and preparation starts with learning about the organization.

## Learning About the Organization

Employers expect serious candidates to demonstrate an understanding of the company's operations, its markets, and its strategic and tactical challenges.[27] You've already done some initial research to identify companies of interest, but when you're invited to interview, it's time to dig a little deeper (see Table 14.3). Making this effort demonstrates your interest in the company, and it identifies you as a business professional who knows the importance of investigation and analysis.

Interviewers expect you to know some basic information about the company and its industry.

In addition to learning about the company, learn as much as you can about the person who will be interviewing you. Search LinkedIn in particular. Think about ways to use whatever information you find during your interview. For example, if an interviewer lists membership in a particular professional organization, you might ask whether the organization is a good forum for people to learn about vital issues in the profession or industry. This question gives the interviewer an opportunity to talk about his or her own interests and experiences for a moment, which builds rapport and might reveal vital insights into the career path you are considering. Just make sure your questions are sincere and not uncomfortably personal.

## Thinking Ahead About Questions

Planning ahead for the interviewer's questions will help you handle them more confidently and successfully. In addition, you will want to prepare insightful questions of your own.

| TABLE 14.3 | Investigating an Organization and a Job Opportunity |
|---|---|

WHERE TO LOOK AND WHAT YOU CAN LEARN

- *Company website, blogs, and social media accounts such as LinkedIn:* Overall information about the company, including key executives, products and services, locations and divisions, employee benefits, job descriptions
- *Competitors' websites, blogs, and social media accounts:* Similar information from competitors, including the strengths these companies claim to have
- *Industry-related websites and blogs:* Objective analysis and criticism of the company, its products, its reputation, and its management
- *Marketing materials (print and online):* The company's marketing strategy and customer communication style
- *Company publications (print and online):* Key events, stories about employees, new products
- *Your social network contacts:* Names and job titles of potential contacts within a company
- *Periodicals (newspapers and trade journals, both print and online):* In-depth stories about the company and its strategies, products, successes, and failures; you may find profiles of top executives
- *Career centre at your college:* A wide array of information about companies that hire graduates
- *Current and former employees:* Insights into the work environment

POINTS TO LEARN ABOUT THE ORGANIZATION

- Full name
- Location (headquarters and divisions, branches, subsidiaries, or other units)
- Ownership (public or private; whether it is owned by another company)
- Brief history
- Products and services
- Industry position (whether the company is a leader or a minor player; whether it is an innovator or more of a follower)
- Key financial points (such as stock price and trends, if a public company)
- Growth prospects (whether the company is investing in its future through research and development; whether it is in a thriving industry)

POINTS TO LEARN ABOUT THE POSITION

- Title
- Functions and responsibilities
- Qualifications and expectations
- Possible career paths
- Salary range
- Travel expectations and opportunities
- Relocation expectations and opportunities

**PLANNING FOR THE EMPLOYER'S QUESTIONS**   Many general interview questions are "stock" queries that you can expect to hear again and again during your interviews. Get ready to face these five at the very least:

> You can expect to face a number of common questions in your interviews, so be sure to prepare for them.

- **What is the hardest decision you've ever had to make?** Be prepared with a good example (that isn't too personal), explaining why the decision was difficult, how you made the choice you made, and what you learned from the experience.
- **What is your greatest weakness?** This question seems to be a favourite of some interviewers, although it probably rarely yields useful information. One good strategy

is to mention a skill or attribute you haven't had the opportunity to develop yet but would like to in your next position.[28]

- **Where do you want to be five years from now?** This question tests (1) whether you're merely using this job as a stopover until something better comes along and (2) whether you've given thought to your long-term goals. Your answer should reflect your desire to contribute to the employer's long-term goals, not just your own goals. Whether this question often yields useful information is also a matter of debate, but be prepared to answer it.[29]

- **What didn't you like about previous jobs you've held?** Answer this one carefully: the interviewer is trying to predict whether you'll be an unhappy or difficult employee.[30] Describe something that you didn't like in a way that puts you in a positive light, such as having limited opportunities to apply your skills or education. Avoid making negative comments about former employers or colleagues.

- **Tell me something about yourself.** One good strategy is to *briefly* share the "story of you" (see page 340), quickly summarizing where you have been and where you would like to go—in a way that aligns your interests with the company's. Alternatively, you can focus on a specific skill that you know is valuable to the company, share something business-relevant that you are passionate about, or offer a short summary of what colleagues or customers think about you.[31] Whatever tactic you choose, this is not the time to be shy or indecisive, so be ready with a confident, memorable answer.

Continue your preparation by planning a brief answer to each question in Table 14.4. You can also find typical interview questions at websites such as Quintessential Careers (**www.quintcareers.com/interview_question_database**).[32]

As you prepare answers, look for ways to frame your responses as brief stories (30 to 90 seconds) rather than simple declarative answers.[33] Cohesive stories tend to stick in the listener's mind more effectively than disconnected facts and statements.

> Look for ways to frame your responses as brief stories rather than as dry facts or statements.

**PLANNING QUESTIONS OF YOUR OWN**   Remember that an interview is a two-way conversation; the questions you ask are just as important as the answers you provide. By asking insightful questions, you can demonstrate your understanding of the organization, you can steer the discussion into areas that allow you to present your qualifications to best advantage, and you can verify for yourself whether this is a good opportunity. Plus, interviewers expect you to ask questions and tend to look negatively on candidates who don't have any questions to ask. For a list of good questions that you might use as a starting point, see Table 14.5.

> Preparing questions of your own sends an important signal that you are truly interested.

## Bolstering Your Confidence

Interviewing is stressful for everyone, so some nervousness is natural. However, you can take steps to feel more confident. Start by reminding yourself that you have value to offer the employer, and the employer already thinks highly enough of you to invite you to an interview. Instead of dwelling on your weaknesses, focus on your strengths. Instead of worrying about how you will perform in the interview, focus on how you can help the organization succeed. As with public speaking, the more prepared you are, the more confident you'll be.

## Polishing Your Interview Style

Competence and confidence are the foundation of your interviewing style, and you can enhance them by giving the interviewer an impression of poise, good manners, and good judgment. You can develop an adept style by staging mock interviews with a friend or using an interview simulator. Record these mock interviews so you can evaluate yourself. Your college's career centre may have computer-based systems for practising interviews as well (see Figure 14.4).

> Staging mock interviews with a friend is a good way to hone your style.

| TABLE 14.4 | 25 Common Interview Questions |
| --- | --- |

QUESTIONS ABOUT COLLEGE OR UNIVERSITY

1. What courses did you like most? Least? Why?
2. Do you think your extracurricular activities were worth the time you spent on them? Why or why not?
3. When did you choose your major? Did you ever change your major? If so, why?
4. Do you feel you did the best scholastic work you are capable of?
5. How has your education prepared you for this position?

QUESTIONS ABOUT EMPLOYERS AND JOBS

6. What jobs have you held? Why did you leave?
7. What percentage of your post-secondary expenses did you earn? How?
8. Why did you choose your particular field of work?
9. What are the disadvantages of your chosen field?
10. What is your management style?
11. What important trends do you see in our industry?
12. Why do you think you would like this particular type of job?

QUESTIONS ABOUT WORK EXPERIENCES AND EXPECTATIONS

13. Do you prefer to work in any specific geographic location? If so, why?
14. What motivates you? Why?
15. What do you think determines a person's progress in a good organization?
16. Describe an experience in which you learned from one of your mistakes.
17. Why do you want this job?
18. What have you done that shows initiative and willingness to work?
19. Why should I hire you?

QUESTIONS ABOUT WORK HABITS

20. Do you prefer working with others or by yourself?
21. What type of boss do you prefer?
22. Have you ever had any difficulty getting along with colleagues or supervisors? With instructors? With other students?
23. What would you do if you were given an unrealistic deadline for a task or project?
24. How do you feel about overtime work?
25. How do you handle stress or pressure on the job?

*Source:* Adapted from Alison Green, "The 10 Most Common Job Interview Questions," *U.S. News & World Report,* 24 January 2011, http://money.usnews.com; "Most Common Interview Questions," Glassdoor blog, 29 December 2011, www.glassdoor.com; *The Northwestern Endicott Report* (Evanston, Ill.: Northwestern University Placement Center).

| TABLE 14.5 | 10 Questions to Ask the Interviewer |
| --- | --- |

| QUESTION | REASON FOR ASKING |
| --- | --- |
| 1. What are the job's major responsibilities? | A vague answer could mean that the responsibilities have not been clearly defined, which is almost guaranteed to cause frustration if you take the job. |
| 2. What qualities do you want in the person who fills this position? | This will help you go beyond the job description to understand what the company really wants. |

*(continued)*

| QUESTION | REASON FOR ASKING |
|---|---|
| 3. How do you measure success for someone in this position? | A vague or incomplete answer could mean that the expectations you will face are unrealistic or ill defined. |
| 4. What is the first problem that needs the attention of the person you hire? | Not only will this help you prepare, but it can signal whether you're about to jump into a problematic situation. |
| 5. Would relocation be required now or in the future? | If you're not willing to move often or at all, you need to know those expectations now. |
| 6. Why is this job now vacant? | If the previous employee got promoted, that's a good sign. If the person quit, that might not be such a good sign. |
| 7. What makes your organization different from others in the industry? | The answer will help you assess whether the company has a clear strategy to succeed in its industry and whether top managers communicate it to lower-level employees. |
| 8. How would you define your organization's managerial philosophy? | You want to know whether the managerial philosophy is consistent with your own working values. |
| 9. What is a typical workday like for you? | The interviewer's response can give you clues about daily life at the company. |
| 10. What systems and policies are in place to help employees stay up to date in their professions and continue to expand their skills? | If the company doesn't have a strong commitment to employee development, chances are it isn't going to stay competitive very long. |

**FIGURE 14.4** Interview Simulators

*Source:* Perfect Interview LLC.

After each practice session, look for opportunities to improve. Have your mock interview partner critique your performance, or critique yourself if you're able to record your practice interviews, using the list of warning signs shown in Table 14.6. Pay close attention to the length of your planned answers as well. Interviewers want you to give complete answers but they don't want you to take up valuable time chatting about minor or irrelevant details.[34]

Evaluate the length and clarity of your answers, your nonverbal behaviour, and the quality of your voice.

| TABLE 14.6 | Warning Signs: 25 Traits That Interviewers Don't Like to See |
|---|---|

1. Poor personal appearance
2. Overbearing, overaggressive, or conceited demeanour; a "superiority complex"; a know-it-all attitude
3. Inability to express ideas clearly; poor voice, diction, or grammar
4. Lack of knowledge or experience
5. Poor preparation for the interview
6. Lack of interest in the job
7. Lack of planning for career; lack of purpose or goals
8. Lack of enthusiasm; passive and indifferent demeanour
9. Lack of confidence and poise; appearance of being nervous and ill at ease
10. Insufficient evidence of achievement
11. Failure to participate in extracurricular activities
12. Overemphasis on money; interested only in the best dollar offer
13. Poor scholastic record; just got by
14. Unwillingness to start at the bottom; expecting too much too soon
15. Tendency to make excuses
16. Evasive answers; hedging on unfavourable factors in record
17. Lack of tact
18. Lack of maturity
19. Lack of courtesy; being ill-mannered
20. Condemnation of past employers
21. Lack of social skills
22. Marked dislike for schoolwork
23. Lack of vitality
24. Failure to look interviewer in the eye
25. Limp, weak handshake

In addition to reviewing your answers, evaluate your nonverbal behaviour, including your posture, eye contact, facial expressions, and hand gestures and movements. Do you come across as alert and upbeat or passive and withdrawn? Pay close attention to your speaking voice as well. If you tend to speak in a monotone, for instance, practise speaking in a livelier style, with more inflection and emphasis. And watch out for "filler words" such as *uh*, *like*, and *um*. Many people start sentences with a filler without being conscious of doing so. Train yourself to pause silently for a moment instead as you gather your thoughts and plan what to say.

Dress conservatively and be well groomed for every interview.

## Presenting a Professional Image

"Looks count," says Jellinck. "Not in your physical features, but in the way you present yourself."[35] Clothing and grooming are important elements of preparation because they reveal something about a candidate's personality, professionalism, and ability to sense the unspoken "rules" of a situation. Your research into various industries and professions should give you insight into expectations for business attire. If you're not sure what to wear, ask someone who works in the same industry or even visit the company at the end of the day and see what employees are wearing as they leave the office. You don't need to spend a fortune on interview clothes, but your clothes must be clean, pressed, and appropriate (see Figure 14.5). The following look will serve you well in just about any interview situation:[36]

REAL-TIME UPDATES

**Learn More by Reading This Infographic**

**Get a quick reminder of the key steps in preparing for an interview**

Use these tips to refresh your memory before an interview. Go to http://real-timeupdates.com/bce6 and click on Learn More. If you are using MyBCommLab, you can access Real-Time Updates within Business Communication Resources.

- Neat, "adult" hairstyle
- For more formal environments, a conservative business suit (for women, that means no exposed midriffs, short skirts, or plunging necklines) in dark solid colour or a subtle pattern such as pinstripes

| FIGURE 14.5 | Professional Appearance for Job Interviews |

- White shirt for men; coordinated blouse for women
- Understated tie (classic stripes or subtle patterns) for men
- Limited jewellery (men, especially, should wear very little jewellery)
- No visible piercings other than one or two earrings
- No visible tattoos
- Stylish but professional-looking shoes (no extreme high heels or casual shoes)
- Clean hands and neatly trimmed fingernails
- Little or no perfume or cologne (some people are allergic and many people are put off by strong smells)
- Subtle makeup (for women)
- Exemplary personal hygiene

Remember that an interview is not the place to make flamboyant statements or to let your inner rebel run wild. Send a clear signal that you understand the business world and know how to adapt to it. You won't be taken seriously otherwise.

*If you want to be taken seriously, dress and act seriously.*

## Being Ready When You Arrive

When you go to your interview, bring a small notebook, a pen, a list of the questions you want to ask, several copies of your résumé (protected in a folder), an outline of what you have learned about the organization, and any past correspondence about the position. You may also want to take a small calendar, a transcript of your college grades, a list of references, and a portfolio containing samples of your work, performance reviews, and certificates of achievement.[37] Think carefully if you plan to use a tablet computer or any other device for note taking or reference during an interview. You don't want to waste any of the interviewer's time fumbling with it. Also, turn off your mobile phone; in a recent survey of hiring professionals, answering calls or texting while in an interview was identified as the most common mistake job candidates make during their interviews.[38]

*Be ready to go the minute you arrive at the interviewing site; don't fumble around for your résumé or your list of questions.*

Be sure you know when and where the interview will be held. The worst way to start any interview is to be late. Verify the route and time required to get there, even if that means travelling there ahead of time. Plan to arrive early, but don't approach the reception desk until five minutes or so before your appointed time.[39] Chances are the interviewer won't be ready to receive you until the scheduled time.

When you arrive, you may have to wait for a while. Use this time to review the key messages about yourself you want to get across in the interview. Conduct yourself professionally while waiting. Show respect for everyone you encounter and avoid chewing gum, eating, or drinking. Anything you do or say at this stage may get back to the interviewer, so make sure your best qualities show from the moment you enter the premises.

LEARNING OBJECTIVE ④
Explain how to succeed in all three stages of an interview.

# Interviewing for Success

At this point, you have a good sense of the overall process and know how to prepare for your interviews. The next step is to get familiar with the three stages of every interview: the warm-up, the question-and-answer session, and the close.

## The Warm-Up

The first minute of the interview is crucial, so stay alert and be on your best business behaviour.

Of the three stages, the warm-up is the most important, even though it may account for only a small fraction of the time you spend in the interview. Studies suggest that many interviewers, particularly those who are poorly trained in interviewing techniques, make up their minds within the first 20 seconds of contact with a candidate.[40] Don't let your guard down if it appears that the interviewer wants to engage in what feels like small talk; these exchanges are every bit as important as structured questions.

Body language is crucial at this point. Stand or sit up straight, maintain regular but natural eye contact, and don't fidget. When the interviewer extends a hand, respond with a firm but not overpowering handshake. Repeat the interviewer's name when you're introduced ("It's a pleasure to meet you, Ms. Litton"). Wait until you're asked to be seated or the interviewer has taken a seat. Let the interviewer start the discussion, and be ready to answer one or two substantial questions right away. The following are some common openers:[41]

- Why do you want to work here?
- What do you know about us?
- Tell me a little about yourself.

## The Question-and-Answer Stage

Questions and answers usually consume the greatest part of the interview. Depending on the type of interview, the interviewer will likely ask about your qualifications, discuss some of the points mentioned in your résumé, and ask about how you have handled particular situations in the past or would handle them in the future. You'll also be asking questions of your own.

Listen carefully to questions before you answer.

**ANSWERING AND ASKING QUESTIONS** Let the interviewer lead the conversation, and never answer a question before he or she has finished asking it. Not only is this type of interruption rude, but the last few words of the question might alter how you respond. As much as possible, avoid one-word, yes-or-no answers. Use the opportunity to expand on a positive response or explain a negative response. If you're asked a difficult question, pause before responding. Think through the implications of the question. For instance, the recruiter may know that you can't answer a question and only wants to know how you'll respond under pressure.

Whenever you're asked if you have any questions, or whenever doing so naturally fits the flow of the conversation, ask a question from the list you've prepared. Probe for what the company is looking for in its new employees so that you can show how you meet the firm's needs. Also try to zero in on any reservations the interviewer might have about you so that you can dispel them.

**LISTENING TO THE INTERVIEWER**   Paying attention when the interviewer speaks can be as important as giving good answers or asking good questions. Review the tips on listening offered in Chapter 2. The interviewer's facial expressions, eye movements, gestures, and posture may tell you the real meaning of what is being said. Be especially aware of how your answers are received. Does the interviewer nod in agreement or smile to show approval? If so, you're making progress. If not, you might want to introduce another topic or modify your approach.

**HANDLING DISCRIMINATORY QUESTIONS**   A variety of federal, provincial, and local laws prohibit employment discrimination on the basis of race, ethnicity, gender, age, marital status, religion, national origin, or disability. Interview questions designed to elicit information on these topics are potentially illegal.[42] Table 14.7 compares some specific questions that employers are and are not allowed to ask during an employment interview.

If an interviewer asks a potentially unlawful question, consider your options carefully before you respond. Remember that not all interviewers are **trained** interviewers. You can answer the question as it was asked, you can ask tactfully whether the question might be prohibited, you can simply refuse to answer it, or you can try to answer "the question behind the question."[43] For example, if an interviewer inappropriately asks whether you are married or have strong family ties in the area, he or she might be trying to figure out if you're willing to travel or relocate—both of which are acceptable questions. Only you can decide which is the right choice based on the situation.

## The Close

Like the warm-up, the end of the interview is more important than its brief duration would indicate. These last few minutes are your last opportunity to emphasize your value to the organization and to correct any misconceptions the interviewer might have. Be aware that many interviewers will ask whether you have any more questions at this point, so save one or two from your list.

| TABLE 14.7 | Interview Questions That May and May Not Be Asked |
|---|---|

| INTERVIEWERS MAY ASK THIS . . . | BUT NOT THIS |
|---|---|
| What is your name? | What was your maiden name? |
| Are you over 18? | When were you born? |
| Did you graduate from high school? | When did you graduate from high school? |
| [No questions about race are allowed.] | What is your race? |
| Can you perform [specific tasks]? | Do you have physical or mental disabilities? |
| [No questions about drug or alcohol use are allowed.] | Do you have a drug or alcohol problem? Are you taking any prescription drugs? |
| Would you be able to meet the job's requirement to frequently work weekends? | Would working on weekends conflict with your religion? |
| Do you have the legal right to work in Canada? | What country are you a citizen of? |
| Have you ever been convicted of a felony? | Have you ever been arrested? |
| This job requires that you speak French. Do you? | What language did you speak in your home when you were growing up? |

*Source:* Adapted from Dave Johnson, "Illegal Job Interview Questions," CBS Money Watch, 27 February 2012, www.cbsnews.com; "5 Illegal Interview Questions and How to Dodge Them," Forbes, 20 April 2012, www.forbes.com; Deanna G. Kucler, "Interview Questions: Legal or Illegal?" *Workforce Management,* accessed 28 September 2005, www.workforce.com.

Conclude an interview with courtesy and enthusiasm.

**CONCLUDING GRACEFULLY** You can usually tell when the interviewer is trying to conclude the session. He or she may ask whether you have any more questions, check the time, summarize the discussion, or simply tell you that the allotted time for the interview is up. When you get the signal, be sure to thank the interviewer for the opportunity and express your interest in the organization. If you can do so comfortably, try to pin down what will happen next, but don't press for an immediate decision.

If this is your second or third visit to the organization, the interview may end with an offer of employment. If you have other offers or need time to think about this offer, it's perfectly acceptable to thank the interviewer for the offer and ask for some time to consider it. If no job offer is made, the interview team may not have reached a decision yet, but you may tactfully ask when you can expect to know the decision.

Research salary ranges in your job, industry, and geographic region before you try to negotiate salary.

**DISCUSSING SALARY** If you receive an offer during the interview, you'll naturally want to discuss salary. However, let the interviewer raise the subject. If asked your salary requirements during the interview or on a job application, you can say that your requirements are open or negotiable or that you would expect a competitive compensation package.[44] Remember that you're negotiating a business deal, not asking for personal favours, so focus on the unique value you can bring to the job. The more information you have, the stronger your position will be.

## Interview Notes

Keeping careful record of your job interviews is essential.

Maintain a notebook or simple database with information about each company, interviewers' answers to your questions, contact information for each interviewer, the status of thank-you notes and other follow-up communication, and upcoming interview appointments.

**LEARNING OBJECTIVE** 5
Identify the most common employment messages that follow an interview and explain when you would use each one.

# Following Up After an Interview

Staying in contact with a prospective employer after an interview shows that you really want the job and are determined to get it. Doing so also gives you another chance to demonstrate your communication skills and sense of business etiquette. Following up brings your name to the interviewer's attention once again and reminds him or her that you're actively looking and waiting for the decision.

Any time you hear from a company during the application or interview process, be sure to respond quickly. Companies flooded with résumés may move on to another candidate if they don't hear back from you within 24 hours.[45]

## Thank-You Message

A thank-you message is more than a professional courtesy; it's another chance to promote yourself to an employer.

Write a thank-you message within two days of the interview, even if you feel you have little chance of getting the job. In addition to demonstrating good etiquette, a thank-you message gives you the opportunity to reinforce the reasons you are a good choice for the position and lets you respond to any negatives that might've arisen in the interview.[46] Acknowledge the interviewer's time and courtesy, convey your continued interest, reinforce the reasons that you are a good fit for the position, and ask politely for a decision (see Figure 14.6). Email is usually acceptable for follow-up messages, unless the interviewer has asked you to use other media.

## Message of Inquiry

Use the model for a direct request when you write an inquiry about a hiring decision.

If you're not advised of the interviewer's decision by the promised date or within two weeks, you might make an inquiry. A message of inquiry (which can be handled by email if the interviewer has given you his or her email address) is particularly appropriate if you've received a job offer from a second firm and don't want to accept it before

## FIGURE 14.6 Thank-You Message

you have an answer from the first. The following message illustrates the general model for a direct request:

> When we talked on April 7 about the fashion coordinator position in your North York showroom, you indicated that a decision would be made by May 1. I am still enthusiastic about the position and eager to know what conclusion you've reached.
>
> To complicate matters, another firm has now offered me a position and has asked that I reply within the next two weeks.
>
> Because your company seems to offer a greater challenge, I would appreciate knowing about your decision by Thursday, May 12. If you need more information before then, please let me know.

*Identifies the position and introduces the main idea*

*Places the reason for the request second*

*Makes a courteous request for specific action last, while clearly stating a preference for this organization*

## Request for a Time Extension

If you receive a job offer while other interviews are still pending, you can ask the employer for a time extension. Open with a strong statement of your continued interest in the job, ask for more time to consider the offer, provide specific reasons for the request, and assure the reader that you will respond by a specific date (see Figure 14.7).

## Letter of Acceptance

When you receive a job offer that you want to accept, reply within five days. Begin by accepting the position and expressing thanks. Identify the job that you're accepting. In the next paragraph, cover any necessary details. Conclude by saying that you look forward to reporting for work. As always, a positive letter should convey your enthusiasm and eagerness to cooperate:

> I'm delighted to accept the graphic design position in your advertising department at the salary of $3875 per month.

*Use the model for positive messages when you write a letter of acceptance.*

*Confirms the specific terms of the offer with a good-news statement at the beginning*

---

**FIGURE 14.7** **Request for a Time Extension**

From: Chang Li <ChangLi46@gmail.com> -ChangLi46@gmail.com

To: frank.lapuzo@**wholefoods.com**

Subject: Request for Extension

Dear Mr. Lapuzo:

*Begins with a strong statement of interest in the job* →

The e-commerce director position at Whole Foods is an exciting challenge and a great opportunity. I'm very pleased that you offered it to me.

*Emphasizes specific reasons for preferring the first job offer to help reassure the reader of sincerity* →

Because of another commitment, I would appreciate your giving me until January 25 to make a decision. Before our interview, I scheduled a follow-up interview with another company. I'm interested in your organization because of its commitment to quality and team-based management style, but I do feel obligated to keep my appointment.

← *Stresses a professional obligation as the reason for the request, rather than the desire to learn what the other company may offer*

If you need my decision immediately, I'll gladly let you know. However, if you can allow me the added time to fulfill the earlier commitment, I'd be grateful. Please let me know at your earliest convenience.

← *Closes with an expression of willingness to yield or compromise, while conveying continued interest in the position*

Sincerely,

Chang Li
1448 W15th Avenue
Vancouver, BC V5Z 3B5
(604) 266-6897

---

*Covers miscellaneous details in the middle*

*Closes with another reference to the good news and a look toward the future*

→ Enclosed are the health insurance forms you asked me to complete and sign. I've already given notice to my current employer and will be able to start work on Monday, January 16.

→ The prospect of joining your firm is exciting. Thank you for giving me this opportunity, and I look forward to making a positive contribution.

*Written acceptance of a job offer can be considered a legally binding contract.*

Be aware that a job offer and a written acceptance of that offer can constitute a legally binding contract, for both you and the employer. Before you send an acceptance letter, be sure you want the job.

## Letter Declining a Job Offer

*If you decide to decline a job offer, do so tactfully, using the model for negative messages.*

After all your interviews, you may find that you need to write a letter declining a job offer. Use the techniques for negative messages (see Chapter 8): open warmly, state the reasons for refusing the offer, decline the offer explicitly, and close on a pleasant note that expresses gratitude. By taking the time to write a sincere, tactful letter, you leave the door open for future contact:

*Uses a buffer in the opening paragraph*

→ One of the most interesting interviews I have ever had was the one last month at your Markham facility. I'm flattered that you would offer me the computer analyst position that we talked about.

*Precedes the bad news with tactfully phrased reasons for the applicant's unfavourable decision and leaves the door open*

→ I was fortunate to receive two job offers during my search. Because my desire to work abroad will be fulfilled at another company, I have accepted that job offer.

*Lets the reader down gently with a sincere and cordial ending*

→ I deeply appreciate the time you spent talking with me. Thank you again for your consideration and kindness.

## Letter of Resignation

If you get a job offer while currently employed, you can maintain good relations with your current employer by writing a thoughtful letter of resignation to your immediate supervisor. Follow the advice for negative messages and make the letter sound positive, regardless of how you feel. Say something favourable about the organization, the people you work with, or what you've learned on the job. Then state your intention to leave and give the date of your last day on the job. Be sure you give your current employer at least two weeks' notice.

> Letters of resignation should always be written in a gracious and professional style that avoids criticism of your employer or your colleagues.

My sincere thanks to you and to all the other Emblem Corporation employees for helping me learn so much about serving the public these past two years. You have given me much appreciated help and encouragement.

*← Uses an appreciative opening to serve as a buffer*

You may recall that when you first interviewed me, my goal was to become a customer relations supervisor. Because that opportunity has been offered to me by another organization, I am submitting my resignation. I will miss all of you, but I want to take advantage of this opportunity.

*← States reasons before the bad news itself, using tactful phrasing to help keep the relationship friendly, should the writer later want letters of recommendation*

I would like to terminate my work here two weeks from today but can arrange to work an additional week if you want me to train a replacement.

*← Discusses necessary details in an extra paragraph*

My sincere thanks and best wishes to all of you.

*← Has a cordial close*

---

# LEARNING OBJECTIVES: Check Your Progress

**❶ OBJECTIVE Explain the purposes of application letters and describe how to apply the AIDA organizational approach to them.**

The purposes of an application letter are to introduce your résumé, persuade an employer to read it, and request an interview. With the AIDA model, get attention in the opening paragraph by showing how your work skills could benefit the organization, by explaining how your qualifications fit the job, or by demonstrating an understanding of the organization's needs. Build interest and desire by showing how you can meet the job requirements and, near the end of this section, refer your reader to your résumé. Finally, motivate action by making your request easy to fulfill and by including all necessary contact information.

**❷ OBJECTIVE Describe the typical sequence of job interviews, the major types of interviews, and what employers look for during an interview.**

The typical sequence of interviews involves three stages. During the screening stage, employers filter out unqualified applicants and identify promising candidates. During the selection stage, the pool of applicants is narrowed through a variety of structured and unstructured interviewing methods. In the final stage, employers select the candidates who will receive offers and, if necessary, promote the benefits of joining the company.

Interviews can be distinguished by the way they are structured (structured or unstructured interviews), the number of people involved (one-on-one, panel, or group interviews), and the purpose of the interview (behavioural, situational, working, or stress interviews). The behavioural interview, probably the most common in terms of purpose, requires candidates to use their own experiences and attributes to craft answers. The situational interview is similar, but instead of using incidents from the candidate's past, it explores how the candidate would respond to hypothetical situations in the future.

Employers look for two things during an employment interview. First, they seek evidence that an applicant is qualified for the position. Second, they seek reassurance that an applicant will be a good fit with the "personality" of the organization and the position.

**3 OBJECTIVE List six tasks you need to complete to prepare for a successful job interview.**

To prepare for a successful job interview, (1) complete the research you started when planning your résumé, (2) think ahead about questions you'll need to answer and questions you'll want to ask, (3) bolster your confidence by focusing on your strengths and preparing thoroughly, (4) polish your interviewing style, (5) present a professional image with businesslike clothing and good grooming, and (6) arrive on time and ready to begin.

**4 OBJECTIVE Explain how to succeed in all three stages of an interview.**

All employment interviews have three stages. The warm-up stage is the most important because first impressions greatly influence an interviewer's decision. The question-and-answer stage, during which you will answer and ask questions, is the longest. The close is your final opportunity to promote your value to the organization.

**5 OBJECTIVE Identify the most common employment messages that follow an interview and explain when you would use each one.**

Following an interview, send a *thank-you message* to show appreciation, emphasize your strengths, and politely ask for a decision. Send an *inquiry* if you haven't received the interviewer's decision by the date promised or within two weeks of the interview—especially if you've received a job offer from another firm. You can *request a time extension* if you need more time to consider an offer. Send a *letter of acceptance* after receiving a job offer that you want to take. Send a *letter declining a job offer* when you want to refuse an offer tactfully. Finally, if you are currently employed, send a *letter of resignation* after you have accepted the offer of another job.

MyBCommLab®

Go to MyBCommLab for everything you need to help you succeed in the job you've always wanted! Tools and resources include the following:
- Writing Activities    • Document Makeovers
- Video Exercises    • Grammar Exercises—and much more!

# Practise Your Grammar

Effective business communication starts with strong grammar skills. To improve your grammar skills, go to MyBCommLab, where you'll find exercises and diagnostic tests to help you produce clear, effective communication.

# Test Your Knowledge

To review chapter content related to each question, refer to the indicated Learning Objective.

1. What are three ways you can get attention in the opening of a letter of application? L.O.**1**
2. What should your objective be for an interview during the selection stage? L.O.**2**
3. How does a structured interview differ from an open-ended interview? L.O.**2**
4. Why are the questions you ask during an interview as important as the answers you give to the interviewer's questions? L.O.**3**
5. What are the three stages of every interview, and which is the most important? L.O.**4**

## Apply Your Knowledge

To review chapter content related to each question, refer to the indicated Learning Objective.

1. How can you distinguish yourself from other candidates in a screening interview and still keep your responses short and to the point? Explain. L.O.❷

2. How can you prepare for a situational or behavioural interview if you have no experience with the job for which you are interviewing? L.O.❷

3. If you want to switch jobs because you can't work with your supervisor, how can you explain this situation to a prospective employer? L.O.❹

4. If you lack one important qualification for a job but have made it past the initial screening stage, how should you prepare to handle this issue during the next round of interviews? Explain your answer. L.O.❸

5. What is an interviewer likely to conclude about you if you don't have any questions to ask during the interview? L.O.❹

## Practise Your Skills

### ACTIVITIES

Each activity is labelled according to the primary skill or skills you will need to use. To review relevant chapter content, you can refer to the indicated Learning Objective. In some instances, supporting information will be found in another chapter, as indicated.

1. **Message Strategies: Employment Messages** L.O.❶ Revise this message so that it follows this chapter's guidelines.

> I'm writing to let you know about my availability for the brand manager job you advertised. As you can see from my enclosed résumé, my background is perfect for the position. Even though I don't have any real job experience, my grades have been outstanding considering that I went to a top-ranked business school.
>
> I did many things during my undergraduate years to prepare me for this job:
> * Earned a 3.4 out of a 4.0 with a 3.8 in my business courses
> * Elected representative to the student governing association
> * Selected to receive the Lester Pearson Award
> * Worked to earn a portion of my tuition
>
> I am sending my résumé to all the top firms, but I like yours better than any of the rest.

> Your reputation is tops in the industry, and I want to be associated with a business that can say it's the best.
>
> If you wish for me to come in for an interview, I can come on a Friday afternoon or anytime on weekends when I don't have classes. Again, thanks for considering me for your brand manager position.

2. **Message Strategies: Employment Messages** L.O.❶ Revise this message so that it follows this chapter's guidelines.

> Did you receive my résumé? I sent it to you at least two months ago and haven't heard anything. I know you keep résumés on file, but I just want to be sure that you keep me in mind. I heard you are hiring health-care managers and certainly would like to be considered for one of those positions.
>
> Since I last wrote you, I've worked in a variety of positions that have helped prepare me for management. To wit, I've become lunch manager at the restaurant where I work, which involved a raise in pay. I now manage a waitstaff of 12 girls and take the lunch receipts to the bank every day.

*(continued)*

Of course, I'd much rather be working at a real job, and that's why I'm writing again. Is there anything else you would like to know about me or my background? I would really like to know more about your company. Is there any literature you could send me? If so, I would really appreciate it.

I think one reason I haven't been hired yet is that I don't want to leave Edmonton. So I hope when you think of me, it's for a position that wouldn't require moving. Thanks again for considering my application.

3. **Career Management: Preparing for Interviews** L.O.❷ Google yourself, Bing yourself, scour your social networking profiles, review your Twitter messages, and explore every other possible online source you can think of that might have something about you. If you find anything potentially embarrassing, remove it if possible. Write a summary of your search-and-destroy mission in a report to your instructor.

4. **Career Management: Researching Target Employers** L.O.❸ Select a large company (one on which you can easily find information) where you might like to work. Use online sources to gather some preliminary research on the company; don't limit your search to the company's own website.
   a. What did you learn about this organization that would help you during an interview there?
   b. What internet sources did you use to obtain this information?
   c. Armed with this information, what aspects of your background do you think might appeal to this company's recruiters?
   d. If you choose to apply for a job with this company, what keywords would you include on your résumé? Why?

5. **Career Management: Interviewing** L.O.❸ Prepare written answers to 10 of the questions listed in Table 14.4.

6. **Career Management: Interviewing** L.O.❸ Write a short email message to your instructor, discussing what you believe are your greatest strengths and weaknesses from an employment perspective. Next, explain how these strengths and weaknesses would be viewed by interviewers evaluating your qualifications and what you can do about the weaknesses.

7. **Career Management: Interviewing; Collaboration: Team Projects** L.O.❹, **Chapter 2** Divide the class into two groups. Half the class will be recruiters for a large chain of national department stores, looking to fill 15 manager-trainee positions. The other half of the class will be candidates for the job. The company is specifically looking for candidates who demonstrate these three qualities: initiative, dependability, and willingness to assume responsibility.
   a. Have each recruiter select and interview an applicant for 10 minutes.
   b. Have all the recruiters discuss how they assessed the applicant in each of the three desired qualities. What questions did they ask or what did they use as an indicator to determine whether the candidate possessed the quality?
   c. Have all the applicants discuss what they said to convince the recruiters that they possessed each of the three desired qualities.

8. **Message Strategies: Interviewing, Practising Answering Behavioural Interview Questions** L.O.❹ In the following activity, use the four-step method to develop your answer:
   1. Describe a specific situation (from work, education, volunteering, or extracurricular activities).
   2. Tell what your role was.
   3. Tell what action you took.
   4. Describe the positive result.

### Part A

Below are five behavioural interview questions. Write a response to one of them.
   a. Describe a situation in which you were able to use persuasion to successfully convince someone to see things your way.
   b. Describe an instance when you had to think on your feet to extricate yourself from a difficult situation.
   c. Give a specific example of a time when you used good judgment and logic in solving a problem.
   d. Describe a time when you were faced with problems or stresses that tested your coping skills.
   e. Give an example of a time in which you had to be relatively quick in coming to a decision.

### Part B

Pick a partner and take turns answering the question you selected in Part A. Give the presenter feedback on:
- The content of the answer
- Use of the four-part response
- The delivery manner
- The nonverbal message sent by the speaker

**Part C**

Revise your answer based on your partner's feedback and submit it to your instructor. Find more practise sample answers at www.quintcareers.com/sample_behavioral.html.

9. **Message Strategies: Interviewing: Writing Case Questions Designed to Find Out How You Would Behave in Difficult Situations L.O.4** With a partner, describe a difficult situation you might face in a particular job that you would like to have. For example, what difficulties might arise in your position as an accountant for a film production company or as an administrator on a construction site?

After you have written your scenario, apply the four-step process to develop a suitable answer. Be prepared to share your scenario and your ideas on how to answer the question with the class.

10. **Message Strategies: Preparing for Behavioural Interview Questions L.O.4** Visit www.quintcareers .com and search "Interview Questions" to find a link to "Job Interview Questions Database." Select 10 questions, prepare your answers, and compare them to the sample answers provided on the website. Write a short summary explaining how your answers compared to the samples given. What should you add or leave out of your answers?

11. **Message Strategies: Employment Messages L.O.5** Revise this message so that it follows this chapter's guidelines.

Thank you for the really marvellous opportunity to meet you and your colleagues at Starret Engine Company. I really enjoyed touring your facilities and talking with all the people there. You have quite a crew! Some of the other companies I have visited have been so rigid and uptight that I can't imagine how I would fit in. It's a relief to run into a group of people who seem to enjoy their work as much as all of you do.

I know that you must be looking at many other candidates for this job, and I know that some of them will probably be more experienced than I am. But I do want to emphasize that my two-year stint in the Navy involved a good deal of engineering work. I don't think I mentioned all my shipboard responsibilities during the interview.

Please give me a call within the next week to let me know your decision. You can usually find me at my dormitory in the evening after dinner (phone: 877-9080).

12. **Message Strategies: Employment Messages L.O.5** Revise this message so that it follows this chapter's guidelines.

I have recently received a very attractive job offer from the Warrington Company. But before I let them know one way or another, I would like to consider any offer that your firm may extend. I was quite impressed with your company during my recent interview, and I am still very interested in a career there.

I don't mean to pressure you, but Warrington has asked for my decision within 10 days. Could you let me know by Tuesday whether you plan to offer me a position? That would give me enough time to compare the two offers.

13. **Message Strategies: Employment Messages L.O.5** Revise this message so that it follows this chapter's guidelines.

I'm writing to say that I must decline your job offer. Another company has made me a more generous offer, and I have decided to accept. However, if things don't work out for me there, I will let you know. I sincerely appreciate your interest in me.

14. **Message Strategies: Employment Messages; Communication Ethics: Resolving Ethical Dilemmas L.O.5, Chapter 1** You've decided to accept a new position with a competitor of your company. Write a letter of resignation to your supervisor, announcing your decision. In an email message to your instructor, address the following questions:
a. Will you notify your employer that you are joining a competing firm? Explain.
b. Will you use the direct or indirect approach? Explain.
c. Will you send your letter by email, send it by regular mail, or place it on your supervisor's desk?

15. **Message Strategies: Exploring LinkedIn** L.O.➎ Visit LinkedIn Jobs at www.linkedin.com/jobs (open a free LinkedIn account if required) to find a job that interests you. Next, look up the company and using whatever medium your instructor requests, write a brief summary (no more than one page) of what you learned. If you find that you were not qualified for the position, identify what types of education or experience you would need to add to apply for this job in the future.

# CASES

**Apply the three-step writing process to the following cases, as assigned by your instructor.**

▌ **Writing Application Letters** ▌ **Email Skills**
### 1. Message Strategies: Employment Messages L.O.➊

Use one of the websites listed in Table 13.3 to find a job opening in your target profession. If you haven't narrowed down to one career field yet, choose a business job for which you will have at least some qualifications at the time of your graduation.

**YOUR TASK** Write a letter of application as if you were applying for this job. Base your letter on your actual qualifications for the position, and be sure to "echo" the requirements listed in the job description. Include the job description with your letter when you submit it to your instructor.

▌ **Microblogging Skills**
### 2. Message Strategies: Employment Messages L.O.➊

If you want to know whether job candidates can express themselves clearly on Twitter, why not test them as part of the application process? Rather than having job candidates use conventional application methods, some companies ask intern candidates to tweet their applications in 13 messages.[47]

**YOUR TASK** Find a job opening on Twitter by searching on any of the following hashtags: #hiring, #joblisting, or #nowhiring.[48] Next, write an "application letter" composed of 13 individual tweets (140 characters maximum). If your class is set up with private Twitter accounts, go ahead and send the tweets. Otherwise, email them to your instructor or post them on your class blog, as your instructor indicates.

▌ **Email Skills**
### 3. Message Strategies: Employment Messages L.O.➊

Finding job openings that align perfectly with your professional interests is wonderful, but it doesn't always happen. Sometimes you have to widen your search and go after whatever opportunities happen to be available. Even when the opportunity is not ideal, however, you still need to approach the employer with enthusiasm and a focused, audience-centric message.

**YOUR TASK** Find a job opening for which you will be qualified when you graduate (or close to being qualified, for the purposes of this activity), but make it one that is outside your primary field of interest. Write an email application letter for this opening, making a compelling case that you are the right candidate for this job.

▌ **Interviewing** ▌ **Blogging Skills** ▌ **Team Skills**
### 4. Career Management: Researching Target Employers L.O.➌

Research is a critical element of the job search process. With information in hand, you increase the chance of finding the right opportunity (and avoiding bad choices), and you impress interviewers in multiple ways by demonstrating initiative, curiosity, research and analysis skills, an appreciation for the complex challenges of running a business, and willingness to work to achieve results.

**YOUR TASK** With a small team of classmates, use online job listings (see Table 13.1) to identify an intriguing job opening that at least one member of the team would seriously consider pursuing as graduation approaches. (You'll find it helpful if the career is related to at least one team member's major or on-the-job experience so that the team can benefit from some knowledge of the profession in question.) Next, research the company, its competitors, its markets, and this specific position to identify five questions that would (a) help the team member decide if this is a good opportunity and (b) show an interviewer that you've really done your homework. Go beyond the basic and obvious questions to identify current, specific, and complex issues that only deep research can uncover.

For example, is the company facing significant technical, financial, legal, or regulatory challenges that threaten its ability to grow or perhaps even survive in the long term? Or is the market evolving in a way that positions this particular company for dramatic growth? In a post for your class blog, list your five questions, identify how you uncovered the issue, and explain why each is significant.

**▌Team Skills**
**5. Career Management: Interviewing** L.O.❹

Interviewing is a skill that can be improved through practice and observation.

**YOUR TASK**  You and all other members of your class are to write letters of application for an entry-level or management-trainee position that requires an engaging personality and intelligence but a minimum of specialized education or experience. Sign your letter with a fictitious name that conceals your identity. Next, polish (or create) a résumé that accurately identifies you and your educational and professional accomplishments.

Now, three members of the class who volunteer as interviewers divide up all the anonymously written application letters. Then each interviewer selects a candidate who seems the most convincing in his or her letter. At this time, the selected candidates identify themselves and give the interviewers their résumés.

Each interviewer then interviews his or her chosen candidate in front of the class, seeking to understand how the items on the résumé qualify the candidate for the job. At the end of the interviews, the class decides who gets the job and discusses why this candidate was successful. Afterward, retrieve your letter, sign it with the right name, and submit it to your instructor.

**▌Team Skills**
**6. Career Management: Interviewing** L.O.❹

Select a company in an industry in which you might like to work and then identify an interesting position within the company. Study the company and prepare for an interview with that company.

**YOUR TASK**  Working with a classmate, develop a list of questions, including at least three behavioural or situational questions, then take turns interviewing each other for your chosen positions. Interviewers should take notes during the interview. When the interview is complete, critique each other's performance. (Interviewers should critique how well candidates prepared for the interview and answered the questions; interviewees should critique the quality of the questions asked.) Write a follow-up letter thanking your interviewer and submit the letter to your instructor.

**▌Following Up After an Interview ▌Letter Writing Skills**
**7. Message Strategies: Employment Messages** L.O.❺

Due to a mix-up in your job application scheduling, you accidentally applied for your third-choice job before going after the one you really wanted. What you want to do is work in retail marketing with the upscale department store Holt Renfrew in Montreal; what you have been offered is a job with Reitman's, 60 km away in the town of Saint Jerome.

You review your notes. Your Reitman's interview was three weeks ago with the human resources manager, R.P. Bronson, who has just written to offer you the position. The store's address is 27 Rue Baron, Saint Jerome, QC, J1H 5N1. Ms. Bronson notes that she can hold the position open for 10 days. You have an interview scheduled with Holt Renfrew next week, but it is unlikely that you will know the store's decision within this 10-day period.

**YOUR TASK**  Write to Ms. Bronson, requesting a reasonable delay in your consideration of her job offer.

**▌Letter Writing Skills ▌Email Skills**
**8. Message Strategies: Employment Messages** L.O.❺

Fortunately for you, your interview with Holt Renfrew (see Case 7) went well, and you've just received a job offer from the company.

**YOUR TASK**  Write a letter to Ms. R.P. Bronson at Reitmans, declining her job offer, and write an email message to Clarisse Baptiste at Holt's, accepting her job offer. Make up any information you need when accepting the Holt Renfrew offer.

## BUSINESS COMMUNICATION NOTEBOOK

# Workplace Skills

## Interview Strategies: Answering the 15 Toughest Questions

You can expect to face several tough questions during every interview. If you're prepared with thoughtful answers and specific examples, you're bound to make a good impression. Here are 15 tough questions and guidelines for planning answers that put your qualities in the best light.

1. **What was the toughest decision you ever had to make?** Be prepared with a good example, explaining why the decision was difficult and how you decided.

2. **Why do you want to work for this organization?** Show that you've done your homework, and cite some things going on in the company that appeal to you.

3. **Why should we employ you?** Emphasize your academic strengths, job skills, and enthusiasm for the firm. Tie specific skills to the employer's needs, and give examples of how you can learn and become productive quickly. Cite past activities to prove you can work with others as part of a team.

4. **If we hire you, what changes would you make?** No one can know what to change in a position before settling in and learning about the company operations. State that you would analyze first before making recommendations.

5. **Can we offer you a career path?** Reply that you believe so, but you need to know more about the normal progression within the organization.

6. **What are your greatest strengths?** Answer sincerely by summarizing your strong points: "I can see what must be done and then do it," or "I'm willing to make decisions," or "I work well with others."

7. **What are your greatest weaknesses?** Describe a weakness so that it sounds like a virtue—honestly revealing something about yourself while showing how it works to an employer's advantage. If you sometimes drive yourself too hard, explain that it has helped when you've had to meet deadlines.

8. **What didn't you like about previous jobs you've held?** State what you didn't like and discuss what the experience taught you. Avoid making slighting references to former employers.

9. **How do you spend your leisure time?** Mention a cross-section of interests: active and quiet, social and solitary.

10. **Are there any weaknesses in your education or experience?** Take stock of your weaknesses before the interview, and practise discussing them in a positive light.

11. **Where do you want to be five years from now?** This question tests whether you're merely using this job as a stopover until something better comes along and whether you've given thought to your long-term goals.

12. **What are your salary expectations?** If you're asked this at the outset, say, "Why don't we discuss salary after you decide whether I'm right for the job?" If the interviewer asks this after showing real interest in you, speak up. Do your homework, but if you need a clue about salary levels, say, "Can you discuss the salary range with me?"

13. **What would you do if . . . ?** This question tests your resourcefulness. For example: "What would you do if your computer broke down during an audit?" Your answer is less important than your approach to the problem—and a calm approach is best.

14. **Tell me something about yourself.** This is a great chance to sell yourself. Ask what the interviewer wants to know. If this point is clarified, respond. If it isn't, explain how your skills can contribute to the job and the organization.

15. **Do you have any questions about the organization or the job?** Employers like candidates who are interested in the organization. Convey your interest and enthusiasm as you ask your prepared questions.

## Applications for Success

Improve your interviewing skills by visiting Quintessential Careers (www.quintcareers.com/interview_question_database/) and selecting 20 interview questions.

Answer the following questions:

1. Which question seems the toughest to you? In no more than two paragraphs, write out your answer to the question that you think is the toughest of all. Then submit your work to your instructor.

2. When an interviewer asks you a question, what makes one answer more effective than another? Consider some of the ways answers can vary: specific versus general, assertive versus passive, informal versus formal.

# Format and Layout of Business Documents

The format and layout of business documents vary from country to country; they even vary within Canada. In addition, many organizations develop their own variations of standard styles, adapting documents to the types of messages they send and the kinds of audiences they communicate with. The formats described here are more common than others.

## First Impressions

Your documents tell readers a lot about you and about your company's professionalism. So all your documents must look neat, present a professional image, and be easy to read. Your audience's first impression of a document comes from the quality of its paper, the way it is customized, and its general appearance.

### Paper

To give a quality impression, businesspeople consider carefully the paper they use. Several aspects of paper contribute to the overall impression:

- **Weight.** Paper quality is judged by weight. The weight most commonly used by Canadian businesses is 20-pound paper, but 16- and 24-pound versions are also used.
- **Cotton content.** Paper quality is also judged by the percentage of cotton in the paper. Cotton doesn't yellow over time the way wood pulp does, plus it's both strong and soft. For letters and outside reports, use paper with a 25 percent cotton content. For memos and other internal documents, you can use a lighter-weight paper with lower cotton content.
- **Size.** In Canada, the standard paper size for business documents is 8½ by 11 inches. Standard legal documents are 8½ by 14 inches.
- **Colour.** White is the standard colour for business purposes, although neutral colours such as grey and ivory are sometimes used.

### Appearance

Nearly all business documents are produced using an inkjet or laser printer. Certain documents, however, should be handwritten (such as a note of condolence). Be sure to handwrite, print, or type the envelope to match the document. However, even a letter on the best-quality paper with the best-designed letterhead may look unprofessional if it's poorly produced. So pay close attention to all the factors affecting appearance, including the following:

- **Margins.** Companies in Canada make sure that documents (especially external ones) are centred on the page, with margins of at least 2.5 cm (1 inch) all around.
- **Line length.** Lines are rarely right-hand justified because the resulting text looks too formal and can be difficult to read.
- **Character spacing.** Use proper spacing between characters and after punctuation. For example, Canadian conventions include leaving one space after commas, semicolons, colons, and sentence-ending periods. Each letter in a person's initials is followed by a period and a single space. Abbreviations such as USA or MBA may or may not have periods, but they never have internal spaces.
- **Corrections.** Messy corrections are obvious and unacceptable in business documents. Reprint any document requiring a lot of corrections.

## Reports

Enhance your report's effectiveness by paying careful attention to its appearance and layout. Follow whatever guidelines your organization prefers, always being neat and consistent throughout. If it's up to you to decide formatting questions, the following conventions may help you decide how to handle margins, headings, spacing and indention, and page numbers.

### Margins

All margins on a report page are at least 2.5 cm wide. For double-spaced pages, use 2.5-cm margins; for single-spaced pages, set margins between 3 cm and 3.75 cm. The top, left, and right margins are usually the same, but the bottom margins can be one and a half

**FIGURE A.1** Margins for Formal Reports

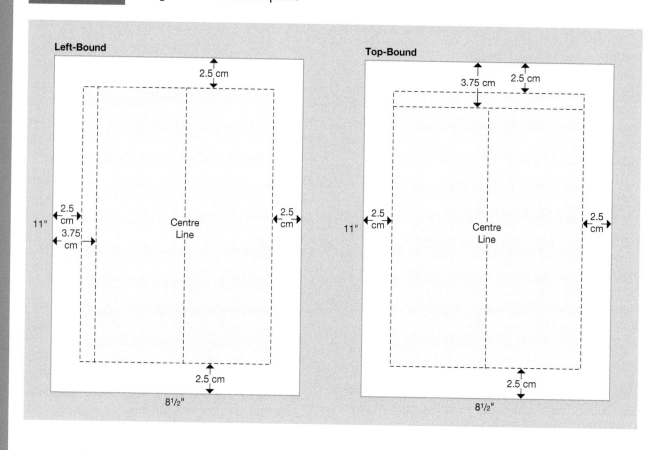

times deeper. Some special pages also have deeper top margins. Set top margins as deep as 5 cm for pages that contain major titles: prefatory parts (such as the table of contents or the executive summary), supplementary parts (such as the endnotes or bibliography), and textual parts (such as the first page of the text or the first page of each chapter).

If you're going to bind your report at the left or at the top, add 1.25 cm to the margin on the bound edge (see Figure A.1). The space taken by the binding on left-bound reports makes the centre point of the text 0.5 cm to the right of the centre of the paper. Be sure to centre headings between the margins, not between the edges of the paper. Computers can do this for you automatically.

## Headings

If you don't have a template supplied by your employer, choose a design for headings and subheadings that clearly distinguishes the various levels in the hierarchy. The first-level headings should be the most prominent, on down to the lowest-level subheading.

## Page Numbers

Remember that every page in the report is counted; however, not all pages show numbers. The first page of the report, the title page, is unnumbered. All other pages in the prefatory section are numbered with a lower case roman numeral, beginning with *ii* and continuing with *iii*, *iv*, *v*, and so on. Start numbering with Arabic numerals (1, 2, and so on) on the first page of the body (normally the Introduction). You have numerous options for placing and formatting page numbers. Position the numbers so they are easy to see as the reader flips through the report.

A sample report page showing headings and layout is shown in Figure A.2.

## Email

Because email messages can act both as memos (carrying information within your company) and as letters (carrying information outside your company and around the world), their format depends on your audience and purpose. You may choose to have your email resemble a letter or you may decide to keep things as

FIGURE A.2 | Sample Report Page: Excerpt from an Internal Report on Recruiting

Paragraphs are single spaced with double spaces between

Specific headings tell what is in each section

Subheadings are distinguished by a different type style

Pages are numbered

### INTRODUCTION

On Feb. 12, you asked our department to look into a way to reduce our company's costs for hiring. Our company currently spends $1340 per new hire for recruiting and interviewing. Three human resource officers work full time to source applicants and arrange interviews. Recent research shows that recruiting over the internet, called "e-cruiting," could not only save us time and money, but also extend the reach of our recruitment.

### USE OF INTERNET FOR RECRUITING

Currently 30 000 to 100 000 internet sites are devoted to recruiting and more than 150 million people are using the internet in North America. Last year, 74 percent of those people over the age of 18 used the internet to look for a job. That number represents a huge pool of potential talent that we might tap. Craigslist is an example of the type of network we could use for advertising and recruitment.

### POTENTIAL FOR COST-SAVING

Using the internet for recruitment has the potential for saving money. The Bank of Montreal is reported to have saved $1 million by relying on e-cruiting this year. Currently only 2 percent of our building-industry competitors are using this new technique to find good employees. We could be among the first in our industry to use the technique.

### TWO WAYS E-CRUITING CAN HELP

E-cruiting can improve our current methods of recruitment in two ways.

#### Faster Access to Available Candidates

We can use software to scan and screen potential candidates from huge online data banks of resumés. We list the qualifications we need, and the job sites send us the resumés of candidates who have those qualifications. This approach will save our company approximately 6 hours of work per hiring. The pre-screening process will already be done—and this service is free.

#### Reduced Costs to Advertise

We can list our job openings on the major career websites such as monster.ca, hotjobs.com, or careermosaic.com for only $100–$300 per month—a lot less than the $1000 we pay for local newspaper advertisements. Plus, the online listing reaches a potentially unlimited audience, and it has no word limit. You can describe the openings in as much detail as you like. This way, we may attract some candidates who don't post their resumés online but who do check the web for job openings.

#### TIME SAVINGS

Bank of Montreal and Hudson's Bay, who use e-cruiting, report they have cut hiring times from six weeks to one hour.

1

---

simple as an interoffice memo. A modified memo format is appropriate for most email messages.[1] All email programs include two major elements: the header and the body (see Figure A.3).

## Header

The email header depends on the particular program you use. Some programs even allow you to choose between a shorter and a longer version. However, most headers contain similar information.

- **To:** Contains the name of the receiver and/or audience's email address. Most email programs also allow you to send mail to an entire group of people all at once by first creating a distribution list.
- **From:** Contains your email address.
- **Date:** Contains the day of the week, date (day, month, year), time, and time zone.

## FIGURE A.3 A Typical Email Message

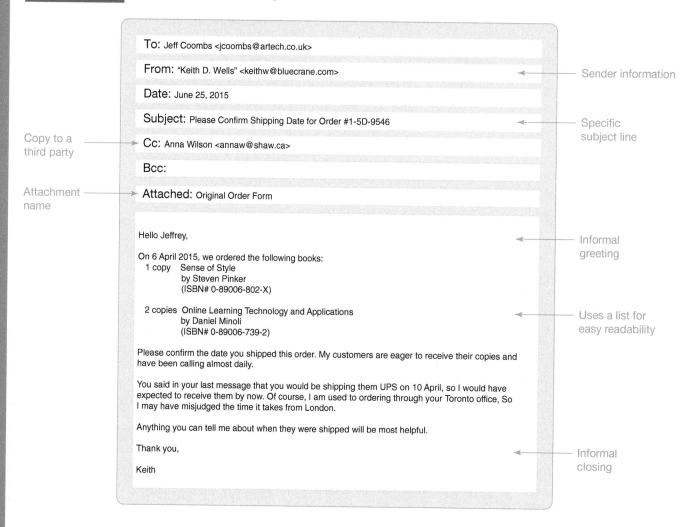

Sender information

Copy to a third party

Specific subject line

Attachment name

Informal greeting

Uses a list for easy readability

Informal closing

---

- **Subject:** Describes the content of the message and presents an opportunity for you to build interest in your message.
- **Cc:** Allows you to send copies of a message to more than one person at a time. It also allows everyone on the list to see who else received the same message.
- **Bcc:** Lets you send copies to people without the other recipients knowing—a practice considered unethical by some.[2]
- **Attachments:** Contains the name(s) of the file(s) you attach to your email message (a document, a picture, an audio or video file, or a spreadsheet).

## Body

The rest of the space below the header is for the body of your message. In the *To:* and *From:* lines, some headers actually print out the names of the sender and receiver (in addition to their email addresses). Other headers do not.

Include a greeting such as "Hello" in your email. Greetings personalize your message. Do not use casual greetings such as "Hey." Leave one line space above and below your greeting to set it off from the rest of your message. You may end your greeting with a colon (formal), a comma (conversational), or even two hyphens (informal)—depending on the level of formality you want.

Your message begins one blank line space below your greeting. Just as in memos and letters, skip one line space between paragraphs and include headings, numbered lists, bulleted lists, and embedded lists when appropriate. Limit your line lengths to a maximum of 80 characters by inserting a hard return at the end of each line.

One blank line space below your message, include a simple closing, often just one word. A blank line space below that, include your signature. Whether you type your name or use a signature file, including your signature personalizes your message.

# Memos

Electronic media have replaced most internal printed memos in many companies, but you may have occasion to send printed memos from time to time. These can be simple announcements or messages, or they can be short reports using the memo format.

On your document, include a title such as *MEMO* or *INTEROFFICE CORRESPONDENCE* (all in capitals) centred at the top of the page or aligned with the left margin.

Also at the top, include the words *To*, *From*, *Date*, and *Subject*—followed by the appropriate information—with a blank line between, as shown here:

```
MEMO
TO:
FROM:
DATE:
SUBJECT:
```

---

**FIGURE A.4** **Sample Memo**

### MEMORANDUM

**To:** Jodie Whitehead, Director of Public Relations

**From:** Jessie Long, Associate Director of Human Resources

**Date:** May 18, 2015

**Re:** **IMPROVING COMPANY RECRUITMENT**

Employee turnover in our company is at 20 percent, and filling these vacancies can take us up to one year. High turnover is costing our company time and money. Giving employees a small amount of company stock could help us reduce our costs by improving retention.

**How the Stock Program Would Work**

Employees would be given $200 worth of stock after the first three months with the company and $500 of stock after they have been with the company for two years. At this point they would also have an option of purchasing additional stock at a 10 percent discount.

Human Resources would track when the stock option should be offered to each employee. The offer would be renewed every five years. The cost of offering this benefit to all our staff is $43 000 for the first seven-year period. The cost of recruitment and hiring is already $35 000 for the previous three years.

**Advantages of Offering Applicants a Stock Bonus**

- We can still honour our internal pay scale
- Employees expecting stock will feel they have more invested in the company.
- When employees realize stock gains, they will be more likely to stay employed.
- We are able to offer a benefit to counter the competitive forces outside our company without hiring additional staff or losing productivity.

**Action**

Is it possible to meet with you on Wednesday, May 23rd, to further discuss ways to decrease employee turnover? Please let me know your thoughts.

You can arrange these four pieces of information in almost any order. The *date* sometimes appears without the heading *Date*. The subject may be presented with the letters *Re:* (in place of *SUBJECT:*) or without any heading (but in capital letters so that it stands out clearly). You may want to include a file or reference number, introduced by the word *File*.

The following guidelines will help you effectively format specific memo elements:

- **Addressees.** When sending a memo to a long list of people, include the notation *See distribution list* or *See below* in the *To* position at the top; then list the names at the end of the memo. Arrange this list alphabetically, except when high-ranking officials deserve more prominent placement. You can also address memos to groups of people—*All Sales Representatives, Production Group, New Product Team*.
- **Subject line.** The subject line of a memo helps busy co-workers quickly find out what your memo is about. Although the subject "line" may overflow onto a second line, it's most helpful when it's short (but still informative).
- **Body.** Start the body of the memo on the second or third line below the heading. Like the body of a letter, it's usually single-spaced with blank lines between paragraphs. Handle lists, important passages, and subheadings as you do in letters.
- **Second page.** If the memo carries over to a second page, head the second page just as you head the second page of a letter.
- **Writer's initials.** Unlike a letter, a memo doesn't require a complimentary close or a signature, because your name is already prominent at the top. However, you may initial the memo—either beside the name appearing at the top of the memo or at the bottom of the memo—or you may even sign your name at the bottom, particularly if the memo deals with money or confidential matters.
- **Other elements.** Treat elements such as reference initials, enclosure notations, and copy notations just as you would in a letter.

Informal, routine, or brief reports for distribution within a company are often presented in memo form (see Chapter 10). Don't include report parts such as a table of contents and appendixes.

# Letters

Canadian businesses commonly use letterhead stationery, which may be either professionally printed or designed in-house using word-processing templates and graphics. The letterhead includes the company's name and address, usually at the top of the page but sometimes along the left side or even at the bottom. Other information may be included in the letterhead as well: the company's telephone number, email address, fax number, website address, product lines, date of establishment, slogan, and symbol (logo). Well-designed letterhead gives readers the company's name and address and often its logo, creating a positive impression.[3]

For as much as it's meant to accomplish, the letterhead should be as simple as possible.

In Canada, businesses always use letterhead for the first page of a letter. Successive pages are usually plain sheets of paper that match the letterhead in colour and quality. Some companies use a specially printed second-page letterhead that bears only the company's name. All business letters have certain elements in common. Several of these elements appear in every letter; others appear only when desirable or appropriate.

## Standard Letter Parts

The letter in Figure A.5 shows the placement of standard letter parts. The writer of this business letter had no letterhead available but correctly included a heading. All business letters typically include the following eight elements.

**HEADING** Letterhead (the usual heading) shows the organization's name, full address, telephone number (almost always), and email address (often). If letterhead stationery is not available, the heading includes a return address (but no name) and starts 13 lines from the top of the page, which leaves a 5-cm top margin.

**DATE** If you're using letterhead, place the date at least one blank line beneath the lowest part of the letterhead. Without letterhead, place the date immediately below the return address. The usual method of writing the date in Canada uses the full name of the month (no abbreviations), followed by the day (in numerals, without *st, nd, rd,* or *th*), a comma, and then the year: July 14, 2012. Some organizations follow other conventions (see Table A.1). To maintain the utmost clarity in international correspondence, always spell out the name of the month in dates.[4]

**INSIDE ADDRESS** The inside address identifies the recipient of the letter. For Canadian correspondence, begin the inside address at least one line below the date. Precede the addressee's name with a courtesy title, such as *Dr., Mr.,* or *Ms.* The accepted courtesy title for women in business is Ms., although a woman known

## FIGURE A.5 Standard Letter Parts

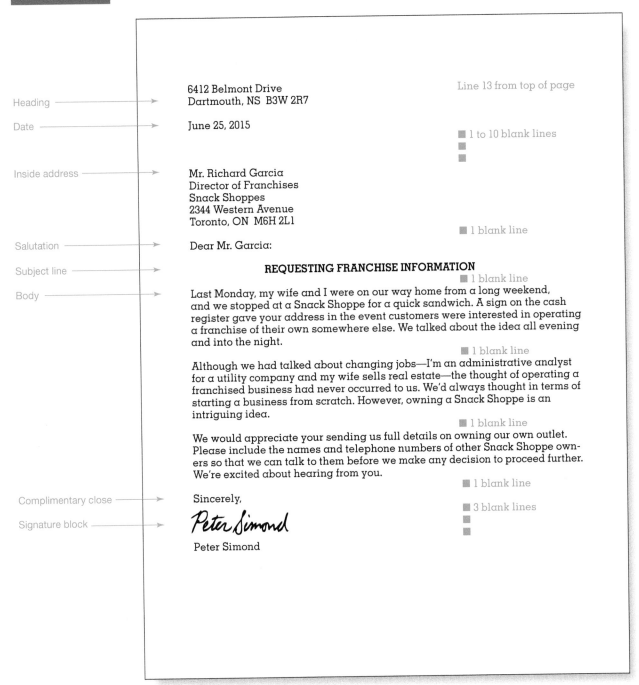

Heading → 6412 Belmont Drive
Dartmouth, NS  B3W 2R7

Line 13 from top of page

Date → June 25, 2015

■ 1 to 10 blank lines
■
■

Inside address → Mr. Richard Garcia
Director of Franchises
Snack Shoppes
2344 Western Avenue
Toronto, ON  M6H 2L1

■ 1 blank line

Salutation → Dear Mr. Garcia:

Subject line → **REQUESTING FRANCHISE INFORMATION**

■ 1 blank line

Body → Last Monday, my wife and I were on our way home from a long weekend, and we stopped at a Snack Shoppe for a quick sandwich. A sign on the cash register gave your address in the event customers were interested in operating a franchise of their own somewhere else. We talked about the idea all evening and into the night.

■ 1 blank line

Although we had talked about changing jobs—I'm an administrative analyst for a utility company and my wife sells real estate—the thought of operating a franchised business had never occurred to us. We'd always thought in terms of starting a business from scratch. However, owning a Snack Shoppe is an intriguing idea.

■ 1 blank line

We would appreciate your sending us full details on owning our own outlet. Please include the names and telephone numbers of other Snack Shoppe owners so that we can talk to them before we make any decision to proceed further. We're excited about hearing from you.

■ 1 blank line

Complimentary close → Sincerely,

■ 3 blank lines
■
■

Signature block → *Peter Simond*

Peter Simond

## TABLE A.1 Common Date Forms

| CONVENTION | ORDER | DATE (MIXED) | DATE (ALL NUMERALS) |
|---|---|---|---|
| Canadian and U.S. standard | Month day year | July 14, 2015 | 7/14/15 |
| Japan | Year month day | 2015 July 14 | 15/7/14 |
| Europe (most countries) | Day month year | 14 July 2015 | 14.7.2015 |
| International (ISO) format | Year month day | 2015 July 14 | 2015-07-14 |

to prefer the title *Miss* or *Mrs.* is always accommodated. If you don't know whether a person is a man or a woman (and you have no way of finding out), omit the courtesy title. For example, *Terry Smith* could be either a man or a woman. The first line of the inside address would be just *Terry Smith*, and the salutation would be *Dear Terry Smith*. The same is true if you know only a person's initials, as in *S. J. Adams*.

Spell out and capitalize titles that precede a person's name, such as *Professor* or *General* (see Table A.2 for the proper forms of address). The person's organizational title, such as *Director*, may be included on this first line

## TABLE A.2  Forms of Address

| PERSON | IN ADDRESS | IN SALUTATION |
|---|---|---|
| **Personal Titles** | | |
| Man | Mr. [first and last name] | Dear Mr. [last name]: |
| Woman (marital status unknown) | Ms. [first and last name] | Dear Ms. [last name]: |
| Woman (single) | Ms. or Miss [first and last name] | Dear Ms. *or* Miss [last name]: |
| Woman (married) | Ms. or Mrs. [wife's first and last name] *or* Mrs. [husband's first and last name] | Dear Ms. *or* Mrs. [last name]: |
| Woman (widowed) | Ms. or Mrs. [wife's first name and last name] | Dear Ms. *or* Mrs. [last name]: |
| Woman (separated or divorced) | Ms. or Mrs. [first and last name] | Dear Ms. *or* Mrs. [last name]: |
| Two men (or more) | Mr. [first and last name] and Mr. [first and last name] | Dear Mr. [last name] and Mr. [last name]: *or* Messrs. [last name] and [last name]: |
| Two women (or more) | Ms. [first and last name] and Ms. [first and last name] *or* Mrs. [first and last name] and Mrs. [first and last name] | Dear Ms. [last name] and Ms. [last name]: *or* Mses. [last name] and [last name]: Dear Mrs. [last name] and Mrs. [last name]: *or* Dear Mesdames [last name] and [last name]: *or* Mesdames: |
| | Miss [first and last name] and Mrs. [first and last name] | Dear Miss [last name] and Mrs. [last name]: |
| One woman and one man | Ms. [first and last name] and Mr. [first and last name] | Dear Ms. [last name] and Mr. [last name]: |
| Couple (married) | Mr. and Mrs. [husband's first and last name] | Dear Mr. and Mrs. [last name]: |
| Couple (married with different last names) | [title] [first and last name of husband] [title] and [first and last name of wife] | Dear [title] [husband's last name] and [title] [wife's first and last name]: |
| Couple (married professionals with same title and same last name) | [title in plural form] [husband's first name] and [wife's first and last name] | Dear [title in plural form] [last name]: |
| Couple (married professionals with different titles and same last name) | [title] [first and last name of husband] and [title] [first and last name of wife] | Dear [title] and [title] [last name]: |
| **Professional Titles** | | |
| President of a college or university (doctor) | Dr. [first and last name], President | Dear Dr. [last name]: |
| Dean of a school of college or university | Dean [first and last name] *or* [title] Miss [first and last name] Dean of [school] | Dear Dean [last name]: *or* Dear [title] [last name] Miss [last name]: |
| Professor | Professor [first and last name] | Dear Professor [last name]: |
| Physician | [first and last name], M.D. | Dear Dr. [last name]: |

(continued)

| TABLE A.2 | (Continued) | |
|---|---|---|
| PERSON | IN ADDRESS | IN SALUTATION |
| **Governmental Titles** | | |
| Prime Minister of Canada | The Prime Minister | Dear Mr. *or* Madam Prime Minister: |
| Member of Parliament | Honourable [first and last name] | Dear Honourable Member of Parliament [last name]: |
| Mayor | Honourable [first and last name] Mayor of [name of city] | Dear Mayor [last name]: |
| Judge | The Honourable [name] | Dear Judge [last name]: |
| **Religious Titles** | | |
| Priest | The Reverend [first and last name], [initials of order, if any] | Reverend Sir: (formal) *or* Dear Father [last name]: (informal) |
| Rabbi | Rabbi [first and last name] | Dear Rabbi [last name]: |
| Minister | The Reverend [first and last name], [title, if any] | Dear Reverend [last name]: |

(if it is short) or on the line below; the name of a department may follow. In addresses and signature lines, don't forget to capitalize any professional title that follows a person's name:

Mr. Ray Johnson, Dean

Ms. Patricia T. Higgins, Assistant Vice-President

However, professional titles not appearing in an address or signature line are capitalized only when they directly precede the name.

President Kenneth Johanson will deliver the speech.

Maria La Mothe, president of ABC Enterprises, will deliver the speech.

The Honourable Elizabeth May, member of Parliament for Saanich and the Islands, will deliver the speech.

If the name of a specific person is unavailable, you may address the letter to the department or to a specific position within the department. Also, be sure to spell out company names in full, unless the company itself uses abbreviations in its official name.

Other address information includes the treatment of buildings, house numbers, and compass directions (see Table A.3). The following example shows all the information that may be included in the inside address and its proper order for Canadian correspondence:

Dr. H. C. Armstrong
Research and Development
Commonwealth Mining Consortiumv
The Chelton Building, Suite 301
585 Second Street SW
Calgary, Alberta T2P 2P5

| TABLE A.3 | Inside Address Information |
|---|---|
| DESCRIPTION | EXAMPLE |
| Capitalize building names. | Welland Building |
| Capitalize locations within buildings (apartments, suites, rooms). | Suite 1073 |
| Use numerals for all house or building numbers, except the number *one*. | One Trinity Lane 637 Adams Avenue, Apt. 7 |
| Spell out compass directions that fall within a street address. | 1074 West Connover Street |
| Abbreviate compass directions that follow the street address. | 783 Main Street, N.E., Apt. 27 |

The order and layout of address information vary from country to country. So when addressing correspondence for other countries, carefully follow the format and information that appear in the company's letterhead. However, when you're sending mail from Canada, be sure that the name of the destination country appears on the last line of the address in capital letters. Use the English version of the country name so that your mail is routed to the right country. Then, to be sure your mail is routed correctly within the destination country, use the foreign spelling of the city name (using the characters and diacritical marks that would be commonly used in the region).

For example, the following address uses Köln instead of *Cologne*:

| | |
|---|---|
| H. R. Veith, Director | Addressee |
| Eisfieren Glaswerk | Company name |
| Blaubachstrabe 13 | Street address |
| Postfach 10 80 07 | Post office box |
| D-5000 Köln I | District, city |
| GERMANY | Country |

Be sure to use organizational titles correctly when addressing international correspondence. Job designations vary around the world. In England, for example, a managing director is often what a Canadian company would call its chief executive officer or president, and a British deputy is the equivalent of a vice-president. In France, responsibilities are assigned to individuals without regard to title or organizational structure, and in China the title *project manager* has meaning, but the title *sales manager* may not.

To make matters worse, businesspeople in some countries sign correspondence without their names typed below. In Germany, for example, the belief is that employees represent the company, so it's inappropriate to emphasize personal names.[5]

**SALUTATION** In the salutation of your letter, follow the style of the first line of the inside address. If the first line is a person's name, the salutation is *Dear Mr.* or *Ms. Name*. The formality of the salutation depends on your relationship with the addressee. If in conversation you would say "Mary," your letter's salutation should be Dear *Mary*, followed by a colon. Otherwise, include the courtesy title and last name, followed by a colon. Presuming to write *Dear Lewis* instead of *Dear Professor Chang* demonstrates a disrespectful familiarity that the recipient will probably resent.

If the first line of the inside address is a position title such as *Director of Personnel*, then use *Dear Director*. If the addressee is unknown, use a polite description, such as *Dear Alumnus, Dear SPCA Supporter*, or *Dear Voter*. If

the first line is plural (a department or company), then use *Ladies and Gentlemen*.

**SUBJECT LINE** The subject line tells recipients at a glance what the document is about (and indicates where to file the letter for future reference). It usually appears below the salutation, either against the left margin, indented (as a paragraph in the body), or centred. It can be placed above the salutation or at the very top of the page, and it can be underscored. Some businesses omit the word *Subject*. The subject line may take a variety of forms, including the following:

Subject: RainMaster Sprinklers

FALL 2015 SALES MEETING

Reference Order No. 27920

**BODY** The body of the letter is your message. Almost all letters are single-spaced, with one blank line before and after the salutation or opening, between paragraphs, and before the complimentary close. The body may include indented lists, entire paragraphs indented for emphasis, and even subheadings. If it does, all similar elements should be treated in the same way. Your department or company may select a format to use for all letters.

**COMPLIMENTARY CLOSE** The complimentary close begins on the second line below the body of the letter. Alternatives for wording are available, but currently the trend seems to be toward using one-word closes, such as *Sincerely*. In any case, the complimentary close reflects the relationship between you and the person you're writing to. Avoid cute closes, such as *Yours for bigger profits*. If your audience doesn't know you well, your sense of humour may be misunderstood.

**SIGNATURE BLOCK** Leave three blank lines for a written signature below the complimentary close, and then include the sender's name (unless it appears in the letterhead). The person's title may appear on the same line as the name or on the line below:

Yours truly,

Raymond Dunnigan

Director of Human Resources

Your letterhead indicates that you're representing your company. However, if your letter is on plain paper or runs to a second page, you may want to emphasize that you're speaking legally for the company. The accepted way of doing that is to place the company's name in capital letters a double space below the complimentary close and then include the sender's name and title four lines below that:

Sincerely,

WENTWORTH INDUSTRIES

(Mrs.) Helen B. Taylor

President

If your name could be taken for either a man's or a woman's, a courtesy title indicating gender should be included, with or without parentheses. Also, women who prefer a particular courtesy title should include it:

Mrs. Nancy Winters

(Miss) Celine Dufour

Ms. Pat Li

(Mr.) Jamie Saunders

## Additional Letter Parts

Letters vary greatly in subject matter and thus in the identifying information they need and the format they adopt. The letter in Figure A.6 shows how these additional parts should be arranged. The following elements may be used in any combination, depending on the requirements of the particular letter:

- **Addressee notation.** Letters that have a restricted readership or that must be handled in a special way should include such addressee notations as *PERSONAL, CONFIDENTIAL,* or *PLEASE FORWARD.* This sort of notation appears a double space above the inside address, in all-capital letters.
- **Attention line.** Although not commonly used today, an attention line can be used if you know only the last name of the person you're writing to. It can also direct a letter to a position title or department. Place the attention line on the first line of the inside address and put the company name on the second.[6] An attention line may take any of the following forms or variants of them:

    Attention: Dr. McHenry

    Attention: Director of Marketing

    Attention: Marketing Department

- **Second-page heading.** Use a second-page heading whenever an additional page is required. Some companies have second-page letterhead (with the company name and address on one line and in a smaller typeface). The heading bears the name (person or organization) from the first line of the inside address, the page number, the date, and perhaps a reference number. Leave one blank line before the body. Make sure that at least two lines of a continued paragraph appear on the first and second pages. Never allow the closing lines to appear alone on a continued page. Precede the complimentary close or signature lines with at least two lines of the body. Also, don't hyphenate the last word on a page. All the following are acceptable forms for second-page headings:

    Ms. Melissa Baker

    May 10, 2015

    Page 2

    Ms. Melissa Baker, May 10, 2015, Page 2

    Ms. Melissa Baker        -2-        May 10, 2015

- **Company name.** If you include the company's name in the signature block, put it all in capital letters a double space below the complimentary close. You usually include the company's name in the signature block only when the writer is serving as the company's official spokesperson or when letterhead has not been used.
- **Reference initials.** When businesspeople keyboard their own letters, reference initials are unnecessary, so they are becoming rare. When one person dictates a letter and another person produces it, reference initials show who helped prepare it. Place initials at the left margin, a double space below the signature block.
- **Enclosure notation.** Enclosure notations appear at the bottom of a letter, one or two lines below the reference initials. Some common forms include the following:

    Enclosure

    Enclosures (2)

    Enclosures: Résumé

        Photograph

- **Copy notation.** Copy notations may follow reference initials or enclosure notations. They indicate who's receiving a *courtesy copy* (*cc*) or they simply use *copy* (*c*). Recipients are listed in order of rank or (rank being equal) in alphabetical order. Among the forms used are the following:

    cc: David Wentworth, Vice-President

    c: Dr. Martha Littlefield

    Copy to Hans Vogel

        748 Chesterton Road

        Kitimat, BC V8C 5V1

FIGURE A.6 Additional Letter Parts

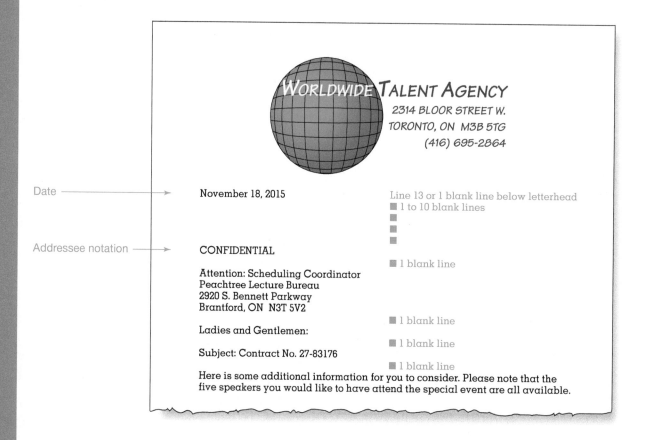

Date

Addressee notation

November 18, 2015

Line 13 or 1 blank line below letterhead
■ 1 to 10 blank lines
■
■
■

CONFIDENTIAL

■ 1 blank line

Attention: Scheduling Coordinator
Peachtree Lecture Bureau
2920 S. Bennett Parkway
Brantford, ON  N3T 5V2

■ 1 blank line

Ladies and Gentlemen:

■ 1 blank line

Subject: Contract No. 27-83176

■ 1 blank line

Here is some additional information for you to consider. Please note that the
five speakers you would like to have attend the special event are all available.

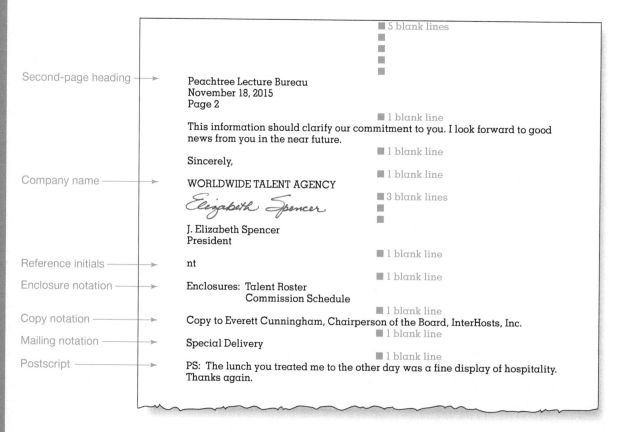

Second-page heading

Company name

Reference initials

Enclosure notation

Copy notation

Mailing notation

Postscript

■ 5 blank lines
■
■
■
■

Peachtree Lecture Bureau
November 18, 2015
Page 2

■ 1 blank line

This information should clarify our commitment to you. I look forward to good
news from you in the near future.

■ 1 blank line

Sincerely,

■ 1 blank line

WORLDWIDE TALENT AGENCY

■ 3 blank lines
■
■

J. Elizabeth Spencer
President

■ 1 blank line

nt

■ 1 blank line

Enclosures:  Talent Roster
             Commission Schedule

■ 1 blank line

Copy to Everett Cunningham, Chairperson of the Board, InterHosts, Inc.

■ 1 blank line

Special Delivery

■ 1 blank line

PS:  The lunch you treated me to the other day was a fine display of hospitality.
Thanks again.

- **Mailing notation.** You may place a mailing notation (such as *Special Delivery* or *Registered Mail*) at the bottom of the letter, after reference initials or enclosure notations (whichever one is last) and before copy notations. Or you may place it at the top of the letter, either above the inside address on the left-hand side or just below the date on the right-hand side. For greater visibility, mailing notations may appear in capital letters.
- **Postscript.** A postscript is an afterthought to the letter, a message that requires emphasis, or a personal note. It is usually the last thing on any letter and may be preceded by *P.S.*, *PS.*, *PS:*, or nothing at all.

## Letter Formats

A letter format is the way of arranging all the basic letter parts. Sometimes a company adopts a certain format as its policy; sometimes the individual letter writer or preparer is allowed to choose the most appropriate format. In Canada, three major letter formats are commonly used:

- **Full block format.** Each letter part begins at the left margin. The main advantage is quick and efficient preparation (see Figure A.7).
- **Modified block format.** Same as block format, except that the date, complimentary close, and signature block start near the centre of the page

---

**FIGURE A.7**  **Block Letter Format**

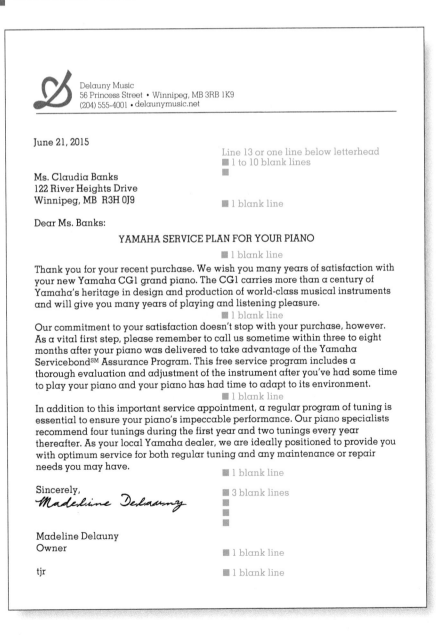

## FIGURE A.8  Modified Block Letter Format

**Greyhound Canada**
P.O. Box 850 • Calgary, AB  T2E 4S7

■ line 13 from top of page          November 3, 2015
■ 1 to 10 blank lines
■

Mrs. Eugenia Preston, President
Drayton Valley High School PAC
P.O. Box 335
Drayton Valley, AB  T7A 1T9
■ 1 blank line
Dear Mrs. Preston:
■ 1 blank line
**TRAVELLING TO EDMONTON**
■ 1 blank line
Thank you for inviting us to participate in your "Government Experience" program. So that your honours students can experience government firsthand, we will be delighted to provide one of our motor coaches next May at a 15 percent discount to transport up to 40 students and 7 teachers from Drayton Valley to Edmonton and back.
■ 1 blank line
Our buses seat 47 passengers, are fully equipped with restrooms and reclining seats, and are climate controlled for year-round comfort. You can rely on us for your charter transportation needs:
■ 1 blank line
• Our intensive, ongoing driver-training program ensures your safety and satisfaction.
• Our competitive pricing allows us to compete both locally and nationwide.
• Our state-of-the-art maintenance facilities are located in all major Canadian cities to ensure quality, reliability, and excellent service.
■ 1 blank line
Please give me a call at (403) 997-4646 to discuss the specific date of your event, departure times, and the discounted price for your trip. Together, we'll make sure your students have a day that's not only fun and educational but safe and secure. I look forward to hearing from you.
■ 1 blank line

                                        Yours truly,
■ 3 blank lines
■
■                                       *Ronald Struthers*

                                        Ronald Struthers
                                        Vice-President, Public Relations
■ 1 blank line
pf
■ 1 blank line
Enclosure

(see Figure A.8). The modified block format does permit indentions as an option. This format mixes preparation speed with traditional placement of some letter parts. It also looks more balanced on the page than the block format does.

• **Simplified format.** Instead of using a salutation, this format often weaves the reader's name into the first line or two of the body and often includes a subject line in capital letters (see Figure A.9). With no complimentary close, your signature appears after the body, followed by your printed (or typewritten) name (usually in all capital letters). This format is convenient when you don't know the reader's name; however, some people object to it as mechanical and impersonal (a drawback you can overcome with a warm writing style). Because certain letter parts are eliminated, some line spacing is changed.

| FIGURE A.9 | Simplified Block Letter Format |

**KELLY**
SERVICES

May 5, 2015

Line 13 from top of page
■ 1 to 10 blank lines
■
■
■

Ms. Gillian Savard, President
Scientific and Technical Contracts, Inc.
6348 Ste-Croix Avenue
Montreal, QC  H3P 1T4

■ 2 blank lines
■

NEW SERVICES

■ 2 blank lines
■

Thank you, Ms. Savard, for your recent inquiry about our services. Our complete line of staffing services offers high-level professionals with the skills you require. From the office to the factory, from the tech site to the trade show, from the law firm to the lab—we can provide you with the people and the expertise you need.

■ 1 blank line

I have enclosed a package of information for your review, including specific information on our engineers, designers/drafters, and engineering support personnel. The package also contains reprints of customer reviews and a comparison sheet showing how our services measure up against those of competing companies. We identify qualified candidates and recruit through a network of professional channels to reach candidates whose skills match the specific engineering disciplines you require.

■ 1 blank line

Please call me with any questions you may have. Whether you need a temporary employee for a day or an entire department staffed indefinitely, our staffing solutions give you the freedom you need to focus and the support you need to succeed. I will be glad to help you fill your staffing needs with Kelly professionals.

■ 3 blank lines
■
■

*Rudy Cohen*

RUDY COHEN
CUSTOMER SERVICE SPECIALIST

■ 1 blank line

jn

■ 1 blank line

Enclosures

999 WEST AVE • MONTREAL, QUEBEC  H3Z 1A4
TELEPHONE (514) 362-444

The most common formats for intercultural business letters are the block style and the modified block style. *Standard punctuation* uses a colon after the salutation (a comma if the letter is social or personal) and a comma after the complimentary close. *Open punctuation* uses no colon or comma after the salutation or the complimentary close.

# Envelopes

For a first impression, the quality of the envelope is just as important as the quality of the stationery. Letterhead and envelopes should be of the same paper stock, have the same colour ink, and be imprinted with the same address and logo. Most envelopes used by Canadian

## FIGURE A.10 Prescribed Envelope Format

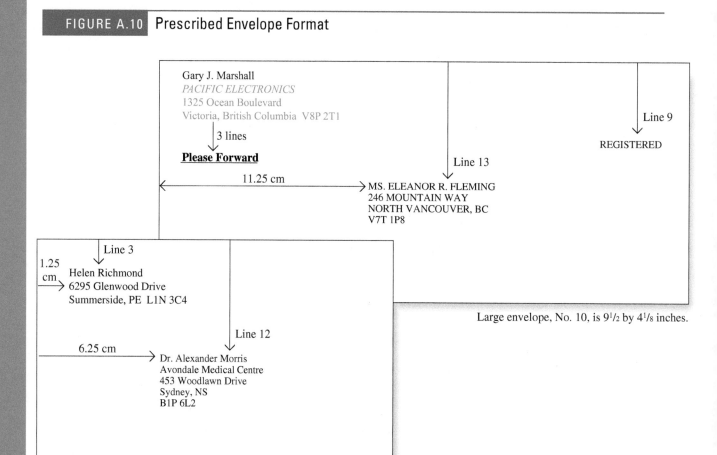

Large envelope, No. 10, is 9½ by 4⅛ inches.

Small envelope, No. 6¾, is 6½ by 3⅝ inches.

businesses are No. 10 envelopes (9½ inches long), which are sized for an 8½-by-11-inch piece of paper folded in thirds. Figure A.10 shows the most common size.

## Addressing the Envelope

The address is always single-spaced with all lines aligned on the left. The address on the envelope is in the same style as the inside address and presents the same information. The order to follow is from the smallest division to the largest:

1. Name and title of recipient
2. Name of department or subgroup
3. Name of organization
4. Name of building
5. Street address and suite number, or post office box number
6. City, province, and postal code
7. Name of country (if the letter is being sent abroad)

Because Canada Post uses optical scanners to sort mail, envelopes for quantity mailings, in particular,

should be addressed in the prescribed format. No punctuation is included, and all mailing instructions of interest to the post office are placed above the address area (see Figure A.10). Canada Post requires that the city is all in capitals, and the postal code is placed on the line below the name of the city. The post office scanners read addresses from the bottom up, so if a letter is to be sent to a post office box rather than to a street address, the street address should appear on the line above the box number. Figure A.10 also shows the proper spacing for addresses and return addresses.

Canada Post Corporation and the U.S. Postal Service have published lists of two-letter mailing abbreviations for provinces, territories, and states (see Table A.4). Postal authorities prefer no punctuation with these abbreviations. Canadian postal codes are alphanumeric, with a three-character "area code" and a three-character "local code" separated by a single space (K2P 5A5). Canadian postal codes may be separated from the province by two spaces or put separately in the bottom line of the address.

| TABLE A.4 | Two-Letter Mailing Abbreviations for Canada and the United States |
| --- | --- |

| PROVINCE/ TERRITORY OR STATE | ABBREVIATION | PROVINCE/ TERRITORY OR STATE | ABBREVIATION | PROVINCE/ TERRITORY OR STATE | ABBREVIATION |
| --- | --- | --- | --- | --- | --- |
| **Canada** | | Delaware | DE | New Jersey | NJ |
| Alberta | AB | District of Columbia | DC | New Mexico | NM |
| British Columbia | BC | Florida | FL | New York | NY |
| Manitoba | MB | Georgia | GA | North Carolina | NC |
| New Brunswick | NB | Guam | GU | North Dakota | ND |
| Newfoundland and Labrador | NL | Hawaii | HI | Ohio | OH |
| Northwest Territories | NT | Idaho | ID | Oklahoma | OK |
| Nova Scotia | NS | Illinois | IL | Oregon | OR |
| Nunavut | NU | Indiana | IN | Pennsylvania | PA |
| Ontario | ON | Iowa | IA | Puerto Rico | PR |
| Prince Edward Island | PE | Kansas | KS | Rhode Island | RI |
| Quebec | QC | Kentucky | KY | South Carolina | SC |
| Saskatchewan | SK | Louisiana | LA | South Dakota | SD |
| Yukon Territory | YT | Maine | ME | Tennessee | TN |
| | | Maryland | MD | Texas | TX |
| **United States** | | Massachusetts | MA | Utah | UT |
| Alabama | AL | Michigan | MI | Vermont | VT |
| Alaska | AK | Minnesota | MN | Virginia | VA |
| American Samoa | AS | Mississippi | MS | Virgin Islands | VI |
| Arizona | AZ | Missouri | MO | Washington | WA |
| Arkansas | AR | Montana | MT | West Virginia | WV |
| California | CA | Nebraska | NE | Wisconsin | WI |
| Colorado | CO | Nevada | NV | Wyoming | WY |
| Connecticut | CT | New Hampshire | NH | | |

# Documentation of Report Sources

By providing information about your sources, you improve your own credibility as well as the credibility of the facts and opinions you present. Documentation gives readers the means for checking your findings and pursuing the subject further. Also, documenting your report is the accepted way to give credit to the people from whose work you have drawn.

Experts recommend various forms, depending on your field or discipline. Business writers do not all use the same style. Whatever style you choose, be consistent within any given report, using the same order, punctuation, and format from one reference citation or bibliography entry to the next.

A wide variety of style manuals provide detailed information on documentation. Here is a brief annotated list:

- American Psychological Association, *Publication Manual of the American Psychological Association*, 6th ed. (Washington, DC: American Psychological Association, 2010). Details the author-date system, which is preferred in the social sciences and often in business as well. For updates on citing electronic references, see **www.apastyle.org**.
- *The Chicago Manual of Style*, 16th ed. (Chicago: University of Chicago Press, 2010). Often referred to only as *Chicago* and widely used in the publishing industry; provides detailed treatment of source documentation.
- Joseph Gibaldi, *MLA Style Manual and Guide to Scholarly Publishing*, 7th ed. (New York: Modern Language Association, 2008). Serves as the basis for the note and bibliography style used in much academic writing and is recommended in many university and college textbooks on writing term papers; provides a lot of examples in the humanities.

Although many schemes have been proposed for organizing the information in source notes, all of them break the information into parts: (1) information about the author (name); (2) information about the work (title, edition, volume number); (3) information about the publication (place, publisher); (4) information about the date (5); and information on relevant page ranges.

The following sections summarize the major conventions for documenting sources in three styles: the *Publication Manual of the American Psychological Association* (APA), *The Chicago Manual of Style* (Chicago), and the *MLA Style Manual* (MLA).

# APA Style

The American Psychological Association (APA) recommends the author-date system of documentation, which is popular in the physical, natural, and social sciences, and in business. When using this system, you simply insert the author's last name and the year of publication within parentheses following the text discussion of the material cited. Include a page number if you use a direct quotation. This approach briefly identifies the source so that readers can locate complete information in the alphabetical reference list at the end of the report. The author-date system is both brief and clear, saving readers time and effort.

## In-Text Citation—APA Style

To document report sources in text using APA style, insert the author's surname and the date of publication at the end of a statement. Enclose this information in parentheses. If the author's name is referred to in the text itself, then the name can be omitted from parenthetical material.

> Some experts recommend both translation and back-translation when dealing with any non-English-speaking culture (Assira, 2012).

> Toller and Fielding (2012) make a strong case for small companies succeeding in global business.

Personal communications and interviews conducted by the author would not be listed in the reference list at all. Such citations would appear in the text only.

> Increasing the role of cable companies is high on the list of Georgia Stainer, general manager at Day Cable and Communications (personal communication, March 2, 2011).

## List of References—APA Style

For APA style, list only those works actually cited in the text (so you would not include works for background or for further reading). Report writers must choose their references judiciously. Following are the major conventions for developing a reference list according to APA style (see Figure B.1):

- Format entries in alphabetical order as hanging indents, using double spacing.
- List all author names in reversed order (last name first), and use only initials for the first and middle names.

## FIGURE B.1  Sample References—APA Style

**REFERENCES**

| | |
|---|---|
| Online magazine article | Babauta, L. (2010, November 14). 17 tips to be productive with instant messaging. *Web Worker Daily*. Retrieved from http://webworkerdaily.com |
| Brochure | BestTemp Staffing Services. (2011). *An employer's guide to staffing services* (2d ed.) [Brochure]. Denver: BestTemp Information Center. |
| Online encyclopedia article, no author | Capitalism. (2013). In *Encyclopædia Britannica Online*. Retrieved from http://www.britannica.com/EBchecked/topic/93927/capitalism |
| Journal article with volume and issue numbers | Clifton, J. (2012). Beyond taxonomies of influence. *Journal of Business Communication, 46*(1), 57. |
| Webpage (no date, no author) | Company history. (n.d.). Retrieved from  http://about.hbc.com/aboutus/company hist/ companyhist.asp. |
| Magazine article | Dolan, K. A. (2013, June 2).  A whole new crop. *Forbes*, 72–75. |
| Television broadcast | Han, D. (2013, March 5). Trade wars heating up around the globe. *CNN Headline News*. [Television broadcast]. Atlanta, GA: CNN. |
| Book, component parts | Kuntz, S. (2001). Moving beyond benefits. In R. Jacobson (Ed.), *Our changing workforce* (pp. 213–227). New York: Citadel Press. |
| Newspaper article, no author | Might be harder than it looks. (2009, January 30). *The Globe & Mail*, p. A22. |
| Unpublished dissertation or thesis | Morales, G. H. (2009). *The economic pressures on industrialized nations in a global economy* (Unpublished doctoral dissertation). University of Toronto. |
| Paper presented at a meeting | Myers, C. (2007, August). *HMOs in today's environment*. Paper presented at the Conference on Medical Insurance Solutions, Chicago, IL. |
| Blog post | Scott, D. (2013, August 9). Offering unique experiences generates attention for nonprofits. Retrieved from http://www.webinknow.com. (2013, August 16). |
| Newspaper article, one author | Standish, E. (2012, January 19). Global market crushes OPEC's delicate balance of interests. *Report on Business, pp.* 43–45. |
| Book, two authors | Toller, M., & Fielding, J. (2012). *Global business for smaller companies*. Rocklin, CA: Prima Publishing. |
| Government publication | U.S. Department of Defense. (2010). *Stretching research dollars: Survival advice for universities and government labs*. Washington, DC: U.S. Government Printing Office. |
| Annual report | The Walt Disney Company. (2014). *2013 Annual Report*. Burbank, CA.: The Walt Disney Company. |
| Interview | *Cited in text only, not in the list of references.* |

- Arrange entries in the following general order: (1) author name, (2) date, (3) title information, (4) publication information, (5) periodical page range.
- Follow the author name with the date of publication in parentheses.
- List titles of articles from magazines, newspapers, and journals without underlines or quotation marks. Capitalize only the first word of the title, any proper nouns, and the first word to follow an internal colon.
- Italicize titles of books, capitalizing only the first word, any proper nouns, and the first word to follow a colon.
- Italicize names of magazines, newspapers, journals, and other complete publications—capitalizing all the important words in the title.
- For journal articles, include the volume number (in italics) and, if necessary, the issue number (in parentheses). Finally, include the page range of the article: *Journal of Business Communication, 36*(4), 72–81.

(In this example, the volume is 36, the issue number is 4, and the page range is 72–81.)

- Include personal communications (such as letters, memos, email, and conversations) only in text, not in reference lists.
- Electronic references include author, date of publication, title of article, name of publication (if one), volume, and the source.
- For electronic references, indicate the actual year of publication.
- For webpages with extremely long URLs, use your best judgment to determine which URL from the site to use. For example, rather than giving the URL of a specific news release with a long URL, you can provide the URL of the "Media relations" webpage.
- APA citation guidelines for social media are still evolving. For the latest information, visit the APA Style Blog at http://blog.apastyle.org/apastyle.
- For online journals or periodicals that assign a digital object identifier (DOI), include that after the volume or issue, noted as doi:1234 instead of a conventional URL. If no DOI is available, include the URL of the publication's home page (such as www.theglobeandmail.com for *The Globe & Mail*).
- Do not use periods after either DOIs or URLs.

# Chicago Humanities Style

*The Chicago Manual of Style* recommends two types of documentation systems. The *documentary-note*, or *humanities*, style gives bibliographic citations in notes—either footnotes (when printed at the bottom of a page) or endnotes (when printed at the end of the report). The humanities system is often used in literature, history, and the arts. The other system strongly recommended by *Chicago* is the *author-date* system, which cites the author's last name and the date of publication in the text, usually in parentheses, reserving full documentation for the reference list (or bibliography). For the purpose of comparing styles, we will concentrate on the humanities system, which is described in detail in *Chicago*.

## In-Text Citation—Chicago Humanities Style

To document report sources in text, the humanities system relies on superscripts—standard numerals placed just above the line of type at the end of the reference:

> Toward the end of his speech, Myers sounded a note of caution, saying that even though the economy is expected to grow, it could easily slow a bit.[10]

The superscript lets the reader know how to look for source information in either a footnote or an endnote (see Figure B.2). Some readers prefer footnotes so that they can simply glance at the bottom of the page for information. Others prefer endnotes so that they can read the text without a clutter of notes on the page. Also, endnotes relieve the writer from worrying about how long each note will be and how much space it will take away from the page. Both footnotes and endnotes are handled automatically by today's word processing software.

For the reader's convenience, you can use footnotes for **content notes** (which may supplement your main text with asides about a particular issue or event, provide a cross-reference to another section of your report, or direct the reader to a related source). Then you can use endnotes for **source notes** (which document direct quotations, paraphrased passages, and visual aids). Consider which type of note is most common in your report, and then choose whether to present these notes all as endnotes or all as footnotes. Regardless of the method you choose for referencing textual information in your report, notes for visual aids (both content notes and source notes) are placed on the same page as the visual.

## Bibliography—Chicago Humanities Style

The humanities system may or may not be accompanied by a bibliography (because the notes give all the necessary bibliographic information). However, endnotes are arranged in order of appearance in the text, so an alphabetical bibliography can be valuable to your readers. The bibliography may be titled *Bibliography, Reference List, Sources, Works Cited* (if you include only those sources you actually cited in your report), or *Works Consulted* (if you include uncited sources as well). Following are the major conventions for developing a bibliography according to *Chicago* style (see Figure B.3):

- Exclude any page numbers that may be cited in source notes, except for journals, periodicals, and newspapers.
- Alphabetize entries by the last name of the lead author (listing last name first). The names of second and succeeding authors are listed in normal order. Entries without an author name (or issuing organization) are alphabetized by the first important word in the title.
- Format entries as hanging indents (indent second and succeeding lines three to five spaces).
- Arrange entries in the following general order: (1) author name, (2) title information, (3) publication information, (4) date, (5) periodical page range.

| FIGURE B.2 | Sample Endnotes—*Chicago* Humanities Style |

NOTES

Journal article with volume and issue numbers

1. Jonathan Clifton, "Beyond Taxonomies of Influence," *Journal of Business Communication* 46, no. 1 (2012): 57–79.

Brochure

2. BestTemp Staffing Services, *An Employer's Guide to Staffing Services,* 2d ed. (Denver: BestTemp Information Center, 2011), 31.

Newspaper article, no author

3. "Might Be Harder Than It Looks," *The Globe & Mail,* 30 January 2009, sec. A, p. 22.

Annual report

4. The Walt Disney Company, *2013 Annual Report* (Burbank, CA: The Walt Disney Company, 2014), 48.

Magazine article

5. Kerry A. Dolan, "A Whole New Crop," *Forbes,* 2 June 2013, 72–75.

Television broadcast

6. Daniel Han, "Trade Wars Heating Up Around the Globe," *CNN Headline News* (Atlanta: CNN, 5 March 2013).

Webpage (no date, no author)

7. HBC, "Company History," Hbc.com (accessed 16 August 2013).

Book, component parts

8. Sonja Kuntz, "Moving Beyond Benefits," in *Our Changing Workforce,* ed. Randolf Jacobson (New York: Citadel Press, 2001), 213–27.

Unpublished dissertation or thesis

9. George H. Morales, "The Economic Pressures on Industrialized Nations in a Global Economy" (Ph.D. diss., University of Toronto, 2009), 32–47.

Paper presented at a meeting

10. Charles Myers, "HMOs in Today's Environment" (paper presented at the Conference on Medical Insurance Solutions, Chicago, IL, August 2007), 16–17.

Online magazine article

11. Leo Babauta, "17 Tips to Be Productive with Instant Messaging," in *Web Worker Daily* [online] (San Francisco, 2010 [updated 14 November 2010; cited 14 February 2011]); available from http://webworkerdaily.com.

Online encyclopedia

12. "Capitalism," *Encyclopædia Britannica Online* http://www.britannica.com/EBchecked/topic/93927/capitalism (accessed 16 August 2013).

Interview

13. Georgia Stainer, general manager, Day Cable and Communications, interview by author, Topeka, KS, 2 March 2011.

Newspaper article, one author

14. Evelyn Standish, "Global Market Crushes OPEC's Delicate Balance of Interests," *Report on Business,* 19 January 2012, 43–45.

Book, two authors

15. Miriam Toller and Jay Fielding, *Global Business for Smaller Companies* (Rocklin, CA: Prima Publishing, 2012), 102–3.

Government publication

16. U.S. Department of Defense, *Stretching Research Dollars: Survival Advice for Universities and Government Labs* (Washington, DC: GPO, 2010), 126.

Blog post

17. David Meerman Scott, "Offering Unique Experiences Generates Attention for Nonprofits," WebInkNow [blog], 9 August 2013, http://www.webinknow.com.

- Use quotation marks around the titles of articles from magazines, newspapers, and journals—capitalizing the first and last words, as well as all other important words (except prepositions, articles, and coordinating conjunctions).

- Use italics to set off the names of books, newspapers, journals, and other complete publications—capitalizing the first and last words, as well as all other important words.

- For journal articles, include the volume number and the issue number (if necessary). Include the year of publication inside parentheses and follow with a colon and the page range of the article: *Journal of Business Communication* 36, no. 4 (2014): 72. (In this source, the volume is 36, the issue number is 4, and the page is 72.)

- Use brackets to identify all electronic references: [Online database] or [Blog].

- Explain how electronic references can be reached: Available from **www.spaceless.com/WWWVL**.

- Give the citation date for online references: Accessed 23 August 2010.

**FIGURE B.3** Sample Bibliography—*Chicago* Humanities Style

| | |
|---|---|
| | **BIBLIOGRAPHY** |
| Online magazine article | Babauta, Leo. "17 Tips to Be Productive with Instant Messaging," In *Web Worker Daily* [online], San Francisco, 2010 [updated 14 November 2010, cited 14 February 2011]. Available from http://webworkerdaily.com. |
| Brochure | BestTemp Staffing Services. *An Employer's Guide to Staffing Services.* 2d ed. Denver: BestTemp Information Center, 2011. |
| Online encyclopedia | "Capitalism," *Encyclopædia Britannica Online,* http://www.britannica.com/EBchecked/topic/93927/capitalism (accessed 16 August 2013). |
| Journal article with volume and issue numbers | Clifton, Jonathan. "Beyond Taxonomies of Influence." *Journal of Business Communication* 46, no. 1 (2012): 57–79. |
| Website | "Company History," HBC (accessed 16 August 2013) http://www.hbc.com. |
| Magazine article | Dolan, Kerry A. "A Whole New Crop," *Forbes,* 2 June 2013, 72–75. |
| Television broadcast | Han, Daniel. "Trade Wars Heating Up Around the Globe." *CNN Headline News.* Atlanta: CNN, 5 March 2013. |
| Book, component parts | Kuntz, Sonja. "Moving Beyond Benefits." In *Our Changing Workforce,* edited by Randolf Jacobson. New York: Citadel Press, 2001. |
| Newspaper article, no author | "Might Be Harder Than It Looks." *The Globe & Mail,* 30 January 2009, sec. A, p. 22. |
| Unpublished dissertation or thesis | Morales, George H. "The Economic Pressures on Industrialized Nations in a Global Economy." Ph.D. diss., University of Toronto, 2009. |
| Paper presented at a meeting | Myers, Charles. "HMOs in Today's Environment." Paper presented at the Conference on Medical Insurance Solutions, Chicago, IL, August 2007. |
| Blog post | Scott, David Meerman. "Offering Unique Experiences Generates Attention for Nonprofits," WebInkNow [blog], 9 August 2013, http://www.webinknow.com. |
| Interview | Stainer, Georgia, general manager, Day Cable and Communications. Interview by author. Topeka, KS, 2 March 2011. |
| Newspaper article, one author | Standish, Evelyn. "Global Market Crushes OPEC's Delicate Balance of Interests." *Report on Business,* 19 January 2012, sec. A, p. 1. |
| Book, two authors | Toller, Miriam, and Jay Fielding. *Global Business for Smaller Companies.* Rocklin, CA: Prima Publishing, 2012. |
| Government publication | U.S. Department of Defense. *Stretching Research Dollars: Survival Advice for Universities and Government Labs.* Washington, DC: GPO, 2010. |
| Annual report | The Walt Disney Company, *2014 Annual Report,* Burbank, CA: The Walt Disney Company, 2013. |

# MLA Style

The style recommended by the Modern Language Association of America is used widely in the humanities, especially in the study of language and literature. Like APA style, MLA style uses brief parenthetical citations in the text. However, instead of including author name and year, MLA citations include author name and page reference.

## In-Text Citation—MLA Style

To document report sources in text using MLA style, insert the author's last name and a page reference inside parentheses following the cited material:

(Matthews 63). If the author's name is mentioned in the text reference, the name can be omitted from the parenthetical citation: (63). The citation indicates that the reference came from page 63 of a work by Matthews. With the author's name, readers can find complete publication information in the alphabetically arranged list of works cited that comes at the end of the report.

Some experts recommend both translation and back-translation when dealing with any non-English-speaking culture (Assira 72).

Toller and Fielding make a strong case for small companies succeeding in global business (102–03).

## List of Works Cited—MLA Style

The *MLA Style Manual* recommends preparing the list of works cited first so that you will know what information to give in the parenthetical citation (for example, whether to add a short title if you're citing more than one work by the same author, or whether to give an initial or first name if you're citing two authors who have the same last name). The list of works cited appears at the end of your report, contains all the works that you cite in your text, and lists them in alphabetical order. Following are the major conventions for developing a reference list according to MLA style (see Figure B.4):

- Format entries as hanging indents.
- Double space inside and between entries.

- Arrange entries in the following general order: (1) author name, (2) title information, (3) publication information, (4) date, (5) periodical page range, (6) medium of publication (print, web, CD-ROM, etc).
- List the lead author's name in reverse order (last name first), using either full first names or initials. List second and succeeding author names in normal order.
- Use quotation marks around the titles of articles from magazines, newspapers, and journals—capitalize all important words.
- Italicize the names of books, newspapers, journals and other complete publications, capitalizing all main words in the title.

---

**FIGURE B.4** Sample Works Cited—MLA Style

### WORKS CITED

Online magazine article

Babauta, Leo. "17 Tips to Be Productive with Instant Messaging," *Web Worker Daily* 14 Nov. 2010. 14 Feb. 2011. <http://webworkerdaily.com>.

Brochure

BestTemp Staffing Services. *An Employer's Guide to Staffing Services*. 2d ed. Denver: BestTemp Information Center, 2011.

Journal article with volume and issue numbers

Clifton, Jonathan. "Beyond Taxonomies of Influence." *Journal of Business Communication* 46.1 (2012): 57–79. Print.

Webpage (no date, no author)

"Company History." *Hbc.com*. HBC, n.d. 16 Aug. 2013. Web.

Magazine article

Dolan, Kerry A. "A Whole New Crop." *Forbes*, 2 June 2013: 72–75. Print.

Television broadcast

Han, Daniel. "Trade Wars Heating Up Around the Globe." *CNN Headline News*. CNN, Atlanta. 5 Mar. 2013. Television.

Book, component parts

Kuntz, Sonja. "Moving Beyond Benefits." *Our Changing Workforce*. Ed. Randolf Jacobson. New York: Citadel Press, 2001. 213–27. Print.

Newspaper article, no author

"Might Be Harder Than It Looks." *The Globe & Mail*, 30 Jan. 2009: A22. Print.

Unpublished dissertation or thesis

Morales, George H. "The Economic Pressures on Industrialized Nations in a Global Economy." Diss. U of Toronto, 2009. Print.

Paper presented at a meeting

Myers, Charles. "HMOs in Today's Environment." Conference on Medical Insurance Solutions. Chicago. 13 Aug. 2007. Address.

*(continued)*

**FIGURE B.4** (Continued)

Blog post

Scott, David. "Offering Unique Experiences Generates Attention for

Nonprofits." WebInkNow.com. WebInkNow, 16 Aug. 2013. Web.

Interview

Stainer, Georgia, general manager, Day Cable and Communications. Telephone

interview. 2 Mar. 2011.

Newspaper article, one author

Standish, Evelyn. "Global Market Crushes OPEC's Delicate Balance of Interests."

*Report on Business,* 19 Jan. 2012: 43–45. Print.

Book, two authors

Toller, Miriam, and Jay Fielding. *Global Business for Smaller Companies.* Rocklin,

CA: Prima Publishing, 2012. Print.

Government publication

United States. Department of Defense. *Stretching Research Dollars: Survival Advice*

*for Universities and Government Labs.* Washington: GPO, 2010. Print.

Annual report

The Walt Disney Company; *2013 Annual Report.* CA: The Walt Disney Company,

2014. Print.

- For journal articles, include the volume number and the issue number (if necessary). Include the year of publication inside parentheses and follow with a colon, the page range of the article, and the publication medium: *Journal of Business Communication* 36.4 (2009): 72–76. Print. (In this source, the volume is 36, the issue number is 4, the page range is 72–76, and the researcher read the source in print form.)

- Electronic sources are less fixed than print sources, and they may not be readily accessible to readers.

- The date for electronic sources should contain both the date assigned in the source and the date accessed by the researcher (if no date is shown, write "n.d.").

- The URL must be as accurate and complete as possible, from access-mode identifier (http, or ftp) to all relevant directory and file names. If the URL is extremely long, however, use the URL of the website's home page or the URL of the site's search page if you used the site's search function to find the article. The *MLA Style Manual* no longer requires writers to include URLs for materials retrieved online. However, follow whatever guidelines your instructor gives you in this regard.

- MLA style requires you to indicate the medium of publication. For most sources, this will be "Web" or "Print," but you may also cite "CD-ROM" and other media, as appropriate.

# Correction Symbols

Instructors often use these short, easy-to-remember correction symbols and abbreviations when evaluating students' writing. You can use them too, to understand your instructor's suggestions and to revise and proofread your own letters, memos, and reports.

## Content and Style

| | |
|---|---|
| Acc | Accuracy. Check to be sure information is correct. |
| ACE | Avoid copying examples. |
| ACP | Avoid copying problems. |
| Adp | Adapt. Tailor message to reader. |
| App | Approach. Follow proper organizational approach. (Refer to Chapter 4.) |
| Assign | Assignment. Review instructions for assignment. |
| AV | Active verb. Substitute active for passive. |
| Awk | Awkward phrasing. Rewrite. |
| BC | Be consistent. |
| BMS | Be more sincere. |
| Chop | Choppy sentences. Use longer sentences and more transitional phrases. |
| Con | Condense. Use fewer words. |
| CT | Conversational tone. Avoid using overly formal language. |
| Depers | Depersonalize. Avoid attributing credit or blame to any individual or group. |
| Dev | Develop. Provide greater detail. |
| Dir | Direct. Use direct approach; get to the point. |
| Emph | Emphasize. Develop this point more fully. |
| EW | Explanation weak. Check logic; provide more proof. |
| Fl | Flattery. Avoid compliments that are insincere. |
| FS | Figure of speech. Find a more accurate expression. |
| GNF | Good news first. Use direct order. |
| GRF | Give reasons first. Use indirect order. |
| GW | Goodwill. Put more emphasis on expressions of goodwill. |
| H/E | Honesty/ethics. Revise statement to reflect good business practices. |
| Imp | Imply. Avoid being direct. |
| Inc | Incomplete. Develop further. |
| Jar | Jargon. Use less specialized language. |
| Log | Logic. Check development of argument. |
| Neg | Negative. Use more positive approach or expression. |

| | |
|---|---|
| Obv | Obvious. Do not state point in such detail. |
| OC | Overconfident. Adopt humbler language. |
| OM | Omission. |
| Org | Organization. Strengthen outline. |
| OS | Off the subject. Close with point on main subject. |
| Par | Parallel. Use same structure. |
| Pom | Pompous. Rephrase in down-to-earth terms. |
| PV | Point of view. Make statement from reader's perspective rather than your own. |
| RB | Reader benefit. Explain what reader stands to gain. |
| Red | Redundant. Reduce number of times this point is made. |
| Ref | Reference. Cite source of information. |
| Rep | Repetitive. Provide different expression. |
| RS | Resale. Reassure reader that he or she has made a good choice. |
| SA | Service attitude. Put more emphasis on helping reader. |
| Sin | Sincerity. Avoid sounding glib or uncaring. |
| SL | Stereotyped language. Focus on individual's characteristics instead of on false generalizations. |
| Spec | Specific. Provide more specific statement. |
| SPM | Sales promotion material. Tell reader about related goods or services. |
| Stet | Let stand in original form. |
| Sub | Subordinate. Make this point less important. |
| SX | Sexist. Avoid language that contributes to gender stereotypes. |
| Tone | Tone needs improvement. |
| Trans | Transition. Show connection between points. |
| UAE | Use action ending. Close by stating what reader should do next. |
| UAS | Use appropriate salutation. |
| UAV | Use active voice. |
| Unc | Unclear. Rewrite to clarify meaning. |
| UPV | Use passive voice. |
| USS | Use shorter sentences. |
| V | Variety. Use different expression or sentence pattern. |
| W | Wordy. Eliminate unnecessary words. |
| WC | Word choice. Find a more appropriate word. |
| YA | "You" attitude. Rewrite to emphasize reader's needs. |

# Grammar, Mechanics, and Usage

| | |
|---|---|
| Ab | Abbreviation. Avoid abbreviations in most cases; use correct abbreviation. |
| Adj | Adjective. Use adjective instead. |
| Adv | Adverb. Use adverb instead. |
| Agr | Agreement. Make subject and verb or noun and pronoun agree. |
| Ap | Appearance. Improve appearance. |
| Apos | Apostrophe. Check use of apostrophe. |
| Art | Article. Use correct article. |
| BC | Be consistent. |
| Cap | Capitalize. |
| Case | Use cases correctly. |
| CoAdj | Coordinate adjective. Insert comma between coordinate adjectives; delete comma between adjective and compound noun. |
| CS | Comma splice. Use period or semicolon to separate clauses. |
| DM | Dangling modifier. Rewrite so that modifier clearly relates to subject of sentence. |
| Exp | Expletive. Avoid expletive beginnings, such as *it is*, *there are*, *there is*, *this is*, and *these are*. |
| F | Format. Improve layout of document. |
| Frag | Fragment. Rewrite as complete sentence. |
| Gram | Grammar. Correct grammatical error. |
| HCA | Hyphenate compound adjective. |
| lc | Lower case. Do not use capital letter. |
| M | Margins. Improve frame around document. |
| MM | Misplaced modifier. Place modifier close to word it modifies. |
| NRC | Nonrestrictive clause (or phrase). Separate from rest of sentence with commas. |
| P | Punctuation. Use correct punctuation. |
| Par | Parallel. Use same structure. |
| PH | Place higher. Move document up on page. |
| PL | Place lower. Move document down on page. |
| Prep | Preposition. Use correct preposition. |
| RC | Restrictive clause (or phrase). Remove commas that separate clause from rest of sentence. |
| RO | Run-on sentence. Separate two sentences with comma and coordinating conjunction or with semicolon. |
| SC | Series comma. Add comma before *and* or *or* in a list. |
| SI | Split infinitive. Do not separate *to* from rest of verb. |
| Sp | Spelling error. Consult dictionary. |
| S-V | Subject-verb pair. Do not separate with comma. |
| Syl | Syllabification. Divide word between syllables. |
| WD | Word division. Check dictionary for proper end-of-line hyphenation. |
| WW | Wrong word. Replace with another word. |

# Proofreading Marks

| Symbol | Meaning | Symbol Used in Context | Corrected Copy |
|---|---|---|---|
| ≡ | Align horizontally | meaningful result | meaningful result |
| \|\| | Align vertically | 1. Power cable<br>2. Keyboard | 1. Power cable<br>2. Keyboard |
| ≣ | Capitalize | Pepsico, Inc. | PepsiCo, Inc. |
| ⊐⊏ | Centre | ⌐Awards Banquet⌐ | Awards Banquet |
| ◡ | Close up space | self- confidence | self-confidence |
| ℓ | Delete | harrassment and abuse | harassment |
| (ds) | Double-space | text in first line<br>text in second line (ds) | text in first line<br><br>text in second line |
| ⋀ | Insert | tirquoise shirts (u) (and white) | turquoise and white shirts |
| ⋁ | Insert apostrophe | our teams goals | our team's goals |
| ⋀ | Insert comma | a, b and c | a, b, and c |
| = | Insert hyphen | third quarter sales | third-quarter sales |
| ⊙ | Insert period | Harrigan et al | Harrigan et al. |
| ⋁ ⋁ | Insert quotation marks | This team isn't cooperating. | This "team" isn't cooperating. |
| # | Insert space | real estate test case | real estate test case |
| / | Lower case | TULSA, South of here | Tulsa, south of here |
| ⌞ ⌟ | Move down | Sincerely, | Sincerely, |
| ⊏ | Move left | Attention: ⊏ Security | Attention: Security |
| ⊐ | Move right | February 2, 2015 ⊐ | February 2, 2015 |
| ⌐ ⌐ | Move up | THIRD-QUARTER SALES | THIRD-QUARTER SALES |
| (STET) | Restore | staff talked openly and frankly (STET) | staff talked openly |
| ⌇ | Run lines together | Manager,<br>Distribution | Manager, Distribution |
| (ss) | Single space | text in first line<br>text in second line (ss) | text in first line<br>text in second line |
| ⬭ | Spell out | (COD) | cash on delivery |
| (sp) | Spell out | (sp) Assn. of Biochem. Engrs. | Association of Biochemical Engineers |
| ⌐ | Start new line | Marla Fenton, Manager, Distri-bution | Marla Fenton,<br>Manager, Distribution |
| ¶ | Start new paragraph | ¶The solution is easy to determine but difficult to implement in a competitive environment like the one we now face. | The solution is easy to determine but difficult to implement in a competitive environment like the one we now face. |
| ∼ | Transpose | airy, light, casual tone | light, airy, casual tone |
| (bf) | Use boldface | Recommendations (bf) | **Recommendations** |
| (ital) | Use italics | Quarterly Report (ital) | *Quarterly Report* |

# Endnotes

## PREFACE

1. Iain Black, *Sounding Board*, Vancouver Board of Trade, Volume 53, no. 11 (November 2013), 11.

## CHAPTER 1

1. Conference Board of Canada, *Employability Skills 2000+* [accessed 13 June 2003], www.conferenceboard.ca/nbec.
2. Julie Connelly, "Youthful Attitudes, Sobering Realities," *New York Times*, 28 October 2003, E1, E6; Nigel Andrews and Laura D'Andrea Tyson, "The Upwardly Global MBA," *strategy+business* 36, 60–69; Jim McKay, "Communication Skills Found Lacking," *Pittsburgh Post-Gazette*, 28 February 2005 [accessed 28 February 2005], www.delawareonline.com.
3. Brian Solis, *Engage!* (Hoboken: John Wiley & Sons, 2010), 11–12; "Majority of Global Companies Face an Engagement Gap," Internal Comms Hub website, 23 October 2007 [accessed 5 July 2008], www.internalcommshub.com; Gary L. Neilson, Karla L. Martin, and Elizabeth Powers, "The Secrets to Successful Strategy Execution," *Harvard Business Review*, June 2008, 61–70; Nicholas Carr, "Lessons in Corporate Blogging," *BusinessWeek*, 18 July 2006, 9; Susan Meisinger, "To Keep Employees, Talk—and Listen—to Them!" *HR Magazine*, August 2006, 10.
4. Richard L. Daft, *Management*, 6th ed. (Cincinnati: Cengage South-Western, 2003), 147.
5. Richard Edelman, "Teaching Social Media: What Skills Do Communicators Need?" in *Engaging the New Influencers; Third Annual Social Media Academic Summit* (white paper) [accessed 7 June 2010], www.newmediaacademicsummit.com; "CEOs to Communicators: 'Stick to Common Sense'," Internal Comms Hub website, 23 October 2007 [accessed 11 July 2008], www.internalcommshub.com; "A Writing Competency Model for Business," BizCom 101.com, 14 December 2007 [accessed 11 July 2008], www.business-writing-courses.com; Sue Dewhurst and Liam FitzPatrick, "What Should Be the Competency of Your IC Team?" (white paper, 2007) [accessed 11 July 2008], http://competentcommunicators.com.
6. Paul Martin Lester, *Visual Communication: Images with Messages* (Belmont, Calif.: Cengage South-Western, 2006), 6–8.
7. Anne Field, "What You Say, What They Hear," *Harvard Management Communication Letter*, Winter 2005, 3–5.
8. Ben Hanna, *2009 Business Social Media Benchmarking Study* (published by Business.com), 2 November 2009, 11.
9. Michael Killian, "The Communication Revolution—'Deep Impact' About to Strike," Avaya Insights blog, 4 December 2009 [accessed 2 June 2010], www.avayablog.com.
10. Thomas Young, "Ethics in Business: Business of Ethics," *Vital Speeches*, 15 September 1992, 725–730.
11. Philip C. Kolin, *Successful Writing at Work*, 6th ed. (Boston: Houghton Mifflin, 2001), 17–23.
12. Michael Oliveira, "Netflix Apologizes for Using Actors to Meet Press at Canadian Launch," *Globe and Mail*, 22 September 2010, www.theglobeandmail.com.
13. Robert Plummer, "Will Fake Business Blogs Crash and Burn?" BBC News, 22 May 2008 [accessed 3 June 2010], http://news.bbc.co.uk.
14. Linda Pophal, "Tweet Ethics: Trust and Transparency in a Web 2.0 World," *CW Bulletin*, September 2009 [accessed 3 June 2010], www.iabc.com.
15. Daft, *Management*, 155.
16. Based in part on Robert Kreitner, *Management*, 9th ed. (Boston: Houghton Mifflin, 2004), 163.
17. Alan Kline, "The Business Case for Diversity," *US Banker*, May 2010, 10–11.
18. Podcast interview with Ron Glover, IBM website [accessed 17 August 2008], www.ibm.com.
19. "Culture Influences Brain Function, Study Shows," *Science Daily*, 13 January 2008 [accessed 5 June 2010], www.sciencedaily.com; Tracy Novinger, *Intercultural Communication: A Practical Guide* (Austin: University of Texas Press, 2001), 15.
20. Arthur Chin, "Understanding Cultural Competency," *New Zealand Business*, December 2010/January 2011, 34–35; Sanjeeta R. Gupta, "Achieve Cultural Competency," *Training*, February 2009, 16–17; Diane Shannon, "Cultural Competency in Health Care Organizations: Why and How," *Physician Executive*, September–October 2010, 15–22.
21. Geneviève Hilton, "Becoming Culturally Fluent," *Communication World*, November/December 2007, 34–35.
22. Mary O'Hara-Devereaux and Robert Johansen, *Global Work: Bridging Distance, Culture, and Time* (San Francisco: Jossey-Bass, 1994), 55, 59.
23. Edward T. Hall, "Context and Meaning," in *Intercultural Communication: A Reader*, 6th ed., edited by Larry A. Samovar and Richard E. Porter (Belmont, Calif.: Wadsworth, 1991), 34–42.
24. Daft, *Management*, 459.
25. Shital Kakkar Mehra, "Understanding Cultures," *The Economic Times* (India), 21 September 2007 [accessed 27 January 2008], http://economictimes.indiatimes.com.
26. O'Hara-Devereaux and Johansen, *Global Work: Bridging Distance, Culture, and Time*, 55, 59.
27. Linda Beamer, "Teaching English Business Writing to Chinese-Speaking Business Students," *Bulletin of the Association for Business Communication* 57, no. 1 (1994), 12–18.
28. Charley H. Dodd, *Dynamics of Intercultural Communication*, 3rd ed. (Dubuque, Iowa: Brown, 1991), 69–70.
29. Daft, *Management*, 459.
30. "Different Personalities Can Create Culture Clashes, Study Warns," Internal Comms Hub website, 27 February 2007 [accessed 25 January 2008], www.internalcommshub.com.
31. Hannah Seligson, "For American Workers in China, a Culture Clash," *New York Times*, 23 December 2009 [accessed 5 June 2010], www.nytimes.com.
32. Hannah Seligson, "For American Workers in China, a Culture Clash," *New York Times*, 23 December 2009, www.nytimes.com.

33. Linda Beamer and Iris Varner, *Intercultural Communication in the Workplace*, 2nd ed. (New York: McGraw-Hill Irwin, 2001), 230–233.

34. Ed Marcum, "More U.S. Businesses Abandon Outsourcing Overseas," *Seattle Times*, 28 August 2010, www.seattletimes.com.

35. Guo-Ming Chen and William J. Starosta, *Foundations of Intercultural Communication* (Boston: Allyn & Bacon, 1998), 288–289.

36. Anne Howland, "Mix of Age Groups Can Cause Friction," *Vancouver Sun*, 26 May 2007.

37. Steff Gelston, "Gen Y, Gen X and the Baby Boomers: Workplace Generation Wars," *CIO*, 30 January 2008, www.cio.com.

38. Peter Coy, "Old. Smart. Productive." *BusinessWeek*, 27 June 2005 [accessed 24 August 2006], www.businessweek.com; Linda Beamer and Iris Varner, *Intercultural Communication in the Workplace*, 2nd ed. (New York: McGraw-Hill Irwin, 2001), 107–108.

39. John Gray, *Mars and Venus in the Workplace* (New York: HarperCollins, 2002), 10, 25–27, 61–63.

40. Joanna Barsh and Lareina Yee, "Changing Companies' Minds About Women," *McKinsey Quarterly* 4 (2011): 48–59; Jennifer Luden, "Ask for a Raise? Most Women Hesitate," NPR, 14 February 2011, www.npr.org.

41. Mark D. Downey, "Keeping the Faith," *HR Magazine*, January 2008, 85–88.

42. Jensen J. Zhao and Calvin Parks, "Self-Assessment of Communication Behavior: An Experiential Learning Exercise for Intercultural Business Success," *Business Communication Quarterly* 58, no. 1 (1995), 20–26; Dodd, *Dynamics of Intercultural Communication*, 142–143, 297–299; Stephen P. Robbins, *Organizational Behavior*, 6th ed. (Paramus, N.J.: Prentice Hall, 1993), 345.

43. Lillian H. Chaney and Jeanette S. Martin, *Intercultural Business Communication*, 4th ed. (Upper Saddle River, N.J.: Pearson Prentice Hall, 2007), 9.

44. Mona Casady and Lynn Wasson, "Written Communication Skills of International Business Persons," *Bulletin of the Association for Business Communication* 57, no. 4 (1994), 36–40.

45. "Brain Overload Causing Loss of Deep Thinking: Study," ZeeNews, 14 December 2009 [accessed 5 June 2010], www.zeenews.com; Tara Craig, "How to Avoid Information Overload," *Personnel Today*, 10 June 2008, 31; Jeff Davidson, "Fighting Information Overload," *Canadian Manager*, Spring 2005, 16+.

46. Robert X. Cringely, "Let's Get Small," I, Cringely blog, 26 May 2010 [accessed 5 June 2010], www.cringely.com.

47. "Many Senior Managers Communicate Badly, Survey Says," Internal Comms Hub website, 6 August 2007 [accessed 25 January 2008], www.internalcommshub.com.

48. Mike Schaffner, "Step Away from the Computer," *Forbes*, 7 August 2009 [accessed 5 June 2010], www.forbes.com.

49. Cory Edwards, "Panel Presentation on Social Media Strategies at the International Association of Business communicators World Conference," *New York City*, June 26, 2013.

50. The concept of a four-tweet summary is adapted from Cliff Atkinson, *The Backchannel* (Berkeley, Calif.: New Riders, 2010), 120–121.

CHAPTER 2

1. James Manyika, Kara Sprague, and Lareina Yee, "Using Technology to Improve Workforce Collaboration," What Matters (McKinsey & Company), 27 October 2009, http://whatmatters.mckinseydigital.com.

2. Courtland L. Bovée and John V. Thill, *Business in Action*, 3rd ed. (Upper Saddle River, N.J.: Pearson Prentice Hall, 2005), 175.

3. Aliza Sherman, "5 Reasons Why Virtual Teams Fail," GigaOM, 20 April 2011, http://gigaom.com.

4. "Five Case Studies on Successful Teams," *HR Focus*, April 2002, 18+.

5. Stephen R. Robbins, *Essentials of Organizational Behavior*, 6th ed. (Upper Saddle River, N.J.: Prentice Hall, 2000), 98.

6. Max Landsberg and Madeline Pfau, "Developing Diversity: Lessons from Top Teams," *strategy+business*, Winter 2005, 10–12.

7. "Groups Best at Complex Problems," *Industrial Engineer*, June 2006, 14.

8. Alex "Sandy" Pentland, "The New Science of Building Great Teams," *Harvard Business Review*, April 2012, 60–70; Nicola A. Nelson, "Leading Teams," *Defense AT&L*, July–August 2006, 26–29; Larry Cole and Michael Cole, "Why Is the Teamwork Buzz Word Not Working?" *Communication World*, February–March 1999, 29; Patricia Buhler, "Managing in the 90s: Creating Flexibility in Today's Workplace," *Supervision*, January 1997, 241; Allison W. Amason, Allen C. Hochwarter, Wayne A. Thompson, and Kenneth R. Harrison, "Conflict: An Important Dimension in Successful Management Teams," *Organizational Dynamics*, Autumn 1995, 201.

9. Geoffrey Colvin, "Why Dream Teams Fail," *Fortune*, 12 June 2006, 87–92.

10. Vijay Govindarajan and Anil K. Gupta, "Building an Effective Global Business Team," *MIT Sloan Management Review*, Summer 2001, 631.

11. Louise Rehling, "Improving Teamwork Through Awareness of Conversational Styles," *Business Communication Quarterly*, December 2004, 475–482.

12. Andy Boynton and Bill Fischer, *Virtuoso Teams: Lessons from Teams That Changed Their Worlds* (Harrow, UK: FT Prentice Hall, 2005), 10.

13. Jon Hanke, "Presenting as a Team," *Presentations*, January 1998, 74–82.

14. William P. Galle, Jr., Beverly H. Nelson, Donna W. Luse, and Maurice F. Villere, *Business Communication: A Technology-Based Approach* (Chicago: Irwin, 1996), 260.

15. Mary Beth Debs, "Recent Research on Collaborative Writing in Industry," *Technical Communication*, November 1991, 476–484.

16. Rob Koplowitz, "Building a Collaboration Strategy," *KM World*, November/December 2009, 14–15.

17. Eric Knorr and Galen Gruman, "What Cloud Computing Really Means," *InfoWorld* [accessed 11 June 2010],

www.infoworld.com; Lamont Wood, "Cloud Computing Poised to Transform Communication," LiveScience, 8 December 2009 [accessed 11 June 2010], www.livescience.com.

18. Richard McDermott and Douglas Archibald, "Harnessing Your Staff's Informal Networks," *Harvard Business Review*, March 2010, 89–89.

19. "Lululemon in the Community," lululemon website [accessed 24 March 2011], www.lululemon.com/community/blog.

20. Chuck Williams, *Management*, 2nd ed. (Cincinnati: Cengage South-Western, 2002), 706–707.

21. Ron Ashkenas, "Why We Secretly Love Meetings," *Harvard Business Review* blogs, 5 October 2010, http://blogs.hbr.org.

22. Douglas Kimberly, "Ten Pitfalls of Pitiful Meetings," *Payroll Manager's Report*, January 2010, 1, 11; "Making the Most of Meetings," *Journal of Accountancy*, March 2009, 22.

23. Roger O. Crockett, "The 21st Century Meeting," *BusinessWeek*, 26 February 2007, 72–79.

24. Steve Lohr, "As Travel Costs Rise, More Meetings Go Virtual," *New York Times*, 22 July 2008 [accessed 23 July 2008], www.nytimes.com.

25. GoToMeeting website [accessed 3 May 2012], www.gotomeeting.com; "Unlock the Full Power of the Web Conferencing," CEOworld.biz, 20 November 2007, www.ceoworld.biz.

26. IBM Jam Events website [accessed 10 June 2010], www.collaborationjam.com; "Big Blue Brainstorm," *BusinessWeek*, 7 August 2006 [accessed 15 August 2006], www.businessweek.com.

27. Nick Morgan, "How to Conduct a Virtual Meeting," *Harvard Business Review* blogs, 1 March 2011, http://blogs.hbr.org; "17 Tips for More Productive Conference Calls," AccuConference website [accessed 30 January 2008], www.accuconference.com.

28. Judi Brownell, *Listening*, 2nd ed. (Boston: Allyn & Bacon, 2002), 9, 10.

29. Carmine Gallo, "Why Leadership Means Listening," *BusinessWeek*, 31 January 2007 [accessed 29 January 2008], www.businessweek.com.

30. Augusta M. Simon, "Effective Listening: Barriers to Listening in a Diverse Business Environment," *Bulletin of the Association for Business Communication* 54, no. 3 (September 1991): 73–74.

31. Robyn D. Clarke, "Do You Hear What I Hear?" *Black Enterprise*, May 1998, 129.

32. Dennis M. Kratz and Abby Robinson Kratz, *Effective Listening Skills* (New York: McGraw-Hill, 1995), 45–53; J. Michael Sproule, *Communication Today* (Glenview, Ill.: Scott Foresman, 1981), 69.

33. Brownell, *Listening*, 230–231.

34. Kratz and Kratz, *Effective Listening Skills*, 78–79; Sproule, *Communication Today*.

35. Tyner Blaine, "Ten Supercharged Active Listening Skills to Make You More Successful," Tyner Blain blog, 15 March 2007 [accessed 16 April 2007], http://tynerblain.com/blog; Bill Brooks, "The Power of Active Listening," *American Salesman*, June 2003, 12; "Active Listening," Study Guides

and Strategies website [accessed 5 February 2005], www.studygs.net.

36. Bob Lamons, "Good Listeners Are Better Communicators," *Marketing News*, 11 September 1995, 13+; Phillip Morgan and H. Kent Baker, "Building a Professional Image: Improving Listening Behavior," *Supervisory Management*, November 1985, 35–36.

37. Clarke, "Do You Hear What I Hear?"; Dot Yandle, "Listening to Understand," *Pryor Report Management Newsletter Supplement* 15, no. 8 (August 1998): 13.

38. Brownell, *Listening*, 14; Kratz and Kratz, *Effective Listening Skills*, 8–9; Sherwyn P. Morreale and Courtland L. Bovée, *Excellence in Public Speaking* (Orlando, Fla.: Harcourt Brace, 1998), 72–76; Lyman K. Steil, Larry L. Barker, and Kittie W. Watson, *Effective Listening: Key to Your Success* (Reading, Mass.: Addison-Wesley, 1983), 21–22.

39. Patrick J. Collins, *Say It with Power and Confidence* (Upper Saddle River, N.J.: Prentice Hall, 1997), 40–45.

40. Madelyn Burley-Allen, *Listening: The Forgotten Skill* (New York: Wiley, 1995), 70–71, 119–120; Judi Brownell, *Listening: Attitudes, Principles, and Skills* (Boston: Allyn & Bacon, 2002); 3, 9, 83, 89, 125; Larry Barker and Kittie Watson, *Listen Up* (New York: St. Martin's, 2000), 8, 9, 64.

41. Morreale and Bovée, *Excellence in Public Speaking*, 296.

42. Dale G. Leathers, *Successful Nonverbal Communication: Principles and Applications* (New York: Macmillan, 1986), 19.

43. Gerald H. Graham, Jeanne Unrue, and Paul Jennings, "The Impact of Nonverbal Communication in Organizations: A Survey of Perceptions," *Journal of Business Communication* 28, no. 1 (Winter 1991), 45–62.

44. Bremer Communications website [accessed 28 January 2008], www.bremercommunications.com.

45. Danielle S. Urban, "What to Do About 'Body Art' at Work," *Workforce Management*, March 2010 [accessed 11 June 2010], www.workforce.com.

46. Virginia P. Richmond and James C. McCroskey, *Nonverbal Behavior in Interpersonal Relations* (Boston: Allyn & Bacon, 2000), 153–157.

47. Joe Navarro, "Body Language Myths," *Psychology Today*, 25 October 2009 [accessed 11 June 2010], www.psychologytoday.com; Richmond and McCroskey, *Nonverbal Behavior in Interpersonal Relations*, 2–3.

48. John Hollon, "No Tolerance for Jerks," *Workforce Management*, 12 February 2007, 34.

49. "Use Proper Cell Phone Etiquette at Work," Kelly Services website [accessed 11 June 2010], www.kellyservices.us.

50. J. J. McCorvey, "How to Create a Cell Phone Policy," *Inc.*, 10 February 2010 [accessed 11 June 2010], www.inc.com; "Use Proper Cell Phone Etiquette at Work," Kelly Services website.

51. Alan Cole, "Telephone Etiquette at Work," Work Etiquette website, 14 March 2012, www.worketiquette.co.uk; Alf Nucifora, "Voice Mail Demands Good Etiquette from Both Sides," *Puget Sound Business Journal*, 5–11 September 2003, 24; Ruth Davidhizar and Ruth Shearer, "The Effective Voice Mail Message," *Hospital Material Management Quarterly*, 45–49; "How to Get the Most Out of Voice Mail," *The CPA Journal*, February 2000, 11; Jo Ind,

"Hanging on the Telephone," *Birmingham Post,* 28 July 1999, PS10; Larry Barker and Kittie Watson, *Listen Up* (New York: St. Martin's Press, 2000), 64–65; Lin Walker, *Telephone Techniques,* (New York: Amacom, 1998), 46–47; Dorothy Neal, *Telephone Techniques,* 2nd ed. (New York: Glencoe McGraw-Hill, 1998), 31; Jeannie Davis, *Beyond "Hello"* (Aurora, Col.: Now Hear This, Inc., 2000), 2–3; "Ten Steps to Caller-Friendly Voice Mail," *Managing Office Technology,* January 1995, 25; Rhonda Finniss, "Voice Mail: Tips for a Positive Impression," *Administrative Assistant's Update,* August 2001, 5.

52. Dana May Casperson, *Power Etiquette: What You Don't Know Can Kill Your Career* (New York: AMACOM, 1999), 10–14; Ellyn Spragins, "Introducing Politeness," *Fortune Small Business,* November 2001, 30.

53. Tanya Mohn, "The Social Graces as a Business Tool," *New York Times,* 10 November 2002, sec. 3, 12.

54. Casperson, *Power Etiquette,* 44–46.

55. Casperson, *Power Etiquette,* 109–110.

56. Nick Wingfield, "Oh, for the Good Old Days of Rude Cellphone Gabbers," *New York Times,* 2 December 2011, www.nytimes.com.

57. "Are You Practicing Proper Social Networking Etiquette?" *Forbes,* 9 October 2009 [accessed 11 June 2010], www.forbes.com; Pete Babb, "The Ten Commandments of Blog and Wiki Etiquette," *InfoWorld,* 28 May 2007 [accessed 3 August 2008], www.infoworld.com; Judith Kallos, "Instant Messaging Etiquette," NetM@anners blog [accessed 3 August 2008], www.netmanners.com; Michael S. Hyatt, "E-Mail Etiquette 101," From Where I Sit blog, 1 July 2007 [accessed 3 August 2008], www.michaelhyatt.com.

58. Dan Schawbel, "5 Lessons Celebrities Can Teach Us About Facebook Pages," Mashable, 15 May 2009 [accessed 13 June 2010], http://mashable.com.

## CHAPTER 3

1. Carol Kinsey Gorman, "What's So Great About Face-to-Face?" *Communication World,* May–June 2011, 38–39.

2. Linda Duyle, "Get Out of Your Office," *HR Magazine,* July 2006, 99–101.

3. Liz Lockhard, "How to Make Your First Infographic," website [accessed 12 July 2013], http://www.lizlockhard.com/create-your-first-infographic/.

4. Caroline McCarthy, "The Future of Web Apps Will See the Death of E-Mail," Webware blog, 29 February 2008 [accessed 25 August 2008], http://news.cnet.com; Kris Maher, "The Jungle," *Wall Street Journal,* 5 October 2004, B10; Kevin Maney, "Surge in Text Messaging Makes Cell Operators :-)," *USA Today,* 28 July 2005, B1–B2.

5. David Kirkpatrick, "It's Hard to Manage if You Don't Blog," *Fortune,* 4 October 2004, 46; Lee Gomes, "How the Next Big Thing in Technology Morphed into a Really Big Thing," *Wall Street Journal,* 4 October 2004, B1; Jeff Meisner, "Cutting Through the Blah, Blah, Blah," *Puget Sound Business Journal,* 19–25 November 2004, 27–28; Lauren Gard, "The Business of Blogging," *BusinessWeek,* 13 December 2004, 117–119; Heather

Green, "Online Video: The Sequel," *BusinessWeek,* 10 January 2005, 40; Michelle Conlin and Andrew Park, "Blogging with the Boss's Blessing," *BusinessWeek,* 28 June 2004, 100–102.

6. Presslite website [accessed 28 June 2010], www.presselite.com; Neville Hobson, "Augmented Reality: Overlay Your World," Neville Hobson blog, 27 July 2009 [accessed 28 June 2010], www.nevillehobson.com.

7. Kevin Shively, "The Data Behind 5 Brands Using Instagram Video," 27 June 2013, Simply Measured.com [accessed 10 July 2013], http://simplymeasured.com/blog/2013/06/27/the-data-behind-5-brands-using-instagram-video/.

8. Berk and Clampitt, "Finding the Right Path in the Communication Maze."

9. Samantha R. Murray and Joseph Peyrefitte, "Knowledge Type and Communication Media Choice in the Knowledge Transfer Process," *Journal of Managerial Issues,* Spring 2007, 111–133.

10. Raymond M. Olderman, *10 Minute Guide to Business Communication* (New York: Alpha Books, 1997), 19–20.

11. Mohan R. Limaye and David A. Victor, "Cross-Cultural Business Communication Research: State of the Art and Hypotheses for the 1990s," *Journal of Business Communication,* Summer 1991, 277–299; "Doing Business with Americans? Use E-mail or Voicemail," *Canadian Press Newswire,* 4 August 2000; "Netiquette," *Financial Post* (*National Post*) 29 September 1999, C8.

12. Steve Tobak, "How to Be a Great Storyteller and Win Over Any Audience," BNET, 12 January 2011, www.bnet.com.

13. Chip Heath and Dan Heath, *Made to Stick: Why Some Ideas Survive and Others Die* (New York: Random House, 2008), 206.

## CHAPTER 4

1. Martin Shovel, "How to Be an Outstanding Communicator," CreativityWorks blog, 16 May 2011, www.creativityworks.net; "About Us," CreativityWorks, 16 May 2011, www.creativityworks.net.

2. Annette N. Shelby and N. Lamar Reinsch, Jr., "Positive Emphasis and You Attitude: An Empirical Study," *Journal of Business Communication* 32, no. 4 (1995): 303–322.

3. Sherryl Kleinman, "Why Sexist Language Matters," *Qualitative Sociology* 25, no. 2 (Summer 2002): 299–304.

4. Judy E. Pickens, "Terms of Equality: A Guide to Bias-Free Language," *Personnel Journal,* August 1985, 24.

5. Biography of Ursula M. Burns, Xerox website [accessed 25 June 2010], www.xerox.com; biography of Shelly Lazarus, Ogilvy & Mather website [accessed 25 June 2010], www.ogilvy.com; biography of Andrea Jung, Avon website [accessed 25 June 2010], www.avoncompany.com.

6. Lisa Taylor, "Communicating About People with Disabilities: Does the Language We Use Make a Difference?" *Bulletin of the Association for Business Communication* 53, no. 3 (September 1990): 65–67.

7. Susan Benjamin, *Words at Work* (Reading, Mass.: Addison-Wesley, 1997), 136–137.

8. Plain Language website [accessed 28 June 2010], www.plainlanguage.gov.

9. Plain English Campaign website [accessed 28 June 2010], www.plainenglish.co.uk.

10. Plain Language website; Etzkorn, "Amazingly Simple Stuff."

11. Susan Jaderstrom and Joanne Miller, "Active Writing," *Office Pro*, November/December 2003, 29.

12. Portions of this section are adapted from Courtland L. Bovée, *Techniques of Writing Business Letters, Memos, and Reports* (Sherman Oaks, Calif.: Banner Books International, 1978), 13–90.

13. Catherine Quinn, "Lose the Office Jargon; It May Sunset Your Career," *The Age* (Australia), 1 September 2007 [accessed 5 February 2008], www.theage.com.au.

14. Visuwords website [accessed 12 July 2013], www.visuwords.com.

15. Food Allergy Initiative website [accessed 23 September 2006], www.foodallergyinitiative.org; Diana Keough, "Snacks That Can Kill; Schools Take Steps to Protect Kids Who Have Severe Allergies to Nuts," *Plain Dealer*, 15 July 2003, E1; "Dawdling Over Food Labels," *New York Times*, 2 June 2003, A16; Sheila McNulty, "A Matter of Life and Death," *Financial Times*, 10 September 2003, 14.

16. Denise Faguy, "Subtle Differences: Inside Canada's Aftermarket," *Aftermarket Insider* 15 (2002): 1 [accessed 2 June 2003], www.aftermarket.org/Information/Aftermarket_Insider/canada.asp; Lori Doss, "Tim Hortons Makes Plans to Roll out Hundreds of New Branches," *Nation's Restaurant News*, 10 June 2002, 95–96; Hollie Shaw, "Tim Hortons in Push to Overtake McDonald's: Plans More Outlets," *National Post*, 24 May 2002, FP1; Tim Hortons website [accessed 2 June 2003], www.timhortons.com.

17. Inspired by Inglesina website [accessed 14 March 2008], www.inglesina.com and BestBabyGear website [accessed 14 March 2008], www.bestbabygear.com.

**CHAPTER 5**

1. Leo Babauta, "Edit to Done: Revision and the Art of Being Concise," Write to Done blog, 1 January 2008 [accessed 29 June 2010], www.writetodone.com.

2. Natalie Canavor and Claire Meirowitz, "Good Corporate Writing: Why It Matters, and What to Do," *Communication World*, July–August 2005, 30–33.

3. "Revision in Business Writing," Purdue OWL website [accessed 8 February 2008], http://owl.english.purdue.edu.

4. Holly Weeks, "The Best Memo You'll Ever Write," *Harvard Management Communication Letter*, Spring 2005, 3–5.

5. Lynn Gaertner-Johnston, "Best Practices for Bullet Points," Business Writing blog, 17 December 2005 [accessed 8 February 2008], www.businesswritingblog.com.

6. Deborah Gunn, "Looking Good on Paper," *Office Pro*, March 2004, 10–11.

7. Jacci Howard Bear, "Desktop Publishing Rules of Page Layout," About.com [accessed 22 August 2005], www.about.com.

8. Jacci Howard Bear, "Desktop Publishing Rules for How Many Fonts to Use," About.com [accessed 22 August 2005], www.about.com.

**CHAPTER 6**

1. Glen Korstom, "Debt Low, Maintenance High. Hotel Owners Say Investing in Sustainability and Monitoring Social Media Have Been Successful Strategies," *Business in Vancouver, The Black Edition: Profitability*, March 2011, 4–5.

2. Angelo Fernando, "Content Snacking—and What You Can Do About It," *Communication World*, January–February 2011, 8–10.

3. Jennifer Van Grove, "Social Networking on Mobile Devices Skyrockets," Mashable, 20 October 2011, http://mashable.com.

4. Angelo Fernando, "Social Media Change the Rules," *Communication World*, January/February 2007, 9–10; Geoff Livingston and Brian Solis, *Now Is Gone: A Primer on New Media for Executives and Entrepreneurs* (Laurel, Md.: Bartleby Press, 2007), 60.

5. Don Tapscott and Anthony D. Williams, *Wikinomics: How Mass Collaboration Changes Everything* (London: Portfolio, 2006), 216–217; Dan Schawbel, "Why Social Media Makes It Possible for Gen-Y to Succeed," Personal Branding blog, 12 December 2007 [accessed 14 February 2008], http://personalbrandingblog.wordpress.com.

6. Richard Edelman, "Teaching Social Media: What Skills Do Communicators Need?" in *Engaging the New Influencers; Third Annual Social Media Academic Summit* (white paper) [accessed 7 June 2010], www.newmediaacademicsummit.com.

7. Catherine Toole, "My 7 Deadly Sins of Writing for Social Media—Am I Right?" Econsultancy blog, 19 June 2007, www.econsultancy.com; Muhammad Saleem, "How to Write a Social Media Press Release," Copyblogger [accessed 16 September 2008], www.copyblogger.com; Melanie McBride, "5 Tips for (Better) Social Media Writing," Melanie McBride Online, 11 June 2008, http://melaniemcbride.net.

8. Christian Pieter Hoffmann, "Holding Sway," *Communication World*, November–December 2011, 26–29.

9. Jon Russell, "Why 'Going Global' Makes No Sense for China's Social Networks—for Now," The Next Web, 14 May 2012, http://thenextweb.com.

10. H. James Wilson, P.J. Guinan, Salvatore Parise, and Bruce D. Weinberg, "What's Your Social Media Strategy?" *Harvard Business Review*, July–August 2011, 23–25.

11. Patrick Hanlon and Josh Hawkins, "Expand Your Brand Community Online," *Advertising Age*, 7 January 2008, 14–15.

12. Christopher Swan, "Gamification: A New Way to Shape Behavior," *Communication World*, May–June 2012, 13–14.

13. Samantha Murphy, "Why Mobile Commerce Is on the Rise," Mashable, 7 March 2012, http://mashable.com.

14. Todd Wasserman, "What Drives Brand Sociability?" Mashable, 12 October 2011.

15. Toyota Facebook page [accessed 3 June 2012], www.facebook.com/toyota; General Motors Facebook page [accessed 3 June 2012], www.facebook.com/generalmotors; Ford Facebook page [accessed 3 June 2012], www.facebook.com/ford; B.L. Ochman, "Doing It Wrong: 11 Boring Things GM Posted on Facebook," *Ad Age*, 18 May 2012.

16. "Shaking Things Up at Coca-Cola," *Harvard Business Review*, October 2011, 94–99.

17. Alex Wright, "Mining the Web for Feelings, Not Facts," *New York Times*, 23 August 2009, www.nytimes.com.

18. Hoffmann, "Holding Sway"; Josh Bernoff, "Social Strategy for Exciting (and Not So Exciting) Brands," *Marketing News*, 15 May 2009, 18; Larry Weber, *Marketing to the Social Web* (Hoboken, N.J.: Wiley, 2007), 12–14; David Meerman Scott, *The New Rules of Marketing and PR* (Hoboken, N.J.: Wiley, 2007), 62; Paul Gillin, *The New Influencers* (Sanger, Calif.: Quill Driver Books, 2007), 34–35; Jeremy Wright, *Blog Marketing: The Revolutionary Way to Increase Sales, Build Your Brand, and Get Exceptional Results* (New York: McGraw-Hill, 2006), 263–365.

19. Sonia Simone, "What's the Difference Between Content Marketing and Copywriting?" Copyblogger [accessed 4 June 2012], www.copyblogger.com.

20. Matt Rhodes, "Build Your Own Community or Go Where People Are? Do Both," FreshNetworks blog, 12 May 2009, www.freshnetworks.com.

21. Brian Solis, *Engage!* (Hoboken, N.J.: Wiley, 2010), 13.

22. Zachary Sniderman, "5 Ways to Clean Up Your Social Media Identity," 7 July 2010, Mashable, http://mashable.com.

23. HP company profiles on LinkedIn and Facebook [accessed 6 June 2012], www.facebook.com/hp and www.linkedin.com.

24. Vanessa Pappas, "5 Ways to Build a Loyal Audience on YouTube," Mashable, 15 June 2010 [accessed 21 July 2010], www.mashable.com.

25. Tamar Weinberg, *The New Community Rules: Marketing on the Social Web* (Sebastapol, Calif.: O'Reilly Media, 2009), 288.

26. "About Us," Yelp, accessed 6 June 2012, www.yelp.com; Lisa Barone, "Keynote Conversation with Yelp Chief Operating Officer Geoff Donaker," 5 October 2010, http://outspokenmedia.com.

27. Rohit Bhargava, "How Curation Could Save the Internet (and Your Brand)," *Communication World*, January–February 2012, 20–23.

28. Reid Goldborough, "More Trends for 2009: What to Expect with Personal Technology," *Public Relations Tactics*, February 2009, 9.

29. Michelle V. Rofter, "If Tim Try Has His Way, He'll Eradicate Email for Good," *Workforce Management*, 24 April 2012, www.workforce.com.

30. Matt Cain, "Managing E-Mail Hygiene," ZD Net Tech Update, 5 February 2004 [accessed 19 March 2004], www.zdnet.com.

31. Hilary Potkewitz and Rachel Brown, "Spread of E-Mail Has Altered Communication Habits at Work," *Los Angeles Business Journal*, 18 April 2005 [accessed 30 April 2006], www.findarticles.com; Nancy Flynn, *Instant Messaging Rules* (New York: AMACOM, 2004), 47–54.

32. Mary Munter, Priscilla S. Rogers, and Jone Rymer, "Business E-Mail: Guidelines for Users," *Business Communication Quarterly*, March 2003, 26+; Renee B. Horowitz and Marian G. Barchilon, "Stylistic Guidelines for E-Mail," *IEEE Transactions on Professional Communication* 37, no. 4 (December 1994): 207–212.

33. Steve Rubel, "Tip: Tweetify the Lead of Your Emails," The Steve Rubel Stream blog, 20 July 2010 [accessed 22 July 2010], www.steverubel.com.

34. Judith Newman, "If You're Happy and You Know It, Must I Know, Too?" *New York Times*, 21 October 2011, www.nytimes.com.

35. Michal Lev-Ram, "IBM: Instant Messaging Has Replaced Voicemail," CNNMoney, 31 May 2011, http://tech.fortune.cnn.com; Robert J. Holland, "Connected—More or Less," Richmond.com, 8 August 2006, www.richmond.com.

36. Vayusphere website [accessed 22 January 2006], www.vayusphere.com; Christa C. Ayer, "Presence Awareness: Instant Messaging's Killer App," *Mobile Business Advisor*, 1 July 2004 [accessed 22 January 2006], www.highbeam.com; Jefferson Graham, "Instant Messaging Programs Are No Longer Just for Messages," *USA Today*, 20 October 2003, 5D; Todd R. Weiss, "Microsoft Targets Corporate Instant Messaging Customers," *Computerworld*, 18 November 2002, 12; "Banks Adopt Instant Messaging to Create a Global Business Network," *Computer Weekly*, 25 April 2002, 40; Michael D. Osterman, "Instant Messaging in the Enterprise," *Business Communications Review*, January 2003, 59–62; John Pallato, "Instant Messaging Unites Work Groups and Inspires Collaboration," *Internet World*, December 2002, 14+.

37. Paul Mah, "Using Text Messaging in Business," Mobile Enterprise blog, 4 February 2008 [accessed 16 September 2008], http://blogs.techrepublic.com.com/wireless; Paul Kedrosky, "Why We Don't Get the (Text) Message," *Business 2.0*, 2 October 2006 [accessed 4 October 2006], www.business2.com; Carpenter, "Companies Discover Marketing Power of Text Messaging."

38. Mark Gibbs, "Racing to Instant Messaging," *NetworkWorld*, 17 February 2003, 74.

39. "E-Mail Is So Five Minutes Ago," *BusinessWeek*, 28 November 2005 [accessed 31 July 2009], www.businessweek.com.

40. "*SANS Top-20 2007 Security Risks*," SANS Institute [accessed 16 September 2008], www.sans.org; Tom Espiner, "Spim, Splog on the Rise," CNET News, 6 July 2006 [accessed 16 September 2008], http://news.cnet.com; Anita Hamilton, "You've Got Spim!" *Time*, 2 February 2004 [accessed 1 March 2004], www.time.com; Elizabeth Millard, "Instant Messaging Threats Still Rising," Newsfactor.com, 6 July 2005 [accessed 5 October 2006], www.newsfactor.com.

41. Clint Boulton, "IDC: IM Use Is Booming in Business," InstantMessagingPlanet.com, 5 October 2005 [accessed 22 January 2006], www.instantmessagingplanet.com; Jenny Goodbody, "Critical Success Factors for Global Virtual Teams," *Strategic Communication Management*, February/March 2005, 18–21; Ann Majchrzak, Arvind Malhotra, Jeffrey Stamps, and Jessica Lipnack, "Can Absence Make a Team Grow Stronger?" *Harvard Business Review*, May 2004, 131–137; Christine Y. Chen, "The IM Invasion," *Fortune*, 26 May 2003, 135–138; Yudhijit Bhattacharjee, "A Swarm of Little Notes," *Time*, September

2002, A3–A8; Mark Bruno, "Taming the Wild Frontiers of Instant Messaging," *Bank Technology News*, December 2002, 30–31; Richard Grigonis, "Enterprise-Strength Instant Messaging," Convergence.com, 10–15 [accessed March 2003], www.convergence.com.

42. Leo Babauta, "17 Tips to Be Productive with Instant Messaging," Web Worker Daily, 14 November 2007 [accessed 14 February 2008], http://webworkerdaily.com; Pallato, "Instant Messaging Unites Work Groups and Inspires Collaboration."

43. "State of the Blogosphere 2011," Technorati, 4 November 2011, http://technorati.com.

44. Marcus Sheridan, "5 Reasons Your Business Should Be Blogging," Social Media Examiner, 2 December 2011, www.socialmediaexaminer.com; Stephen Baker, "The Inside Story on Company Blogs," *BusinessWeek* 14 February 2006, www.businessweek.com; Jeremy Wright, *Blog Marketing* (New York: McGraw-Hill, 2006), 45–56; Paul Chaney, "Blogs: Beyond the Hype!" 26 May 2005, http://radiantmarketinggroup.com.

45. Solis, *Engage!*, 314.

46. Diane Culhane, "Blog Logs a Culture Change," *Communication World*, January/February 2008, 40–41.

47. Solis, *Engage!*, 86.

48. Weinberg, *The New Community Rules: Marketing on the Social Web*, 89.

49. "IBM Social Computing Guidelines," IBM Website [accessed 5 June 2012], www.ibm.com.

50. Joel Falconer, "Six Rules for Writing Great Web Content," Blog News Watch, 9 November 2007 [accessed 14 February 2008], www.blognewswatch.com.

51. Dion Hinchcliffe, "Twitter on Your Intranet: 17 Microblogging Tools for Business," ZDNet, 1 June 2009 [accessed 22 July 2010], www.zdnet.com.

52. Hinchcliffe, "Twitter on Your Intranet: 17 Microblogging Tools for Business."

53. B.L. Ochman, "Why Twitter Is a Better Brand Platform Than Facebook," Ad Age, 1 June 2012, *Ad Age*, http://adage.com.

54. Leon Widrich, "4 Ways to Use Twitter for Customer Service and Support," Social Media Examiner, 12 April 2012, www.socialmediaexaminer.com.

55. Paul André, Michael Bernstein, and Kurt Luther, "What Makes a Great Tweet," *Harvard Business Review*, May 2012, 36–37.

56. André et al., "What Makes a Great Tweet."

57. Interview with Cliff Ravenscraft in Michael Stelzner, "Podcasting for Business: What You Need to Know," Social Media Examiner, 23 December 2011, www.socialmediaexaminer.com.

58. "Set Up Your Podcast for Success," FeedForAll website [accessed 4 October 2006], www.feedforall.com.

59. Nathan Hangen, "4 Steps to Podcasting Success," Social Media Examiner, 14 February 2011, www.socialmediaexaminer.com.

60. Shel Holtz, "Ten Guidelines for B2B Podcasts," Webpronews.com, 12 October 2005 [accessed 9 March 2006], www.webpronews.com.

61. Martin Turcotte, "Ethical Consumption," 2010, Statistics Canada [accessed 1 February 2011], http://www.statcan.gc.ca/pub/11-008-x/2011001/article/11399-eng.pdf.

## CHAPTER 7

1. Courtland L. Bovée, John V. Thill, Barbara E. Schatzman, and Jean A. Scribner, *Business Communication Essentials*, 1st Canadian ed. (Toronto: Pearson, 2005), 148.

2. Fraser P. Seitel, *The Practice of Public Relations*, 9th ed. (Upper Saddle River, N.J.: Prentice Hall, 2004), 402–411; *Techniques for Communicators* (Chicago: Lawrence Ragan Communication, 1995), 34, 36.

3. David Meerman Scott, *The New Rules of Marketing and PR* (Hoboken, N.J.: Wiley, 2007), 62.

4. Shel Holz, "Next-Generation Press Releases," CW Bulletin, September 2009 [accessed 9 August 2010], www.iabc.com; Steph Gray, "Baby Steps in Social Media News Releases," Helpful Technology blog, 15 May 2009 [accessed 9 August 2010], http://blog.helpfultechnology.com.

5. Pat Cataldo, "Op-Ed: Saying 'Thank You' Can Open More Doors Than You Think," Penn State University Smeal College of Business website [accessed 19 February 2008], www.smeal.psu.edu.

6. Jackie Huba, "Five Must-Haves for Thank-You Notes," Church of the Customer Blog, 16 November 2007 [accessed 19 February 2008], www.churchofthecustomer.com.

7. Mary Mitchell, "The Circle of Life—Condolence Letters," ULiveandLearn.com [accessed 18 July 2005], www.liveandlearn.com; Donna Larcen, "Authors Share the Words of Condolence," *Los Angeles Times*, 20 December 1991, E11.

8. Adapted from Vancouver International Wine Festival website [accessed 5 February 2011], http://www.playhousewinefest.com/.

9. Adapted from Mountain Equipment Co-op website [accessed 7 February 2011], www.mec.ca.

10. Adapted from Grasshopper Solar website [accessed 18 July 2013], www.grasshoppersolar.com.

11. Carolyn A. Emery et al., "Risk of Injury Associated with Body Checking," *Journal of the American Medical Association*, 2010, 303: 2265–2272; Mark A. Halstead and Kevin D. Walter, "Sport-Related Concussions in Children and Adolescents," *Pediatrics* 126 (2010): 597–615; Brent Hagel et al., "Effect of Body Checking on Injury Rates Among Minor Ice Hockey Players," *Canadian Medical Association Journal* 175 (2006): 155–160; Carol DeMatteo et al., "My Child Doesn't Have a Brain Injury, He Only Has a Concussion," *Pediatrics* 125 (2010): 327–334.

## CHAPTER 8

1. Matt Rhodes, "Social Media as a Crisis Management Tool," Social Media Today blog, 21 December 2009 [accessed 8 July 2010], www.socialmediatoday.com.

2. Katie Grasso, "Deliver Bad News to Workers Face-to-Face, with Empathy," *Courier-Post* (Camden, New Jersey), 8 February 2006 [accessed 14 May 2006], www.courierpostonline.com.

3. Ian McDonald, "Marsh Can Do $600 Million, but Apologize?" *Wall Street Journal*, 14 January 2005, C1, C3; Adrienne Carter and Amy Borrus, "What if Companies Fessed Up?" *BusinessWeek*, 24 January 2005, 59–60; Patrick J. Kiger, "The Art of the Apology," *Workforce Management*, October 2004, 57–62; British Columbia, *Apology Act*, S.B.C. 2006, c. 19; Nova Scotia, *Apology Act*, S.N.S. 2008, c. 34; Newfoundland and Labrador, *Apology Act*, S.N.L. 2009, c. A-10.1; Manitoba, *Apology Act*, C.C.S.M., c. A98; Ontario, *Apology Act*, 2009, S.O., c. 3; Nunavut, *Legal Treatment of Apologies Act*, S. Nu. 2010, c.12.

4. "The Power of Apology: Removing the Legal Barriers," A Special Report by the Ombudsman of the Province of British Columbia, February 2006 [accessed 14 May 2006], www.bcombudsperson.ca/; Ameeta Patel and Lamar Reinsch, "Companies Can Apologize: Corporate Apologies and Legal Liability," *Business Communication Quarterly*, March 2003 [accessed 1 December 2003], www.elibrary.com.

5. John Guiniven, "Sorry! An Apology as a Strategic PR Tool," *Public Relations Tactics*, December 2007, 6.

6. Omowale Casselle, "Really, You Want ME to Write YOU a LinkedIn Recommendation," RecruitingBlogs, 22 April 2010, www.recruitingblogs.com.

7. "LinkedIn Profiles to Career Introductions: When You Can't Recommend Your Friend," *Seattle Post-Intelligencer* Personal Finance blog, 16 November 2010, http://blog.seattlepi.com.

8. Neal Schaffer, "How Should I Deal with a LinkedIn Recommendation Request I Don't Want to Give?" Social Web School, 20 January 2010, http://humancapitalleague.com.

9. Christopher Elliott, "7 Ways Smart Companies Tell Customers 'No'," CBS Money Watch, 7 June 2011, www.cbsnews.com.

10. Matt Rhodes, "Build Your Own Community or Go Where People Are? Do Both," FreshNetworks blog, 12 May 2009 [accessed 14 July 2010], www.freshnetworks.com.

11. Andy Blatchford and Paola Loriggio, "50 feared dead in Lac-Megantic; railway suspends employee," *Montreal Gazette*, July 10, 2013 [accessed 18 July 2013], www.montrealgazette.com/mobile/news/national-news/Head+railway+whose+train+exploded+LacMegantic+visit+town/8639379/story.html.

12. "Gulf of Mexico Response," BP website [accessed 14 July 2010], www.bp.com.

13. David Meerman Scott, "The US Air Force: Armed with Social Media," WebInkNow blog, 15 December 2008 [accessed 14 July 2010], www.webinknow.com; Matt Rhodes, "How to React if Somebody Writes About Your Brand Online," FreshNetworks blog, 9 January 2009 [accessed 14 July 2010], www.freshnetworks.com; Rhodes, "Social Media as a Crisis Management Tool."

14. Adapted from Pui-Wing Tam, Erin White, Nick Wingfield, and Kris Maher, "Snooping E-Mail by Software Is Now a Workplace Norm," *Wall Street Journal*, 9 March 2005, B1+.

15. Adapted from "Bathtub Curve," *Engineering Statistics Handbook*, National Institute of Standards and Technology website [accessed 16 April 2005], www.nist.gov; Robert Berner, "The Warranty Windfall," *BusinessWeek*, 20 December 2004, 84–86; Larry Armstrong, "When Service Contracts Make Sense," *BusinessWeek*, 20 December 2004, 86.

16. Adapted from Twitter/JetBlue website [accessed 15 July 2010], http://twitter.com/JetBlue; and from Twitter West-Jet website [accessed 31 March 2011], http://twitter.com/westjet.

17. Adapted from Lee Valley website [accessed 29 October 2008], www.leevalley.com.

18. Adapted from Wolf Blitzer, "More Employers Taking Advantages of New Cyber-Surveillance Software," *CNN.com*, 10 July 2000 [accessed 11 July 2000], www.cnn.com/2000/US/07/10/workplace.eprivacy/index.html.

19. Adapted from Courtland L. Bovée and John Thill, *BusinessCommunication Essentials*, 2nd US ed. (New Jersey: Pearson Education, 2006), p. 23; adapted from Sean Doherty, "Dynamic Communications," *Network Computing*, 3 April 2003, 14, no. 6:26 [accessed 24 July 2003], http://search.epnet.com/direct.asp?an-9463336&db=tg=AN; R.P. Srikanth, "IM Tools Are the Latest Tech Toys for Corporate Users," *Express Computer*, 2 July 2002 [accessed 21 July 2003], www.expresscomputeronline.com/20020701/indtrend1.shtml.

20. Adapted from "Mass Alert Notification System Goes Online," press release, 6 March 2008, Simon Fraser University website [accessed 6 March 2008], www.sfu.ca/pamr/media_releases/media_releases_archive/media_release03060801.html.

21. Adapted from Associated Press, "Employers Restricting Use of Cell Phones in Cars," CNN.com/Sci-Tech, 27 August 2001 [accessed 27 August 2001], www.cnn.com/2001/TECH/08/27/cellphones.cars.ap/index.html; Julie Vallese, "Study: All Cell Phones Distract Drivers," CNN.com/U.S., 16 August 2001 [accessed 7 September 2001], www.cnn.com/2001/US/08/16/cell.phone.driving/index.html.

22. Adapted from "Recall Safety Notice," Bombardier Recreational Products website, 10 September 2008 [accessed 30 October 2008], www.brp.com; Bombardier Recreational Products website [accessed 30 October 2008], www.brp.com.

CHAPTER 9

1. Sonia Simone, "The #1 Conversion Killer in Your Copy (And How to Beat It)," Copyblogger, [accessed 21 June 2012], www.copyblogger.com.

2. Jay A. Conger, "The Necessary Art of Persuasion," *Harvard Business Review*, May–June 1998, 84–95; Jeanette W. Gilsdorf, "Write Me Your Best Case for . . ." *Bulletin of the Association for Business Communication* 54, no. 1 (March 1991): 7–12.

3. "Vital Skill for Today's Managers: Persuading, Not Ordering, Others," *Soundview Executive Book Summaries*, September 1998, 1.

4. Mary Cross, "Aristotle and Business Writing: Why We Need to Teach Persuasion," *Bulletin of the Association for Business Communication* 54, no. 1 (March 1991): 3–6.

5. Robert B. Cialdini, "Harnessing the Science of Persuasion," *BusinessWeek*, 4 December 2007 [accessed 4 March 2008], www.businessweek.com.

6. Wesley Clark, "The Potency of Persuasion," *Fortune*, 12 November 2007, 48; W. H. Weiss, "Using Persuasion Successfully," *Supervision*, October 2006, 13–16.

7. Tom Chandler, "The Copywriter's Best Friend," The Copywriter Underground blog, 20 December 2006 [accessed 4 March 2008], http://copywriterunderground.com.

8. John D. Ramage and John C. Bean, *Writing Arguments: A Rhetoric with Readings*, 3rd ed. (Boston: Allyn & Bacon, 1995), 430–442.

9. Philip Vassallo, "Persuading Powerfully: Tips for Writing Persuasive Documents," *et Cetera*, Spring 2002, 65–71.

10. Dianna Booher, *Communicate with Confidence* (New York: McGraw-Hill, 1994), 102.

11. Conger, "The Necessary Art of Persuasion."

12. Courtland L. Bovée, John V. Thill, Barbara E. Schatzman, and Jean A. Scribner, *Business Communication Essentials*, 1st Canadian ed. (Toronto: Pearson, 2005), 211.

13. "Social Factors in Developing a Web Accessibility Business Case for Your Organization," W3C website [accessed 17 July 2010], www.w3.org.

14. Weinberg, *The New Community Rules: Marketing on the Social Web*, 22, 23–24, 187–191; Larry Weber, *Marketing to the Social Web* (Hoboken, N.J.: Wiley, 2007), 12–14; David Meerman Scott, *The New Rules of Marketing and PR* (Hoboken, N.J.: Wiley, 2007), 62; Paul Gillin, *The New Influencers* (Sanger, Calif.: Quill Driver Books, 2007), 34–35; Jeremy Wright, *Blog Marketing: The Revolutionary Way to Increase Sales, Build Your Brand, and Get Exceptional Results* (New York: McGraw-Hill, 2006), 263–365.

15. Gilsdorf, "Write Me Your Best Case for . . ."

16. "How to Comply with the Children's Online Privacy Protection Rule," U.S. Federal Trade Commission website [accessed 17 July 2010], www.ftc.gov; "Frequently Asked Advertising Questions: A Guide for Small Business," U.S. Federal Trade Commission website [accessed 17 July 2010], www.ftc.gov; "Consumer Handbook," Canada Business website [accessed 4 April 2011], http://www.canadabusiness.ca/eng/89/903/; "Safety Tips for Tweens and Teens," OnGuard Online website [accessed 4 April 2011], http://www.onguardonline.gov/topics/safety-tips-tweens-teens.aspx.

17. Adapted from Whole Foods Market website [accessed 19 July 2010], www.wholefoodsmarket.com.

18. Kevin M. Savetz, "Preventive Medicine for the Computer User," *Multimedia Online* 2, no. 2 (June 1996): 58–60.

19. Adapted from Margo Kelly, "The Emerging Green Economy," *CBC News*, 10 March 2008 [accessed 15 March 2008], www.cbc.ca/news/goinggreen/greenrush.html.

20. Charlene Li and Josh Bernoff, *Groundswell* (Boston: Harvard Business Press, 2008), 104–106.

21. Adapted from WestJet website [accessed 9 July 2008] http://c5dsp.westjet.com/guest/contacts/donationRequest.jsp;jsessionid=R91LLzNGyqY7Z6RkM1KvQx3bnHQqVQgGgfp0 21dVvKGPTn7ZqH2Q!-1595351148.

CHAPTER 10

1. Courtland L. Bovée, Michael J. Houston, and John V. Thill, *Marketing*, 2nd ed. (New York: McGraw-Hill, 1995), 194–196.

2. Legal-Definitions.com [accessed 17 December 2003], www.legal-definitions.com.

3. Lynn Quitman Troyka, *Simon & Schuster Handbook for Writers*, 6th ed. (Upper Saddle River, N.J.: Prentice Hall, 2002), 481.

4. Fair Dealing in Canadian law, Wikipedia [accessed 6 July 2013], http://en.wikipedia.org/wiki/Fair_dealing_in_Canadian_copyright_law; Giuseppina D'Agostino, "Healing Fair Dealing? A Comparative Copyright Analysis of Canada's Fair Dealing to U.K. Fair Dealing and U.S. Fair Use," McGill Law Journal, (53) 336 [accessed 7 July 2013], http://lawjournal.mcgill.ca/documents/dAgostino.pdf.

5. Adapted from BCIT Library Electronic Resources Databases & Indexes, "Business" [accessed 2 June 2003], www.lib.bcit.ca/eResources/databases/subject.php?sybhect=Business; interview with Linda Matsuba, Business Librarian, B.C. Institute of Technology, 2 June 2003.

6. AllTheWeb.com advanced search page [accessed 27 August 2005], www.alltheweb.com; Google advanced search page [accessed 27 August 2005], www.google.com; Yahoo! advanced search page [accessed 27 August 2005], www.yahoo.com.

7. Christina Warren, "Yolink Helps Web Researchers Search Behind Links," Mashable, 24 July 2010 [accessed 26 July 2010], http://mashable.com.

8. Naresh K. Malhotra, *Basic Marketing Research* (Upper Saddle River, N.J.: Prentice-Hall, 2002), 314–317; "How to Design and Conduct a Study," *Credit Union Magazine*, October 1983, 36–46.

9. A. B. Blankenship and George Edward Breen, *State of the Art Marketing Research* (Chicago: NTC Business Books, 1993), 136.

10. Tesco website [accessed 25 July 2010], www.tesco.com.

11. Reid Goldsborough, "Words for the Wise," *Link-Up*, September–October 1999, 25–26.

12. Julie Rohovit, "Computer Eye Strain: The Dilbert Syndrome," Virtual Hospital website, [accessed 9 November 2004], www.vh.org.

13. Nick Usborne, "Two Pillars of a Successful Site," Excess Voice, May 2004, www.excessvoice.com.

14. Shel Holtz, "Writing for the Wired World," International Association of Business Communicators, 1999, 6–9.

15. Holtz, "Writing for the Wired World," 28–29.

16. Jakob Nielsen, "How Users Read on the Web" [accessed 11 November 2004], www.useit.com/alertbox/9710a.html.

17. Reid Goldsborough, "Words for the Wise," *Link-Up*, September–October 1999, 25–26.

18. Rohovit, "Computer Eye Strain."

19. Usborne, "Two Pillars of a Successful Site."

20. Holtz, "Writing for the Wired World," 6–9.

21. Holtz, "Writing for the Wired World," 28–29.

22. Adapted from Kate Sangha, conversation, 9 May 2008.

23. Adapted from Bob Smith, "The Evolution of Pinkerton," *Management Review*, September 1993, 54–58.

24. Adapted from Air-Trak website [accessed 26 July 2010], www.air-trak.com.

## CHAPTER 11

1. Courtland L. Bovée, John V. Thill, Barbara E. Schatzman, and Jean A. Scribner, *Business Communication Essentials*, 1st Canadian ed. (Toronto: Pearson, 2005), 276.

2. Qvidian website, [accessed 26 June 2012], www.qvidian.com.

3. "Web Writing: How to Avoid Pitfalls," *Investor Relations Business*, 1 November 1999, 15.

4. Jakob Nielsen, "How Users Read on the Web" [accessed 11 November 2004], www.useit.com/alertbox/9710a.html; Patsi Krakoff, "Writing on the Web: Letting Go of the Words," *Writing on the Web* blog, 15 April 2010 [accessed 28 July 2010], http://writingontheweb.com.

5. Paul Boag, "10 Harsh Truths About Corporate Websites," *Smashing Magazine* blog, 10 February 2009 [accessed 28 July 2010], www.smashingmagazine.com.

6. "Codex: Guidelines," WordPress website [accessed 16 February 2008], http://wordpress.com; Michael Shanks, "Wiki Guidelines," Traumwerk website [accessed 18 August 2006], http://metamedia.stanford.edu/projects/traumwerk/home; Joe Moxley, M. C. Morgan, Matt Barton, and Donna Hanak, "For Teachers New to Wikis," Writing Wiki [accessed 18 August 2006], http://writingwiki.org; "Wiki Guidelines," PsiWiki [accessed 18 August 2006], http://psi-im.org.

7. "Codex: Guidelines," WordPress website [accessed 28 July 2010], http://wordpress.com.

8. Alexis Gerard and Bob Goldstein, *Going Visual* (Hoboken, N.J.: Wiley, 2005), 18.

9. Gerard and Goldstein, *Going Visual*, 103–106.

10. Edward R. Tufte, *Visual Explanations: Images and Quantities, Evidence and Narrative* (Cheshire, Conn.: Graphics Press, 1997), 82.

11. Joshua David McClurg-Genevese, "The Principles of Design," *Digital Web Magazine*, 13 June 2005 [accessed 23 November 2006], www.digital-web.com.

12. Charles Kostelnick and Michael Hassett, *Shaping Information: The Rhetoric of Visual Conventions* (Carbondale, Ill.: Southern Illinois University Press, 2003), 17.

13. Edward R. Tufte, *The Visual Display of Quantitative Information* (Cheshire, Conn.: Graphic Press, 1983), 113.

14. Stephen Few, "Oracle—Have You No Shame?" Visual Business Intelligence blog, 29 April 2010 [accessed 29 July 2010], www.perceptualedge.com.

15. "Pyramid Perversion—More Junk Charts," Stubborn Mule blog, 12 March 2010 [accessed 29 July 2010], www.stubbornmule.com.

16. Stephen Few, "Save the Pies for Dessert," *Visual Business Intelligence Newsletter*, August 2007 [accessed 29 July 2010], www.perceptualedge.com.

17. Maria Popova, "Data Visualization: Stories for the Information Age," *BusinessWeek*, 12 August 2009 [accessed 29 July 2010], www.businessweek.com.

18. "Data Visualization: Modern Approaches," *Smashing Magazine* website, 2 August 2007 [accessed 15 March 2008], www.smashingmagazine.com; "7 Things You Should Know About Data Visualization," Educause Learning Initiative [accessed 15 March 2008], www.educause.edu; TagCrowd website [accessed 15 March 2008], www.tagcrowd.com.

19. Angelo Fernando, "Killer Infographic! But Does It Solve TMI?" *Communication World*, March–April 2012, 10–12.

20. Based in part on Tufte, *Visual Explanations: Images and Quantities, Evidence and Narrative*, 29–37, 53; Paul Martin Lester, *Visual Communication: Images with Messages*, 4th ed. (Belmont, Calif.: Cengage Wadsworth, 2006), 95–105, 194–196.

21. John Morkes and Jakob Nielsen, "Concise, Scannable, and Objective: How to Write for the Web," UseIt.com [accessed 13 November 2006], www.useit.com.

22. Martin James, "PDF Virus Spreads Without Exploiting Any Flaw," IT Pro, 8 April 2010, www.itpro.co.uk.

23. Adapted from Ieva M. Augstumes, "Buyers Take the Driver's Seat," *Dallas Morning News*, 20 February 2004 [accessed 30 June 2004], www.highbeam.com; Jill Amadio, "A Click Away: Automotive Web Sites Are Revved Up and Ready to Help You Buy," *Entrepreneur*, 1 August 2003 [accessed 30 June 2004], www.highbeam.com; Dawn C. Chmielewski, "Car Sites Lend Feel-Good Info for Haggling," *San Jose Mercury News*, 1 August 2003 [accessed 30 June 2004], www.highbeam.com; Cromwell Schubarth, "Autoheroes Handle Hassle of Haggling," *Boston Herald*, 24 July 2003 [accessed 30 June 2004], www.highbeam.com; Rick Popely, "Internet Doesn't Change Basic Shopping Rules," *Chicago Tribune*, 28 February 2004 [accessed 30 June 2004], www.highbeam.com; Matt Nauman, "Walnut Creek, Calif., Firm Prospers as Online Car Buying Becomes More Popular," *San Jose Mercury News*, 21 June 2004 [accessed 30 June 2004], www.highbeam.com; Cliff Banks, "e-Dealer 100," *Ward's Dealer Business*, 1 April 2004 [accessed 30 June 2004], www.highbeam.com; Cars.com website [accessed 30 June 2004], www.cars.com; CarsDirect.com website [accessed 30 June 2004], www.carsdirect.com.

24. WorkSafeBC, *Backgrounder: Training and Orientation for Young and New Workers*, WorkSafeBC Publications (pamphlet), 2007; WorksafeBC, *Three Steps to Effective Worker Education and Training 2007 Edition*, WorksafeBC Publications, 2007.

## CHAPTER 12

1. EZspeech website, [accessed 19 March 2008], www.ez-speech.com; Marc S. Friedman, "Use Visual Aids, Not Visual Crutches," Training, 24 December 2007, www.presentations.com.

2. Nancy Duarte, *Slide:ology: The Art and Science of Creating Great Presentations* (Sebastopol, Calif.: O'Reilly Media, 2008), 13.

3. Amber Naslund, "Twebinar: GE's Tweetsquad," 4 August 2009 [accessed 3 August 2010], www.radian6.com/blog.

4. Carmine Gallo, "How to Deliver a Presentation Under Pressure," *BusinessWeek* online, 18 September 2008 [accessed 15 August 2009], www.businessweek.com.

5. Sarah Lary and Karen Pruente, "Powerless Point: Common PowerPoint Mistakes to Avoid," *Public Relations Tactics*, February 2004, 28.

6. Garr Reynolds, *Presentation Zen: Simple Ideas on Presentation Design and Delivery* (Berkeley, Calif.: New Riders, 2008), 66.

7. Reynolds, *Presentation Zen: Simple Ideas on Presentation Design and Delivery*, 39–42.

8. Sherwyn P. Morreale and Courtland L. Bovée, *Excellence in Public Speaking* (Fort Worth, Tex.: Harcourt Brace College Publishers, 1998), 234–237.

9. John Windsor, "Presenting Smart: Keeping the Goal in Sight," *Presentations*, 6 March 2008 [accessed 19 March 2008], www.presentations.com.

10. Morreale and Bovée, *Excellence in Public Speaking*, 241–243.

11. Adapted from Eric J. Adams, "Management Focus: User-Friendly Presentation Software," *World Trade*, March 1995, 92.

12. Carmine Gallo, "Grab Your Audience Fast," *BusinessWeek*, 13 September 2006, 19.

13. Walter Kiechel III, "How to Give a Speech," *Fortune*, 8 June 1987, 180.

14. *Communication and Leadership Program* (Santa Ana, Calif.: Toastmasters International, 1980), 44, 45.

15. Reynolds, *Presentation Zen: Simple Ideas on Presentation Design and Delivery*, 10.

16. Cliff Atkinson, "The Cognitive Load of PowerPoint: Q&A with Richard E. Mayer," Sociable Media [accessed 15 August 2009], http://www.sociablemedia.com/articles_mayer.htm.

17. "The Power of Color in Presentations," 3M Meeting Network [accessed 25 May 2007], www.3m.com/meetingnetwork/readingroom/meetingguide_power_color.html.

18. Duarte, *Slide:ology: The Art and Science of Creating Great Presentations*, 118.

19. Sarah Lary and Karen Pruente, "Powerless Point: Common PowerPoint Mistakes to Avoid," *Public Relations Tactics*, February 2004, 28.

20. Reynolds, *Presentation Zen*, 85.

21. Reynolds, *Presentation Zen*, 66.

22. Reynolds, *Presentation Zen*, 208.

23. Richard Zeoli, "The Seven Things You Must Know About Public Speaking," *Forbes*, 3 June 2009 [accessed 2 August 2010], www.forbes.com; Morreale and Bovée, *Excellence in Public Speaking*, 24–25.

24. Jennifer Rotondo and Mike Rotondo, Jr., *Presentation Skills for Managers* (New York: McGraw-Hill, 2002), 9.

25. Rick Gilbert, "Presentation Advice for Boardroom Success," *Financial Executive*, September 2005, 12.

26. Rotondo and Rotondo, *Presentation Skills for Managers*, 151.

27. Teresa Brady, "Fielding Abrasive Questions During Presentations," *Supervisory Management*, February 1993, 6.

28. Robert L. Montgomery, "Listening on Your Feet," *The Toastmaster*, July 1987, 14–15.

29. Cliff Atkinson, *The Backchannel* (Berkeley, Calif.: New Riders, 2010), 17.

30. Atkinson, *The Backchannel*, 51, 68–73.

31. Olivia Mitchell, "10 Tools for Presenting with Twitter," Speaking About Presenting blog, 3 November 2009 [accessed 3 August 2010], www.speakingaboutpresenting.com; Atkinson, *The Backchannel*, 51, 68–73, 99.

32. SlideShare website [accessed 3 August 2010], www.slideshare.net.

33. Adapted from PechaKucha20x20 website [accessed 4 August 2010], www.pecha-kucha.org; Reynolds, *Presentation Zen: Simple Ideas on Presentation Design and Delivery*, 41.

34. Adapted from Foursquare website [accessed 4 August 2010], http://foursquare.com; Christina Warren, "Foursquare Reaches 100 Million Checkins," Mashable, 20 July 2010 [accessed 4 August 2010], http://mashable.com.

## CHAPTER 13

1. Camille DeBell, "Ninety Years in the World of Work in America," *Career Development Quarterly* 50, no. 1 (September 2001): 77–88.

2. John A. Challenger, "The Changing Workforce: Workplace Rules in the New Millennium," *Vital Speeches of the Day* 67, no. 23 (15 September 2001): 721–728.

3. Marvin J. Cetron and Owen Davies, "Trends Now Changing the World: Technology, the Workplace, Management, and Institutions," *Futurist* 35, no. 1 (March/April 2001): 27–42.

4. Courtland L. Bovée and John V. Thill, *Business in Action*, 5th ed. (Upper Saddle River, N.J.: Pearson Prentice Hall, 2010), 18–21; Randall S. Hansen and Katharine Hansen, "What Do Employers Really Want? Top Skills and Values Employers Seek from Job-Seekers," QuintCareers.com [accessed 17 August 2010], www.quintcareers.com.

5. Iain Black, *Sounding Board*, Vancouver Board of Trade, Volume 53 #11, November 2013, p. 11 [accessed January 3, 2014].

6. Nancy M. Somerick, "Managing a Communication Internship Program," *Bulletin of the Association for Business Communication* 56, no. 3 (1993): 10–20.

7. Crowdsourcing.org website, [accessed 2 August 2011], www.crowdsourcing.org.

8. Jeffrey R. Young, "'E-Portfolios' Could Give Students a New Sense of Their Accomplishments," *The Chronicle of Higher Education*, 8 March 2002, A31.

9. Brian Carcione, e-portfolio [accessed 20 December 2006], http://eportfolio.psu.edu.

10. Mohammed Al-Taee, "Personal Branding," Al-Taee blog [accessed 17 August 2010] http://altaeeblog.com.

11. Pete Kistler, "Seth Godin's 7-Point Guide to Bootstrap Your Personal Brand," Personal Branding blog, 28 July 2010 [accessed 17 August 2010] www.personalbrandingblog; Kyle Lacy, "10 Ways to Building Your Personal Brand Story," Personal Branding blog, 5 August 2010 [accessed 17 August 2010] www.personalbrandingblog; Al-Taee, "Personal Branding"; Scot Herrick, "30 Career Management Tips—Marketing AND Delivery Support Our Personal Brand," Cube Rules blog, 8 September 2007 [accessed 17 August 2010] http://cuberules.com; Alina Tugend, "Putting Yourself Out There on a Shelf to Buy," *New York Times*, 27 March 2009 [accessed 9 August 2009] www.nytimes.com.

12. Anne Fisher, "How to Get Hired by a 'Best' Company," *Fortune*, 4 February 2008, 96.

13. Eve Tahmincioglu, "Revamping Your Job-Search Strategy," MSNBC.com, 28 February 2010 [accessed 5 August 2010], www.businessweek.com.

14. Jessica Dickler, "The Hidden Job Market," CNNMoney.com, 10 June 2009 [accessed 6 August 2010], http://money.cnn.com.

15. Tara Weiss, "Twitter to Find a Job," *Forbes*, 7 April 2009 [accessed 6 August 2010], www.forbes.com.

16. Miriam Saltpeter, "Using Facebook Groups for Job Hunting," Keppie Careers blog, 13 November 2008 [accessed 6 August 2010], www.keppiecareers.com.

17. Anne Fisher, "Greener Pastures in a New Field," *Fortune*, 26 January 2004, 48.

18. Liz Ryan, "Etiquette for Online Outreach," Yahoo! Hotjobs website [accessed 26 March 2008], http://careers.yahoo.com.

19. Eve Tahmincioglu, "Employers Digging Deep on Prospective Workers," MSNBC.com, 26 October 2009 [accessed 10 August 2010], www.msnbc.com.

20. Career and Employment Services, Danville Area Community College website [accessed 23 March 2008], www.dacc.edu/career; Career Counseling, Sarah Lawrence College website [accessed 23 March 2008], www.slc.edu/occ/index.php; Cheryl L. Noll, "Collaborating with the Career Planning and Placement Center in the Job-Search Project," *Business Communication Quarterly* 58, no. 3 (1995): 53–55.

21. Randall S. Hansen and Katharine Hansen, "What Résumé Format Is Best for You?" QuintCareers.com [accessed 7 August 2010], www.quintcareers.com.

22. Hansen and Hansen, "What Résumé Format Is Best for You?"

23. Katharine Hansen, "Should You Consider a Functional Format for Your Resume?" QuintCareers.com [accessed 7 August 2010], www.quintcareers.com.

24. Kim Isaacs, "Resume Dilemma: Criminal Record," Monster.com [accessed 23 May 2006], www.monster.com; Kim Isaacs, "Resume Dilemma: Employment Gaps and Job-Hopping," Monster.com [accessed 23 May 2006], www.monster.com; Susan Vaughn, "Answer the Hard Questions Before Asked," *Los Angeles Times*, 29 July 2001, W1–W2.

25. "How to Ferret Out Instances of Résumé Padding and Fraud," *Compensation & Benefits for Law Offices*, June 2006, 1+.

26. "Resume Fraud Gets Slicker and Easier," CNN.com [accessed 11 March 2004], www.cnn.com.

27. Cari Tuna and Keith J. Winstein, "Economy Promises to Fuel Résumé Fraud," *Wall Street Journal*, 17 November 2008 [accessed 8 August 2010], http://online.wsj.com; Lisa Takeuchi Cullen, "Getting Wise to Lies," *Time*, 1 May 2006, 59; "Resume Fraud Gets Slicker and Easier"; Employment Research Services website [accessed 18 March 2004], www.er-services.com.

28. "How to Ferret Out Instances of Résumé Padding and Fraud."

29. Jacqueline Durett, "Redoing Your Résumé? Leave Off the Lies," *Training*, December 2006, 9; "Employers Turn Their Fire on Untruthful CVs," *Supply Management*, 23 June 2005, 13.

30. Cynthia E. Conn, "Integrating Writing Skills and Ethics Training in Business Communication Pedagogy: A Résumé Case Study Exemplar," *Business Communication Quarterly*, June 2008, 138–151; Marilyn Moats Kennedy, "Don't Get Burned by Résumé Inflation," *Marketing News*, 15 April 2007, 37–38.

31. Rockport Institute, "How to Write a Masterpiece of a Résumé" [accessed 9 August 2010], www.rockportinstitute.com.

32. Lora Morsch, "25 Words That Hurt Your Resume," CNN.com, 20 January 2006 [accessed 20 January 2006], www.cnn.com.

33. Liz Ryan, "The Reengineered Résumé," *BusinessWeek*, 3 December 2007, SC12.

34. Katharine Hansen, "Tapping the Power of Keywords to Enhance Your Resume's Effectiveness," QuintCareers.com [accessed 7 August 2010], www.quintcareers.com.

35. Hansen, "Tapping the Power of Keywords to Enhance Your Resume's Effectiveness."

36. Anthony Balderrama, "Résumé Blunders That Will Keep You from Getting Hired," CNN.com, 19 March 2008, www.cnn.com; Michelle Dumas, "5 Résumé Writing Myths," Distinctive Documents blog, 17 July 2007, http://blog.distinctiveweb.com; Kim Isaacs, "Résumé Dilemma: Recent Graduate," Monster.com, [accessed 26 March 2008], http://career-advice.monster.com.

37. Rockport Institute, "How to Write a Masterpiece of a Résumé."

38. "Résumé Length: What It Should Be and Why It Matters to Recruiters," *HR Focus*, June 2007, 9.

39. John Hazard, "Resume Tips: No Pictures, Please and No PDFs," Career-Line.com, 26 May 2009 [accessed 10 August 2010], www.career-line.com; "25 Things You Should Never Include on a Resume," HR World website, 18 December 2007 [accessed 25 March 2008], www.hrworld.com.

40. John Sullivan, "Résumés: Paper, Please," *Workforce Management*, 22 October 2007, 50; "Video Résumés Offer Both Pros and Cons During Recruiting," *HR Focus*, July 2007, 8.

41. Rachel Louise Ensign, "Is the Paper Résumé Dead?" *Wall Street Journal*, 24 January 2012, http://online.wsj.com.

42. Nancy M. Schullery, Linda Ickes, and Stephen E. Schullery, "Employer Preferences for Résumés and Cover Letters," *Business Communication Quarterly*, June 2009, 163–176.

43. VisualCV website [accessed 10 August 2010], www.visualcv.com.

44. Elizabeth Garone, "Five Mistakes Online Job Hunters Make," *Wall Street Journal*, 28 July 2010 [accessed 10 August 2010], http://online.wsj.com.

45. "10 Reasons Why You Are Not Getting Any Interviews," *Miami Times*, 7–13 November 2007, 6D.

46. "Protect Yourself from Identity Theft When Hunting for a Job Online," *Office Pro*, May 2007, 6.

47. Jessi Hempel, "How LinkedIn Will Fire Up Your Career," *Fortune* 161, no. 5 (04 December 2010), 74–82 [accessed 14 January 2013]; Harvey Schacter, "LinkedIn: The under-the-radar recruiting tool," *The Globe and Mail*

[Toronto, Ontario], (16 July 2012): B7 [accessed 08 January 2014].

48. Olga Kharif, "Recruiters eschew job boards to find talent on LinkedIn," *Leader Post* [Regina, Saskatchewan] (05 January 2013): B5 [accessed 08 January 2014]; Olga Kharif, "Job recruiters turn to LinkedIn; Newer social media gain upper hand," *The Ottawa Citizen* [Ottawa, Ontario] (19 December 2012): F4 [accessed 08 January 2014].

49. Olga Kharif, "Recruiters eschew job boards to find talent on LinkedIn."

50. Lou Adler, "Job-seekers: The Power of Networking," *LinkedIn.com*, 17 February 2013 [accessed 14 January 2014] online article.

51. Robin M. Hensley, "LinkedIn Tips for CPAs," *Journal of Accountancy*, March 2011, 44–47 [accessed 14 January 2014], www.journalofaccountancy.com.

**CHAPTER 14**

1. Matthew Rothenberg, "Manuscript vs. Machine," The Ladders, 15 December 2009 [accessed 13 August 2010], www.theladders.com; Joann Lublin, "Cover Letters Get You in the Door, So Be Sure Not to Dash Them Off," *Wall Street Journal*, 6 April 2004, B1.

2. Lisa Vaas, "How to Write a Great Cover Letter," The Ladders, 20 November 2009 [accessed 13 August 2010], www.theladders.com.

3. Allison Doyle, "Introduction to Cover Letters," About.com [accessed 13 August 2010], http://jobsearch.about.com.

4. Doyle, "Introduction to Cover Letters"; Vaas, "How to Write a Great Cover Letter"; Toni Logan, "The Perfect Cover Story," *Kinko's Impress* 2 (2000): 32, 34.

5. Lisa Vaas, "How to Follow Up a Résumé Submission," The Ladders, 9 August 2010 [accessed 12 August 2010], www.theladders.com.

6. Alison Doyle, "How to Follow Up After Submitting a Resume," About.com [accessed 13 August 2010], http://jobsearch.about.com; Vaas, "How to Follow Up a Résumé Submission."

7. Anne Fisher, "How to Get Hired by a 'Best' Company," *Fortune*, 4 February 2008, 96.

8. Fisher, "How to Get Hired by a 'Best' Company."

9. Sarah E. Needleman, "Speed Interviewing Grows as Skills Shortage Looms; Strategy May Help Lock in Top Picks; Some Drawbacks," *Wall Street Journal*, 6 November 2007, B15.

10. Scott Beagrie, "How to Handle a Telephone Job Interview," *Personnel Today*, 26 June 2007, 29.

11. John Olmstead, "Predict Future Success with Structured Interviews," *Nursing Management*, March 2007, 52–53.

12. Fisher, "How to Get Hired by a 'Best' Company."

13. Erinn R. Johnson, "Pressure Sessions," *Black Enterprise*, October 2007, 72.

14. "What's a Group Interview?" About.com Tech Careers [accessed 5 April 2008], http://jobsearchtech.about.com.

15. Fisher, "How to Get Hired by a 'Best' Company."

16. Katherine Hansen, "Behavioral Job Interviewing Strategies for Job-Seekers," QuintCareers.com [accessed 13 August 2010], www.quintcareers.com.

17. Hansen, "Behavioral Job Interviewing Strategies for Job-Seekers."

18. Chris Pentilla, "Testing the Waters," *Entrepreneur*, January 2004 [accessed 27 May 2006], www.entrepreneur.com; Terry McKenna, "Behavior-Based Interviewing," *National Petroleum News*, January 2004, 16; Nancy K. Austin, "Goodbye Gimmicks," *Incentive*, May 1996, 241.

19. William Poundstone, "Beware the Interview Inquisition," *Harvard Business Review*, May 2003, 18+.

20. Peter Vogt, "Mastering the Phone Interview," Monster.com [accessed 13 December 2006], www.monster.com; Nina Segal, "The Global Interview: Tips for Successful, Unconventional Interview Techniques," Monster.com [accessed 13 December 2006], www.monster.com.

21. Segal, "The Global Interview: Tips for Successful, Unconventional Interview Techniques."

22. Barbara Kiviat, "How Skype Is Changing the Job Interview," *Time*, 20 October 2009 [accessed 13 August 2010], www.time.com.

23. HireVue website [accessed 4 April 2008], www.hirevue.com; in2View website [accessed 4 April 2008], www.in2view.biz; Victoria Reitz, "Interview Without Leaving Home," *Machine Design*, 1 April 2004, 66.

24. Gina Ruiz, "Job Candidate Assessment Tests Go Virtual," *Workforce Management*, January 2008 [accessed 14 August 2010], www.workforce.com; Connie Winkler, "Job Tryouts Go Virtual," *HR Magazine*, September 2006, 131–134.

25. Jonathan Katz, "Rethinking Drug Testing," *Industry Week*, March 2010, 16–18; Ashley Shadday, "Assessments 101: An Introduction to Candidate Testing," *Workforce Management*, January 2010 [accessed 14 August 2010], www.workforce.com; Dino di Mattia, "Testing Methods and Effectiveness of Tests," *Supervision*, August 2005, 4–5; David W. Arnold and John W. Jones, "Who the Devil's Applying Now?" *Security Management*, March 2002, 85–88; Matthew J. Heller, "Digging Deeper," *Workforce Management*, 3 March 2008, 35–39.

26. Frederick P. Morgeson, Michael A. Campion, Robert L. Dipboye, John R. Hollenbeck, Kevin Murphy, and Neil Schmitt, "Are We Getting Fooled Again? Coming to Terms with Limitations in the Use of Personality Tests in Personnel Selection," *Personnel Psychology* 60, no. 4 (Winter 2007): 1029–1049.

27. Austin, "Goodbye Gimmicks."

28. Rachel Zupek, "How to Answer 10 Tough Interview Questions," CNN.com, 4 March 2009 [accessed 13 August 2010], www.cnn.com; Barbara Safani, "How to Answer Tough Interview Questions Authentically," The Ladders, 5 December 2009 [accessed 13 August 2010], www.theladders.com.

29. Nick Corcodilos, "How to Answer a Misguided Interview Question," *Seattle Times*, 30 March 2008 [accessed 5 April 2008], www.seattletimes.com.

30. Katherine Spencer Lee, "Tackling Tough Interview Questions," *Certification Magazine*, May 2005, 35.

31. Scott Ginsberg, "10 Good Ways to 'Tell Me About Yourself,'" The Ladders, 26 June 2010 [accessed 13 August 2010], www.theladders.com.

32. Quintessential Careers Website [accessed August 8, 2011], www.quintcareers.com.

33. Joe Turner, "An Interview Strategy: Telling Stories," Yahoo! HotJobs [accessed 5 April 2008], http://careers.yahoo.com.

34. "A Word of Caution for Chatty Job Candidates," *Public Relations Tactics*, January 2008, 4.

35. Interview with Caroline Jellinck, 1 March 2011.

36. Randall S. Hansen, "When Job-Hunting: Dress for Success," QuintCareers.com [accessed 5 April 2008], www.quintcareers.com; Alison Doyle, "Dressing for Success," About.com [accessed 5 April 2008], http://jobsearch.about.com.

37. William S. Frank, "Job Interview: Pre-Flight Checklist," *The Career Advisor* [accessed 28 September 2005], http://careerplanning.about.com.

38. "Employers Reveal Outrageous and Common Mistakes Candidates Made in Job Interviews, According to New CareerBuilder Survey," CareerBuilder.com, [accessed 24 March 2011], www.careerbuilder.com.

39. Alison Green, "10 Surefire Ways to Annoy a Hiring Manager," *U.S. News & World Report* [accessed 24 July 2012], http://money.usnews.com.

40. T. Shawn Taylor, "Most Managers Have No Idea How to Hire the Right Person for the Job," *Chicago Tribune*, 23 July 2002 [accessed 29 September 2005], www.ebsco.com.

41. "10 Minutes to Impress," *Journal of Accountancy*, July 2007, 13.

42. Steven Mitchell Sack, "The Working Woman's Legal Survival Guide: Testing," FindLaw.com [accessed 22 February 2004], www.findlaw.com.

43. Todd Anten, "How to Handle Illegal Interview Questions," Yahoo! HotJobs [accessed 7 August 2009], http://careers.yahoo.com.

44. "Negotiating Salary: An Introduction," *InformationWeek* online [accessed 22 February 2004], www.informationweek.com.

45. Lisa Vaas, "Resume, Meet Technology: Making Your Resume Format Machine-Friendly," The Ladders [accessed 13 August 2010], www.theladders.com.

46. Joan S. Lublin, "Notes to Interviewers Should Go Beyond a Simple Thank You," *Wall Street Journal*, 5 February 2008, B1.

47. Tiffany Hsu, "Extreme Interviewing: Odd Quizzes, Weird Mixers, Improv Pitches. Can You Get Past the Hiring Gatekeepers?" *Los Angeles Times*, 19 February 2012, B1.

48. From Ritika Trikha, "The Best Tips for Tweeting Your Way to a Job," *U.S. News & World Report*, 24 July 2012, http://money.usnews.com.

## APPENDIX A

1. Renée B. Horowitz and Marian G. Barchilon, "Stylistic Guidelines for E-Mail," *IEEE Transactions on Professional Communications*, 37, no. 4 (1994): 207–212.

2. Horowitz and Barchillon, "Stylistic Guidelines for E-Mail," 207–212.

3. "When Image Counts, Letterhead Says It All," *Stamford (Conn.) Advocate and Greenwich Times*, 10 January 1993, F4.

4. Mary A. De Vries, *Internationally Yours* (Boston: Houghton Mifflin, 1994), 8.

5. Lennie Copeland and Lewis Griggs, *Going International: How to Make Friends and Deal Effectively in the Global Marketplace*, 2nd ed. (New York: Random House, 1985), 24–27.

6. De Vries, *Internationally Yours*, 8.6; U.S. Postal Service, *International Mail Manual*, Issue 34, 14 May 2007 [accessed 23 October 2007], www.usps.com.

# Credits

## PHOTO CREDITS

**1** WavebreakMediaMicro/Fotolia. **24** Chagin/Fotolia. **32** Peter Wynn Thompson/The New York Times/Redux. **47** Pressmaster/Fotolia. **69** Imtmphoto/Shutterstock. **71** Microsoft Corporation. **84** Ignite Social Media. **94** StockLite/Shutterstock. **117** Ambrophoto/Shutterstock. **149** Pressmaster/Fotolia. **174** Wavebreakmedia/Shutterstock. **199** Wavebreakmedia/Shutterstock. **225** Zurijeta/Shutterstock. **257** Rido/Fotolia. **308** WavebreakMediaMicro/Fotolia. **318** Left: Sergey Nivens/Shutterstock; Right: Szefei/Shutterstock. **336** Monkey Business Images/Shutterstock. **370** Racorn/Shutterstock. **385** Merzzie/Shutterstock.

## LITERARY CREDITS

**1** Judi Hess, vice president, Eastman Kodak general manager, Enterprise Solutions. **3** Based on Brian Solis, *Engage!* (Hoboken: John Wiley & Sons, 2010), 11–12; "Majority of Global Companies Face an Engagement Gap," Internal Comms Hub website, 23 October 2007 [accessed 5 July 2008], www .internalcommshub.com; Gary L. Neilson, Karla L. Martin, and Elizabeth Powers, "The Secrets to Successful Strategy Execution," *Harvard Business Review*, June 2008, 61–70; Nicholas Carr, "Lessons in Corporate Blogging," *BusinessWeek*, 18 July 2006, 9; Susan Meisinger, "To Keep Employees, Talk—and Listen—to Them!" *HR Magazine*, August 2006, 10. **5** Based on Richard Edelman, "Teaching Social Media: What Skills Do Communicators Need?" in *Engaging the New Influencers*; Third Annual Social Media Academic Summit (white paper) [accessed 7 June 2010], www.newmediaacademicsummit.com; "CEOs to Communicators: 'Stick to Common Sense'," Internal Comms Hub website, 23 October 2007 [accessed 11 July 2008], www.internalcommshub.com; "A Writing Competency Model for Business," BizCom 101.com, 14 December 2007 [accessed 11 July 2008], www.business-writing-courses.com; Sue Dewhurst and Liam FitzPatrick, "What Should Be the Competency of Your IC Team?" (white paper, 2007) [accessed 11 July 2008], http://competentcommunicators.com. **10** Thomas Young, "Ethics in Business: Business of Ethics," *Vital Speeches*, 15 September 1992, 725–730; Philip C. Kolin, *Successful Writing at Work*, 6th ed. (Boston: Houghton Mifflin, 2001), 17–23. **11** Based in part on Robert Kreitner, *Management*, 9th ed. (Boston: Houghton Mifflin, 2004), 163; Gord Nixon, CEO of Royal Bank of Canada. **12** Charley H. Dodd, *Dynamics of Intercultural Communication*, 3rd ed. (Dubuque, Iowa: Brown, 1991), 69–70. **13** Hannah Seligson, "For American Workers in China, a Culture Clash," *New York Times*, 23 December 2009 [accessed 5 June 2010], www.nytimes.com; Guo-Ming Chen and William J. Starosta, *Foundations of Intercultural Communication* (Boston: Allyn & Bacon, 1998), 288–289. **15** Based on Jensen J. Zhao and Calvin Parks, "Self-Assessment of Communication Behavior: An Experiential Learning Exercise for Intercultural Business Success," *Business Communication Quarterly* 58, no. 1 (1995), 20–26; Dodd, *Dynamics of Intercultural Communication*, 142–143, 297–299; Stephen P. Robbins, *Organizational Behavior*, 6th ed. (Paramus, N.J.: Prentice Hall, 1993), 345; Adapted from Mona Casady and Lynn Wasson, "Written Communication Skills of International Business Persons," *Bulletin of the Association for Business Communication* 57, no. 4 (1994), 36–40. **18** Cory Edwards, panel presentation on social media strategies at the International Association of Business Communicators World Conference, New York City, June 26, 2013, www.slideshare.net/RebeccaJarvis2/adobe-coryedwards-ub-socialoct2013. **24** Tony Martino, vice president, Human Resources, Communication, and Corporate Affairs, Xerox Canada; Tony Martino, president, JTX Inc. **25** Stephen R. Robbins, *Essentials of Organizational Behavior*, 6th ed. (Upper Saddle River, N.J.: Prentice Hall, 2000), 98. **26** Andy Boynton and Bill Fischer, *Virtuoso Teams: Lessons from Teams That Changed Their Worlds* (Harrow, UK: FT Prentice Hall, 2005), 10; Mary Beth Debs, "Recent Research on Collaborative Writing in Industry," *Technical Communication*, November 1991, 476–484. **35** Based on Judi Brownell, *Listening: Attitudes, Principles, and Skills* (Boston: Allyn & Bacon, 2002), 14; Kratz and Kratz, *Effective Listening Skills*, 8–9; Sherwyn P. Morreale and Courtland L. Bovée, *Excellence in Public Speaking* (Orlando, Fla.: Harcourt Brace, 1998), 72–76; Lyman K. Steil, Larry L. Barker, and Kittie W. Watson, *Effective Listening: Key to Your Success* (Reading, Mass.: Addison-Wesley, 1983), 21–22. **40** Based on "Are You Practicing Proper Social Networking Etiquette?" *Forbes*, 9 October 2009 [accessed 11 June 2010], www.forbes.com; Pete Babb, "The Ten Commandments of Blog and Wiki Etiquette," *InfoWorld*, 28 May 2007 [accessed 3 August 2008], www.infoworld.com; Judith Kallos, "Instant Messaging Etiquette," *NetM@nners* blog [accessed 3 August 2008], www.netmanners.com; Michael S. Hyatt, "E-Mail Etiquette 101," *From Where I Sit* blog, 1 July 2007 [accessed 3 August 2008], www.michaelhyatt.com. **47** Aaron Brindle, public affairs manager, Google Canada. **61** Steve Tobak, "How to Be a Great Storyteller and Win Over Any Audience," *CBS MoneyWatch*, 12 January 2011, www.cbsnews.com/news/how-to-be-a-great-storyteller-and-win-over-any-audience. **69** Martin Shovel, writer, speech writer, illustrator, and cofounder of CreativityWorks, May 16, 2011, published in "How to Be an Outstanding Communicator," *Chartered Institute of Internal Auditors Magazine*, August 2010. **76** Plain English Campaign website [accessed 28 June 2010], www.plainenglish.co.uk. **90** Based on Inspired by Inglesina website [accessed 14 March 2008], www.inglesina.com, and BestBabyGear website [accessed 14 March 2008], www.bestbabygear.com. **94** Leo Babauta, author and blogger, *WritetoDone.com: Revision and the Art of Being Concise*. **117** Mandy Farmer, president, Accent Inns; Glen Korstom, "Debt Low, Maintenance High: Hotel Owners Say Investing in Sustainability and Monitoring Social Media Have Been Successful Strategies," *Business in Vancouver, The Black Edition:*

*Profitability*, March 2011, 4–5. **122** Richard Edelman, "Teaching Social Media: What Skills Do Communicators Need?" in *Engaging the New Influencers*; Third Annual Social Media Academic Summit (white paper) [accessed 7 June 2010], www.newmediaacademicsummit.com. **124** Adi Ignatius, "Shaking Things Up at Coca-Cola," *Harvard Business Review*, October 2011, 94–99. **125** Based on Sonia Simone, "What's the Difference Between Content Marketing and Copywriting?" *Copyblogger* [accessed 4 June 2012], www.copyblogger.com; Matt Rhodes, "Build Your Own Community or Go Where People Are? Do Both," *FreshNetworks* blog, 12 May 2009, www.freshnetworks.com; Brian Solis, *Engage!* (Hoboken, N.J.: Wiley, 2010), 13; Zachary Sniderman, "5 Ways to Clean Up Your Social Media Identity," 7 July 2010, *Mashable*, http://mashable.com; HP company profiles on LinkedIn and Facebook [accessed 6 June 2012], www.facebook.com/hp and www.linkedin.com. **128** Michelle V. Rafter, "If Tim Fry Has His Way, He'll Eradicate Email for Good," *Workforce Management*, 24 April 2012, www.workforce.com. **132** Based on Leo Babauta, "17 Tips to Be Productive with Instant Messaging," *Web Worker Daily*, 14 November 2007 [accessed 14 February 2008], http://webworkerdaily.com; Pallato, "Instant Messaging Unites Work Groups and Inspires Collaboration." **133** Based on Marcus Sheridan, "5 Reasons Your Business Should Be Blogging," *Social Media Examiner*, 2 December 2011, www.socialmediaexaminer.com; Stephen Baker, "The Inside Story on Company Blogs," *BusinessWeek*, 14 February 2006, www.businessweek.com; Jeremy Wright, *Blog Marketing* (New York: McGraw-Hill, 2006), 45–56; Paul Chaney, "Blogs: Beyond the Hype!" 26 May 2005, http://radiantmarketinggroup.com; Solis, *Engage!*, 314. **149** Fred G. Withers, managing partner, Ernst & Young. **160** Based on Fraser P. Seitel, *The Practice of Public Relations*, 9th ed. (Upper Saddle River, N.J.: Prentice Hall, 2004), 402–411; *Techniques for Communicators* (Chicago: Lawrence Ragan Communication, 1995), 34, 36; David Meerman Scott, *The New Rules of Marketing and PR* (Hoboken, N.J.: Wiley, 2007), 62. **174** Matt Rhodes, digital director, FreshMinds, "Social Media as a Crisis Management Tool." **178** "Companies Can Apologize: Corporate Apologies and Legal Liability," *Business Communication Quarterly*, 66.1 (March 2003): 9. **188** Based on David Meerman Scott, "The US Air Force: Armed with Social Media," *WebInkNow* blog, 15 December 2008 [accessed 14 July 2010], www.webinknow.com; Matt Rhodes, "How to React if Somebody Writes About Your Brand Online," *FreshNetworks* blog, 9 January 2009 [accessed 14 July 2010], www.freshnetworks.com; Rhodes, "Social Media as a Crisis Management Tool." **196** Adapted from Associated Press, "Employers Restricting Use of Cell Phones in Cars," CNN.com/Sci-Tech, 27 August 2001 [accessed 27 August 2001], www.cnn.com/2001/TECH/08/27/cellphones.cars.ap/index.html; Julie Vallese, "Study: All Cell Phones Distract Drivers," CNN.com/U.S., 16 August 2001 [accessed 7 September 2001], www.cnn.com/2001/US/08/16/cell.phone.driving/index.html. **199** Sonia Simone, cofounder and chief marketing officer of Copyblogger Media, *The #1 Conversion Killer in Your Copy (and How to Beat It)*, 2013. **205** John D. Ramage and John C. Bean, *Writing Arguments: A Rhetoric with Readings*, 3rd ed. (Boston: Allyn & Bacon, 1995),

430–442. **206** Conger, *The Necessary Art of Persuasion* (Boston, Mass.: Harvard Business Press, 2008); Courtland L. Bovée, John V. Thill, and Barbara E. Schatzman, *Business Communication Today*, 7th ed. (Upper Saddle River, N.J.: Prentice Hall, 2003), 264. **213** Based on Weinberg, *The New Community Rules: Marketing on the Social Web*, 22, 23–24, 187–191; Larry Weber, *Marketing to the Social Web* (Hoboken, N.J.: Wiley, 2007), 12–14; David Meerman Scott, *The New Rules of Marketing and PR* (Hoboken, N.J.: Wiley, 2007), 62; Paul Gillin, *The New Influencers* (Sanger, Calif.: Quill Driver Books, 2007), 34–35; Jeremy Wright, *Blog Marketing: The Revolutionary Way to Increase Sales, Build Your Brand, and Get Exceptional Results* (New York: McGraw-Hill, 2006), 263–365. **214** Based on "How to Comply with the Children's Online Privacy Protection Rule," U.S. Federal Trade Commission website [accessed 17 July 2010], www.ftc.gov; "Frequently Asked Advertising Questions: A Guide for Small Business," U.S. Federal Trade Commission website [accessed 17 July 2010], www.ftc.gov; "Consumer Handbook," Canada Business website [accessed 4 April 2011], www.canadabusiness.ca/eng/89/903/; "Safety Tips for Tweens and Teens," OnGuard Online website [accessed 4 April 2011], www.onguardonline.gov/topics/safety-tips-tweens-teens.aspx. **225** Gerry Roy, chief corporate officer and legal counsel, Inuvialuit Corporate Group; Gerry Roy, chief corporate officer and legal counsel, Inuvialuit Corporate Group. **236** Based on Naresh K. Malhotra, *Basic Marketing Research* (Upper Saddle River, N.J.: Prentice-Hall, 2002), 314–317; "How to Design and Conduct a Study," *Credit Union Magazine*, October 1983, 36–46. **239** David McCandless, "The Beauty of Data Visualization," TED website, http://bit.ly/sHXvKc. **257** Sidney Sawyer, manager, Community Programs, Vancity Community Foundation; Sidney Sawyer. **265** Based on "Codex: Guidelines," WordPress website [accessed 16 February 2008], http://wordpress.com; Michael Shanks, "Wiki Guidelines," Traumwerk website [accessed 18 August 2006], http://metamedia.stanford.edu/projects/traumwerk/home; Joe Moxley, M. C. Morgan, Matt Barton, and Donna Hanak, "For Teachers New to Wikis," *Writing Wiki* [accessed 18 August 2006], http://writingwiki.org; "Wiki Guidelines," *PsiWiki* [accessed 18 August 2006], http://psi-im.org. **308** Dr. Marc S. Friedman, public speaking coach, "Use Visual Aids, Not Visual Crutches," December 24, 2007. **312** Sherwyn P. Morreale and Courtland L. Bovée, *Excellence in Public Speaking* (Fort Worth, Tex.: Harcourt Brace College Publishers, 1998), 234–237. **314** Sherwyn P. Morreale and Courtland L. Bovée, *Excellence in Public Speaking* (Fort Worth, Tex.: Harcourt Brace College Publishers, 1998), 241–243. **315** Based on Eric J. Adams, "Management Focus: User-Friendly Presentation Software," *World Trade*, March 1995, 92. **318** Reynolds, *Presentation Zen: Simple Ideas on Presentation Design and Delivery*, 10. **322** Duarte, *Slide:ology: The Art and Science of Creating Great Presentations*, 118. **324** Reynolds, *Presentation Zen: Simple Ideas on Presentation Design and Delivery*, 66. **327** Based on Richard Zeoli, "The Seven Things You Must Know About Public Speaking," *Forbes*, 3 June 2009 [accessed 2 August 2010], www.forbes.com; Morreale and Bovée, *Excellence in Public Speaking*, 24–25. **328** Cliff Atkinson, *The Backchannel* (Berkeley, Calif.: New Riders, 2010), 17; Based on

Olivia Mitchell, "10 Tools for Presenting with Twitter," *Speaking About Presenting* blog, 3 November 2009 [accessed 3 August 2010], www.speakingaboutpresenting.com; Atkinson, *The Backchannel*, 51, 68–73, 99. **334** Carol Channing quoted in Leon Fletcher, *How to Speak Like a Pro* (New York: Random House Publishing Group, 2010). **336** Stephanie Sykes, president and owner, Stephanie Sykes HR Solutions Inc.; Stephanie Sykes. **337** Based on Courtland L. Bovée and John V. Thill, *Business in Action*, 5th ed. (Upper Saddle River, N.J.: Pearson Prentice-Hall, 2010), 18–21; Randall S. Hansen and Katharine Hansen, "What Do Employers Really Want? Top Skills and Values Employers Seek from Job-Seekers," QuintCareers.com [accessed 17 August 2010], www.quintcareers.com. **340** Mohammed Al-Taee, "Personal Branding," *Al-Taee* blog [accessed 17 August 2010], http://altaeeblog.com; Based on Pete Kistler, "Seth Godin's 7-Point Guide to Bootstrap Your Personal Brand," *Personal Branding* blog, 28 July 2010 [accessed 17 August 2010], www.personalbrandingblog.com; Kyle Lacy, "10 Ways to Building Your Personal Brand Story," *Personal Branding* blog, 5 August 2010 [accessed 17 August 2010], www.personalbrandingblog.com; Al-Taee, "Personal Branding"; Scot Herrick, "30 Career Management Tips—Marketing AND Delivery Support Our Personal Brand," *Cube Rules* blog, 8 September 2007 [accessed 17 August 2010], http://cuberules.com; Alina Tugend, "Putting Yourself Out There on a Shelf to Buy," *New York Times*, 27 March 2009 [accessed 9 August 2009], www.nytimes.com. **342** Anne Fisher, "How to Get Hired by a 'Best' Company," *Fortune*, 4 February 2008, 96. **351** Based on Kim Isaacs, "Resume Dilemma: Criminal Record," Monster.com [accessed 23 May 2006], www.monster.com; Kim Isaacs, "Resume Dilemma: Employment Gaps and Job-Hopping," Monster.com [accessed 23 May 2006], www.monster.com; Susan Vaughn, "Answer the Hard Questions Before Asked," *Los Angeles Times*, 29 July 2001, W1–W2. **370** Caroline Jellinck, partner, Odgers Berndtson; Caroline Jellinck. **372** Based on Doyle, "Introduction to Cover Letters"; Vaas, "How to Write a Great Cover Letter"; Toni Logan, "The Perfect Cover Story," *Kinko's Impress* 2 (2000): 32, 34. **375** Based on Alison Doyle, "How to Follow Up After Submitting a Resume," About.com [accessed 13 August 2010], http://jobsearch.about.com; Vaas, "How to Follow Up a Résumé Submission." **378** Based on Jonathan Katz, "Rethinking Drug Testing," *Industry Week*, March 2010, 16–18; Ashley Shadday, "Assessments 101: An Introduction to Candidate Testing," *Workforce Management*, January 2010 [accessed 14 August 2010], www.workforce.com; Dino di Mattia, "Testing Methods and Effectiveness of Tests," *Supervision*, August 2005, 4–5; David W. Arnold and John W. Jones, "Who the Devil's Applying Now?" *Security Management*, March 2002, 85–88; Matthew J. Heller, "Digging Deeper," *Workforce Management*, 3 March 2008, 35–39. **384** Interview with Caroline Jellinck, 1 March 2011; Based on Randall S. Hansen, "When Job-Hunting: Dress for Success," QuintCareers.com [accessed 5 April 2008], www.quintcareers.com; Alison Doyle, "Dressing for Success," About.com [accessed 5 April 2008], http://jobsearch.about.com. **386** "10 Minutes to Impress," *Journal of Accountancy*, July 2007, 13. **387** Todd Anten, "How to Handle Illegal Interview Questions," Yahoo! HotJobs [accessed 7 August 2009], http://hotjobs.yahoo.com.

# Index